Public Information Technology and E-Governance: Managing the Virtual State

G. David Garson, PhD

North Carolina State University

Raleigh, North Carolina

World Headquarters

Jones and Bartlett Publishers
40 Tall Pine Drive
Sudbury, MA 01776
978-443-5000
info@jbpub.com
www.jbpub.com

Jones and Bartlett Publishers
Canada
6339 Ormindale Way
Mississauga, ON L5V 1J2
Canada

Jones and Bartlett Publishers
International
Barb House, Barb Mews
London W6 7PA
United Kingdom

Jones and Bartlett's books and products are available through most bookstores and online booksellers. To contact Jones and Bartlett Publishers directly, call 800-832-0034, fax 978-443-8000, or visit our website at www.jbpub.com.

Substantial discounts on bulk quantities of Jones and Bartlett's publications are available to corporations, professional associations, and other qualified organizations. For details and specific discount information, contact the special sales department at Jones and Bartlett via the above contact information or send an email to specialsales@jbpub.com.

ISBN-13: 978-0-7637-3468-8
ISBN-10: 0-7637-3468-3

Library of Congress Cataloging-in-Publication Data

Garson, G. David.
  Public information technology and e-governance : managing the virtual state / by G. David Garson.—1st ed.
       p. cm.
  Includes bibliographical references and index.
  ISBN 0-7637-3468-3 (pbk.)
  1. Internet in public administration—United States. 2. Internet in public administration—United States—Case studies. 3. Information technology—Management. 4. Information technology—Management—Case studies. 5. Information technology—Government policy—United States. I. Title.
  JK468.A8G35 2006
  352.3'8—dc22
  6048   2005018958

Production Credits
Executive Editor: David Cella
VP of Manufacturing and Inventory Control: Therese Connell
Production Director: Amy Rose
Production Editor: Carolyn F. Rogers
Editorial Assistant: Katilyn Crowley
Marketing Manager: Emily Ekle
Associate Marketing Manager: Laura Kavigian
Composition: Auburn Associates, Inc.
Cover Design: Timothy Dziewit
Printing and Binding: Malloy, Inc.
Cover Printing: Malloy, Inc.

Printed in the United States of America
10 09 08 07 06   10 9 8 7 6 5 4 3 2

Table of Contents

Preface

This work is an attempt to fill the need for a comprehensive textbook on policy and management issues that arise when considering information technology in the public sector. The chapters in Parts I and II cover policy issues, including privacy, access, security, and regulation. The chapters in Part III and IV cover management topics, including business plans, strategic planning, project management, and program evaluation. A final chapter relates organization theory and organization behavior to the study of public information systems.

An attempt has been made to present a balanced view. Public information technology is presented neither as a panacea leading to a future in which most human problems are solved, nor as a malevolent tidal force leading to control and oppression. Instead, at the end of each chapter four theoretical perspectives are considered and evaluated in terms of the chapter topic. The four perspectives are those of (1) technological determinism, which gives primacy to technology as a force for change in its own right; (2) sociotechnical theory, which emphasizes the critical role of human factors in technological change; (3) systems theory, which emphasizes the drive for integration as the essential dynamic of information systems; and (4) reinforcement theory, which sees information technology as a tool and, as such, primarily serving powers that have the most resources to employ tools of any kind.

To reveal the conclusion here at the beginning, it will be found that each of these four theoretical perspectives has much to offer, though some more than others. The role of theory is not so much to provide the "correct" view of a complex topic as it is to direct us toward interesting questions. By counterposing theories, we ask these questions from a variety of viewpoints that, it is hoped, will enrich our analysis in the process. Still, the core content of this text is not primarily theoretical. Rather the focus of this work is on the political issues raised by information policy in the public sector and on the administrative issues that managers may anticipate in governing the *virtual state*.

Some use the term *virtual state* to refer to that ideal typical or future time when the brick-and-mortar institutions of government will have disappeared, replaced by online networks and services accessed by citizens, businesses, and other agencies from millions of decentralized locations—even from home. In this book, however, the term *virtual state* is used to refer to the present-day reality that information technology and networking infuse every level of government and every domain of government service. More and more, effectively managing public agencies occurs only to the extent that the heads of agencies are able to mobilize information technology resources and integrate them with human, financial, and policy resources. Managing the virtual state refers to this process of mobilization and integration.

Each chapter presents an introduction to the topic, sections covering its main dimensions, and a summary that relates the topic to each of the four major theoretical perspectives on public information technology. Additionally, a glossary and discussion questions follow each chapter. As an addition to the text, case studies contributed by other authors also follow each chapter in Parts II, III, IV, and V. These case studies offer concrete examples of many of the subjects presented in the chapter as well as present additional coverage and differing perspectives useful for discussion of the chapter topics.

The book begins and ends on a theoretical note, perhaps unexpected by believers in the myth that public administration is a theory-poor discipline. The first chapter, "The Vision of E-Governance," begins with the notion from 40 years ago of the emerging "global village" and moves through later concepts of the *network nation*, the *electronic cottage*, the *network society*, *smart communities*, and *digital places* to present-day concepts of *electronic government*. The purpose of this intellectual history is to show that public information technology is not merely a technical or administrative subject, but rather is closely caught up in the hopes and dreams of a better future by recent generations of thoughtful observers. These topics are approached not at a highly generalized and untestable level, as is so often the case, but rather are resolved into midrange theories. While these midrange theories may fall short of constituting a "unified field theory of public information systems," they have the advantage of being amenable to empirical assessment, exploring such questions as whether information systems are changing the structure of public organizations and whether telecommuting may deterritorialize public work, to name two of several midrange theories that are discussed.

In Part II, policy issues are treated, starting with a brief history of public-sector information technology policy from its origins in the Cold War through governmental sponsorship of the creation of the Internet to contemporary policies and legislation affecting access, privacy, and other aspects of e-government. Chapter 3 treats e-democracy, including e-activism, e-campaigning, e-voting, e-legislating, and other dimensions of e-participation in government. Chapter 4 covers the issue of information equality and the *digital divide,* examining gender, race, income, and age differences. Chapter 5 covers freedom of information policy, access issues, and the concept of governmental transparency, as well as the trade-offs of these with security and privacy values. Chapter 6 treats the privacy issue in much more detail, exploring computer surveillance, data sharing and matching, the national ID controversy, and many related issues. Security policy is the topic of Chapter 7, treating homeland security, national infrastructure protection, encryption, and much more. The last policy chapter, Chapter 8, covers regulatory and taxation issues, including Internet taxation, regulation of the information technology sector and e-commerce, as well as issues pertaining to computer crime, intellectual property rights, and regulation of such e-vices as pornography and gambling on the Web.

Part III of this text treats managerial issues, starting with the explanation of e-government business models in Chapter 9. Chapter 10 discusses partnering, outsourcing, contracting, and procurement issues in the context of Bush administration policies aimed at increasing the role of the private sector in government. Planning for public information systems is the topic of Chapter 11, which covers the changing role of federal chief information officers, strategic planning, portfolio management, risk management, and records management. Chapter 12 covers a lower level of planning concerns, including needs assessment, business process analysis, feasibility studies, and project management.

In Part IV, causes of information technology failure in the public sector are explored in Chapter 13, which also covers the large literature on implementation success factors. The final chapter in Part IV is on the critical topic of evaluating information technology projects, including evaluation of public Web portals.

A decade ago I would have written, "Knowledge of the policy and management issues is quickly becoming as essential to the public executive as is knowledge of policy, financial, and human resource management." Today it is safe to replace "is quickly becoming" with simply "is." The public executive who is unprepared to integrate information technology resources with the agency's operations and financial systems is one who operates at a severe disadvantage. Unfortunately, such executives remain common. It does not help that schools of public administration have been slow to move information technology into their required core curricula. In an era when public managers are under severe pressure to outsource many agency operations to the private sector and to retrench on what remains because of budgetary austerity, knowledge of public information technology policies and management has become essential to preserve public administration as an endeavor that provides effectiveness and accountability in the context of serving the public interest.

G. David Garson
Raleigh, North Carolina
June 2005

Contributor List

Dennis Betz, BA
Community Development Specialists, Inc.
Client Referral Network
Newland, NC

Loreen Marie Butcher-Powell, ABD
College of Business
Bloomsburg University of Pennsylvania
Bloomsburg, PA

Charles N. Davis, PhD
School of Journalism
University of Missouri
Columbus, MO

Paul K. Dezendorf, PhD, MBA, MSW
Social Work Department
Winthrop University
Rock Hill, SC

William L. Dougan
Department of Management
University of Wisconsin—Whitewater
Whitewater, WI

G. David Garson, PhD
Department of Political Science and Public Administration
North Carolina State University
Raleigh, NC

James Patrick Glasson, MA
The Praxis Network
Beaufort, SC

Randolph Hawkins, PhD
Department of Sociology
University of South Carolina
Beaufort, SC

Charles Christopher Hinnant, PhD
School of Public and International Affairs
The University of Georgia
Athens, GA

Tracy Leigh Jenkins
Social Work Department
Winthrop University
Rock Hill, SC

Sandra Jones, PhD, MA, MEd, DipEd
School of Management
Royal Melbourne Institute of Technology
Melbourne, Australia

Ronnie L. Korosec, PhD, MA
Department of Public Administration
University of Central Florida
Orlando, FL

Jennifer Kurtz, MBA, BA
Center for Education and Research in
    Information Assurance and Security
Purdue University
Lafayette, IN

**Owen Lockwood, Masters of Enterprise
Innovation, Graduate Degree in Risk
Management, Graduate Degree in
Maintenance**
School of Management
Royal Melbourne Institute of
    Technology
Melbourne, Australia

Todd Loendorf, ABD
Department of Political Science and
    Public Administration
North Carolina State University
Raleigh, NC

Lynn M. Mulkey, PhD
Department of Sociology
University of South Carolina
Beaufort, SC

Dale K. Nesbary, PhD, MPA, BA
Director, Master of Public
    Administration Program
Oakland University
Rochester, MI

Alana Northrop, PhD, MA
Division of Political Science and
    Criminal Justice
University of California—Fullerton
Fullerton, CA

Costas Panagopoulos, PhD, MA
Department of Politics
New York University
New York, NY

Jennifer Powers, PhD
School of Information Science and
    Policy
State University of New York at Albany
Albany, NY

Tracey E. Rizzuto, PhD, MS
Department of Psychology
Louisiana State University
Baton Rouge, LA

Steve Sawyer, DBA
School of Information Sciences and
    Technology
The Pennsylvania State University
University Park, PA

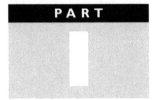

Introduction

The Vision of E-Governance

When Vannevar Bush, President Franklin Roosevelt's science director, penned a visionary essay titled, "As We May Think," General Douglas MacArthur was landing in Japan to attend the formal surrender ceremony of that nation, marking the end of World War II. Science had contributed mightily to the successful conclusion of the military campaign. Bush himself had coordinated the efforts of over 6,000 scientists in the war effort. With that purpose accomplished, Bush now set himself to the task of establishing a new agenda to rally scientists in the emerging postwar era. In World War II, science had created the greatest engine of destruction that had ever been known. In the new era, science would create the greatest engine of knowledge that the earth had ever witnessed. He called that engine *the memex*. The memex embodied a striking vision of the information society which was to come into being by the end of the century in which Bush lived.

At the end of World War II, powerful forces were coming together that would make possible what was once only dreamed. Two centuries earlier, Bush noted, Leibnitz had invented the calculating machine, but it could not come into use because in his day the labor it saved would be outweighed by the labor needed to create and maintain it. Now, however, the invention of the means of mass production had changed that calculus. Two hundred years earlier, complexity was inextricably linked to unreliability, but now modern production had broken that link, enabling complexity also to be reliable. "The world has arrived at an age of cheap complex devices of great reliability; and something is bound to come of it," Bush wrote (Bush, 1945; Nyce & Kahn, 1991).

Models of reliable complexity already existed in 1945: the automatic telephone exchange, the gossamer webs of metal thread embedded in vacuum tubes to drive radio communications, devices to count cosmic rays by electronic means at the rate of 100,000 per second, and of course, the atomic bomb, radar, and all the science of war. Moreover, instructions to such machines could be programmed, as on control cards, and carried out simply by feeding keyboard punches into their enormous appetites. The new mission for science was to create programmed information machines that would transform how humans handled knowledge, multiplying the power of information and accelerating the development of society.

Bush coined the term *memex* to refer to an imagined device for storing knowledge—for storing all of an individual's books, records, letters, and data. The individual would be able to consult his electronic knowledge base rapidly and flexibly, supplementing his memory, yet the memex would be simple enough to operate at his desktop or even from a distance. With translucent screens and keyboards, the memex would be an information machine like no other. It is true that some of Bush's vision was rooted in 1945, with references to storing data on "improved microfilm," but even these references were a precursor to scanners that would record photographs, longhand notes, and all manner of visual information using a "transparent platen."

In "As We May Think," Bush also envisioned what is now called hypertext—the complex interactive linking of terms. He wrote that the user would be able to consult a book in the memex, then enter a code on the keyboard to see related information for any indexed term, leaving one page in place while simultaneously viewing another, consulting or adding marginal notes and speeding forward or backward in text. Users would, he wrote, build trails through information, storing them exactly as if the gathered items formed a new book, as it were. Any item could be joined to numerous trails. The student of the bow and arrow, for instance, would be linked to comparisons of the short Turkish bow with the English long bow, and to information on battles of the Crusades, and to the physics of elasticity, tables of physical constants, and to a trail through the maze of all things related to bows and arrows. Even several years later, the user would be able to resume his journey through these same stored trails. Vendors would sell whole new forms of encyclopedias, with preestablished meshes of associative trails through their topic of concern, whether medical information for the physician or scientific information for the chemist or chronological information for the historian. Moreover, great minds would create their own associative works, transmitting knowledge from master to student in this manner.

Vannevar Bush concluded his visionary statement with this thought:

> The applications of science have built man a well-supplied house, and are teaching him to live healthily therein. They have enabled

him to throw masses of people against another with cruel weapons. They may yet allow him truly to encompass the great record and to grow in the wisdom of race experience. He may perish in conflict before he learns to wield that record for his true good. Yet, in the application of science to the needs and desires of man, it would seem to be a singularly unfortunate stage at which to terminate the process, or to lose hope as to the outcome (Bush, 1945, p. 108).

From the perspective of the close of the greatest war in history, the vision of harnessing all the complexity of human knowledge was a bright hope for science, for government, and for the world. It was what Bush called the "Endless Frontier" in a report to President Roosevelt, writing in the era of the ENIAC computer, used by the Army for ballistic calculations. Less than a decade later, the Census Bureau purchased the first UNIVAC computer. By the Korean War, IBM 701 computers became widespread in the federal government. When the Soviet Union launched Sputnik in 1957, the federal government established the Advanced Research Projects Agency (ARPA) within the Department of Defense to promote defense technology. Twelve years later, ARPAnet went online as the predecessor of the modern Internet. Half a century after Vannevar Bush wrote "As We May Think," his vision became reality. We start with the concept of the *global village* and work through other visions such as the *network nation* and conclude with a discussion of *electronic governance.*

COMPETING THEORIES OF INFORMATION TECHNOLOGY AND CHANGE

Before turning to a survey of important visions of our electronic future, it is worth taking a moment to consider the theoretical framework within which they may fit. Four theories of information technology (IT) and social change seek to provide the context for the development of IT and for its public-sector manifestations, such as e-government.

Technological determinism holds that IT is an unstoppable force in its own right, reshaping the world in profound ways, and government along with it. Although policy makers may be able to shape the particular enactment of technology in particular situations, and may even block its advance in some instances, technology has an inner *telos*, or DNA if you will, that wants to be manifested in ways that undercut traditional bureaucratic forms. Like the child trying to build walls to protect his sandcastle against the advancing tide, the administrator who opposes technology finds himself in a futile struggle against a fated outcome.

Reinforcement theory holds that IT is a tool like any other. Like other tools, it tends to reinforce the structural position of the powers that be. Dissidents in Tiénnamen Square may use the Internet, but their efforts pale in contrast to the benefits the state derives from its dominance of electronic media. Activists may use telecommunications to mobilize to oppose globalization at meetings of the World Trade Organization, but global finance built on new ITs is the force reshaping international economics. Computer technocrats function as the hired guns of the electronic frontier, answerable to the masters who pay them. These masters were once those who controlled the means of production. Today they are those who control the means of information, and thus this perspective is also called *control theory*. (The term *reinforcement theory* rather than *control theory* is used in this text because the latter is an ambiguous term that can also be cast in terms of systems theory, discussed below.)

Sociotechnical theory holds that the development of IT is relatively unconstrained by technological determinism or by extant power structures, as the previous two theories respectively hold. Instead systems design is paramount. In design theory, ITs may be created to support centralization or decentralization, autocracy or participation, hierarchy or adhocracy, and, indeed, whatever the designer may imagine can be brought into being. A pluralism of designers leads to diversity of outcomes, whether in corporate settings or in public information systems. While not denying the influence of chief executive officers and politicians emphasized by reinforcement theory, sociotechnical theory gives a great role to the designer—whether consultant, technocrat, or innovative manager—as an agent of change. It also gives great importance to the role of stakeholders and human factors in the design of managerial systems that rely on IT.

Systems theory holds that technological factors, not human factors, are paramount in design (in contrast to sociotechnical theory), though design is not technologically determined (in contrast to technological determinism). Organizational problems can be addressed through engineering methodologies to achieve ever higher levels of efficiency and effectiveness. Organizations are transformed, not through the humanistic interventions of a change agent, but through the logic of knowledge engineering and its institutionalization in control systems. Implicit in this perspective is a great role for systems engineers and the technocratic infrastructure that supports their work. Outcomes are what systems engineers perceive as efficient solutions to the problems of the organizational environment within which they work.

These four theories of the nature of information systems and change can be viewed in terms of a *factor environment matrix* in which one dimension has to do with the relative importance of technological versus human factors and the other dimension has to do with whether the environment is perceived as relatively constrained or unconstrained (see Figure 1-1).

For the technological determinist, change is highly constrained by technological factors, which are paramount. For the student of reinforcement theory, change is highly constrained by human factors (power structure), which are dominant. For sociotechnical systems analysis, however, change outcomes are relatively unconstrained, though human factors are foremost. And for systems theorists, change outcomes are also relatively unconstrained, but technical (engineering) factors are considered most important.

In the real world, IT authors rarely articulate a pure version of any of these four theories. Rather, while often tending to favor one perspective or another, they frequently acknowledge elements of all theories. Indeed, a reason why each of these has been so prominent is that each contains acknowledged truths. In the remainder of this chapter, and in this book generally, the four theoretical perspectives of the factor environment matrix will be used as a framework for understanding many of the approaches to IT found in the popular, academic, and managerial literatures.

THE GLOBAL VILLAGE (1964)

The concept of *the global village* was developed and popularized by Canadian academic and student of communications technology, Marshall McLuhan (1911–1980), who directed the University of Toronto's Center for Culture and Technology in the 1960s. Where Karl Marx had argued that control of the means of production was the primary factor for understanding the nature of social change, McLuhan argued that technological innovation in its own right was dominant. In this, his work can be associated with technological determinist theory. McLuhan set forth the concept of the global village in *Gutenberg Galaxy* (1962) but developed it

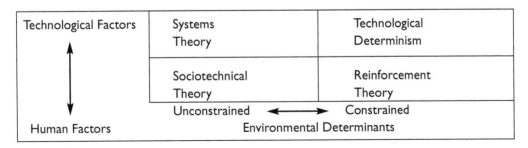

Figure 1-1 The Factor Environment Matrix

further in *Understanding Media* (1964) and later in *The Medium is the Message* (1967), arguing that society would be transformed as television and electronic IT displaced newspapers and print media.

Central to McLuhan's argument was the concept of the global village. The global village was created as electronic media displaced print media. McLuhan foresaw that in the near future one might live anywhere on Earth and still communicate interactively with anyone else on Earth. Events on one part of the planet could be experienced in real time by individuals located on another part of the planet. The immediacy of events in the village could be recreated electronically on a global basis, restoring worldwide the intimacy that had been lost with the passing of village life as the center of human existence. Before the Internet, even before its predecessor, ARPAnet, McLuhan foresaw the globalizing effects of the creation of a worldwide electronic nervous system. He foresaw global integration at the organizational level and global liberation at the personal level.

Yet the creation of the global village was not entirely liberating in McLuhan's analysis. Television was a "cool medium," by which McLuhan meant that it was soporific, encouraging passivity among its viewers (McLuhan & Powers, 1989). It is difficult to say if he would see differences with the Internet as a more interactive medium, coming into its own a quarter century later. McLuhan was generally positive about the technological transformation of society that he saw and foresaw, but he also worried about the potential of the new media to fall into manipulative advertising and perversion of social culture.

In terms of the theory of IT and change, it must be acknowledged that McLuhan's work preceded the Internet and focused on television as the prime example of electronic media. However, McLuhan's analysis of how technology relates to societal change is generalizable. He believed all innovations were associated with the four processes of retrieval, enhancement, obsolescence, and reversal (see Table 1-1).

We may speculate about the implications of these four processes for the contemporary world of the Internet and e-government. Perhaps McLuhan would observe that much of what passes for e-government is less revolutionary than advertised, instead based on retrieval of traditional bureaucratic elements. He might acknowledge the efficiencies of providing governmental services through the Internet, a form of enhancement, and he would predict the gradual shift of public resources from traditional to electronic forms as traditional forms come to be seen as obsolescent (something that still lies largely in the future). Finally, he might predict that the public sector would eventually overinvest in e-government, dazzled by its benefits but overlooking its costs, until a reaction set in to

Table 1-1   McLuhan's Inventory of Technological Change Processes

Change Processes and Their Meanings	
Retrieval	New technologies draw from and contain elements from the existing cultural inventory of the society.
Enhancement	New technologies supercede the old in terms of performance.
Obsolescence	Old technologies wither in the face of the new.
Reversal	New technologies are pursued past the optimal benefit point, eventually leading to the need to reverse direction.

reverse direction and restore to some degree face-to-face interactions and street-level bureaucracy.

THE NETWORK NATION (1978)

The Network Nation was the title of an influential book by Roxanne Starr Hiltz and Murray Turoff (1978) in which they argued that the revolution in information systems could lead to a new epoch of decentralization and democratization. Hiltz and Turoff believed that technological change could potentially have profound social and political impacts that, in theory, could democratize decision making at organizational, civil, and even national levels. Like McLuhan, implicit in the work of Hiltz and Turoff was a technological determinist belief in the inevitability of socio-organizational change forced by technology change.

Turoff worked for the Institute for Defense Analysis during the late 1960s, where he helped develop the Delphi protocol for achieving expert consensus through serial surveys, voting, and feedback. In 1971 he was commissioned by the U.S. Office of Emergency Preparedness to automate EMISARI, the Emergency Management Information and Reference System, resulting in one of the first model computer conferencing systems. EMISARI incorporated online notebooks, channeling of text threads into "conferences," keyword search of archives, Delphi-like voting on alternatives, and a system of electronic mail, all available for either real-time synchronous or asynchronous conferencing. Turoff then was hired by the New Jersey Institute of Technology, where he developed the Electronic Information Exchange System (EIES) conferencing system in 1975.

Hiltz's studies of users of the EIES conference system showed that as participants became heavy users of computer conferencing, a substitution effect occurred, marked by diminished telephone usage. But what Hiltz and Turoff were observing was more than the displacement of old technologies by new. They were observing a shift from direct communication (voice to voice) toward computer-mediated communication

(CMC). Their research strongly suggested that CMC would have major impacts on patterns of group communication and therefore on organizational processes. In particular, CMC obscured status and position cues in communication and therefore diminished the ability of a single person at the top to dominate meetings and other decision processes. At the same time, CMC created a literal marketplace of information that empowered the individual and the work group, altering traditional hierarchical organizational processes.

In arguing for the decentralizing and democratizing effects of information technology, Hiltz and Turoff were following Marshall McLuhan, who had written of computerization, "At the same time it dissolves hierarchy in favor of centralization. . . . Any business corporation requiring the use of computers for communication and record keeping will have no other alternative but to decentralize" (McLuhan & Powers, 1989, p. 103).

Hiltz and Turoff (1993, p. 141) went beyond McLuhan, however, spelling out what they believed to be the specific nature of the democratic change forced by new electronic technology.

> You change the communications structure of an organization. You inevitably change also the nature of the decision-making process within it and the kinds of decisions that are likely to result. Ultimately, you change the form of the organization itself. . . . We predict that by the 1990s, we may see the emergence of a kind of internal marketplace within the organization. Individual employees may offer portions of their available time and allocate it to the highest internal bidder. . . . Supply and demand would govern the allocation of information workers and the production of information services within the organization (Turoff, Hiltz, & Mills, 1989; Turoff, 1985).

That is, organizational hierarchies would dissolve into a democratic marketplace of online marketing of professional services.

Hiltz and Turoff made 14 other predictions:

- Computerized conferencing will be a prominent form of communications in most organizations by the mid-1980s.
- By the mid-1990s, it will be as widely used in society as the telephone today.
- It will offer a home recreational use that will make significant inroads into TV viewing patterns.
- It will have dramatic psychological and sociological impacts on various group communication objectives and processes.
- It will be cheaper than postal mail or long-distance telephone voice communications.

- It will offer major opportunities to disadvantaged groups in the society to acquire the skills and social ties they need to become full members of the society.
- It will have dramatic impacts on the degree of centralization or decentralization possible in organizations.
- It will become a fundamental mechanism for individuals to form groups having common concerns, interests, or purposes.
- It will facilitate working at home for a large percentage of the work force during at least half of their normal work week.
- It will have a dramatic impact upon the formation of political and special interest groups.
- It will open the doors to new and unique types of services.
- It will indirectly allow for sizable amounts of energy conservation through substitution of communication for travel.
- It will dramatically alter the nature of social science research concerned with the study of human systems and human communication processes.
- It will facilitate a richness and variability of human groupings and relationships almost impossible to comprehend.

In the 1993 revision of *The Network Nation*, Hiltz and Turoff acknowledged that while CMC had increased dramatically:

> The first edition had one major mistake: overoptimism about the speed at which computer-mediated communication would be adopted around the world, to create a "network nation" that spans political and social boundaries. At the time we so readily perceived and experienced the benefits of the technology that we seriously underestimated the time it would take for it to spread (Hiltz & Turoff, 1993, p. xxix).

However, they believed that the prevalence of the personal computer and the near-universal spread of the Internet meant that "There is thus a new and pervasive technological foundation for the growth of the Network Nation" (Hiltz & Turoff, 1993, p. xxxi).

As found in a survey by Kling and Iacono (1988), many social scientists in the 1980s shared with Hiltz and Turoff the common underlying belief that as computerization increases, more and more opportunities would arise by which organizations would be remade, largely in a spontaneous, decentralized manner benefitting everyone. On the other hand, the revolutionary predictions of organizational democracy through networks and computer-supported cooperative work by other researchers in the 1980s (Kraemer & King, 1986) showed that the organization's top management was, if anything, strengthened by firm and growing central control over new ITs (the reinforcement theory perspective). Similarly, Kraut (1987) found that telecommuting reinforced existing office structures and was not leading to structural change and innovation. If the network nation was coming, it was coming much more slowly than Hiltz and Turoff predicted and with far fewer revolutionary consequences.

THE ELECTRONIC COTTAGE IN THE INFOSPHERE (1980)

In his book *The Third Wave* (1980), Alvin Toffler wrote, "What is inescapably clear, whatever we choose to believe, is that we are altering our infosphere fundamentally. . .we are adding a whole new strata of communication to the social system. The emerging Third Wave infosphere makes that of the Second Wave era—dominated by its mass media, the post office, and the telephone—seem hopelessly primitive by contrast" (Toffler, 1980, p. 172). In Toffler's Third Wave, organizations would be recast in decentralized form. In our lifetimes, organizational change centers on the conflict between those who would hold onto the hierarchical forms of the Second Wave and those in the Third Wave who are displacing them.

In Toffler's theories, social change proceeds by "waves." The First Wave was the agricultural era, shifting civilization from hunting and gathering to living in villages and raising crops. The Industrial Revolution was the Second Wave, shifting civilization away from the culture of the agrarian village to living in cities and working in factories. The Third Wave is the information age, which, with the rise of the *infosphere*, separated work from location. Toffler forecast a vast expansion of personal freedom arising from work at home rather than in the office or factory. This was not a new prediction, even in 1980. Jack Nilles, a California consultant, coined the term *telecommuting* in 1973. He predicted that by 1993 it would cease to be an aberration and become a mainstream practice (Furger, 1989, p. 45). Through advances in technology, Toffler foresaw the rise of the home office, which he called the *electronic cottage*.

The Third Wave is characterized by replicable rather than finite resources (the home office worker cannot make a Second Wave Ford automobile, but he may create and replicate Third Wave software systems); individuation rather than standardization (the home worker can quickly customize graphic designs for different outlets); and demassified niche culture erodes mass culture (the home worker can belong to specialized electronic interest groups that support his work). The management implication was that the centralized management of the Second Wave was giving way to the decentralization, delegation of authority, and empowerment of self-managing teams of the Third Wave.

Toffler's vision of the electronic cottage in the infosphere was essentially another in the series of technological determinist theories we have been discussing in this chapter. Compared to the global village or the network nation, the electronic cottage placed more emphasis on the demassifying and individuating effects of technology and made stronger predictions about telecommuting. From a management point of view, it called attention to the executive's role as a facilitator of innovation and a coordinator of decentralization.

THE NETWORK SOCIETY (1996)

If the global village, network nation, and electronic cottage were visions of the future rooted in technological determinist theories, a contrast may be found in the vision of Maurice Castells' *network society*, which is based on a version of the reinforcement theory of IT. In 1996, Castells published *The Information Age: Economy, Society and Culture. Vol I: The Rise of Network Society*, followed by additional volumes in 1997 and 1998. In this much-acclaimed trilogy, he presented a grand theory, backed by an enormous diversity of historical and empirical research, interpreting the modern era in terms of a dialectic between the *informational capitalism* of networked international corporations on the one hand, and social movements and regional efforts to assert unique cultural identities on the other.

Castells' thesis is cast as a prophetic warning. He wrote, "The rise of informationalism in this end of the millennium is intertwined with rising inequality and social exclusion throughout the world" (1998, p. 70). International inequalities grow, particularly at the extremes, and groups are systematically denied the resources for meaningful survival of their cultural identity. "Black holes of information capitalism" appear, from which there is no empirically evident means to escape poverty and de-identification. The political dynamics of the age are not class based or even nationalist, as a century ago, but rather involve the conflict of one set of informational capitalists against another (e.g., the United States versus the Pacific Rim versus the European Union), and against the new international criminal economy, and against regional pockets of resistance to the full impact of informational capitalism on cultural identity.

Castells' theory of IT and change is part of the school of thought called critical theory, which has five general themes (Coyne & Wiszniewski, 1999):

1. Whereas computer networks are presented as providing opportunity for access and to restore an informed and active citizenry, overcom-

ing social barriers, in reality there is a digital divide that inhibits equal access and that means that IT, including the Internet, is dominated by and is primarily in the service of economically advantaged groups and nations.

2. The presentation of IT is characterized by deception: the claims of egalitarian access and the necessity, inevitability, and desirability of growth in IT conceals other agendas associated with the growth of big business, globalization, control, and the preparation of a yet more compliant consumer culture.

3. Computer simulation (in the form of virtual reality, game playing, virtual communities, computerized theme parks, and so on) functions to present the unreal as real, and to mask the true reality of everyday existence in a consumer culture.

4. IT functions to set the terms of discourse and to undercut dissent by concealing domination under the legitimating cloak of metanarratives of logic, order, rule, and objective reasoning, whereas they are unmasked by critical theory, which shows them to be a form of symbolic hegemony by the powerful.

5. IT cannot be analyzed in isolation from the social system of consumers, advertisers, developers, designers, manufacturers, educators, mass media, and lawmakers, because the function of IT is not primarily technological at all, but rather to perpetuate the dominant social system.

Uniting all five themes of critical theory is the premise of reinforcement theory: IT is a formidable tool wielded with great effect by the powers that be.

Castells' work is hardly a management text, but it does have clear implications for the management of IT. Neither labor nor management can afford to ignore the deeply political aspects of the design of information systems, which are not merely means to achieve efficiencies but are even more importantly means to define organizational goals and objectives. These become embedded in planning and performance measurement systems that track goal achievement of the organization's units and its individual workers. IT is also the basis for the localized fragmentation of work (e.g., home offices, just-in-time hiring, expansion of part-time work) and for global outsourcing of jobs, ending the traditional countervailing power balance between capital and labor decisively to the disadvantage of the latter.

The Industrial Revolution, in what Toffler called the *Second Wave*, took the atomized artisans of the agrarian First Wave and consolidated them into a homogenous work force. Castells' theory describes how the network society reverses the process. The traditional full-time worker of the past century is replaced by the more mobile worker of the new millennium, more educated to meet the demands of the information economy, more likely to be self-employed or working for a number of corporations, constantly struggling to stay on the cutting edge of what Castells calls the *New Economy*.

In his 2001 book *The Internet Galaxy: Reflections on the Internet, Business, and Society,* Castells addressed the public sector specifically. In this work Castells acknowledges that e-governance has, in theory, provided for greater accountability, transparency, and information access. However, after tracing the roots of the free culture of the Internet in academia and hacker culture, Castells then documents how cyberliberty is becoming eroded as nation states and their networked corporate allies seek to reassert control. Among the tendencies that Castells discerns are the creation of the *electronic panopticon*, referring to what others have called the surveillance society; the digital divide, which has exacerbated the gulf between economically powerful nations and economically disadvantaged nations; and use of the Internet as an engine of state and corporate propaganda, as has happened in traditional media according to scholars such as Noam Chomsky (1992, 1994, 1996). In Castells' analysis, the Internet is both the centerpiece of freedom and the central battleground for the struggle to control the New Economy and to reassert the sovereignty of the state.

SMART COMMUNITIES (1997)

The origin of the concept of *smart communities* is difficult to identify with a single author, but it is clearly associated with the establishment of the World Foundation for Smart Communities (WFFSC) in 1997, under the presidency of John Eger, who has also written prolifically on the subject (Eger, 1997).[1] In its emphasis on community transformation through humanistic design principles based on adapting IT to serve human needs, the smart communities movement is implicitly associated with the sociotechnical theory of IT and change. That is, it assumes a relatively unconstrained environment in which to focus on human factors as the key to IT progress.

Canada, in particular, has become a leader in the smart communities movement. The WFFSC Demonstration Projects initiative was a $60 million 1999–2002 Canada-wide competition to select one world-class Demonstration Project in each province, one in the North and one in an Aboriginal community. Created and administered by Industry Canada, the goal was to help Canada become a world leader in the use of information and communication technologies for economic, social, and cultural purposes. The projects are the Kuh-ke-nah Network of Smart First Nations (aboriginal), the Calgary INFOPORT Community Empowerment Project (Alberta), and several others.

To take just one of these examples, the Calgary INFOPORT Community Empowerment Project helps frontline storefront agencies assist at-risk individuals to get computer-related training at drop-in centers; a directory at informcalgary.org offers a directory of community, health, and social services; the Calgary Housing Registry has information on city housing; nextSteps.org offers free employment services to Calgary and area youth; the Learning Resources website assists with adult education needs; and the most ambitious component is establishment of an extranet to provide rapid access to information about social service providers, integrating databases across social service agencies. In summary, for Alberta, smart communities means using public funds to subsidize the IT capabilities and integration of social service agencies.

Relating this concrete example back to IT theory, the Calgary smart communities initiative can be seen as a counterexample to technological determinism (it was created through community will and was not technologically inevitable) and to reinforcement theory (it is not in the service of the powerful). Rather, it is an example of sociotechnical theory at work: designing information services to serve social needs by emphasizing the human factor.[2] The smart communities movement calls on communities to make a conscious effort to apply IT to bring transformative progress to life and work in the region, usually through the incremental efforts of local projects that have strong community involvement. This progress is brought about not in some diffuse, inevitable way, but rather through the overt choice of communities to act as catalysts for IT-based social change in their areas.

Smart community advocates argue that smart communities provide regions with an economic competitive advantage by creating an advanced telecommunications infrastructure. In addition, the argument is made that smart communities are more ecologically friendly (e.g., less car pollution due to increased telecommuting and teleconferencing) and more empowering to citizens (e.g., convenient electronic access to community-wide services).

The *community* term in *smart communities* has been chosen with forethought. It is meant to convey two important ideas. First, regional change is thought to be best, and perhaps only, accomplished by mobilization of and alliance among many heterogenous groups representative of the area. Second, regional transformation is seen as something to cut across municipal functions, being community wide, rather than simply being automation of this or that city function or creating a city website. Rather, the goal is creating a virtual community that changes and improves the quality of life for all the inhabitants of the region.

Some of the specific objectives of a smart communities plan to create a virtual community are provision of governmental services through the Internet (as with e-government, discussed below), but also linking and integrating nonprofit and private-sector services as well. The plan may include creation of electronic marketplaces that bring supply and demand together in a way that overcomes the digital divide and equalizes access for all citizens. For John Eger and at least some of the advocates of smart communities, the concept also involves the idea of cities as engines of civilization, taking on the responsibility to integrate culture, commerce, and civic life. For Eger, the late industrial age led to the decay and death of cities, whereas the information age will revive them as the smart communities movement takes hold.

Transportation plays a central role in the smart communities vision. Eger traces the decay of cities in no small part to the sprawl created by the automobile culture. In smart communities, in contrast, telecommunications becomes a substitute for transportation. Eger foresees a new breed of architects and city planners who will rethink civic life and who will implement smart growth for smart communities under the banner of "the new urbanism" (Katz, 1993). This view has been forcefully stated in *City of Bits* (1996) by William Mitchell, Dean of the School of Architecture and Urban Planning at Massachusetts Institute of Technology. Mitchell predicts cities will abandon the buildings and places where face-to-face encounters now occur in favor of digital means of communicating and interacting. Thus consumers will order goods online. Online banking and small ATM machines will lead to the disappearance of large banking establishments. Doctors will diagnose and give prescriptions, even conduct surgery, using the Internet, digital cameras, and robotic tools. Legislators will debate and vote without leaving their homes. Even prisoners will spend their sentences in electronic home arrest. The revolution in transportation, or perhaps what might be called the revolution against transportation, will be a centerpiece of advanced smart communities.

The smart communities movement reflects what Eger calls the "reverse flow of sovereignty," in which local governments assume more responsibility than ever before for their residents' well-being. The nation–state, too large and distant to solve local problems, is at the same time too small to solve the borderless problems of globalization. In this world, smart communities are like a revival of the city–states of ancient Greece, in Eger's view, creating self-sustaining economies that can effectively compete on a global basis.

Collaboratories are the new model, Eger believes, for successful urban organization of smart communities in the age of globalization. He points to Smart Valley and San Diego as examples where collaboration among government, business, academia, nonprofit organizations, and others, and across jurisdictions within a region, has created globally competitive urban regions. Such success stories are far from being technologically determined. Rather, communities must come together with a compelling vision to create the electronic infrastructure that mobilizes all partners in the collaboratory for economic development and improved quality of life.

DIGITAL PLACES (2000)

The concept of digital places, associated for instance with Thomas Horan's *Digital Places: Building Our City of Bits* (2000a), is a similar but more moderate version of smart communities. Unlike some smart communities advocates, Horan does not predict that digital places will displace traditional forms of community interaction, or even become primary. Rather, he sets forth a continuum of three levels of digital places, from *unplugged designs* at the low end, to *adaptive designs* in the middle, to smart communities-like *transformative designs* at the high end. Although Horan does advocate smart growth at the regional level, he is anxious to emphasize the human need to attach meaning to physical places as part of their culture (Horan, 2000b).

Horan discusses, for instance, the relative failure of electronic distance education to supplant the brick-and-mortar university. In general, the challenge for those who advocate digital places is not to advocate the overthrow of the old but rather to develop new combinations of electronic and physical space (Horan, 2000a, p. 118). The digital university is a new layer overlaying the brick-and-mortar university, not replacing it but requiring new campus architectures to support both old and new functions.

The concept of digital places is similar to that of smart communities in also reflecting assumptions of sociotechnical theory. It casts architects and city planners as change agents operating in a relatively unconstrained frontier of opportunity in which success and progress depend upon sensitivity to human factors and social needs, and failure is associated with unthinking imposition of sheer technology in a top-down technocratic manner that is the opposite of "smart."

E-GOVERNMENT AND E-GOVERNANCE (2000–2002)

With the foregoing background, we may now discuss the vision of e-governance as the "next American revolution" (Ronen, 2000) and relate this explicitly to public-sector visions, such as the Office of Management and Budget's (OMB's) paradigm of the five stages of e-governance. In this discussion, *digital government* is the umbrella term that comprises all uses of information and telecommunications technologies in the public sector. *E-government* refers to one aspect of digital government: the provision of governmental services by electronic means, usually over the Internet. *E-governance*, in contrast, refers to a vision of changing the nature of the state. Under e-governance, networks rather than agencies become primary. Moreover, networks blur the lines separating governmental, nonprofit, and private-sector actors.

Jane Fountain has examined e-governance in what is a contemporary version of sociotechnical theory that she labeled *technology enactment theory* in her book, *Building the Virtual State* (2001). Though Fountain advanced her theory as wholly novel, as Carl Grafton (2003) has observed, it is a restatement and updating of the sociotechnical viewpoint. Technology enactment theory holds that technological possibilities are enacted into technological realities in ways strongly affected by organizational, political, and cultural environments, with nondeterministic results that cannot be predicted from technological considerations alone. This view contrasts sharply with simplistic versions of technological determinism and, for that matter, with systems theory assumptions of OMB implementation of e-government, to be discussed in a later chapter.

In terms of e-governance, Fountain saw FirstGov.gov and other Quicksilver initiatives as part of a transformation of governance. (Quicksilver was the OMB's label for major e-government projects under President Bush's President's Management Initiative.) The old public administration was agency centered, containing IT in a "stovepipe" manner, in ways that prevented cross-agency integration. The old public administration used IT to automate existing practices, not to reinvent government. The old public administration was bureaucracy centered, not client centered. Above all, the old public administration relied on offices, whereas the future lay in networks.

The "virtual state," the building of which was seen by Fountain as the central public administration challenge of our times, is epitomized by the one-stop portal, where the citizen can access cross-agency services online in a customer-friendly way. The citizen would log onto, say, a jobs site, enter a profile one time, and be presented with an individualized Web portal connecting him or her to employment resources from not only a variety of federal agencies, but also state and local agencies, nonprofit groups, and private-sector firms. Information entered one time in the profile would elicit appropriate responses from multiple service providers. The old public administration was about the dispensing of agency services; the new governance was about the mobilization of cross-agency, cross-jurisdiction, cross-sector resources in an individualized manner through networked systems.

The cross-cutting aspect of networked systems envisioned by Fountain is at the heart of the distinction between e-government and e-governance. This difference was articulated by Donald F. Kettl in his book, *The*

Transformation of Governance (2002), which distinguished *government* from *governance*. Kettl's historical analysis of American public administration defined government as the collection of institutions that act with the authority of society to translate politics into legislated policies. Governance, in contrast, Kettl defined as the outcome of the interaction of the public sector and its broader environment—administrative, political, and social. Kettl argued that linking government and governance is the foundation for effective public management in 21st-century America.

Digital government has been around since the 1950s. E-government has been around since the 1980s. For instance, voice mail, computers, interactive cable television, touch-screen kiosks in malls, and electronic bulletin boards were in use by local governments in Kansas City, Missouri; Mercer Island, Washington; Pasadena, California; and by the New York Municipal Management Association since the 1980s (Public Management, 1989). Early efforts at e-governance included the California General Assembly's "Capitol Connection" electronic bulletin board with access to legislative issues and a forum for discussion of policy issues with legislative staff and with other citizens (Fredell, 1987). In the 1980s the City of New Orleans also experimented with a human services-oriented public data access system operating in conjunction with that city's cable television system (Ruberg, 1989). The People's Electronic Exchange of Somerville, New Jersey, provided a medium for online classified ads and community announcements (Balas, 1990). Public Technology, Inc., and IBM supported 24-hour city hall projects placing electronic kiosks in over a dozen municipalities.

A survey of these early experiments with e-government by Dutton (1992) found that digital and electronic government initiatives at the local level fell into five general categories:

1. Broadcasting (e.g., touch-screen multimedia PCs used to disseminate civic information)
2. Transaction processing (e.g., use of magnetic smart cards in the New York City food stamp program)
3. Public records access (e.g., dial-up electronic bulletin boards in the Pasadena, CA, PARIS/PALS program)
4. Interpersonal communication (e.g., computer conferencing in the Santa Monica, CA, PEN system)
5. Surveying and monitoring (e.g., electronic surveillance, as in Caltran's experiments with toll collections).

Although the experiments of the 1980s added up to something less than a comprehensive approach, e-government was given a powerful public symbol in 1993 when the White House announced the availability of direct electronic mail access to President Clinton and Vice President Gore. As will be discussed in the next chapter, the Clinton–Gore administration played a critical role in developing and implementing the concept of e-government, and did so in a bipartisan manner that was adopted by President George W. Bush as Point 4 of his President's Management Agenda (PMA) in 2001 (OMB, 2001), when the OMB was directed to oversee 21 Quicksilver e-government initiatives (this later grew to 25 initiatives), marking the beginning of the era of full-scale e-government at the federal level.

As articulated in the PMA, the e-government strategy was premised on the belief that IT had contributed 40% of the increase in private-sector productivity growth, but that the $45 billion federal IT expenditures had not produced measurable gains in public-sector productivity. Echoing statements of the Clinton administration, the Bush PMA argued that the reason for the lack of productivity impact was that government agencies were using IT to automate existing processes rather than creating new and more efficient processes. Whereas IT offered opportunities to break down obsolete bureaucratic divisions, managers resisted cross-agency integration and instead pursued redundant IT investments, each creating separate financial, procurement, personnel, and other systems (OMB, 2001, p. 23).

The Bush PMA promised to:

> Advance e-government strategy by supporting projects that offer performance gains across agency boundaries, such as e-procurement, e-grants, e-regulation, and e-signatures. It will manage e-government projects more effectively by using the budget process to insist on more effective planning of IT investments by government agencies. A task force of agency personnel in coordination with OMB and the President's Management Council will identify e-government projects that can deliver significant productivity and performance gains across government. . . . The task force will work to create easy-to-find single points of access to government services for individuals (OMB, 2001, p. 24).

The symbol of the PMA e-government initiative was the expansion and upgrading of the FirstGov (www.FirstGov.gov) website as the premier national point of citizen entry to federal services.

The OMB report "Implementing the President's Management Agenda for e-government" (OMB, 2003a) listed as examples these Quicksilver e-government initiatives under the PMA, in addition to the FirstGov portal:

- Volunteer.gov: Supports the President's USAFreedomCorps initiative allowing citizens to volunteer for more than 100,000 openings at national parks, veteran hospitals, and other federal facilities.
- Recreation.gov: Provides citizens with one-stop online access to over 2500 national parks and public recreation area sites.
- GovBenefits.gov: One-stop access to information and services from over 400 government programs representing more than $2 trillion in annual benefits.
- Internal Revenue Service (IRS) free filing: Over 78 million Americans were eligible to file their taxes online for free.
- Integrated Acquisition Environment: IAE launched a number of key websites and tools, including the Past Performance Information Retrieval System (www.PPIRS.gov), which provided a single search and retrieval of contractor past performance information; and the Federal Technical Data System (www.FedTeDS.gov), which provided for the secure transmission and dissemination of sensitive acquisition material.
- BusinessLaw.gov: BusinessLaw.gov is an online resource guide designed to provide small businesses quick access to legal and regulatory information, compliance assistance tools, and the ability to perform online transactions.
- Regulations.gov: Regulations.gov was estimated to save $94 million by creating a single system supporting the rule-making process.
- GoLearn.gov: This online training initiative in 2003 was the most visited e-training site in the world, with more than 60 million hits for information on over 2000 e-training courses, e-books, and career development resources. GoLearn.gov has over 45,000 registered users who can receive training at a cost of pennies per course—training that would not have been possible prior to the launch of GoLearn.
- E-Payroll: The initiative consolidated government payroll processing centers from 22 to 2 payroll provider partnerships (DoD/GSA and USDA/DOI).
- E-Clearance: E-Clearance deployed an integrated database to help enable reductions in the security clearance backlog.

A 2004 Government Accountability Office (GAO) audit of the QuickSilver e-government initiatives defined some 91 specific objectives for the 25 projects. Of these, the GAO found 33 had been fully or substantially achieved; 38 had been partially achieved; and for 17, no significant progress had been made. In addition, 3 of the objectives no longer applied because they had been found to have been impractical or inappropriate. Only 2 of the 25 initiatives (Grants.gov and the IRS Free File initiative) had achieved all original objectives. For another 5, a majority of objectives had been met. For most, however, objectives were either not achieved or only partially achieved. The GAO called it "a mixed picture" (GAO, 2004a, p. 2).

Jeffrey Seifert (2003) of the Congressional Research Service has summarized the stages of development of e-government as described in numerous statements, reports, and guidelines issued by the OMB, the GAO, the federal Chief Information Officers Council, and others active in federal e-government, based on Gartner Group work, an IT consulting firm (Baum & Di Maio, 2000). In this quasi-official schema, there are four stages of e-governance:

1. Presence
   This stage is typified by a simple information-providing Web site of a passive nature, sometimes described as "brochureware," indicating the same level of functionality as a paper brochure.
2. Interaction
   The interaction stage offers simple interactions between government and citizen (G2C), government to business (G2B), or government agency to government agency (G2G). Interaction stage Web sites provide e-mail contact and interactive forms that generate informational responses.
3. Transaction
   The transaction stage enables transactions such as paying for license renewals online, paying taxes or fees, or submitting bids for procurement contracts.
4. Transformation
   The highest stage, most closely aligned with the concept of *governance*, involves a reinvention of how government functions are conceived and organized. Seifert (2003, p. 14) elaborated:

   The goal is a seamless flow of information and collaborative decision making between federal, state, local, public, and private partners. In other words, transformative e-government initiatives often seek to remove the organizational barriers that promote agency-centric solutions and, instead, promote customer-centric solutions. Some advocates suggest that, at its most advanced level, e-government could potentially reorganize, combine, and/or eliminate existing agencies and replace them with virtual organizations.

Current federal efforts are largely concentrated on achieving level 3 (the transaction stage). Although some e-government portals such as Recreation.gov do link federal, state, local, public, and private partners, at this time such efforts cannot be said to be seamless and, indeed, many of these linkages are at level 1 (brochureware). Nonetheless, the vision of progression through these four levels until virtual government is achieved at level 4 is a common gospel for the OMB spokesperson for e-governance strategy.

SUMMARY

The vision of e-governance has been over half a century in the making. Vannevar Bush's famous 1945 essay, "As We May Think," proved prophetic in many ways. Over this half century, many popular visions have been put forth. Many of the earliest visions were rooted in technological determinist theory, predicting that the tide of technology would brush aside all before it. Marshall McLuhan's global village was primarily a positive vision centering on how IT may restore the intimacy of the village and liberate the individual. Many other positive predictions were associated with the network nation vision of Hiltz and Turoff, which focused on the decentralizing and democratizing effects of new information and communication technologies.

Some visions were more extreme. Alvin Toffler's electronic cottage emphasized the demassifying and individuating effects of IT, leading to predictions of the displacement of hierarchical organization in favor of home offices and virtual networks. In a more recent and more cautionary vision, Castells' network society drew on reinforcement theory to provide a global picture of IT as a tool making the powerful more so, within the organization and among nations.

More optimistically, the smart communities movement of John Eger and others has led to widespread government activity to leverage information technology for regional development and to improve social services and the quality of community life. Drawing on sociotechnical theory like smart communities, the digital places and new urbanism concepts rally architects, city planners, and urban decision makers to more fully integrate the possibilities of IT within traditional forms.

E-government begins to come on the scene in the 1980s, but does not flower until the dawn of the new century. While many of its actual achievements are modest, the vision is not. The vision is one of progression from passive, informational e-government to interactive, transformative e-governance. The holy grail of the envisioned virtual state is the cross-agency, cross-jurisdiction, cross-sector mobilization of resources in an individualized manner through networked systems, fundamentally and forever changing the way government works.

DISCUSSION QUESTIONS

1. McLuhan introduced the concept of the global village in the 1960s in response to what he foresaw occurring as electronic media (television) replaced printed media. Give one present-day example for each of the four change processes shown in Table 1-2 and explain your reasoning.

2. McLuhan's concept of the global village and Hiltz and Turoff's concept of a network nation shared common assumptions but also differed in important respects. What were the similarities and differences?

3. In Hiltz and Turoff's 1993 revision of *The Network Nation,* they acknowledged one major mistake. What was that mistake? How would things be different if they had been correct in their original assumption?

4. Has Toffler's vision of the electronic cottage come to fruition? What is the implication of the electronic cottage in terms of mass culture? In terms of organizational management?

5. According to Castells, why is it important for both labor and management to pay attention to the design of information systems? Use the five general themes of critical theory to help explain.

6. Eger points to urban sprawl as leading to the decay of cities. How do smart communities address this problem? How effective are they, in your opinion?

7. Horan emphasizes the importance humans place on attaching meaning to physical places. With this in mind, what are the implications for the design of digital places?

8. What is the difference between e-government and e-governance? How does public administration change with the advent of e-governance according to Jane Fountain?

9. President Bush's President's Management Agenda initiative found that the $45 billion of federal IT expenses had not produced measurable gains in public-sector productivity. What reason did they attribute to this? What remedy was promoted by this initiative?

10. Describe the four stages of e-governance as described by Seifert and the Gartner Group.

GLOSSARY

Collaboratories: Combining the terms *collaboration* and *laboratory,* collaboratories are a model for virtual organization of smart communities, encouraging collaboration among government, private, nonprofit, and academic entities stemming from a shared vision for an electronic infrastructure to serve and develop the community.

Electronic cottage: The electronic cottage is a term used by Alvin Toffler to describe home offices made possible by the Third Wave infosphere, which is dissolving the linkage connecting work functions with physical work spaces associated with an organization.

Global village: The global village is a concept developed by Marshall McLuhan. According to McLuhan, a global connectedness emerges, restoring the immediacy and intimacy of village life as print media is replaced with electronic media bringing information to a worldwide audience in real time.

Infosphere: The infosphere is a construct offered by Alvin Toffler to denote the emerging information environment by which humans receive information and communicate. Toffler argues that revolutionary changes in the infosphere lead to a corresponding revolution in the structure of social life (the creation of the new sociosphere).

Reinforcement theory: Reinforcement theory is one of four general theories of information technology and social change discussed in this book. It holds that information technology is a tool, not a force in its own right (as in technological determinist theory). Its development has the general tendency of reinforcing the existing power structure of organizations, communities, and nations.

Smart communities: Smart communities provide an advanced communication and information infrastructure that enable and empower the residents and organizations. Such infrastructure is "smart" to the extent that it is interactive and transactional (not just passive, one-way electronic dissemination of information, for example). This concept is associated with a movement in city planning, architecture, and allied fields.

Sociotechnical theory: Sociotechnical theory is one of four general theories of information technology and social change discussed in this book. It holds that information technology is limited only by the constraints of the designer, not existing power structures or technological determinism, and that human factors are central to the design of information systems. It is associated with a participative approach to systems design.

Systems theory: Systems theory is one of four general theories of information technology and social change discussed in this book. Developed from the 1940s to the 1970s primarily from an engineering and scientific disciplinary base, systems theory advances 19th-century scientific management by focusing on interdependent complexity. The solution to problems marked by complex interdependence requires expert systems engineering, and efficient solutions are unlikely to come about by sheer force of technology, or by undue influence of human factors, or deference to considerations of organizational power.

Technological determinism: Technological determinism is one of four general theories of information technology and social change discussed in this book, associated with the belief that information technology is an organic force that evolves according to its own inner *telos* or direction, and as such is a powerful force in its own right, significantly altering how humans receive, process, and disseminate information.

ENDNOTES

[1]The WFFSC operates in partnership with the California Institute for Smart Communities at San Diego State University. The institute organized the first City of the Future initiative (1992), issued a *Smart Communities Guidebook*, and in 1996 developed the Smart Communities Program for the state of California in 1996.

[2]For further information, see smartcommunities.ic.gc.ca.

A Brief History of Public-Sector Information Technology Policy

In 1813, a year before the British burned the buildings of the nation's capital in "Mr. Madison's War," Congress made provision for the protection of state documents. In what may be considered the beginning of federal information policy, it was mandated that one copy of the House and Senate journals along with certain other legislative documents be made available by the secretary of state to selected universities, state libraries, and historical societies. By the 1840s, the Depository Library program was promoting the practice of agencies making their publications available to the public. The Printing Act of 1852 established the office of the Superintendent of Public Printing under the Secretary of the Interior, who in 1857, became responsible for distribution to depository libraries. On the day Abraham Lincoln was inaugurated, the Government Printing Office (GPO) was established, displacing the private printing companies serving the government at that time. The Office of the Superintendent of Documents was created in 1869, and under the Printing Act of 1895 the Depository Library program was taken over by the GPO and the *Monthly Catalog* of GPO publications was launched. There is a direct line of development of federal information policy from the wartime concerns of 1813 to the launch of electronic publication formats in the 1990s, but by then the scope of governmental publications had grown exponentially and all agencies, not just the GPO, had become outlets for federal information, often via the Internet.

The first depository library shipment under the 1895 act was sent out to 420 libraries on July 17, 1895. It contained only 11 publications of Congress. By 1922, however, depository libraries were receiving so many publications that they complained about lack of space and staff, particularly in view of relative lack of use of government documents. The GPO ended the practice of sending every library every publication and instead developed the *Classified List of United States Government Publications,* allowing libraries to select desired holdings. Only 48 of the 418 depository libraries existing in 1923 opted to continue to receive all publications. Still, by 1945, the GPO was doing eight mailings a day per library. Libraries were overwhelmed, complaining about being unable to maintain comprehensive records, to ensure documents were actually shelved, and to cope with the perishable stock paper on which documents were printed. Eventually, under the Depository Library Act of 1962, libraries were relieved of the obligation to retain forever documents they had agreed to receive; instead, 53 regional depositories were named to receive all government publications, but even they could dispose of documents after 5 years (McGarr, 2000).

During the 1980s and 1990s, governmental efforts to reduce paperwork combined with sharp cutbacks in funding for printing meant a noticeable decline in the number of federal publications in print. Information dissemination on microfiche, which the GPO had seen as a solution to the information explosion, now became viewed as outdated technology as libraries, universities, and the media retooled for the computer age. Many government publications became issued only in electronic format, abandoning print altogether. As this occurred, the GPO, which for over 100 years had been the dominant agency for information dissemination by the federal government, now became one among a larger number of players in the arena of federal information policy. The National Technical Information Service, the National Archives, the Smithsonian Institution, the office of the president, and of course the agencies themselves all have become major direct providers of federal information in electronic format. In 2004 the GPO, having already cut its consumption of paper in half in the 1992–2003 period and mounted over a quarter million free digital documents by 2004, drew up a 3-year plan to transform itself from a printing office to a manager of digital documents (Menke, 2004a).

The federal Depository Library program and the GPO were pioneers establishing the principle of information access for all Americans. At the dawn of this new century, however, information access has come to transcend the concept of document dissemination. Moreover, since the 1970s, new information policy issues have come to the fore as well, including the government's role in developing the infrastructure for information and communications technologies (ICT); leveraging information technology (IT) to promote public-sector productivity and to reinvent the way government does business; information security, particularly after the terrorist attack of September 11, 2001; and any number of regulatory issues arising from the coming of age of cyberspace.

WAR AND COLD WAR: ORIGINS OF INFORMATION TECHNOLOGY INFRASTRUCTURE IN THE UNITED STATES

In Chapter 1 we discussed the vision of the digital future foreseen by Vannevar Bush, who directed the Office of Scientific Research and Development for Franklin Delano Roosevelt. It was no accident that Bush had overseen the effort to mobilize scientists in support of military objectives in World War II, and that he was also in the best position to see and understand the potential of new electronic technologies for the future. The origins of widespread use of IT and, indeed, of the Internet itself, were inextricably linked to military uses.

The first programmable computer in the world was the Colossus, created in 1943 and in service until 1946 as a code-breaking machine built for the British war effort by Max Newman and others (Cragon, 2003; Hinsley & Stripp, 2001). There had been other earlier computers, such as Bell Lab's Z3 computer based on electromagnetic relays, but Colossus was the first digital all-electronic programmable machine, based on vacuum tube technology. It was designed and used successfully to break German military codes, which were based on teletype-like electromechanical devices built by Siemens. By the end of the war, 10 Colossus computers were in operation.

Because of the secrecy associated with the development and use of the Colossus computer, its influence on postwar IT was limited. A greater role can be ascribed to the ENIAC computer, developed between 1942 and 1946 by J. Presper Eckert and John W. Mauchly at the University of Pennsylvania for the U.S. Army, which employed it for ballistic calculations. ENIAC, which stood for *Electronic Numerical Integrator And Computer,* was a gigantic machine using more than 18,000 vacuum tubes and weighing some 30 tons.

Eckert and Mauchly went on to develop a successor computer, the UNIVAC 1 (Universal Automatic Computer 1), constructing it under the auspices of their own company. The UNIVAC 1 used 13,000 fewer vacuum tubes than the ENIAC, reducing the size of the computer by over two-thirds but still weighing eight tons! Eckert and Mauchly sold their technology to Remington Rand in 1950, and in 1951 Remington Rand sold the first UNIVAC computer to the Census Bureau, making it the first commercially available computer. It was also the first alphanumeric computer, capable of handling text for government and business. The U.S. Navy and the Atomic Energy Commission bought the second and third UNIVACs. The first private sector purchaser was General Electric, which bought the eighth UNIVAC 3 years later in 1954. UNIVACS were phased out, however, in the mid 1950s.

The advent of widespread mainframe computing in the federal government was associated with IBM's 701 computer, which was sold starting in 1952–1953 for defense purposes during the Korean War. IBM, in an alliance with Harvard University, had developed the Mark 1 computer in 1944, but it had been a relay computer, relying on decimal storage wheels and rotary dial switches. IBM chief Thomas Johnson Watson had the 701 developed specifically for the Korean War effort, as a "defense calculator." Early 701s were sold to the U.S. Navy, the Department of Defense, aircraft companies, atomic research laboratories, and other government agencies.

A new level of computer use in government was achieved by the IBM 7090, introduced in 1960 as the first commercial transistorized computer and the world's fastest. With the 7090 and its upgrades, IBM dominated the mainframe world of computing in the 1960s and 1970s. Then, in the face of competition by Apple Computer's revolutionary desktop microcomputer, IBM introduced the IBM PC in 1981. Intended as a personal computer for use in the home and not competitive with IBM's mainframe computers for business, the PC soon came into general governmental and business use, eventually ending the stand-alone mainframe architecture for IT.

In 1957 as IBM's 701 computers were coming into widespread use in the federal government, the Soviet Union launched the world's first artificial satellite, Sputnik-1. In direct response, that same year the federal government established the Advanced Research Projects Agency (ARPA) within the Department of Defense to promote defense technology. Over the next 12 years, major governmental initiatives reconstructed telecommunications infrastructure and created the predecessor of the modern Internet.

Some of these initiatives were specifically military. Semi-Automatic Ground Environment and the related Whirlwind project (1958), for instance, represented major advances in data communications technology and were used in the service of air defense. In 1960, President Eisenhower placed the National Aeronautics and Space Administration (NASA) in charge of communications satellite development. Echo, NASA's first satellite, was launched August 12 and functioned to reflect radio waves back to earth. The Communications Act of 1962 combined the efforts of AT&T, NASA, and the Department of Defense to create Comsat on February 1, 1963. In 1964, led by Comsat, a consortium of 19 nations formed IntelSat with the purpose of providing global satellite coverage and interconnectivity. IntelSat in 1965 launched the Early Bird satellite, the world's first commercial communications satellite, serving the Atlantic Ocean Region. Global satellite coverage was achieved by IntelSat 7 years later, in 1969.

In an effort that predated the modern Internet by decades, in 1965 ARPA sponsored a study of the "cooperative network of time-sharing computers." The Massachusetts Institute of Technology's Lincoln Lab and the System Development Corporation in Santa Monica, California, were directly linked via a dedicated 1200 bps phone line. Finally, in 1969 ARPAnet, the predecessor of the Internet, went online with four nodes. It reached 15 nodes by 1971, had e-mail in 1972, and international connections in 1973, the year in which Bob Kahn started the "internetting" research program at ARPA, working with others to develop many of the fundamental concepts on which the Internet rests. ARPAnet initiated online discussion lists in 1975 and suffered its first viruses in 1980 (an accidental status message virus). ARPAnet was not phased out until 1990, having performed its function as the test bed of the Internet.

ESTABLISHING THE ARCHITECTURE OF FEDERAL INFORMATION POLICY, 1946–1980

Although not directed specifically toward IT, the postwar period saw the emergence of several pillars of federal information policy.

The Administrative Procedures Act of 1946. The earliest of these critical pieces of legislation was the Administrative Procedures Act of 1946 (APA), which required agencies responsible for proposing new rules and regulations to publish them in the *Federal Register,* which developed an electronic version in 1993. More significantly, the APA required hearings and public participation in regulatory rule making. In the late 1990s the APA became a legal basis for electronic public participation in e-rulemaking.

The Federal Records Act of 1950. Four years later, the Federal Records Act of 1950 (FRA, amended 1964), mandated agencies to preserve "adequate and proper documentation of the organization, functions, policies, decisions, procedures, and essential transactions of the agency." Combined with the 1966 Freedom of Information Act and the 1996 Electronic Freedom of Information Act, the FRA became the legal basis for the mandate that federal agencies make information available online.

The Freedom of Information Act of 1966. This act, known as FOIA, established the right of public access to government information. Agencies were required to make information available automatically at their own initiative or in response to individual requests. FOIA specified certain exemptions, including classified defense and foreign policy matters, internal agency personnel rules and practices, information protected by other laws (e.g., many contractor bids), commercial trade secrets and financial information, documents normally privileged in the civil discovery context, personal information affecting an individual's privacy, investigatory records compiled for law enforcement purposes, information that might reasonably be construed to interfere with law enforcement or deprive a person of a fair trial, information revealing the identity of a confidential source, information needed to protect the safety of individuals, records of financial institutions, and geographical information on oil wells. Three decades later, the Electronic Freedom of Information Act Amendment of 1996 (EFOIA) updated the Freedom of Information Act for the digital era.

The Technology Assessment Act of 1972. This act created the Office of Technology Assessment (OTA), later disbanded as other IT agencies superceded it. The OTA, along with the Congressional Research Service (reconstituted and expanded by the Legislative Reorganization Act of 1970) and the Congressional Budget Office (created by the Budget Impoundment Act of 1974) became major users of FOIA to access executive agency data.

The Federal Advisory Committee Act of 1972. FACA was an elaboration of the 1966 FOIA legislation. It required timely notice in the *Federal Register* of advisory committee meetings. FACA also required agencies to allow interested parties to appear or file written statements and mandated that advisory committees keep detailed minutes (to include a record of the persons attending, documents received, documents issued, and documents approved by committees). These materials and all other advisory committee minutes, transcripts, reports, and studies were required to be available for public inspection.

The Privacy Act of 1974. This act protected the privacy of individuals identified in information systems maintained by federal agencies. The collection, maintenance, use, and dissemination of information were regulated. The Privacy Act forbade disclosure of any record containing personal information, unless released with the prior written consent of the individual. Agencies were also mandated to provide individuals with access to their records.

The Government in the Sunshine Act of 1976. This was another elaboration of the 1966 FOIA. It established the principle that the public is entitled to the fullest practicable information regarding the decision-making processes of federal agencies.

The Presidential Records Act of 1978. This post-Watergate legislation changed the legal ownership of the official records of the president from private to public, further expanding public access to federal information.

The Paperwork Reduction Act of 1980. The PRA mandated an information resource management (IRM) approach to federal data. This important piece of legislation was the culmination of a decade of information policy discussion and debate and represented the first truly unified policy framework for IRM at the federal level. The director of the Office of

Management and Budget (OMB) was given responsibility for developing a policy for treating information as a resource and for overseeing the implementation of an IRM plan. A major revision of the PRA in 1995 made strategic planning for IRM a federal mandate.

Thus, by the end of the 1970s, the federal government had moved from data management to IRM and had put in place the legal infrastructure to ensure both public access to federal information and also the protection of individual privacy. As later chapters will discuss, this legislation was less than effective in rendering its lofty ideals into satisfactory practice. Moreover, these acts were the architectural underpinning for what was to come, but they were written before the full impact of the IT revolution in the two decades that followed. That impact ensured that policies associated with the legislation enumerated above would continue to require revisitation for the remainder of the century and, indeed, to the present day.

FROM BITNET TO FIRSTGOV: GROWTH OF THE INTERNET, 1981–2000

The last two decades of the 20th century witnessed the coming of age of the Internet, which in turn breathed life into visions of e-governance discussed in Chapter 1. In 1981 there was no Internet. By 2000, the federal government had established an impressive presence on the Web—a presence that many thought would change everything.

The year 1981 saw the establishment of BITNET, the *Because It's Time NETwork*. This important forerunner of the Internet was initiated as a cooperative network at the City University of New York. It provided electronic mail, file transfer, and discussion list functionality. In 1986 the National Science Foundation (NSF) funded NSFNet as a backbone network. In 1987, NSF signed a cooperative agreement to manage NSFNet in cooperation with IBM, MCI, and Merit Network. By the end of 1987 there were 10,000 Internet hosts. Together, the military's ARPAnet, academia's BITNET, and the government's NSFNet formed the triad of networks that melded to become the modern Internet.

By 1984 computer networking had advanced to the point where a formally administered system of addresses was necessary. The domain name system (DNS) was established that year, allowing users to employ mnemonic Internet addresses (URLs—uniform resource locator addresses, such as www.nsf.gov) instead of numeric Internet provider (IP) addresses. The translation between URLs and their IP numeric counterparts was first done through a single lookup file, hosts.txt, maintained by UCLA's Jon Postel, on a Department of Defense contract. Later, a company called SRI maintained the lookup file, transferring it by file transfer protocol (a way to transfer computer files over networks) to server administrators around the country and around the world. In 1984, USC's Information Sciences Institute devised the modern DNS, in which DNS address information is spread out across the Internet. Maintenance of DNS administration remained under Department of Defense contract until 1991, when the NSF took over the nonmilitary portion. In 1992, NSF contracted with Network Solutions, Incorporated (NSI) to perform this function. Later, the government-created Internet Corporation for Assigned Names and Numbers assumed responsibility for the DNSs and related Internet infrastructure functions, though the military remains responsible for the .mil sector, the federal government for the .gov sector, and foreign governments for their own domains.

By 1989, the number of Internet hosts reached 100,000, and the following year ARPAnet was phased out, eclipsed by NSFNet. When the Clinton administration took office, the growing significance of the Internet was already clear. Vice President Al Gore had been a champion of the High Performance Computing Act of 1991, which authorized the creation of a "national high-performance computing program" for high-speed networking and established the National Research and Education Network. A year later the number of Internet hosts had reached one million, the first Web browser software was released (Mosaic, created by Tim Berners-Lee), and the age of Web surfing was launched. The same year, 1992, the first White House Web page was put up, and in 1993 public e-mail to the president and vice-president was inaugurated.

Up to 1992, access to the Internet backbone was limited by the NSF's "Acceptable Use Policy." This restriction, instituted by the National Science Foundation Act, prohibited commercial traffic on the Internet. Up to 1992, all Internet traffic had to be educational, scientific, or research oriented. With the support of Congressman Rick Boucher (D, VA), Chairman of the Science Subcommittee of the House Committee on Science, Space, and Technology, legislation was passed and in November 1992 President Bush signed new legislation that repealed the Acceptable Use Policy, replacing it with language that permitted commercial traffic on the Internet backbone. The effects were profound and immediate.

The commercialization of the Internet was given a further accelerant in 1992, when the Supreme Court in *Quill Corporation v. North Dakota* chose to uphold the precedent of its *Bellas Hess V. Illinois State Department of Revenue* (1967) case. These principles prohibited Internet sales taxation, overruling a North Dakota Supreme Court finding that technology had made the 1967 ruling obsolete. The tax prohibition applied to vendors with no physical presence in the state. In 1996, the World Trade Organization (WTO), meeting in Singapore, reduced tariffs on IT trade items, thereby encouraging global Internet commercial development. And in 1998, the Internet Tax Freedom Act of 1998 (ITFA) imposed a 3-year moratorium on state and local taxation of Internet access—a moratorium that was subsequently renewed.[1] The overall effect of Supreme Court, congressional, and WTO actions was to open up e-commerce as a very attractive milieu for doing business.

By the time federal funding of the Internet ended in 1993, the Internet had become a private-sector entity. Routing began through private providers in 1994. NSFNet reverted to being a limited research network. But the commercialization of the Internet did not mean the federal government had lost interest in promoting IT infrastructure—far from it. The National Information Infrastructure Act of 1993 mandated funding priority in federal research and development efforts be given to accelerated development of high-performance computing and high-speed networking services.

The federal government also became more sensitive to social problems associated with the growth of the Internet in this period. The Commerce Department's 1995 National Telecommunications and Information Administration's report, "Falling Through the Net," brought widespread public attention to the issue of the *digital divide*. In reaction, the Telecommunications Act of 1996 provided for a Universal Service Fund fee (a telephone tax, also known as the "E-rate" fund or fee), part of which became used on a Clinton administration initiative to provide modem-based Internet access to schools, libraries, Indian reservations, and other digital divide target groups.

At the start of the new millennium, on June 24, 2000, President Clinton made the first presidential Internet address to the nation, calling for the establishment of the FirstGov.gov portal, a consumer-oriented one-stop Web address leading to all that the federal government had to offer. It was seen by some as the start of building the virtual state. FirstGov.gov was launched September 22, 2000, as a Clinton management initiative that provided a gateway to 47 million federal government Web pages. FirstGov.gov also linked state, local, DC, and tribal government pages in an attempt to provide integrated service information in particular areas, such as travel. It was managed by the Office of Citizen Services and Communications within the General Services Administration (GSA). It fell short of some aspirations for it, but FirstGov.gov marked a tremendous milestone in federal IT policy.

POLICY ISSUES IN THE INFORMATION AGE, 1986–2005

The coming of the information age brought with it several policy issues, all having the common theme of applying long-standing social principles to new situations created by the possibilities of ICT. These issues included guaranteeing public access to electronic information, promoting public participation in e-government, ensuring accessibility for the disabled, protecting individual privacy, modernizing education, securing intellectual property, and, more recently, implementing electronic voting and stopping the export of American IT jobs.

Public access to electronic information. EFOIA extended the right of citizens to access executive agency records, updating FOIA rights to include access to electronic formats and mandating agencies to provide online opportunities for public access to agency information. EFOIA officially defined a *record* in very broad terms. Release of information had to be in a format convenient to the user instead of the agency's choosing, as previous case law had held. Agencies were required to make "reasonable efforts" to search electronic databases for records. Electronic reading rooms were required to have available "policy statements, administrative rulings and manuals, and other materials that affect members of the public." In 1998, the National Archives and Records Administration (NARA), in *Bulletin 98-02: Disposition of Electronic Records*, reminded agencies of their obligations under federal law to provide documentation of agency activities, including website pages and records.

Public participation in e-government. Toward the end of the last decade of the century, e-government advocates increasingly emphasized the need to go beyond passive information provision and instead actively involve citizens in agency decision processes. In 1997, the U.S. Department of Agriculture became the first federal agency to engage in e-rulemaking, soliciting Web-based comments on rules for organic foods. This initiative won the 1998 Government Technology Leadership Award. A few other agencies followed suit, but implementation of this type of initiative did not become widespread until management of e-rulemaking became one of the two dozen Quicksilver e-government projects of the Bush administration's President's Management Agenda in 2001. In 2002 the OMB called for a uniform protocol for e-rulemaking by the end of 2003. Finally, Regulations.gov was launched as a new one-stop Web portal in late 2002, part of the Bush administration e-government initiatives. On this site, citizens could find, review, and submit comments on federal documents that are open for comment and published in the *Federal Register*.[2]

Accessibility for the disabled. The Rehabilitation Act Amendments of 1986 (sometimes called the Rehabilitation Act of 1986) added Section

508 to the Rehabilitation Act of 1973. Section 508 required federal agencies to establish guidelines for making IT accessible to the disabled. Agency accessibility evaluations were mandated, and the attorney general was charged with compliance evaluation. The 1998 Amendments to the Rehabilitation Act of 1973 required federal agencies to make their electronic information, including their Internet pages, available to people with disabilities. This strengthened the Section 508 disability access standards mandated, by the 1986 amendments, though a significant loophole allowed federal agencies to be exempted from Section 508 implementation where the disability initiative in question would constitute an undue burden.

Individual privacy. Privacy in cyberspace has been a continuing congressional priority as federal IT has become pervasive, though implementation has been weak, as later chapters discuss. The Computer Matching and Privacy Protection Act of 1988 was an amendment to the Privacy Act of 1974 that extended Privacy Act protections to most forms of computer matching of individual records across agencies. However, in 1996 the Personal Responsibility and Work Opportunity Reconciliation Act, also known as welfare reform, required interstate and intergovernmental coordination for the matching of records to ensure that no individual exceeded the allotted 5-year lifetime cap on assistance. Moreover, many IT initiatives after the terrorist strike of September 11, 2001, were based on creating new levels of computer matching of individual records, often in secret and rarely with individual consent.

President Clinton, in his presidential memorandum of May 14, 1998 (*Privacy and Personal Information in Federal Records*), directed federal agencies to review their compliance with the Privacy Act of 1974. Each agency was to designate a senior official for privacy policy. Each agency was required to conduct a Privacy Act compliance review. This requirement was generalized under the Bush administration, when in 2003 the OMB required privacy assessments as part of the FY 2005 budget process. For the first time agencies were required to submit privacy assessments of major IT systems as part of their annual business case submissions. This implemented privacy provisions detailed in the E-Government Act of 2002, which included sections on privacy assessments and Web site privacy statements.

Modernizing education. In the 1990s, the federal government increased its support for modernizing technology infrastructure in public education. The Information and Technology Act of 1992 promoted technology development in public education, health care, and industry and called on NSF to fund efforts to connect K–12 classrooms to NSFNet. And, as mentioned above, the Telecommunications Act of 1996 provided for the "E-rate" telephone tax to fund Internet access for schools, libraries, and others. Likewise, the Library Services and Technology Act of 1996 provided additional IT funding for public libraries. Finally, the New Millennium Classrooms Act of 2000 provided tax incentives to corporations to donate up-to-date computers and related technology to schools and libraries.

Regulating e-vice. The dark side of the Internet also came under congressional scrutiny in the 1990s. The Communications Decency Act of 1996 (CDA) prohibited Internet distribution of "indecent" materials. A few months later a three-judge panel issued an injunction against its enforcement on grounds of vagueness. The Supreme Court unanimously ruled most of the CDA unconstitutional in 1997. Subsequently, the Child Online Protection Act of 1998 (COPA) established $50,000 fines for commercial Web publishers who knowingly used the Web to allow children to view pornography. It also required adults to have to use access codes or other registration procedures before being allowed to see objectionable material online. The American Civil Liberties Union (ACLU) took the position that COPA criminalized free speech. In the last case of its term, by a five to four vote, in the case of *Ashcroft v. the ACLU* (2004), in July 2004 the Supreme Court ruled that COPA "likely violates the First Amendment" and that the government had not shown that its more restrictive approach was more effective than less restrictive approaches such as filtering software. The case was remanded to the lower courts, where the Bush administration was expected to continue to defend the law as of this writing.

The Child Pornography Prevention Act of 1996 (CPPA) sought to outlaw digitally altering images of nude adults to make them appear to be children. This was overturned by the Supreme Court in 2002 on grounds it unduly censored artistic expression. Congress then reworded its legislation and passed the Prosecutorial Remedies and Tools Against the Exploitation of Children Today Act of 2003 (PROTECT). This also outlawed adult images being digitally altered to appear as if children were having sex and prohibited use of misleading domain names that tempt children to access pornography. An amendment to PROTECT is the Child Obscenity and Pornography Prevention Act of 2003 (confusingly also called COPPA, the same acronym as the 1998 act discussed below), which addressed the Supreme Court's 2002 decision by not mentioning artistic morphing of images at all, but instead simply outlawed solicitation to buy or sell child pornography. The ACLU found PROTECT to be a considerable improvement over the CPPA, but still found it fell short of free speech standards.

The Children's Online Privacy Protection Act of 1998 (COPPA, not to be confused with COPA, above) made it illegal to collect, use, or disclose personal information from children under 13. Enforced by the Federal Communications Commission, COPPA required those who collect data from children under 13 to first obtain parental permission. Chat rooms and similar websites were also prohibited from collecting data on children as a prerequisite for access to the sites. COPPA legal action has centered on nonpornographic commercial sites such as GirlsLife.com and Toysmart.com, which became entangled in COPPA-related Federal Trade Commission (FTC) fines and litigation. COPPA has been much less controversial than other legislation mentioned in this section and is thought to be unlikely to be overturned by the Supreme Court.

The Protection of Children from Sexual Predators Act of 1998, in its Title X, Section 604, made it the responsibility of Internet service providers (ISPs) to report to law enforcement authorities any information pertaining to child pornography, child prostitution, or child abuse. The great majority of reporting under this act has been in the first category, child pornography.

The Children's Internet Protection Act of 2000 (CIPA) was an amendment to an omnibus appropriations bill for the departments of Labor, Education, and Health and Human Services. It required use of filter software by schools and libraries that received federal funds. Part of CIPA was the Neighborhood Children's Internet Protection Act, which required schools and libraries to post Internet safety guidelines. The American Library Association and the ACLU challenged the constitutionality of CIPA, the former on digital divide grounds (poorer citizens who can only get Internet access through libraries would be restricted to a smaller, inferior subset of the Web) and the latter on traditional free speech grounds. Supreme Court upheld CIPA in a 6-3 decision on June 23, 2003.

In 2002, Congress passed the Dot Kids Implementation and Efficiency Act, creating a new .kids domain, similar to .com and .edu. This domain was to be a child-friendly space constituting a safe zone for children, monitored for content, safety, and from which all objectionable material would be removed. Online chat rooms and instant messaging were prohibited unless they could be certified as safe. The websites under this new domain would not connect a child to other online sites outside the child-friendly zone. While representing a novel approach to the issue of child protection on the Internet, as of this writing the .kids domain remains relatively unpopulated and unused.

The Controlling the Assault of Non-Solicited Pornography and Marketing Act of 2003 (CAN-SPAM) gave the FTC, state attorneys general, and

ISPs the power to enforce rules requiring senders of marketing e-mail to include pornography warnings, to offer opt-out methods, and to not use false or deceptive information in e-mail subject lines. The law became effective January 1, 2004, and authorized the FTC to impose fines up to $250 per e-mail, with a cap of $2 million for initial violations and $6 million for repeat violations (these caps do not apply to e-mail using false/deceptive subject lines). There were also criminal penalties including up to 5 years of prison. The FTC was mandated to develop a plan for a national do-not-spam registry and was authorized to launch the list after filing its report.

A 2004 study found that most spammers were ignoring the CAN-SPAM law. However, it was only in April 2004 that the first CAN-SPAM prosecutions took place against operations promoting diet patches and human grown hormone pills. In May 2004, the FTC required that the term *SEXUALLY-EXPLICIT:* appear in the subject line of sexually oriented commercial e-mail. In June 2004, the FTC advised Congress that the proposed no-spam national registry could not be implemented until technology emerged that could verify the origin of e-mail.

Securing intellectual property. Largely in response to demands from the entertainment industry, Congress moved to protect intellectual property rights through the Digital Millennium Copyright Act of 1998 (DMCA), which extended copyrights to digital media, but the "Fair Use Doctrine" was retained to promote the rights of universities, libraries, and other occasional users of intellectual property. The act also prohibited removal of *copyright management information* from electronic media, outlawing the circumvention of antipiracy access controls. The DMCA implemented the 1996 World Intellectual Property Organization (WIPO) Copyright Treaty of 1996 and the WIPO Performances and Phonograms Treaty of the same year. The next year, the Trademark Cyberpiracy Prevention Act of 1999 outlawed cybersquatting, giving corporations and others protection against those who register well-known domain names as a means of extorting fees from existing trademark owners.

Electronic voting. The "hanging chad" controversy over voting in the 2000 presidential elections motivated passage of the Help America Vote Act of 2002 (HAVA). HAVA funded replacement of lever and punch card voting technologies with new electronic systems. By January 1, 2004, states had to submit plans to switch to electronic voting machines for use in the 2006 national elections. However, since 2002, numerous issues have emerged about the security and integrity of existing electronic voting systems from Diebold and other vendors, bringing implementation into question and raising fears of litigation.

Regulating the outsourcing of IT jobs. The faltering performance of the economy and the approaching 2004 presidential elections brought another IT policy issue to national center stage: the offshoring of IT jobs to countries such as India and Ireland, where lower wages prevailed. This also raised information security issues in the case of federal IT work, as well as issues of enforcement of privacy protection legislation when work is performed abroad. Passed in January 2004, a provision of the omnibus budget bill barred companies that win federal jobs through A-76 competitions from shifting the work to other countries. The measure, known as the Thomas-Voinovich Amendment (after its two Republican sponsors), prohibited for one year any work won by a vendor from being "performed by the contractor at a location outside the United States," unless the work is already being done overseas by government employees. The bill reflected growing congressional opposition to outsourcing IT work, especially overseas.

In summary, the period from 1986 to the present has brought IT policy from the sidelines to the forefront of congressional attention. Policies have been formed and implemented in a wide variety of arenas that affect the way government does business and the rights of all Americans. The policy issues raised in each arena are far from resolved; in most cases the legislated solutions are less than effective, and much more political and agency activity may be anticipated in the future.

SECURING E-GOVERNMENT, 1986–2005

Even before the 9/11 terrorist attack on the World Trade Center, guaranteeing the security of cyberspace was emerging as a central concern for those involved in public IT policy. After 9/11, security emerged as the number one priority of federal information officers, and IT budgets were reallocated to reflect its heightened importance.

In the 1980s, security was seen primarily in terms of computer crime. The Computer Fraud and Abuse Act of 1986 imposed fines and imprisonment up to 20 years for various types of unauthorized computer access and fraud. A 1996 amendment extended coverage to all computers involved in interstate commerce and communications. The Electronic Communications Privacy Act of 1986 updated wiretap laws for the digital era and also criminalized the unauthorized capture of telecommunications between network points. The Computer Security Act of 1987 (CSA) mandated that the National Institute of Standards and Technology (NIST) develop security standards and guidelines for federal computer systems. The CSA also required that all federal agencies and their contractors establish computer security plans.

In the 1990s, the Clinton administration began to put into place the architecture for securing cyberspace against foreign and domestic enemies. In 1994, reflecting FBI support, Congress passed the Digital Telephony Act, requiring telecommunications carriers to design systems that would be tappable by law enforcement authorities. In 1998, in his Presidential Decision Directive 63 (*Protecting America's Critical Infrastructures*), based on recommendations of the President's Commission on Critical Infrastructure Protection, President Clinton set forth the goal of establishing an integrated, secure IT infrastructure by 2003. A national center to warn of infrastructure attacks was established in the National Infrastructure Protection Center. Agencies were required to establish performance measures of website security.

The Government Information Security Reform Act of 2000 (GISRA; part of the FY 2001 Defense Authorization Act) amended the PRA by enacting a new subchapter on "Information Security." Sometimes called the Security Act, this legislation required the establishment of agency-wide information security programs, annual agency program reviews, annual independent evaluations of agency programs and practices, agency reporting to OMB, and OMB reporting to Congress. GISRA covered programs for both unclassified and national security systems but exempted agencies operating national security systems from OMB oversight.

The terrorist attack of 9/11 brought an escalation of activity to the security arena. The centerpiece legislation was the Homeland Security Act of 2002, which established a chief information officer (CIO) for the new Department of Homeland Security (DHS). The CIO was to oversee the largest consolidation of federal databases in U.S. history. Other provisions of Title 2 (the Information Analysis and Infrastructure Protection title):

- Section 201—The Office of Under Secretary for Information Analysis and Infrastructure Protection was created to receive and integrate security information, design and protect the security of data, and issue security advisories to the public.
- Section 202—Transferred these units to DHS: the National Infrastructure Protection Center of the FBI (other than the Computer Investigations and Operations Section), the National Communications System of the Department of Defense, the Critical Infrastructure Assurance Office of the Department of Commerce, the Computer Security Division of NIST, the National Infrastructure Simulation and Analysis Center of the Department of Energy, and the Federal Computer Incident Response Center of the GSA.
- Section 203—This section established the secretary of homeland security's entitlement to receive intelligence and other information from agencies.
- Section 204—Allows the federal government to deny FOIA requests regarding information voluntarily provided by nonfederal parties to the DHS.

Also following 9/11, Executive Order 13231 (*Critical Infrastructure Protection in the Information Age*) created the President's Critical Infrastructure Protection Board. The board was intended to be the central executive branch policy body for cyberspace security. It was composed of senior officials from more than 20 departments and agencies.

Better known by the general public, the USA Patriot Act of 2001 became law on October 26 of that year. It gave government investigators greater authority to track e-mail and to eavesdrop on telecommunications. In September 2002, the court of review interpreted the USA Patriot Act to mean that surveillance orders under the Foreign Intelligence Surveillance Act could apply to criminal as well as terrorist cases, meaning that U.S. citizens could suffer electronic eavesdropping on a less protected basis than hitherto.

A spate of new cybersecurity legislation followed on the heels of the Patriot Act. The Cyber Security Research and Development Act of 2002 authorized funding for new computer and network security research and grant programs and shielded ISPs from customer lawsuits when they reveal customer information to law enforcement authorities. The Federal Information Security Management Act of 2002 strengthened the information security program, evaluation, and reporting requirements of federal agencies. In 2003, President Bush dissolved the Critical Infrastructure Protection Board, placing its functions in the new Homeland Security Council, which was charged with coordinating cybersecurity policy. Early strategy emphasized public- and private-sector best practices and downplayed enforcement of security policies on the private sector.

For consumers, an amendment to the Fair Credit Reporting Act strengthened laws to prevent identity theft, improve resolution of consumer disputes, improve the accuracy of consumer records, and make improvements in the use of, and consumer access to, credit information. Called the Fair and Accurate Credit Transactions Act of 2003, the law required credit reporting firms to give consumers free copies of their credit reports and the opportunity to correct them. Also, the law required that credit card receipts be shortened so as not to disclose consumer names and full credit card numbers. A National Fraud Alert System was also set up to alert businesses of accounts suspected of being involved with identity theft.

In 2004, the OMB formed the Information Systems Council (ISC) to coordinate the sharing of terrorist information. This was seen as an implementation of an August 2004 executive order by President Bush (*Strengthening the Sharing of Terrorism Information to Protect Americans*) and partially implementing recommendations of the 9/11 commission. The ISC included representation from the departments of

Commerce, Defense, Energy, Homeland Security, Justice, State, and Treasury, and the CIA, FBI, and National Counterterrorism Center. The ISC's role was to coordinate what types of information systems were deployed in these 10 agencies for purposes of antiterrorism.

Finally, the much-publicized recommendations of the 9/11 commission, centering on how to avoid future terrorist attacks, included the long-proposed establishment of a separate, secure network for federal information sharing. The McCain-Lieberman bill (for Senators Joseph Lieberman, D-Conn., and John McCain, R-Ariz.) proposed such a network in September 2004 for the dissemination of homeland security information, in spite of some criticism that the plan would reduce redundancy and increase the incentive for targeted hacking of federal information. Their bill also called for establishment of a national intelligence authority and creation of a national counterterrorism center.

BUILDING THE VIRTUAL STATE, 1990–2005

In terms of building e-government itself, one of the first important pieces of legislation in the recent period (since 1990), was the Chief Financial Officers Act of 1990 (CFOA). The CFOA called for (1) complete and timely information prepared on a uniform basis and that is responsive to the financial information needs of agency management; (2) the development and reporting of cost information; (3) the integration of accounting and budgeting information; and (4) the systematic measurement of performance. These four objectives required development of a financial information system and networked access to it, as well as a computerized performance tracking system—all central components of e-government.[3]

Political clout was given to the movement toward e-government by the establishment of the National Performance Review (NPR) on March 3, 1993. (NPR was later renamed the National Partnership for Reinventing Government). NPR represented the Clinton administration's belief in IT as a tool to reform government. Under the leadership of Vice President Al Gore, the NPR report, *Creating a Government that Works Better and Costs Less: Reengineering Through Information Technology,* signified a watershed in thinking among governmental reformers. The reinventing government movement, originated with a focus on decentralization/devolution, by 1993 had come to see e-government as a major means of leveraging reform. The Government Information Technology Services Board was created in 1993 to help implement NPR in IT arenas.

Three other developments also made 1993 a watershed year for e-government. The Government Performance and Results Act of 1993 required agencies to prepare multiyear strategic plans that described agency mission goals and approaches for reaching them. The act also required agencies to prepare annual program performance reports to review progress toward annual performance goals, which, of course, included IT goals. Executive Order 12862 (*Setting Customer Service Standards, 1993*) mandated that all agencies, including IT agencies, identify their customers, customer needs, and set standards and benchmarks for customer service, laying the basis for a policy of customer orientation as a keystone of e-government later in the decade. Finally, the Government Information Locator System (GILS) was announced February 22, 1993, as an Internet index to all federal materials. It reflected a decision of the Clinton administration to support direct agency release of electronic information, reversing a Reagan-era policy that held release should be contracted through private third parties.

The 1995 amendment to the PRA established strategic planning principles for IRM, designated senior information resources manager positions in major federal agencies, and created the Office of Information and Regulatory Affairs (OIRA) within OMB to provide central oversight of IT activities across the federal government. OIRA was mandated to "develop and maintain a government-wide strategic plan for information resources management." The OIRA director became, in principle, the main IT advisor to the director of the OMB. The PRA also called on agencies to "ensure that the public has timely and equitable access to the agency's public information," including electronically. Agency use of GILS (an Internet index to federal information) was mandated. In these ways the PRA created the control structure for implementing the e-government initiatives that were to come. To implement the PRA, the OMB's 1996 issue of Circular A-130 mandated life cycle information management planning and work process redesign.

The most important IT legislation of the decade was the Clinger-Cohen Act of 1996 (originally named the Information Technology Management Reform Act of 1996, an amendment to the PRA of 1980), which established a CIO in every federal agency, making agencies responsible for developing an IT plan that relates IT planning to agency missions and goals. The Clinger-Cohen Act also mandated top management involvement in IT strategic planning, using IT portfolio management approaches. The oversight role of the director of the OMB was strengthened. The Clinger-Cohen Act also accomplished the following:

- Encouraged federal agencies to evaluate and adopt best management and acquisition practices used by private and public sector organizations
- Required agencies to base decisions about IT investments on quantitative and qualitative factors related to costs, benefits, and risks, and to

use performance data to demonstrate how well the IT expenditures support improvements to agency programs through such measures like reduced costs, improved productivity, and higher client satisfaction

- The Clinger-Cohen Act also streamlined the IT acquisition process by ending the GSA's central acquisition authority. It placed procurement responsibility directly with federal agencies and encouraged adoption of smaller, more modular IT projects.

Later, when e-government became a priority, the existence of the CIO strategic planning structure was an important element facilitating e-government implementation at the federal level. President Clinton in 1996 issued Executive Order 13011, a companion to the Clinger-Cohen Act, creating the CIO Council, an advisory body from 28 federal agencies plus senior OMB/OIRA personnel. The CIO Council was intended to be the central interagency forum for improving agency IT practices. EO 13011 represented the presidential "seal of approval" for e-government. In practice the CIO Council was eclipsed by initiatives from the OMB itself and did not become a major generator of IT initiatives under the subsequent Bush administration.

The next major building block of IT policy was the Government Paperwork Elimination Act of 1998 (GPEA), which authorized the OMB to acquire alternative ITs for use by executive agencies (Sec. 1702); provided support for electronic signatures (Sections 1703–1707); and provided for the electronic filing of employment forms (Sec. 1705). Electronic filing of most forms was required to be in place by October 21, 2003. The GPEA was the legal framework for accepting electronic records and electronic signatures as legally valid and enforceable and also represented congressional endorsement of the e-government strategy.[4]

At the same time, advocates of privatization and outsourcing of governmental activities were making serious inroads in the world of public IT. The Federal Activities Inventory Reform Act of 1998 (FAIR) required agencies to inventory and report to the OMB all of their commercial activities. The FAIR Act then established a two-step administrative challenge and appeals process under which an interested party could challenge the omission or the inclusion of a particular activity on the inventory as a "commercial activity." Although the FAIR Act did not require agencies to privatize, outsource, or compete its commercial activities, subsequent OMB guidelines required that nonexempt commercial activities undergo a cost evaluation for a "make or buy" decision. Each time a federal agency head considers outsourcing to the private sector, a competitive process is required. FAIR put pressure on agencies to outsource IT operations. Though core operations were not to be outsourced, CIOs sometimes felt the core was encroached upon and that it was difficult to establish effective performance standards with vendors.

President Clinton endorsed the concept of a federal government-wide Internet portal, Firstgov.gov, in his Presidential Memo of December 17, 1999 (*Electronic Government*). The President announced 12 steps agencies could take, including getting forms online by December 2000, posting online privacy policies, posting e-mail contact information, and identifying e-gov "best practices." In the same year, the President's Management Council adopted digital government as one of its top three priorities. On June 24, President Clinton made the first Internet address to the nation by a president of the United States. On September 22, 2000, the FirstGov.gov portal was launched. In the 2000 election, both candidates (Gore and Bush) advocated expansion of digital government.

Though not limited to IT, the little-known Data Quality Act of 2000 (DQA, aka Information Quality Act) was significant as an example of federal policy aimed at information control. This one-paragraph provision was added without debate or hearings as Section 515a of the Treasury and General Government Appropriations Act of 2000. It charged OMB with the task of developing government-wide guidelines to ensure and maximize the quality of information disseminated by agencies. Each agency must develop an administrative mechanism whereby affected parties can request that agencies correct poor-quality information (that is, an appeals process was mandated). The practical effect of the DQA was to give primarily industry complainants the basis for holding up environmental or other reports by objecting to individual statistics, requiring agencies to provide evidence for every statistic and statement in a report recommending some action.[5]

The incoming Bush administration issued its core document, *The President's Management Agenda*, in August 2001 (OMB, 2003a). This document committed the Bush administration to five major management objectives, one of which was electronic government. In June 2001, the OMB created the position of Associate Director for Information Technology and E-Government. This gave the OMB a "point man" to give higher priority to IT initiatives, particularly the goal of creating a *citizen-centric government* through e-government. Mark Forman was the first to serve in this position.

The OMB issued the cornerstone document *E-Government Strategy* on February 17, 2002 (OMB, 2002). This document set forth the three fundamental Bush administration e-government principles: citizen-centric, results oriented, market based.[6] It also called for increased cross-agency data sharing. Some 34 specific projects were identified for funding, including the 23 (eventually 25) in the Quicksilver initiative announced in October 2001:

- Government to citizen
  - USA Service (GSA)
  - EZ Tax Filing (Treasury)
  - Online Access for Loans (DoEd)
  - Recreation One Stop (Interior)
  - Eligibility Assistance Online (Labor)
- Government to business
  - Federal Asset Sales (GSA)
  - Online Rulemaking Management (DOT)
  - Simplified and Unified Tax and Wage Reporting (Treasury)
  - Consolidated Health Informatics (HHS)
  - Business Compliance One Stop (SBA)
  - International Trade Process Streamlining (Commerce)
- Government to government
  - E-Vital (SSA)
  - E-Grants (HHS)
  - Disaster Assistance and Crisis Response (FEMA)
  - Geospatial Information One Stop (Interior)
  - Wireless Networks (Justice)
- Internal effectiveness/efficiency
  - E-Training (OPM)
  - Recruitment One Stop (OPM)
  - Enterprise HR Integration (OPM)
  - Integrated Acquisition (GSA)
  - E-Records Management (NARA)
  - Enterprise Case Management (Justice)

In 2002, the first Chief Technology Officer for the federal government was appointed. This officer was to oversee the implementation of e-government initiatives. Casey Coleman, heading up the GSA's Office of Citizen Services, was appointed July 25. Although coordination of implementation was shared with the GSA and CIO Council, the OMB retained primary responsibility for IT and e-government policy at the federal level.

Under the Bush administration, a performance engineering (systems analysis) approach to public IT and e-government became ascendant. Acting on a February 2002 recommendation from the Federal CIO Council, the OMB established the Federal Enterprise Architecture Program Management Office (FEAPMO) on February 6, 2002. In 2002 FEAPMO issued The Business Reference Model Version 1.0, which created a functional (not department-based) classification of all government services with a view to its use by OMB for cross-agency reviews to eliminate redundant IT investments and promote reusable

IT components. A Performance Reference Model (Fall 2002) set general performance measurement metrics. A Data and Information Reference Model was issued to set uniform guidelines for data needed to support Enterprise Architecture. Overall, this was reminiscent of 1960s program planning and budgeting systems (PPB): functional instead of line item budgeting, emphasis on empirical measurement of performance, strengthening top management oversight capabilities. Other 2002 developments included improvements in e-procurement and geospatial recordkeeping.[7]

Perhaps the best-known piece of 2002 IT legislation was the Electronic Government Act of 2002 (EGA), passed November 15 and signed by the president on December 16. The act was sponsored by Senator Joe Lieberman (D, Conn.) and was intended to promote e-government in all federal agencies. In essence, the EGA formalized much of what had been done by the OMB's Associate Director for IT and E-Government:

- The EGA established an Office of Electronic Government (OEG) within the OMB. The head of this office was to be appointed by the president and report to the OMB director. In essence, this formalized the administrative setup established by the OMB in 2001 under Mark Forman, making the OEG head the federal CIO and the new OEG the overseer of setting cross-agency standards, including privacy standards, and ensuring new e-government initiatives were cross-agency in nature. As such the EGA represented a direct attack on the agency-centric "stovepipe" approach to IT of prior years.
- The EGA required regulatory agencies to publish all proposed rules on the Internet and to accept public comments via e-mail as part of *e-rulemaking*.
- All information published in the *Federal Register* was now to be published on the Web also.
- The federal courts were required to publish rulings and other information on the Web.
- Privacy protections were added, prohibiting posting of personally identifiable information. Privacy notices are required, codifying a 3-year-old OMB directive to agencies.
- The EGA also promoted better recruiting and training of federal IT officers. Each agency head was required to establish an IT training program. Public–private employee exchange programs were also authorized.
- Share-in-savings IT contracting was authorized and the Federal Acquisition Regulations were changed accordingly.
- Common standards for geographic information systems (GIS) information were mandated.
- The OMB's prime role in overseeing IT security was reaffirmed, to be coordinated with the NIST's role in setting security technical standards.

The EGA authorized $45 million available to the OMB for e-government projects in the fiscal year 2003, $50 million in FY 2004, and $250 million in each of FY 2005 and 2006. However, actual appropriations deleted $40 million of the authorized $45 million, forcing the OMB to implement e-gov strategy from mostly departmental budgets. Subsequent appropriations were also far lower than originally planned.[8]

In 2003, the OMB announced "Round 2" of its e-government initiatives in March, looking beyond the initial 24 Quicksilver initiatives. Round 2 was to focus on six areas: data and statistics, criminal investigations, financial management, public health monitoring, and monetary benefits to individuals. The OMB was trying to force joint projects (e.g., Justice, Treasury, and the Environmental Protection Agency to have one criminal investigation system instead of three separate ones). However, funding of e-government initiatives for FY 2004 was cut to $1 million, far short of the $50 million over 5 years initially announced. OMB's head of the OEG, Mark Forman, quit, departing for the private sector. Future growth of e-government was called into question, at least temporarily, and agencies were forced to look largely to internal resources to implement e-government. This became increasingly difficult as spending for IT security trumped e-government priorities in the post-9/11 period.

Nonetheless, in 2004 the OMB forged ahead with an ambitious agenda for public IT and e-government. A key priority was systems consolidation. As part of FY 2005 planning, the OMB directed agencies to list human resources or financial IT systems that are in planning or acquisition stages, with a view to redirecting redundant spending and moving toward government-wide combined HR–financial applications. Also as part of FY 2005 planning, the OMB required agencies to sign fee-for-service agreements with Recruitment One-Stop, E-Training, Grants.gov, and Geospatial One-Stop portals, attempting to institutionalize an internal market to fund these e-government initiatives from departmental budgets. And in the third prong of 2004 OMB IT policy, the OMB required agencies in their FY 2005 requests to integrate security plans with IT systems proposals, providing business cases that incorporate security in life cycle planning. Starting in 2004, the OMB demanded agencies not only report security incidents but break reporting down by certified versus noncertified systems, and to identify causes of incidents, creating additional pressure on agencies to meet security standards. The OMB implemented red–yellow–green ratings of each major agency on a variety of IT dimensions, including both e-government and security. To get green, agencies must attain security certification for 90% of their IT systems.

Most recently, the Bush administration has pushed ahead with its privatization and outsourcing agenda. This agenda is implemented directly in the OMB's A-76 guidelines for competing federal jobs as discussed in Chapter 10 and indirectly through the General Services Administration Modernization Act of 2005 (GSAMA), which is pending and expected to pass at this writing. GSAMA promotes partnering and outsourcing by permitting public- and private-sector acquisition staff to work in each other's organizations for a period of time. The GSAMA also makes permanent controversial share-in-savings contracting and requires agencies to use commercially available online procurement services. All this is to be overseen by a new Federal Acquisition Service, which incorporates the former Federal Technology Service and Federal Supply Service.

SUMMARY

From the War of 1812 to the war on terrorism, federal information policy has been influenced by military events. From the protection of national records in 1813 to the protection of the nation's electronic infrastructure in 2004, the underlying continuity of policy has been national action to establish and safeguard information as a national resource. The great achievement of the 19th century was the creation of the GPO under the Superintendent of Documents, with distribution through the Federal Depository Library Program.

In the aftermath of World War II, Vannevar Bush laid out the vision of what was to one day be called the Internet, calling for the mobilization of science to serve the goal of expanding human knowledge. Government subsidy and direction marked the advent of the computer age, with the first mainframe computers being created for the military, and later, used by large federal agencies such as the U.S. Census. The origins of the Internet may be traced to the ARPA of the Department of Defense and to NSFNet, and federal subsidy did not end until the early 1990s. Even the commercialization of the Internet came about through legislation.

Several important lines of policy making mark the study of modern IT policy in the United States:

- Increasing public access to information, from the FOIA of 1966 to the launch of FirstGov.gov in 2000
- Increasing public participation, from the APA of 1946 to the launch of Regulation.gov in 2002
- Protecting citizen rights, from the Privacy Act of 1974 to the OMB requirement of privacy assessments in 2003
- Establishing a comprehensive approach to the management of public information systems, from the PRA of 1980 to the Clinger-Cohen Act of 1996 and the EGA of 2002

- Securing the infrastructure of cyberspace, from the Computer Fraud and Abuse Act of 1986 to the Homeland Security Council of 2003 and the ISC of 2004.

Along the way, information policy has expanded into such issues as providing accessibility for the disabled, modernizing education, securing intellectual property, implementing electronic voting, and stopping the export of American IT jobs, to name a few.

Today, in the first years of the 21st century, the evolution of information policy is at a crossroads. E-government struggles to expand in an era of budgetary austerity. The protection of citizen rights struggles to survive in an age of counterterrorist surveillance. Efforts to expand public participation face the long-term trend of increasing levels of nonvoting and disbelief in the efficacy of government. Sociotechnical approaches to IT, emphasizing the human factor, find diminishing leeway as systems management becomes the dominant theoretical foundation of those charged with implementing federal information policy. And the core IT capabilities of federal agencies are stretched to the limit by the privatization and outsourcing of their former functions.

In the adverse setting that faces much of the public IT world, the good news is that citizens and presidents alike believe in the efficacy of IT solutions to the problems governments face. Whether from resignation to technological determinism or systems theory assumptions that IT methods equate to efficiency or, for that matter, from actively embracing the belief that IT will reinforce their power, political leaders are more prone than ever to give priority to legislation and executive branch actions that advance public IT policies.

DISCUSSION QUESTIONS

1. What were some of the hurdles the federal government had to clear with respect to saving and sharing information with the public between 1813 and 1945? How have these hurdles changed since entering the electronic age?
2. How has the national defense sector influenced the development of electronic communications?
3. The Internet has not always been open for commercial use. What events occurred to change the Internet from a strictly educational, scientific, and research-oriented tool to what it is today?
4. The move to privatization and commercialization of the Internet provided new challenges for the government with respect to social issues. What is the *digital divide*, and what actions have been taken by the federal government to bridge it?

5. What steps have been taken by Congress, the FTC, and Internet providers to stop SPAM? What barriers remain in the way of effectively regulating SPAM?
6. Pre-Internet computer crime legislation dealt mainly with fraud and unauthorized access. With the advent of the Internet how has computer crime changed, and what steps have been taken to curb it?
7. How have counterterrorism efforts of the federal government impacted citizen's rights?
8. The outsourcing of IT positions is currently a controversial issue. Discuss pro and con arguments for outsourcing and for associated legislation.
9. What steps have been taken to move federal government away from providing purely passive information on the Internet to actively involving citizens in electronic rulemaking?
10. The funding of federal IT projects remains a challenge. What has the OMB required of participating agencies in order to continue funding in recent years?

GLOSSARY

Administrative Procedures Act of 1946: This act required the publication of proposed federal rules and regulations in the *Federal Register*. It also required agencies to hold hearings and ensure public participation as part of agencies' rule-making processes. In 1993 an electronic version of the *Federal Register* was created. The APA laid the legal basis for e-regulation.

Clinger-Cohen Act of 1996: Also known as the Information Technology Management Reform Act of 1996, this act was an amendment to the Paperwork Reduction Act of 1980. It established a chief information officer within each federal agency, responsible for developing an agency IT plan that incorporated the agency's missions and goals. The act also mandated top management involvement in IT strategic planning, encouraged the evaluation and adoption of private- and public-sector best management practices, required qualitative and quantitative information to be used in IT investment decision making, and streamlined the IT acquisition process.

Computer Fraud and Abuse Act of 1986: This act imposed fines and imprisonment on those found guilty of such computer crimes as unauthorized computer access and fraud. The 1996 amendment extended the legislation to cover all computers involved in interstate commerce and communication.

Electronic Government Act of 2002: This act promoted e-government for federal agencies. It established an Office of Electronic Government within the Office of Management and Budget to oversee the setting of cross-agency standards and to make sure new e-government initiatives adhered to the standards. The act also formalized prior OMB directives that required regulatory agencies to publish proposed rules on the Internet and to accept electronic public comments.

FirstGov.gov: This Internet portal, launched on September 22, 2000, was the product of a Clinton administration management initiative to improve public access to federal information and services. At its inception, this consumer-oriented portal provided access to 47 million federal government, tribal government, state, and District of Columbia Web pages. The portal was expanded under the Bush administration.

Freedom of Information Act of 1966 (FOIA):   This act established the right of the public to have access to federal information. Agencies were directed to make available, either automatically or upon an individual's request, their information with several exemptions for law enforcement, military, intelligence, and other agencies. Also exempted was information pertaining to internal rules and personnel issues, trade secrets, individual privacy, items protected by existing laws, information that could affect law enforcement or trials, and geographical information on oil wells. Thirty years later FOIA was amended to reflect the rising influence of the Internet. The 1996 E-FOIA directed executive agencies to provide electronic information in a format most convenient for the user, and electronic reading rooms were mandated.

Homeland Security Act of 2003:   This act was created in the aftermath of September 11; this legislation established a chief information officer for the new Department of Homeland Security, responsible for the largest consolidation of federal databases in the history of the United States as well as several changes in data storage, sharing, and accessibility. This included the right of the federal government to deny FOIA requests on information provided voluntarily by nonfederal parties to the Department of Homeland Security for reasons of homeland security.

Information Systems Council of 2004:   Created under the Office of Management and Budget, this body coordinates the sharing of terrorist information between agencies. The council was created in part in accord with the recommendations of the 9/11 commission. Representatives from 10 federal agencies presented a plan in December 2004 detailing what information systems should be deployed.

Paperwork Reduction Act of 1980 (PRA):   This act mandated the first unified policy framework for information resource management within the federal government. The PRA required that the director of the OMB develop a resource management plan for information and to oversee its implementation. In 1995 the PRA was revised to require strategic planning for information resources management at a federal level.

Privacy Act of 1974:   This act regulated the collection, maintenance, use, and dissemination of federal information in order to protect the privacy of any individuals identified there within. Any disclosure of private information required prior written consent from the individual. The act was amended by the Computer Matching and Privacy Protection Act of 1988 to extend the protections of the act to most computer matching of individual records across agencies.

Regulations.gov: This Internet portal provided an electronic space for citizens to review and then provide feedback on proposed rules and regulations from the *Federal Register*. It was launched in late 2002 as a product of the Bush administration's e-government initiative to provide active electronic opportunities for public participation in rule making.

ENDNOTES

[1] President Bush signed the Internet Access Taxation Moratorium on November 28, 2001, extending the 1998 ITFA to November 1, 2003. The moratorium on Internet taxation was seen by the Bush administration as an economic stimulus as well as a promotion of Internet industries, but state governments feared significant revenue losses. The Bush administration supported a permanent extension of the moratorium, which passed the House, but the Senate voted only for an additional four years in April 2004. At this writing, the two versions had not been reconciled.

[2] The URL is http www.regulations.gov.

[3] The Federal Financial Management Improvement Act of 1996 (FFMIA) required agency financial management systems to comply with federal financial management system requirements, applicable federal accounting standards, and the *U.S. Government Standard General Ledger*. To the extent that federal accounting standards specify IT aspects, the FFMIA requires uniformity of IT accounting across the federal government.

[4] The IRS Restructuring and Reform Act of 1998. Section 2001c promoted electronic filing of tax returns. Section 2003d required the IRS to establish that all forms, instructions, publications, and other guidance be available via the Internet. Section 2003e provided for tax return preparers to be authorized electronically to communicate with the IRS. Section 2005 provided taxpayers electronic access to their accounts by 2006. In 1998 also, the Postal Service launched e-commerce, selling stamps via the Web. The Check Clearing for the 21st Century Act of 2003 allowed the substitutability of electronic images of checks for physical transfer of printed checks among banks. It did not mandate electronic check clearance but made it legally equivalent.

[5] Jim J. Tozzi, former Reagan administration head of the Office of Information and Regulatory Affairs, later turned lawyer-lobbyist for chemical, rubber, pesticides, agriculture, and other industries, challenged the EPA's regulation of the chemical atrazine on the ground that since there were opposing findings in the literature, the information used by the EPA could not be said to be reliable since the same findings could not always be reproduced. The *Washington Post* quoted Natural Resources Defense Council scientist Jennifer Sass as saying the act has "hamstrung EPA's ability to express anything that it couldn't back up with a mountain of data. It basically blocked EPA scientists from expressing an expert opinion." Atrazine was eventually given the go-ahead as a hormone blocker

sprayed on corn, in spite of considerable but not universal evidence that it might cause cancer (Weiss, 2004, p. 7).

[6]President Bush issued a Presidential Memo on the Importance of E-Government in July 2002, stating, "My administration's vision for government reform is guided by three principles. Government should be citizen-centered, results oriented, and market based."

[7]The General Services Administration and the Office of Federal Procurement Policy, with involvement from DOD, NASA, and NIH, advanced e-procurement by establishing the Past Performance Information Retrieval System in 2002 to give online access to past vendor performance records. Also in 2002, the OMB issued a revision of Circular A-76 in October, replacing lowest-cost acquisition with best-value acquisition, a goal long sought by CIOs. The circular also encouraged outsourcing, in line with the Bush administration's goal to outsource 15% of "noninherently governmental jobs."

The OMB issued a revision of OMB Circular A-16 in August 2002 setting guidelines for standardizing GIS data collection records. This laid the basis for its Geospatial One Stop portal, one of 24 OMB e-government Quicksilver initiatives. Circular A-16 was originally issued in 1953 to give OMB authority over surveying and mapping.

[8]The GSA was also authorized $8 million for digital signatures and $15 million for maintenance and improvement of FirstGov.gov and other portals. FirstGov.Gov will be improved by adding a subject directory so pages can be accessed by topic rather than by agency.

Politics & Policy

3

E-Democracy

E-democracy may seem to be a strange topic in a book about management. E-democracy may seem, well, too political. Certainly, when we think of e-activism, from Internet use by the prodemocracy demonstrators in Tiénnamen Square to terrorists' use of the Internet in the post-9/11 world, the notion of e-democracy seems remote from the day-to-day concerns of public managers. True, the wise public sector leader is attuned to the reality that agency budgetary success rests on coalition building, and in today's world, electronic outreach to online groups is something ignored at the administrator's political peril. However, e-democracy goes far beyond e-activism.

E-activism can be seen as the outer circle of a half dozen layers of e-democracy, as illustrated in Figure 3-1. At the center of Figure 3-1 is e-participation, a dimension of e-democracy that is implemented by managers and that impacts them directly. At the periphery is e-activism, which affects the political environment of the agency. In between are other layers that also affect what public managers do, some directly, some indirectly. The two inner layers are not optional for federal managers but are mandated by law.

What are each of these six layers of e-democracy and how are they related to the role of the manager?

E-participation. This layer refers to use of electronic means to encourage public participation in governmental decision making or agency rule making. As mentioned in Chapter 2, public participation has been an agency mandate since the Administrative Procedures Act of 1946. E-rulemaking was a priority under Bush's President's Management Agenda initiative, and since 2002 has been a subject of Office of Management and Budget (OMB) guidance for federal departments.

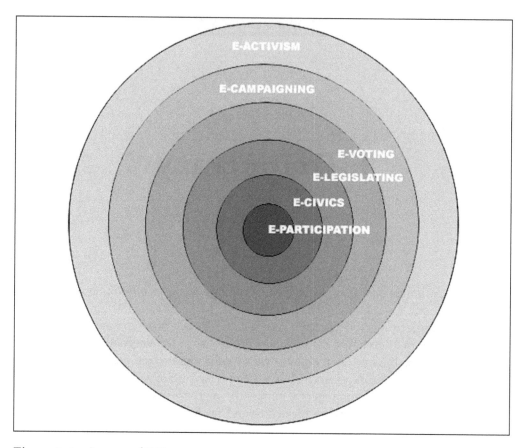

Figure 3-1   Layers of E-Democracy.

E-civics. *This* refers to the use of electronic means to provide citizens access to agency information. As also mentioned in the previous chapter, public access to agency information has been a mandate for federal managers since the Federal Depository Library Program in the 1800s, a requirement applied specifically to electronic documents and digital information by the Electronic Freedom of Information Act of 1996.

E-legislating. This layer refers to the use of electronic means to enhance the legislative process. Because agencies themselves are important actors in the policy networks that are associated with setting agendas and legislation, this layer of e-democracy, while not mandated in the case of most agencies, is an increasingly significant part of the agency environment and provides an avenue both for legislative oversight of the bureaucracy and for agency influence on the legislative process.

E-voting. This refers to the use of electronic means to implement voting or polling processes, not necessarily limited to traditional political elections. The primary managerial potential for e-voting lies in the area of securing participation and feedback from stakeholder groups and from the public on agency priorities and actions, though it could be used internally for purposes of organizational development.

E-campaigning. This layer refers to the use of electronic means to mobilize volunteers, raise funds, disseminate information, and otherwise pursue the various functions of running for elective office. Public managers are prohibited under the Government Ethics Code Act of 1992 and other legislation from campaigning using agency funds, equipment, or time, but it is not unusual for incumbent political leaders to promote agency information that is favorable to their agendas, including promotion by electronic means.

E-activism. This refers to the use of electronic means to mobilize volunteers, raise funds, disseminate information, and otherwise pursue the various functions of interest groups that seek to influence public policy. Although sometimes thought of in terms of peace groups, environmental groups, or protest groups, most e-activism is associated with labor and especially with business interest groups, if only because of their greater resources. Although outside the public sector, interest groups are part of the agency's environment, and public managers may wish to take a proactive, coalition-building stance toward them, understanding the importance of alliances in promoting agency objectives.

The six layers of e-democracy entail many new roles for public managers, many new challenges, and many new opportunities.

In terms of theories of information technology (IT) and social change discussed in Chapter 1, technological determinists often foresee the most sweeping effects, concentrating on the outer layers of e-democracy and forecasting revolutionary dispersion of power through e-activism, a new grassroots politics through e-campaigning, and a new era of revitalized governance through direct e-voting by citizens on policy issues. Technological determinists tend to believe that today's technological possibilities will become tomorrow's sociopolitical realities.

Sociotechnical theorists, who at one time concentrated on intraorganizational processes of team building around the introduction of information systems, now have expanded their horizons to apply the same arguments about team building, organization development, and human factors, to the extraorganizational environment in relation to creating digital places, smart communities, and a participative approach to e-governance. Sociotechnical theorists tend to emphasize building collaboratories in the e-activism layer with a view to implementing creative, participative systems in the inner two layers (the e-civics and e-participation layers).

Systems theorists tend to focus on engineering approaches to managerial systems issues. The outer layers of e-democracy are generally not their concern, except insofar as they may be called upon to design electronic voting machinery, develop mass e-mailing databases for campaigns, or some other component of one of these layers. Their concern is more likely to be reflected in the attempt to apply best business systems practices to e-government, such as in the OMB's performance engineering guidelines for IT planning or in risk management for complex systems (Moynihan, 2004). The practical focus tends to be on such objectives as elimination of system redundancy (e.g., replacing multiple agency payroll systems with a single cross-agency system), establishing standards (e.g., e-authentication standards for citizen transactions), or creating appropriate electronic infrastructure (e.g., the OMB's information architecture guidelines). That is, the main thrust of systems theory in public information systems applications is toward an ever more comprehensive and integrated e-civics, with the corresponding electronic back-office support for it, with only occasional forays into the other dimensions of e-democracy.

Reinforcement theorists, of course, play the role of critics (hence, *critical theory*), emphasizing the imbalance in e-activism, favoring well-financed and politically more powerful interest groups, and likewise favoring the dominant parties in e-campaigning, e-voting, and e-legislating. They view attempts at e-civics and e-participation as efforts to reinforce existing power structures, not truly democratize them, much less overturn traditional hierarchies. Reinforcement theorists would find no surprise in the fact the military sector is by far the largest investor in e-systems of all sorts, from e-surveillance to e-propaganda to e-logistics. They would find no surprise in the dominance of Internet culture by the most powerful nations, or, at the organizational level, they find no surprise that predictions of "an end to hierarchy" have come to naught in the information age. Information tools serve hierarchy in the view of reinforcement theory, in each of the six domains of e-democracy.

E-ACTIVISM

If the Internet had military origins, by the 1990s e-activism had become a strategy of a wide variety of interest groups. Many of the early examples were protest groups, which fit in with the views of certain technological determinists who believed that new IT would lead to a profound democratization of political life. HandsNet (www.handsnet.org), for instance, was founded in 1987 as an online network for human services activists, and it served to bring thousands of organizations online, providing information, training, strategic planning seminars, and content services, all in the cause of social change in health, poverty, housing, and other areas of social concern. Likewise, the Institute for Global Communications (IGC; www.igc.org/) became host to EcoNet, PeaceNet,

WomensNet, and AntiRacismNet (Vance, 1991). Also founded in 1987, the IGC was the original host to LaborNet (www.labor net.org), which became independent in 1991, and to ConflictNet, which has ceased to exist. At its peak in 1998, IGC had a full-time staff of over three dozen. As of 2004, over 250 nonprofit groups hosted their websites through the IGC. Early e-activism in community organizing and social change is detailed in Mizrahi, Downing, Fasano, et al. (1991), and more recent experiments are treated in N. Roberts (2004).

The 1980s and 1990s also witnessed the community computing movement, part of whose ideology was "empowering the powerless." Some of the empowerment rhetoric is illustrated by Kolleck (1993, p. 463), who argued that "The powers which are in new techniques have to be given back to the people to help them stand on their own and act responsibly." Often empowerment had to do with job training or personal skill improvement, not political action. Kolleck, for instance, was advocating computer courses in youth centers and using the Internet for counseling the disadvantaged, not for organizing protests.

The community computing movement was (and is) just that, a movement, not a specific organization. Labels associated with this movement are civic networks, community networks, community computing centers, and public access networks. Many were organized under the National Public Telecomputing Network (NPTN), a nonprofit organization coordinating dozens of "Free-Net" projects in the United States and abroad.[1] Perhaps the earliest specific community computing movement project was Community Memory, in Berkeley, California, founded in the 1970s explicitly as a model of how computing could transform a community. Locations included libraries, community centers, and laundromats, and activities centered on reading and contributing to forums ranging from organizing anti-Vietnam marches to discussing the lunch menu at senior citizens' centers. Other later examples included Paying to Win, started in Harlem in 1981 and spreading to 50 cities, focusing on computer literacy and economic self-sufficiency for low-income residents; the New York Youth Network, established in 1987 by social service agencies promoting online discussions about gangs, teen pregnancy, and social problems; and the Big Sky Telegraph project, founded in 1988 to promote rural development.

Innovative communities also experimented with e-activism in the 1980s. The most publicized example was the Public Electronic Network (PEN) sponsored in the late 1980s by the city of Santa Monica, California. PEN hosted discussion forums similar to some community computing movement projects, but it also had heavy doses of e-civics (e.g., access to governmental information such as city council reports and the library online catalog) and touches of e-participation (e-mail to city officials and access to the city council's agenda). Although city politicians found it lacking as a participative forum (too many unrepresentative hecklers, activists, and political junkies), it was a pioneering example of e-civics that was a model for other communities.

Among the most successful efforts at community e-activism was the Cleveland Free-Net, an "electronic city" with tens of thousands of members and representation from hundreds of community organizations, ranging from Alcoholics Anonymous to the Lesbian/Gay Community Service Center to the United Way and the Cleveland Institute of Music. Each group maintained information in its own area, though there were common forums and other forms of e-activity. However, the Cleveland Free-Net closed down in 1999, as did many other community computing projects as functions such as provision of community forums, access to civic information, computer literacy training, and networking among socially concerned groups became institutionalized in other venues. NPTN went bankrupt. The Akron Free-Net was absorbed by the city's public library. Santa Monica's PEN evolved into a very conventional municipal home page (pen.ci.santa-monica.ca.us/).

Although there have been some successes, and the community computing movement is alive and well, if one goes back a decade to read the enthusiastic literature about e-activism, one cannot help but be struck by the fact that most of the great success stories of the day have now either disappeared or have had only marginal impact. In an empirical study of some 40 information networks of the type associated with the community computing movement discussed above, Tonn, Zambrano, and Moore (2001, p. 201) concluded bluntly, "It does not appear that, either individually or in combination, the websites are working to strengthen the social capital of the communities they serve." In many cases, the business model for community computing and e-activism was shaky at best, leaving pioneers without an adequate revenue stream to fund their vision. Often that vision was quite conventional, and the envisioned functions were taken over and institutionalized by city governments, public libraries, Internet service providers, and activist and interest groups themselves.

Of course, examples can be cited where e-activism has been a powerful tool of radical protest. During the prodemocracy upheavals in China in 1989, computer networks played a key role in providing news about protests alternative to state-controlled broadcasts (Leitschuh, 1989; Lyons, 1989). Ganley (1991) detailed how information access through computer media has played a critical role in such modern events as the 1978–1979 Islamic revolution in Iran, the 1986 unseating of Ferdinand Marcos in the Philippines, the 1987–1988 attempt to remove General Manuel Noriega as leader of Panama, the 1988 efforts of opposition parties to obtain independent voting results in the Chilean plebiscite, and the 1989 prodemocracy movement in the People's Republic of China. The activist network EcoNet was instrumental in promoting Earth Day around the world (Richardson, 1990), and the women's movement was advanced by various online services (Atkinson & Hudson, 1990). In 1994, skillful mobilization of worldwide Internet-based support for the Zapatistas in Chiapas, Mexico, led to unanticipated concessions by the Mexican government to the Zapatistas (Ronfeldt & Arquilla, 1998; McGirk, 1999). More recently there was the gathering of e-petitions contributing to the removal of Philippine President Joseph Estrada from office in 2000 (CNN, 2000; Bagalawis, 2001). To this day, NetAction.org provides online training materials on how to be a virtual activist (see www.netaction.org/). Internet activism is still important in China (Amnesty International, 2004), and recent international protests against meetings of the World Trade Organization would probably be impossible without the Internet. Nonetheless, in spite of the assertions of some (e.g., Downing, 1989) that activist networks such as Peacenet in the United States are new options for democracy, such examples are dwarfed by conventional system-maintaining uses by mainstream institutions. This prevents one from characterizing information and communications technologies as a whole as instruments of disruption, empowerment, or structural change, though occasionally they are.

Back in 1986, one commentator on Berkeley's "radical" Community Memory experiment wrote that community computing could:

> point to the potential for political participation and organization through networks of computers connected by phone lines; the ability of individuals and small groups to gain access to and manipulate data, do typesetting, and perform other tasks that previously required large and costly machines; and, perhaps most important, the demystification of computers themselves (Siegel, 1986, p. 116).

Two decades later, computers were largely demystified, online publishing was routine in an era of blogs and e-zines, electronic access to data was official government policy, individuals could connect for free through Yahoo! Groups and similar venues and political parties and interest groups were spending millions to secure citizens' political participation.

If e-activism has not revolutionized American politics, it has transformed the way interest groups do their business. Visit the website of almost any well-heeled interest group, and one will find concerted efforts to use ITs to mobilize members and supports. For instance, the website of the American Association of Retired Persons (AARP) at www.aarp.org, an organization with nearly 36 million members, features e-mail subscription to its newsletter, an opportunity to join message boards of one of its online communities (e.g., there's one for educators), online subscription and renewal of membership, online periodicals in English and Spanish, online press releases and an opportunity to subscribe to them electronically (also in two languages), online solicitation of funds for its foundation, online solicitation of volunteers, online learning opportunities, online publications of its Public Policy Institute, Web links to allied groups, online solicitation to become an advocate "and make your voice heard in Washington," and much more. Various links from its home page target not only seniors, but also others the AARP seeks to influence on behalf of its members: journalists and media representatives, researchers, and educators. To take an entirely different arbitrary example, the National Pork Producers Council (www.nppc.org), an organization whose members are 44 state-level pork associations, has such e-activism features as an online Legislative Action Center that guides users both to elected representatives and to congressional agendas; a "tell a friend" feature for easy e-mailing with the default message "I just took action on this issue and thought you might find it interesting too"; the opportunity to download a "Write to Congress" Web sticker for one's own website; online news releases, policy reports, and publications; pork industry-related screensavers and e-postcards; an e-mail list for pork recipes; links to allied groups like Pork4Kids and PorkTimes; and much more. Although political activist groups such as Econet provide online membership, solicitation of volunteers, online fund-raising, Web publications, and online advocacy tips, in general the e-activism of protest groups pales in comparison with the e-activism of resource-advantaged interest groups.

This brings us back to the role of public managers. At first consideration, e-activism might seem to be far removed from the functions of the public administrator. However, almost every public agency exists in an environment that includes interest groups focused on policies with which the agency deals. Increasingly these interest groups are using various forms of e-activism to influence public opinion and legislation that affects the agency. Although many public managers assume a passive posture toward these developments, others do not. Proactive strategies of managers include (1) publicizing friendly e-activism sites (e.g., as the Environmental Protection Agency does[2]); (2) reprinting supportive e-activism online publications on agency websites (e.g., the Department of Health and Human Services publicizes the AARP's Public Policy Institute reports[3]); and (3) engaging in agency e-activism of their own (e.g., the Department of Housing and Urban Development has created online message boards for insurance underwriters rather than just leaving such online community formation to the insurance industry alone.[4]

E-CAMPAIGNING

E-campaigning first came to widespread public attention in the 1992 presidential election campaign, when it was endorsed by independent candidate Ross Perot. Hundreds of private electronic bulletin boards figured heavily in the Perot campaign. Also in 1992, for the first time a major Democratic candidate (Jerry Brown) campaigned on electronic bulletin board system (BBS) services like CompuServe instead of just on television, radio, and the press (Higgins, 1992).

Among the most notable examples of e-campaigning is MoveOn.org, an online fundraising and political mobilization group that claims two million activist supporters. In Campaign 2000, MovOn.org raised over $3 million to elect four new senators and five new house members. In 2003, MoveOn.org raised $700,000 for Minnesota Senator Paul Wellstone after he voted against the Iraq War resolution, then another $200,000 in two hours for his replacement when Wellstone was killed in an airplane crash (Packer, 2003). Its 2003 "Virtual March on Washington" resulted in over a million phone calls and faxes against the war in Iraq. In 2004, MoveOn.org mobilized a half million volunteers in its "Bake Back the White House" campaign of 1100 bake sales to raise funds in Campaign 2004.

MoveOn offered to advise the nine Democratic candidates in Campaign 2004 about use of e-campaigning, but only the campaign of Howard Dean accepted the offer, perhaps because he had been front-runner on a MoveOn online presidential preference poll. Dean did not get the Democratic presidential nomination, but he was an early front-runner who emerged from obscurity through a dramatic mobilization of money and volunteers, largely through the Internet and partly through the help of MoveOn. This model was widely noted by other candidates and by both parties. It is certain to be widely imitated in future American politics (Rivero, 2004). The success of MoveOn was implicitly acknowledged when, in 2004, President Bush called for a prohibition against political activities of 527 organizations, referring to Section 527 of the IRS Code, under which MoveOn operates in conformity with the McCain-Feingold campaign finance reform legislation.

Of course, e-campaigning does not always lead to political mobilization. This point was made by Alexis Rice, whose Johns Hopkins University study of the effect of Internet blogs on the 2004 presidential campaign documented that while more citizens use the Internet for purposes of political participation, they are not necessarily more politically active (Williams, 2003). The ease of Internet involvement may work for more Internet use, but to move beyond ease and into actual participation may require stronger motivation, such as anger over actions of an incumbent president, as the MoveOn.org case illustrates.

Moreover, in some ways IT in support of e-campaigning may be working against the spirit of American democracy. Novotny's (2002, p. 65) study of presidential election campaigns and IT noted, for instance, that technology was furthering political disengagement of the citizen: "Where candidates once coveted relationships with voters in their districts, they now purchase lists of these same voters on CD-ROM and data files on the World Wide Web as a part of the new campaign technologies." The personal relationship of the urban resident with the city ward boss is replaced, in this view, by the impersonal relationship of the isolated cybercitizen to an automated e-campaign website.

As the techniques developed by industry to profile consumers are adapted by e-campaigners to profile voters and potential votes, the 19th century issue of buying votes has resurfaced in a new form. A *New York Times* article, for instance, discussed the political consulting firm, Aristotle International (VoterListsOnline.com), which sells personal data from its massive database of over 150 million voters. Dozens of variables are available for each voter, including telephone numbers, ethnicity, car ownership, name of employer, and income. The *New York Times* reported that in the 2000 campaign, two-thirds of House and almost three-quarters of Senate candidates used Aristotle lists, not to mention President George W. Bush (Wayne, 2000). E-campaigning is not primarily a voluntary political activity—rather, it is a business. The firm E-Campaigning.com is one of a great many that sell such services as campaign computer network installation, online fundraising, custom website packages, e-mail/fax campaigns, or you can click a button to invoke "eCampaign Builder" and buy your own custom political campaign. Although campaign consulting has been central to American political campaigns for some time, IT has enhanced its pervasiveness and power in ways hitherto unseen.

With the rise of e-campaigning as a business come privacy issues, which Christopher Hunter has noted:

> Through the use of cookies, online donation forms, and political mailing lists, Internet-based campaigns can now gather tremendous amounts of information about which candidates voters prefer and where they choose to surf. The creation and sale of such detailed voter profiles raises serious questions about the future of political privacy and the democratic electoral process itself (Hunter, 2002a, p. 1).

Moreover, the threat to citizen privacy with regard to e-campaigning databases is rendered even more problematic by stringent Federal Election Commission disclosure rules.

Imagine a society in which e-democracy prevails, from online input into city council meeting on up to e-campaigning and electronic voting. There are many ways one might also imagine such an e-democracy being sabotaged. Political junkies, hecklers, and just plain nuts find it gives them a sense of power and is fun to try to dominate all online discussion forums, which turns off ordinary citizens. Political candidates find it is not worthwhile to expose themselves to the hassle and disengage. Interactive forums cease to be meaningful vehicles for policy discussion. E-campaigning becomes a political consulting profession: people are hired whose sole job it is to bad-mouth the opponents of those who hired them. They rely on facts when they can, innuendo and half-truths when it benefits them. Ordinary citizens do not have time to put in the equivalent effort. Interest groups line up volunteers to swamp e-forums, e-lists, and e-bulletin boards. They find it is a good way to make members feel involved and to lobby. However, this tends to attract activists, who have more extreme views. The overall result is polarization of the discussion. Again, political decision makers come to see e-democracy vehicles as biased and prefer to rely on public opinion polls, which are more representative. Corporate interests and others with access to mass e-mailing lists become disproportionately influential. Average candidates are at a severe disadvantage. The tidal wave of e-mailings, pop-ups, and other electronic information associated with e-democracy comes to be seen by average citizens as annoying spam. Alienation from political processes increases rather than decreases. Political commentators express yearnings for a return to traditional politics, before the information age, arguing that a time-limited, every-four-years media blitz of traditional politics was better than the all-the-time information overload of e-democracy.

From the point of view of public managers, political campaigning, including e-campaigning, is prohibited and thus irrelevant. While certainly this makes the e-campaigning dimension of e-democracy less salient to public management, the one significant connection that exists has to do with the fact that public managers control agency websites, and there is explicit or implicit pressure to make their elected superiors look good. As noted above, it is not unusual for incumbent political leaders to promote agency information that is favorable to their agendas on these websites.

As this is written it is September 17, 2004, in the middle of the U.S. presidential campaign. What do we find if we visit federal departmental website home pages? The Department of the Treasury headlines "Secretary John W. Snow is in Cincinnati today to tour a local business and meet with business leaders on the president's efforts to strengthen the economy," a headline whose context is implicit rebuttal of the major Democratic campaign theme that the Bush administration had been bad for the economy. The Department of State headlined Secretary Powell parroting the Bush line on Iraq, perhaps the leading campaign issue: "[T]he Iraqi Interim Government—President Sheikh Ghazi, and Prime Minister Allawi, and their whole cabinet are determined to go forward. The national council, which is now in place, is determined to go forward. The UN is determined to go forward and have these elections. It is a necessary step toward putting in place a solid democracy in Iraq and allowing that democracy to thrive." The Department of Defense made the uppermost button on its home page "The War on Terror," implicitly supporting the Bush campaign theme that what the military is doing in Iraq is against terrorists, even though the 9/11 commission found no connection between the Iraq regime and the al-Qaeda terrorists. The headline story of the Department of Agriculture was how it was promoting the president's faith-based initiatives, another campaign issue. The Department of Human Services' only picture was of its secretary at a press conference announcing new measures to help seniors get the lowest price possible for their medicines, naturally with no mention of the recent bitter partisan fight over prescription benefits for seniors and the passage of a Bush-backed plan Democrats argued subsidized drug companies and did nothing to lower drug prices. The Department of Transportation's home page featured the "President's Management Agenda Success Stories." The U.S. Department of the Interior headlined how "Secretary Norton has signed an agreement with representatives of Arizona, Nevada, and California to complete an initiative to recover endangered species and protect wildlife habitat," which stood as an implicit rebuttal of Democratic campaign arguments that Bush had a terrible record as a steward of the environment. No agency Web page headlined anything that could be construed as support for Democratic positions in the 2004 campaign; every agency home page had at least some pro-Bush content. It is, of course, hardly surprising that a Republican administration would have websites that take a Republican point of view. However, it must be recognized that this form of participation in e-campaigning is very much part of the public manager's job.

E-VOTING

Electronic voting is a social technology whose time is almost upon us. Election Data Services reported that almost 20 million registered voters used electronic voting systems in the 2000 election. It is expected that electronic voting in the 2004 election will have proved to have been as high as 50 million. Partly electronic voting is a matter of replacing manual and punch card machine devices that had caused an electoral scandal in Florida in the 2000 presidential elections. But e-voting also includes the concept of holding e-referenda on policy issues, greatly increasing the frequency and effect of direct democracy on legislation. Also, e-voting technology can be used at the agency level both externally to poll stakeholder groups or the public at large on policies pertaining to the agency, or it can be used internally, replacing employee surveys and enhancing feedback for purposes of agency policy formulation and decision making.

Many in the public first learned about e-voting in the 1992 presidential campaign, when the independent candidate Ross Perot, who had become wealthy selling computer services to the health industry, advocated a system under which he would hold periodic electronic referenda on such issues as new taxes. More recently, e-voting was widely touted as a solution to the hanging chad scandal in Florida, where failure of voting machinery may have determined the 2000 presidential election. Over $2 billion was appropriated for e-voting machinery under the Help America Vote Act of 2002, passed in the wake of the Florida fiasco. Also in 2002, the Arizona Democratic Party experimented with online voting in primaries and got 50% of voters (about 40,000) to vote online. However, the 4-day election was marred by technical glitches such as problems arising from voters using old, incompatible versions of Web browsers. In January 2000, Alaska's Republican Party sought to have online voting in a presidential straw poll, to reach out to remote residents, but got only 35% participation.

The defense of e-voting is that by automating the process of recording and counting votes, there will be no error, almost instantaneous result reporting, and provision of ability to vote by those who cannot go to polling stations. The criticism of e-voting is that it is insufficiently reliable and lacks an auditable paper trail, as noted by e-voting critic Rebecca Mercuri of Harvard University's John F. Kennedy School of Government and as was reflected in the 2004 presidential elections when some e-voting machines lost votes in North Carolina (Geary, 2005). Some of these criticisms are remediable. California, for instance, has already required e-voting vendors to support a paper audit trail and has provided paper ballots to voters who so request. At this writing, auditable e-voting has not been widely implemented. If it is, it likely will feature voters using smartcards or PIN numbers to authenticate their identity, receiving a paper printout to verify their votes, and only then casting their electronic ballots. Presently, however, e-voting vendors oppose paper audit trails. "We oppose the idea of a voter-verified paper trail," states Harris Miller, president of the trade group Information Technology Association of America, on grounds that it increases costs, slows the voting process, and may reduce reliability (Santosus, 2004).

Parallel to concerns about e-campaigning, there are many fears that e-voting also could be sabotaged. Corporate and other interest groups could mount well-financed e-mail and e-forum campaigns leading up to e-referenda. They could supplement this with TV and media campaigns as well. When the e-referendum took place, many might wonder if the referenda had been bought by massive PR campaigns. Corporate or other interest lobbies might like e-referenda because they might be confident they could prevail. Mussolini, the fascist ally of Hitler, liked referenda as an alternative to representative democracy through legislative bodies precisely because it lent itself to mass persuasion. Moreover, politicians and interest groups might phrase e-referenda and e-discussion forum questions in ways that bias the results. For instance, they may ask "Do you support x?" questions, knowing support diminishes sharply if asked "Do you support x even if the costs mean we cannot do y?" The party in control of the presidency, Congress, or any agency may make it a priority as soon as they come to power to put loyal political appointees in charge of any e-government processes so they can guide e-referenda in a favorable direction. And in a different form of sabotage of e-democracy, hackers paid by powerful interests may find ways to crack e-voting code to enter illegal votes. And even if they don't, suspicions might abound and people might lose confidence in the legitimacy of elections. Such alienation has already surfaced, as in a current political cartoon in which George Bush announces his reelection three months prior to November, is questioned on it by a crony, and replies, "Heard of Diebold?", referring to a vendor of e-voting machines whose voting integrity has been questioned by academics and the press.

Given the state of the art in 2004, many critics feel e-voting is not ready for general use. Rebecca Mercuri,[5] of Harvard's JFK School of Government, a leading scholar of electronic voting systems, examined existing systems and found:

> Proponents of electronic and Web-based voting systems are quick to criticize punch cards and lever machines as being slow and antiquated. Yet numerous studies, including recent data from the California recall election, has revealed that many new computer-based systems are inferior to older mechanical and manual technologies. Furthermore, some electronic systems may compromise voter privacy and recount capability, a fact that many vendors and election officials do not want voters to know (Mercuri, 2003).

At a security conference in Washington, DC, in August 2003, Aviel Rubin reported on his team's examination of voting software. Aviel, technical director of the Information Security Institute, Johns Hopkins University, said that at least one version (Diebold software) was "far below even the most minimal security standards applicable in other contexts" (Walsh, 2003a). Alarmed by the Rubin report, Maryland (which uses Diebold machines) commissioned Raba Technologies to simulate a mock election.

The ensuing Raba report found software problems and revealed that the locked cabinet containing the printer tape, the on/off switch, and the modem could be opened by any one of 32,000 keys issued, and that keys could be duplicated at any hardware store. A Department of Defense evaluation of the Secure Electronic Registration and Voting Experiment[6] (SERVE) to be used for absentee balloting by members of the armed forces in 50 countries, was supportive of the system, but a minority report said it will invite "hackers and even terrorists to interfere with fair and accurate voting" (Jackson, 2004a). Abroad, Ireland cancelled the use of electronic voting machines for the 2004 European elections after an independent commission said the secrecy and accuracy of the voting could not be guaranteed. In 2002 the Irish security firm Zerflow reviewed the machines used in Ireland and concluded that manipulation of the voting process was possible, in part because there was no paper trail (EDRI-news, 2004). Questions about e-voting integrity are deepened by the fact that vendor software code (e.g., Diebold) is proprietary rather than open source, obstructing public scrutiny.

An entirely different problem with IT and voting was raised by electronic vote swapping in the 2000 presidential election campaign. In that campaign, websites supporting independent candidate Ralph Nader created online opportunities whereby Democrats in predominantly Republican states could swap their vote with a Green Party supporter in a swing state. That is, a North Carolina Democrat, knowing the Democrats had not won a presidential election in that state since 1976, would agree to vote for Nader's Green Party, and a Green Party member in Michigan, a swing state, would agree to vote Democratic. The purpose was to allow Nader to gain the needed 5% of votes to be eligible for federal matching funds. Votetrader.org reported that 10 swapping sites registered 35,000 people resulting in 15,000 swaps nationwide, possibly making a difference in the very tight 2000 elections, which was ultimately tipped by only several hundred votes in a single state. Some charged that this vote swapping was sufficient to alter the outcome in Florida, which was the critical state that year (Harris, 2000). Although such vote-swapping could have taken place in the past in principle, the Internet facilitated widespread implementation of the scheme for the first time in U.S. history.

E-voting in national elections is remote from the concerns of most public managers (except those charged with administering elections!). National e-referenda on policy issues might strike closer to home for agencies, but thus far such referenda are mostly only a glimmer in the eye of e-democracy enthusiasts. The real relevance of e-voting comes in nonbinding online voting or online survey initiatives that agencies mount for purposes of public feedback and/or to demonstrate public support for agency activities. The usually nonbinding nature of such e-voting means that the security and audit trail problems discussed above largely are ignored by public managers who, because of this and because the vote-who-may, self-selected participation usual in this type of voting means the sample is unscientific, treat results as a nonbinding straw vote. The lack of universality of computer access generally prevents the use of electronic voting by agencies such as the Department of Agriculture, which still relies on mail and fax voting for binding referenda.[7]

Most forms of e-voting administered by public managers are e-surveys of stakeholder groups or of agency employees, taken to provide feedback for decision making. Innumerable examples exist. The U.S. Department of Education uses online surveys for purposes of "improving the Internet services of the U.S. Department of Education."[8] The Library of Congress uses online surveys to tell which exhibitions citizens have visited and prefer, so it may better develop its Web exhibitions.[9] The Office of Thrift Supervision of the U.S. Department of Treasury uses online surveys of chief executive officers of thrift institutions to gain feedback on its regulatory processes.[10] King County, Washington, uses online surveys to get citizens to vote on alternative funding proposals developed by a county commission.[11] The City of Las Vegas uses online surveys to solicit feedback for improvement of its municipal website.[12] The Recreation Services Department of the City of Milpitas, California, surveys residents online as they "try and plan for future programs, services, and special events."[13] The Rockville, Maryland, police department uses online surveys of residents "to measure our effectiveness and improve our delivery of police service."[14] Thousands of such examples can be cited.

Likewise, examples of public managers using online surveys for internal reasons also abound. The Los Alamos National Laboratories uses online employee surveys through its process improvement team as part of its productivity management program.[15] The State of Washington has used its State Employee Survey online since 1997, because "Obtaining anonymous feedback from employees regarding management and leadership practices is key information for managerial teams to improve productivity."[16] The State of Michigan's Department of Management and Budget uses online employee surveys as a central aspect of its organizational assessment process for state agencies.[17] King County, cited above, also uses online surveys of employees for health policy planning.[18] In 2004, the Government Accountability Office (GAO) reported, "The last four years have seen exponential growth in the use of Web-based surveys to gather data for GAO engagements and for various GAO mission support activities" (*GAO Management News*, 2004). A September 2004 search of .gov public sector websites for the term *online survey* using www.google.com yielded over 59,000 hits, suggesting the use of e-surveys in government is well on the way to becoming standard fare for public agencies and their managers.

E-LEGISLATING

We now turn from the outer three layers of e-democracy (e-activism, e-campaigning, e-voting) to the inner three, which are even more focused on the public sector, starting with the legislative branch. Although popular opinion equates public management with the executive branch of government, the truth is that staff functions reporting to the legislative branch have created large bureaucracies in their own right, including offices that now implement e-legislating, which is, in this sense, a public management function. For the larger number of public managers in the executive branch, e-legislating creates new opportunities and challenges in legislative oversight of the bureaucracy and in agency liaison with legislatures.

In 1996, Washington and Missouri were the first state legislatures to show their committee hearings via the Internet. In 2002, the Center for Digital Government and *Government Technology Magazine* ranked state legislatures on citizen ease of following legislative bills and hearings and supporting online input. The winner was the Arizona legislature, whose Arizona Legislative Information System let the public create a free, individualized bill-tracking system to select bills on which to receive alerts.[19] All bills were online and searchable by keyword, bill number, title, or sponsor. Citizens could find complete e-mail addresses for legislators and could search for representatives by zip code or map, or access streaming video of all committee hearings and legislative floor activities (Peterson, 2002a).

In 2004, Virginia's legislative website, to take another example, had full-text bill lookup, real-time session tracking of legislation, "lobbyist in a box" automatic e-mail notification of bill changes meeting a user-specified profile, online tools to monitor the progress of the state budget as it moves through the legislative process, and a Capitol Classroom set of online activities and information for children.[20] Also in 2004, the New York State Assembly featured online bill searching and legislative information, an online legislative calendar, live coverage of the assembly session, online press releases and legislative reports, online committee updates, and more.[21]

Likewise, e-legislating has been extensively implemented by the Michigan legislature, where all hearings and committee sessions are broadcast in streaming video, live over nine channels. Some 700 legislative staff members now find it crucial, using it to filter committee work while still able to work in their offices. Gene Rose, public affairs director of the National Conference of State Legislatures, stated that by 2002, almost every state broadcast at least some of its hearings over the Web, and a majority broadcast floor sessions (Bhambhani, 2002). The 2003 "Digital Legislatures" report found that all states had online, searchable bill reporting and three quarters supported bill status tracking and session voting records. Almost half also featured real-time alerts to citizens on changes in state laws and administrative codes, and about a third also had e-mail notices available (Center for Digital Government, 2004).

At the national level, the main website of the Congress has been maintained by the Library of Congress since 1995.[22] It features full-text bill search, full-text search of the *Congressional Record*, roll call votes of the House and Senate, online committee reports, and other information. There is also a House of Representatives website,[23] with a "Write Your Representative" feature, online search of the U.S. Code, schedule information, and links to the Web pages of one's representative in Congress. Similar functions are at the U.S. Senate site.[24] The National Archives and Records Administration provides online access of congressional records.[25] The C-Span website provides three live video and one online radio feed, as well as online search of its video and audio archives on topics of greatest public interest.[26] Capitol Hearings, jointly sponsored by C-Span and *Congressional Quarterly*, provides streaming coverage of the committee hearings of the U.S. Congress.[27]

This is not to say that full transparency has been achieved by legislatures or by Congress. West (2000) surveyed e-government and found "There are problems in terms of access and democratic outreach" (p. 2) and that "some states have been slow to put accountability-enhancing material such as legislative deliberations, campaign finance information, and ethics reports online" (p. 5). Legislative websites do not promote e-polling of citizens on upcoming issues, do not host online discussion groups for the public, do not provide for citizen input into committee processes, and do not seek to go beyond traditional political structures.

Interest groups package e-legislative information for their members for purposes of policy-oriented lobbying which, of course, has the potential for direct impact on management of the agencies affected. For instance, the "Electronic Legislature" of the California Truckers' Association (CTA) provides its members with online tracking of legislative information pertaining to that industry.[28] This service is "hugely popular" with CTA members and has been widely imitated by other organizations. Joel Anderson, president of the CTA, writes, "We call on members to be our local contact with elected officials and our local voice with the media. The Internet is among the most important tools we use to make these things happen" (*ComData News*, 2002).[29] The CTA and its associate Caltrux.org website provide a complete lobbying service, from general political analysis of bills to helping members write letters to their state representatives.

Public-sector civil servants also use e-legislative information for lobbying. For instance, the website of the Virginia Coalition of Police and Deputy Sheriffs (VCOPS) notes, "With the advent of the electronic legislature it has become easier and easier for officers to be a part of the system that in many cases determines issues that impact their careers."[30] The VCOPS website tracks legislation affecting law enforcement departments, provides an online forum for policy discussion, and helps members contact representatives in the Virginia General Assembly by e-mail. Similarly, at the national level, the American Federation of State, County, and Municipal Employees union website has a typical "Legislative Action" page, featuring online legislative alerts, a voter's guide, weekly legislative reports, legislative fact sheets, an online find/write to your representative feature, and more.[31]

At the same time that legislatures seek to be transparent through e-legislating, while being e-lobbied by private- and public-sector interest groups, legislatures also use IT to perform the function of legislative oversight of the bureaucracy. A 1986 report of the now-defunct Office of Technology Assessment (OTA) noted, "Congress as a whole has made great strides over the last 10 to 15 years in using information technology with respect to legislative information retrieval, constituent mail and correspondence management, and some administrative functions. However, the use of information technology for direct support of policymaking and oversight is just beginning" (OTA, 1986). Now, almost two decades later, Congress has assembled a powerful e-toolkit to perform its oversight functions.

For example, the Government Performance and Results Act of 1993, discussed in Chapter 2, required agencies to prepare multiyear strategic plans and annual program performance reports to review progress. Inspectors general report findings about waste, fraud, and abuse periodically to agency heads and Congress and, under the Reports Consolidation Act of 2000, inspectors general report agencies' most serious management and performance challenges. Reports from Congress's GAO, the OMB in the executive branch, and from the Office of Government Ethics, as well as from the agencies themselves, are among the hundreds of sources of information directly pertinent to congressional oversight of federal agencies. Almost all of these reports are now electronically searchable and retrievable. The amount of oversight information available to legislators is now exponentially higher than it was only two decades ago.

The Congressional Research Service (CRS) was created by the Legislative Reorganization Act of 1970. Its performance in FY2003 included support for 160 major policy issues and writing and updating more than 900 key reports, all available to members of Congress online through the Current Legislative Issues system on the CRS website. The impressive increases in CRS activity (e.g., a 30% increase in reports during FY2003 compared to FY2002) are made possible in no small part by IT, without which it could not possibly have handled the 875,197 individual information and analysis requests it received that year, managed through its Inquiry Status and Information System. The FY 2003 CRS report discusses how the service "increased its Web services in response to the growing needs of the Congress for electronic transfer of analysis and information" and details the transformation of the CRS through information technology (CRS, 2004, p. 30). Many state legislatures have their own legislative research services, also deeply involved with IT in the service of legislative oversight of executive branch agencies.

In summary, legislative oversight of bureaucracy before the information age was driven by manual correspondence and in-person hearings, an inefficient set of tools that ensured that oversight came only to the most visible agencies and programs. Now, as IT comes into its own in Congress and the nation's legislatures, and as e-governance reforms have forced agencies to become more transparent, the capacity for legislative oversight has become qualitatively greater. IT allows even casual questions from members of Congress to be researched and objective data delivered in a timely fashion. IT allows legislators to be proactive, searching for problems and policy issues that agency data may reveal, not waiting for scandals to force hearings. Above all, e-legislating means that the legislative process has become even more intense in both directions—not only legislative oversight of public management, but also IT-based influences upon the legislative process itself by both private- and public-sector interests.

E-CIVICS

E-civics refers to the use of electronic means to provide citizens access to agency information. E-civics now involves most Americans. The Pew Internet & American Life Project reported in 2004 that 97 million American adults accessed e-government services in 2003, a 50% growth over 2002! ICT such as Internet websites, e-mail, electronic bulletin boards and discussion lists, computerized voice mail, and touch-screen kiosks in malls are routine for most American citizens, who now assume a much higher level of access and agency transparency than their parents did.

The e-civics dimension of e-democracy centers on information provision, using IT as a "tool of governance." In an early example, in the 1980s the City of New Orleans experimented with a public data access system for human services (Ruberg, 1989). At the same time, libraries around the country began offering online access to their card catalogs as well as adult education listings, city and school board meeting calendars and minutes, and other civic information (Mallory, 1991). The 1991 Electronic Democracy Conference in Sacramento, California, highlighted the creation of "24-hour city halls" to make government data available to the public. Public Technology, Inc., and IBM supported 24-hour city hall projects, placing electronic kiosks in over a dozen municipalities.

A survey by Dutton (1992) found that electronic democracy initiatives of local governments in this period fell into five general categories: broadcasting (e.g., touch-screen multimedia PCs used to disseminate civic information), transaction processing (e.g., use of magnetic smartcards in the New York City food stamp program), public records access (e.g., dial-up electronic bulletin boards in the Pasadena, California, PARIS/PALS program), interpersonal communication (e.g., computer conferencing in the Santa Monica, California, PEN system), and surveying and monitoring (e.g., electronic surveillance as in Caltrans experiments with toll collections in California).

E-civics is necessarily limited by the very propensity of online communications to dramatically increase the volume of information flow. This was illustrated when in 1993 the White House announced the availability of direct electronic mail access to President Clinton and Vice President Gore. Part of the Americans Communicating Electronically project of several federal agencies to increase information access, White House e-mail did not mean Bill Clinton read your message. Rather, the White House selected from among several software packages that "read" e-mail and responded with the electronic equivalent of form letters. Although form letter responses had long dominated White House mail operations, up to then at least some human being had actually examined each incoming letter. The new online system increased access to the White House, but that access was reduced to poll-like tally results calculated by e-mail software.

Largely in the last decade, e-civics expanded from information provision to transactional processing of forms for such things as licenses, permits, and fees. The Government Paperwork Elimination Act of 1998 mandated that all federal agencies have their forms online by October 2003. Only about half met the deadline (Miller, 2003a). The OMB reported that by the end of 2003, 57% of all federal agencies' transactions were online (Michael, 2004). The Taubman Center for Public Policy at Brown University likewise reported that 56% of federal and state websites had at least one fully executable online transaction service as of summer 2004 (West, 2004). Informational Web pages by then were nearly universal at all levels of government and, at the federal level, an explicit, legislatively mandated responsibility of public managers.

E-civics has substantially lowered the cost of governmental information. Reschenthaler and Thompson (1996) are among the public administrationists who have theorized that the effects of reduced information costs are:

1. Increased efficacy of market mechanisms becomes more efficient than direct provision of governmental services or than governmental regulation.
2. Decentralized allocation of resources becomes more efficient than centralized and before-the-fact controls, pushing decision making as low in the organization as possible.
3. Job-oriented process structures become more efficient than the functional structures of traditional bureaucracy (e.g., multidisciplinary teams working holistically rather than functional departments working sequentially).

These proponents of "the new public management" argue, for instance, that the information explosion in the financial sector lessens the need for governmental financial regulations to protect investors, that advances in information processing allow such things as pollution rights or airport landing rights to be securitized and bought and sold on the market, and that technology-based improvements in costing and pricing transportation and telecommunications services justified the deregulation of these industries.

Reschenthaler and Thompson conclude with the argument that the information revolution requires a radical governmental restructuring (cutting back to core functions), reinvention through a customer-oriented product-market strategy, actual devolution to market mechanisms, reengineering (creating new processes rather than incrementally adjusting existing bureaucratic ones), rethinking (creating an adaptive information culture throughout the organization), and realigning (ensuring that organizational structure matches the new information culture).

It is true that the rise of e-civics has corresponded with an era of privatization of governmental functions, but whether this is made possible by or caused by the lowering of costs of governmental information is questionable. It is also true that e-civics involves a certain degree of customer-oriented rethinking and reengineering of agency processes, though there has been relatively little realigning of government structures. E-civics has been an extension of the existing bureaucracy, not a radical democratization of it as activists have wanted, nor a conservative dismantling of it as the so-called new public management movement has sometimes envisioned.

In a recent issue of the *Public Administration Review*, it was asserted that there were four models of electronic democracy: electronic bureaucracy, information management, populist, and civil society (Kakabadse, Kakabadse, & Kouzmin, 2003). Strategies for reinventing democratic governance were presented, including accommodating critical debate and providing access for citizen participation in policy discussions. E-civics has little to do with such objectives, instead being a tame and largely passive approach to providing public access to governmental information and some transactions. Many have criticized various levels of government for becoming stuck in the e-civics layer and not proceeding to e-participation, which is seen as the core of e-democracy.

The history of access legislation was discussed in Chapter 2, and access will be treated at length in Chapter 5.

E-PARTICIPATION

E-participation is the use of electronic means to allow the public or stakeholder groups to participate in the policy decision-making processes of the agency. It is not simply taking citizen surveys as discussed in the previous section on e-voting and it is not simply allowing citizens to make online transactions as in the preceding section on e-civics. Rather, it takes three forms:

1. Decision-making transparency, which refers to timely electronic provision of information on upcoming agency policy decisions and their associated options
2. E-mail, proactively inviting electronic correspondence with agency officials on policy matters
3. E-regulation, which is providing an electronic equivalent to hearings, allowing citizens, interest groups, or corporations to make input to the agency prior to the issuance of rules and regulations. (Often *e-regulation* refers only to a subset of the bureaucracy, the regulatory agencies, but here we use it to refer to the establishment of similar participative electronic mechanisms with regard to the decisions of any type of agency.)

Transparency is the prerequisite to any form of e-participation. Unless the public and stakeholders are apprised of upcoming agency decisions and of alternatives being considered, the availability of even the simplest e-participation options such as e-mail to agency directors is meaningless. A full-blown system of e-regulation builds in e-notification of decisions as well as electronic posting of stakeholder responses, including ability of stakeholders to read the input of others as well as agency responses.

The U.S. Information Agency promotes e-government transparency as evidence that the government in the United States is evolving to ever more democratic heights (Porter, 2003). The Intergovernmental Advisory Board of the Federation of Government Information Processing Councils (FGIPC) asserts, "The use of E-Gov can be an important tool of democratic governance, facilitating the transparent, two-way, open communication that makes government-of-the-people possible" (FGIPC, 2003). The same assertions are heard at the local government level as well: "E-Government services are seen to help local government in a positive way—website resources boost transparency, increase access to policy making, and increase accountability from government leaders" (Collins, 2002).

Transparency has become a popular catchword among e-democracy advocates. One governmental agency defines transparency this way:

> Transparency can be defined as practical and easy access to the rules, procedures, and basic data needed to conduct business; access to the grounds for administrations' decisions and choices; and the possibility for those potentially affected by plans to modify the regulatory environment to take part (access to information and the possibility to make proposals) in the decision-making process, in order to state their needs and defend their interests (ITU, 2003, p. 42).

If we agree that true e-participation is built on transparency in government, this definition calls attention to specific conditions. Access must be easy. Agencies must put online information pertaining not only to decisions, but also must lay out the choices and the grounds for these choices. This must be done well in advance of decisions so as to permit stakeholders and the public to express their needs and make proposals. To this definition, the author would add one additional condition: comments and proposals made as part of the e-participation process must be incorporated by the agency as a significant part of the decision-making process.

E-mail appears to be a widely utilized vehicle for e-participation. A 2002 report from the Pew Internet and American Life Project found 42 million Americans had used government websites to research public policy issues, and 23 million had used the Internet to send comments to public officials about policy choices. The report found that these e-citizens were satisfied (80% find what they are looking for on the Web) and more favorable to government as a result (60% say e-government has improved their interactions with at least one level of government) (Larsen & Rainie, 2002a).

Although e-mail is widely used, it is not clear that officials are as responsive to citizen e-mail as might be thought. A related Pew report based on a survey of mayors and city council members found some 88% of local elected officials used e-mail and the Internet in their official duties and 79% reported receiving e-mail from citizens or local groups about civic issues (Larsen & Rainie, 2002b). About 25% stated they received e-mail from constituents every day. The report concluded, however that "While the use of e-mail adds to the convenience and depth of civic exchanges, its use is not ushering a revolution in municipal affairs or local politics" (p. 2). At this time, traditional communications media, notably the telephone, constitute more important links between local officials and citizens. Only 14% of officials said that they assigned a significant amount of weight to e-mail. Silicon Valley lobbies still urge supporters to contact Congress by fax, not e-mail, because e-mail seems to make no impact on congressmen (Levy, 2002, p. 42). Another study found that while 68% of governmental websites did post e-mail addresses so citizens could interact in this way, only 15% provided for posting of citizen comments (West, 2000).

In terms of e-mail participation, the nation's premiere exemplar of e-government, the FirstGov.gov portal, as of September 2004, did have a Contact Your Government section with an E-mail option, but it led to an online form and notice that "a member of our Citizen Response Team will respond to you within two business days." Hunting through FirstGov.gov to make input to a particular agency, the U.S. Department of Transportation (DOT), led to a similar message: "Please send your suggestions, comments or questions, as well as e-mail for the Secretary and other Department of Transportation officials, to dot.comments@ost.dot.gov. A team of information specialists answer every message sent from this home page." That is, what is solicited through FirstGov.gov e-mail forms is not participation in policy decision processes but simply the opportunity to pose questions to a public relations specialist.

E-regulation in regulatory agencies has provided somewhat more meaningful e-participation at the federal level. By the 1990s, several agencies were experimenting with electronic feedback for the rule-making process. The DOT developed the first federal agency-wide docket-based e-rulemaking information system (Perritt, 1995). In 1997 the DOT received some 3000 online responses with regard to 155 proposed rules. By 2000, it was receiving 63,000 online comments regarding a smaller number of proposed rules. In 2002 the U.S. Department of Housing and Urban Development tested online forums to seek public comments (Vasishtha, 2002b). Also in 2002, the Environmental Protection Agency publicly launched its E-Docket system which, being newer than that of the DOT, became the model for a government-wide system launched the following year.

Regulations.gov, created under Section 206 of the E-Government Act of 2002 and formally launched in January 2003, was touted as a reform to make the federal rule-making process more accessible and enable citizens and small businesses to access and comment on proposed rules. On this site, one could find, review, and submit comments on federal documents that are open for comment and published in the *Federal Register*. OMB Director Mitchell E. Daniels Jr. stated, "E-rulemaking will democratize an often closed process and enable every interested citizen to participate in shaping the rules which affect us all" (OMB, 2003b). The motive for establishment of Regulations.gov was not simply the promotion of public participation. Some form of citizen input to the regulatory process was required under the Administrative Procedures Act of 1946, and creating a single electronic system for the entire federal government was estimated to save $94 million. Administration officials also emphasized that Regulations.gov was a Bush administration response to small business concerns about excessive governmental regulation, providing an avenue to protest or suggest modifications to regulations before they took effect.

Regulations.gov seeks to create a one-stop government-wide centralized docket system for all federal agencies, such that any citizen can access and search all publicly available regulatory material as well as view and comment on proposed rules. A docket system includes all the materials referenced in the *Federal Register* document announcing a proposed rule or regulation, any public comments received, as well as any other information used by decision makers. It is administered by the Environmental Protection Agency (EPA) in coordination with the Department of Health and Human Services/Food and Drug Administration, the National Archives and Records Administration/Federal Register, and the Government Printing Office (GPO). Specifically, the GPO hosts Regulations.gov and the EPA's National Computing Center provides back-end support for collection and dissemination of comments.

A spot check by the author on September 21, 2004, revealed there were 486 proposed regulations available for comment on Regulations.gov, including 9 added that day. At any given time, up to 500 rules may be open for public comment from over 160 federal rule-making agencies. However, full docket materials were often not conveniently available on this date. Rather one was apt to find only a statement such as, "Comments and submissions will be posted on OSHA's Web page (http://www.osha.gov). Contact the OSHA Docket Office for information about materials not available on OSHA's Web page and for assistance in using the Web page to locate docket submissions." Retrieval from the referenced Web pages were often incomplete and sometimes hard to find at all. The expected "other information used by decision makers" was generally absent. Most materials were highly technical and, more important, were presented devoid of the policy context.

While Regulations.gov certainly is an important step toward transparency as well as ease of public comment on proposed regulations, it is also far from being a forum for informed public debate on public policy or even reportage on how decision makers select among policy alternatives and reach an outcome. A GAO report in late 2003 found that only 2 of 411 rule-making events in the period studied cited input from Regulations.gov, bringing into question the meaningfulness of this form of e-participation (GAO, 2003a). It should be noted, though, that Regulations.gov is just the first of three planned phases to implement e-rulemaking. The second phase, to be completed in 2005, is intended to facilitate viewing of supporting regulatory documents not now accessible. The future third phase will introduce a "Regulation Writers' Workbench," automating internal agency processes for developing and reviewing new rules. It remains to be seen if these future phases will substantially change the limited nature of participation presently seen under Regulations.gov.

SUMMARY

E-democracy is an umbrella term that means many things to many people, ranging from revolutionary democratization of traditional hierarchies to all-too-tame municipal postings of basic city service information to a website. In this chapter we have treated the six dimensions of e-democracy. Two of these dimensions, e-civics and e-participation, are direct public management responsibilities now mandated by federal law. However, the other four dimensions (e-activism, e-campaigning, e-voting, and e-legislating) form important parts of the new environment of public agencies in the information age. Proactive public managers wishing to gain external support, form alliances, and anticipate legislative mandates need to be cognizant of the outer layers of e-democracy as well as the core layers.

It is unlikely that American governance will ever reach a point where decisions are made by citizens in e-referenda, with Congress relegated to merely overseeing this electronic decision process. Most public administrationists would emphatically deny this is even a desirable goal, contrary to the more extravagant visions of some e-democracy advocates. Still, short of such a radical vision, there is a lively debate over the impact of ICT on governance. Will ICT prove to be "the great equalizer" (Rheingold, 1991) ushering in a revitalization of American democracy? Or will computerized telecommunications be an incremental improvement, not a revolution, much as cable television extended commercial broadcasting but failed to live up to early promises of interactive wired cities once predicted to transform American democracy (Smith, 1972)?

The tendency of information systems to reinforce existing structures of power is widely noted in everyday life. The intense debate of the 1980s over whether centralization or decentralization was given life by the prospect that distributed microcomputing would shatter the structure of centralized IT departments. Now, in a new era dominated by enterprise architectures, the triumph of such departments and the near ubiquity of powerful new offices of chief information officers in both the private and public sectors have decisively resolved this debate in favor of the view that computing reinforces central control. To take another example, IT has reinforced the role of libraries rather than replaced them as once predicted (McDonald, 2002). At a societal level, IT also has reinforced considerably the capacity of national authorities to regulate specific industries (e.g., Commission of the European Communities, 2003).

The evidence on IT and power tends to lie in the direction of reinforcement theory. At the organizational level, this was widely understood by researchers two decades ago. As summarized by Kraemer and King (1986, 1987), the organization's top management is strengthened by its firm and growing central control over new ITs. Danziger (1986) also undertook a survey of research on computing, telecommunications, and politics that showed little evidence of significant impact. Another survey of the literature on information systems, power, and centralization/decentralization in 1992 also found that computers reinforce the power of the already potent players (Bloomfield & Coombs, 1992). Of course, IT is closely associated with change, and although most changes serve the goals of the powerful and reinforce existing structures, as a survey of the literature on IT and power 10 years later noted, IT can be used to create symbols and meaning that reinforce current power structures *or* to mold altered structures (Jasperson, Butler, Carte, et al., 2002). Individuals and groups may leverage IT to political advantage within organizations, communities, and nations and may indeed create change. Overall, however, there is little evidence that the impact of IT is revolutionary with respect to existing power structures at any of these levels. Although IT has deeply impacted the mechanisms of democracy, as yet it has not fundamentally changed the nature of democracy. E-democracy looks a lot like democracy.

DISCUSSION QUESTIONS

1. E-democracy can be described as a sphere with six layers. The outer layer, e-activism, affects the political environment of an agency. How do the other five layers affect public managers?

2. The 1980s and 1990s saw the rise of the community computing movement— "empowering the powerless." What happened to the community computing movement as technology has improved? Have aspects of the community computing been replaced by others?

3. What strategies would a proactive public manager take in an environment of increasing e-activism? What do you think the results of these strategies would be?

4. Argue both sides of the e-campaigning issue that a) e-campaigning strengthens democratic ideals, and b) e-campaigning furthers the disengagement of citizens. Consider both immediate and long-term effects of the e-campaigning strategies listed in the text.

5. The author gives examples of indirect support for e-campaigning evidenced on many federal Web pages to further the position of the incumbent president. Can you find your own similar examples on the Web at the federal level? At the state or local level?

6. E-voting seems to be in the near future for the United States. What are the benefits and the risks associated with e-voting? If all technological impediments were removed, how do you think e-voting would affect the voting habits of the public? Would it advantage one political party more than another?

7. What e-legislation steps have been greatly utilized so far by the federal government? What exists in your state?

8. E-civics has been evolving fairly rapidly over the last 15 years. What are some of the major developments? What are some of the benefits for both the public and the government?

9. Why is transparency necessary for successful e-participation? The text cites a government agency for the definition of *transparency*. One very important condition has been omitted. What is that final condition? What could happen if it continued to be neglected?

10. What is Regulations.gov? What was the motivation for creating it? Has it been perfected? Go to this website and assess its citizen friendliness as an instrument of e-democracy.

GLOSSARY

Blog: *Blog* is an abbreviated form of *Web log*. Blogs are electronic journals published on the Internet, usually on a free, noncommercial basis. Blogging describes the author's act of updating a blog.

Community computing movement: The community computing movement gained strength in the 1980s and 1990s, generally promoting information equity, often for disadvantaged groups but also for citizens at large. Practical activities included computer and network access, job training, skill building, and literacy building. Some but by no means all community computing groups were associated with the National Public Telecomputing Network, a nonprofit organization coordinating dozens of "Free-Net" projects in the United States and abroad.

E-activism: E-activism refers to activities promoting a cause through electronic means, often on behalf of an interest group. Activities may include fund-raising, activist enlistment, information dissemination, and other methods of influencing policy. E-activism refers to methods that may be used not only by protest or social activism groups but also by large interest groups or corporations.

E-campaigning: E-campaigning refers to carrying out the functions of campaigning-volunteer motivation, voter motivation, fund raising, and information dissemination through electronic means.

E-civics: E-civics refers to the provision of public access to governmental information through electronic means. Federal agencies have operated under mandates to provide public access to information since the Federal Depository Library Program in the early 1800s. The 1996 Electronic Freedom of Information Act applied access mandates to the electronic sphere.

E-democracy: E-democracy is an umbrella term given to any of six democratic activity dimensions carried out through electronic means. The six activities are e-activism, e-campaigning, e-civics, e-legislating, e-participation, and e-voting. The degree to which these are utilized is dependent upon such variables as resource availability, public desire, and governmental will.

E-legislating: E-legislating is the enhancement of the legislative process through electronic means. Activities in this dimension generally are not mandated for most agencies but they provide an avenue for both legislative oversight of bureaucracy and for agency influence on the legislative process.

E-participation: E-participation is public participation in governmental decision making or rule making through electronic means.

E-referenda: E-referenda refers to polling the electorate directly on a specific legislative or constitutional issue or set of issues by electronic means. It is a subset of e-voting.

E-voting: E-voting refers to voting or polling through electronic means, not necessarily limited to traditional voting but also including internal and external agency surveys.

ENDNOTES

[1]The NPTN went bankrupt and dissolved in 1996, but many of its functions were assumed by the Organization for Community Networks (www.ofcn.org/).

[2]Yosemite National Park website. Retrieved 9/15/04, from http://yosemite.epa.gov/water/surfnote.nsf/FTsearchForm?readform&Limit=300&Query=Field+State+Contains+Field+State+Contains+'Texas.'

[3]AOA website. Retrieved 9/15/04, from http://www.aoa.gov/prof/transportation/research/aarp.asp.

[4]HUD website. Retrieved 9/15/04 from http://www.hud.gov/offices/hsg/sfh/hecm/snahech.cfm.

[5]Rebecca Mercuri is a leading scholar of electronic voting systems, affiliated with the JFK School of Government, Harvard University. Her Electronic Voting website at http://www.notablesoftware.com/evote.html is a rich resource for this topic. Her paper, "A Better Ballot Box?" is at http://www.spectrum.ieee.org/WEBONLY/publicfeature/oct02/evot.html.

6SERVE relies on digital certificates embedded by Common Access smart cards issued to military personnel for authentication purposes. Voters log onto www.serveusa.gov, see the ballots for their county, cast, and have a second chance to confirm their vote, and then Accenture sends the ballot to the county for tallying.

SERVE is massively more comprehensive than the 100 military users in a 2002 prototype voting experiment, but SERVE is still limited to 50 U.S. counties in 10 states. SERVE was mandated by Congress in the Uniformed and Overseas Citizens Absentee Voting Act of 2002. For more information, see www.fvap. gov.

7For example, see http://www.ams.usda.gov/fv/rpdockets/fv01706fr.pdf, where the USDA considered and rejected electronic voting in 2002 for reasons of lack of universal access.

8See http://www.ed.gov/help/support/survey/index.html, retrieved 9/17/04.

9See http://www.loc.gov/exhibits/exhiform.html, retrieved 9/17/04.

10See http://www.ots.treas.gov/docs/2/25203.pdf, retrieved 9/17/04.

11See http://www.metrokc.gov/exec/mptf/survey/index.cfm, retrieved 9/17/04. The site deals with "ideas developed by the Metropolitan King County Parks Task Force to generate new savings and revenue for funding King County Parks. Please take a moment to share your thoughts about the ideas by voting *favor* or *oppose* next to each idea."

12See http://www.lasvegasnevada.gov/websurvey/, retrieved 9/17/04.

13See http://www.ci.milpitas.ca.gov/citydept/planning/recreation/survey/default. wasp, retrieved 9/17/04.

14See http://www.rockvillemd.gov/residents/police/forms/survey.html, retrieved 9/17/04.

15See http://www.lanl.gov/worldview/news/director/AskDirector/Part40.html, retrieved 9/17/04.

16See http://www.dis.wa.gov/bestpractices/bestpracticessurvey.htm, retrieved 9/17/04.

17See http://www.michigan.gov/documents/August_71157_7.pdf, retrieved 9/17/04.

18See http://www.metrokc.gov/exec/news/2004/041904emp.htm, retrieved 9/17/04.

19See http://www.azleg.state.az.us.

20See http://legis.state.va.us/, retrieved 9/18/04.

21See http://assembly.state.ny.us/, retrieved 9/18/04.

22See http://thomas.loc.gov/.

23See http://www.house.gov/.

24See http://www.senate.gov/.

25See http://www.archives.gov/records_of_congress/index.html.

26See http://www.c-span.org/.

27See http://www.capitolhearings.org/.

28See http://www.caltrux.org/, retrieved 9/18/04.

29See http://www.comdata.com/cn0401-sap.html, retrieved 9/18/04.

30See http://www.virginiacops.org/GenAssemb/Howtouse.htm. retrieved 9/18/04.

31See http://www.afscme.org/action/index.html, retrieved 9/18/04.

CASE STUDY
Virginia.gov: The Official Homepage of the Commonwealth of Virginia

Todd Loendorf

The Commonwealth of Virginia has become a national leader in e-democracy activities. The commitment, which is being made at every corner of the state, is best illustrated by the results of the 2004 survey conducted by the Center for Digital Government (CenterDigitalGov.com). The survey is a comprehensive study on best practices, policies, and progress made by state and local governments across the United States in their use of digital technologies to better serve their citizens. Virginia ranked third just behind Michigan and Washington, and the following cities were recognized:

- Virginia Beach; 1st place; 250,000 or more population
- Hampton; 2nd place; 125,000–249,999 population
- Norfolk; 5th place; 125,000–249,999 population
- Chesapeake; 7th place; 125,000–249,999 population
- Roanoke; 5th place; 75,000–124,999 population
- Blacksburg; 2nd place; 30,000–74,999 population
- Lynchburg; 4th place; 30,000–74,999 population
- Charlottesville; 5th place; 30,000–74,999 population

Perhaps the most impressive example of the commitment being made in Virginia to bring citizens, businesses, and government closer together can be found at Virginia.gov, the state's official home page.

Origins

Established in 1996, The Virginia Information Providers Network (VIPNet) was created to make interacting with government easier for residents and businesses. The team at VIPNet knew that using a standards-based approach would be the best way to develop the site; however, the skills needed to create portals were not part of the core competency of their technical staff. VIPNet decided to partner with NIC Inc. (NICUSA.com) in an effort to provide consistent, easy-to-use online services for the citizens of Virginia. Founded in 1991, NIC Inc. is a leading provider of government portals in the United States and has provided e-government related services to 17 state governments including the official home page for the Commonwealth of Virginia, Virginia.gov (www.virginia.gov, www.state.va.us, or www.vipnet.org). Understanding that the success of any development project requires the participation and buy-in of potential end users, the VIPNet–NIC team included key business leaders, educators, and citizens in the development process. This strategy, viewed by many as a model of public–private cooperation, produced a portal that provides a blueprint for others in their e-democracy efforts. In 2003, VIPNet and all other state technology functions were consolidated into a new agency, the Virginia Information Technologies Agency, or VITA. As of 2005, VIPNet remains a separate entity within VITA.

Virginia.gov

Launched in March 1998, Virginia.gov quickly began delivering on the promise of providing citizens and businesses with a single gateway to all government-related information and services. This includes links to all state agencies, elected officials, local governments, colleges and universities, K–12 schools, libraries, and museums. Today, Virginia.gov receives more than 28 million hits per month and has evolved into a world-class portal that not only delivers information but it allows citizens to customize their view of Virginia.gov. "By making a series of content and linkage selections, a citizen may tailor the exact type of information and services to be displayed on his or her Virginia.gov home page" (Virginia.gov, 2005). This type of technology is typically referred to as *push* technology because information is sent (*pushed*) from a central information server based on user preferences. The use of this technology will keep Virginia.gov on the cutting edge and prepare them for future features such as the ability to request electronic notification of registration, license, and permit renewals. Virginia.gov has also paved the way for those using wireless technology with the introduction of My Mobile Virginia, the nation's first wireless state portal. As impressive as this new functionality is, a closer look at the long list of core features available at Virginia.gov really illustrates the power of this portal. By grouping the features into those that help citizens participate (E-Participation), those that provide citizens with access to agency information and services (E-Civics), those that bring citizens closer to the legislative process (E-Legislation), and those that help citizens vote (E-Voting), one can see both the breadth and depth of functionality available at Virginia.gov.

E-Participation

Virginia.gov provides citizens of all ages the opportunity to participate in the democratic process. One of the more distinctive features of the site is Virginia Communities. Virginia Communities (http://www.vipnet.org/community/hub_page.htm) is an online database that helps citizens by providing an organized way of accessing the services and resources they need to live, do business, and interact with government. A great example of these communities can be found at the homepage for Smart Region Hampton Roads (SmartRegion.org).

Known simply as Smart Region, Smart Region Hampton Roads was created to help citizens, businesses, and government cross barriers that have traditionally inhibited the flow of information and suppressed the exchange of ideas. "Smart Region envisions Hampton Roads as a *virtual region* in which borders and distance pose no barriers to the flow of ideas, information, and commerce, and where sharing, collaboration, and the promotion and use of best practices is common among the governmental, educational, and business organizations in Hampton Roads" (SmartRegion.org, 2005).

Another interesting feature that is designed to help get young citizens interested and involved is the Kids Commonwealth website (KidsCommonwealth.Virginia.gov). The site provides "fun-filled" online environment where children can find information and learn about Virginia's economy, political processes, and notable places and people.

E-Civics

From its inception, Virginia.gov was created to deliver community services, driver and vehicle services, education services, employment services, tax services, and legal information to citizens and businesses. Today the list of services available is staggering. Some of the services include:

- Community services
  - Child care database, hunting and fishing licenses online, birth certificates, restaurant inspection reports.
  - Assistance eligibility screener—This service can help you find out if you are eligible to receive temporary cash or food stamps.

continues

- Online Crime Victims' Compensation Fund payment—The Crime Victim's Compensation Fund was created by the Virginia General Assembly in 1977 to pay unreimbursed expenses of victims who suffer personal physical injury or death as a result of a crime. The fund is administered by the Virginia Workers' Compensation Commission.
- Driver and vehicle services
  - Address change, driver's license replacement, insurance verification, organ donor status change
  - Sample knowledge exam—The sample knowledge exam shows you how well you know Virginia's motoring laws and safe driving techniques.
  - Prospective purchaser inquiry—Allows you to check DMV's records before purchasing a vehicle.
- Education Services
  - Find It Virginia—You can research any topic online with a valid Virginia public library card.
- Employment Services
  - CareerConnect—CareerConnect is a customer service network designed to assist workers, students, individuals seeking employment, and employers with an abundance of educational, employment, and career-related information.
  - Virginia Employment Commission continued claim for benefits—You can file a weekly continued claim for benefits over the Internet.
- Tax Services
  - iFile for Individuals—Allows individuals to file their Virginia taxes online.
- Legal information for public use
  - Sex Offender and Crimes against Minors Registry—Violent sex offender's database offered through the Virginia State Police.
  - Case management system—The Supreme Court of Virginia offers circuit court searches and district court searches.

Based on citizen and business feedback, the list of services will continue to evolve to meet the changing needs of Virginians.

E-Legislation

Although Virginia.gov does provide legislative information to citizens in the form of citizen bill tracking, a legislation information system, and a searchable database of the Code of Virginia, it is not clear if these efforts really help bring citizens closer to the legislative process. The site does provide links to every legislator in the state, but it is difficult to know if contacting a legislator, typically done through e-mail, has any real effect on the outcome of legislation. The concept of e-legislation is challenging and should continue to provide Virginia.gov with a great opportunity for enhancement.

One very nice and unique feature is the lobbyist-in-a-box. By partnering with the Virginia General Assembly's Division of Legislative Automated Systems, VIPNet created a user-friendly, online interface for professional lobbyists and legislators to track bills during the Virginia legislative session. This concept has been extended to allow normal citizens the ability to track up to five bills at any given time.

E-Voting

E-voting provides another opportunity for advancement. Currently, the risk associated with information security breaches is too great to consider allowing citizens to vote online. Unless the correct precautions are taken, an experienced hacker could easily alter the outcome of any election. A hacker is a person that uses electronic means to break into a computer system for which they have no authorization or intentionally overstep their bounds on systems for which they do have legitimate access. Hackers may or may not have destructive intentions when they compromise a system. A person who does have harmful intentions is typically referred to as a *cracker*. Whether a person is a hacker or a cracker is of little concern because the act of compromising a system that is being used in the electoral process would be enough to raise questions into the accuracy of the election results. The task of staying ahead of any set of criminals, especially hackers, is very challenging. Even if a reasonable amount of protection is implemented, criminals always find a way to beat the system. For this reason, Virginia.gov provides only basic voting information and services such as absentee ballot status lookup, election results, polling place lookup, voter registration information and verification, election calendars, and election schedules.

Moving Forward

The team at Virginia.gov has done a fantastic job building a portal that is both user-friendly and useful. Since it was created, the site has been recognized on a consistent basis for the different services that help bring government and citizens together. As time pushes forward, they are well prepared to continue to add relevant services; however, to remain on the cutting edge and continue to be viewed as an innovator in the world of e-democracy, Virginia.gov will have to pursue activities that allow citizens and businesses to become more directly involved with the political decision-making process. As mentioned earlier, there are many challenges to face in regards to bringing the legislative and electoral processes online. One simple first step could be to provide one central interface for users to send suggestions and comments to their legislator or to a list of legislators. This would help standardize the process and keep the users from having to follow links to every specific site for every different legislator. In addition to making the process easier for the user, it would provide the team at Virginia.gov with a much easier infrastructure from which they could set up a way to measure the effectiveness of the site. The suggestions could be published on the site, and a linkage to any legislation that was created or affected by the suggestion could be highlighted. Additionally, the time it takes for the legislative staff to respond to the person making the suggestion could also be measured. The ability to measure the effectiveness of the site should be viewed as a critical factor leading toward the growth and acceptance of more complex activities. By cashing in on successes along the way, the team at Virginia.gov will continue to evolve on the leading edge of e-democracy.

References

CenterDigitalGov.com, [http://www.centerdigitalgov.com/], accessed May 13, 2005.

KidsCommonwealth.Virginia.gov, [http://www.kidscommonwealth.virginia.gov/home/], accessed May 11, 2005.

NICUSA.com, [http://www.nicusa.com/html/index.html], accessed May 16, 2005.

SmartRegion.org, [http://www.smartregion.org/], accessed May 20, 2005.

Virginia.gov, [www.virginia.gov], accessed May 11, 2005.

Information Equality and the Digital Divide

In the basic sense of access to computers and the Internet, information equity is important to public managers because the less information equity exists, the less agencies can rely on information and communications technologies (ICT) as a vehicle for dissemination of official information. Also, the less the information equity, the lower the proportion of the citizens who will engage in electronic transactions with the government. When information equity is low, agencies are often forced to provide parallel services, one traditional and one electronic. Electronic services, instead of serving to make government more efficient, in some cases become add-on costs because of the need for duplication of electronic and traditional functions. Moreover, of course, information equity is widely perceived to be the basis for informed choice in modern democracies, and its assurance is in the civic interest, which is in turn based on democratic cultural values that public managers share with the rest of society.

The debate over information equity has centered around the concept of the *digital divide*. Some scholars think that the digital divide was once important, but as Internet access has become widespread, if not at home then at least in schools and libraries, the digital divide has closed and information equity should no longer be a priority in public policy making. Some say the digital divide may be relatively trivial within the United States or other advanced democracies, but that there is an international digital divide with profound consequences. Others say that the optimists who think the digital divide issue has gone away are simply measuring it incorrectly, and that information equity must be thought of as more than simple access to the Internet.

The policy answers public managers arrive at in this arena have much to do with how the digital divide is defined in the first place:

- Dichotomous access—Some define the digital divide as the gap among income, racial, ethnic, regional, or other groups in terms of differential access to the Internet, where access is considered a dichotomous variable (you have it or you don't). This definition is the one to select if one wishes to minimize the digital divide as a policy issue, though even in this definition one will find substantial disparities.

- Continuous access—A broader definition identical to the preceding one, except access is defined as a continuous variable that may vary from none to a great deal, depending on such component items as convenience of access (home, school, library), speed of access (28 KB modem to T1 line), time for access (discretionary time for access provided at work and home), cost of access, and/or other direct access factors. The digital divide for African-Americans, for instance, appears much wider for continuous access than for dichotomous access.

- Skilled access—A yet broader definition that defines the digital divide as the gap among groups in terms not only of physical access but also in terms of competencies for use of information technology (IT). Proponents of this type of definition point out, for instance, that public schools in the United States are notorious for funding computer hardware that sits unutilized in the back of the classroom because of lack of teacher training and staffing resources. Schools show a small or no digital divide in terms of dichotomous access but may exhibit a relatively large digital divide in terms of skilled access.

Few doubt that information equity is potentially a significant policy issue for managers. As discussed in Chapter 2, the history of information policy goes back to the 1800s and is, broadly speaking, a history of progress toward ever more equitable and widespread access to public information. At the federal level, numerous laws mandate equitable information access. What is debated often centers on whether the marketplace can provide that equity, or whether information access is one of those arenas where profit principles do not yield optimal outcomes, and affirmative action is needed by governments and by public managers to do what the market on its own cannot.

THE AMERICAN DIGITAL DIVIDE IN INFORMATION ACCESS BY GROUP

Between 1995 and 2000, the National Telecommunications and Information Administration of the U.S. Department of Commerce published an influential series of reports titled *Falling through the Net*.[1] These included "A Survey of the 'Have Nots' in Rural and Urban America (1995), "New Data on the Digital Divide" (1998), "Defining the Digital Divide" (1999), and "Toward Digital Inclusion" (2000). Although the first of these reports publicized the digital divide as a policy issue, the 2000 report came to relatively optimistic conclusions:

- The overall level of U.S. digital inclusion is rapidly increasing.
- By 2000, more than half of all households had computers.
- By 2001, more than half of all households would be using the Internet.
- The digital divide had diminished markedly for rural residents, blacks, Hispanics, and other "have-not" groups.

The 2000 report concluded, "The rapid uptake of new technologies is occurring among most groups of Americans, regardless of income, education, race or ethnicity, location, age, or gender, suggesting that digital inclusion is a realizable goal. Groups that have traditionally been digital 'have nots' are now making dramatic gains" (U.S. Department of Commerce, 2000).

In February 2002, the Commerce Department issued an even rosier view of evidence for the disappearance of the digital divide, titled "A Nation Online: How Americans Are Expanding Their Use of the Internet" (2002). This report noted that over half the population then used the Internet. It found that Internet use was increasing regardless of income, education, age, races, ethnicity, or gender. The executive summary of this report, somewhat at odds with the statistics buried in its back pages, was decidedly slanted to emphasize the view taken in March 2002, when Commerce Secretary Donald Evans said, "With the expansion of the Internet and related technologies into all sectors of society, the administration believes federal subsidies are no longer justified to prove the usefulness of such technologies" (Jackson, 2002a). A number of academics have also made arguments along the same lines, seeing the digital divide as having faded away or being about to disappear (Compaine, 2001).

Looking selectively at these reports and the data on which they were based, the incoming Bush administration based its information equity policies on the assumption that the digital divide issue was becoming irrelevant in an era of ubiquitous computing and Internet usage. Presidents Bush's FY 2003 budget proposed to eliminate two critically important Clinton-era information equity programs: the Technology Opportunities Program (TOP), administered by the Department of Commerce, to provide matching grants to bring the benefits of innovative digital network technologies to underserved communities across the United States; and the Community Technology Center (CTC) initiative, a competitive grant program administered by the Department of Education, which provided a broad range of services in locations convenient to underserved and disenfranchised individuals. Congress, however, chose not to defund TOP[2] or the CTC,[3] though FY 2004 CTC funding was only one-sixth the level of FY 2001.

As information equity policy has become more controversial and politi-
cized, Bush administration policy seems to be that the digital divide is
a thing of the past and therefore e-government (one of five major initiations of the President's Management Agenda) may proceed with little
worry for bias based on inequalities of information access. Whether the
assumptions of this policy are true or not makes a difference for public
managers, since it is they who must decide if information bias affects
their agencies. In this section we consider the extent to which the
assumptions of this policy are valid.

The Digital Divide by Gender

Cooper and Weaver (2003), based on their survey of two decades of
research studies, have documented the propensity of males to enjoy using
computers more than females, that males have less computer anxiety, have
a higher sense of computing competency, spend more time using computers, enroll more in computer classes, and more often select IT careers, in
spite of widespread general introduction to computing in schools. Females
are found to prefer traditional learning tools with frequent verbal feedback
and a noncompetitive format free of noise (e.g., not explosive sounds, pre-
ferred by young males). Females more knowledgeable about gender stereotypes of computer use had far less positive attitudes toward computer use.
Computer performance of females suffers most in mixed gender groups. In
general, early socialized stereotypes about computing and gender become
self-fulfilling prophecies to the detriment of female computer usage.

Computing history includes notable role models for women. A woman,
Grace Hopper, created Common Business-Oriented Language, the first
major computer language for business applications. Also, computing has
been used on a widespread basis for the last two decades to advance
women's issues (Eastman, 1991). However, for the general population,
computer-related gender bias against women started in childhood and
has continued right on through life. Early research showed that in each
of four major institutional arenas (leisure industry, media, education,
and the family) males received greater support and encouragement to be
computer users (Reisman, 1990).

In this early research, various authors (Demetrulias & Rosenthal, 1985;
Marshall & Bannon, 1988; Ware & Stuck, 1985) documented gender bias
in computer advertising. When women were illustrated, it was often as
clerical workers, sex objects, or in other passive roles. Only women were
shown in roles rejecting computer technology, whereas males were over-
represented in roles such as managers, experts, and repair technicians.
Other early obstacles to computer involvement for women included lack
of role models, gender bias in software, and sexual harassment in a
male-dominated curriculum and profession (Frenkel, 1988).

Only a decade and a half ago, researchers were finding that while as many girls as boys liked computers, many more girls ardently disliked them (Hattie & Fitzgerald, 1987). Women were also less willing to purchase a computer than were males (Morahan-Martin, Olinsky, & Schumacher, 1992). It was found that 85% of children using computers in schools were males (Erdman & Foster, 1988). Although more than one-third of undergraduate degrees in computer science were awarded to women, only 10% of doctorates went to women (Snyder, 1988). In summary, early research showed lack of experience was both a cause and effect of women having significantly less favorable attitudes toward computers (Badagliacco, 1990; Griswold, 1985; Kay, 1989).

Early researchers also noted, however, that once women became involved in computing, there was evidence that they did not evaluate computing less favorably than males (Shields, 1985). At least one study found that even controlling for occupational status, women might be much more satisfied with their experiences in computerized offices than men (Gutek & Bikson, 1985). Temple and Lips (1989) studied university students and found that while men had taken more computer science courses, men and women did not differ in their reported personal interest in and enjoyment of computers. Likewise, Chen (1986) found that when amount of computer experience was controlled, attitudes toward computing were similar between men and women.

These more positive studies suggested that as computing and the Internet became more universal, there would be no inherent gender bias and that the digital divide gender gap seen in the 1980s might disappear. Not everyone agreed. Frenkel (1988), for instance, noted that her studies showed female students were, if anything, losing interest in computing. Likewise, Smith's longitudinal study of journalism students showed the gender gap on computer use and attitudes had worsened significantly between 1989 and 1992 (Smith, 1993). Now, a decade and a half later, we are in a better position to judge which speculation was correct.

There is a persisting gender gap in the IT profession. A Harvard research project on gender trends found that at the turn of the century, women were still lagging behind men in terms of advancing in technology fields, with only 20% of IT professionals being women. Although the percentage of women receiving graduate degrees is increasing in most fields, it is not in computer science. The Harvard research also shows that the number of females enrolled in advanced computer classes in high school and college is actually falling (Grant-Lewis & Wood, 2000). The percentage of undergraduate computer science majors who are women peaked back in the 1980s and has since declined in spite of major efforts to remediate the gender gap in that discipline (Wulf, 2000).

Unfortunately similar adverse trends can be observed with respect to Internet usage by women. A survey of surveys on Internet usage in the United States taken between 1997 and 2001 showed that in terms of dichotomous access (use/no use), the gender gap evident in the early to mid 1990s had largely disappeared by the end of the period studied (Ono & Zavodny, 2002). However, in terms of continuous access, defined by use frequency and use intensity, the authors found that a gender gap remains. In a more recent comparative study based on 2002–2003 data, UCLA's World Internet Project researched Internet use in the United States and 13 other countries and found that in every country, more men use the Internet than women (*Business Journal*, 2004). The gender gap in Internet use averaged about 8% for the countries studied, though it was half that in the United States. Contrary to theories that economic development would be associated with greater equality, the UCLA study found the widest gender gap in Italy (20%) and least in Taiwan (2%), suggesting the gap might be more cultural than economic in nature.

The implication for public managers is that sole reliance on Internet distribution of agency information will have outcomes marked by moderate but predictable gender bias. It may be that affirmative agency steps to reach out to women as a population group, as by targeted advertising of Web site addresses or placement of appropriate articles in women's periodicals, can compensate for this gender bias. However, research to support this speculation does not as yet exist. In its absence, the gender gap remains a significant problem for public managers interested in information equity as it pertains to their agency.

The Digital Divide by Race

As with gender, early research linked race and ethnicity to holding less favorable attitudes toward and having less experience with computers (Badagliacco, 1990). Dutton, Blumler, and Kraemer (1987) found that formal education, which was significantly lower among minorities, was a strong factor in explaining the adoption and use of computers in the home. Race also appeared as a correlate of computing experience in other early studies (Gattiker & Nelligan, 1988; Platter, 1988).

Two major reasons were advanced to account for these findings of racial bias in IT matters. One line of reasoning held that it was a remediable matter of investing more in schools in minority neighborhoods. In addition to racial differentials in home computer ownership, wealthy school districts were thought to familiarize white students with IT more than could be done in poor inner-city districts disadvantaged by lack of computer equipment and staff (Ibrahim, 1985). A second line of reasoning emphasized a vicious self-perpetuating cultural cycle. "The fact that computer-related activities are seen as white and male may influence and

discourage women and minorities from making an academic commitment to careers for which high-technology skills are essential," Joanne
Badagliacco (1990, p. 42) wrote, predicting the formation of a "technological underclass" (p. 59) of women and minority workers in terms of
use of computer technology.

During the 1980s over a billion dollars was invested in helping public
schools compete technologically. As a result, sharp racial and income
disparities noted early in the 1980s seemed to have diminished
markedly by 1990. In the 1990s, further governmental efforts to mod-
ernize education have impacted information equity issues. The Telecommunications Act of 1996 (provided for an *E-rate* telephone tax to
fund Internet access for schools and libraries), the Library Services and
Technology Act of 1996 (provided additional IT funding for public
libraries), and the New Millennium Classrooms Act of 2000 (gave tax
breaks to corporations to donate computers) have combined, along with
state and local efforts, to make the existence of computer hardware
widespread in American education, even in low-income areas. This
increased the proportion of African-Americans who had some Internet
access, even if not at home. By 2000 the U.S. Department of Education's
National Center for Education Statistics reported that 98% of all U.S.
public schools had Internet access (NUA eMarketer, 2001). Although
some as a result proclaimed an end to the digital divide by race, school
access has not solved the problem of racial information inequality.

In 2000, Jupiter Communications reported a survey of 30,000 households,
finding that 60% more white households were online than African-
American households, though Jupiter predicted the gap would close by
two-thirds by 2005 (Fridman, 2000). More recently, according to Nielsen
NetRatings, as of January 2003, over 10 million African-Americans used
the Internet. They spent a total of 44 hours on the Web, initiated 42 sessions, and viewed 1186 pages.[4] Nonetheless, African-American usage of
the Internet remains less than that of whites. The total online population
in the United States spent more than 50 hours surfing the Net, logged 52
sessions, and viewed 1444 pages (Nielsen NetRatings, 2003), and according to the Pew Internet & American Life Project, 58% of the general population was using the Internet in 2003 (Stone, 2003) compared to the 29%
for African-Americans as reported in the Nielsen report.

Put another way, the Pew report found "Despite making up 13 percent
of the nation's population, blacks account for just 8 percent of all
Internet users" (About.com, 2003). The National Urban League's report,
"State of Black America," 2004, reported an "equality gap in technology," with African-American ownership of home computers being only
59% that of whites, and Internet access only 51% that of whites
(National Urban League, 2004, p. 5). African-Americans are less likely to

have home computers or Internet access, even controlling for rural residence and gender. However, African-Americans are also more likely to know of public computing facilities in their area; controlling for the same variables, this suggests the importance of digital divide programs operated through public libraries and schools (Wilson, Wallin, & Reiser, 2003). The percentages vary by survey and trends are toward improvement, but for now public managers must assume that a significant racial digital divide persists in terms of usage of the Web.

The Digital Divide by Income

Even though costs came down dramatically since the introduction of microcomputers in 1979, it is still not cheap to own and maintain a computer in the home. The Jupiter Communications research report cited above found that income was the most significant digital divide factor, more so than race or gender (Fridman, 2000). A 2003 detailed study of the digital divide in Detroit, Michigan, likewise found that for the Detroit area, which is one of the most racially segregated areas of the United States, differences in computer usage were based on disparities in income, not race (DeGroat, 2004). In that study, three times as many high-income households (over $50,000) connected to the Internet than did the lowest income group (under $20,000). Nationally, among the very poor (under $5,000), some 25% do not even have the possibility of Internet service because they lack telephones according to Federal Communications Commission (FCC) data.[5]

In 2002, the Consumer Federation of America (CFA) reported that fewer than 25% of the one-third of Americans with incomes below $25,000 had the Internet at home, while more than 75% of the one-third of Americans with incomes above $50,000 did. Moreover, the gap is wider when speed of connection is taken into account. The CFA found that the percent of upper-income households (over $75,000) that already had high-speed Internet in 2002 was as large as lower income households (below $25,000) that had dial-up Internet connections at home. Based on these data, the CFA report concluded, "Lower income households have fallen a full generation of technology behind" (Cooper, 2002, p. 5). The Annie E. Casey Foundation reported that 68% of U.S. children from households that earned $75,000 a year or more had access to the Internet compared to just 14% of children in households earning less than $15,000 (NUA eMarketer, 2002). Likewise, a 2002 survey of Temporary Assistance for Needy Families recipients showed only 15.8% of welfare recipients had some sort of computer in the home (Larrison, Nackerud, Risler, & Sullivan, 2002). Clearly, the digital divide is alive and well for public managers whose agencies deal with poverty and welfare programs.

Income and education are closely linked. For instance, in the Detroit study cited above, over 90% of college graduates were found to be computer and Internet users, compared to under 50% of high school graduates. While scholars argue the exact relationships among income, race, education, and jobs, there is agreement that employment is often tied to education, and educated applicants for employment have disproportionately used and benefited from the use of computers and are therefore more likely to receive higher salaries. That is, the digital divide by income is an obstacle to income mobility.

In an address to the Washington chapter of the American Society for Public Administration, Patricia Wood, in a presentation on "People, Politics, and Technology: Public Service in the 21st Century," cited the digital divide as one of the "major technical and management challenges" faced by public managers (Wood, 2000). Although the United States is not truly a classless society, the norms of public management as a field are set by the constitutional ideal of equality before the law, regardless of income group. Equality before the law in turn means that governmental services should not be rendered, at least not without offsetting approaches, in a manner that is biased by income group, which IT is.

The Digital Divide and Senior Americans

Early research established that computer and Internet use by senior Americans would be particularly beneficial. The American Association of Retired Persons surveys indicates that seniors held positive attitudes toward computing (Edwards & Englehardt, 1989). Controlled experiments demonstrated the computer capabilities of older Americans (Ogozalek, 1991). And it was found that nursing home residents benefited from feelings of mastery resulting from use of computers, not to mention benefits in the form of computerized health care technology (Levy & Gordon, 1988; Weisman, 1983).

In spite of long-demonstrated benefits, actual use of computers and the Internet by senior Americans has lagged. Jupiter Communications, a New York research firm, reported from its 2000 survey of 30,000 households that only 16% of seniors then used the Internet (Fridman, 2000). Data from 2002 in a University of California - Los Angeles report found that more than four in five Americans between 12 and 35 used the Internet, compared to only one-third of those over 65 (UCLA, 2003). A Pew Internet & American Life Project study covering 2000 to 2004 found that only 22% of Americans 65 or older had Internet access, much lower than any other age group (Fox, 2004).

Research to the present day (Fox, 2004) shows that the aged who do have access benefit greatly from it and in particular use Internet searching to find health-related information, often from governmental websites. On the other hand, for public managers in agencies that deal with senior citizens, the message is clear. Although information equity by age may exist sometime in the future, at the present time the digital divide is very pronounced for the aged and sole reliance on electronic dissemination of information and provision of services would be biased and a form of age discrimination.

The American Digital Divide: Summary

IT has great potential as a tool for public managers. However, information inequality by gender, race, income, and age remain significant problems at present. To break the circle of IT bias requires affirmative public policies rather than simple reliance on marketplace forces. Although public policy has been successful in aiding the diffusion of computer hardware and Internet connections for schools and libraries, this does not resolve digital divide issues. Indeed, the success in making Internet connections universal in American public schools combined with the fact that the digital divide remains significant in many dimensions suggests that the digital divide cannot be addressed solely as a matter of dichotomous access. Rather, psychosocial and cultural factors need to be taken into account, as a number of authors have emphasized (Stanley, 2003). Some authors argue that even as Internet access continues to become more equal in terms of connectivity, the differential in terms of access skills and usage is likely to increase (van Dijk & Hacker, 2003). Although treating the digital divide has waned in terms of American public policy (Wilhelm, 2003), this makes the challenges for the public manager even greater as the potentially discriminatory biases of IT endure.

THE INTERNATIONAL DIGITAL DIVIDE IN INFORMATION ACCESS

There is a pronounced global digital divide between the developed and the developing worlds. The 2004 report of Internet World Stats revealed this distribution of percentages of national populations having access to the Internet.

As can be seen in Table 4-1, gross global disparities in Internet access exist. In 2004, a North American was about 10 times more likely to have Internet access than a citizen of China, and almost 50 times more likely than an African. On the other hand, in the short 4-year period between 2000 and 2004, the number of individuals on a worldwide basis with Internet access more than doubled.

The Nielsen corporation, which rates television viewership in the United States, now also assesses Internet viewership from a media standpoint. As of February 2003, Nielsen-Netratings found that over half a billion people worldwide then had Internet access. Of this, the United States accounted for 29% of global Internet access, followed by Europe

Table 4-1   Percent of Individuals with Internet Access[6]

	2000	2004
North America	41%	68.3%
Western Europe	19%	
Eastern Europe	3%	
Europe		31.6%
Worldwide	5%	12.7%
Latin America	3%	10.3%
Asia/Pacific	2%	7.1%
Middle East	1%	6.7%
Africa	0%	1.4%

with 23%, Asia-Pacific with 13%, and Latin America with 2% (NUA, 2003a). That is, the Nielsen study findings indicated that the digital divide between developed and developing nations was as wide as ever. Fewer than 10% of the world's Internet users were based in Latin America, the Middle East, and Africa combined. However, Nielsen also predicted the doubling of viewership by 2005, so such percentages are moving targets. Nothing like the saturation penetration that has occurred in the United States is expected on a global basis, however, and some form of global digital divide will remain for the foreseeable future.

There is some progress even in Africa, which is the worst case region in terms of the digital divide. Corporate networks, cyber cafes, university connections, and other peepholes into the worldwide information society exist even in Africa. A notable development is the African Virtual University (AVU), a "university without walls" that uses modern ICT to give the countries of sub-Saharan Africa direct access to high-quality academic faculty and learning resources throughout the world. AVU's initial project was an online degree in computer science. However, it is still true that when the more developed South Africa and northern Africa are excluded, only one in 250 Africans uses the Internet, compared to more than one out of every two in North America and Europe (NUA, 2003b).

Many have argued that the digital divide perpetuates poverty within the information have-not nations. One website, for instance, examines how the digital divide and poverty go hand in hand on an international level.[7] The poor cannot afford to have access to the Internet and the digital world. People who do not have access to the digital world fall farther behind economically because of the shift toward a digital economy. The website quotes the prime minister of China making the statement that it should be up to the wealthy people of each country and the wealthy countries of the world to help provide technology access to those who are poor.

There is resistance on the part of developed nations to fund efforts to attack the global digital divide. The United Nations' World Summit on the Information Society (WSIS),[8] meeting in Geneva in December 2003, saw wealthy nations such as the United States, Japan, and many European nations rejecting the call of Mali, Senegal, Mozambique, and other poorer nations to create a special fund, with funding from richer nations and from IT companies, to subsidize hardware and software for poorer nations. A WSIS task force will review funding issues and reports back at the 2005 WSIS summit, to be held in Tunis (*The Economist*, 2003a).

The global digital divide is not simply a matter of funding and economics. As Drori and Jang (2003) have noted, connectedness in the global village depends not only on financial or even on political forces, but also on culture as reflected in the permeation of science. International contact and intercourse may be as or more important. For instance, Wilson (2004) studied the information revolution in Brazil, China, and Ghana. Like Drori and Jang, Wilson showed that the information revolution is rooted in societal dynamics, political interests, and social structure. His research documented how local apathy and vested interests opposed to reform must be overcome by information activists who need to fight to revise laws regulating telecommunications, found Internet companies, and involve nongovernmental organizations in social strategies for addressing digital divide issues. Another study of Egypt likewise found that seeking to use technology as a panacea for development does not work when technology is thrust on top of a dysfunctional system rather than being used to transform that system (Warschauer, 2003). That is, the international digital divide is a cultural as well as technological one.

The global distribution of information assets has significant implications for U.S. foreign policy, global competitiveness, and ultimately for the life of public managers in the developed and developing worlds alike. These implications involve not only the possibility of cyberterrorism, but other less-publicized but more important trends:

- The possibilities of cultural hegemony by content-producing nations applies to the Internet, as to movies, television, and other media. This in turn creates possibilities of backlash against digital globalization as well as Internet-based countermedia.
- Information access and assets come to be seen as "tickets to development" and securing them becomes a point of contention between developed and developing nations.
- Regulation of national economies becomes more difficult as the Internet facilitates the international transfer of funds and even of productive work itself. While undermining governance in developed countries as well, this trend makes developing nations feel even more disempowered.

- The spread of the Internet promotes transparency in government which, while desirable, can be a destabilizing factor for formerly closed societies.
- The World Wide Web increases professionalism in government as training becomes available inexpensively, immediately, and globally, and this too can pose problems for local elites.

Through these trends, public managers who deal directly with foreign policy are forced to move toward more responsive organizational structures, to work to a greater degree in partnership with global corporations and nongovernmental organizations, and to upload some regulatory functions to international organizations.

BEYOND ACCESS: DEEPER FORMS OF INFORMATION EQUALITY

Realizing the potential of the Internet requires much more than simple access as defined in current government policy. When one considers Internet applications such as telemedicine, for instance, implementation requires far more than plunking down computer machinery or even providing relevant content. It requires cultivating human capacity and changing ways in which both professionals and citizens behave (Wilhelm, 2003). That is, it requires organizational development, professional development, and social change. While market forces can accomplish some of this, government intervention is usually necessary as well.

Many now argue that access to IT equipment alone will do little to change people's lives (van Dijk & Hacker, 2003). Even with saturation of simple Internet access, large gaps in IT skill and usage will remain. This different type of but very real digital divide should be the focus of future public policy, it is argued. Investment in policies to enhance IT skill and usage is part of building *information capital*, which is a critical type of social capital needed by nations seeking to maintain and improve global competitiveness.

In terms of going beyond simple access, it should be noted that information equity also raises the issue of literacy as it is traditionally understood. To take an obvious example, a large proportion of the Internet is in English, placing speakers of other languages at a distinct disadvantage. Even for English speakers, simple literacy remains a significant problem even in the United States. Add to this the professional jargons of medical communities, financial communities, or other communities of expertise, and true access may require intermediaries who filter expert knowledge for general use. Market forces have already provided many such intermediaries, but at a price that raises information equity issues. What is the role of government in providing free or subsidized information services, continuing the tradition of free public libraries for print information?

PUBLIC POLICIES TO REMEDIATE INFORMATION INEQUALITY

The most significant public effort to remediate information inequality in the United States has been the E-Rate program created under the Telecommunications Act of 1996. Technically known as the Schools and Libraries Universal Service Support Mechanism, a Universal Service Fund was created based on funds collected from customers of telephone and telecommunications companies. In effect, the E-Rate is a publicly mandated, privately collected telecommunications tax earmarked for the purchase of computing and telecommunications equipment by public schools and libraries.

The Universal Service Fund reimburses from 20% to 90% of the cost of selected school and library acquisitions of computer and telecommunications hardware. This program is credited with the fact that by 2002, some 99% of U.S. schools and 92% of classrooms had Internet access according to the National Center for Education Statistics (2003). Differentials in school computer use by income level of the student was small (ranging from 80% for the poorest to 90% for the wealthiest students) and by race almost nonexistent.[9] This very success, combined with certain accusations of fraud and waste, led the Bush administration to the view that the digital divide issue was something of the past and no longer merited funding. In 2003 a Republican member of the House of Representatives, Tom Tancredo (R-CO), introduced the E-Rate Termination Act. Although this act has not passed as of this writing, many consider the E-Rate program's days numbered and, at this writing, funding has been suspended, prompting a congressional hearing, but resumption is promised (Funds for Learning, 2004).

The E-Rate program has provided up to $2.25 billion in annual discounts for telecommunications services and Internet access and, when funds permitted, for internal connection products and services. The highest priority has been given to the neediest applicant schools, based on the percentage of students in the National School Lunch Program, which was taken as a measure of need. This needs-based system led to some abuses where equipment was ordered more frequently than necessary by high-priority schools and disbursed to less needy schools in the same jurisdiction. New FCC regulations issued in 2003 and 2004 are designed to prevent such program distortions.

Although the E-Rate program is generally considered a success, a notable problem has been that it has funded only hardware and connections, not the personnel and educational support resources needed to go along with the equipment. The consequence has been that many schools have unused or underutilized computing and Internet capacity due to lack of computer resource teachers and lack of teacher training. As one local school system noted, "Experts and experienced practitioners in educational technology recommend that at least 30% of the total technology budget be targeted for staff development. While staff development choices are many for the teachers, true integration of technology has not been present in the classroom, due to the lack of support and resources at the school level" (Winston-Salem/Forsyth County Public Schools, 2001, p. 10).

At the other end of the spectrum from the E-Rate program are community-based initiatives addressed to handle the domestic digital divide. The community computing movement, discussed in the previous chapter, creates local facilities for Internet access, computer training, and development of information literacy. Community initiatives have a mixed record, and turnover of projects has been high. The FreeNet never quite became the national network of vibrant community networks that activists once hoped. In a case study of the Family Technology Resource Centers Program of 14 community technology centers operated by the Dekalb County School System in Atlanta, Georgia, O'Neil and Baker (2003) found that organizations seeking to mount community-based computing initiatives face major obstacles. They also found the best strategy for addressing these obstacles was through a participatory approach to community development.

Finally, it should be noted that the United Nations (UN) and other international bodies have developed a variety of programs to diminish the global digital divide. High investment costs mean the global digital divide will exist for the foreseeable future. National cultural differences obstruct regulation, and many scholars have called for a transnational effort (Ferguson, 1998; Gattiker, 2001; Norris, Bennett, & Entman, 2001). An example of digital divide policy in the international arena is the Alliance for the Information Society, a cooperation program started by the European Commission in 2001 with Latin American nations, aiming to promote the information society and fight the digital divide throughout Latin America.

As early as 1998 the UN General Assembly expressed "its grave concern over the generally widening technological gap between the developed and developing countries, particularly in the area of ICT (information and communications technology), which is shaping the contours of globalization." This marked the debut of the digital divide in the UN, which called a high-level panel to address it (Schölvinck, 2001). In 2000 a UN panel met, chaired by Jose Maria Figueres Olsen, former President of

Costa Rica, and issued a report identifying ICT as critical to addressing poverty, health care, education, and other global development needs and setting up a UN ICT Task Force and Trust Fund. In the same period, the Secretary-General's Millennium Report created three initiatives: (1) the United Nations Information Technology Service (UNITeS) to provide Internet training in developing countries[10]; (2) the Health Inter Network, seeking to create 10,000 hospital-based Internet connections in developing countries with access to up-to-date medical information[11]; and (3) the First on the Ground disaster response initiative, based on satellite and microwave technology for humanitarian relief workers.

In 2002, UN Secretary-General Kofi Annan called for a world summit on the information society, discussed above. It was at this 2003 summit that developed and developing nations reached an impasse over the questions of establishing a fund to attack the global digital divide in a far more dramatic way than the 2000 UN initiatives. The summit will meet again in Tunis in 2005. In the meantime, UNITeS continues to coordinate worldwide volunteer efforts addressing digital divide issues, as well as provide news resources on the subject.[12]

SUMMARY

There are several reasons why public managers must be concerned with issues of information equality and the digital divide. In immediate terms, to the extent to which digital access is not truly universal for the clients an agency serves, e-government will be undermined and the agency may even be forced to provide costly, duplicative services in both digital and brick-and-mortar modes. Beyond this, and more significantly, equality before the law is guaranteed by the Bill of Rights and the Fourteenth Amendment, making provision of equal services a constitutional obligation. In a democratic society, differentials in achievement and outcomes are accepted, but there is a strong presumption in favor of a "level playing field" in terms of equality of opportunity in such areas as access to education. Access to the information society is widely perceived to be in the same category.

Interest in developing computer skills is positively associated with digital citizenship. Viewing technology as a source of informational power is positively related to support for digital government and to support for computer access equity, research has demonstrated (Shelley et al., 2004). Not surprisingly, information "haves" are more complacent about issues of information inequality than are the "have-nots." The same study found, for instance, that nonwhites were more likely than whites to agree that technological information is key to citizen empowerment, and that computers should be accessible to all citizens, and to report increased interest in learning computer skills. Likewise, on a global basis, the call for funding an attack on the remaining digital divide is heard most loudly from the developing nations. For public managers who see a relationship between governance and the creation of a digital citizenry, the policy implications are clear.

Even as national and international organizations struggle with digital divide issues, market forces are deemphasizing the role of the state, the Keynesian social contract, and the idea of the public sphere in favor of an emphasis on privatization, commodification, and commercialization of institutions, resulting in a widening of the global digital divide (Stolfi & Sussman, 2001). Current U.S. national policy likewise is based on the assumption that market forces are solving all problems of information inequality. In spite of some notable international efforts, the bottom line at present is that wealthier nations have spurned the call to establish a global fund to attack information inequality, and this refusal, too, is partly based on the belief that market forces will remedy the problem. However, as data in this chapter show, even in the United States, information inequalities exist on a massive scale, such that public managers in many instances must assume that full realization of digital governance for their agencies must lie in the indefinite future. As Malina (1999) has warned, public managers who ignore the digital divide in their pursuit of e-government may well wind up widening the divide, making matters worse.

DISCUSSION QUESTIONS

1. The debate over information equity centers on the concept of the digital divide. However, how we define the digital divide has an impact on our public policies for information access. What are the three main definitions of digital divide, how do they relate, and how are they different? Which would you use, and why?

2. The G.W. Bush administration holds the belief that the digital divide in the United States has generally closed. What actions were taken because of this belief? What difference does the administration's view on the digital divide make to public managers?

3. According to the studies cited in this chapter, how relevant is the stereotype that women are less likely to be computer savvy? Explain your reasoning.

4. There are two major reasons that account for the racial bias within information technology issues. What are they? What has been done to correct them, and has it helped?

DISCUSSION QUESTIONS continued

5. According to a report by Jupiter Communications, income was the most significant digital divide factor, even controlling for race and gender (Fridman, 2000). What agencies would be most concerned by this finding? How does education relate to the digital divide by income?

6. Does information equity exist for senior citizens in the United States? Do you think this will change? Why or why not?

7. Some argue that the international digital divide perpetuates poverty in developing countries. Would technology funding from developed countries such as Japan and the United States be effective in closing the digital divide? Why or why not? Why should information equity within other countries concern us?

8. The E-Rate program provided up to $2.25 billion in annual discounts for telecommunication services and Internet access, mostly for schools. Although the program is generally considered a success, where has it failed? What are the short- and long-term results of this failure?

GLOSSARY

Continuous access: One of three main bases for defining the digital divide. The digital divide in this definition is a gap among income, racial, ethnic, or other groups where access to information technology is considered a continuous variable—one may have no, little, or a great deal of access, depending on components such as convenience of access, speed of access, cost of access, and so on.

Dichotomous access: One of three main bases for defining the "digital divide." The digital divide in this definition is a gap among income, racial, ethnic, or other groups where access to information technology is considered a dichotomous variable—one either has access or does not have access. This view minimizes the digital divide as a policy issue.

Gender, digital divide by: One of many components in the digital divide. Gender has been found in numerous studies to impact the degree to which individuals are comfortable and successfully utilize computers. Early research revealed that a lack of experience was both a cause and effect of women having significantly less favorable attitudes toward computers (Badagliacco, 1990; Griswold, 1985; Kay, 1989).

Global digital divide: Global statistics reveal that gross disparities exist in Internet access. Across nations there are several reasons for this, including the lack of affordable access in some populations, political will, cultural beliefs, and literacy (the Internet is predominantly biased toward English speakers).

Income, digital divide by: One of many components in the digital divide. Income is correlated with information technology access. Those with lower incomes are less likely to own a personal/home computer or to be connected to the Internet (many do not have telephones).

Race and ethnicity, digital divide by: One of the many components in the digital divide. Ethnic minority groups have been linked to holding less favorable attitudes toward and less experience with computers (Badagliacco, 1990). Two main reasons were found for this race/ethnicity connection: (1) schools in wealthy districts have more technology available to them as well as sufficient staffing and training, and (2) the view that computer-related tasks are generally white male endeavors may discourage women and ethnic minority groups from utilizing computers (Badagliacco, 1990).

Senior Americans, digital divide by: One of the many components in the digital divide. Senior citizens in the United States are less likely than younger age groups to make use of information technology resources. While many online resources, especially regarding health care, could benefit the elderly, the lack of access should be an information equity concern for agencies. This will change as those individuals using computers today replace current seniors.

Skilled access: One of three main bases for defining the digital divide. The digital divide in this definition is a gap among groups dependent upon competencies for use of information technologies as well as physical access.

ENDNOTES

[1]See http://www.ntia.doc.gov/ntiahome/digitaldivide/.

[2]See http://www.ntia.doc.gov/top/whoweare/whoweare.htm.

[3]See http://www.ed.gov/programs/comtechcenters/index.html.

[4]The most visited site by African-Americans was BlackPlanet.com, which had started with support for personal Web pages and later added matchmaking, job postings, African-American news, opinion polls, and discussions on political and social issues.

[5]See http://www.edu-cyberpg.com/Teachers/telephone.html.

[6]See http://internetworldstats.com/stats.htm. Retrieved 10/14/04.

[7]See http://www.idg.net/idgns/2002/09/03/DigitalDividePerpetuatesPoverty AsianLead.shtml. Retrieved 8/12/03.

[8]The WSIS website is at http://www.itu.int/wsis.

[9]See http://nces.ed.gov/programs/digest/d02/tables/dt428.asp. Sept. 2001 data.

[10]See http://www.unites.org.

[11]See http://www.healthinternetwork.net.

[12]See http://http://www.unites.org/html/news/news.htm.

CASE STUDY
Bridging the Digital Divide in America: E-Rate Program

Costas Panagopoulos
Yale University

The Telecommunications Act of 1996 codified lawmakers' commitment to ensuring universal service in the provision of telecommunications services. This legislation added a section (Section 254) to the Communications Act of 1934 to expand the principles of universal service in various ways, including that elementary schools—both classrooms and libraries—should have access to telecommunications services for educational purposes at discounted rates. The Federal Communications Commission (FCC) was charged with implementation starting in May 1997, and Congress directed the FCC to create competitively neutral rules to, "enhance, to the extent technically feasible and economically reasonable, access to advanced telecommunications and information services for all public and nonprofit elementary and secondary school classrooms, health care providers and libraries" (Section 254(h)(2)(A)).

As part of the universal service principles outlined in the 1996 Act, the FCC established a discount program for eligible schools and libraries, partly aimed to ensure availability of communications services to low-income and rural communities. The program has become known as the education rate or E-Rate program. E-Rate is available only to public and private nonprofit elementary and secondary schools with endowments below $50 million, public libraries, independent research libraries, elementary and secondary school libraries, and certain private libraries.

Initially, the FCC created the Schools and Libraries Corporation (SLC), an independent, not-for-profit corporation, to administer the E-Rate program. In 1999, an FCC reorganization dismantled the SLC as an independent entity and incorporated it into the Universal Service Administrative Company (USAC), a not-for-profit subsidiary of the National Exchange Carrier Association, where it has operated as the Schools and Libraries Division (SLD).

The E-Rate program permits eligible schools and libraries to obtain telecommunications services, Internet access, and internal connections at discounted rates that can range from 20% to 90%. Discount rates depend upon each school's percentage of pupils from low-income families and the urban/rural location of the school. (Income is measured as a percent of students eligible for the National School Lunch program.) If the percentage of students in the school who qualify for free or reduced price lunch ranges from 20% to 34%, for example, and the school is located in a rural location, the school is eligible to receive an E-Rate discount of 60%. (The E-Rate discount for a similar school in an urban location is 50%.) Individual schools and libraries are responsible to pay nondiscount costs.

To apply for E-Rate, schools and libraries are required to submit a technology plan detailing how technology will be integrated into the curriculum and professional development to improve education. Applicants are required to include several components in the plan, outlining clear goals and strategies for implementation, an assessment of necessary services, software and hardware, a budget, and an evaluation mechanism that enables schools to monitor progress. Technology plans must be approved by an independent state agency.

Despite the fact that E-Rate is a federal program, it receives no funding directly from the government. Instead, the program is funded by mandatory contributions from interstate telecommunications service providers. Congress requires all interstate telecommunications providers to contribute to the program, and contributions are based on a percentage of both interstate and international revenues. The FCC's Common Carrier Bureau calculates providers' contribution amounts quarterly.

The FCC caps funding for the E-Rate program at $2.25 billion annually. During the first six years of the program (January 1998 through June 2004), $12.9 billion of funds were committed. Since its inception, the E-Rate program has proven to be popular, and demand for funds typically exceeds availability. The funding ceiling has not been raised, however. During the filing window for 2003, for example, 41,146 applicants requested an estimated $4.7 billion. As of July 2004, $2.6 billion had been committed to 33,887 applicants. Similarly, 39,785 applicants requested an estimated $4.3 billion in 2004. According to estimates of funded applications, 29% were from schools, 53% from school districts, 17% from libraries or library consortia, and 2% from school/library consortia.

The E-Rate program remains popular on Capitol Hill, yet it is not without its critics. Opponents find the program to be controversial and too costly and suggest that funds are being used to purchase sophisticated equipment that goes beyond the provisions enacted by Congress. Many question the need for the program altogether and argue that it seriously duplicates or overlaps other federal programs. Others believe voluntary private sector initiatives adequately address the same shortcomings the E-Rate program was designed to ameliorate. Moreover, critics assert that the program's strong hardware orientation is unmatched by teacher support, creating waste and lack of effectiveness. Still others condemn the program's funding mechanism and propose alternatives including a state block grant program or funding the program from the federal telephone excise tax.

Recently, charges of abuse and fraud have generated potent attacks and caused the program to come under increased congressional and regulatory scrutiny. A report issued by the Inspector General for the FCC in 2002 showed that $8 million of E-Rate funds were erroneously disbursed. Other failures also surfaced. Allegations range from an incident in the Chicago public school system, where $5 million worth of equipment was purchased at E-Rate discounts but remains uninstalled, to a $50 million dollar case in San Francisco. In 2004, the Department of Justice indicted five people for fraudulently collecting $1.2 million from the program. The House Energy and Commerce Committee and the Commerce Subcommittee on Oversight and Investigations initiated investigations into several allegations of abuse or other improprieties. Hearings to investigate fraud, waste, and abuse have also been held in the Senate.

These criticisms have inspired lawmakers to review the E-Rate program and to consider changes. One extreme measure, H.R. 1252 introduced by Representative Tancredo in the 108th Congress, seeks to eliminate the program entirely. No action was taken on the measure. Senate Commerce Committee Chairman McCain introduced S. 1264 that called for additional scrutiny, review, and audit of the program. Senator McCain also asked the General Accounting Office to conduct a formal investigation and audit of the program. The GAO assessment, released at a Senate Commerce Committee hearing in July 1998, identified several administrative shortcomings and suggested a number of recommendations to address these concerns. Additional recommendations followed subsequent GAO investigations.

Concern over implementation failures have prompted the FCC and the USAC to respond. E-Rate administrators announced their intent to comply with GAO recommendations and have taken steps to improve E-Rate implementation. New FCC rules to improve the E-Rate program were adopted in 2003 and still further improvements are expected.

Despite these challenges, E-Rate proponents argue that the program effectively helps to bridge the digital divide by ensuring access to communities that would otherwise be disadvantaged. The findings of a report prepared by the Urban Institute and issued by

continues

the U.S. Department of Education Office of Educational Technology in 2000 provides some support for their arguments. The report documents that the E-Rate program targets the neediest schools and confirms that these benefit most from the program. It finds, for example, that the poorest schools (greater than 50% of students eligible for free and reduced lunch) represent only 25% of public school students but receive 60% of funds. Seventy-five percent of districts with 75% or more students eligible for free or reduced lunch applied for the E-Rate and received 14% of the total E-Rate funds even though they represent only 4% of the total number of students. The report showed that the poorest districts receive almost 10 times as much per student compared to the wealthiest districts; per student funding ranges from $109 per student in the poorest districts (75% or more eligible for free and reduced lunch) to $12 in the wealthiest districts (1–20% eligible for free and reduced lunch).

The report also provides evidence that the E-Rate program benefits public schools most: 90% of E-Rate funds are typically allocated to public schools and districts at an average per student funding level of $41. It also reveals that over 70% of rural schools typically participate in the program, and that 95% of libraries that applied for an E-Rate discount were funded.

These findings may be both a blessing and a curse for the E-Rate program. On the one hand, the evidence that the E-Rate initiative is helping to bridge the digital divide is hopeful. But what if E-Rate and similar projects have been too successful, effectively contributing to eradicating any disparities in equitable access to telecommunications? Would they still be necessary? The Bush administration, guided by FCC Chairman Michael Powell, is convinced this is the case, contending that the digital divide has virtually vanished (if it ever existed at all) and moving, consequently, to dismantle federal programs aimed at bridging the digital gap. Critics charge, however, that the administration's conclusions may be flawed, or, at best, premature. A report issued by the Consumer Federation of America, for example, finds empirical evidence of a persisting digital divide and claims that, "A close look at the data shows that the perception that the digital divide has disappeared is simply wrong (Cooper, 2002: 2). The report goes on to warn that, "Americans cut off from the benefits of digital technology will be severely disadvantaged in the new economy" (2002, p. 2) and calls for the continuation of policies designed to close the gap.

This discussion of the E-Rate program describes the intent of the initiative and suggests that, despite the controversies, criticisms, complexities, and imperfections, the program appears to be achieving, at least to some extent, its goal of helping to bridge the digital divide in the provision of advanced telecommunications services.

Costas Panagopoulos is a postdoctoral fellow at the Institution for Social and Policy Studies at Yale University. He may be reached via email at costas@post.harvard.edu.

References

Cooper, M. (2002). *Does the Digital Divide still exist? Bush administration shrugs, but evidence says 'Yes'*. Consumer Federation of America Report. May 30.

Gilroy, A. A. (2004). *Telecommunications discounts for schools and libraries: The "E-Rate" program and controversies* (CRS Report No. IB98040). Washington, DC: Congressional Research Service.

Jackson, C. (2004). *The E-Rate program: Universal Service Fund telecommunications discount for schools* (CRS Report RL32018). Washington, DC: Congressional Research Service.

McGuire, D. (2003, July 17). Fraud issue could undermine E-Rate program. *Washington Post.*

United States Department of Education, Office of the Under Secretary, Planning and Evaluation Service, Elementary and Secondary Education Division. (2000). E-Rate and the Digital Divide: A preliminary analysis from the Integrated Studies of Educational Technology. Washington, DC: Author.

Information Access and Governmental Transparency

Information access has two sides. One side has to do with whether citizens have physical access to computers, network access to the Internet, and the computer literacy and cultural motivation to seek government information, as discussed in Chapter 4. However, all the hardware, network connections, and computer competence in the world will mean little if the government is not able and willing to provide electronic information in a usable form. In this chapter we examine this second side of the information access issue, an issue many have discussed under the banner of *transparency*.

Transparency in government has become a buzzword, even a policy movement. Transparency is seen as an engine of development, creating an environment of good government in which business may prosper, the economy thrive, and governments advance.[1] The transparency movement does not have radical origins in protest groups, though protest groups do in fact benefit from governmental transparency. Rather, the main impetus comes from the private sector, where it has been argued persuasively that transparency is the prerequisite making possible the global economy and its efficient functioning (Oliver, 2004).

Global corporations, like all corporations, are beholden to investors. Investors, in turn, need transparency to "see through" market-relevant information to test the validity of investment strategies and financial assumptions. Corporations that are transparent are thought to be able to leverage this attribute for competitive advantage. Transparent corporations give investors and shareholders confidence in the company's operations and profit statements. Transparency is also said to promote employee loyalty and productivity, and to enable corporate managers to engage in strategic and tactical planning under sound and well-defined assumptions and policies.

At the same time transparency was becoming a widely held value in global finance and commerce, students of international affairs were also taking note of the phenomenon. The coming of the age of the Internet and of global media made information available to policy makers and ordinary citizens, to presidents and protest groups, to bureaucrats and legislators throughout the world. The new transparency, it was hoped, would increase global integration, diminish conflict, and promote economic development (Finel & Lord, 2002). A World Bank publication noted that institutions that support transparency are essential to sound economic development (World Bank, 2002). The World Bank specifically noted that "freedom of information law can signal the government's commitment to transparency" (p. 12), whereas lack of transparency "raises the price of information by inducing more voters who do not have special interests not to participate actively" (p. 10), creating governments dominated by special interests . . . a situation harmful to economic development. An example of governmental promotion of transparency is the municipality of Seoul, Korea, which as early as 1999 placed online all civil applications for permits, registrations, procurements, contracts, and approvals as part of an anticorruption campaign (Cho & Choi, 2004).

The same arguments about transparency applied in the private sector and the international sphere are also made about the United States. We find arguments such as this: "Representative democracies require competition for elected office allowing citizens to choose from among alternative candidates and parties. Multiple sources of information should he available in civic society so that citizens can . . . have their preferences weighted equally in the conduct of government. Transparency in government decision making, where it is clear who is responsible for what, promotes accountability via the ballot box" (Norris, Bennett, & Entman, 2001, p. 102). The rise of the Internet is seen as the driver of greater transparency and openness in American government, as it is in other countries and in corporations. The Internet can also allow wider and more informed public participation in policy decision making, more interactive communication between citizens and their government, and more pluralistic competition in the political marketplace.

Unfortunately, from a public management viewpoint, *transparency* is more of a banner or slogan than it is a set of directly implementable policy guidelines. It is true that the concept of transparency is entering the legislative sphere, affecting some segments of public management directly. The 108th Congress considered or passed the Government Settlement Transparency Act of 2003, the Mutual Fund Transparency Act of 2003, the Accountability and Transparency in Federal Campaigns Act of 2003, and the Tax Shelter Transparency and Enforcement Act, among others. Nonetheless, it is still true that there is no general

"Transparency in Government Act." Rather, public managers must assemble agency policy based on the Freedom of Information Act of 1966 (FOIA), discussed below, along with a large collection of other statutes affecting data collection, data transfer, and information access. Along with freedom of information, public managers must also wrestle with disability access and with trade-offs among information access, security, privacy, outsourcing, and a variety of other policy variables discussed below.

FREEDOM OF INFORMATION

The two pieces of federal legislation most directly related to the obligations of public managers to provide public access to government information in the United States are FOIA and its extension 30 years later in the Electronic Freedom of Information Act of 1996 (EFOIA). Hammitt (2000) has detailed the history of these three decades. Though largely forgotten now, it is meaningful to recall that Americans have not always enjoyed freedom of information. Freedom of information was a political movement before it was a law. The freedom of information movement originated in the resistance of reporters and editors to abuses of governmental control of information at the height of the McCarthy era. These abuses were justified in the name of antiterrorism, providing parallels a half century later, as McCarthy and his largely Republican allies sought to provide homeland security by seeking to root out all vestiges of communism in America (though opponents saw the motive more as political self-aggrandizement than actual homeland security).

Although the Administrative Procedures Act of 1946 (APA, Section 3) had stipulated that all matters of official record should be made available to the public, in fact agency managers were permitted to withhold information for "good cause." Moreover, under the APA, requests for information were limited to those deemed by public managers to be properly and directly concerned with the issue about which information was sought. For these reasons, the APA did little to help reporters, public interest groups, and ordinary citizens pry needed information from the hands of government bureaucrats.

The freedom of information movement was already beginning to crystallize, when it was rallied by Harold Cross's book, *The People's Right to Know* (1953). Cross had been hired as legal counsel for the American Society of Newspaper Editors in their fight against government secrecy. The freedom of information movement found a champion in Representative John E. Moss (D-CA). When the Civil Service Commission had declined Moss's request for data on the number of postal employees fired due to alleged Communist affiliations, Moss became upset. He used his position as chair of the Special Subcommittee on Government Information to hold Congressional hearings on freedom of information issues.

A survey of some 60 federal agencies by the Special Subcommittee polled public managers about the legal authority they claimed under which they were withholding information. When there was any authority cited at all, the most frequent response cited the Housekeeping Statute of 1789. Although Moss was able to get an amendment to the Housekeeping Statute in 1958, specifying that "this section does not authorize the withholding of information from the public," the Special Subcommittee found in a follow-up survey the following year that agencies had not modified their information-withholding behavior.

Between 1959 and 1966, freedom of information issues were taken up by Congressional committees. Hearings centered not so much on the principle of free public access to information as they did on the question of just which exceptions to the rule should be authorized. From the beginning, trade-offs were recognized between information access on the one hand and national security and individual privacy on the other.

FOIA owed its passage in no small part to a large number of compromises about exceptions to its provisions. The initial exemptions allowed withholding of records for reasons of national security, invasion of personal privacy, or if prohibited by another statute. Additional exemptions were passed to protect business trade secrets, geologic information important to the extractive industries, and financial records important to the banking industry. More exemptions safeguarded personnel files and agency memoranda.

On Independence Day, 1966, on signing FOIA, President Lyndon Johnson stated, "A democracy works best when the people have all the information that the security of the nation permits. No one should be able to pull curtains of secrecy around decisions which can be revealed without injury to the public interest." The president then ordered "every official in this administration to cooperate to this end and to make information available to the full extent consistent with individual privacy and with the national interest" (Public Citizen, 2004).

FOIA required each federal agency to designate an official to handle requests for information. All data that could be obtained with "reasonable effort" were to be made available. However, those requesting data were required to formulate specific requests, and this was often difficult when a journalist or interest group did not know what information might be available. Also, those requesting data could be charged "reasonable costs" set by the very agencies that might not be friendly to information requests. No time limits were specified for agency response to information requests. Requesters had no rights of appeal. And most important of all, there were no penalties for agency noncompliance with FOIA processes. The cause of freedom of information was not helped when in 1973, in *EPA v. Mink*, the Supreme Court held that the national security exemption applied to all classified records, meaning in practice that any agency with a "classified" stamp could withhold any records on an unchallenged, unappealable basis.

Congressional advocates of freedom of information took note of the many shortcomings of the 1966 act and, on the tide of public revulsion against government secrecy in the Watergate scandal, were able to pass a variety of reforms in the FOIA Amendments of 1974. Under these amendments, agencies were forbidden to assess FOIA requests for any charges other than the direct costs of searching and duplicating records. When it was necessary to go into litigation to obtain information via FOIA, successful litigants would receive legal fees. Time limits were set giving agencies 10 days to respond to FOIA requests and 20 days to respond to appeals. Authority to impose sanctions for agency noncompliance was given to the Civil Service Commission. The 1974 amendments were vetoed by President Gerald Ford on national security grounds and because the time limits were too short, he argued. His veto was overridden by Congress.

The FOIA Amendments of 1974 opened the floodgates for information requests that had been suppressed by shortcomings of the 1966 law. Unfortunately from the point of view of freedom of information, 1974 saw new obstacles imposed from a different direction. The Privacy Act of 1974 stipulated that federal records could not be disseminated without prior consent. In spite of the fact that the Privacy Act exempted information required to be disclosed under FOIA, the Ford Justice Department construed the act to mean all personally identifying records had to be withheld. In effect, this created an additional exemption to FOIA. Although this restrictive interpretation was protested by Senator Edward Kennedy (D-MA) and other freedom of information advocates, it was not until a decade later, with the CIA Information Act of 1984, that Congress clarified that the Privacy Act could not be cited as a FOIA exemption.

During the 1980s, in the years of the Reagan administration, freedom of information took further setbacks. The CIA Information Act of 1984 made records of that agency virtually unobtainable through FOIA. Law enforcement exemptions to FOIA were broadened by the Freedom of Information Act Reform Act of 1986. Federal agencies launched widespread computer matching of personal data, as of welfare recipients and income tax statements, enabled because the Privacy Act was interpreted to withhold data from the public but not from other federal agencies.

Finally, in *Department of Justice v. Reporters' Committee* (1989), the Supreme Court ruled that when privacy issues pertained to personally identifiable information, the requestor of information had to demonstrate that disclosure was necessary to shed light on government activities. Since this was difficult to demonstrate, particularly in advance of having the data, this 1989 court decision had the effect of further elevating privacy over access for personally identifiable information.

More damaging to the cause of freedom of information was an earlier Supreme Court decision, in *Chrysler Corporation v. Brown* (1979), which upheld "reverse-FOIA" lawsuits in which corporations sued agencies to block government release of data affecting them. Businesses previously had often lost such lawsuits, but President Ronald Reagan's Executive Order 12600 in 1987 changed that by requiring agencies to notify businesses when information was to be released, to give the right to corporate comment, to notify businesses of agency decisions about information release, and to delay actual release of information to give corporations time to file reverse-FOIA lawsuits.

President Bill Clinton championed an explicit "openness in government" information policy, encouraging agencies to provide data online and by CD-ROM. His Circular A-130 of 1993 reversed Reagan policy and mandated that agencies release information directly, not through contractors, who were less accountable. In the same year, Clinton's attorney general, Janet Reno, issued a FOIA memorandum that noted the purpose of FOIA was "achieving maximum responsible disclosure of government information," and encouraged agencies to disclose public information "whenever possible" without "foreseeable harm." Also, a system was created in 1993 to index all federal information (the Government Information Locator System), making information searching much more feasible. In 1994, the Department of Energy conducted national stakeholder meetings to declassify its data in accord with the Clinton program for openness in government.[2] Most important, during the Clinton administration the freedom of information movement succeeded in extending FOIA rights to the digital world.

EFOIA was passed in 1996, requiring agencies to make records available in electronic form in user-friendly formats, to create "electronic reading rooms" for public access, to issue handbooks on how to obtain information, and to make available indexed lists of what digital information is available. The act also provided for expediting FOIA processing for media representatives in matters of "urgency to inform the public." With the "urgency" exception, the time by which agencies had to respond was doubled from 10 to 20 days, but backlog was no longer to be considered an acceptable excuse.

In spite of good intentions, an analysis by Lewis (2000b) concluded that EFOIA made little difference for freedom of information. One reason was the EFOIA exception, which stated that agencies had to make reasonable efforts to search for electronic records "except where such efforts would significantly interfere with the operation of the agency's automated information system." Also, Congress provided agencies with no additional funding for the processing of EFOIA requests for records, and EFOIA was given no enforcement provisions to deal with noncomplying agencies. A 1997 Office of Management and Budget study cited by Lewis concluded that of 57 agencies studied, only the National Aeronautics and Space Administration (NASA) was in full compliance. Only 73% displayed any FOIA compliance at all, and in general, federal information was still hard to find on agency websites. A 1998 study by the Public Citizens Litigation Group complained of two "crippling failures" in EFOIA: lack of usable directories of federal records and long delays in making records available. Another 1998 study by the Reporters Committee for Freedom of the Press concluded that agencies that were responsive to FOIA requests before EFOIA (for example, the Environmental Protection Agency [EPA] and Department of Transportation) continued to be responsive, but lagging agencies did not improve in processing time or affording expedited review for reporters due to the passage of EFOIA.

Although in 1998 the Justice Department required all federal agencies to insert an EFOIA link on their home pages, a quick survey by the author in October 2004 found that many have not, including the Defense Department, the State Department, the Department of Education, and the White House itself. Those that do often have a link that leads to difficult-to-read information that only lawyers would consider user-friendly. Likewise, the level of information in the required "electronic reading rooms" varies widely, with some agencies listing only their mandated FOIA annual report. The required expedited processing for reporters also was perhaps not what one would expect. The Department of Health and Human Services, for instance, received 66 requests for expedited processing in 2003 and granted only 16.

After the terrorist attack of 9/11/2001, many agencies limited freedom of information. The Nuclear Regulatory Commission pulled its entire website. The U.S. Geological Survey removed maps of open water spaces. The EPA eliminated data on toxic waste sites needed by community groups to identify chemical hazards. The Department of Energy removed information about environmental impacts of nuclear plants and information on which communities are traversed by trucks carrying hazardous materials—information previously used by public interest groups. According to the nonpartisan Working Group on Community Right-to-Know, more than 6000 public documents were removed from websites of over a dozen federal agencies after 9/11. While some of this has been restored, there is little doubt that the United States now operates with less freedom of information than prior to 9/11. The EPA, for instance, denied twice as many FOIA requests in 2003 as it had in 2001. In terms of legislation, the Critical Infrastructure Information Security Act of 2001 exempted from FOIA disclosure any "critical infrastructure information that is voluntarily submitted" to one of 13 covered federal agencies (such as the EPA), and this has been cited as constituting a major new exemption to FOIA rights.

Immediately after the 9/11 tragedy, Bush's attorney general, John Ashcroft, issued a memorandum to all federal agency heads outlining how FOIA was to be implemented. Whereas Clinton and his attorney general had instructed agencies to promote freedom of information and to release documents even if they might arguably have been exempted under a FOIA exceptions clause, the Ashcroft memorandum reversed this policy. The new policy became one of encouraging agencies to look for reasons to deny access to information, and to expand secrecy in government by utilizing FOIA's exceptions as a way of denying access even beyond formal classification of documents. Moreover, public managers were assured that the resources of the Justice Department would be made available to them to defend refusals of FOIA requests should litigation occur (Public Citizen, 2004).

The Bush administration in 2002 resurrected the Eisenhower-era Office of Strategic Information (OSI) as part of the administration's antiopenness strategy to handle what some called "misinformation" to U.S. and foreign journalists and to citizens of Afghanistan (Shah, 2004). While deliberate misinformation has long been a weapon of information warfare, this marked a departure in expanding the strategy to an agency targeting American journalists and the American public, not just foreign enemies. In its short life, the OSI disseminated widely influential but false stories, such as a notable one about Iraqi soldiers yanking premature babies from their cribs and dashing them to the floor (Morano, 2002).

Then in 2002 the Homeland Security Act (HSA) was passed, called by Senator Patrick Leahy (D-VT), the "most severe weakening of the Freedom of Information Act in its 36-year history." In order to withhold information from terrorists, the HSA also denied to American citizens access to vital information about the public's health and security. Leahy noted, "Behind closed doors they jettisoned a bipartisan compromise on a responsible FOIA exemption and replaced it with a big-business wish list gussied up in security garb" (Reporters' Committee for Freedom of the Press, 2002). Moreover, the HSA added an element of intimidation, providing fines and imprisonment for any public manager who "publishes, divulges, discloses, or makes known in any manner" information concerning critical "infrastructure." Given the vagueness of *infrastructure*, the HSA and Bush administration policy was well designed to encourage the public manager to err on the side of information withholding and secrecy.

Environmental information has been a particular object of secrecy in the name of national defense under the Bush administration, which has encouraged federal agencies to resist FOIA requests. In late 2001, the Natural Resources Defense Council (NRDC) had undertake a FOIA lawsuit to obtain documents related to Vice President Richard Cheney's 2001 energy task force, "in which high-ranking administration officials met with representatives from utilities and the oil, gas, coal, and nuclear power industries to formulate national energy policy. The Bush administration ultimately turned over about 13,500 pages—less than half of NRDC's FOIA request" (*Greenwatch Today*, 2004; see also Nakashima, 2002). With the NRDC lawsuit's partial success, the Bush administration moved to close information access at the EPA. In May 2002, President George W. Bush's Executive Order 12958 gave the EPA the authority to classify documents as "secret" or "confidential." Once classified, these documents can be accessed by citizens only after the request is reviewed by an agency head or his or her designee, the citizen signs a nondisclosure agreement, and the citizen is able to establish a "need-to-know" to the satisfaction of agency officials, who may or may not grant the information request.

Writing of the unprecedented level of secrecy in the administration of George W. Bush, John Dean, former counsel to President Richard Nixon, wrote to Karl Rove, Bush's chief political strategist, "The continuing insistence on secrecy by your White House is startlingly Nixonian. I'm talking about everything from stiffing Congressional requests for information and witnesses, to employing an executive order to demolish the 1978 law providing public access to presidential papers, to forcing the Government Accountability Office to go to court to obtain information on how the White House is spending tax money when creating a pro-energy-industry Vice Presidential task force. The Bush administration apparently seeks to reverse the post-Watergate trend of open government" (Dean, 2004, pp. 12–13). Of the Bush administration, Dean wrote, "Government under a virtual gag order became their standard operating procedure" (Dean, 2004, p. xv).

Bush administration undermining of freedom of information principles led to opposition, even within the Republican Party (Nakashima, 2002; Schmitt & Pound, 2003). In 2004, a bipartisan group led by Senators Trent Lott (R-MS) and Ron Wyden (D-OR) proposed establishment of an Independent National Security Classification Board, which might function as a check on overclassification of federal documents. Bush's National Security Advisor Condoleeza Rice and Budget Director Joshua

Bolten wrote to House–Senate conferees on the bill, "The administration . . . opposes section 226 of S. 2845, which would . . . create a Congressional right to appeal classification decisions made by an executive agency with respect to national security information" (Federation of American Scientists, 2004).

A 2004 survey of open government laws by Rep. Henry A. Waxman (D-CA) concluded that under the Bush administration there had been a consistent pattern of undermining laws designed to promote public access, while laws that authorize the government to withhold information or to operate in secret were expanded. Waxman called the result "an unprecedented assault on the principle of open government" (Government Reform Minority Office, 2004). Specifically, the Waxman committee found that Bush

- had limited the scope of FOIA and had used procedural tactics and delays to resist information requests
- had issued an executive order undermining the law making presidential records available to historians and the public
- had evaded and undermined the Federal Advisory Committee Act, which requires openness and a balance of viewpoints on government advisory bodies
- had reversed Clinton efforts to declassify information
- had instead expanded the classification powers of executive agencies, resulting in a dramatic increase in the volume of classified government information
- had expanded the definition of "sensitive security information" to allow the withholding of information about the safety of any mode of transportation
- had proposed a pending directive to allow the Department of Homeland Security to conceal information about environmental impacts of its activities
- had expanded authority to conduct law enforcement operations in secret with limited or no judicial oversight through the USA Patriot Act and through new interpretations of existing law
- had repeatedly refused to provide members of Congress, the Government Accountability Office (GAO), and congressional commissions with information needed for meaningful congressional oversight
- had repeatedly challenged the authority of the GAO to review federal records or investigate federal programs
- had resisted providing information to senior committee members of Congress and to the National Commission on Terrorist Attacks.

The Waxman report concluded, "The Bush administration has systematically sought to limit disclosure of government records while expanding its authority to operate in secret. Taken together, the administration's actions represent an unparalleled assault on the principle of open government" (Government Reform Minority Office, 2004).

In 2005, Rep. Waxman also spoke out against the unusual decision of the Bush administration to suppress the State Department's *Patterns of Global Terrorism* report, even though the report was mandated under a law that requires it to be submitted to the House and to the Senate Foreign Relations Committee. The report, published and released publicly each year since 1986, detailed on a country-by-country basis all known incidents of terrorism. When the 2005 report covering 2004 revealed that there were more incidents of terrorism in 2004 than at any time since 1985,[3] facts that implied criticism of Bush policy, the Bush administration suddenly declared the methodology of the report to be "flawed" and ordered the State Department's National Counterterrorism Center to stop publishing the report. "This is the definitive report on the incidence of terrorism around the world," Waxman stated. "It should be unthinkable that there would be an effort to withhold it—or any of the key data—from the public" (Landay, 2005). However, Bush administration information policy centered on control, not access.

COMMERCIAL ACCESS RIGHTS

While in general the public supports access rights, there is one form of Internet access that is almost universally despised: spam. When in the fall of 2002 the Internet reached 50% spam traffic, this issue moved from a matter of personal annoyance to being a subject for public policy (McCarthy, 2002). By 2004, spam was averaging almost two-thirds of all e-mail (Wagner, 2004). In spite of widespread dislike of spam, however, the Supreme Court has protected commercial speech as part of free speech, albeit with some greater restriction. Commercial groups have argued that there is a free-speech right to access the Internet for purposes of transmitting commercial information.

The spam issue raises innumerable policy issues. Should AOL and other intermediaries have a right not to deliver spam? Should there be fines for spammers? If so, how are spammers to be differentiated from legitimate advertisers? Should there be fines for businesses that advertise via spamming services? Should companies, universities, AOL, and other mail directory hosts be required to install software to shield mail directories from bots, which read e-mail addresses and send them back to spamming services? Should government agencies or others be required not to list e-mail contact addresses as text but instead to have all listings as graphics? Should it be illegal to send e-mail with a spoof rather than real "from" address? Are we as citizens willing to pay extra taxes to pay for policing spam? Is spam control hopeless in any event in view of the fact that spamming services are often offshore?

A common inclination is to distinguish between legitimate advertising the recipient has requested and illegitimate spam that has not been requested but that is forced into the user's e-mailbox. Unfortunately, however, the "user asked for mail" criterion is, in practice, not very effective as a definition. All it takes is forgetting to uncheck a radio button on some purchase or other form for the user to have granted access rights. Moreover, those rights may have been given to a vendor of lists, who will resell the address to many more spammers, all of whom will claim to be sending advertising "with the user's consent."

A second possible solution is to allow spamming but require advertisers to run a clickable response form that lets users be removed from the list for future e-mailings. This solution has three flaws, however. Much spam comes from outside the United States and is not subject to U.S. law. It would be very expensive, if possible at all, to enforce that every e-mailing had a list-exemption response form that was present, working, and actually was utilized by the advertiser. And third, list exemption from a particular advertiser is virtually useless when rights have been given to a list vendor who does not itself do e-mailings and therefore offers no list exemption response forms. That list vendor will continue selling rights to its e-mail lists to thousands of other advertisers, making the voluntary response form exemption fatally flawed as a solution.

In 2003, under considerable public pressure and with the precedent of establishment of a no-call registry for commercial solicitation by telephone, Congress passed the Controlling the Assault of Non-Solicited Pornography and Marketing Act of 2003 (CAN-SPAM). While ballyhooed by the Bush administration as a piece of consumer legislation that would significantly restrict spam, other consumer groups have viewed it as a formal legalization of spam. The CAN-SPAM Act prohibits only fraudulent unsolicited commercial e-mail and in this aspect is redundant with previous, more general, fair-trade legislation against fraudulent advertising. No national antispam registry was created by this act. Moreover, CAN-SPAM superceded state antispam laws, preempting more consumer-oriented efforts such as California's.

CAN-SPAM does:

- Prohibit e-mail containing false or fraudulent headers
- Require spam containing advertisements for sexually oriented material to be so labeled
- Require commercial e-mail to contain an opt-out button for consumers wishing not to be contacted again
- Prohibit spammers from using false or misleading identification

CAN-SPAM does not:

- Stop users from having to go through 20 pages of advertisements to find an opt-out link
- Stop users from having to opt-out on each and every subdivision of a spamming company
- Prohibit spammers from creating new subdivisions on a daily basis to repeat spam in spite of opt-outs from previous subdivisions
- Give consumers the right to sue spammers (authority to take action under CAN-SPAM is given only to Internet Service Providers, state attorneys general, and the Federal Trade Commission [FTC]). Moreover, caps are placed on damages spammers could pay due to litigation.
- Apply to unsolicited commercial e-mail unless the "primary purpose" is commercial advertisement

The FTC's website at http://www.ftc.gov/spam/ urges consumers to report fraud to the FTC for storage in a database it states is used for litigation. The site also instructs consumers on how to suppress pop-up ads in their Web browsers and how to set e-mail software to attempt to filter spam. Other advice to businesses describes how to secure servers from being captured and used by spam software. Advertisers are warned about fraudulent, deceptive, and unfair business practices, which specifically includes having nonworking opt-out buttons in spam mailings. Nothing suggests that nonfraudulent spam is illegal because, indeed, CAN-SPAM recognizes the legality of unsolicited commercial e-mail. As President Bush's press release on CAN-SPAM noted, the law "provides greater certainty in interstate commerce for businesses that would otherwise face a wide diversity of state laws on spam" (Office of the Press Secretary, 2004). That is, the CAN-SPAM act must be viewed primarily as legislation to regularize the practice of mass unsolicited commercial access to the Internet.

DISABILITY ACCESS

New technology now makes possible creative ways for people with disabilities to access information. For instance, in 2003 the Internal Revenue Service (IRS) enabled some 50 forms to "talk" in order to provide visually impaired users with access. Forms include the widely used income tax forms 1040, 1040A, and 1040EZ (Vasishtha, 2002a).[4] Nonetheless, access to the Internet by the disabled remains a serious problem in America, with implications specific to public management. For instance, a 2003 survey of 100 social service agency websites found, for instance, that an overwhelming majority of websites failed one or more accessibility measures (multilingual access, reading simplicity, reading comprehension [grade level], disability access), creating substantial barriers for service consumers (Vernon & Lynch, 2003). Nationally—using data from summer 2004, gathered by Darrell M. West, director of the Taubman Center for Public Policy—Brown University researchers studied 1,873 sites maintained by the 70 largest city governments in the country as well as sites at the state and federal levels. The researchers found only 21% of city sites, 37% of state sites, and 42% of federal websites complied with disability access standards as measured by automated Bobby software created by Watchfire Inc. to assess disability compliance. This was little changed from the previous year (Brown University, 2004). That is, the majority of governmental websites do not meet national disability access standards in spite of this having been a requirement for public managers for years.

In 1965 Congress created the National Commission on Architectural Barriers to Rehabilitation of the Handicapped. Its 1968 report led to the passage of the Architectural Barriers Act of 1968 (ABA). Shortcomings in compliance with the ABA led Congress to pass the Rehabilitation Act of 1973. Section 502 created the Access Board, an independent federal agency that was originally responsible for disabilities standards in architecture and transportation but was later responsible for developing and maintaining accessibility requirements for information technology (IT) and telecommunications as well.

The Access Board is governed by a board of federal departmental representatives and public members appointed by the President. The Rehabilitation Act Amendments of 1974 gave the Access Board the authority to withhold federal funds from noncomplying state and local agencies. The Rehabilitation Act Amendments of 1978 gave the Access Board a technical assistance role in disability compliance, including assistance to the private sector. Throughout the 1980s, focus was primarily on the disability compliance of physical architecture and transportation with the ABA.

The passage of the Americans with Disabilities Act of 1990 (ADA) substantially increased the scope of disability compliance concerns, specifically mandating that governmental telecommunications services be disability compliant. The Telecommunications Act of 1996 included provisions that recognized the importance of disability compliance in the telecommunications sector. The Access Board was given the mandate to develop guidelines for making telecommunications products manufactured in the private sector accessible.

President Clinton signed the Rehabilitation Act Amendments of 1998, which strengthened Section 508 access to electronic technology and IT provided by the federal government. This gave the Access Board the responsibility to develop disabilities standards for federal procurement of IT equipment and required purchasing compliance by all federal agencies unless there was "undue burden." The Access Board created the Electronic and Information Technology Access Advisory Committee to assist in the formulation of standards, which were released in December 2000.

The U.S. Department of Justice provides a variety of detailed guidelines for public managers wishing to mount a disabilities-compliant website.[5] Rehabilitation Act Section 508 is the legal authority for mandated disabilities access to governmental websites, and guidance for public managers mounting websites is maintained by the Access Board (www.access-board.gov; guide at www.access-board.gov/sec508/guide/1194.22.htm). The General Services Administration also runs an online course for Web developers interested in accessible Web design (www.section508.gov). Private sector organizations also provide ADA guidance (see www.w3c.org/WAI/Resources). Also, declining vision may impede access to the Web for some seniors unless Web designers follow guidelines published by the National Institute on Aging (Becker, 2004).

Among the managerial guidelines promoted by the Department of Justice are having a formal, written disabilities access policy; making the disabilities plan public and inviting public participation by the disabled and groups representing them; training in-house staff in disabilities awareness as it pertains to Web access; requiring that contractors be responsible for ADA compliance for web-related products; and providing a posted telephone number and e-mail address for disabled citizens seeking assistance in gaining access. Managers should also enlist disability groups to test agency pages for ease of use on a periodic basis.

OBSTACLES TO INFORMATION ACCESS: SECURITY

The classifying and withholding from the public of information deemed important to national security is a long-standing and widespread practice that is largely accepted by public managers without controversy. National security reasons are an explicit exception written into FOIA. Security, moreover, goes beyond the military and is defined more broadly than commonly realized. A study by Brown University's Center for Public Policy studied 1,265 federal and state websites. Some 6% had restricted areas requiring a password to enter, an increase reflecting post-9/11 attention to security (Sweeney, 2002). At the federal level, a report by the Information Security Oversight Office (ISOO) found that in 2003, the federal government made over 14 million decisions to declare information and files "confidential," "secret," or "top secret" (Carr & Duffy, 2004). The rapid growth in the federal classification system under the Bush administration, up 40% between 9/11 and the end of

2003, prompted ISOO Director Bill Leonard to warn that the public's democratic right to obtain information about government activities was threatened.

In 2004, the GAO undertook an inventory of major government networks supporting homeland security functions. Of the 34 major systems identified, costing about $1 billion annually to maintain, eight were classified, 18 were sensitive but unclassified, and only eight were unclassified. Moreover, the GAO indicated that there were additional classified networks whose very existence was not publicly acknowledged and that therefore were not reported (Dizard, 2004a).

The burgeoning classification system is not accompanied by an equivalent expansion of attention and oversight from senior officials. On the contrary, public managers feel under substantial pressure to classify any sort of information that might in some way relate to the war on terrorism. Fear of reprimand or even prosecution is a motivation for mid-level officials to err on the side of classification of information, according to Steven Aftergood, director of the Federation of American Scientists' Project on Government Secrecy.

In this context, civil libertarians complain that the abuses of the Patriot Act cannot be investigated empirically because the data are secret. Environmentalists complain that toxic waste site and nuclear accident information is no longer made available, charging this is less part of the war on terrorism than it is undermining the ability of public interest groups to oppose public policies.[6] Should civil liberties and environmental groups have access to the public information they seek? For that matter, should ordinary citizens have access to data on juvenile crimes in their neighborhood? Should citizens have access to data on criminal suspects not yet convicted in a court of law? Should labor unions be allowed to access IRS data about corporations whose workers they represent, to better assess the ability of employers to make concessions? Should sociologists be able to access data about suicides in the military? These and thousands more questions form the grist with which civilian and military public managers must deal as they seek to walk the line between their obligation to provide access to government information and their obligations to follow security and privacy regulations.

Of course security is not limited to matters of defense. There is a trade-off between security and access in all information systems, from CIA computers to campus computer labs. The rise of computer viruses and hacking, to be discussed in Chapter 8, has profoundly changed the nature of networking (Jackson, 1988), forcing IT managers to invest heavily in security and to create less-than-user-friendly but more secure systems. The federal IT security budget is orders of magnitude larger than all e-government access programs combined, creating direct resource competition between security and access advocates. Clear, written policies on both security and access help public agencies to deal with the inevitable trade-off from undermining the legitimate goals of each.

OBSTACLES TO INFORMATION ACCESS: PRIVACY

A great deal of government information is about us. We fear the rise of the "surveillance society," and we fear equally the loss of our privacy in the name of freedom of information. Privacy issues of IT are explored in more detail in Chapter 6. For now it simply may be noted that there is a trade-off between access and privacy, just as there is between access and security. The public manager is under dual mandates to make government information available and yet also protect individual privacy rights.

Some have responded to this duality by arguing for even more transparency and access. Brin (1999), for instance, has argued that the issue is not surveillance—that is inevitable and growing quickly. The real issue, Brin contends, is who will have access to information? Who will be able to view the cameras that may come to every corner? Even greater freedom would result, he says, if we all had access to public surveillance and public information, so long as surveillance did not intrude into our own homes. In this view, privacy undercuts accountability, eroding the foundation of a free society. He cited examples including access to police cameras to tell which areas are safe, and access to surveillance of gay pride events in Arizona. Brin, a futurist, made the case that universal access enhances freedom. The real danger to freedom, he contended, are "privacy" policies that restrict surveillance information to the eyes of an elite few. The path of openness raises issues about individual privacy; the path of privacy raises the issue of who watches the watchers, an issue that Brin argued is far more intractable and fraught with danger for a free society.

Brin's *The Transparent Society* (1999) carries the logic of freedom of information to its conclusion: the choice between (1) restricted information with our privacy protected (we think, but cannot truly know) by legislative prohibitions on to whom and how information may be released; or (2) an open society where citizens, watchdog groups, public interest lobbies, news media, and everyone would be able to access information to provide a check on the abuse of society. The actual policies pursued by public managers fall between these two extremes, but it may be helpful to note that complete protection of privacy would mean a society where agencies could gather data on citizens but citizens could not effectively hold government accountable for that information. On the other hand, complete freedom of information would be exploited more by corporate marketers, credit institutions, the major political parties, and other elites with greater resources to throw into the task than could the lowly average citizen. The public manager must be concerned with both dangers: the danger abuse of information by politicians above the agency or by bureaucrats within, and the danger of the agency becoming the pawn of information exploitation by elites. The prevailing solution is a middle course, providing some, but not unlimited, information access while establishing some, but limited, privacy rights.

OTHER OBSTACLES TO INFORMATION ACCESS

Literature from transparency-in-government advocates often creates a simple equation: records = transparency = accountability = good government. However, one has only to look at the history of public management in developing countries to see that this equation rests heavily on cultural assumptions. For instance, in sub-Saharan Africa the implementation of financial information systems has not checked corruption (Barata & Cain, 2001). For electronic access to records to lead to accountability, accurate recordkeeping must be in place. This in turn requires accurate source data, payment of record-keeping staff at market rates, realistic backup and storage, realistic targets and project management, and a public management commitment to undertake organizational development and change to create a *culture of openness*.

To create a culture of openness within one's agency, the public manager must overcome many additional obstacles and challenges beyond those already mentioned in this chapter. The manager must be in control of the agency's information resources, including intellectual property rights; must be able to communicate with the public in language that fits the agency's clientele; and must have the resources to avoid the problem of information obsolescence.

- Outsourcing—An open agency must retain control over its information resources, either directly or through contractual agreements. The rampant growth of outsourcing of government functions, discussed in Chapter 10, threatens agency information control and thus access. Agencies must undertake affirmative efforts to retain information control. For instance, Federal Reserve Board guidelines on outsourcing specifically note that arrangements "must not hinder the ability of the institution to comply with all applicable U.S. laws and regulations, including, for example, requirements for accessibility and retention of records" (Federal Reserve, 2000).
- Intellectual property rights—The era of public–private partnership has brought a mixing of public and private information resources.

Intellectual property rights owned by private-sector firms may prevent public access to databases that would have been open under previous all-public arrangements. Intellectual property issues have been raised in relation to access to data from the Human Genome Project, images in government-owned museums, software developed in part with federal funds, biotechnology data, and even Supreme Court transcripts. While agencies often can find solutions that preserve both access and intellectual property rights, this can be challenging and at times may even involve litigation, particularly when the agency has not been skilled in contract-writing for outsourced work.

- Literacy—An open agency must provide information at a literacy level compatible with the populations it serves. A 2003 Brown University study found that 63% of federal websites had a 12th-grade average readability level, while the average American citizen reads at or below the 8th-grade level. This literacy gap significantly limits the utility of federal Web services. The report noted that 90 million adult Americans have low literacy, 53 million have some level of disability, including blindness, and 25 million primarily speak a language other than English (West, 2003a).
- Technical issues—Technology changes quickly, leaving behind obsolete data formats as well as equipment. Agencies that do not invest in updating information resources risk finding that their data can no longer be read, at least not conveniently, by current technology. Data on old media can also decay if not renewed. This is not merely a theoretical possibility. Some 20% of NASA's 1976 Viking Mars landing data are now said to be completely unreadable and lost forever. Likewise, the 1960 U.S. Census was stored on now-obsolete computer tapes that can be read only by one computer, now located in the Smithsonian Institution (Elgan, 1999).

There are, of course, numerous additional obstacles to creating a culture of openness and providing freedom of information to citizens. The most important have been mentioned in this chapter, and they constitute a formidable challenge for the public manager who is committed to transparency in government. As the reversal of information openness policy by the present Bush administration shows, managers cannot assume a unilinear march toward ever-greater freedom of information. In the arena of information, as in other arenas, freedom must be fought for and won, and then defended.

SUMMARY

In his last major work before his death in 2003, Senator Daniel Patrick Moynihan (D-NY) wrote *Secrecy: The American Experience* (1998), in which he advocated a culture of openness in decision making. Based on his chairmanship of the bipartisan Commission on Protecting and Reducing Government Secrecy, in this work Moynihan traced governmental secrecy since World War I through the failure to predict the collapse of the Soviet Union, arguing that many tragedies resulting from events he describes could have been prevented had the issues been clarified in an open exchange of ideas. Likewise, as this chapter is being written, the *New York Times* is quoting federal officials as saying that the 2004 scandals in the military justice system—abuses that severely damaged the credibility of American foreign policy—"are rooted in the secretive and contentious process from which it emerged" (Golden, 2004). Freedom of information, transparency, and openness in government are not niceties of a democratic society; they are fundamental to its survival and a major reason for the effectiveness of the democratic form of government.

Defending democracy against fascism and communism, Karl Popper argued in *The Open Society and Its Enemies* (1945), that open societies are superior because they are better able to adapt to change and to new technologies. Transparency or lack of it is not technologically determined. While reinforcement theory might predict current reversals of transparency brought against the public interest by political powers that be, it is more important to recognize that transparency in government is a force for feedback in systems analysis terms, and feedback is the engine of system adaptation, providing a competitive advantage for the agency. Creating the organizational culture of openness requires organization development using the stakeholder- and employee-centered approaches of sociotechnical theory.

The Information and Privacy Commissioner for Ontario has given these guidelines for creating a culture of openness in a government agency (Wright, 1996).

- Involve staff from all areas of the organization in developing an access strategy.
- Study, examine, and review Freedom of Information requests for purposes of identifying trends, patterns, and problems; then identify solutions.
- Be access-conscious when designing agency forms. For example, keep personally identifiable information separate.
- Use training situations as an opportunity for staff to identify information that can be routinely disclosed or actively disseminated.
- Invest in ongoing staff awareness, orientation, training, and education efforts.
- Partner with other agencies to regularly share ideas about improving access.

The Canadian government has been a leader in both freedom of information and in privacy protection, demonstrating that the two can be compatible. However, compatibility does not occur without planning. It is instructive that in the list above, participative strategic planning is placed first.

Among the similar guidelines of the U.S. GAO for total quality management in federal agencies are these rules for strategic planning:[7]

- Start with the client and end with the client.
- Build consensus by involving all parties.
- Focus on strategic results.
- Use the plan as a framework for all other organizational decisions.
- Publish the plan for transparency reasons.

At the micro level, the principles of freedom of information and transparency in government are widely accepted and frequently acted upon. At the macro level, however, in matters ranging from energy policy to health policy to decision making about the Iraq War, there is a great gap between the principles of open government and its practice in the American setting. Public managers are not policy makers, at least not in the main, but precisely because of the gap between principle and practice, individual public managers face challenging choices when implementing legislation mandating freedom of information.

DISCUSSION QUESTIONS

1. What brought about the Freedom of Information Act of 1966? What changed in how the federal government handled information requests and what were shortcomings of the act?

2. The Homeland Security Act of 2002 was created to prevent events similar to those of 9/11 from happening again. However, it has altered how citizens can access information and agencies can distribute information. What important federal activities have been kept from public view due to this act? How does this impact public health, environmental issues, etc.?

3. Spam has become a nuisance for many. Congress passed the CAN-SPAM Act of 2003 in an effort to curb unsolicited commercial e-mail. However, many consumer groups believe that the act is a formal legalization of spam. Why? How could the act have been more effective?

4. In an effort to overcome information access barriers for those with disabilities, the Department of Justice provides guidelines for managers as they develop and

DISCUSSION QUESTIONS continued

implement disability policy. What are some of their suggestions? Can you think of any other beneficial actions that managers could take?

5. How could one know if the government overclassifies information, preventing access? Would you support an independent review commission with powers to declassify as many documents as possible? If so, what would your arguments be against those, such as the Bush administration, who disagree?

6. Access and privacy policies sometimes constitute a trade-off. What are the two choices Brin sets forward in *The Transparent Society*? What are the benefits and costs of each?

7. Creating a culture of openness presents a host of obstacles for the public manager. Name at least two obstacles. What can managers do to overcome the obstacles you cite?

8. What actions can be taken at a managerial level to close the gap between the principle of transparency in government and its actual practice?

GLOSSARY

Classification: Government agencies under the authority of the president can be granted the authority to label certain information as "secret" or "confidential," thus removing it from the body of information accessible to citizens under FOIA requests.

FOIA requests: The Freedom of Information Act (FOIA) provided specific rights and guidance regarding citizens' requests for information from agencies. The agencies, in turn, were given restrictions on how to process these requests.

Openness in government: President Clinton energetically encouraged agencies to provide as much information as possible within the bounds of FOIA, especially through the Internet and on CD-ROM. This was termed "openness in government" information policy and stands in contrast to unprecedented secrecy during the ensuing Bush administration.

Overclassification: Overclassification refers to the classification of information by government agencies beyond the stated objective of the classification, usually for unstated reasons of protection of the agency and/or political leaders from criticism, or for sheer bureaucratic reasons.

Reverse FOIA: Reverse FOIA refers to lawsuits in which corporations take action against the federal government to block agencies from releasing data that could affect their business practices and sales.

Spam: Spam refers to unsolicited messages sent to Internet users via e-mail from legitimate or illegitimate commercial entities.

Transparency: In the context of electronic information access, transparency is the willingness and ability of government to provide usable and reliable information to citizens on all matters of policy importance.

ENDNOTES

[1]United Nations Development Programme, www.undp.org/oslocenter/access_pos.htm.

[2]http://www.osti.gov/html/osti/opennet/document/press/pc2.html.

[3]There were 625 reported terrorist attacks. The report did not include attacks on U.S. troops in Iraq.

[4]Access required users to own and have installed a speech synthesizer compatible with Microsoft Active Accessible software.

[5]For instance, see U.S. Department of Justice, Civil Rights Division, Disability Rights Section (2003). *Accessibility of State and Local Government Websites to People with Disabilities.* Washington, DC: USGPO. This document suggests the following specific ADA guidelines for agency websites:

1. When navigation links are used, people who use a screen reader must listen to all the links before proceeding. A "skip navigation link" function provides a way to bypass the row of navigation links by jumping to the start of the Web page content.
2. All images and graphics need to have an alt tag or long description.
3. Use alt tags for image maps and for graphics associated with the image map so a person using a screen reader will have access to the links and information.
4. Some photos and images contain content that cannot be described with the limited text of an alt tag. Using a long description tag provides a way to have as much text as necessary to explain the image so it is accessible to a person using a screen reader but not visible on the Web page.
5. Text links do not require any additional information or description if the text clearly indicates what the link is supposed to do. Links such as "click here" may confuse a user.
6. When tables with header and row identifiers are used to display information or data, the header and row information should be associated with each data cell by using HTML so a person using a screen reader can understand the information.
7. A link with contact information provides a way for users to request accessible services or to make suggestions.

The Department of Justice has further information about accessible Web page design in an April 2000 report, available at www.usdoj.gov/crt/508/report/content.htm.

[6]The EPA has removed risk management plans and other information pertaining to hazardous waste sites from its website, citing risk of terrorism outweighing the right of citizens to know hazardous waste risks near their homes, workplaces, and schools (Lais, 2002).

[7]http://www.gao.gov/cghome/tqmsai/text4.html.

CASE STUDY
Obstacles or Access: Reconsidering Anonymous Access to Government Information in a Post-September 11 Environment

Charles N. Davis
University of Missouri

Introduction

The terrorist attacks of the early twenty-first century altered forever the delicate balance between security and liberty, between freedom and safety that for generations had served the constituents of the United States. The relationship between governed and governor, honed over decades by courts and legislatures wary of intrusive central governments, now faces unsettling challenges new to transparent democracies the world over.

Central to that balance is the transparency personified by federal information regimes like the Environmental Protection Agency's Toxic Release Inventory (TRI) and its Risk Management Program (RMP), data sets born of tragedy that have become synonymous with progressive information policy.

One of the sad byproducts of the September 11, 2001, terrorist attacks is the axiomatic secrecy that has plagued government. The shift of military, diplomatic, and political inertia demanded by the threat of terrorism has ushered in a reexamination of some of democracy's core values. Access to governmental information, long thought to serve an invaluable societal purpose, must now be justified against the reality that the free flow of information may also provide support to terrorists. Although certain sensitive information disclosed by the state under access laws may be important for public safety, other information obtained through the laws could also put society at risk.

Some of the conflicts inherent in informing the public and communicating risk have been highlighted by the terrorist attacks of 2001. Officials reacted quickly by "scrubbing" their websites, removing a vast array of information, presumably for homeland security reasons. The public interest group OMB Watch, a nonprofit monitoring agency, has tracked the website removals following September 11. Although no agency removed its entire website, OMB Watch found that information was removed from sites of the Department of Energy; the Interior Department's Geological Survey; the Federal Energy Regulatory Commission; the Environmental Protection Agency; the Federal Aviation Administration; the Department of Transportation's Office of Pipeline Safety and its Bureau of Transportation Statistics' Geographic Information Service; the National Archives and Records Administration; the NASA Glenn Research Center; the International Nuclear Safety Center; the Internal Revenue Service; the Los Alamos National Laboratory; and the National Imagery and Mapping Agency.[1]

The EPA, like most other government agencies, revisited its information policy in the wake of the terrorist attacks. Its policies have changed relatively little, but its actions illustrate the pressures facing those charged with protecting the public from a variety of risks and the effect of the emergent risk of terror on information policy.

Among the principles of freedom of information currently undergoing reexamination in light of the terrorist threat is the notion of anonymous access to some types of governmental information, including sensitive chemical data. This case study examines the balancing of interests driving information disclosure decisions using the EPA's TRI data as a timely example of the values at stake.

The EPA's Access Policies and 9/11

There is no doubt that access is still a fundamental democratic value, and that access far more often than not furthers the public interest. In the past two years alone, public requests under the Freedom of Information Act (FOIA) have yielded important public safety information—from reports about excessive levels of mercury in canned tuna to details about the presence of anthrax spores in a Washington, DC, mail facility and several stories about the failures of homeland security initiatives designed to protect the nation from would-be terrorists.

The many benefits of access to information—hundreds and hundreds of examples produced annually—must now be weighed against a single inescapable truth: U.S. troops discovered "detailed maps and drawings of sensitive infrastructure locations" in caves in Afghanistan and in al-Qaeda training camps. Once an assumed good, access now poses very real dangers, if only in isolated examples involving a small subset of governmental information, and must be defended with the understanding that information itself can be used for good and for ill. Information—historically viewed as an unqualified good—must now confront the very real threat that it could be used to plot terror.

Among the first documents to face reexamination after the terrorist attacks of 2001 were the Environmental Protection Agency's TRI and RMP programs, national databases born from the political fallout of one of the world's worst manufacturing disasters.

The impetus for the TRI, as it is widely known, began on Dec. 3, 1984, when a deadly cloud of methyl isocyanate gas drifted over a cluster of shanties around a pesticide plant in Bhopal, India. In minutes, 25 tons of deadly gas leaking from a ruptured storage plant killed more than 2,000 people and injured 10,000 more. The Bhopal leak has secured an ignoble position in world history as the worst industrial disaster ever, more deadly than even Chernobyl.[2]

Reports after the fact underscored the utter lack of public knowledge of the risks posed by the plant, even as company officials and regulators knew very well that the plant had ample reason to worry about safety.[3]

Back in the United States, the Bhopal tragedy renewed public pressure on Washington to confront growing fears about toxic chemicals. Eight months after the Bhopal leak, another leak—this time at a Union Carbide pesticide plant in West Virginia—injured 135 people and raised the political stakes even higher. What was once a distant disaster became a potent rallying cry for reform. At the heart of that reform was the idea of a "right to know" about everyday risks. Concerns over a more deadly accident led Congress, in 1986, to enact the Emergency Planning and Community Right-to-Know Act (EPCRA), which requires, among other things, that industrial facilities report on the types and quantities of toxic chemicals they release annually into the land, air, and water. This information is then entered in the Toxics Release Inventory (TRI), a national, publicly accessible, electronic data bank.[4]

Public access to information about environmental risks at the time was fragmentary at best, nonexistent at worst. Information required by government regulators was seldom shared with the public, and when it was, it was in piecemeal fashion, as no aggregate data existed.

Congress moved swiftly to require systematic disclosure of toxic releases, passing legislation in 1986 that required standardized reporting of routine, intended releases of

continues

toxic chemicals.[5] Political compromise inevitably weakened the final product some-what, but the result was a dramatic improvement in every way.

The new law required manufacturers to report annually their routine and accidental releases of toxic chemicals to land, air, and water to state officials and the EPA. Releases had to be reported, chemical by chemical, and facility by facility, if a company used more than 10,000 pounds of the chemical or manufactured or processed 25,000 pounds or more annually.[6]

To streamline this staggering pile of data, the EPA created the TRI, a national database that included the maximum amounts present of all chemicals over the thresholds at each facility during the year, the waste treatment or disposal methods employed, an estimate of treatment efficiency achieved, and the annual amount of the chemical released to the air, water, or land.[7]

The EPA made the reports available in paper reports, electronic files, and on the agency's website, meaning that seemingly overnight, interested citizens could access information on their communities.[8] Initially, however, the clunky nature of the EPA's electronic dissemination made accessibility limited in practice, so environmental groups, led by the Working Group on Community Right to Know, joined together to improve by building their own database of TRI reports, the RTK Net.[9]

As access to the TRI data eased, the first reports of toxic release data began to make national news. In May 1989, when the first full set of national reports was made public, toxic chemicals made headlines day after day. The National Wildlife Federation's report *The Toxic 500* ranked the communities with the most toxic pollution, generating even more attention to the issue.[10]

USA Today's award-winning series included this memorable line: ". . .a whopping 7 billion pounds of toxic chemicals—a veritable witches' brew of poisons—were pumped into the air, land, and water by 19,278 factories."[11]

The publicity created by the release of TRI data forever changed the posture of the chemical industry toward toxic releases, writes Graham in *Democracy by Disclosure*. Faced with daily reports linking toxic releases to a variety of health threats, the industry began to act. Richard J. Mahoney, chief executive officer of Monsanto, shocked his peers by announcing plans to cut toxic air releases by 90% in less than 5 years. "We don't think our emissions represent any hazard," he said. "But the public has spoken, and it's unmistakable that they will no longer tolerate toxic emissions. Might as well get on with it."[12]

And get on with it they did: As Graham notes, chemical facilities reduced total releases by 45.5% between 1988 and 1999, from 3.2 billion pounds to 1.5 billion pounds. Air emissions dropped 60%, and surface water emissions dropped by 66%.[13]

As Graham notes:

> No other environmental law had been associated with such dramatic results. The unexpected lesson that would ultimately reverberate throughout govern-ment, particularly as information technology created new possibilities for com-munication, was that the systematic disclosure of standardized information concerning private sector performance could be a powerful inducement for companies to improve environmental practices.[14]

TRI's close cousin, the RMP, is a data set listing each facility that uses or stores extremely hazardous chemicals, the measures each facility takes to prevent an acci-dental release, and its response plans to protect human health and the environment in the event of a release. Also included in each plan is an evaluation of the potential effects of an accidental release, including worst-case scenario information.[15] However,

Congress decided to restrict access to this information, making it available only in 50 "reading rooms" around the country; it has never been available on the Web, even before Sept. 11.

Between RMP and TRI, what began as a right-to-know law had become an effective regulatory measure. Today, thousands of citizens, environmental groups, academic researchers, and other interest groups access millions of TRI records annually, anonymously, 24 hours a day on the RTK site and at libraries across the nation.

Despite disclosure's many expected and unexpected benefits, opposition to it mounted as trade groups representing major industrial sectors formed the Coalition for Effective Environmental Information. Its members include the American Chemical Council, the American Petroleum Institute, and the Automobile Manufacturers Association, among others. The coalition began to question the way in which the EPA was assembling and reporting data, and complained to industry-friendly representatives about the undue burden of reporting placed on their industries.[16]

Simultaneously, industry groups sought to broaden protections for trade secrets in the federal Freedom of Information Act and other statutes. The new arguments reflected the rise of the Internet: Industry argued that the ease with which vast amounts of information could be aggregated on the Internet gave rise to fear that competitors could now construct a "mosaic" revealing corporate secrets. An industry study found that the EPA's website could be used to create a mosaic containing a plant's physical layout, chemical reaction sequences, and production capabilities.[17] Fears of corporate espionage, coupled with the rise of the competitive intelligence sector, which uses legal methods to obtain information about competitors from public sources, began to have real consequences. By the late 1990s, the EPA abandoned plans to require disclosure of toxic chemicals used in production or embedded in products, largely in response to industry concerns over trade secrets.

Like trade secrets, national security issues began to concern industry officials and policy makers as it became clear that the Internet revolutionized the dissemination of environmental information. The "mosaic" of information that frightened industry groups in the context of trade secrets was doubly troubling in the context of national security. The first discussion of conditional access in the context of environmental information appeared within the broader debate over national security raised by worst-case scenarios in chemical accidents in the RMP program, which Congress had ordered as part of risk-management plans to aid responses to chemical emergencies. The EPA initially announced that the scenarios would be posted on the Internet beginning in 1999, but those plans met consistent resistance from industry representatives.[18]

Industry representatives argued that while much of the worst-case scenario information was available through repository libraries and often from the companies themselves, Internet dissemination could make it far easier for would-be terrorists to maximize destruction by targeting the most vulnerable locales. While concluding that such risks were remote in 1996, the EPA nevertheless estimated that the risks were twice as high if data were posted on the Internet because of the efficiency with which far-flung researchers could hone the data to isolate particular plants.[19] Access advocates argued that rather than reduce the flow of information, regulators should redouble their efforts to reduce hazards, but the EPA ultimately decided not to post worst-case scenarios on the Internet. When right-to-know groups vowed to post the information themselves, Congress took the debate into its own hands, enacting legislation to remove public access to worst-case scenarios.

The law did not prohibit non-profits from releasing the information directly to individuals, however, and so RTK Net began obtaining the scenarios from the EPA and post-

continues

ing them on the Internet. The EPA eventually posted limited risk management plans on the Internet, but after the attacks of 9/11, removed them altogether. Today the EPA's plans are available in federal reading rooms.

A Policy Dilemma: Does Secrecy Equal Safety?

To question the EPA's policy with regard to information access on worst-case scenarios is not to deny that such documents might pose a serious threat to homeland security. Quite the contrary: The worst-case scenarios offer a timely criticism of the formulaic equivalency of safety and secrecy.

The EPA has estimated that at least 123 plants store toxic chemicals that, if released through explosion, accident, or terrorist attack, could result in scenarios that would put 1 million or more people at risk. In the U.S. Army Medical Department's worst-case scenario estimate, a terrorist attack on such a chemical plant would lead to about 2.5 million deaths.[20]

However, as former Clinton administration Chief of Staff John Podesta notes in a 2004 essay, of some 75,000 chemicals stored in more than 20,000 facilities across the nation, a small fraction of the whole—probably fewer than two dozen—are potentially lethal enough to be of keen interest to would-be terrorists.[21] It is thus possible to narrow the range of documents requiring restricted or conditional access to a small universe of records.

As Podesta notes, the administration's initial stance was one of risk reduction, whereby homeland security officials (the EPA has no authority to ask industry what voluntary steps it has taken to enhance security) would isolate the worst threats and then take steps to reduce unnecessary risk and increase public safety. Under intense pressure from the chemical industry, the regulatory stance has shifted to voluntary efforts by the industry—stronger fences, guard dogs, and increased physical security instead of actual risk reduction. Homeland Security Department officials are not even requiring that companies report to the government the voluntary steps they have taken to improve physical security, meaning that federal regulators lack the information needed to address the issue. The public—often living near these critical facilities—now has even less access to information about the risk levels in their own backyard. The formulaic equivalency of safety and secrecy has triumphed, altering the disclosure regime ushered in following the Bhopal disaster from a right-to-know stance to what looks more like a need-to-know stance.

To its credit, the EPA has not wavered on access to TRI data; complaints over TRI lie mainly in issues of timing (dissemination of TRI data lags far behind what users of the data would prefer). Worst-case scenario information is still available, but in an onerous and time-consuming way: Those interested in reading it must go to an EPA reading room, where they can read them, several at a time. No copies are allowed. The steps taken to prevent wholesale reproduction of worst-case data certainly make it more difficult for would-be terrorists to compile target information through RMP. However, that which makes it difficult for would-be terrorists makes it equally difficult for environmentalists, journalists, and others. Without access to worst-case scenario information, the benefits of disclosure are replaced by information policy that makes it difficult, if not impossible, for public pressure to mount in ways that foster change.

The parameters of this debate are illustrated by the testimony of Amy E. Smithson, director of the chemical and biological nonproliferation project at the security-oriented Henry L. Stimson Center, before the House Subcommittee on Water Resources and Environment. "The quicker a decision is made" to keep the "website permanently shuttered, the better," Smithson told the committee.

Rather than give the citizenry access to risk assessments, Smithson said that signs of contamination should come from the telltale birds dropping from the sky. "If an intentional or accidental disaster occurred at a chemical plant, small animals, such as birds, would be the first to be affected," she testified. "Put another way, if birds are dropping from the sky . . . people in the area should get inside as quickly as possible, shut the doors, and turn off all ventilation systems."

Certainly, the threat of terrorism should not be discounted. Smithson was in no way advocating censorship of EPA data; her testimony was made in the context of the ease with which anyone can access national data and urged the EPA to rein in ubiquitous Internet-enabled access. The threat of terrorism has moved to the forefront, and information policy must reflect that reality. Yet in making decisions to withhold information, policy makers must not lose sight of why it was made widely available in the first place. Surely the public must be provided with better means of risk assessment than birds falling from the sky.[22]

There is no question that the availability of EPA data has provided important incentives to make real improvements in public health and safety. Empowered by information, community organizations, and environmental groups, the press and citizens were able to expose toxic dangers in their communities, and the resultant publicity created a demand for action. In the 11 years after facilities began reporting under TRI, toxic releases declined by nearly 50%, in large measure due to public pressure, resulting from an increased awareness of toxic dangers.

While the utility of RMP data to terrorists is tenuous, the usefulness to the public is much more clear. The public is able to hold facilities accountable to make upgrades and to keep communities aware of the risk level in their neighborhoods.

Conclusion

On March 23, 2005, hazardous chemicals at BP Amoco's Texas City refinery exploded, killing 15 and injuring over 100. The massive explosion destroyed buildings and vehicles, and shook residents' homes up to five miles away.

A news event of that magnitude leads journalists, activists, neighborhood associations, and other stakeholders to attempt to gain a clearer picture of the plant's past activities, its run-ins with regulators, and its potential for future disaster.

The March 2005 incident was not the first time this facility has released hazardous chemicals into the community. Over the course of the previous six years, BP Amoco's Texas City facility reported over 100 incidents to the National Response Center (NRC), which tracks unverified initial reports of spills, releases, and other accidents ranging from minor to serious.

The EPA's data show that the accident could have been much worse. BP Amoco has reported to EPA that it stores 800,000 pounds of hydrofluoric acid onsite at its Texas City facility. The company has estimated that over half a million people live within the facility's 25-mile "vulnerability zone." Should an accident or explosion cause the full release of this toxic chemical, thousands could be injured or killed.

Such incidents raise a multitude of questions about environmental and information policy. Could the devastating effects of this accident have been lessened even before the accident occurred? Was there a safer technology or chemical that BP Amoco could have been using at the facility? Is such an incident a road map for would-be terrorists? Or does the community face a greater risk of the less dramatic, but equally deadly, mishap from mishandling the chemicals?

continues

Disclosure of risk scenarios through the EPA data was designed to give the public centralized access to information in order to create avenues for creating ongoing accountability and, in many cases, economic and political impetus for change. Mary Graham of the Brookings Institution traces this idea back to Louis D. Brandeis, the pre- and post-Depression Era reformer, who in 1932 called for "letting in the light of day on issues of securities, foreign and domestic, which are offered for sale to the investing public."[23]

Brandeis believed that disclosure of information could reduce social risks in a wide variety of settings; his vision extended far beyond the stock market into all areas of government-business relations.[24] In the wake of the Crash of 1929, Congress followed Brandeis' lead, as Franklin D. Roosevelt adopted his agenda, passing dozens of laws requiring companies that sold securities to the public to reveal detailed information about their earnings and operations, but also about their liabilities and potential risks.

The rise of the administrative state ushered in scores of rules and penalties, but many also required organizations to produce standardized reports at regular intervals. Today, just as investors long have been able to compare corporate earnings reports, travelers can compare airline safety records, bidders for government contracts can examine past winning bids, and community residents can compare toxic releases from nearby factories.[25] Disclosure has become the norm, the presumption of openness of information kept by government the standard.

Until recently, few questioned the assumption that the public enjoyed complete, anonymous access to information, or at least information that did not fall within a statutory exemption such as trade secrets or personal privacy. So long as the information was deemed public, no barriers to access were created by policymakers. Access was viewed as a universal good.

The rise of personal computing and the Internet transformed disclosure into what Graham calls "technopopulism": Acceptable levels of risk are established by the actions of millions of ordinary citizens, armed with factual information, instead of closed-door meetings of regulators.[26]

Such a transformation creates new challenges, however. Disclosure is always a product of political compromise between advocates of greater access and members of the regulated industry. Access often collides with other values, such as trade secrets, personal privacy and now, national security. The risks created by disclosure must be viewed in light of the changing geopolitical landscape, most notably by the intense interest in homeland security and counterterrorism in the post-September 11 landscape.

Such a fundamental shift in information policy requires the strictest of scrutiny, for conditional access is not without great costs, both in terms of dollars and in terms of the ease and practicality of access. A disclosure regime built on the principle of universal access cannot simply convert wholesale to one where records custodians routinely demand identification, for such requests can quickly lead to real or perceived intimidation and even reprisal. Imagine an investigative journalist seeking reports at the local library being asked for a copy of his driver's license, and one can easily see the potential for abuse. Thus, conditional access must be examined in light of the costs to the overall value of disclosure.

In times of great national risk, the temptation to equate secrecy with security runs strong. The conditions of access demand careful reflection as to the appropriate national policy regarding public information, and information policy must serve democratic principles, lest information technology become a tool for social control. The uniqueness of the moment—in which the promise of great advances in technology shares the stage with the looming threat of global terrorism—offers stark choices between empowerment and control, between liberty and surveillance.

It is important to note that public information policy and technology policy are intertwined. Decisions made about information policy all have impact on the degree to which we remain an open society in terms of information access, and technological standards, pricing for information services, and conditions placed on access all have much to say about the quality and breadth of our information society. Indeed, the active engagement of citizens in political life made possible through information technology already has demonstrated the potential to reenergize the democracy. Thus, in developing policy for information access, we should be especially careful to avoid approaches that would impede democratic participation.

Endnotes

[1]*Homefront Confidential*, at 22.

[2]David Sarokin, "Environmentalism and the Right-to-Know: Expanding the Practice of Democracy," *Ecological Economics* (1991), p. 176.

[3]Stuart Diamond, "The Bhopal Disaster: How It Happened," *New York Times*, Jan. 28, 1985, p. A1.

[4]Sidney M. Wolf, "Fear and Loathing about the Public Right to Know: The Surprising Success of the Emergency Planning and Community Right-To-Know Act," 11 *Journal of Land Use & Environmental Law*, 217, 230 (1996).

[5]*Emergency Planning and Community Right-to-Know Act of 1986*, 42 U.S.C. 11023(j),

[6]Ibid., 42 U.S.C. 11023 (b).

[7]42 U.S.C. § 7412(r) (2000).

[8]Sidney M. Wolf, "Fear and Loathing about the Public Right to Know: The Surprising Success of the Emergency Planning and Community Right-To-Know Act," 11 *Journal of Land Use and Environmental Law*, 217, 230 (1996).

[9]Michael Shapiro, "Toxic Substances Policy," in Paul R. Portney, ed., *Public Policies for Environmental Protection* (Resources for the Future, 1993), pp. 195–206.

[10]Norman L. Dean, Jerry Poje, and Randall J. Burke, *The Toxic 500: The 500 Largest Releases of Toxic Chemicals in the U.S., 1987* (National Wildlife Federation, August 1989).

[11]Rae Tyson and Julie Morris, "The Chemicals Next Door," *USA Today*, July 31, 1989, p. A1.

[12]"Air Pollution: It's All Legal," *Newsweek*, July 24, 1989, p. 28.

[13]Mary Graham, *Democracy by Disclosure*, pp. 44–45.

[14]Ibid., p. 45.

[15]See 42 U.S.C. § 7412(r) (West 2002).

[16]Ibid., p. 55.

[17]Kline & Co., "Economic Espionage: The Looting of America's Economic Security in the Information Age" (Chemical Manufacturers Association, 1997).

[18]U.S. Environmental Protection Agency, Security Study: An Analysis of the Terrorist Risk Associated with the Public Availability of Offsite Consequence Analysis Data under EPA's Risk Management Program Regulations (1997).

[19]Ibid.

[20]John Podesta, "Need to Know: Governing in Secret," in *A Little Knowledge: Privacy, Security and Public Information after September 11*, Peter M. Shane, John Podesta and Richard C. Leone, eds. (Century Foundation, 2004), pp. 17–18.

[21]Ibid., pp. 17–18.

[22]See testimony before the House Subcommittee on Water and the Environment, http://www.house.gov/transportation/water/11-08-01/11-08-01memo.html.

[23]Graham, p. 2.

[24]Louis D. Brandeis, *Other People's Money*, 2d ed. (Frederick A. Stockes Co., 1932), pp. 92–108.

[25]Graham, p. 3.

[26]Graham, pp. 5–7.

Information Technology and Privacy

Privacy raises all kinds of interesting policy issues. For instance, a Silicon Valley community installed video surveillance cameras in public spaces. One Michael Naimark found that he could disable the camera temporarily by aiming an inexpensive laser pointer at it. He planned to publish how to do it on the Internet. Should Mr. Naimark have been surveilled and did he have the right to disable surveillance? To publicize the method? In New York City, the Surveillance Camera Players, a guerrilla theater troupe, posted locations of surveillance cameras on the Internet. Should this be legal? A man sued Marriott Hotels for $1.5 million because there was a surveillance camera in a bathroom light fixture. Should the courts award damages?

These surveillance issues are just a small part of much broader issues pertaining to information policy and privacy. For instance, do data warehousing and profiling operations under the USA Patriot Act violate freedom of privacy? Was it OK for the Internal Revenue Service (IRS) to make 3.7 billion disclosures of tax return information for tax and nontax law enforcement and statistical purposes, as it did in 2003? Was it OK for the Census Bureau to disclose to Homeland Security personal data about Arab-Americans, as it did in 2004?[1] Are protections such as the Privacy Act effective? And what are the obligations of the public manager toward the privacy rights of the citizen?

Privacy is a major concern in a society in which every transaction, phone call, vote, border crossing, and application registers into some computer (Alderman & Kennedy, 1997; Lyon, 1994). The Fourth Amendment, protecting against unreasonable searches and seizures, does not necessarily protect you as a citizen from having your e-mail read, your online transactions monitored, your cell phones audited, your eyes scanned at airports, your rental car tracked by Global Positioning System (GPS), your commuting monitored by E-Z Pass tollbooth records, your purchases databased by credit cards, and even your house penetrated by unobtrusive electronic eavesdropping from vans on public streets, however "unreasonable" you may feel such searching is. In the aftermath of 9/11 and as is typical of wartime, as Rosen (2004) and others have noted, Americans are poised to trade privacy for allegedly increased security. In addition to terrorism, the rise of identity theft contributes to growing public support for biometric surveillance, for instance (Hastings Group, 2003). While public surveillance has been around since pre-Civil War slavery days (Parenti, 2003), the present-day increased threat to privacy and public support for eroding privacy rights make the issue all the more important for public policy makers charged with defending the long-term interests of a free society.

Public managers find themselves on both sides of the privacy issue. Among the federal agencies that engage in electronic surveillance, not counting the Department of Defense, National Security Agency, Central Intelligence Agency (CIA), or Department of Homeland Security (DHS), are the

- Drug Enforcement Administration;
- Federal Bureau of Investigation (FBI);
- Customs Service;
- National Park Service;
- IRS;
- Criminal Division of the Department of Justice;
- Forest Service;
- Office of the Inspector General of the Department of Agriculture;
- Agricultural Stabilization and Conservation Service;
- Fish and Wildlife Service;
- Marshals Service;
- Mint; and
- Bureau of Alcohol, Tobacco, and Firearms.

While all federal agencies are constrained by privacy legislation and directives discussed in this chapter, few are able to decline demands to share data with agencies engaged in electronic surveillance and investigation and many additional federal, state, and local agencies do so, agency privacy policies notwithstanding.[2]

The public sector must also be concerned with the formulation of policy and legislation affecting privacy practices in the private sector. The American Management Association (AMA) has regularly surveyed workplace surveillance, documenting its rapid escalation in recent years. Of its 2003 book on the subject (Lane, 2003), the AMA stated, "the state of employee investigation and surveillance in the United States would shock even Orwell," author of the totalitarian vision of surveillance in the novel *1984.*[3] Lane documented for the AMA the proliferation of such new technologies as GPS for tracking all company vehicles; "smart" uniforms that track employee locations as well as health and even emotions; and company cell phones used to monitor employee purchasing habits and leisure activities. Lane also documented the widespread nature of such privacy violations as covertly obtaining job applicants' credit reports, driving records, and medical histories; and secret genetic and medical testing on urine, saliva, and blood samples required of employees in order to reduce health and liability insurance costs for the company. All these raise the possibility of public regulation of private-sector privacy practices and, indeed, Lane has proposed a Bill of Employee Privacy Rights. Likewise the Electronic Privacy Information Center (EPIC) cites public opinion polls supporting public regulation of private-sector privacy rights, including majorities in favor of requiring opt-in principles (companies should have to obtain affirmative consent before collecting or sharing data), giving users the right to sue over privacy violations, disciplining privacy violators, and replacing the present system of self-regulation with comprehensive regulation.[4]

Surveillance studies and *privacy law* are becoming major fields of study and policy activity. Privacy law now ranges from issues of genetic privacy to employee monitoring to applications of the Freedom of Information Act (FOIA), Children's Online Privacy Protection Act, European Union Data Protection Directive, Electronic Communications Privacy Act of 1986 (ECPA), and much more (Solove & Rotenberg, 2003). Smith's *Compilation of State and Federal Privacy Laws* (2004a) lists over 700 federal and state laws pertaining to privacy, covering bank records, credit bureaus, criminal records, electronic surveillance, employment, government agencies, identity theft, libraries, medical records, Social Security numbers, student records, telephone services, telephone sales calls, and testing in employment.[5]

As with so many topics in public information technology (IT) studies, the discussion of privacy policy could well be a book unto itself. In this chapter we restrict discussion to highlighting the topics of computer surveillance, privacy legislation, and executive actions with regard to privacy policy, agency data sharing and matching, privacy impact statements, the national ID controversy, and issues in privacy, governmental outsourcing, and private-sector data mining.

COMPUTER SURVEILLANCE

At one time, the main protection of the privacy of Americans was the sheer cost, inconvenience, and—frequently—the practical impossibility of surveillance (Davis, 2003). Where the "surveillance society" was once a matter for speculation and science fiction, today the rapid acceleration of surveillance systems is proceeding at an astonishing pace in both the public and private sectors. As a result of escalating change, privacy policies of the past are rapidly rendered moot. While survey data show that the majority of Americans are very concerned about privacy and do not trust their government to protect them,[6] privacy as a policy issue simply has not had the political importance of other matters such as the economy, the environment, education, and foreign policy, to name a few.

The central, unaddressed policy issue of electronic surveillance is not simply the intrusion of law enforcement agencies and others into the lives of private individuals. The central issue has to do with how laws are enforced. The traditional model of law enforcement was that evidence of crime would emerge, law enforcement officials would investigate, and if needed, they would secure warrants from judges authorizing surveillance of particular individuals—surveillance that in the absence of judicial authorization would be considered a violation of the individual's privacy rights. Surveillance in the traditional model would be of particular individuals for good cause. Although in certain limited public settings, such as roadblocks, police might search everyone for alcohol or for an escaped criminal, under the traditional model it would not have been considered constitutional to have door-to-door searches of entire neighborhoods or even to stop random individuals on roadways without cause simply on the basis of profiling them by their race or some other attribute. While private conversations outside the home were not protected if overheard, in practical terms privacy was easily obtained in public places and communications within the home itself were considered fully protected from eavesdropping and unwarranted wiretapping, which were considered crimes against privacy.[7]

Without adequate public discussion and formulation of new policy, the traditional model of law enforcement has been radically altered by the emergence of electronic surveillance techniques. Lyon (2002) has called the new model "surveillance as social sorting." That is, online profiling, smart cards, biometrics, intelligent transportation systems, closed-circuit television (CCTV), and other technologies are creating a new model of law enforcement. In this model, although there is no evidence of a crime, law enforcement officials who are interested in a type of crime and know its correlates conduct electronic surveillance on a mass basis looking for these correlates. By a process of social sorting (filtering, profiling) they identify specific suspects, who become targets of more intensive surveillance. Mass surveillance is conducted on a warrantless basis since, by definition, it cannot be warranted by a judge for particular, individual cause. Even intensive surveillance of a particular suspect may not require a warrant under the Patriot Act and other recent legislation and precedents. That is, law enforcement through individual warranted surveillance is being replaced by law enforcement through mass unwarranted surveillance—largely, technological determinists would delight to say, through the force of technology in its own right without real societal decision underpinning this radical shift in models.

Computer surveillance issues arise in all public agencies, not just law enforcement. Notably, the rise of e-mail as a standard method of communication has raised serious issues of workplace privacy. An AMA survey of 1,100 U.S. companies shows 52% monitor e-mail, 22% have terminated an employee for violating e-mail policy, and 14% have been ordered by a court or regulatory body to produce employee e-mail (*Government Technology*, 2003). There appear to be no corresponding public-sector data, but there is little doubt that parallel trends exist with regard to employee monitoring. For instance, American Canyon, CA, a city of only 12,000, uses Sentian software to monitor its employees' use of the Internet. The system generates an access profile for each employee, sends warnings to users that a site is being monitored, and provides monthly reports "for each employee, showing who has been where for how long, and whether any of the sites were monitored or blocked" (Walsh, 2003b).

In general, employees do not have a right to privacy in workplace e-mail. In fact, e-mail is a "public record" that may be subject to FOIA information requests from reporters or the public. Though courts have almost always upheld the right of managers in both the public and private sectors to examine employee e-mail, that right is even more defensible in court if the public manager has taken the standard precautions of informing employees that workplace e-mail is not private and searching only on a limited basis for specific cause. In the case of sexually harassing e-mail, which may constitute a hostile work environment, managers are legally required to take affirmative steps to investigate and remedy the situation. An increasing number of governmental jurisdictions fulfill this responsibility by running porn-scanning software. The Fourth Amendment protection against unreasonable searches does not protect the privacy of e-mail unless the employee has been given a reasonable expectation of privacy by an agency policy statement, but even then management searches for good cause are permissible (Prysby & Prysby, 2003).

Philosophers Jeremy Bentham and Michel Foucault developed the concept of the "panopticon," an ideal prison where compliance with rules would be guaranteed through inescapable surveillance of prisoners on the periphery by a centrally located guard who had a clear view of every activity of every inmate. Writers such as Whitaker (2000), Blanchette and Johnson (2002), and Parenti (2003) see a revival of "panopticism" in the underlying philosophy of the new model of law enforcement and, for that matter, in electronic customer targeting by corporations. The difference, of course, is that now all citizens, not just inmates, lack privacy on the periphery while the guard at the center has been replaced by a rather large number of separate public and private organizations that hold resources for electronic rather than visual surveillance, and do so largely in secret, without those who are surveilled being aware of it, much less having the means to hold the watchers accountable.

PRIVACY LEGISLATION AND EXECUTIVE ACTIONS

The traditional, predigital view of privacy rights was expressed by the Supreme Court in *Katz v. United States* (1967). This case held that general long-term surveillance was an unconstitutional invasion of privacy rights in violation of the Fourth Amendment. However, short-term focused surveillance with judicial approval in advance was held to be constitutional. In general, the Fourth Amendment was meant to protect citizens against unreasonable searches of their homes, and court rulings suggest that networked information submitted through a third party has less privacy protection than, say, postal mail in individuals' home mailboxes because the "home" connection is not integral to networked data. Much of the history of political battles over privacy in the past four decades has been about revision of these constitutional standards in the light of new technological developments.

Privacy emerged as a major public policy issue in the 1970s. A variety of reasons have been ascribed for this, including the Supreme Court's assertion of constitutional privacy rights in the abortion case of *Roe v. Wade* (1973); concern for public records in the aftermath of the Watergate scandal of 1973, which toppled President Nixon; and the proliferation of mainframe computing and electronic networking in government, which had prompted Congress to create the Office of Technology Assessment in 1972.

The major legislation of this period, the Privacy Act of 1974, sought to protect the privacy of individually identifiable information maintained by federal agencies. The collection, maintenance, use, and dissemination of information were regulated. The Privacy Act forbade disclosure of any record containing personal information, unless released with the prior written consent of the individual. Individuals were also given rights to regulate to whom their personal data might be given. Agencies were mandated to provide individuals with access to their records and a right to appeal errors. The Privacy Act of 1974 in draft form would have established a national Privacy Protection Commission, but this provision did not become law.

Although the Privacy Act said records could not be disclosed without prior consent, an exception was made for information required to be disclosed under the FOIA. However, the Justice Department interpreted the Privacy Act to mean that all personally identifiable records had to be withheld and were an *additional* exemption to FOIA. Senator Edward Kennedy (D-MA) protested this construction of the Privacy Act, but the matter was not settled until the passage of the CIA Information Act of 1984, which clarified that the Privacy Act could not be claimed as a FOIA exemption. The Privacy Act of 1974 was often honored in the breach. The U.S. Office of Technology Assessment in 1986 found that the Privacy Act afforded almost no protection against computer matching. While effective in blocking nongovernmental access to personally identifiable information, it did not restrain intra-governmental access.

In the 1980s, computer matching came to the fore as a national issue. In 1977, in an effort to control welfare fraud, Congress had mandated that state welfare agencies cross-reference state income data from tax records. Computer matching efforts were promoted by President Reagan's Council on Integrity and Efficiency in 1981. In 1982, the Office of Management and Budget (OMB) issued computer-matching guidelines. Then in 1984, Congress enacted legislation that authorized computer matching for all need-based programs, requiring states to implement matching as a condition for receiving federal welfare funds. Finally, the Computer Matching and Privacy Protection Act of 1988 introduced privacy protections, requiring agencies to notify those affected by computer matching; requiring agencies to have written agreements when exchanging information for matching; requiring a data integrity board to review written agreements; requiring a cost–benefit analysis of matching programs to determine if they are justified; and requiring civilian notification procedures and an appeals process. Also required was a 30-day notice prior to cutting off benefits after computer matching indicated the need to do so (Shattuck, 1996).

In the case of *Reporters' Committee v. Department of Justice* (1989), the Supreme Court ruled that when privacy issues pertained to personally identifiable information, the requestor of information had to establish that disclosure was necessary to shed light on government activities. This test was a stringent one, difficult to prove, and thus served to further restrict access to personally identifiable information. The *Reporters' Committee* decision greatly narrowed the scope of FOIA (Davis, 2003).

In the late 1980s, the FBI's Library Awareness Program created a privacy controversy as agents tried to enlist librarians in reporting "suspicious" activities by foreigners such as seeking assistance in gathering online information (Database Searcher, 1988, p. 37). In late 1989 Patricia Berger, president of the American Library Association (ALA), revealed based on agency documents that the FBI had "misrepresented their activities by conducting background investigations of librarians who refused to cooperate" (*Information Today*, 1989, p. 7). Whereas the ALA had been assured by the FBI that the Library Awareness Program visits to libraries had stopped in December 1987, new documents revealed that continuing contacts occurred at least through 1989.

The ECPA was intended to give electronic interception the same status as wiretapping. The ECPA does protect against third parties intercepting the e-mail of government employees. However, it does not protect such employees from their own employer reading their e-mail or, for that matter, third parties obtaining e-mail records through FOIA requests. In any event, managers' reading e-mail archive files is not considered analogous to interception of telephone messages through wiretapping. The Electronic Frontier Foundation and other critics have noted that the ECPA has had little effect on privacy rights.

In the 1990s, various pieces of legislation sought to protect privacy in specific circumstances. For instance, the Drivers Privacy Protection Act of 1994 prohibited states from disclosing motor vehicle records, sales of which had demonstrated state-level willingness to sacrifice privacy in favor of securing an additional agency revenue source. Also, the Children's Online Privacy Protection Act of 1998, which went into effect in 2000, protected the personal information of minors from collection and misuse by commercial websites.

In May 1998 President Clinton issued a memorandum, "Privacy and Personal Information in Federal Records," to all federal agency heads requiring agencies to appoint a senior official responsible for privacy policy. Although the Privacy Act had already mandated privacy officers, these officers had only been required to monitor agency compliance with the Act. Publicized as "an electronic bill of rights for the information age," the new policy made privacy officers responsible for privacy as related to all present and future statutes and to all ITs related to "agency use, collection, and disclosure of personal information" (Reporters Committee for Freedom of the Press, 1998).

According to the Center for Democracy and Technology, only one-third of federal agencies had posted privacy policy notices on their sites as of the spring of 1999. In this setting, the OMB followed up on the Clinton memo by requiring all federal agencies to post clearly labeled and easily accessible privacy policies on their websites by September 1, 1999. By December 1, 1999, there was supposed to be a similar posting on all Web pages collecting personal information from the public and on all other high-traffic areas of agency websites. The OMB stipulated that posted policies had to inform citizens of what information is collected about individuals, the reason why the information is collected, and how the information would be used. An interagency committee on federal privacy policies also posted model policy statements as examples.

In the aftermath of the 9/11 terrorist strike on the World Trade Center, Congress literally rushed to pass the USA Patriot Act (the Uniting and Strengthening America by Providing Appropriate Tools Required to Intercept and Obstruct Terrorism Act), signed into law on October 26, 2001. Passed largely without debate, this act had profound privacy and civil liberties implications (see Brasch, 2005). It partially repealed legislation passed in the 1970s prohibiting domestic spying, and it greatly expanded the surveillance powers of law enforcement, permitting federal and state officials to monitor individuals' Web surfing, to oversee the records of Internet Service Providers, and to use roving wiretaps to monitor phone calls.

Not restricted to matters of terrorism, as is popularly thought, USA Patriot Act powers can be used to monitor legitimate protest groups, spy on suspected computer trespassers (which requires spying on all computer traffic) without court order, to take DNA samples of any individual convicted of any crime of violence (for example, scuffling in a protest march), and wiretapping anyone suspected of violating the Computer Fraud and Abuse Act—a mandate that might allow spying on any computer user, the Electronic Frontier Foundation has asserted. Also, the Patriot Act authorizes "sneak and peek" search warrants for any federal crime, even misdemeanors, allowing law officers to enter private premises without informing occupants or obtaining permission, and even without letting occupants know a search had been conducted. Under the Patriot Act, the lower privacy standards of the Foreign Intelligence Surveillance Act may now be applied domestically to U.S. citizens.

The Patriot Act has also been used to access statistical records for which privacy and nondissemination were promised to individual respondents at the time of data collection based on a statutory guarantee of confidentiality, as in the case of records of the National Center for Educational Statistics (Gellman, 2002c). Although a court order is required to open these records for investigative uses, the courts are obliged to issue the order if the government certifies there are facts leading investigators to believe that the statistical records are relevant to their investigation. That is, the Patriot Act has been used to override statutory guarantees of privacy and to do so retroactively, breaking federal confidentiality promises made to citizens.

In October 2004, a federal court ruled unconstitutional the part of the Patriot Act that required Internet Service Providers and phone companies to comply with secret FBI orders to turn over subscriber information, including phone calls made, e-mail subject lines, and logs of websites visited. The basis for the decision was the holding that a mandatory gag provision prevented companies from ever informing customers or others that their privacy had been breached. The court held the gag orders were an unconstitutional violation of free speech rights under the First Amendment (McCullagh, 2004b). Also in 2004, international criticism of the Patriot Act rose, with Latin American countries objecting to providing voter and census data to U.S. law enforcement officials and Canada warning that Patriot Act compliance would violate that nation's constitution. At this writing, some 50 bills that would extend antiterrorism measures were before the new 109th Congress. Both the House and Senate voted in July 2005 to reauthorize the Patriot Act itself, including controversial sections allowing roving wiretaps, search of medical records, and secret access to library and bookstore records. Whether reauthorization is to be permanent in most cases and for 10 years for some sections (House version) or merely extended for 4 years (Senate version) is to be debated in the fall of 2005, when the two reauthorization bills are reconciled.

Section 208 of the E-Government Act of 2002 was the first major reformulation of federal privacy policies since the Privacy Act of 1974. Section 208 mandated that privacy impact assessments be performed for all information systems and programs. It also wrote into law previous OMB directives requiring agencies to post clearly marked privacy policies on agency websites. OMB guidelines issued in 2003 required agencies to tell website visitors when information collection was voluntary, how to grant consent for the use of personal data, and their rights under the Privacy Act and other legislation. Agency websites were also required to disclose the nature of information collected, the purpose of information collection, with whom the information would be shared, and what privacy safeguards were applied to the data (Miller, 2003c).

The E-Government Act of 2002 also stipulated that agencies post privacy policies in machine-readable form compatible with the P3P initiative of the World Wide Web Consortium's Platform for Privacy Preferences project. The P3P initiative enabled user Web browsers to detect automatically the level of privacy afforded by an agency website, and to warn the user when a website's policies did not meet user-set privacy standards set by the user within his or her Web browser. At this writing, however, the P3P initiative has not impacted privacy in government significantly because it has proven difficult for the OMB to implement on the government end, and user interest and demand have been low. Critics say P3P is too complex (Gellman, 2003b) and in any event when users go to a government site, unlike the private sector, they cannot go to a "competitor" site if they do not like the privacy policies they encounter.

Critics soon questioned the meaningfulness of the E-Government Act privacy reforms, however. Commentator Robert Gellman wrote, "The legislation directs the Office of Management and Budget to provide guidance to and oversight of the privacy impact assessment process. Congress used that model in the Privacy Act of 1974, too. If we've learned anything after all these years, it's that OMB does not care about privacy. Repeatedly Congress has asked OMB to focus on privacy but has been disappointed" (Gellman, 2003a). Gellman also objected to the E-Government Act's wording, under which public input to privacy assessments might come only *after* the report is completed and released by the agency chief information officer. Filing a privacy assessment report was required, but the agency was not required to take any specific action based on the report.

Between 1999 and 2004, the issue of identity theft came to the forefront of policy agendas as this form of crime against privacy increased dramatically in scale. The Fair and Accurate Credit Transactions Act of 2003 was passed by Congress to help protect citizens against identity theft. It provides for implementation of a National Fraud Alert System by credit reporting agencies so consumers can place a fraud alert on their credit files, and it requires that credit reporting agencies not report allegedly fraudulent account information when a consumer establishes that he or she has been the victim of identity theft.

In the 1990s, police started monitoring chat rooms for purposes of identifying potential child abusers. Authorities are now exploring automated monitoring on a mass basis. According to contracts obtained by a FOIA request by EPIC, in 2003 the National Science Foundation channeled CIA funds to Rensselaer Polytechnic Institute and others to develop automated monitoring and profiling of the conversations of chat-room users (McCullagh, 2004c).

In May 2004, Democrats introduced the Shield Privacy Act (Strengthening Homeland Innovation by Emphasizing Liberty, Democracy, and Privacy Act) which would create an OMB "privacy czar," appointed by the president, chief privacy officers in each federal agency, and a two-year Privacy Commission to report on privacy implications of new homeland security technologies. The bill had 25 Democratic and no Republican cosponsors and died in committee in the 108th Congress and as of fall 2005, had not been reintroduced in the 109th Congress. Reformers have likewise suggested state-level privacy clearinghouses, review boards, or data-protection commissions with powers ranging from advisory to authority to overrule agencies in privacy matters (Duncan & Roehrig, 2003).

After 9/11, some proposed creation of a new domestic-oriented security police force, and this was featured in the 2004 elections. Such a domestic spy agency, separate from the FBI, might be modeled on the United Kingdom's Security Service, commonly known as MI5. MI5 has emphasized infiltration of suspect groups and cooperation with local civilian police in enhanced surveillance, as part of a philosophy of terrorism prevention and a model favored in a recent RAND Corporation study (Chalk & Rosenau, 2004). However, privacy scandals arose in the 1970s and 1980s when MI5 spied on nonviolent peace groups and even members of Parliament, while FBI infiltration of civil rights and peace groups in the 1960s and later was equally controversial. Similar infiltration and Homeland Security-inspired civilian police activities in the post-9/11 period also were publicized and condemned in Michael Moore's hit documentary, *Fahrenheit 9/11* (2004). The proposal of a once-unthinkable domestic spy agency was considered seriously but ultimately rejected by the 9/11 Commission, which opted instead for reforming the FBI to handle similar functions. In the 2004 elections, both President Bush and Democratic challenger John Kerry endorsed the 9/11 Commission in this decision (in spite of Democratic vice presidential candidate John Edwards's 2002 endorsement of a national domestic spy agency).

AGENCY DATA SHARING AND MATCHING

While most Americans are unaware of agency data sharing and matching, there are cases that rise to the level of public attention. In one such case an Alabama state prison escapee, Bernard McKandes, obtained the birth certificate of one Terry Dean Rogan. Although Rogan had reported his identification papers missing, McKandes frequently used Rogan's name in his criminal undertakings. This led the Los Angeles Police Department (LAPD) to enter Rogan's name in the National Crime Information Center (NCIC) database for many of McKandes's crimes. As a consequence Rogan was arrested no fewer than five times. This was not a unique case: fugitive Richard Skar was also confused by the NCIC with a UCLA professor (Richards, 1989). Did the police have the right to issue arrest warrants for McKandes in Rogan's name? Or was this a violation of Rogan's rights? The U.S. District court agreed with Rogan, holding the LAPD liable. After the courts granted a monetary award to Rogan, the NCIC decided to add a new field for "use of stolen identification" to the Most Wanted file in its database. Under this principle Rogan was not entitled to prevent the police from listing his name in the database records pertaining to McKandes but he could insist that the same record contain clarifying information. Thus, the issue of privacy can involve too little data in computer records as well as too much data about individuals (McGraw, 1988, p. 88).

Some agencies are specifically prohibited by legislation from disseminating individual-level data, including the Bureau of the Census (Title 13 of the U.S. Code), the IRS (Section 6108(c) of the Internal Revenue

Code of 1986), and the Social Security Administration (Section 1106 of the Social Security Act). Many more agencies are constrained only by general legislation, such as the Privacy Act.

Agencies sometimes purposely disseminate individually identifiable data in order to shame citizens into activity or to inform and protect neighbors, as in the case of posting names and addresses of pedophiles. Although these practices are criticized by civil libertarians and arguably contravene state privacy legislation, they are widely accepted as exceptions. For instance, delinquent state income taxpayer lists now appear on the revenue department websites in California, Colorado, Georgia, Illinois, Louisiana, Maryland, Minnesota, New Jersey, North Carolina, Rhode Island, South Carolina, and Washington (Fang, 2004). Sarah Kaufman, director of communications at the Connecticut Department of Revenue Services, observed, "It's amazing what a little embarrassment will do. Of the more than 2200 accounts that have been eligible to be published, we have cleared over 1800" (Perry, 2004, p. 3). Since criminal records are considered to be public data, not only do states publish information on sex offenders, but personally identifiable data are readily available from online services such as www.childsafe network.org, www.nationalalertregistry.com, and www.criminalscreen. com, to name a few. In 2005, the Justice Department announced it was creating a searchable nationwide sex offender database, unifying 48 state systems (Dizard, 2005c).

In spite of such exceptions, the main thrust of agency privacy objectives are set forth under now widely accepted principles of data management and data sharing, which were articulated by the Organization for Economic Co-operation and Development (OECD) in 1980, in an international agreement to which the United States is a signatory.[8] The OECD rules, based on a "code of fair information practices" developed in the United States in the 1970s, encompass eight principles, about which the OECD states: "These guidelines should be regarded as minimum standards which are capable of being supplemented by additional measures for the protection of privacy and individual liberties" (OECD, 1980).

1. Collection Limitation Principle—There should be limits to the collection of personal data and any such data should be obtained by lawful and fair means and, where appropriate, with the knowledge or consent of the data subject.
2. Data Quality Principle—Personal data should be relevant to the purposes for which they are to be used, and, to the extent necessary for those purposes, should be accurate, complete, and kept up-to-date.
3. Purpose Specification Principle—The purposes for which personal data are collected should be specified not later than at the time of data

collection and the subsequent use limited to the fulfillment of those purposes or such others as are not incompatible with those purposes and as are specified on each occasion of change of purpose.

4. Use Limitation Principle—Personal data should not be disclosed, made available, or otherwise used for purposes other than those specified in accordance with Paragraph 9 (the Purpose Specification Principle) except: a) with the consent of the data subject; or b) by the authority of law.

5. Security Safeguards Principle—Personal data should be protected by reasonable security safeguards against such risks as loss or unauthorized access, destruction, use, modification, or disclosure of data.

6. Openness Principle—There should be a general policy of openness about developments, practices, and policies with respect to personal data. Means should be readily available of establishing the existence and nature of personal data, and the main purposes of their use, as well as the identity and usual residence of the data controller.

7. Individual Participation Principle—An individual should have the right:
   a. To obtain from a data controller, or otherwise, confirmation of whether or not the data controller has data relating to him;
   b. To have communicated to him data relating to him within a reasonable time; at a charge, if any, that is not excessive; in a reasonable manner; and in a form that is readily intelligible to him;
   c. To be given reasons if a request made under subparagraphs (a) and (b) is denied, and to be able to challenge such denial; and
   d. To challenge data relating to him and, if the challenge is successful, to have the data erased, rectified, completed, or amended.

8. Accountability Principle—A data controller should be accountable for complying with measures that give effect to the principles stated above.

While in principle the U.S. government subscribes to all eight principles of fair information practice, and while the wording of one or another principle may find its way into the privacy statement of a particular agency, there is no systematic enforcement of these principles within public management in the United States, and many practices are sanctioned that violate one or more principles.

The "Stated Purpose" Rule

One attempt to provide protection for personally identifiable information has been the promulgation of the concept that data should be used only for the purpose described to the user at the time of collection, and data should be retained only so long as needed for the original purpose. This corresponds roughly with Principle 3 (Purpose Specification) of the OECD guidelines above. Ron Brown, Secretary of Commerce under the Clinton administration, for instance, said that agreed-upon international privacy principles included the principles that:

- Personal data should be collected only for specified, legitimate purposes;
- The dissemination, sharing, and reuse of information should be compatible with the purposes for which it was originally collected (Brown, Irving, Prabhakar, & Katzen, 1994).

In practice, the "stated purpose" rule is widely disregarded by public agencies. An example is the E-Z Pass tollbooth system used by Maryland and other states. Under this system, a radio frequency identification chip is attached to commuters' cars, automatically charging their accounts when they go through tollbooths. In practice, E-Z Pass records are not deleted after accounts are charged but, in Maryland, are stored up to 2 years and used for law enforcement tracking of the spatial movements of suspects (McKay, 2004a). Private Citizen, a privacy advocacy group, calls this an abuse of privacy rights since data are not used for the stated purposes. Likewise, the Electronic Frontier Foundation objects to personal information being kept longer than needed for its original purpose.

"Safe Harbor" Principles and the European Union Data Protection Directive

As noted above, Europe has higher privacy standards than prevail in the United States, a fact that has sometimes gotten American companies such as Microsoft in trouble.[9] While of greater concern to the private sector than the public, European Union (EU) countries are obliged by the EU Data Protection Directive not to share data with countries that do not meet certain standards with respect to data privacy and protection. The U.S. State Department in 2000 negotiated certain "safe harbor" principles to clarify the conditions under which data may be shared between the United States and the EU. The "safe harbor" protocol calls for individuals to be notified about collection and use of personal data, gives individuals the right to refuse to allow information about them to be transferred, requires that the agency receiving the data must agree to safe harbor principles, gives individuals the right to access their own information, and provides for enforcement with sanctions for violations of privacy policy.

"Safe harbor" principles are of special importance to U.S. companies that wish to import personally identifiable information about their European customers. Conformity to the necessary privacy principles may involve extensive alteration of existing business practices and restructuring of data protection systems in U.S. companies (Crutchfield George,

Lynch, & Marsnick, 2001). For this reason, most U.S. firms have not adopted the safe-harbor protocol (Duncan & Roehrig, 2003).

Customer Relations Management

New software encourages the databasing and multiple reuse of personally identifiable information. Customer relationship management (CRM) is tracking software used in the private sector to keep tabs on prospective customers and tailor advertising and products to them based on this information. However, under the banner of being "customer oriented," there has been significant recent interest by federal agencies in CRM software. Accenture, a leading management consulting firm that often advises public sector clients, issued a report, *CRM in Government: Bridging the Gaps* (2003). The report documents increased public sector interest in CRM and calls, in a nutshell, for larger and more integrated databases tracking the attributes of an agency's "customers," ostensibly for better outreach purposes. This is seen as a logical extension of e-government, as the public sector strives to be more proactive and more customized to the individual.[10] Although in some ways worthy in its objective, CRM software also tempts the public manager to reuse personally identifiable information for purposes other than that for which it was collected, in possible violation of fair information practices codes regarding privacy.

Methods of Data Sharing with Privacy

Deidentification of Data

Agencies that collect personally identifiable data are prohibited by the Privacy Act and other legislation from sharing it with researchers, journalists, and others. However, there are numerous exceptions at law, including most court and criminal records, motor vehicle records, and property parcel records. Other types of records, such as those of the IRS, are barred by legislation from most data sharing even with other agencies, let alone with the public. Where neither open records nor proscribed or classified records are involved, data sharing is normally implemented through deidentification. Deidentified data sets are those from which Social Security numbers (SSNs) or other identifying fields have been removed, even though each row in the data set represents an individual. Using deidentified data sets, researchers can still investigate individual-level correlations among variables, but they cannot identify any particular individual.

The Reidentification Problem

While agencies may release data stripped of personally identifiable information but having a link field, a second file may share that field with the first. While the original file separately may maintain privacy, it may be possible using two data files relationally to identify particular individuals. For example, a health agency data set may contain confidential fields about subjects with sexually transmitted diseases (STDs) and a second may contain public voter registration data, containing names, addresses, and phone numbers. By using ZIP codes, birth dates, and gender data available in both data sets, a researcher may well be able to reidentify the subjects with STDs, even though the health agency had promised anonymity and stripped the first database of names, addresses, and SSN identifiers. In principle, agencies should anticipate and prevent this, but in practice this sophistication often is ignored. For purposes of federal agency sharing of personally identifiable data with researchers, Government Accountability Office (GAO) guidelines suggest various techniques such as signed consent forms, secure data centers where researchers analyze linked data under controlled conditions, and masked data sharing (such as list inflation, third-party linkage, or grouped linkage) (GAO, 2001a, p. 6):

1. List Inflation—The Drug Treatment Agency wants School Agency data. The School Agency is willing to share, but the Drug Treatment Agency wants its survey data private. The schools are sent an inflated list including people both in and not in drug treatment, so the school does not know who has received drug treatment. The School Agency matches on SSNs and adds its educational fields. When the data are returned to the Drug Treatment Agency, the agency uses the SSN field to deflate the list to just the individuals who have received drug treatments.

2. Third-Party Linkage—The Drug Treatment Agency is willing to let the School Agency know the SSNs of individuals and also a second agency-generated ID code, but not answers to its survey questions. The Drug Treatment Agency wants to make the data available to the School Agency for statistical analysis as long as personal identifiers are removed. The Drug Treatment Agency sends just the SSNs and code numbers to the School Agency, which matches on SSN and adds its educational data, strips off the SSNs, and sends the coded-only school data to trusted Agency 3. The Drug Treatment Agency sends coded-only drug survey data to Agency 3 (also no SSNs). Agency 3 matches the School Agency educational fields and the Drug Treatment Agency survey fields using the code as a link field, then strips the code from the file. The result is a matched drug survey/education database with no individual identifiers, which can be given to the School Agency or others on a deidentified basis for research purposes.

3. Grouped Linkage—The Drug Treatment Agency is willing to let the School Agency know the SSNs of individuals, but neither agency is willing to share individual-level data with the other. Both are willing

to just know group-level differences, such as average school gradua-
tion rates by drug treatment type. The Drug Treatment Agency groups
its survey data into aggregates (for example, by drug treatment type).
The Drug Treatment Agency tells the School Agency the SSNs of people in each group and asks for aggregated school data for each group,
not telling the School Agency the meaning of each group, only an
arbitrary group code number. The School Agency matches on name
or SSN, computes group averages, and sends back the averages for
each arbitrarily coded group. The Drug Treatment Agency uses the
arbitrary codes to match the grouped School Agency data to its
grouped survey results, sharing the results with the School Agency.

Controlled access is probably more common than any of these three
methods of data masking for privacy purposes. Under controlled access,
researchers with security-clearance status are given direct access to
databases of the Drug Treatment Agency and the School Agency. They
do the matching and generate a statistical report without individual-
level identifiers. The matched data file is erased. The analysts are
trusted not to abuse their temporary access to linked data and have the
incentive to protect privacy so as to retain security clearances and research privileges for the future.

PRIVACY IMPACT STATEMENTS

Countries that have had strong leadership in privacy protection policy,
such as Canada (see Treasury Board of Canada Secretariat, 2002), require
privacy impact assessments in conjunction with the institution of new IT
systems. This reform was incorporated in the E-Government Act of 2002.
In 2003, the OMB issued implementing guidelines designed for the FY
2005 budget process. Whereas in 2003 for FY 2004 privacy assessments
were merely "recommended," with few agencies doing them, starting in
2004 for FY 2005, all federal agencies were required to submit privacy
assessments of major IT systems as part of their annual business case submissions.

It is now the responsibility of the public manager at the federal level to
undertake a privacy analysis for each IT system in development or
under procurement. This applies to any IT system that collects, maintains, or disseminates information in a personally identifiable form that
contains data from or about members of the public. Privacy assessments
are required whenever the agency initiates electronic collection of information for 10 or more individuals (Miller, 2003b, 2003c, 2003d).

How do privacy impact assessments work? Consider one example: the
assessment for the Transportation Security Administration's (TSA) test

of the Secure Flight program for screening airline passengers (Transportation Security Administration, 2004). In January 1998, the TSA initiated the Computer-Assisted Passenger Pre-Screening (CAPPS) program, created in response to the crash of TWA 800 in 1996 and terrorist threats. CAPPS screened airline passengers using a database with address, travel history, criminal record, and other information. How effective CAPPS was is not known, but clearly it did not stop terrorists on 9/11. In November 2002, the TSA deployed CAPPS II, a more sophisticated passenger profiling system with a database of thousands of variables, not just a dozen as with CAPPS I. Partly due to civil liberties concerns and probably more due to airline efficiency motives, in early 2004 Homeland Security chief Tom Ridge announced that CAPPS II would be phased out in favor of a new system, Secure Flight.

Under the Secure Flight program, the TSA compares passenger information against consolidated watch lists held in the Terrorist Screening Database maintained by the Terrorist Screening Center to identify known or suspected terrorists. Input was solicited from Congress, the public, privacy and civil liberties groups, airline passengers, and the airline industry. Part of the system is using data from commercial data aggregators who currently provide services to the banking, home mortgage, and credit industries. The accuracy of these commercial data, the privacy assessment notes, is being tested because accuracy is not assumed. The privacy impact assessment addresses the following questions as per OMB guidelines for privacy impact reports (questions and answers are summarized):

1. *What information is to be collected?* Personally identifiable information includes passenger names, contact phone numbers, mailing addresses, and travel itineraries.
2. *Why is the information being collected and who will be affected?* The purpose is to enhance the security of domestic air travel by identifying only those passengers who warrant further scrutiny.
3. *What notice or opportunities for consent are provided?* Notice is via the Privacy Impact Assessment itself and the publication of a Privacy Act System of Records Notice. The report acknowledges these notices do not afford the opportunity for a passenger to provide consent in advance of data collection. Information, the report notes, will be shared not only with TSA employees but also contractors "who have a need to know."
4. *What security protocols are in place?* Data are safeguarded in accordance with the Federal Information Security Management Act of 2002 (Pub. L., pp. 107–347), which established government-wide computer security and training standards. Data are protected by a system of passwords, security clearances, and locked file cabinets for hard copy.

5. *Does this program create a new system of records under the Privacy Act?* Yes. Notification is given in the *Federal Register.*
6. *What is the intended use of the information?* Testing the Secure Flight program.
7. *Will the information be retained and, if so, for what period of time?* TSA will retain these records for a sufficient period of time to conduct and review the Secure Flight test and in the event where a request for redress must be resolved.
8. *How will the passenger be able to seek redress?* By sending a written request to the TSA's privacy officer.
9. *What databases will the names be run against?* A consolidated, comprehensive watch list of known or suspected terrorists based on information contributed by the Departments of Homeland Security, Justice, and State, and by the intelligence community.
10. *Privacy Effects and Mitigation Measures.* Testing follows the recommendations of the National Commission on Terrorist Attacks Upon the United States (9/11 Commission) that "improved use of 'no-fly' and 'automatic selectee' lists should not be delayed." Moreover, by focusing solely on potential terrorism and not other law enforcement purposes, Secure Flight addresses concerns raised by privacy groups and others about the potential for "mission creep" by TSA. Secure Flight will mitigate impact on personal privacy because of its limited purpose and anticipated limited retention period.

In summary, the TSA privacy impact assessment provides assurance that there is an agency privacy plan, and the OMB's list of required questions to be answered ensures that the agency will have at least considered privacy policy issues, such as why data are being collected, with whom data are to be shared, how long records are to be retained, and how citizens may seek redress. However, the impact assessment process does not provide assurance that the agency is prohibited from sharing data beyond its stated purpose later on, does not restrict with whom data may be shared, does not require any particular data retention period, and does not require that citizens receive prior notification or have a channel of redress independent of the agency itself.

The OMB rules implementing the E-Government Act do not apply to IT systems that do not contain personally identifiable data, even if there are significant indirect privacy impacts, as is the case with many systems that support electronic surveillance but do not themselves house collected personally identifiable information. Also, as noted above, critics such as Gellman (2003a) have objected that the act makes no provision for *prior* public input to privacy assessments, necessary to allow the public to have any impact on outcomes. Then too, although agencies must file privacy impact reports, they are not required to take any specific action based on these reports nor is there any systematic provision for penalizing agencies with regard to shortcomings in matters related to privacy reports.

A 2004 review of agency compliance with the new E-Government Act privacy assessment requirements found "few agencies have adequately considered how new or upgraded systems could compromise the privacy of citizens who submit personal information." (Miller, 2004a, p. 1). Very few agencies had made their privacy impact assessments public. While a number of agencies now issue privacy handbooks (e.g., Wartell & McEwan, 2001), as of 2004 only Homeland Security was required by statute to have a privacy office. Some witnesses in recent Congressional hearings have suggested that other departments be so required in order to bring greater priority to privacy protection within federal agencies.

THE NATIONAL ID CONTROVERSY

National ID cards have been suggested as a solution to providing better security at airports and points of entry to the country, as well as authentication for all manner of government and commercial transactions. Traditionally, the idea of having a national ID card was associated with apartheid in South Africa and with totalitarian regimes. It is still an unpopular idea. A national Hart-Teeter poll in 2004 showed only 16% of Americans favored having a national ID system (Council for Excellence in Government, 2004). The media and academia have been skeptical too. For instance, in his book, *A National ID Card: A License to Live* (2002), privacy advocate Robert Ellis Smith called the proposal for a national ID card one of the greatest threats to privacy in the next few years.

It could be asked whether existing governmental ID systems do not suffice. Why not just have a higher-security version of the SSN, for example? The answer is that SSNs are low in security, often stolen, and there are some 10 million duplicate numbers used by different people, according to Social Security Administration estimates. Moreover, SSNs are only for citizens, and national ID advocates want IDs for legal aliens as well, leading to the question, "Why not rely on visas and passports?" The answer is that visas and passports are foreign-issued and provide too low a level of security for such purposes as homeland defense. What about state driver's licenses? Although not yet a reality, state departments of motor vehicles have been collaborating since 2002 on plans to implement a standardized national driver's license, based on interstate agreements on uniform identification requirements (Divis & Horrock,

2002). However, history suggests that data sharing based on state compacts is spotty and is associated with low data quality.

There are practical problems to national IDs. For instance, if establishing identities were to take a public manager just 15 minutes to affirm—the average the Immigration and Naturalization Service takes for documentation on the Mexican border—then 30,000 new federal employees would be required to work for a year to provide national ID authentication for the entire U.S. population. Similarly, a 1997 Social Security Administration report estimated it would cost $10 billion and 10 years to issue secure Social Security cards with pictures, fingerprints, work histories, and earnings for Social Security accounts (Divis & Horrock, 2002).

In spite of practical problems, the main obstacle to having a national ID system is that numerous policy problems would need to be resolved first. Kent and Millett (2002) list these:

1. How intrusive will national IDs be?
   - Just be for authentication, with no retention of information?
   - At other extreme, to track and remember every single interaction an individual ever has with any government agency?
   - Could a national ID be demanded at airports, hotels, when purchasing weapons, perhaps at banks, or, indeed, in any commercial transaction?
2. Who could use the data?
   - Agencies? Corporations? Individual members of the public?
   - Would we outsource management of the national ID system, as we have many other IT functions, and how would we hold management accountable?
3. Would it be voluntary or mandatory to have an ID?
   - Voluntary but if you want to pass through the airport line quicker, you'll want one.
   - If mandatory, would you have to carry your ID with you? What if you refuse to show it?
4. What rights would exist to see your data and to have it corrected?
5. What penalties would exist for abuse of the system?
6. How could we prevent forging national IDs, given that currency and passports are forged now?

These and many other policy issues have yet to enter into serious national dialog, let alone have answers representing a national consensus. It is not yet clear that Americans even want the data integration national IDs could bring.

Nonetheless, at this writing a bill (HR 5111, the Illegal Immigrant Enforcement and Social Security Protection Act of 2004) by Rep. David

Dreier (R-CA), would force all Americans to carry a national ID card (McCullagh, 2004a).[11] Employers could hire only people who held a new federal ID card with their photograph, SSN, and an "encrypted electronic strip" with additional information. To prevent forgery, every time the card is swiped, it would match its data against an employment eligibility database containing Homeland Security and Social Security data. That is, unlike driver's licenses, Social Security cards, and other current government ID systems, the Dreier bill would create serious privacy issues by creating a back-end database for authentication purposes to track an individual whenever the federal ID card is swiped.

PRIVACY, GOVERNMENTAL OUTSOURCING, AND PRIVATE-SECTOR DATA MINING

While most Americans, when they think of violation of privacy rights at all, think of the intrusion of government bureaucrats, in fact all that government does in this regard pales before faceless corporations that trade SSNs, purchasing patterns, and all manner of personal information just like anything else is bought and sold (see Garfinkel, 2001). Even leading defenders of national ID cards, reading of e-mail to fight terrorists, and other pro-security measures, such as the communitarian scholar Amitai Etzioni (2000), have less trust in the respect profit-driven corporations might have for privacy in their pursuit of electronic surveillance of customers and computerized marketing. Moreover, much in privacy legislation does not apply to the private sector, and access to individually identifiable court and other public records is not a legal issue. Commercial services such as www.Intelius.com and www.lawresearchservices.com routinely search public individual data on vital statistics, criminal records, lawsuits, address history, property liens, assets, and much more.

At times, private surveillance may take on public functions. Hunter (2002b), for instance, relates the story of a man who was fined $450 for driving his rental car beyond the speed limit and who was caught not by the police but by the rental car company's GPS system, embedded in the car. This example pales, however, before the vision of "e-vigilantism" advocated by some, such as the proposed Japanese "e-Vigilante Network" of camera-equipped home computers networked in community watches (Fujii, Yoshiura, & Ohta, 2005).[12]

The commoditization of personal information is, of course, made possible by IT. For instance, it is now possible to match your visits to websites against commercial databases containing over 100 million names and associated data on your lifestyle characteristics. In fact, in 1999 Cogit allied with Polk, a worldwide supplier of demographic and lifestyle data and database-marketing services, to accomplish precisely that, launching Cogit.com in 2000. Polk's database includes personal information on your income, net worth, bankruptcies, home value, cars owned, religion, ethnic group, "inferred lifestyles" (such as investments), and many other variables.

A competing commercial service, DoubleClick, was investigated by the Federal Trade Commission (FTC) in the same period, following a complaint by the EPIC, which sought to prohibit the firm from collecting personal information using cookies (cookies are stored by websites on visitors' computers to record data about viewer preferences and attributes) without an individual's informed consent (Livingston, 2000). The FTC held hearings in 1999 and issued a report to Congress about online profiling in 2000. In the report the FTC noted that DoubleClick, the largest network advertising company, estimated that it serves an average of 1.5 billion ads each day, for an average of approximately 45 billion ads per month. The next largest network advertisers, Engage and 24/7 Media, served approximately 8.6 billion ads per month and 3.3 billion ads per month respectively (Federal Trade Commission, 2000). A search of the FTC website in late 2004 for "online profiling" revealed 124 hits, all dealing with the 1999 hearing and the 2000 report, with no further activity. The FTC accepted industry plans for self-regulation and issued no regulations of its own. Its official view was, "The Commission believes that self-regulation is the least intrusive and most efficient means to ensure fair information practices online, given the rapidly evolving nature of the Internet and computer technology" (Federal Trade Commission, 1999).

As of this writing, the FTC has brought only a dozen cases involving the privacy of consumer information under Section 5 of the FTC Act.[13] The first Internet privacy case involving a formal FTC complaint against a private-sector company was the GeoCities case in 1998, where the Web hosting firm was accused of deceptively collecting personal information. The case ended when Geocities agreed to post a privacy policy and not collect data on children under 13 without parental permission. In 1999 the FTC brought charges against Liberty Financial Companies, Inc., for making false promises about the anonymity of personal information collected from children and teens. In the settlement, Liberty Mutual agreed not to make false statements about anonymity, to post a privacy policy, and not to collect information from children under 13 if Liberty Financial had actual knowledge that the child did not have a parent's permission to provide the information.

A 2000 FTC case against ReverseAuction.com dealt with hijacking personal identifying information from e-Bay, then sending deceptive spam claiming their e-Bay IDs were about to expire. In the settlement,

ReverseAuction.com agreed to notify people that their e-Bay IDs were not about to expire, to delete e-mail addresses hijacked from e-Bay from their database, and to post a privacy notice. Also in 2000, ToySmart.com was charged with violating its own privacy policy by selling personally identifiable information, including data on children under 13. The settlement restricted sale of that information by the company, which was going bankrupt at the time for other reasons. In another 2000 case, a group of online pharmacies was charged with making false medical claims for Viagra and Propecia; in the settlement the company agreed to rephrase advertising to be nondeceptive, to post a notice that "Dispensing a prescription drug without a valid prescription is a violation of federal law," and to post a privacy policy.

In 2001, the first year of the Bush administration, there were no FTC privacy cases brought at all, but in 2002 the Eli Lilly company was charged with disclosing 669 e-mail addresses to its Prozac Reminder Service. The company agreed to take appropriate security measures. In 2002 Microsoft Passport was charged with making deceptive statements about the level of security for personal data it took in; it too agreed to take appropriate security measures and to reword its statements. A 2003 charge was that the National Research Center for College & University Admissions, after promising data would be shared only with educational institutions, in fact shared the data with commercial establishments. The firm agreed to stop doing this or to revise its privacy statement to reflect its practices. Another 2003 case against Educational Research Center of America, Inc., was on similar charges with a largely similar outcome. In 2003 also, designer clothing and accessory marketer Guess was charged with misrepresenting the security of personal information it took in online; the company agreed to improve security and eliminate deceptive wording. In 2004, the FTC brought charges against Tower Records because security flaws exposed personal data to other Web users. Tower agreed to improve security and not to misrepresent the level of privacy it afforded. In the most recent FTC privacy case at this writing, also in 2004, Gateway Learning Inc. ("Hooked on Phonics") was charged with renting out personal information it had pledged to keep private. The company agreed to end deceptive practices.

These 12 cases have been enumerated to make the following points about federal regulatory actions against corporate violations of individual privacy in the course of commercial data mining: Action has been taken only against a handful of companies. FTC actions bring no financial penalty, let alone criminal liability, but are routinely settled by modest improvements in security policy and wording of privacy statements. In the rare event that action is taken, it is taken against deceptive and unfair trade practices, not against invasion of privacy. For instance, in the most recent case, Gateway Learning, the company revised its privacy policy to state that "from time to time" Gateway Learning would provide consumers' personal information to "reputable companies" whose products or services consumers might find of interest. Under this improved wording, the company could continue the practices that were the subject of FTC charges. What was deemed illegal was earlier wording not apprising users of the release of information, and the unfair trade practice of applying the new policy retroactively to users whose data had come in under earlier wording. The key to successful commercial exploitation of personal data is having nondeceptive wording buried in a posted privacy statement written by the company's lawyer and assented to in most cases by a user's click of the mouse, usually without reading, or if read, assented to anyway in order to receive the desired service or goods.

Today, most Americans seem ready to give up their privacy rights to a government-corporate data alliance if it is done in the name of national security. When asked in a 2004 Hart-Teeter poll, "Should the government have access to personal information that companies collect about consumers if there is any chance it will help prevent terrorism?" some 60% of the 1633 Americans polled said yes. National schizophrenia on privacy was shown when, in the same poll, in response to the question, "Do you trust government to use personal information properly?" some 72% answered only "some" or "very little" (Council for Excellence in Government, 2004).

Corporate data mining can also be used to allow government to do what it would not be allowed to do in its own right. Though Congress forbade the Department of Defense to continue with its Total Information Awareness, which would have integrated credit, banking, travel, criminal, and other corporate and governmental databases for purposes of surveillance, in the present age of outsourcing IT functions, there is no prohibition against achieving the same ends through private sector data mining. This is examined further in the next chapter.

SUMMARY

On a global basis, privacy does not rank high on the policy agenda. A 2003 study of 2166 government websites in 198 countries by Darrell M. West of the Taubman Center for Public Policy at Brown University found that only 12% even posted privacy policies, let alone had comprehensive or effective ones (West, 2003b). This percentage was down from 14% in 2002, indicating privacy policy may be a long time coming on a worldwide basis. Moreover, West found that the posting of privacy policies was concentrated. The countries most likely to show privacy policies were Australia and Dominica (each with 100% of its sites), followed by Canada (97%), Singapore (93%), China (83%), the

United States (75%), St. Lucia (50%), New Zealand (47%), Great Britain (45%), and Taiwan (42%). Most other countries did not offer privacy statements online at all.

Privacy is important. George Washington University law professor Jeffrey Rosen, in his book *The Unwanted Gaze,* states that "Privacy protects us from being misdefined and judged out of context in a world of short attention spans, a world in which information can easily be confused with knowledge" (2001, p. 8). For those Americans who—through ignorance, trust in government, or for other reasons—do not care whether they are surveilled, sacrifice of privacy seems a cheap price to pay for increased security. As Simson Garfinkel noted in his book *Database Nation* (2001), however, the Americans who do care and are skeptical of the purported benefits, the choice seems to be between allowing their personal data to rest in the public domain or becoming hermits without credit cards, without online transactions, without video rentals or library borrowing, and indeed, without participation in much of life in the digital era. In this regard, Garfinkel discussed the case of an insurance claim form, where the citizen is given the choice of signing a blanket authorization for the insurance company to access all personal records (not just medical) or of not signing and thereby forfeiting reimbursement of expenses. The literature of public management has frequently focused on such negative privacy impacts of IT (Danziger & Andersen, 2002). For their part, hospital administrators and other public managers are often placed in the position of enforcing the surveillance and dataveillance regime even when the security and other benefits do not seem to measure up to the privacy costs.

Many privacy-eroding measures taken in the name of security are not effective or necessary, yielding modest results that could be achieved by alternative methods that do not lessen the freedom of privacy. For instance, a massive CCTV effort in the United Kingdom photographs the average citizen of that country with 300 security cameras every day. Partly motivated by terrorism from the Irish Republican Army, the United Kingdom has invested in 4 million CCTV, making it the most-surveilled nation in the world (Carlile, 2004). Yet a recent case study by Rosen (2004) found that although the system has been used to solve particular cases, data failed to show that CCTV surveillance had done anything at all to reduce overall levels of crime or terrorism. Critics charge that the system does not actually prevent crime or terrorism but does give citizens a false sense of security, and that an equivalent investment in conventional law enforcement would actually solve more crimes as well, all the while protecting privacy rights that are now lost.

Matthew Brzezinski (2004), nephew of former national security adviser Zbigniew Brzezinski, has studied recent antiterrorist efforts under the new DHS. Brzezinski's interviews revealed that DHS employees complained about resource shortages everywhere because, he documented, the DHS budget was not the dramatic increase over pre-9/11 the public supposed it to be but rather merely lumped together the 22 existing budgets of constituent agencies comprising the new department. Brzezinski attributed the lack of adequate additional resources in part to the costs of a war in Iraq that, in terms of terrorism, made matters worse rather better. For Brzezinski, priorities are not well set by the TSA, for instance, which employs thousands to make travelers take their shoes off while only 2% of cargo on passenger planes is screened. Likewise, the question may be raised whether security might not be better increased through protection of chemical plants (the vulnerability of which was documented on a November 2003 *60 Minutes* story) or inspection of cargo containers in American ports (only 5% are screened now), rather than by expensive intrusions into the privacy of individuals, particularly when the quality of information retrieved is low, resulting—in Brzezinski's view—in the sweeping up and secret imprisonment of hundreds of aliens based on ethnic and religious profiles without evidence of specific terrorist involvements.

To take another example, in April 2004 the advocacy group Privacy International released a report based on a study of national ID cards (Privacy International, 2004). The report had been undertaken in response to attempts by the United Kingdom and Canadian governments to introduce biometric ID cards. The report analyzed the 25 countries that have been most affected by terrorism since 1986 and concluded that the presence of an ID card appears to have made no significant impact on prevention of these attacks. Privacy International noted that terrorists have used tourist visas (as in 9/11) or have legitimate ID cards (as in the Madrid bombings). The research was unable to uncover any instance where the presence of an identity card system was seen as a significant deterrent to terrorist activity. To deter a terrorist, the terrorist would have to be eligible to receive an ID card, willing to register for one, and intelligence data would have to cross-reference the identity on the ID card. Again, it is far from clear that the sacrifice of privacy involved in national identity cards would, in fact, bring greater security.

Public managers are legally responsible to ensure privacy in their electronic transactions. Perhaps more important, however, is the fact that privacy assurance is essential to the effective implementation of electronic public services and to the growth of e-government. Failure to have well-designed privacy systems in place beforehand was a significant obstacle to information sharing in the response to the 9/11 terrorist attack on the World Trade Center (Dawes, Cresswell, & Cahan, 2004). The potential threat to privacy has been one of the significant barriers to progress in providing consumers with electronic health services, for instance (Anderson, 2004). Nearly half of Americans presently believe that if they submit personal information to government websites, it may risk the security and privacy of their personal information. A majority (54%) think that government should proceed slowly in relying on the Internet for communication between citizens and government (Council for Excellence in Government, 2003). Until policy leaders and public managers do a better job on privacy protection, the full potential of electronic government will never be reached.

DISCUSSION QUESTIONS

1. What are the reasons for surveillance in public spaces? Do you agree with these reasons?
2. How does "surveillance by social sorting" threaten to change the traditional model of law enforcement? Is this a significant threat to privacy?
3. Why is the USA Patriot Act criticized on privacy grounds? Why was the portion of the act that dealt with turning over subscriber information from Internet service providers and phone companies ruled unconstitutional?
4. What is "computer matching?" What impact did the Computer Matching and Privacy Protection Act of 1988 have on the sharing of personally identifiable information?
5. Give an example of how data matching and sharing has negatively impacted individuals?
6. What are some of the actions taken or rules created by private and public entities to provide protection for personally identifiable information?
7. What is a "privacy impact assessment?"
8. What is the goal behind a national ID card? What are the pros and cons to a national ID card system? Are there alternatives?
9. Profit-driven corporations are frequent users of personal information to enhance sales through targeted marketing. The FTC rarely brings cases involving consumer privacy invasion but when it does, what actions are usually taken? Is the public sector subject to FTC rules?
10. What is data mining and how has it been used by the public sector?

GLOSSARY

Biometrics: *Biometrics* refers to recognition and authentication software based on the scanning of fingerprints, eyes, faces, or other human attributes.

CCTV: Closed-circuit television (CCTV) with linked monitors and cameras can be used in visual surveillance systems in a variety of environments.

Cost–benefit analysis: A method of gauging the efficiency of a proposed or existing program or policy based on the associated benefits and costs.

Computer matching: *Computer matching* or *data matching* involves the comparison of data tables containing personally identifiable data in machine-readable format in order to target a group or individual for enforcement, notification, research, or other purposes.

Dataveillance: *Dataveillance* is the surveillance of individuals through personally identifiable information contained in constantly updated databases, rather than through visual or auditory monitoring.

GPS: Global positioning systems (GPS) use coded satellite signals to ascertain location. GPS can be used in vehicles, clothing, and other objects for surveillance purposes.

P3P Initiative: The Privacy Preferences Project (P3P) was developed by the World Wide Web Consortium in an effort to grant Internet users greater control over the transference of personal information through websites. Users set privacy preferences in their Web browsers, which notify them of any discrepancies when entering a P3P-compliant website.

Reidentification: Recovering the personal identity associated with a record by matching fields in two or more related databases.

ENDNOTES

[1]The Census Bureau has since revised its data-sharing rules.

[2]For instance, the EPA did not want to release survey data on corporations but was sued by the Antitrust Division of the Department of Justice and was forced to release the data (Duncan & Roehrig, 2003).

[3]Quoted in an AMA press release retrieved 10/28/04 from http://www.amanet. org/books/catalog/0814471498_pressrelease.htm.

[4]http://www.epic.org/privacy/survey/.

[5]For a ranking of states by privacy law protections, see Smith (2004b).

[6]A 2000 Fox News/Opinion Dynamics poll found 69% of Americans were "very concerned" about online privacy (Fox News, 2000). An even larger percentage (86%) do not want identifiable government records like driving records, marriage records, real estate purchases, and court cases available on the Web (ABC News, 2000).

[7]Warrantless wiretapping became illegal in 1967.

[8]The Code of Fair Information Practice was established by the U.S. Department of Health, Education, and Welfare in a report titled *Records Computers and the Rights of Citizens* (1973). The (U.S.) Business Roundtable endorsed the code in the 1970s. As reprinted in the *Privacy Journal* (2004), the code set forth these model policies:

1. Organizations establishing privacy policies should incorporate the elements of the widely accepted Code of Fair Information Practice:
   - The existence of all data systems with personal information in them should be publicly disclosed, and the purpose for which information is

gathered about people should be disclosed. This is the principle of openness or transparency.

- There must be a way for an individual to find out what information about him or her is in a record and how it is used.
- There must be a way for an individual to prevent information about him or her that was obtained for one purpose (which was stated when the information was gathered) from being used or made available, either within the organization or outside, for a purpose that is incompatible with the original purpose, without getting the consent of the individual. This is the principle of secondary use.
- There must be a way for an individual to correct or amend a record that contains information that is identifiable to him or her.
- The organization creating, maintaining, using, or disseminating records of identifiable personal data must ensure the reliability, accuracy, security, and timeliness of the data. In other words, the custodian of information that is disseminated has an obligation to the individual to make sure it is accurate, secure, and not misused. This obligation should not be delegated to another entity.

2. An organization must make sure that other entities handling personal information on behalf of the first organization are bound by these same principles.

3. An organization must conduct periodic risk assessments, balancing the possibility or probability of unauthorized access or disclosure against the cost of security precautions and the expected effectiveness of the precautions. In some cases, it will be necessary to establish an audit trail so that records are kept of disclosures of personal information, both within the organization and outside.

4. Organizations must take special precautions in collecting and using personal information about children, both those 13 or younger and those 18 or younger.

5. An organization should openly disclose its policies and practices with regard to electronic surveillance of its employees' and customers' telephone calls, electronic mail, Internet usage, changing rooms, and restrooms. It must articulate in advance the reasons for the surveillance.

6. An organization should collect only that personal information that is *proportional* to the purpose of the information. It must scrutinize each demand for information to determine that it is relevant and necessary.

7. An organization should designate an individual or office (whether full-time or part-time) to handle privacy issues by: (a) acting as an ombudsman for customers or employees, (b) assessing the privacy impact of new undertakings, (c) assuring that the organization complies with all laws and trade-association standards, and (d) informing the organization of the latest technology and policies that affect the privacy of customers or employees. An organization, if it utilizes "opt-out" for customers to stay out of certain uses of their information, should make exercising this option as easy as clicking a button or checking a box, without the need to write a letter or to communicate with another office.

8. An organization should conduct periodic training of its employees (and volunteers) to ensure that they know (1) applicable laws on confidentiality that govern the organization, (2) the organization's policies and actual practices, (3) the rationale for protecting confidentiality and the sensitivity of personal information, (4) the ability to recognize possible breaches and to report them to the proper person. An organization may

choose to certify that employees who handle personal information are properly trained.

[9]Passport is an e-authentication system pushed by Microsoft to manage passwords across websites. In January 2003, the European Union found Passport violated several data protection rules. Specifically, Microsoft was forced to modify Passport to comply with EU law, including giving users the right to specify on a site-by-site basis which personal information they want to enter.

[10]http://www.accenture.com/xd/xd.asp?it=enweb&xd=industries%5Cgovern ment%5Cinsights%5Ccrmgov.xml.

[11]As of late 2004, HR 5111 was still in committee.

[12]The authors' e-vigilante software is available for download at http://www.ev. gunma-u.ac.jp/Download_e.html.

[13]http://www.ftc.gov/privacy/privacyinitiatives/promises_enf.html.

CASE STUDY
The Mother Robinson Black Beaufort Cares Network: Security, Privacy, and Confidentiality in a Shared Human Service Information System

James P. Glasson, Lynn M. Mulkey, and Randolph Hawkins
University of South Carolina, Beaufort

Dennis Betz
Client Referral Network

William Dougan
University of Wisconsin, Whitewater

This case study accounts for the development of a human services database that provides Web-based, shared information and enables application and referral for services in Beaufort County, South Carolina. It covers the period from March 2002 to April 2005. The case reveals how a consortium of a local government, nonprofit agencies, and community-based and faith-based organizations grappled with the issues of privacy, confidentiality, and security while sharing client information in what is now called the Mother Robinson Black Beaufort Cares Network (hereafter referred to as the Mother Black Network, or MBN).

In this case, virtual network governance helps solve problems associated with historically rooted limitations in the delivery of human services. These problems derive from demographic growth and the complexities of a thriving capitalistic economy, which have produced income inequalities and accompanying populations of need. The provision of managed care for clients who suffer from deficits in resources such as income, housing, education, physical and mental health, protection from crime and abuse, has changed from a system of essentially independent providers into an integrated delivery system. Moreover, integrated systems are enhanced by virtual technologies but are challenged and plagued by issues surrounding ethical and legal matters of security, privacy, and confidentiality. MBN is offered as an example from which readers are invited to apply the lessons learned to information systems in other sectors and to subject those lessons to further theoretical scrutiny.

We begin with a brief outline of the social and economic context, followed by history of the effort to develop the network. We then discuss some solutions that were crafted to solve the demanding problems of security, privacy, and confidentiality associated with creating the network.

A Brief Portrait of Beaufort County

Beaufort County, South Carolina (population 130,000), is located in the scenic, coastal low country in the state's southeast corner and is composed of more than 100 sea islands. This picturesque setting contrasts starkly with some of the prevailing social conditions for a number of citizens. As with many Southern, sea-island locales, Beaufort County is a study in differences and disparities. On the one hand, Beaufort is South Carolina's fastest growing county and has its highest median income. Its marshes, tidal creeks, warm climate, and beaches have made the county (specifically Hilton Head Island) a popular tourist and retirement destination. These tourists have generated investments in world-class resorts containing exclusive accommodations, restaurants, and golf and tennis facilities. On the other hand, Beaufort County has been characterized by one local health official as, "A community consisting of pockets of wealth surrounded by poverty." Recent data support this view. For example:

- 23% of children in the county live in poverty.
- Another 13% of children live within $5,000 of poverty.
- 46% of students in Beaufort County schools qualify for free or subsidized meal programs.
- 18% of families have a yearly combined income of $25,000 or less.
- The median price of a house is $124,000.
- An income of at least $35,000 is required for an $80,000 mortgage.
- Approximately 3469 households received food stamps (December 2004).
- More than 3 million pounds of food were distributed by the Lowcounty Food Bank and Second Helping (2004).
- 46% of the adults in the county function at the lowest two levels of literacy and are thus functionally illiterate.

The combination of high property values and the influx of what locals call *come yas* (the "come heres" or newcomers) has created an economy where the *from yas* (the "from heres" or lifelong residents) experience significant levels of underemployment in service occupations that typically offer minimum wage compensation. These conditions place significant economic pressures on lower-, working-, and middle-class families. These economic conditions generate social conditions that involve a significant need for social services in the county.

Attempts by human service agencies to respond to local needs have unearthed a number of problems in service delivery. While many of these agencies collect information from clients, this information has seldom been shared between service providers. Thus, providers have been unable to track outcomes systemwide. When referrals are made, the referring agency seldom knows if the referral is actually executed. Clients must repeatedly complete applications soliciting exactly the same information when they are applying for services.

continues

A Brief History of the MBN

The story of the development of the community response to the problems of coordination began on March 23, 2002. A local community-based organization, the Sheldon Township Community Support Partnership, was conducting focus groups in its community, which is the poorest census tract in Beaufort and one of the poorest in South Carolina. The agenda of the focus group was to solicit the views of mothers and grandmothers from Sheldon Township regarding what the community could do for young children. Attending this meeting was Edgelee Robinson Black, a Sheldon resident, a mother and grandmother, an active member of the Canaan Missionary Baptist Church, and a recognized community leader. In her roles as a leader in her church and community, Ms. Robinson Black, had earned the honorific title of "Mother," which is bestowed by the local Gullah population when a woman nurtures not only her children or grandchildren, but also all the children with whom she has contact. Ms. Robinson Black was fondly and reverently known in her community as Mother Black.

During the discussion, Ms. Robinson Black indicated that what she wanted for the children of her community was that "they all should be accounted for." Mother Black's statement precipitated a groundswell of community effort to provide the support and services that Mother Black had verbalized.

Five days later, another meeting took place. This meeting brought together high-level county professionals from organizations serving young children, including the superintendent of schools, the director of the local Department of Social Services, the director of the local Health Department, the president of the county United Way (representing the Success by 6 Program), and the executive directors of the local Head Start, First Steps, and Healthy Families America organizations. They met with an agenda to improve the way they worked together to increase school readiness and improve the well-being of children in Beaufort County.

The outcome of this and subsequent meetings was the creation of the Beaufort County Early Childhood Coalition (ECC) and the development of a vision, mission, and strategic plan to address the needs of young children and their families. As a part of this process, the coalition developed these priorities:

- Reducing childhood poverty
- Expanding family support services
- Improving child care quality, affordability, and accessibility
- Improving emergent literacy resources and services
- Improving child health, safety, and nutrition
- Expanding child advocacy, volunteerism, and community support for young children
- Identifying who and where our children are, what services they receive, and the effectiveness of these services. (Mother Black's vision and wisdom are strongly encapsulated in this final priority.)

The strategic, visioning, and planning process was facilitated by the same human services professional who had facilitated the focus group in the Sheldon Township meeting at which Mother Black had shared her original vision. When the plans were introduced to the group, a buzz of excitement occurred. The most creative and exciting priorities expressed Mother Black's precipitating statement.

In June 2002, the newly formed ECC submitted a grant proposal to the U.S. Department of Health and Human Services Child Care Bureau under the Early Learning Opportunities Act. Included in this grant proposal was a provision for funding to create an electronic, Web-based database that would allow the ECC to create an online information and referral system. This system would also track services delivery and enable a single, uniform application common to all services. The grant was selected for funding in September 2002. The ECC received $850,000 for emergent literacy services, and approximately $300,000 was allocated to begin the Mother Black Network. In 2004, ECC received a grant of $124,000 from the federal department of Housing and Urban Development (HUD) to include the tracking of homeless services and expand the system to Jasper, Hampton, and Colleton counties. Thus, these grants gave the ECC sufficient resources to make Mother Black's vision into a reality.

After an extensive search for a qualified and experienced vendor, the ECC entered into a contract with Community Development Specialists, Inc. (CDS), a software developer that had created a program called the Client Referral Network and had employed it effectively in counties in eastern North Carolina and Arkansas. CDS also had the experience of working with a variety of agencies and organizations to develop protocols, procedures, and policies to address three major concerns regarding electronic information sharing: security, confidentiality, and privacy.

Challenges for the MBN Relating to Security, Privacy, and Confidentiality

Privacy concerns the withdrawal of information from public view and the protection of the rights of clients regarding data sharing. High levels of staff turnover in human service agencies can lead to inadequate training and inconsistent enforcement of privacy protection policies.

Confidentiality concerns a client's right to privacy of any personal information communicated in confidence to a case manager (or other agency staff) that is stored on an information system. Confidentiality breaches can happen regularly in human service agencies (via conversation, faxes, phone, paper records, e-mail) but they are not desirable.

Security refers to the protection of stored client and program information from unauthorized access, use, or modification. Most security breaches are carried out by authorized users of client record systems.

In South Carolina, participating agencies such as the Department of Health and Environmental Control and the Department of Social Services maintain local offices that may participate in network governance, but authority typically lies with a state-level agency. Each group had to be engaged and to approve privacy and confidentiality models and a scope of participation. The proposed MBN members had no formal agreement for data sharing.

The MBN included agencies that supported child-abuse victims and victims of sexual assault. The extremely sensitive data associated with these services demanded even more restrictive information policies. There was a need for these agencies to follow up on referrals made to other agencies and to receive referrals but for all of the actions to maintain client anonymity among those agencies with no need to be aware of the identity of a client as a victim of those types of experiences.

A number of other questions were posed during discussions with CDS: How would client-level data be protected in an electronic case-management system? Because the system was Web-based, how could client data be secured on a central server? How could a system be designed so domestic-violence care providers would participate? What were state and federal (HIPAA, 42 CFR Part 2) laws pertaining to information about substance abuse, HIV/AIDS, domestic violence, etc.?

Another set of policy issues concerned the human commitment and action to the process. These questions involved three types of issues:

continues

- Participation—How would the universe be defined? In other words, what geographic area(s) would be covered? What types of programs would be included (target population)? Would participation be voluntary or mandatory and what incentives or resources would be available?
- Survey of Programs and Services—What was the technical capacity to implement the system? What were the available hardware and networking resources currently used in the community? What was the computer familiarity of staff?
- Design Options—Community needs and technical capacity inform software design options. One option is to upgrade an existing system (and integrate if there is more than one). The other is to develop or purchase a new system (including vendor-developed products).

Procedures were also necessary to define network operations and maintenance. The following is a list of such issues:

- Creating and maintaining user access to the system
- Maintaining client confidentiality
- Authorization and release of information
- Determining appropriate access to client records
- Creating and executing referral protocols
- Resolving issues involving two or more agencies
- Processes for entering and exiting the MBN
- Determination of the ownership and control of records
- System downtime procedures
- Provision for easy case management
- Physical security of servers

CDS was required to work closely with a local staff member assigned to the project by the Early Childhood Coalition. CDS used three main approaches in addressing these challenges:

1. Building a shared vision among users of the system
2. Developing shared policies and procedures to govern the use of the system
3. Developing technological solutions to achieve the goals of the system subject to the identified constraints.

Vision, Policy, and Technical Solutions

The vision-building and development of shared policies and procedures occurred by bringing the various stakeholders together. These first two strategies were by far the most labor intensive and time-consuming since they required meetings and the building of consensus among service providers who were very skeptical at first. The fact that we could tell Mother Black's story and her concern for our children gave us a powerful vision that service providers quickly shared. This allowed us to move on to the challenges of developing shared policies. Mother Black allowed us to put a very human face on technology that is often intimidating to those working in the human-services arena.

A governance model was present for the MBN from the beginning of CDC's association with the project. The proposed network members had no formal agreement in place for data sharing. Again, the development of agreements took on a twofold negotiation—one by the agency state-level authority and a concurrent effort by local stakeholders.

State templates were used where appropriate and adapted to be relevant to other network agencies. The documents defined the roles and responsibilities of each agency and the users within each agency. To further define relationships and responsibilities, MBN policies and procedures were developed in joint design sessions. The procedures address how network users are maintained, client confidentiality and release of information, appropriate access to client records, referral protocols, resolving issues, entering and exiting the MBN, record ownership, system downtime procedures, and other operating procedures.

After we negotiated the policies and procedures, we formalized them into a Memorandum of Understanding that included the agreed-upon policies and procedures. The inclusion of constituent agencies built confidence in the database.

Then the agreement was put into action. Numerous features have been incorporated into the current software to support rigid security standards for Web-based applications. Users are given unique identification and authentication with login names and passwords. The security model in the application controls the view of data by roles and ensures that only need-to-know information is available for each identified role (intake, complete application, referral, case management, etc.). Other environmental and procedural security features include these provisions:

- Servers are housed in a secure environment at the Beaufort County Government Management Information Systems Department.
- Servers are placed behind an industry-approved firewall.
- Data transmission to and from the application is encrypted.
- Data backups are performed daily.
- Data entered by the user are validated by the application prior to transmission to the data base(s).

While security is a primary function of software and hardware safeguards, confidentiality and privacy are largely a function of the business process and internal controls. Two inputs were used to define privacy and confidentiality issues: network governance and network authority. In addition to the authentication module control, a control within the software is set so that all sessions time out after a predetermined number of minutes and the computer reverts to the login screen. This control prevents unauthorized users from entering into an authorized user's session. As a condition of participation, each agency must have internal policies defining other environmental procedural controls which are in place to prevent third parties from viewing client data screens or printed data. As a result of this project, the *exclude client* logic was improved. The former logic allowed for a worker to exclude a client's record from the view of one, some, or all other agencies when information regarding a client was generally released to other agencies in the network. The state authority requested that this logic be reversed—that all agencies initially are excluded and a recorded action is taken to un-exclude the record from view. A daily management report of un-excluding actions is available. A more restrictive Private Agency view logic was developed, and a business model that limited sensitive information sharing was implemented to prevent inadvertent release of information regarding populations of clients who require anonymity.

In sum, the technological protections of the system include using encryption technology and firewalls to protect the data and the server for the network, which is housed by the county government's Management of Information Services Department.

continues

Technical solutions also include authentication, public key infrastructure, and penetration testing.

Today, more than 25 agencies have been trained and are using the system. The system is also being considered for use by three neighboring counties. Unfortunately, Mother Black was unable to see the system become operational since she passed away in December 2003. However, the legacy of her vision and wisdom continues, and we now call our human services database the Mother Robinson Black Beaufort Cares Network.

Security Policy

Security is necessary to preserve the integrity of government data systems from computer fraud and electronic crimes, political and industrial espionage, sabotage, user error, and natural disaster. When those data systems concern a domain like voting, security is fundamental to democracy itself. Consider security issues surrounding the U.S. Department of Defense's (DOD's) Secure Electronic Registration and Voting Experiment (SERVE), constructed to allow servicemen to vote in the nation's elections. SERVE and similar direct-recording electronic voting systems have been criticized for security vulnerabilities, inadequate software certification, using proprietary software that is difficult to prove secure, lacking a paper audit trail, being open to attacks by insider programmers, and being particularly vulnerable when Internet-based. Internet-based software may be the target of denial-of-service attacks, viral attacks, automated vote buying and trading, spoofing, and insider attacks. Such attacks could be mounted by a well-funded foreign organization or by a disaffected single hacker. The results could be disastrous, including mass voter disenfranchisement or, in some ways worse, selective voter disenfranchisement, not to mention invasion of privacy, selling of voter information, and lowering of public confidence in the democratic process.

One may contrast the SERVE system with new, more secure, electronic voting systems that require voting at polling locations, accept votes by touchscreen, then issue an encrypted double receipt with a serial number. One paper receipt is retained by election officials for purposes of audits and recounts, while the other allows the voter to access an online database that verifies the citizen's vote has been counted for the proper candidates. While no successful attack occurred in the 2004 elections, the danger is that this itself will encourage officials to proceed with an inadequately secure system that at some future point could even reverse the result of an American national election. The 2004 success, some observe, could be "the top of a slippery slope toward even more vulnerable systems in the future" (Jefferson, Rubin, Simons, & Wagner, 2004).

Public managers should be concerned with security not only because it is important but also as a matter of law and policy, at least at the federal level. For instance, the Office of Personnel Management (OPM) requires agencies to identify employees with significant security responsibilities and to provide role-specific training to them, and to provide at least annual security awareness training to all employees (Miller, 2003k). OPM guidelines also call for security training for all program managers. The Government Accountability Office (GAO) regularly assesses the security of agency information systems, as it did for the Internal Revenue Service (IRS) in 2005, finding severe security problems (GAO, 2005). Federal legislation and Office of Management and Budget (OMB) directives require all federal agencies to assess risks, set security priorities for their agency, and develop comprehensive security plans.

LEGISLATION AND EXECUTIVE BRANCH ACTIONS

Initially, Congress perceived information technology (IT) in terms of the first generation of computers, which were developed for wartime purposes of sending encoded messages. Early legislation concerning the security aspects of IT included the International Traffic in Arms Regulation Act of 1943, which defined cryptographic software as "munitions" and thus subject to export controls. Along the same lines, the National Security Act of 1947 legislated that the federal government has formal secrecy rights in cryptographic technology. The National Security Agency (NSA), established in 1952, was given the mission of protecting U.S. cryptography and of cracking cryptography of other nations.

Later, in the 1980s, when mainframe computing was finally well established within the federal government, efforts were made to ensure that software was secure. The "Orange Book" (Department of Defense Trusted Computer System Evaluation Criteria) was the nickname for a work containing "Trusted Computer System Evaluation Criteria" (Department of Defense, 1985). It was used in the 1980s to encourage private systems firms to create more secure software. The systems produced were slower and less functional than nonsecure off-the-shelf software and for this reason were not bought, even by government agencies, in spite of the federal government being the impetus behind them (Computer Science and Telecommunications Board, 2002).

A different, less voluntary approach was embedded in the Computer Security Act of 1987 (CSA), which gave the National Institute of Standards and Technology (NIST) the mission of developing security standards and guidelines for federal computer systems. All federal agencies and their contractors were required by the CSA to establish computer system security plans. In addition, the CSA mandated that security features of information systems applications had to be certified and that agencies had to conduct security awareness training. Some provision was also made in the CSA for partnering with the private sector on security issues.[1]

The Government Information Security Reform Act of 2000 (GISRA) did not replace but complemented the CSA.[2] Sometimes simply called the *Security Act,* GISRA required federal agencies to establish agency-wide information security programs. These programs were required to include annual agency program reviews on security matters and annual independent evaluations of agency security practices by the Inspector General. OMB was given oversight of GISRA, with agencies reporting to the OMB and OMB reporting to Congress. GISRA covered programs for both unclassified and classified systems but exempted agencies operating national security systems (such as the Central Intelligence Agency [CIA] and the NSA) from OMB oversight. Other actions in 2000 included security directives to agencies from the President's Chief of Staff (February), formal OMB guidance to agencies on incorporating and funding IT security (February), and a presidential memo to agency heads on their renewing efforts to guard their websites against Internet denial-of-service attacks (March).

The terrorist attacks of September 11, 2001, led to computer security receiving high budgetary priority and major new political attention. In 2002, the Transportation Security Administration's passenger profiling system, Computer-Assisted Passenger Pre-Screening (CAPPS), was upgraded to version II, since CAPPS-I had clearly failed in 9/11, as discussed in the previous chapter. To create a central focus in the Executive Branch for the security of cyberspace, President Bush issued Executive Order 13231, titled "Critical Infrastructure Protection in the Information Age." This executive order created the President's Critical Infrastructure Protection Board (CIPB) in October 2001, composed of senior officials from more than 20 departments and agencies. In February 2003, President Bush dissolved the CIPB, placing its functions in the new Homeland Security Council, which was charged with coordinating cybersecurity policy. Early strategy emphasized public- and private-sector best practices and downplayed enforcement of security policies vis-a-vis the private sector.

The Homeland Security Act of 2002 (HSA), among other things, established a chief information officer (CIO) in the new Department of Homeland Security (DHS). The CIO was charged with overseeing the largest consolidation of federal databases in U.S. history, and to do so under the banner of security. HSA's Title 2, Section 201, created the Office of Undersecretary for Information Analysis and Infrastructure Protection, to receive and integrate security information, to design and protect the security of data, and to issue security advisories to the public. HSA's Title 2, Section 202, also consolidated under the DHS several formerly separate agencies concerned with national infrastructure security.

Federal coordination with lower levels of government was a major issue in the 9/11 attacks and one addressed in the aftermath. The Federal Bureau of Investigation's (FBI's) National Infrastructure Protection Center (NIPC) formerly sent security alerts to heads of state police, who often did not pass the alerts on to state CIOs. Under a 2002 agreement of the NIPC with the National Association of State Chief Information Officers (NASCIO), state CIOs started getting security alerts directly. The change required top NASCIO officials to receive security clearances to handle classified data. NASCIO also initiated an Interstate Information Sharing and Analysis Center information sharing program with the NIPC, which had become part of the DHS's Information Analysis and Infrastructure Protection Directorate, a unit that channels cyber and physical threat information to the state CIOs.

The Federal Information Security Management Act of 2002 (FISMA) superceded the CSA and incorporated and made permanent most elements of GISRA, which had had a two-year sunset provision.[3] FISMA strengthened information security programs, including training, evaluation, and reporting requirements. FISMA again gave the OMB oversight regarding federal security practices and again mandated the NIST to establish benchmark security standards. The NIST standards-setting function had been opposed in 2002 by interest groups such as the Business Software Alliance, which had argued that formal benchmarks limited the development of software in a fast-changing technological environment (Emery, 2002). Though FISMA set a December 17, 2003, deadline for agencies to secure their information systems, progress was slow, with most agencies far behind meeting this deadline. Some complained that FISMA reporting requirements interfered with spending time and resources on actual security projects. "Challenged with finite resources, they must trade off between implementing real security projects and wrestling the paper tiger of FISMA reporting," one reporter noted (Tracy, 2003). By spring 2004, agencies had spent some $300 million on new security IT to meet FISMA requirements, but experts charged the money had not, in fact, yielded secure systems (Olsen, 2004). In 2005, officials charged with overseeing federal cybersecurity stated that much of the progress reported on federal IT security in 2004 could be illusory, due to questionable FISMA reporting (Jackson, 2005a). At this writing, most agencies claimed they would be FISMA-compliant by the end of 2005.

Also in 2002, the Cyber Security Research and Development Act of 2002 authorized $800 million in funding for new computer and network security research and grant programs and $300 million for cybersecurity training. The act also protected commercial Internet service providers from consumer lawsuits when Internet Service Providers (ISPs) revealed customer information to law enforcement authorities.

On the consumer front, Congress passed the Fair and Accurate Credit Transactions Act of 2003 (FACTA). This law amended the Fair Credit Reporting Act, to "prevent identity theft, improve resolution of consumer disputes, improve the accuracy of consumer records, make improvements in the use of, and consumer access to, credit information, and for other purposes."[4] FACTA, some provisions of which did not take effect until December 1, 2004, required credit reporting firms to provide consumers with a free copy of their credit reports, allowing consumers to discover errors and identify fraudulent uses of their accounts. A National Fraud Alert System was established to alert businesses to accounts suspected of being involved with identity theft. Also, the law required that card receipts be truncated so as not to disclose consumer names and full credit card numbers.

In February 2003 it was revealed that the Bush administration intended the new Terrorism Threat Integration Center (TTIC), charged with maintaining and providing access to a database of known and suspected terrorists, to be located at the CIA, not the DHS. Critics wondered if the TTIC would be redundant with the existing CIA Counterterrorism Center and the FBI Counterterrorism Division, with which it had a cooperation agreement. Gordon England, deputy DHS secretary, acknowledged that the DHS would primarily rely on the CIA and FBI for intelligence. Some members of Congress expressed the view that this violated the will of Congress in setting up the DHS and its Intelligence Analysis and Infrastructure Protectorate Division as an independent entity (Dizard, 2003b).

In terms of public outreach, the DHS in March 2003 unveiled its new Web portal, Ready.gov. Most of the content was drawn from the Federal Emergency Management Agency (FEMA), the Red Cross, and the military. The focus was on highly general information about how citizens might put together an emergency kit and what to do in the event of various types of emergencies. For business, the emphasis was on encouraging businesses to develop security and emergency continuity plans, to involve employees, and to provide for cyber as well as physical security. Although initial plans called for integration with state and local website resources, as of late 2004, this had not occurred.

On December 17, 2003, President Bush issued the Homeland Security Presidential Directive HSPD-7, "Critical Infrastructure Identification, Prioritization, and Protection." By HSPD-7 agencies were directed to prepare plans for identifying and protecting cyber and physical infrastructure. The directive also included guidance on how agencies were to submit critical infrastructure protection (CIP) plans, which in turn would prioritize agency protection objectives as well as develop plans of action where current capabilities are lacking. CIPs were to be reviewed by an interagency review panel coordinated by DHS, which was to use this input to develop the National Infrastructure Protection Plan.

Earlier, in September 2003, the DHS had named a new "cybersecurity czar," Amit Yoran, formerly vice president of worldwide managed security services at Symantec Corporation. DHS simultaneously announced it would work with Carnegie Mellon University's CERT Coordination Center to create U.S. CERT, a system to coordinate responses to cyberterrorism attacks and to undertake preventative measures. U.S. CERT was to consolidate four separate older cyberterror watch efforts (FedCIRC, the National Communications System, the former NIPC, and the DHS Watch Center) (Dizard & Emery, 2003). As of early 2005, however, DHS IT projects were in flux, as most of the first generation of IT leadership resigned, as discussed below.

HOMELAND SECURITY

In 2003, in violation of its stated privacy policies, JetBlue Airways secretly gave the names, addresses, and telephone numbers of over a million of its passengers to the government for homeland security reasons. Subsequently the Electronic Privacy Information Center filed a complaint with the Federal Trade Commission, charging that the private data aggregating firm Acxiom and defense contractor Torch Concepts, which had matched JetBlue passenger data with Social Security and other information, had also violated their respective Web-posted privacy statements. Privacy activist Edward Hasbrouck noted, however, that giving out customer data to officials and even other airlines was common in the industry. Hasbrouck said, "The abuse of privacy by JetBlue was not unusual. What was unusual is JetBlue actually having a privacy policy" (Reuters, 2003). Intrinsic to many homeland security functions is the electronic surveillance of American citizens, sometimes, as in this instance, in violation of acknowledged privacy rights.

The Total Information Awareness Project

In 2002 it was reported that the Pentagon's Defense Advanced Research Projects Agency (DARPA) was developing a "Total Information Awareness System" (TIA) which would use IT to create a virtual database with instant access to information on an individual's phone call records, e-mail transcripts, Web search histories, financial records, store purchases, health prescriptions and medical records, educational records, travel history, and all transactions involving passports and driver's licenses. Part of the TIA project incorporated technology for extracting information about people from e-mail and other message traffic, raising the specter of "Big Brother" reading all your mail. The effort, later renamed the "Terrorism Information Awareness" project to make it more politically palatable, was initially budgeted for $10 million in FY 2003 and headed by Bush administration official John Poindexter. That Poindexter had been involved in the 1980s Iran-Contra scandal and had been found guilty of obstruction of justice and destruction of evidence did nothing to increase confidence in the Bush administration's commitment to protection of privacy under the TIA program.

Criticism of the TIA came not only from the expected civil liberties direction (ACLU, 2002), but also from the conservative think tank, the CATO Institute (Onley, 2002a). CATO Director of Technology Studies Wayne Crews argued that the TIA was "bad on three fronts: civil liberties, compromising the future of electronic commerce, and it's bad for security." That is, the TIA was seen as bad for business because consumers would be wary of making electronic purchases, knowing this information was given to the government for secret domestic surveillance purposes. The CATO Institute also put forward the secondary argument that by consolidating information in a single system, the TIA database would become a prime target for hackers and thus the TIA would actually weaken security.

By January 2003 the combination of civil liberties and business criticism of the TIA project led Congress to begin defunding the effort. A rider to the Senate bill providing funding for the TIA made funding dependent on a report on the project's civil liberties aspects, to come later in 2003. In the meantime, the TIA continued anyway with funds under the discretion of President Bush. The July 2003 TIA report from the Pentagon emphasized that the Palo Alto Research Center, Inc., had been awarded a $3.5 million contract to develop *privacy appliance* software as a filtering gateway to TIA databases, blocking unauthorized access and preventing the release of individually identifiable data. Civil libertarians were not satisfied. Even if DOD or other analysts were required to have a court order for each access to individually identifiable data (mentioned as a possibility but not promised and not deemed practical), noted David Sobel, general counsel for Washington's Electronic Privacy Information Center, even with the "privacy appliance" the system would be "completely alien to our judicial system" because it would involve court-ordered surveillance for a crime that had not actually been committed

(Jackson, 2003a, p. 32). Unmoved by the DOD report, Congress voted to defund the TIA project in September 2003.

As one TIA critic, Erick Schonfeld, noted, defunding the TIA did not stop similar efforts in the private sector, nor governmental access to and utilization of them. He wrote, "Commercial data aggregators such as Accurint, Acxiom, and Choicepoint bring together hundreds of publicly and privately available databases filled with information on people's addresses, phone numbers, driver's licenses, bankruptcy histories, accident histories, and property. These databases are used by police departments and debt collectors to find deadbeats and crime suspects, as well as their assets. And while the technologies they use are primitive versions of what Poindexter wants to create, they are pretty far-reaching nevertheless. For instance, a search in one of those databases for 'John M. Poindexter' comes up with the address of his house in Rockville, Md.; how much he paid for it on March 30, 1971 ($42,000); its assessed value today ($269,050); his known associates (mostly family members), along with their current addresses and phone numbers; and the hull number of his 42-foot boat, the Bluebird. I could go on. But even Poindexter deserves some privacy" (Schonfeld, 2003).

Commenting on the TIA defunding vote, DARPA chief Anthony Tether blamed the decision to appoint the controversial figure of John Poindexter to head the project and also blamed the secretive "need to know" processes surrounding the TIA, arousing public and Congressional suspicion. Tether noted, however, that Congress's Joint Inquiry into 9/11 had called for data mining of the TIA type and that this mandate to the DOD and other federal agencies was still there (Levy, 2003). Although the TIA was dropped from the DOD's appropriations bill, the *Government Computer News* reported that the defunding bill "still states that a similar system could be used to collect data on non-U.S. citizens or residents for counterterrorism and intelligence purposes. That seems to leave wiggle room for grabbing data from any source if it seems important enough" (McCarthy, 2004). In this context, it may be noted that the TIA project involved eight modules created by 23 companies that received awards to build elements of the system (Jackson, 2003b):

1. Genysis database integration
2. Genysis privacy protection system
3. Evidence extraction and link discovery, to relate people to activities
4. Scalable social network analysis, to distinguish terrorist cells from legitimate groups
5. Misinformation detection, to detect lies
6. Human identification at a distance, using biometrics

7. Activity recognition and monitoring, to automate detection of activities observed during surveillance
8. Next-generation face recognition, to improve facial recognition technology

Although the TIA was defunded as an integrated program, components continued in development. Overlapping efforts under the Transportation Security Agency also continued being funded as has been MATRIX (Multistate Anti-Terrorism Information Exchange), a 2003 state-level program to use public and private sector databases to search for profile patterns that conceivably might indicate terrorist or criminal activity. In 2004 it was revealed that MATRIX was under the managerial control of the DHS (ACLU, 2004). Under pressure from privacy advocates, several states withdrew from MATRIX, leaving only five of the original 13 participating states as of March 2004. In 2005, MATRIX was canceled. However, as mentioned above, private data-integration efforts accessed by government agencies have expanded unabated.

Department of Homeland Security IT

A major Bush administration response to the terrorist attack of 9/11 was endorsement of the creation of the DHS. The 9/11 Commission had criticized the government for relying on a hodgepodge of homeland security networks, which hindered information sharing. Predictably, the political desire to integrate information so there would be coordinated and timely warning translated into the management reality of trying to integrate the many IT systems of DHS's 22 constituent units. A 2004 GAO study of DHS IT policy criticized enterprise-wide management of IT in the department. The GAO audit noted the "daunting challenge" of the cross-agency data integration goal, urging DHS to "strike a balance" between unified systems and having a family of more differentiated systems that would "optimally support department-wide operations and mission performance" (Roberts, 2004).

DHS's first "cybersecurity czar," Amit Yoran, resigned suddenly in October 2004, complaining how low Bush administration support for cybersecurity prevented him from being effective in his position. As of January 2005, most of the top IT leadership of DHS had resigned, some for private firms contracting with DHS, raising questions about the effectiveness of DHS's first generation of IT leadership (Dizard, 2005a).

Even if DHS were to force its formerly independent units to accept one-size-fits-all information systems, there would still not be complete data integration. A 2004 GAO inventory of major government networks supporting homeland security functions identified 34 major systems costing about $1 billion annually, run by nine agencies: DHS, but also Agriculture, Defense, Energy, Health and Human Services, Justice, State, Treasury, and the Environmental Protection Agency (Dizard, 2004c).

The response to the 9/11 terrorist attack on the World Trade Center revealed that data issues (quality, access, use, sharing, security) far outweighed technology problems and were harder to solve. Indeed, the naive belief of some that technology "band-aids" could overcome underlying organizational and data quality problems was itself an obstacle to effective information sharing and integration. Other lessons included the need for more redundancy of systems, more planning for business recovery, the need to have well-designed security and privacy systems in place beforehand, the need for interoperability of systems used by responders, and in general the need for more planning, including practice (Dawes, Cresswell, & Cahan, 2004).

While DHS concentrated on unification of databases and other priorities, IT infrastructure protection itself was of low priority (as discussed further in the following section). James Lewis of the Center for Strategic and International Studies called the Bush National Strategy to Secure Cyberspace about "as useful as a paperweight" (Menke, 2003). Business representatives opposed both national efforts like the proposal to create a secure government-only network and also opposed new state laws like California's Database Security Breach Information Act. Lobbyists opposed government initiatives to protect the nation's IT infrastructure as "regulation creep," insisted that industry get liability protection for companies that comply with any new security regulations, and argued that DHS should best function simply to help coordinate research and planning for cybersecurity and to encourage operating systems developers and ISPs to do a better security job. The view that IT homeland security was best achieved through private-sector self-regulation and voluntary public–private cooperative efforts became the prevailing Bush administration policy.

INFRASTRUCTURE PROTECTION AND CYBERCRIME

There is growing concern about the use of electronic communications for criminal activities and the appropriateness of the countermeasures that are being adopted by law enforcement agencies (Thomas & Loader, 2000). At the same time, the public has reason to be concerned with the growth of cyberattacks and cybercrime, all the more so since they are international in nature (see Sofaer & Cuellar, 2001). Since the first Internet worm in 1988, America's data infrastructure has been experiencing more attacks that are more automated and more directed at financial e-crime. The primary organization tracking the number of security incidents reported by public or private sector organizations has been the CERT Coordination Center of the Software Engineering Institute at Carnegie Mellon University. CERT has kept track of security incidents since 1988 (see Table 7-1).

In Table 7-1, the escalating number of reported security incidents partly reflects the rise of automated attack tools. In spite of sharply increased computer security after 9/11, computer attacks continued to escalate. Moreover, Table 7-1 figures greatly understate attacks, since the GAO estimates that 80% of incidents are not reported because the organization was unable to recognize it had been attacked or was reluctant to report vulnerability (GAO, 2003b).

Because an "incident" might involve a single site at a single time point or might involve thousands of sites over a period of time, in 2004 CERT replaced its incident reporting system with the "E-CrimeWatch Survey," undertaken in cooperation with the U.S. Secret Service and *CSO* magazine.[5] The 2004 survey revealed that 43% of respondents reported an increase in e-crimes and intrusions compared to 2003, and 70% reported at least one e-crime or intrusion against their organization. The average number of individual e-crimes and intrusions per organization

Table 7-1   Number of Security Incidents, 1988–2003

Year	Number of Incidents
1988	6
1989	132
1990	252
1991	406
1992	773
1993	1334
1994	2340
1995	2412
1996	2573
1997	2134
1998	3734
1999	9859
2000	21,756
2001	52,658
2002	82,094
2003	137,529

Source: http://www.cert.org/stats/cert_stats.html. Special permission to reproduce "CERT/CC Statistics 1988–2005," © 2005 by Carnegie Mellon University, is granted by the Software Engineering Institute.

was 136. Of the 70% of organizations able to answer, attacks came from the outside rather than from insiders in 71% of the cases (CERT, 2004).

Another 2004 security threat report from the Symantec Corporation, compiled on a different basis, found that the number of threats had leveled off but that there had been a dramatic shift in hacker activity as the number of remotely controlled networks of compromised computers increased from fewer than 2,000 to over 30,000. Hackers use *bot* networks as platforms for launching attacks on other computers or for sending spam. The Symantec report also found a shift toward a higher percentage of attacks being for financial gain (for example, identity theft) rather than hacking as an illicit sport (Jackson, 2004b).

Ultimately, the protection of electronic infrastructure against attack rests with cooperation between the public and private sectors. The National Infrastructure Protection Board (NIPB) was created by the FBI to investigate threats to and to protect the data infrastructure of the nation, public or private. O'Neil and Dempsey (2000) have argued that the NIPB had two roles, which were in conflict: (1) The role of getting voluntary business cooperation on data protection; and (2) the FBI enforcement role and possibly taking criminal action against business regarding possible uses of data obtained by terrorists. In February 2003 the Bush administration dissolved the NIPB as part of a merger with the White House's Critical Infrastructure Protection Board and the Commerce Department's Critical Infrastructure Assurance Office. The functions of these groups were placed under the DHS. With this reorganization, worries persisted about dual helping and punishing roles, but actual practice of the Bush administration lay very heavily in the direction of voluntary cooperation, making the issue moot.

A greater problem was that the above-mentioned reorganization left no one official responsible for national cyber-security strategy, as Richard Clarke had been in the 2001–2003 period before leaving for the private sector. The year 2004 saw three successive "cybersecurity czars" quit (Schmidt, Beers, Yoran), all amid strong speculation that the resignations were due to the relatively low priority given by the Bush administration to IT security (Leyden, 2004). Meanwhile, however, in 2005 the DHS was able to move ahead at the level of information gathering. DHS funded the new Cyber Incident Detection Data Analysis Center at the University of Pennsylvania's Institute of Strategic Threat Analysis and Response, to monitor in real time and report cyberattacks against computer networks related to critical infrastructure (Lipowicz, 2005).

In summary, fears of cyberterrorism have raised the public's level of concern about computer security and infrastructure protection. Recent popular books have sensationalized computer security issues, using phrases like *techno-terror, info warfare, electronic doomsday,* and *cyber meltdown* (Schwartau, 2002). The reality is that the Internet is hard to attack at the "meltdown" level. There are a dozen or more nodes in larger cities around the United States, which in principle could become targets of terrorism. However, the nodes are not necessarily in single locations. They are networked, and there are many paths through the network. Simulated Internet attacks indicate that the aftermath of an attack might leave the Internet still functioning in large cities, though outlying areas might be affected because of lack of redundancy in those areas (McKay, 2004b, p. 26). The Committee on Science and Technology in Countering Terrorism of the National Research Council (NRC) looked into this question in a 2002 report (NRC, 2002), finding an attack on most networking infrastructure targets would have only a local impact and confirming that the decentralized nature of the Internet makes it difficult to bring down. Also, key infrastructure like banking has its own separate, even more secure networks. Likewise, the power grid network is separate and secure. While some fears were expressed about Trojan horse attacks planted by foreign contract programmers, the committee considered physical attacks (as on a nuclear plant) a much more serious danger than cyber attacks. For its part, the first Bush administration has not given electronic infrastructure protection high policy priority.

ENCRYPTION

Encryption of data is important in many systems of authenticating the identity of individuals for purposes of online government transactions, discussed below. In this context perhaps the most common method of encryption in the public sector is PKI (public key infrastructure). PKI software may be based on the freeware program PGP, though there are other implementations of PKI. The general method is this:

1. The user applies to a *certificate authority*, which issues a digital certificate after verifying the user's credentials in some manner.
2. The certificate authority creates a *public key* for the user and stores it in a public registry.
3. The certificate authority also issues the user a matching private key, to be stored on the user's computer or on a *smart card* (discussed below).
4. The user can employ the private key to send encrypted messages. These can be decrypted using the public key. When the user sends an encrypted message, the user's private key authenticates who the user is.

5. The user can decrypt messages others send to the user by employing the user's public key, but senders cannot decrypt even their own messages.

PKI-based security is the usual strategy behind digital signatures.

Digital signatures are now legally binding under federal law. In the private sector, software reduces a purchase order to a *hash function*, which is a number unique to that document. Any alteration of the document would generate a different hash function. The purchaser, using his or her PKI private key to encrypt the hash function of his or her purchase order, sends the order along with the encrypted hash function and his or her public key to the vendor. The vendor generates a hash code for the purchase order and also uses the purchaser's public key to decrypt the hash code the purchaser sent. If the two hash codes match, then the vendor knows (1) the purchase order was not altered in transit, and (2) the same person sent the order as sent the public key. In actual practice, all this is usually embedded in software and hidden from the user.

VeriSign or other companies or agencies that are certificate authorities may issue digital certificates. These can be used to authenticate the sender's identity with respect to any document, such as e-mail. A digital certificate usually contains: (1) a PKI digital signature, (2) certificate authority information, (3) the user's public key, and (4) the user's name. The entire system assumes that the certificate authority is truly trustworthy, that it has followed sound procedures to verify the identity of those to whom it issues certificates, that private keys are secure from capture by third parties, and that nonencrypted data such as message headers and subject lines do not matter.

Public key encryption was proposed in 1997 by the President's Commission on Critical Infrastructure Protection. Under the proposal, the code-breaking key to read encrypted text would be held by a third party. Commercial encryption software would have to support this system. Then, when a government agency wanted to read an encrypted document, it would have to present justification to the third party, then would get the key and read the document. Civil libertarians felt this plan provided inadequate protection against unwarranted release of information. Businesses felt they might be at a disadvantage since foreign encryption software had true encryption and was seemingly more secure. In contrast, the Electronic Communications Privacy Act of 1986 required a judicial warrant for agencies to look at private e-mail. Warrants are required to show probable cause, which is a higher level of protection than envisioned by the public key encryption system.

The use of PKI in government was given a big boost in the spring of 2004 when the DOD set a deadline of April 1, 2004, for vendors to register for encryption certificates if they wanted to contract with the DOD, as did some 350,000 businesses at the time. The DOD approved three certificate vendors: VeriSign, Digital Signature Trust, and Operational Research Consultants (Onley, 2004a). As discussed below, the Department of Health and Human Services (DHHS) had already committed to PKI security in 2003, and the Government Printing Office (GPO) established a PKI-based system for authentication of documents in 2004. For the foreseeable future, PKI is apt to remain the basis for authentication of identities in public information systems.

AUTHENTICATION

Shortly after inauguration in January 2001, the incoming Bush administration made the promotion of e-government one of five main dimensions of its "Presidential Management Initiative." Some two dozen "Quicksilver" initiatives were launched, such as EZ Tax Filing online services from the IRS and Grants.gov on federal grant applications. In this context, authentication to government websites was widely seen as a cornerstone to their expansion. That is, if it were possible to verify the identity of individuals visiting government websites, then a far wider variety of government-to-citizen (and for that matter, government-to-business and government-to-government) transactions could be supported within an e-government framework.

In May 2003 the OMB started processing some transactions for the 24 Quicksilver e-government projects using an e-authentication gateway. Users connected to a project, and if it required authentication they were redirected to an authentication gateway where they had to present a credential. Initially credentials could include personal identification numbers (PINs), passwords, and PKI certificates. After authentication, users were returned to the e-government project site for the actual transaction. The authentication gateway itself stored no user information related to the projects (Jackson & Miller, 2003).[6] By September, the Social Security Administration, DHHS's E-Grants program, the General Services Administration's (GSA's) E-Travel project, and FEMA's Disaster Management Initiative had joined the authentication gateway system, toward which each agency was to pay $400,000 annually (Miller, 2003f).

Critics were quick to question the new authentication gateway system (Holden, 2003). There were fears agencies would be coerced into giving up the use of simple credentials like PINs in favor of more challenging methods such as PKI certificates. Some wondered if the OMB intended to overrule agency business decisions on the assurance levels needed to authenticate various classes of visitors to websites. Then there was the matter of financing the authentication gateway from agency budgets that had not necessarily been increased for that purpose. An October 2003 report by the GAO found limited e-authentication progress, with essential activities such as developing authentication profiles not completed by most Quicksilver e-government projects. The GAO report also pointed out that GSA had yet to define user requirements, achieve interoperability among available authentication products, or fully address funding, security, and privacy issues (Miller, 2003g).

The federal-wide authentication gateway had hardly been given policy guidance by the GSA when the plug was pulled in October 2003, when the OMB announced that the federal e-authentication gateway was to be scrapped, in spite of its having been seen as the cornerstone of e-government a year earlier and in spite of an investment of almost $2 million dollars (Miller, 2003i). Instead, the OMB decided to pursue an authentication system similar to verification systems in use in finance and business. This new "federated model" approach was based on reliance on third-party credential providers[7] to validate transactions between agencies and the public (Miller, 2003j).

An example of the federated model was announced in November 2003, as the DHHS awarded a $4.5 million contract with Digital Signature Trust Company of Salt Lake City to administer a public-key infrastructure that would issue 100,000 PKI certificates to employees, contractors, public health personnel, researchers, and some volunteers over the next 4 years (Jackson, 2003d). Users would be verified in person, then allowed to download their digitally signed certificate (containing their separate PKI keys for encryption).

When OMB guidance for e-authentication systems finally came out in May 2004, it centered on helping agencies identify appropriate assurance levels for each of their e-government initiatives. After deciding upon the assurance level needed, based on risk assessment, agencies were to choose an e-authentication provider from an OMB-approved list that matched the assurance level selected. Then the agency was to pick an authentication product from that vendor (Miller, 2004a). For instance, DHHS's Grants.gov Quicksilver project used as the provider Operational Research Consultants and the product for authentication was Security Assertion Markup Language 1.0 (SAML). Under this system, the vendor maintained a database of user PINs and password credentials, and SAML was used to verify the credentials, between Grants.gov and the vendor's database. Other federal agencies were expected to follow similar strategies for authentication, albeit with various vendors.

While *authentication* normally refers to the authentication of people to agencies, it can refer also to the authentication of documents or e-mail.

The GPO in 2004 launched the federal government's first major use of digital signatures for document authentication. Contracting through Entrust, Inc., the GPO system attached a digital signature to all documents submitted through its website, www.gpoaccess.gov. Using PKI technology, the document was then authenticated by matching the document digital certificate with the embedded hash signature in the document itself, using free, downloadable software that supports the S.509 protocol for digital signatures. The databases for the certificate directory, certificate authority, and the registration authority for the PKI system all resided on GPO servers (Miller, 2004b). A more generalized government-wide system for authenticating documents, the National Archives and Records Administration's Electronic Records Archive Project, is still underway as of this writing.

FEDERAL ID CARDS

While there is still opposition to having a national system of electronic identity cards for American citizens, the nation is very close to having an identity card system for all federal employees and contractors. Such a system is now expected to be in place by 2006. Identity cards, usually called *smart cards*, contain verified identifying information such as a PIN and biometric fingerprint data on a microchip. They also usually include anticounterfeit protection, such as holographs and microprinting. Smart cards can be used in conjunction with entrance readers and visitor identification validation systems to gain access to government facilities anywhere, as well as used for electronic access to government computers, websites, or digital resources. Smart cards are also used for digital signatures in conjunction with PKI encryption, discussed above.

There has been almost no opposition to increasing security through federal identity cards. The main obstacle has been ensuring that all smart cards meet government-wide interoperability standards. The Federal Identity Credentialing Committee (FICC) was charged in 2003 with developing standards for machine-readable IDs. Created in June 2003 by the Federal PKI Steering Committee and the Federal Smart Card Managers Committee, FICC standards represented an alternative to the earlier Federal Bridge Certification Authority, by being based on services of standards-compliant private vendors rather than being based on a government-run system. Also, by being vendor-based, the prospect is raised that standards-compliant ID systems will be implemented at the state level and perhaps even by other nations, such as Canada (Jackson, 2003c).

In September 2003, the GSA contracted with BearingPoint, Inc., to provide 14,000 smart cards to GSA employees by the beginning of 2004, with cards for GSA contractors to follow (Miller, 2003e). On a larger scale, in November 2003, the DOD announced that it would be distributing some 4 million Common Access cards in 2004 (Onley, 2003). By late 2004, some 3.5 million cards had actually been distributed (Menke, 2004b).

In August 2004, President Bush issued Homeland Security Presidential Directive HSPD-12, Policy for a Common Identification Standard for Federal Employees and Contractors. This directive declared it a federal policy to promote a federal identity system "by establishing a mandatory, Government-wide standard for secure and reliable forms of identification issued by the Federal Government to its employees and contractors (including contractor employees)." The Secretary of Commerce, through NIST, was ordered to promulgate appropriate standards by early 2005, in consultation with the Department of State, DOD, the Attorney General, DHS, the OMB, and the Director of the Office of Science and Technology Policy.

Draft NIST standards for federal smart card IDs were released in November 2004. The new standard (Federal Information Processing Standard [FIPS] 201, which became final in February 2005) requires federal smart cards to contain right and left index fingerprint information, embedded chips, PKI certificates, and a cryptographic algorithm. PINs, bar codes, and magnetic stripe features were to remain optional with agencies, which were to bring their smart cards into FIPS 201 compliance by June 2005, requiring upgrading more than 4 million ID cards, including 3.5 million DOD cards and 90,000 National Aeronautics and Space Administration cards. By fall 2005, agencies must, to "the maximum extent practicable," require the use of identification by federal employees and contractors that meets the FIPS 201 standard in gaining physical access to federally controlled facilities (to be listed and identified to the OMB) and logical access to federally controlled information systems. The OMB is to oversee agency compliance.[8] The Center for Democracy and Technology (CDT) has criticized the Bush federal employee ID plan for a rush to implementation before an adequate policy framework for privacy and data misuse had been debated and established (CDT, 2005).

At the state level, the driver's license remains the primary governmental ID. Richard Outland, the assistant chief of forensic services for the Secret Service, was recently quoted as saying that "Fake IDs are becoming as prevalent as fake currency was back in 1865, when the Secret Service was established to fight counterfeiting" (Menke, 2004c). At that time, about one-third of all currency was counterfeit. Today, the problem is counterfeit traveler's checks, credit cards, and "breeder documents" such as birth certificates, which let counterfeiters obtain genuine driver's licenses and other valuable credentials. To fight this, the Secret Service has joined with 19 federal agencies and 70 vendors to form the Document Security Alliance to police how driver's licenses are issued. Recommended security practices include not handing driver's licenses out over the counter but only mailing them to authenticated addresses, centralizing driver's license bureaus to reduce personnel exposed to bribery attempts, and in addition to a photograph, having a bar code and magnetic strip, heavy polycarbonate lamination, laser engraving, ultraviolet and infrared images, digital signatures and watermarks, holograms, kinegrams, and ghosted duplicate images to prevent photo swapping.

At this writing (May 2005), the Real ID Act of 2005 had been passed by the House and was pending in the Senate. Its Title II established minimum requirements for driver's licenses and state-issued ID cards. These requirements specify that name, address, identification number, and digital photo be put in a machine-readable format. However, there was no provision at this writing for encryption or other security, leaving open the possibility that this form of national identification card could be an invitation to identity theft. The security risk might be all the greater because data would be shared in database form among states, with no security requirements in the Real ID Act. Richard Hunter, research director of the Gartner Group, an IT consulting firm, termed the cards an "ID theft kit" (Jackson, 2005a).

AGENCY-LEVEL SECURITY POLICIES

Security threats to agencies include *keyloggers* that record the keystrokes of employees unbeknown to them, *Trojan horses* that insert secret programs in agency computers, network and wireless eavesdropping that listen in on agency messages, basic input/output system (BIOS) passwords that support cyberattacks, and simply breaking into a building or pilfering an agency-owned notebook computer (McNamara, 2003). Federal agencies are required to take computer security seriously. Starting in 2004, the OMB required agencies to report security incidents broken down by certified vs. noncertified systems, as a way to pressure agencies to get all of their IT systems certified. The OMB uses red-yellow-green ratings of each agency on a variety of IT dimensions, one of which is security. To get green, agencies must attain security certification for 90% of their IT systems. Then, in their FY 2005 budget requests, agencies were required to integrate security plans with all IT systems and agency business cases to incorporate security life-cycle planning.

Agency-level security problems are legendary. Employees put passwords on Post-it notes or use as passwords their birthdates or children's names. Some purposely defeat security programs, thinking, for instance, that antivirus software on their machine is slowing it down. Users open unsolicited e-mail attachments, which may introduce viruses. They lose laptops with agency data. The software they run on their networked PCs may not be updated to protect against hackers. Not long ago *Government Computer News* published a long list of federal agencies whose websites reveal which operating system they use and which server software version is in use. With this information "and a few Web addresses such as the CERT Coordination Center site, CERT.org, or a subscription to a bugtraq mail list, anyone with moderate computer skills can quickly learn which attacks are likeliest to succeed against a particular site" (McCormick, 2003, p. 10).

Agencies at all levels of government are moving toward more and more support for wireless computing. An attack scenario recently detailed exactly what publicly available hacking software can be used to intercept wireless data. Kismet software, for instance, can give a hacker media access control (MAC) addresses of wireless access points, the intended employee-victim's MAC address, the access point's current channel, and the wireless LAN's service set identifier—all the tools needed by a data hijacker. This publicly available article even details which wireless cards are easiest for attempting security breaches (Soto, 2003). In a survey of 100 public sector IT managers, 69% saw security concerns as the biggest hurdle in implementing wireless technology. Some 63% answered "no" to the question, "Are you comfortable with the level of security for wireless products?" Nonetheless, in 2003 some 20% had wireless technology already and another 21% planned to implement it in the next 24 months (Walker, 2003a).

In 2004 a hacker found a security hole in the unsecured computer of a researcher at the University of California, Berkeley, accessed the computer, and may have stolen 1.4 million names, addresses, phone numbers, Social Security numbers, birth dates, and other information that had been under the data stewardship of the California Department of Social Services. This followed on the heels of an incident in which the California Employment Development Department may have exposed 55,000 names due to inadequate security. In a third incident, a laptop of a UCLA researcher was stolen, exposing personal data from another 145,000 individuals. In an era of increasing identity theft, such breakdowns in security not only may violate individual privacy rights but may expose individuals to substantial loss. With 80% of the American public concerned about identity theft in some polls, public agencies are under more pressure than ever to get their security acts together (Lemos, 2004).

A notable public-sector example of what can go wrong due to poor security policies occurred in the U.S. Department of Interior (DOI). In December 2001, U.S. District Judge Royce C. Lamberth ordered all DOI systems disconnected from the Internet because security weaknesses could undermine the integrity of America Indian trust accounts. By fall 2002 most DOI systems had been reconnected, but not those of the Bureau of Indian Affairs (Dizard, 2002a). After over 2 years of additional DOI work on computer security failed to improve matters, the U.S. District Court for the District of Columbia, in the case of *Cobell v. Norton* (2004), ordered nine agencies disconnected from the Internet, finding that American Indian trust data still could be easily hacked over the Internet. The new disconnect order, which came after that a judge's employee was able to hack into computer systems at Interior, applied agency-wide, even to systems not holding Department of Indian Affairs data, including EdNet, an educational network serving Bureau of Indian Affairs schools. The 2004 court ruling followed DOI getting a grade of "F" on systems security from the House Government Reform Subcommittee on Technology, Information Policy, Intergovernmental Relations, and the Census (Dizard, 2004b). Nor was this highly unusual: seven other Cabinet agencies also received "F" grades from the subcommittee. Though a higher court subsequently overturned the DOI disconnect order later the same month (Sternstein, 2004), the fact remains that the underlying class action suit against DOI has dragged on for 8 years, has disrupted DOI services, and has reflected security practices that seem to have exasperated judges and alienated Indian clients.

Agency security planning must be multidimensional. The 2003 FBI Computer Crime and Security Survey of 490 organizations found viruses (82%) and insider abuse of net access (80%) to be the most-reported security problems, followed by lost or stolen laptops (59%), unauthorized insider network access (45%), denial-of-service attacks (42%), system penetration (36%), theft of proprietary information (21%), sabotage (21%), and financial fraud (15%) (*State Tech,* 2004). No single security strategy can address the many forms of security breach an agency may encounter.

While security planning is an acknowledged need and at the federal level is mandated by law, particular security strategies vary from agency to agency. A 2004 CERT survey of public and private organizations found that the most common methods used to combat e-crime were firewalls (98%), physical security systems (94%), and manual patch management (91%). Other security methods included encryption of data in transit, encryption of data in storage, regular security audits, and recording and reviewing employee communications. Firewalls were ranked the most effective and manual patch management the least effective method (CERT, 2004). What follows is a brief discussion of strategies agencies use as part of their overall security planning.

Security Governance and Reporting

Fundamental to security is simply knowing the situation and having a structure to take appropriate steps. The OMB rates the security programs of federal agencies largely on this basis: having complete inventories of IT assets, having complete listings of critical infrastructure and mission-critical systems, having strong incident identification and reporting procedures, having tight oversight over what contractors are doing, and having strong plans for reporting security problems. Security risks should be reported to senior management, listing each type of risk and assessing how compliant the organization is to the corresponding security plan element and listing planned actions to become compliant (or a statement of organizational willingness to accept the risk). Business managers should be taking primary responsibility for the security plan, with IT professionals only in an advisory role.

Physical Security Systems

When computer security is mentioned, most think of computer viruses or other types of cyberattack. However, simple physical security is a major problem deserving high priority in agency security plans. Computer centers themselves should be catastrophe-proof, with backup, and secure from theft and loss. In actuality, lapses in physical security abound. The Inspector General of the Treasury Department had to chastise the IRS in 2002 for losing track of 6600 desktop and notebook computers it had loaned to volunteers to help low-income, disabled, and senior citizens prepare income tax returns, having failed to first remove 2001 Social Security data from them (Vasishtha, 2002c). Similarly, in 2002 it was reported that the Justice Department had been unable to account for more than 400 missing notebook computers and 775 missing weapons over the previous 2 years (Dizard, 2002b). When in 2003 Los Alamos National Laboratory, a weapons research and development facility, lost 79 computers, the director and deputy director of security were assigned nonmanagement jobs (Daukantas, 2003a).

Security Checks and Clearances

A neglected security problem is *hacking out* rather than *hacking in*. So-called *180-degree hacking* involves planting a physical device (a notebook, a hard drive, even a game console) on a network, which then searches information behind the firewall and dials data out, since many security systems do not check for outgoing traffic. Security checks of personnel is a necessary component of a comprehensive security plan in agencies where data must be protected. In comprehensive plans, usually personnel are assigned an appropriate clearance level, limiting their access to data and systems. Network traffic, including e-mail, may be monitored for unusual patterns. Where a more aggressive approach is needed, Forensic Recovery and Evidence Devices (FRED) are becoming more widely used in the public sector, allowing investigators to plug an employee's computer into a FRED to recover financial records, e-mail, images, and other information that users may have thought were deleted or overwritten on hard drives, CD-ROMs, DVDs, ZIP disks, and other media.

Firewalls

Firewalls are considered central to agency network defense, though they vary considerably in performance and the types of attacks they can fend off. A firewall consists of one or more dedicated computers that filter Internet traffic, blocking such things as unauthorized outside requests to access the agency's computers, printers, or other network devices. Hardware firewalls use packet filtering, screening packet headers to compare source and destination information with predefined or user rules for handling incoming traffic. Alternatively, particularly for home use, firewalls can be run in software. Software firewalls insert themselves between one's network card and one's operating system, intercepting denial-of-service and other attacks. Firewalls are not foolproof and must be used by agencies as just one component of an overall security strategy.

Passwords and PINs

The simplest form of authentication is that of passwords or PINs. Particularly in the case of passwords, agencies often allow users to set their own. This creates security problems because users may post passwords in plain view, lend out passwords, allow people to look over their shoulder, may be tricked by persons masquerading as help desk technicians, or use too-common passwords like names of children, birthdays, or pet names. A common proposed solution is computer-generated passwords, longer passwords, or case-sensitive passwords with upper and lower case letters as well as numbers. However, these solutions do not prevent loss of passwords to packet-sniffing software, which filters all network transmissions. At the same time, they are not user-friendly and increase the costs of user support and may be self-defeating, making users *more* likely to put complex passwords on Post-it notes on their computers. Also, since brute force software can apply as many as a million passwords a second against a known username, even computer-generated passwords may fail. A better level of security is achieved when login attempts are restricted to a finite number (for example, three) and all passwords are encrypted before being transmitted on a network. An alternative is represented by Bell Labs software, which gives users a one-time disposable password for each transaction. A comprehensive security policy also involves security checks on password administrators themselves.

Biometrics

In motion pictures, biometric technologies like iris scanning and facial recognition are portrayed as the future of security. As mandated by the USA Patriot Act of 2001, however, NIST conducted an evaluation of biometric technology in 2002, coming to four preliminary conclusions: (1) iris scans relied on proprietary technology, making it difficult to evaluate; (2) fingerprints worked well but accuracy needed improvement before widespread use; (3) facial recognition technologies were not mature yet; and (4) no biometric technology was sufficiently reliable to be trusted when used by itself (Jackson, 2002a). The 2003 NIST survey still found facial recognition deficient (the best brand had under 72% accuracy, though with only .01% false positives). The best fingerprint identification system, from NEC Technologies, was 99.9% accurate on four-print sets and had only .01% false positives (Jackson, 2004c). Accordingly, when used as one strategy in multiple identification, biometric technology is taking hold in U.S. agencies. The Computer Science and Telecommunications Board (2002) has taken a policy stand favoring combining smart cards with biometrics in national ID systems, and this is beginning to take hold in government:

1. In 2004 the GSA issued employee "smart card" IDs with fingerprint recognition (Miller, 2003e).
2. Also in 2004, DHS's Transportation Security Administration began prototype testing of its biometric identity card for workers in maritime, rail, aviation, and truck commerce.
3. Government agencies are beginning to use keyboards that incorporate a smartcard reader and fingerprint ID, preventing computer use except by biometric match (intruders cannot swap in an alternate keyboard either).[9]

Configuration Management

As noted, manually installing security patches in software used by the agency is one of the most common security strategies, and one judged least effective. The Computer Science and Telecommunications Board (2002) also addressed this strategy in its call for investment in configuration management tools. If every employee's computer is configured differently, security compliance must be handled on a manual machine-by-machine basis. Configuration management software provides the capacity to install and update software on all machines via a network. In an ideal world, it might be possible to update millions of computers almost instantly when DHS or some other agency deemed it necessary.

For the moment, however, configuration management software is in its infancy.

Secure System Design

A security strategy must plan not only for methods by which attacks might be prevented but it also must provide for the inevitable "day after" when security breaches do occur. Partly this is handled through redundant backup of databases in physically and electronically secure locations. However, the backup strategy may be an "all or nothing" approach that assumes an entire IT system would be shut down when successful attacks occur. An ideal alternative, advocated by the Computer Science and Telecommunications Board (2002), is software design for "graceful degradation." That is, IT software would be designed in layers of functionality, with the capacity to shut individual layers down or turn them back on.

Red Teams

Red teams is a designation for experts, usually consultants rather than in-house agency personnel, who are hired to try to break into agency security systems in order to determine points of vulnerability. Since the best-designed system rarely anticipates everything, regular red team attacks can be an irreplaceable part of agency security strategy. For instance, Forensic Tec Solutions broke into dozens of military computers containing information on radio encryption, Social Security numbers, and other sensitive data in June 2002, notifying the military of the vulnerabilities discovered and precipitating a security review (Onley, 2002b). The Computer Science and Telecommunications Board (2002) recommends red teams be part of the agency's normal security plan as part of a strategy to go beyond "defensive security."

Honey Pots

Like red teams, *honey pots* are a proactive security strategy. In this strategy, the agency installs a computer (perhaps even an older, unpatched, more vulnerable one) on a network specifically to log access attempts. All traffic to the honey pot is suspect because, while it appears to have useful information, there is no reason for employees to go there or even know about it. The agency uses intrusion detection system packet-sniffing software to log hack attempts on the honey pot machine.

SUMMARY

In spite of huge investments in security, few think that security in IT is today satisfactory. A 2003 study by the GAO of DHS data sharing, for instance, found "no level of government perceived the process as effective." The GAO blamed three factors: lack of integrated databases, lack of federal security clearances among state and local officials, and inability of state and local officials to secure information they received (Dizard, 2003a). Using OMB data, another 2003 report on cybersecurity from the House Government Reform Subcommittee on Technology, Information Policy, Intergovernmental Relations, and the Census, rated 14 of 24 major agencies below a "C" on security, with eight agencies flunking outright (Emery, 2003). That is, few agencies could meet all five OMB security criteria:

1. Complete inventories of IT assets
2. Complete listings of critical infrastructure and mission-critical systems (only 5 of 24 agencies had this)
3. Strong incident identification and reporting procedures
4. Tight controls over contractors
5. Strong plans for finding and eliminating security problems

Disillusionment with the earlier "solution"—creation of the DHS—led in 2004 to calls for yet more security reforms based on the report of the 9/11 Commission, which had been deeply critical of previous security measures.

This is not to say that IT investments have not led to progress. West (2004), for instance, found that in 2004 some 46% of state and federal websites had a visible security policy on the Web, up from 37% in 2003. Still, security is a frustrating responsibility for public managers. The security job is never done. Some liken it to an arms race, with security experts and their hacker enemies in a perpetual game of move and countermove. A politically and economically unrealistic fantasy is that the security responsibility might be offloaded to others, say vendors. Along these lines, the Computer Science and Telecommunications Board has proposed legislation "that would increase the exposure of software and system vendors and system operators to liability for system breaches and mandated reporting of security breaches that could threaten critical societal functions" (Computer Science and Telecommunications Board, 2002). Security breaches are increasingly expensive, and it is not likely vendors will be made to pay for them. The consequence is that the high costs of security come at the expense of the public agency's other IT priorities, such as e-government.

Costs of security are high because there are six types of costs (Irvine, 2000). Acquisition and installation are only the first two, to which must be added the cost of audit and intrusion detection, costs for user training, the cost of decreased system performance due to security procedures, and the cost of hiring security consultants (security is constantly evolving and in-house expertise is never enough). That there is a price to be paid for security is added reason for public agencies to plan carefully before establishing security policies.

Public agencies, at least at the federal level, are required to establish written security policies (GAO, 1998). Their formulation is difficult because it is not the case that "the more security, the better." Too much security may be costly, robbing agencies of programmatic funds. Too much security may unduly trample privacy rights. Too much security may slow agency processes. Too much security may create an employee environment that is perceived as an undesirable or even unprofessional place to work. Too many security requirements can lead to them being ignored. It is better to require key practices, making others recommendations and using regular risk assessment to monitor the situation.

The formulation of agency security plans centers on trade-offs with privacy, productivity, human resource development, and budgetary priorities. As in other planning domains, it is often helpful in security planning to take a participative sociotechnical approach that gives stakeholders on an enterprise-wide basis a hearing and sense of ownership of the security procedures to be put into effect in the agency.

A comprehensive security policy will have the following elements:

- Risk Management Structure—The agency should have a formal organizational structure for security planning, with top management representation and active support as well as its own security budget. The security team should be placed high in the organizational structure. The security team should undertake periodic risk assessment as a prerequisite for setting security goals and priorities.
- Data Stewardship—Information systems and their major databases should be inventoried and specific agency personnel should be given stewardship responsibility for implementing security and privacy policies with respect to each.
- Risk Tracking—The agency should have a formal system for regularly tracking all forms of risk, which in turn means the agency must develop security indicators and measurement procedures (for example, measuring the number of information incidents per month, number of hacker attacks, etc.). Server logs, monitoring software, and incident handling protocols are often part of risk tracking.
- Risk Notification—The agency should not keep risk-tracking data centralized and secret but rather should disseminate risk information (for example, information on viruses) quickly. Notification is an important basis for employee commitment to security implementation. Likewise, risk-tracking data must be given to the risk management structure for analysis and use as part of security strategy-setting, not filed away.

- Authentication—Agencies should have procedures to verify the identity of those with whom it shares information and to support different classes of access for different types of users.
- Encryption—Agencies should have procedures for secure transfer of information, appropriate to the assessed risk level for the type of data.
- Data Security—Agencies should have plans for protecting information from external electronic access and from physical theft or loss. Equally, information should be protected for insider abuse through security checks and clearances of personnel. Particularly critical IT functions should apply the "separation of privileges" principle, requiring the cooperation of two or more personnel to effect an action.
- Data Sharing—The agency should decide how it will handle data requests from other governmental bodies and from the public. These policies should support FOIA access and should protect the privacy of individually identifiable data and protecting ownership rights of intellectual property. Employees, contractors, and all others should be expected to sign acceptable-use policies with regard to data that may be accessed.
- Data Disposal—Agency security plans should specify how and when to dispose of records.
- Security Training—The agency should provide security procedure training for new employees, security awareness training for all employees, and technical security training for its IT staff. The more user-friendly the software and ergonomic the hardware, the easier and more long-lasting the effects of training. IT managers must be trained to be able to make the business case for security as part of selling security priorities to top management. Security cannot be something employees are merely assumed to "know."

Whereas experts often emphasize justifying security as part of the agency's business plan, the Computer Science and Telecommunications Board views this as part of the problem. Many IT operators, they believe, only do as much security as justified on business grounds, but there are national security reasons for going beyond what can be cost-justified (Computer Science and Telecommunications Board, 2002). It would be tempting to categorize this as short-sightedness characteristic of the version of systems theory orientation that looks to the internal processes of the organization, neglecting the large sociopolitical environment. The creation of ever more comprehensive and intensive security systems poses a threat to such values as empowerment, democratization of information, and privacy rights valued by many who approach IT from a sociotechnical viewpoint. In fact, the development of security systems is, if anything, in support of reinforcement theory, where, for instance, computerization of the Social Security Administration generally increased management control over both staff and claimants (Henman & Adler, 2003).

One must be skeptical of claims that the Internet will lead to democratization of regimes like China, or that it creates a "global village" reducing conflict among global subcultures. Rather the Internet is a new mass medium that can be used for various ends, ranging from promotion of democracy to strengthening of nationalism to shoring up authoritarian regimes through misinformation (see Mazarr, 2002). When this is put in the context of the need for IT security, with its nonparticipatory enforcement ethos, its inherent bias against freedom of information, and its massive claims on IT budget resources, the more secure IT systems of the future are likely to be even less hospitable to the democratic visions of some sociotechnical theorists.

DISCUSSION QUESTIONS

1. In the 1980s, when mainframe computing was well established, the government produced the "Orange Book" encouraging private systems firms to create more secure software. What was the result of this effort?
2. The Federal Information Security Act of 2002 (FISMA) superceded the Computer Security Act of 1987. What did FISMA set out to accomplish? Why did some within the software industry dislike formal security benchmarks? Did agencies encounter problems implementing the FISMA security changes?
3. What was the Total Information Awareness Project (TIA)? How would it affect private industry, individuals, and the federal government? What was the fate of the TIA?
4. The FBI, to investigate threats and to protect national data infrastructure, created the National Infrastructure Protection Board (NIPB). However, NIPB had two conflicting roles. What was the conflict? Does it still exist?
5. Fears of cyberterrorism have been elevated in the public's eye. How plausible is a "cyber meltdown?" Why?
6. What safeguards were in place to protect personal information in the public key infrastructure (PKI) system? How is the federal government ensuring the use of PKI systems?
7. What is *e-authentication*? What criticism has this system received from agencies?
8. As part of Homeland Security, secure and reliable forms of identification are required for all federal employees and contractors. Should all individuals in the United States be required to have a national identification card? Why or why not?
9. Security threats within public agencies are not only from viruses. What are some other types of security threats that can be found in a government agency? Are there strategies that can be applied to safeguard the system?
10. What are the basic elements of a comprehensive security policy?

GLOSSARY

Cryptography: The science of encrypting or coding text or messages so only those with knowledge of a code or possession of a decoding device may access the information.

Denial-of-service attacks: This is a specific form of attack whereby the attacker(s) seeks to prevent legitimate website users from access to a service. This can be accomplished through "flooding" a network with a large amount of automatically generated traffic, disruption of the connection among computers, and by finding weaknesses through system or individual targeted disruptions.

Digital signature: This is a unique signifier that is attached to data through a function known as "hashing" to ensure that it has not been altered and that only the authorized individual had access to the data.

Encryption: The application of a specialized code to mask or scramble the meaning of data, protecting it from unauthorized individuals.

Packet: This is a portion of an electronic message that contains the destination address information as well as other data to be transmitted across a network.

Spoofing: The use of created TCP/IP (Transmission Control Protocol /Internet Provider) packets based on another's IP address.

ENDNOTES

[1]A section of the CSA required the federal government "to assist the private sector, upon request, in using and applying the results of the programs and activities under this section." Later, in 1998, Information Sharing and Analysis Centers (ISACs) were established by presidential directive to serve as vehicles for business to share information about cybersecurity threats.

[2]GISRA was Section X, Subtitle G, of the Defense Authorization Act of 2000 (for FY 2001) and amended the Paperwork Reduction Act of 1995 by enacting a new subchapter on Information Security.

[3]FISMA is Title III of the E-Government Act of 2002.

[4]http://thomas.loc.gov/cgi-bin/bdquery/D?d108:35:./temp/~bdjjdW:@@@L& summ2=m&l/bss/d108query.htmll.

[5]On the E-Crime Watch Survey, see http://.www.cert.org/about/ecrime.html.

[6]See http://www.cio.gov/eauthentication, and http://www.cio.gov/eauthentication/library.htm#documents.

[7]For instance, one credentialing system in the federated model was the Liberty Alliance, which included EDS, Lockheed Martin, Sun Microsystems, and Veri-Sign.

[8]HSPD-12 was available on 11/11/04 at http://csrc.nist.gov/policies/Presidential-Directive-Hspd-12.html.

[9]One vendor is http://www.cherrycorp.com .

CASE STUDY
Telework Security

Loreen Marie Butcher-Powell
Bloomsburg University of Pennsylvania

Introduction

The advancements of technology have altered the way many corporations operate in the United States. Not only have many corporations moved toward a global commerce, but they also have employed a telework infrastructure. "Telework refers to an approved working arrangement whereby a teleworker officially performs his/her assigned job tasks on a regular basis in a specified work area including a home, a client's office, a telework center, or on the road" (ITAC, 2004; United States Department of Defense, n.d.). Telework offers substantial savings of physical facility related costs including rent, storage, and electricity. It also enables companies to expand labor pools without geographic restrictions (Carlson, 2000; Hirsch, 2004; Mehlman, 2002; and Motskula, 2001). Approximately, 16.8 million Americans teleworked in 2001, 23.5 million in 2003 (International Telework Association & Council (ITAC), 2004), and it has been predicted that by the end of 2005 more than 60% of the work force will be considered teleworkers (DecisionOne, 2002).

While telework offers substantial benefits for corporations to expand labor pools without geographic restrictions, and to save on physical facility costs including rent, storage, and electricity (Hirsch, 2002; Mehlman, 2002; and Motskula, 2001), it also has the potential to create major security risks for the corporation (Atwood, 2004; Hirsch, 2002; Motskula, 2001; Quirk, 2002; and Rubens, 2004).

Background

Typical Telework Infrastructure

Today, an increasing number of corporations are using telework communications to support their sales and marketing staff in geographically dispersed residential locations. Most telework communication elements include laptop computers, the Internet, a Citrix client, a firewall, and various routers used to access their company's data warehouse server, an AS400, a back office server, or a other types of servers.

Each teleworker is typically provided with a laptop that contains locally installed programs such as Microsoft Office, corporate sales programs, Norton AntiVirus protection, and an Internet browser. Each laptop uses a client and Microsoft's Point-to-Point Transfer Protocol (PPTP) to enable remote access to the corporate network. The client is typically installed and configured to accept TCP/IP connections on the corporate network as needed. The teleworker will be required to obtain an Internet connection for his or her laptop via his or her choice of common public accommodations including a dial-up Internet service provider, a cable modem connection, or a digital subscriber line (DSL).

Once an Internet connection is established, the teleworker executes the client software installed on his or her laptop to begin the authentication process. The client software is designed to authenticate a teleworker's laptop through the corporate network security installations. The client contains a designated Internet protocol (IP) address, and a valid logon password needed to establish a peer-to-peer relationship to

continues

the corporate network. The peer-to-peer relationship is established by utilizing client software to connect to the corporate firewall via tunneling.

Once the client is authenticated, a browser link interface, similar to the one found on in-house corporate workstation desktops, will appear on the teleworker's screen. The browser link interface may contain shortcuts linking to Microsoft Office suite, Microsoft Office Outlook, Instant Messenger, access to onsite corporate printers, as well as access to networked drives including the AS400, a data warehouse server, back office server, or other important servers that are needed for the teleworker to do the job.

The Problem with Typical Telework Infrastructures

The problem with most typical telework networks is that they allow access and transmission of data across the Internet for electronic usages including electronic mail, database access and manipulation, online order processing, Web browsing, and remote file transfer. As a result, an outside intruder may find it simpler to attack a less fortified teleworker's laptop that is logged on to the corporation network rather than directly attacking the corporate network itself (Hirsch, 2002). A small study conducted by Teleworker.org (2004) suggested that teleworkers using a high-speed Internet connection, such as a cable modem or DSL, create an even higher security risk for telework infrastructures. Because high-speed Internet connections are always connected to the network, this will increase the chance of a teleworker's computer being discovered by hackers running automated port scans.

Additionally, research has illustrated that the severity of security threats in a telework infrastructure is often related to the computer literacy of the teleworker accessing the network rather than the actual corporate network (Hirsch, 2002; Mehlman, 2002; and Motskula, 2001). Not all of the corporate teleworkers' laptops are protected at all times by the corporate network. Consequently, if a teleworker's laptop is not connected to the corporate network, it could be used for web surfing, new software programs that are not related to work, old software reconfiguration, opening of e-mail attachments, and downloading of Internet files—thereby decreasing the effectiveness of any security software and increasing the risk of virus infection.

Understanding the security risks of teleworkers is important in order to secure its telework infrastructure. AT&T (2003) conducted a survey of 237 telework corporations. Their study revealed that 49% of telework corporations have security concerns regarding the electronic communication of telework. AT&T, Hirsch (2002), Mehlman (2002), and Motskula (2001) suggested that additional research regarding teleworker vulnerabilities is needed to help secure future telework infrastructures. They also assert that this type of research is critical because, without it, future telework infrastructures may result in corporate failure.

Research

A case study was conducted to better understand how to better secure telework infrastructure. A company located in Northeastern Pennsylvania and recognized for its innovative Internet and corporate network usage supporting internal operations and customer relationships was studied. The company employed over 130 employees and approximately 65% of its employees were teleworkers. The company used telework communications to support its sales and marketing staff in geographically dispersed residential locations along the East Coast.

Methodology

To understand how to better secure the telework infrastructure and its teleworkers, an information security assessment methodology was used. This research used the Operationally Critical Threat, Asset, and Vulnerability Evaluation (OCTAVE) model. The Networked Systems Survivability (NSS) Program in the Software Engineering Institute (SEI) at Carnegie Mellon University developed the OCTAVE. The OCTAVE model is a repeatable methodological approach for identifying and managing information security risks of actual threats including disclosure of a critical asset, modification of a critical asset, loss or destruction of a critical asset, or interruption of access to a critical asset, via an organizational self-assessment (Alberts, Behrens, Pethia, & Wilson, 1999).

The OCTAVE model was chosen for this research because "it is designed to be easily modified to meet the needs of many organizations" (Alberts & Dorofee, 2003, p. 241). Approval was obtained from SEI to study and modify the OCTAVE model to effectively allow for the telework infrastructure. A Delphi process was used to develop and validate a specific set of criteria necessary for the successful inclusion of end-user/telework-based activities.

The modifications made to the OCTAVE model included:

- Phase 1: Build Enterprise-Wide Security Requirements, Process 3: Identify Staff Knowledge, was modified. This research used this process to gather knowledge and security perceptions from the corporation's teleworkers instead of traditional staff.
- Phase 1, 2, and 3 focused on the telework infrastructure and the remote end-user/teleworker-based activities rather than traditional internal network-based activities.

Preliminary Results

While this research is still in progress, preliminary results indicate that almost 97% of the teleworkers assessed in this study were not concerned with maintaining and conducting security procedures that were required by corporate technology policies, such as effectively utilizing virus scanners, backup procedures, firewalls settings, spyware, and the operating system's controls. In fact, when asked in the workshops why they did not comply with corporate standards, the responses included:

- "This is not part of the job. I am a sales rep, not an IT specialist."
- "I was never trained how to complete these tasks."
- "I work over 40 hours with my job as it is. I don't have the time for this nonsense."

One initial response to this problem would be to propose a corporate security plan that included proper education and training for teleworkers on a yearly basis. However, further results of this case study revealed that 79% of teleworkers do not attend corporate education and training sessions. And there is no consequence for not attending these because yearly raises are not based on attending them but rather they are based on the number of sales.

continues

Conclusion

Many corporate infrastructures feature high volumes of sensitive and confidential data relevant to internal and external transactions. Research has shown that not only do the telework connections but the teleworkers lack of IT knowledge put the network at risk for potential for intrusion or eavesdropping resulting from their telework computers (Dhillion & Backhouse, 2000; Myersson, 2002). Every telework computer is susceptible to various computer threats. Threats and risk assessments can be used to list the potential threats for a particular computer. Remote computers require protection; otherwise, sensitive data existing on the remote computer could be disclosed, modified, or made unavailable. Various threats to the remote computer itself include viruses, data modification, Trojan horses, trap doors, sabotage, human error, and scavenging. To proactively develop a security evaluation plan that assesses the teleworker's system and safeguards telework infrastructures, further research needs to be conducted on modifying existing security evaluation models to include the teleworker.

Acknowledgements

Special permission to use the OCTAVE Model © 2004 Carnegie Mellon University, in Loreen Butcher-Powell's study (2002) was granted by the Software Engineering Institute.

References

Alberts, C., Behrens, S. G., Pethia, R. D., & Wilson, W.R. (1999). Operationally critical threat, asset, and vulnerability evaluation (OCTAVE) framework, version 1.0. (CMU/SEI-00-TR-017). Retrieved June 1, 2004, from www.sei.cmu.edu/publications/documents/99.reports/99tr017/99tr017abstract. html.

Alberts, C., & Dorofee, A. (2003). *Managing information security risks: The OCTAVE approach.* Upper Saddle River, NJ: Addison-Wesley.

American Telephone and Telegraph Company [AT&T]. (2003). Remote working in the net-centric organization. Retrieved June 27, 2004, from http://www.business.att.com/content/whitepaper/remote_working_net-centric_org.pdf.

Atwood, S. (2004). Data protection: Protecting your remote office data using replication technologies. *Disaster Recovery Journal, 17*(2), 20.

Carlson, P. A. (2000). Information technology and the emergence of a worker-centered organization. *ACM Journal of Computer Documentation, 24*(4), 204–212.

DecisionOne. (2002). Creating an effective telework plan: What works, what doesn't, and why. Retrieved June 1, 2004, from http://www.decisionone.com/d1m/news/white_papers/white_paper_04.shtml.

Dhillon, G., & Backhouse, J. (2000, July). Information system security management in the new millennium. *Communications of ACM, 3*(7), 125–128.

Herscovitz, E. (1999). Secure virtual private networks: The future of data communications. *International Journal of Network Management, 12*(1), 213–220.

Hirsch, J. (2002). Telecommuting: Security policies and procedures for the "work-from-home" workforce. Retrieved June 1, 2004, from http://www.teleworker.org/articles/telework_security.html.

International Telework Association & Council [ITAC] (2004). About telework. Retrieved February 3, 2004, from http://www.workingfromanywhere.org/resouces/abouttelework.htm.

Mehlman, B. P. (2002). Telework and the future of American competitiveness. Retrieved February 1, 2004, from http://www.technology.gov/Speeches/BPM_020923_Telework.htm.

Motskula, P. (2001). Securing teleworking as an ISP service. Retrieved June 2, 2004, from http://www.telework2001.fi/Motskula.rtf.

Myersson, J. (2002). Identifying enterprise network vulnerabilities. *International Journal of Networking Management, 12*(1), 135–144.

Powell, L. (2002). Telework security: What users don't understand. Proceedings from the Telebalt Conference 2002, Vilnius, Lithuania.

Quirk, K. P. (2002). Telework in the information age. Retrieved June 2, 2004, from http://www. accts.com/telework.htm.

Rubens, P. (2004). What you need to tell teleworkers. Retrieved June 1, 2004, from http://net working. earthweb.com/netsecur/article.php/3306781.

Teleworker.org. (2004). Telecommuting–A security threat? Retrieved June 1, 2004, from http://www. teleworker.org/articles/telecomuting_security.html.

United States Department of Defense (n.d.). Telework policy. Retrieved June 1, 2004, from http:// www.telework.gov/policies/dodpolicy.asp#definitions.

Regulation and Taxation Issues

Taxation of the Internet may be the greatest U.S. fiscal issue of the coming decade as more and more commerce shifts to online stores, presently still free of state taxation. In the information technology (IT) sector, giant firms like IBM and Microsoft have the budgets and manpower of many nations using their products around the world, bringing calls for reining them in. Electronic crimes like identity theft, computer fraud, and cyber-sabotage have changed the landscape of law enforcement. The ease of copying digital materials has raised intellectual property rights issues that have prompted traditional media giants to clamor for government controls. Regulation of the Internet is feared by civil libertarians and lauded by Christian conservatives opposed to online pornography and gambling. The following sections of this chapter deal with these pressing policy issues—with Internet taxation, regulation of the IT sector, regulation of e-commerce and computer fraud, protecting intellectual property, regulation of pornography on the web, and regulation of e-gambling.

INTERNET TAXATION

Whereas the federal government enjoys a relatively sound tax base rooted in the income tax, state and local governments are left to piece together their revenue from a variety of sources, one of the most important of which is the sales tax. With a mounting fiscal crisis characterizing many states in the last decade, the prospect of losing a substantial portion of their revenue stream is threatening to governors—yet that is the prospect posed by the predicted shift of consumer purchases from in-state stores to tax-free out-of-state Internet vendors. The Internet also makes tax avoidance through offshore banking easier (Weissberg, 2003).

The question of Internet taxation is a momentous one, possibly even affecting federalism and the power of the states and of the nation itself.

Though sometimes confused, there are two distinct types of proposed taxation of the Internet: (1) an access tax, akin to a telephone tax, to be paid by individuals, firms, and organizations that connect to the Internet; and (2) a sales tax, to be rebated to the states based on residence of the purchaser, on goods and services sold via the web. Like telephony, information and communications technologies cross state lines and fall under the federal government's constitutional power to regulate interstate commerce. While sales taxes are a state power, states only have the right to tax goods purchased by their citizens on the Internet. However, they do not have the power to regulate interstate commerce by putting demands on out-of-state Internet vendors. Thus one finds, for instance, that the North Carolina state income tax form asks residents to estimate their Internet purchases and pay tax on these purchases. However, from a state viewpoint this is an ineffective, largely voluntary system that is far inferior to proposed but thus far never enacted federal legislation that might require Internet vendors to collect sales taxes themselves and mail the appropriate revenue to the states, making the system largely involuntary from a citizen point of view (Nesbary, 2000). Because such legislation would be a form of regulation of interstate commerce, it would have to be based on federal, not state, law.

The question of taxation of Internet sales (as opposed to access) has been settled in the courts, at least for the present. In *National Bellas Hess, Inc. v. Department of Revenue of Illinois* (1967), the Supreme Court ruled that states could not require an out-of-state mail-order house that had no outlets or sales representatives in the state to collect and pay to the state a use tax on goods purchased for use within that state. In *Bellas Hess* the Supreme Court found that such taxation violated the due process clause of the Fourteenth Amendment and created an unconstitutional burden on interstate commerce. In particular, the Court ruled that a "seller whose only connection with customers in the State is by common carrier or the United States mail" lacked the requisite minimum contacts with the state.

Though dealing with mail order, the principles of *Bellas Hess* were directly applicable to the question of taxing Internet-based commerce. In *Quill Corporation v. North Dakota* (1992), the Supreme Court explicitly upheld *Bellas Hess* principles in prohibiting Internet sales taxation. In this ruling, the Court disagreed with a North Dakota Supreme Court ruling that technology had made the 1967 *Bellas Hess* precedent obsolete. Legislation has been proposed but never passed to overturn *Quill* and allow states to tax Internet sales. The tax prohibition applies to vendors with no physical presence in the state, which is, of course, the common situation.

Congress has been friendly to the concept of the Internet as a tax-free zone. The Internet Tax Freedom Act of 1998 (ITFA) initially imposed a three-year moratorium on state and local taxation of Internet access, and this was extended in 2001 for another two years. The Bush administration viewed the moratorium on Internet taxation as an economic stimulus as well as being a pro-business policy in support of the technology sector and Internet industries. The Internet Tax Non-discrimination Act of 2003 passed the House that year and was passed by the Senate in April 2004, by a vote of 93 to 3, with the Senate bill as amended passed by the House by suspension of the rules and voice vote in November 2004. Originally intended to make permanent the moratorium on taxes on Internet access and multiple and discriminatory taxes on electronic commerce imposed by ITFA, as passed it was amended only to extend the moratorium. It also phased out access taxes on digital subscriber line services and required the comptroller general to study the impact of ITFA on state and local governments and on broadband deployment. Current econometric studies indicate access taxation does not reduce access (Bruce, Deskins, & Fox, 2004). On November 19, 2004, a continuing resolution of Congress extended ITFA until November 1, 2006.

REGULATION OF THE IT SECTOR

Government can be drawn into regulation of the IT sector simply by the need to create order. In the idealistic era of the precommercial Internet, some believed that issues would be settled by professional collegialism and interpersonal networking, without the need for the state. Today's reality is that clashing commercial interests bring to the Internet the same conflicts that have brought legislation and administrative interventions to other policy arenas like global trade or environmental impact.

The domain name system provides an example. Every reader is familiar with domain names, reflected in web addresses. This is the basic naming and addressing system on which navigation on the web depends. But who determines these names? Since 1998, domain names have been under the authority of the Internet Corporation for Assigned Names and Numbers (ICANN). ICANN, in turn, operates under the authority of the U.S. Department of Commerce and has some representation from foreign governments as well. When a massive denial-of-service attack on Internet domain name servers (DNS) overloaded and almost brought down the Internet in October 2002, some blamed lack of regulation of the Internet backbone. Government Computer News columnist John McCormick noted, "If you run a DNS server, there is no real economic incentive to keep it secure." McCormick recommended that the government increase

DNS security by regulation or other forms of intervention (Jackson, 2002b). Increased regulation has thus far been fought relatively successfully by VeriSign, other IT corporations, and by their conservative think-tank supporters such as the Progress and Freedom Foundation.

Referring to Microsoft, VeriSign, and other multinational firms, one commentator on the domain name issue recently wrote, "The Internet has become over the past quarter century so darn expensive that the huge tech multinationals that control the Internet have become the world's new governments in fact. With war chests of billions of dollars in reserve and little debt on their balance sheets, certain ones are wealthier than the countries in which they are domiciled . . . It is governed by a few major multinationals which report to no one but their shareholders" (T1, 2004). On a host of issues ranging from trademark law to enforcing security features of the Internet, even the weak and largely privatized regulatory structure of ICANN has brought it into sharp conflict with multinationals like VeriSign, which prefer unregulated markets.

Because of the U.S. origins and composition of ICANN, there has been mounting international pressure to place coordination of the domain name system under some multilateral body such as the International Telecommunications Union, which is a United Nations (UN) body headquartered in Geneva and which serves to coordinate global telecom networks and services. In 2003 this issue arose at the UN World Summit on the Information Society, where it became clear that many nations, including China and several Middle Eastern and African nations, want more of a say in governance of the Internet. At this meeting, the United States was successful in arguing that multilateralization would imperil technological innovation and free speech on the Internet, a none-too-veiled allusion to the poor record of multilateralization proponents on human rights and transparency in government. In spite of the 2003 victory for the status quo, this is an issue that will not go away. In November 2004, UN Secretary-General Kofi Annan announced the formation of a UN Working Group on Internet Governance, to prepare the second World Summit on the Information Society in 2005, where the issue is sure to be contentious again.

Antitrust Action

Under the Sherman Antitrust Act of 1890 as well as parallel state laws, it is illegal for corporations to engage in monopolistic conduct, come to price-fixing agreements, or otherwise act in restraint of trade. Both IBM, when it dominated the IT sector in the 1970s, and Microsoft Corporation more recently, have come under antitrust actions brought by the U.S. Department of Justice (DOJ) and by rival firms (Baase, 1996).

Early antitrust action against IBM, based on lawsuits in 1932 and 1952, originated when IBM's stock in trade was tabulating machines, not computers. A 1956 consent decree forced IBM to sell its business machines, ending the practice of only leasing them so as to retain monopoly control. As a result, over 100 new firms entered the market, buying and then leasing IBM equipment on competitive terms. The decree also forced IBM to provide training, parts, and service to these new firms on an equitable basis.

Starting in 1968, the IBM Corporation was the target of a dozen antitrust suits centering on its new business, computing (Fisher, McGowan, & Greenwood, 1985). Major antitrust suits were filed by the DOJ, the Telex Corporation, and the Control Data Corporation (Baase, 1974). The federal case in principle could have resulted in breaking the IBM Corporation into independent elements but, after 13 years (1969–1981), the case was never brought to trial. Instead, the incoming Reagan administration, friendly to big business, dismissed the case as being "without merit" in spite of long-documented evidence of price fixing and unfair pricing practices designed to reduce competition in restraint of trade in the nascent computer industry. The IBM antitrust case was not without effects, however, as in the 1970s IBM dropped a number of its monopolistic practices, such as bundling software and service with computer sales so as to make it more difficult for other computer software and service firms to compete.

The European Commission (EC) had been pursuing parallel antitrust action against IBM in the same period. After having themselves dropped the IBM antitrust lawsuit, in 1982 the Reagan administration lobbied to "express concern" about prospective EC actions against IBM. The EC rebuffed pressure to drop its antitrust case but before formal sanctions were imposed, in 1984 the IBM Corporation agreed to a compromise that included providing interface specifications within 120 days of product release and unbundling mainframe products for sales in Europe.

By the 1990s, the IT industry was revolutionized by the rise of personal computing. With the proliferation of competing personal computer (PC) manufacturing firms, software firms, and of course, the Microsoft Corporation, IBM was no longer the monopolistic giant it once had been. Instead, during the 1990s, the DOJ targeted alleged monopolistic practices of the Microsoft Corporation, which published the Windows operating system.

The 1998 *U.S. v. Microsoft* antitrust lawsuit by the DOJ was joined by 20 states and supported by Microsoft competitors such as Novell, Inc., publishers of rival web browsing software. The suit contended that Microsoft engaged in monopolistic practices by bundling its Internet Explorer (IE) web browser with its Windows operating system, suppressing competition from Novell and other firms. It was also charged that Microsoft altered its operating system to favor its IE browser, engaged in restrictive licensing agreements, and otherwise acted in restraint of trade. Microsoft defended itself with arguments that merging Internet access with operating systems was the innovative wave of the future of operating systems, undertaken for reasons of technological progress, not for anticompetitive motives. That is, the essential issue was whether IE was a "product" like the Microsoft Excel spreadsheet that Microsoft had agreed not to tie to the sales of Windows by virtue of a 1994 settlement with the DOJ, or whether IE was a "feature" like Windows Explorer, the file-management component of the Windows operating system, and thus something Microsoft could freely include as part of sales of Windows.

When U.S. District Court Judge Thomas Penfield Jackson ordered Microsoft to produce a version of Windows devoid of IE, Microsoft responded that this would force the company to offer consumers obsolete software. Microsoft also took out full-page newspaper ads and otherwise undertook a public relations campaign to portray itself as an innovative enterprise under attack by heavy-handed government regulators acting on behalf of rivals to suppress competition, precisely and ironically what it itself was accused of doing!

Jackson's 1999 preliminary ruling declared that Microsoft's market position and practices did in fact constitute a monopoly. A follow-up ruling in 2000 reaffirmed that Microsoft had used its monopoly powers to stifle competition and harm consumers, and Jackson ordered Microsoft split into independent operating system and software companies. Though this Microsoft-busting order was overturned on appeal, the finding of monopolistic practices remained. The incoming Bush administration announced it would not seek to reverse the appeal decision and in November 2001, the DOJ reached a proposed settlement agreement with Microsoft. Microsoft was to be required to disclose technical information about its application programming interfaces with third-party software firms. This was to be overseen by a panel that would have full access to Microsoft source code and records for five years. Microsoft, however, was not required to change its code or to separate IE from its Windows software, opening the door to further software integration with Windows in the future. In November 2002, a federal court judgment essentially accepted the proposed DOJ settlement discussed above.

In November 2004, Microsoft reached antitrust settlements with Novell, Inc., and with the Computer and Communications Industry Association (CCIA, dominated largely by Microsoft competitors), the two major players associated with the 1998 DOJ antitrust case against Microsoft. In the settlement, Microsoft agreed to pay Novell over half a billion dollars in damages and to join the CCIA, compensating it for certain legal expenses and agreeing to support CCIA lobbying for federal research and development funding, immigration reform for software developers, and IT security and privacy regulation. Novell and the CCIA agreed to withdraw from antitrust activities against Microsoft in U.S. courts and in Europe. With the Commonwealth of Massachusetts having lost its appeal of the DOJ settlement and deciding not to pursue litigation, the November 2004 settlement seems to have ended the Microsoft antitrust saga in the United States.

It may be noted that the resurgence of U.S. computer global competitiveness under the banner of *Wintelism* (the Microsoft Windows, Intel processor alliance) rested on controlling architectural standards for software and networking (Borrus & Zelman, 1997). Hart and Kim (2002) observe that supportive U.S. government structures involving modified regulation rather than trust-busting and break-up of Microsoft gave the United States a competitive advantage over more state developmental approaches, such as that of Japan. Other countries were forced to abandon state controls in favor of decentralization of their computer and electronics industry to adapt and compete with the Wintel model.

The European Union (EU) took antitrust action against Microsoft over the issues of bundling and non-disclosure. *Bundling* referred to the Microsoft practice of bundling software such as its media player with its Windows operating system, thereby suppressing competition from other software firms (for example, from other media player software firms). The nondisclosure issue referred to the failure of Microsoft to make sufficient technical information available to allow competing software firms to achieve full interoperability with Windows, the dominant PC operating system. In March 2004 the EU fined Microsoft a record $613 million and ordered it to remove media player software from Windows. Following the EC action, Microsoft settled antitrust disputes brought in Europe and paid approximately $1 billion in damages to AOL/Time Warner and Sun Microsystems. At this writing, Microsoft is appealing the EU decision, and a European-based antitrust suit by RealNetworks Inc. remains the sole major unsettled antitrust suit against Microsoft.

The Open Source Debate

Parallel to the decline of antitrust actions against Microsoft has been the rise of the open source debate. This is a marketing campaign by IBM, Hewlitt Packard, Red Hat, and other vendors of the Linux operating system, joined by their supporters in computer science and elsewhere, to persuade corporations and governments that it is in their interest to switch from a Windows-based environment to a Linux-based one. *Open source* refers to the fact that the programming code for the

Linux operating system is openly available, while the code for the Windows operating system is proprietary. The open source campaign is also a matter of public policy because: (1) governments are encouraged to pass legislation requiring "open source code"; and (2) governments are encouraged to use the "power of the purse" to restructure the IT sector through their massive procurements of information systems.

The timeline for the open source campaign goes back a decade. In 1998, the Oracle Corporation announced it would port its Oracle8 database to Linux, partnering with four Linux vendors and giving Linux the credibility that it could be used for major governmental database projects. The following year, other large players like Compaq, Dell, HP, and IBM decided to invest in Linux. Among the first governmental units to switch were city and county jurisdictions using free Linux-based Apache web server software instead of proprietary software, sometimes saving hundreds of thousands of dollars. In 2001, IBM announced it would spend $1 billion on Linux that year. In 2003, Red Hat Advanced Server became the first Linux platform to be certified by the Defense Information Systems Agency. The Department of Defense (DOD) by then had become the leading federal department in terms of open source support. In 2003 also, open source legislation was introduced in Oregon and Texas but did not pass after intense Microsoft lobbying. For the U.S. federal government as of 2004, the spread of Linux open source applications has been slow outside the DOD and the Federal Emergency Management Agency. At the state level, open source is making slow but steady progress, with a 2004 milestone being the Massachusetts Enterprise Open Standards Policy, which requires IT managers to review existing IT systems for open standards compatibility (a looser definition[1] than *open source*) and to select open standards-compliant solutions when new systems are installed or existing ones need major overhaul.

The international story reveals stronger open source inroads. In 2003 Munich and various governments across the world ousted Microsoft Windows in favor of Linux as an operating system. China has been working on a local version of Linux for years, on the grounds of national self-sufficiency, security, and to avoid being too dependent on a single foreign supplier. Politicians in India have called on that country's vast army of programmers to develop open source products for the same reasons. In September 2003, Japan (which allocated ¥1 billion to the project) said it would collaborate with China and South Korea to develop open source alternatives to Microsoft's software (*The Economist*, 2003b). In 2004, another major defection from the Windows world occurred when the United Kingdom's (UK's) National Health Service began deployment of the Sun Microsystem's Java Desktop System (based on open source software) on 5000 of its estimated 800,000 terminals, justifying it on grounds of best value and interoperability. Likewise, in 2004 the Federal German Railways system switched to open source software. The spread of open source in public agencies outside the United States is proceeding at a more rapid clip than within the United States.

Why should governments switch to open source software? It is argued that open source code lets users adapt and improve software, catch bugs, and share programming code. This in turn may mean that applications software evolves at a faster rate, enabling governments to stay on the cutting edge. Then there is the fact that open source code may be free, saving organizations substantial costs (Peterson, 2003). When software is free, procurement can be much faster, resolving a major problem especially characteristic of public information systems.[2] Also, with open systems there is no danger of public data and functions being stranded in proprietary systems dependent for access continuity on the whims of a firm motivated by profit, not public interest. Finally, open source software may be more secure and has been subjected to fewer hacker attacks. In 2004, seven states formed the Government Open Code Collaborative to share open source code.[3]

Microsoft and its allies in and out of government have their own counter-arguments. To the extent that IBM, HP, Red Hat, and other Linux vendors provide support and services, these are not free. Red Hat premium, Sendmail commercial products, MySQL commercial products, StarOffice, and other "open source" software are all fee-based since Linux vendors must make a profit too. While there is lots of free Linux-based applications code, there may be just as much or more free Windows-based applications code. In April 2004, for the first time Microsoft placed source code for a product under Common Public License, allowing free use and modification of code for XML developers (XML is critical to e-government applications). The incentives for government to go to Linux are questionable. If a state or agency invests in open source coding, it has little or no incentive to make it well-commented and documented and generically designed so it can be shared widely. Agencies developing open source software have no funding to provide phone support for users outside the agency, who are largely on their own to handle software issues. In general, the level of vendor and even peer support for open source products may well be less than for popular proprietary products.

It should be noted that software acquisition is typically 3–5% of a new IT system and "free software" savings may be outweighed by costs of support, training, project management, etc. These other cost dimensions may favor proprietary software. For instance, training is a major ongoing cost of information systems. To take a basic example, new clerical workers easily can be hired with skills ready-to-go for Microsoft Office, but if the agency wants to use the open source StarOffice software, it will likely have to train clericals for it. Moreover, clerical workers may be less receptive to such training because the investment of time will have fewer transferable skill payoffs for them should they shift jobs later on, where they are much more likely to need proficiency in Microsoft Office procedures. The same issue is multiplied across software applications. In general, users have tended to find Linux software less user-friendly and more difficult to learn. Full cost accounting, taking training and other life-cycle costs into account, may very well change the cost–benefit equation for a proposed switch to open source applications.

Microsoft, as might be expected, has developed initiatives to counter the open source campaign. Its Shared Source Initiative since 2001 has made Windows source code available to customers, partners, and governments. This initiative shared code with 200,000 developers by early 2003. Shared Source gives hundreds of its most valuable professionals access to all the source code of Windows and Windows Server. Also, most of Microsoft's proprietary software products are customizable using built-in scripting languages. This script is usually freely shareable, and in fact websites for sharing custom script for Windows applications are common.

Legal issues about open source use have also arisen. Microsoft argues that being proprietary, purchasers have the benefit of a clear contract and clear rights of use, whereas, as the 2004 SCO lawsuit of IBM over use of Linux code shows, using "open source" code without contract is legally ambiguous and may expose the organization to risk of litigation.[4] A 2004 Office of Management and Budget (OMB) memo warned federal agencies that open source software has more complex licensing requirements, requiring review by agency general counsel, which also adds to its cost. Citizens Against Government Waste cited the OMB memo in a complaint arguing that because of legal and other costs, open source can be more expensive than proprietary software (Lyman, 2004).

REGULATION OF E-COMMERCE AND COMPUTER FRAUD

By now most readers are familiar with computer crime, because it appears on the national news from time to time. In the late 1990s, hacker Kevin Mitnick was charged with hundreds of millions of dollars in damage to Sun, Motorola, Nokia, Fujitsu, and other corporations. An employee hacked into the Viewsonic Corporation server, destroyed data, and cost the firm an estimated billion dollars in lost revenue. Hackers at the 2004 Republican National Convention conducted a campaign of "electronic civil disobedience" by conducting "an electronic sit-in" against Republican websites, mobilizing supporters to overload servers and cause a slowdown.

According to the 2004 U.S. E-Crime Watch survey, sponsored by *CSO Magazine* in cooperation with the U.S. Secret Service and CMU's CERT

Coordination Center, e-crime robbed American businesses and organizations of some $666 million in 2003. Over half the loss was operational and a quarter was directly financial. While most of the attacks came from outside the organization, almost a third were from employees or former employees. For chief security officers in U.S. organizations, 43% said e-crime was greater in 2003 than 2002, and 70% had experienced at least one e-crime against their organization in 2003 (Continuity Central, 2004). In January 2004, the Federal Trade Commission (FTC) reported 50% of consumer complaints concerned Internet-related fraud.

Hate speech is another much-reported class of computer crime. In 2003, for instance, the UK Home Secretary was asked to take action against an extreme right-wing group whose password-protected website posted a hit list of targets, including social workers, journalists, and politicians. As yet, however, there is no national Internet hate speech legislation in the United States, though Connecticut and Georgia legislation does deal specifically with Internet hate speech. At the Organization for Security and Cooperation in Europe meeting on the "Relationship Between Racist, Xenophobic and Anti-Semitic Propaganda on the Internet and Hate Crimes," in Paris in June 2004, the United States declined to support the Council of Europe's 2003 Additional Protocol to the Convention on Cybercrime Concerning the Criminalisation of Acts of a Racist and Xenophobic Nature Committed Through Computer Systems,[5] on the grounds that regulating the Internet to prohibit hate speech was not a strategy appropriate for the American constitutional system and its free speech protections.

In the past quarter century, a variety of laws directed specifically against e-crime have been enacted. Some of these are listed below. (Legislation on pornography and gambling is discussed separately.)

1. False Identification Crime Control Act of 1982, making it illegal to manufacture, traffic in, or illegally possess federal or foreign identification documents.
2. Credit Card Fraud Act of 1984, part of the Comprehensive Crime Control Act of 1984, made it illegal to use any "access device" for purposes of credit card or debit instrument fraud.
3. Counterfeit Access Device and Computer Fraud and Abuse Act of 1984, which was anti-hacking legislation that criminalized unauthorized access to "protected computers," defined as computers used in interstate or foreign commerce or communication, or by or for a financial institution, or the government of the United States.
4. Computer Fraud and Abuse Act of 1986, which, among other things, prohibited unauthorized attempts to upload information or change or destroy information on websites or networked computers. With 1996 amendments, the act protects against abuse any computer connected to the Internet for purposes of interstate or foreign commerce

as well as all federal computers. Trafficking in passwords and information related to unauthorized access is also criminalized.

5. Major Fraud Act of 1988, which created a new offense of "procurement fraud" for any government contract fraud in excess of $1 million.

6. Major Fraud Act Amendments of 1989, which increased penalties for major fraud.

7. Comprehensive Thrift and Bank Fraud Prosecution and Taxpayer Recovery Act of 1990, which was Title XXV of the Crime Control Act of 1990, increased penalties for banking crimes and gave regulators increased powers.

8. Computer Abuse Amendments Act of 1994, which expanded the Computer Fraud and Abuse Act of 1986 to cover the transmission of viruses and other harmful code.

9. False Statements Accountability Act of 1996, which prohibits anyone from knowingly and willfully making misrepresentations to any of the three branches of the federal government. As such it clarifies Congress's authority to obtain truthful testimony. An amendment, known as the Internet False Identification Prevention Act of 2000, applied to statements via electronic media.

10. The Economic Espionage Act of 1996, which had its first prosecutions in 1999. This was the first major act to protect corporations against theft of trade secrets, but it requires companies to implement reasonable security safeguards, which include computer security measures.

11. Wireless Telephone Protection Act of 1998, against cellular fraud. The act criminalized the use, possession, manufacture, or sale of cloning hardware or software that allows criminals to use cell phones operating on the accounts of legitimate customers.

12. Identity Theft and Assumption Deterrence Act of 1998, which made identity theft a federal crime with penalties of up to 15 years' imprisonment and a maximum fine of a quarter million dollars. The FTC was the clearinghouse for identity theft complaints.

13. Internet False Identification Prevention Act of 2000, which prohibited the transfer of false identification documents by electronic means, and required the Attorney General and Secretary of the Treasury to establish a coordinating committee to ensure that the creation and distribution of false identification documents is vigorously investigated and prosecuted.

14. The USA Patriot Act of 2001, which contains provisions related to computer crime and electronic evidence. It authorizes courts to grant pen register and trap and trace orders that apply to the Internet, not just phone lines. It also allows computer service providers who are victims of attacks by computer trespassers to authorize officials to monitor trespassers on their computer systems. As interpreted in

guidance from Attorney General John Ashcroft, the act permits investigators to obtain senders' and receivers' e-mail addresses as had previously been limited to telephone surveillance. Investigators can subpoena credit card and bank account numbers of suspected terrorists on the Internet, allowing them to identify suspects hiding behind Internet aliases. Title II of the act also expanded authority to intercept wire, oral, and electronic communications relating to terrorism and to computer fraud and abuse offenses.

15. The Homeland Security Act of 2002, Section 225 (known as the Cyber Security Enhancement Act of 2002), was a supplement to the USA Patriot Act that increased penalties for and directed the U.S. Sentencing Commission to reconsider sentencing guidelines for computer crimes. It also protected Internet service providers from being sued when giving subscriber information and communications to law enforcement agents.

16. The Prosecutorial Remedies and Tools Against the Exploitation of Children Today Act of 2003 (PROTECT Act), discussed later in this chapter.

In addition, the FTC applies fair trade practices legislation to electronic crimes involving fraud and deception. FTC actions, for instance, have led to indictments against criminals selling counterfeit luxury goods online, releasing bogus press releases to manipulate stock prices, and for trademark violations in relation to selling Viagra pills.

In addition to laws mentioned above, the United States, along with Canada and European nations, is party to the 2001 Convention on Cyber-Crime of the Council of Europe,[6] which requires signatory states to criminalize unauthorized access to computer systems; unauthorized interception or interference with data transmission; interference with computer systems; misuse of devices designed or adapted to commit computer crime, computer-related fraud, and forgery; child pornography; and offenses related to copyright and intellectual property.

Although the Federal Bureau of Investigation has a Cyber Investigations unit that has conducted Operation Web Snare and other operations against criminal spam, phishing, spoofed or hijacked accounts, international reshipping schemes, cyberextortion, auction fraud, credit card fraud, theft of intellectual property, computer intrusions (hacking), economic espionage, international money laundering, identity theft, and other electronic crimes, the overall picture is that enforcement of electronic crime laws is erratic, especially below the federal level. The National Institute of Justice's (NIJ) Electronic Crime Unit's 2001 Electronic Crime Needs Assessment for State and Local Law Enforcement, for instance, came to the following conclusions, many of which apply to the federal level as well[7]:

- Insufficient resources to establish computer crime units, pursue investigations and prosecutions, and develop tools
- Lack of knowledge on how to structure a computer crime unit
- Lack of uniform training for personnel
- Inability to retain trained personnel
- Lack of knowledge of existing technical tools or other resources
- Insufficient technical tools
- Lack of standards and certification for technical tools
- Lack of standards and certification for training
- Need for updated laws and regulations
- Insufficient cooperation with the private sector and academia

The assessment also noted that the overwhelming majority of law enforcement is at the state and local level. While federal agencies have a major responsibility in combating e-crime, they cannot handle the sheer number of incidents. The NIJ provides support for public managers through its Electronic Crime Partnership Initiative, Forensic Tool Development and Evaluation at the Office of Law Enforcement Standards, and its CyberScience Lab.

Public managers who are not involved in law enforcement do have reason to be knowledgeable about e-crime legislation. It is the other side of the computer security coin, which is a legislatively mandated responsibility of all federal agency heads. When a security breach occurs, the agency head must cooperate with the agency's legal department and the DOJ in bringing prosecution, usually under the Computer Fraud and Abuse Act of 1986 or one of the other pieces of legislation cited above. Reference to the Computer Fraud and Abuse Act and other legislative authority is commonly posted by public managers on agency web pages containing use warnings and disclaimers. For chief financial officers, e-crime training is rapidly becoming required. Legal guidance is available from the DOJ and NIJ and is available to state and local as well as federal public managers.

PROTECTING INTELLECTUAL PROPERTY

The theft of intellectual property is among the most important categories of computer crime. Theft may occur through electronic hacking, reverse software engineering, and by simple misappropriation of content or code, intentional or otherwise. Much of computer law deals with patent, copyright, trademark, and other intellectual property issues (Graham, 1999). The protection of intellectual property is the focus of all that fine print that most users ignore when purchasing software and media products. Public managers have particular reason to be concerned with intellectual property rights because: (1) government is the largest purchaser of software and media, and (2) users often have the mistaken view that whatever the government owns is in the public domain and therefore may be freely appropriated and copied.

The precise wording of purchase agreements and contracts determines what ownership rights are. In general, if the legal agreement specifies that the intellectual property is "work for hire," then it is fully owned by the government and is public property. In many cases, however, software and media content are licensed for use by the government, but the government acquires no right to sell or give the property to others beyond the scope and terms specified in the agreement.

Intellectual property may be placed in the public domain, but it may also have a more restrictive legal status (Coe & Broucek, 2000). A *patent* is a federal grant of rights giving the holder the right to control the use, manufacture, and sale of an invention for a specified time period. To get a patent, the inventor must show the item is novel (not previously invented), useful, and nonobvious. Once secured, a patent's term is normally 20 years. A *trademark* is a federal grant of rights giving the holder the right to control the use of words, designs, color contexts, even sounds or packaging. *Trade dress*, referring to the overall "look and feel" of a product, is also protected by trademarks. For instance, a public manager could not give a local recreation website the same look and feel as the Disneyland website, even though content was not copied. Unlike patents, trademarks have no term limit, provided the trademark holder continues to use the mark and proves use every 10 years when the mark is reregistered. Finally, a *copyright* is a legal right arising from authorship, even if the author has not officially registered the work with the U.S. Copyright Office. Copyrighted work may not be copied and reproduced by others, though "fair use" clauses of copyright legislation allow certain limited forms of copying for educational purposes. Also violations of copyright must show actual copying, not merely identical content (such as lines of computer code) independently arrived at.

The purchase of intellectual property by public managers is regulated by Part 27 of the Federal Acquisitions Regulation (FAR). Weapons systems and some other intellectual property are contracted on terms that give the government exclusive *unlimited rights*. Software created for the federal government is usually under a "for hire" contract giving the government unlimited rights. In general, however, FAR encourages agencies to obtain *limited rights* to intellectual property created under federally funded grants and contracts. Most commercial software contracted by the government, even if customized for specific agency uses, is contracted on a limited rights basis. Limited rights specify that the government has certain named use rights but the author retains ownership of the intellectual property, including the right to sell it to private parties. Typically, however, federal intellectual property contracts contain a "march in" clause, which permits it to take title to the intellectual property if the author fails or ceases to make it available through some form of licensing or sale. Finally, uncustomized off-the-shelf software used by the government usually has *restricted rights* status, meaning the same contractual obligations that any other purchaser would have.

Traditionally, intellectual property owned by the federal government on an unlimited rights basis was in the public domain, unless classified as secret by the DOD or another agency. However, starting in the 1980s, the federal government has encouraged licensing of government-owned computer software and in some cases databases by private parties, with sharing of revenues with the government employees who created it. The purpose of this was to encourage retention of skilled employees who might otherwise leave for the private sector, where author royalties were permitted. Also, in the absence of any clear Congressional legislation defining what is in the public domain, some agencies, such as the Smithsonian Institution, have asserted copyright over their intellectual property and charge fees for its use, creating a revenue stream for the agency. In most other countries, such as the UK, this has not been an issue because there never has been a presumption that government-owned intellectual property was in the public domain.

The *fair use* exception to copyrighted intellectual property allows a work to be copied if "for purposes such as criticism, comment, news reporting, teaching, scholarship, or research" (Coe & Broucek, 2000). Court rulings have determined that *fair use* refers to use in the nonprofit or educational sectors, not use by commercial enterprises. Even within the nonprofit and educational sectors, fair use must be for educational rather than entertainment purposes, must not involve copying a substantial percentage of the work, and must not damage the market value of the work. There is no specific guideline on the percentage of a work that may be copied under fair use, but in general, the more important the work is commercially, the less that may be copied. Copying even a few seconds of a hit song, for instance, may violate fair use, whereas copying many pages of an old book may be entirely acceptable.

The Digital Millennium Copyright Act of 1998 (DMCA) extended the concept of fair use to permit Internet service providers and others to make temporary copies of programs and other intellectual property during the performance of computer maintenance, and also amended the Copyright Act to support Internet broadcasting. Its main provisions, however, prohibited both unauthorized copying of digital media and criminalized the sale of copy-protection-breaking technology. The first indictment under the DMCA came in 2001, against Russian defendants, for trafficking in technology whose primary use was to circumvent copyright protection on Adobe Acrobat e-Book Reader media. Specifically, the defendants had written software to remove all limitations on copying, printing, and having the e-book read audibly by computer. The defendants were found not guilty in 2002, having successfully argued that protection-defeating software could legitimately be used for "fair use" purposes. Because the DMCA has been used to intimidate researchers studying copyright security and to support corporate market segmentation strategies (for example, regional coding of PlayStation games to prevent copies purchased in one part of the world from running on game machines purchased in another part of the world—a strategy also used by DVD publishers) rather than primarily to punish software pirates, the Electronic Frontier Foundation and others are supportive of the Digital Media Consumers' Rights Act (DMCRA), which would clarify and support "fair use" copying technology. The DMCRA was still stalled in Congressional committee as of fall 2005.

Meanwhile, the recording industry and their allies have begun to consider another technology that would restrict access and raise privacy issues. This is digital rights management (DRM) software, which in some versions would contain spyware functionalities embedded in CD-ROMs and DVDs, capable of reporting back to copyright owners the activities of individual users. Reported activities might include not only illegal copying but also consumer music or other preferences and patterns of use for marketing purposes (Cohen, 2003). Neither the Computer Fraud and Abuse Act of 1986 nor the Electronic Communications Privacy Act of 1986 regulate DRM software intrusions on individual privacy, and Congress has yet to address the issue.

Public websites are, of course, constrained by intellectual copyright law. Websites cannot post copyrighted materials or link to copyrighted materials in a way that makes it appear that the material is located on a public website, even if in fact it is not. When agencies link to the pages of others, litigation may ensue if the link is not to the home page. Linking lower down in a nonagency web tree bypasses disclaimers, advertising, and use agreements that the site owner intended visitors to view. Likewise, it is common practice on agency websites to inform users when they are exiting an agency web page and going on to a page hosted by another agency or by a nonprofit or commercial entity.

A variety of international treaties exist, but there is no true international copyright law, let alone effective enforcement. The two most important international agreements are the Berne Convention for the Protection of Literary and Artistic Works (1886, completed in Paris in 1896, with revisions in 1908, 1914, 1928, 1948, 1967, and 1971) and the Universal Copyright Convention, Geneva, 1952 (revised, Paris, 1971). Other agreements include World Trade Organization (WTO) agreements such as the Marrakesh Agreement of 1994 to implement the Uruguay Round Agreements of 1994, which included the Agreement on Trade-Related Aspects of Intellectual Property Rights, the first global trade agreement on intellectual property enforcement standards. Another important agreement was the World Intellectual Property Organization Copyright Treaty, Geneva, 1996, which extended the Berne Convention to cover digital property rights and also gave more protection to sound recordings. Not all countries subscribe to all international copyright conventions and some countries have no real copyright law at all, while others choose to give enforcement low priority. Jayakar (2003) found that nations with strong state-industry linkages were most likely to enforce intellectual property rights, even if they themselves had low levels of innovative intellectual property activity.

REGULATION OF PORNOGRAPHY ON THE WEB

In the summer of 2004, Chinese authorities shut down nearly 700 pornographic websites and arrested some 224 people in a campaign against Internet pornography. In more democratic societies, less autocratic action is possible because concerns must be balanced among prevailing moral standards, freedom of speech, the rights of adults versus children, corporate rights, and a host of other considerations, not the least of which is a public that opposes Internet pornography when asked in opinion polls but creates a market demand for it in actual practice.

The Internet has transformed pornography into a major business with public flotations, professional management, brand equity building, media management, self-regulation, and lobby and trade groups (Cronin & Davenport, 2001), not to mention self-help books on how to get started in the business (Sharlot, 2004). Internet pornography statistics for 2004 document the existence of some 4.2 million pornographic websites (12% of all websites), containing some 372 million web pages. Two out of three visitors are men. Internet search engines are used to seek out pornographic topics some 68 million times a day and constitute a quarter of all search engine requests. There are 2.5 billion pornographic e-mailings a day, constituting 8% of all e-mail traffic and representing over four e-mails per Internet user per day (TopTenReviews, 2004). Some of this e-mail is sent by pornographic spammers who have illicitly enslaved the home computers of unknowing citizens for mail-forwarding purposes (Miller, 2003k). Nielsen NetRatings data suggest that as of 2003, about one in four U.S. Internet surfers visits pornographic websites (Farrar, 2004).

However, in spite of popular perceptions, the Internet pulls in only an estimated $2.5 billion dollars of the $57 billion worldwide pornography industry—about the same as cable and pay-per-view television, half that of sex clubs or phone sex firms, a third that of pornographic magazines, and an eighth that of adult videos. Of the $57 billion, the U.S. share of pornographic demand is an estimated $12 billion (TopTenReviews, 2004). Most pornography is not regulatable within the confines of U.S. borders, yet the Internet brings the world to one's computer at home or work and would continue to do so even if all U.S. pornographic websites were eliminated. Cynics observe that even if U.S. Internet pornography were effectively regulatable, there are economic issues about closing down a $12 billion industry and shipping it overseas, where it would continue to be accessed anyway.

Child pornography is a minor but particularly objectionable portion of Internet pornography. It is estimated that about 100,000 of the 4.2 million pornographic websites contain illegal child pornography. It is also estimated that the average age for a child to first be exposed to Internet pornography is 11 years old, and that by age 16, some 90% will have encountered online pornography, not infrequently in the course of doing homework research. Some one in five youths have received a sexual solicitation on the Internet and 29% of youths 7–17 say they would give out their home address in a chat room or e-mail (TopTenReviews, 2004). The National Juvenile Online Victimization survey in 2002 reported 2577 arrests for sex-related crimes involving a computer.

There are three major legal statuses that may apply to pornography. *Obscene* materials are those that violate contemporary community standards and thus may be censored or prohibited, even from adults. This Supreme Court definition was ambiguous even in the days of print pornography, as the Internet has eroded the meaningfulness of the geographical local community as the appropriate referent. *Child pornography* is the second status, and material in this category is clearly illegal. Child pornography consists of depiction of sexual acts by minors (and by "virtual" minors under the PROTECT Act, discussed later in this chapter) and "lewd" display of genitals by minors. The third legal status is *obscene for minors*, meaning adults have the constitutional right to view freely such erotic materials, although it may be prohibited for minors.

The definition of *child pornography* is largely accepted, apart from policy difference on the treatment of images of "virtual children." Few disagree with the notion that minors should be protected from most pornography that adults may view. However, there is little agreement on strategies for restricting the access of minors. The major options are requiring filtering or nanny software, requiring adult passes, requiring warnings, and imposing fines. Each of these policy options has major problems. Filters are often ineffective. Virtual passes do not rigorously scrutinize the age validity of applicants. Warnings are as much invitation as deterrent. Fines are difficult to enforce and cannot be imposed on out-of-country websites at all.

Congress has moved repeatedly but largely ineffectually to regulate Internet pornography, starting with the Communications Decency Act of 1996 (CDA). The CDA prohibited Internet distribution of "indecent" materials. A few months later a three-judge panel issued an injunction against its enforcement, and in 1997 the Supreme Court unanimously ruled most of the CDA unconstitutional on grounds of vagueness and overbreadth. Likewise, the Child Pornography Prevention Act of 1996 outlawed digitally altering images of nude adults to make them appear to be children, but this was overturned on similar grounds by the Supreme Court in the case of *Ashcroft v. Free Speech Coalition* (2002).

In reaction to the defeat of the CDA in the courts, Congress narrowed the scope of its prohibitions in the Child Online Protection Act of 1998 (COPA), which criminalized actions by commercial web publishers who knowingly used the web to allow children to view pornography. Enforcement of COPA almost immediately fell under court injunction and in 2004, in the case of *Ashcroft v. American Civil Liberties Union*, the Supreme Court upheld the injunction against enforcement. In ruling that COPA was probably unconstitutional, the Court cited parental filtering software as a method of protection superior to the methods contained in COPA, citing findings of the Commission on Child Online Protection, which Congress had established to review alternative strategies for dealing with harmful materials on the Internet.

Filtering (*nanny*) software is an oft-proposed strategy for dealing with Internet pornography, and one cited in court rulings. However, filtering is not particularly effective. A 2002 study in the *Journal of the American Medical Association* tested 3052 health sites and 516 pornography sites using seven common filtering programs. At their least restrictive settings, programs blocked 10% of health sites; at their most restrictive settings, they blocked 24% of health sites. Because legislation forces many libraries and schools to use filtering software, this was seen as a medical issue and an argument against mandated use of filtering software (Sweeney, 2003).

Congress was more successful, as far as constitutionality goes, with other more limited legislation. The Children's Online Privacy Protection Act of 1998 made it illegal to collect, use, or disclose personal information from children under 13. The Children's Internet Protection Act of 2000 (CIPA) required schools and libraries receiving federal funds to use filtering software to protect minors (under 17). CIPA's constitutionality was upheld by the Supreme Court in 2003. And the Dot Kids Implementation and Efficiency Act of 2002 created a new domain, similar to *.com* and *.edu*. The .kids domain was to be a child-friendly space within the Internet with every site monitored for content, and online chat rooms and instant messaging prohibited unless certified as safe. The websites under this new domain would not connect a child to other online sites outside the child-friendly zone. As of late 2004, there were links at www.kids.us to only three dozen domains, including the National Aeronautics and Space Administration and the Smithsonian, but in general the concept had yet to take off.

PROTECT outlawed adult images digitally altered to appear as if children are having sex, and prohibited use of misleading domain names that tempt children to access pornography. The DOJ established a "CyberTipLine" to receive reports of violations of PROTECT and in February 2004, a Manhattan man was sentenced to 30 months in jail under PROTECT provisions for having created pornographic websites with domain names that were minor variations on the spelling of *Disney*, *Bob the Builder*, and other legitimate children's websites. While the domain name abuse provisions of PROTECT are uncontroversial, the American Civil Liberties Union has raised free speech objections to the PROTECT provisions imposing penalties on virtual child images when no actual children can be shown to have been harmed, particularly since PROTECT does not prohibit otherwise similar nonphotographic drawing images.

Finally, the Controlling the Assault of Non-Solicited Pornography and Marketing Act of 2003 was passed in December of that year and, as it pertains to pornography, gave the FTC, state attorneys general, and Internet service providers the power to enforce rules requiring senders of commercial e-mail to include pornography warnings, to offer opt-out methods, and to not use false or deceptive information in e-mail subject lines.

Many of the policy issues surrounding regulation of Internet pornography were explored by the Computer Science and Telecommunications Board and the National Research Council (NRC), which resulted in a report titled, "Youth, Pornography, and the Internet" (Thornburgh & Lin, 2002). The report noted that social science is divided on the effect of viewing sexually explicit materials, ranging from social learning theory that maintains that what is viewed now may be acted out later on in life to psychoanalytic theory that holds that basic sex and aggression drives must be released in some way, and catharsis through erotic fantasy has a positive social effect. The report surveyed the literature, finding some evidence that viewing sexual violence may be desensitizing and may promote promiscuity for young adults, but these effects apply to sexual themes in movies, on television, and other non-Internet media as well and, indeed, go beyond any ordinary definition of pornography. Also, the report noted, older high school students have very different information needs and react to erotic content very differently from elementary students, a difference generally ignored in Congressional legislation pertaining to "child" pornography. Some empirical research has found that younger children are uninterested in pornography and content regulation legislation may be addressed to a nonproblem (Sandvig, 2003).

The NRC report investigated pornographic websites, concluding that this was not a self-regulating industry. Nearly two thirds did not include a notice indicating the adult nature of the site, three quarters displayed adult content on the first page, and only 3% required a credit card or other adult verification to proceed past the first page. FTC regulation was found to be equally peripheral to the problem, limited to a few cases involving deception in use of domain names or fraud in billing. The NRC report (Thornburgh & Lin, 2002, p. 17) recommended not regulation but instead funding more research to study the problem; supporting families' efforts to exercise greater choice, as through parental controls on web browsers and televisions; and educating the upcoming generation in the hopes of reducing the demand for online pornography.

REGULATION OF E-GAMBLING

Like online pornography, Internet gambling has already become big business in the full sense of that term. As of 2003, online gambling revenue was estimated to be $5.7 billion and was projected to triple to $16.9 billion by 2009. Some 12 million people gambled on the Internet in 2003, over a third of them U.S. residents (American Gaming Association, 2004). There are two major schools of policy strategy with regard to online gambling. The first school regards it as an addictive threat to family life and one that should be curtailed through regulation. Moreover, child gambling is seen as a threat analogous to child pornography. A 2002 FTC survey documented that minors are frequently exposed to online gambling advertising and can easily access online gambling sites, in spite of gambling by minors being illegal in every state (Muris, 2003). The second school accepts online gambling as a fact of life and wishes only that it be properly regulated to ensure age requirements, to minimize fraud, and to ensure that taxes are collected. Regulations of Internet gambling draw support from both schools, though for quite different motives.

There are five major policy options that have been considered by governments around the world:

1. Making online gambling illegal, on penalty of jail time for gambling operators or players
2. Making online gambling illegal, on penalty of having assets seized

3. Curtailing gambling opportunity by forbidding financial institutions to honor credit card, debit card, or other banking transactions involving payments to gambling operators
4. Making online gambling legal but taxing it and regulating it to prevent fraud
5. Making online gambling legal and establishing state-run online gambling concessions for revenue purposes

In the view of what may be called the *family values* school, online gambling is an asocial and solitary activity, more so than live gambling, and this makes it doubly addictive. A literature review by Griffiths and Park (2002), however, found that empirical research to date does not support the "worse than regular gambling" position and this has undercut support for policy options (1) and (2) above. It has also been argued that online gambling may become a convenient way to launder criminal revenues, but because evidence is lacking that this is more true of Internet gambling than of other forms of e-commerce, this argument too has had little impact.

For its part, the gaming industry takes the position that Internet gambling is a wonderful boon to the economy, potentially providing an additional $100 billion in federal revenues (*Gamble Tribune*, 2004a). The industry supports option (4): legislation that will bring increased tax revenues and that will regulate the industry for fair trade practices. That is, the lobbying goal of the gaming industry is to regularize gambling and make it a permanent legal activity operating under more or less the same regulatory constraints as other businesses, perhaps along the lines of UK policy, which since 1963 has regulated gambling by enforcing age requirements and requiring assistance be provided to problem gamblers. The industry lobbying group BETonSPORTS has launched a "Right to Wager" television advertising campaign in support of regulated legitimization of online gambling.

In the United States, gambling has traditionally been regulated at the state level. As of 2004, Illinois, Louisiana, Michigan, Oregon, and South Dakota specifically prohibit online gambling. Both Presidents Clinton and Bush have taken the position that online gambling is illegal under the Federal Wire Act of 1961, which prohibited the use of interstate communications lines to transmit or receive bets, and under the Professional and Amateur Sports Protection Act of 1992, which banned sports betting except in states where it already existed (Nevada, Oregon, and Delaware). A federal court in 2002, however, ruled that these laws only prohibit sports betting, not casino gambling online, putting the question of legality into question. Partly in reaction, the U.S. Congress subsequently displayed interest in pursuing punitive policies. The Unlawful Internet Gambling Funding Prohibition Act of 2003 (UIGFPA), which passed the House but never passed in the Senate would have made it illegal to operate an online gaming establishment and would have prohibited credit card and banking payments to online gambling operators, hoping thereby to severely curtail gambling. However, although the UIGFPA has not yet passed, many U.S. credit card issuers already deny online gambling transactions and gambling websites are not given "merchant" status by U.S.-based banks.

Also still in Congressional committee but never passed, was the Internet Gambling Licensing and Regulation Commission Act of 2004 (HR 1223), which would create a commission on Internet gambling licensing and regulation. This would be a federal equivalent to existing state-level gambling commissions that regulate the gaming industry in states that permit it.

In line with the prohibitory rather than regulatory approach, President Bush's Attorney General, John Ashcroft, has taken action against search engine companies and others who accept advertising for online gambling. However, this has been challenged in the courts as an unconstitutional infringement on commercial free speech (*Gamble Tribune*, 2004b). In the meantime, Yahoo! and Google both dropped all gambling advertising in June 2004.

The internationalization of online gambling threatens to make U.S. policy moot. It is estimated that U.S. citizens provide about half of all Internet gambling revenues worldwide (Glasner, 2002). Attempts to regulate Internet gambling within a single country, such as the United States, are frustrated by its being legal in many countries in Asia, the Caribbean, and elsewhere. The UK legalized Internet sports betting in 2002. Brunker (2001) has described how Antigua, once the world capital of Internet gambling, quickly had competitors from Britain, Asia, and elsewhere as international gambling corporations raced for cyber-hegemony. Most online gambling now originates offshore. Moreover, in 2004 the WTO upheld the right of Antigua, Barbuda, and other nations to host Internet gambling operations, overruling U.S. attempts to prevent them from doing so (*Gamble Tribune*, 2004c). The prohibitory policy of the United States finds itself at odds with a growing international consensus under which foreign governments are taking a regulatory approach as favored by the gambling industry.

SUMMARY

Underlying all issues of regulation and taxation in public information management is the question of the scope of government. In IT, as elsewhere, there are broad ideological disagreements about the proper extent of government activity. On the one hand, the United States currently finds itself in a politically conservative period, favoring limited government and outsourcing of government functions (including IT) to the private sector. On the other hand, the dramatic growth of the Internet and of IT have led to an expectation that public managers and elected officials will take a much more active role in technology than has been the case historically, or suffer accordingly. Whether empirically it is true or not that public sector leaders are rewarded for taking on the challenges of technology leadership (the ill-fated example of Vice President Al Gore and his emphasis on Internet technology leadership in the 2000 presidential elections raises questions), the more important point is that IT raises all sorts of policy issues that political leaders perceive as compelling their involvement and activism.

Regulation is not a story of government versus business. On the contrary, many of the strongest proregulation voices come from the private sector, with media companies wanting stronger protection of intellectual property rights, the commercial sector wanting stronger enforcement of e-crime law, the gaming industry wanting the stability of regulation, churches wanting strong antipornography controls, and brick-and-mortar businesses wanting their online competitors to be taxed the way they are. Regulation seeks to find a middle ground between individual and entrepreneurial freedom at one end of the spectrum, and governmental control on the other. Too little regulation and IT is abused; too much regulation and innovation is stifled.

Everywhere policy makers look in cyberspace, there are political issues to resolve, even beyond those discussed in this chapter. Should the government subsidize universal Internet service for the poor, for rural residents, for students? Should state colleges promote e-learning, or is this shifting students into a second-class education? How far should cities go to foot the bill for community computing and local IT infrastructure? What about taxing the Internet? Requiring corporations in critical areas to meet security standards? How much obligation does government have to ensure electronic transparency in its operations? Should the nation's foreign policy seek to promote the interests of IT corporations? Should foreign policy be marshaled to oppose the "information rights" abuses of other countries, as Web Zimbabwe deported journalists for publishing critical stories on the Internet even though not printed in any newspaper in that country? Even the courts are not immune from policy choices, as happened when France attempted to force the U.S.-based Yahoo! corporation to remove a website selling Nazi memorabilia—sales outlawed in France but not in the United States.

Systems theorists would expect regulation to reflect more and more comprehensive and integrated treatment of the policy domains discussed in this chapter, with a closer and closer approach to achieving societal values. The actual picture is mixed. New legislation has largely filled in the holes where traditional laws had not foreseen the world of cyberspace, so in this sense a more comprehensive approach now exists. But in each area it would be hard to say the United States is closer to societal values. The revenue bases of the states are eroded as the powerful e-commerce sectors and their IT supporters fend off taxation, antitrust policy has come to little, e-crime enforcement is spotty at best, and online piracy, pornography, and gambling all seem on the ascendant. As to sociotechnical theory, with its emphasis on the importance of human factors and participatory implementation, most of the outcomes discussed in this chapter have come about based on economic motives without benefit of participatory processes. These outcomes seem more consistent with the technological determinist view, that if it is possible, it will happen, regardless of the powers that be, referring to the limited powers of the state. However, reinforcement theorists, thinking the powers that be may be better thought of as the new electronic elites that finance online enterprises from selling books to selling gambling, perhaps would argue that IT reinforces the power of these elites, who become able to shift their activities around the world so as to avoid the regulatory thumb of even the most powerful nations.

DISCUSSION QUESTIONS

1. Why do states desire the taxation of e-commerce? Is there any precedent for or against e-taxing? How has the federal government reacted to calls for the taxation of Internet sales?

2. What reasons are there for the extension of domain name coordination to international bodies? Should this happen? Why or why not?

3. What are some actions that Microsoft has been accused of under antitrust actions? Have the courts remedied Microsoft's monopolistic characteristics, creating a level playing field for IT competitors? Explain.

4. What are the supposed benefits of open-source code? What are the arguments against governmental units relying on open-source code?

5. The European Union has taken legislative action against hate speech on the Internet. Why has the United States not joined the EU in this battle? What international cyber crime action has the United States participated in?

6. Intellectual property theft is one of the most important types of computer crime. Why is it important for public administrators to be concerned with this? Do you know of any examples of intellectual property crime in your organization or situations where it may become an issue?

7. The Internet has transformed pornography into a major industry. What are the major policy arguments in related U.S. legislation about? Are there multiple means to address the pornography issue? How well do they work?

8. What are the general policy options governments have at their disposal to handle e-gambling? Why would it be virtually impossible to eliminate e-gambling for U.S. citizens? How do you think e-gambling should be addressed? Why?

9. Theoretically, how does e-regulation impact technological innovation? What are the parties generally in favor of e-regulation?

10. How would each—systems theorists, sociotechnical theorists, technological determinists, and reinforcement theorists—feel about e-regulation? What point of view is most aligned with your own beliefs?

GLOSSARY

Bundling: The offering of multiple technological services or products as a packaged purchase, in order to reduce competition from other vendors and enhance a company's sales.

Domain: With regard to the World Wide Web, the domain is part of the web address that indicates the site's position in a system of identifying features (.com, .gov, .edu, etc.). For instance *.gov* indicates the site's relation to a government agency. Similarly, subdomains exist as further mapping such as *nc.gov* to show a site's relation to the government of North Carolina.

Intellectual property: Any idea, concept, invention, and work of human creation that is unique or novel. It is inferred that the intellectual property does or could have value in a market setting.

Internet Tax Moratorium: This is a federal law that bans state taxation of Internet access and online sales.

Source code: This is the set of commands or instructions that make up a program and describe how it operates. Thus, *open source code* refers to computer commands or instructions that are made available for entities other than the creator on a nonproprietary basis.

Script: Script is a small computer program or set of instructions. Scripts are written in a scripting language such as JavaScript. Many applications contain scripting capabilities to allow software customization.

ENDNOTES

[1]Microsoft supports *open standards* in its publications, but not *open source.* Open standards signify widespread technical agreements on achieving interoperability. Open source code may or may not be interoperable with existing software or with open standards software, though arguably when code is open source, it is easier for developers to achieve interoperability. The counterargu-

ment is that proprietary vendors such as Microsoft have an enormous stake in promoting interoperability, sink large scale investments into it, and may deliver solutions that are more interoperable than a smaller scale vendor using open source code can deliver.

[2]The Open Source Initiative website is located at www.opensource.org. See also the Center of Open Source and Government, Cyber Security Policy and Research Institute, George Washington University, at www.egovos.org. Freshmeat.com is a website cataloging open source applications. The Linux Documentation Project is located at www.tlpd.org.

[3]The URL is www.gocc.gov.

[4]SCO sued IBM over IBM use of open source Linux code, claiming Linux copies sections of UNIX code, which SCO holds rights to. One commentator predicted the rise of open source insurance for software companies and users because "Open source provides an area of risk and uncertainty that is much higher than proprietary software" (Krill, 2004).

[5]See http://conventions.coe.int/Treaty/en/Treaties/Html/189.htm.

[6]See http://conventions.coe.int/Treaty/en/Treaties/Html/185.htm.

[7]The list of assessments is from http://www.ojp.gov/nij/sciencetech/ecrime.htm.

CASE STUDY
Tax Policy in the Virtual State:
A Case Study of the Michigan Department of Treasury

by Dale Nesbary, Oakland University

The emergence of personal computer and Internet technology has impacted nearly all governmental activities. Customer service, the approval of legislation, prison security, and tax policy and administration are among the services impacted by these technologies. At the state level, tax administration has moved from a largely paper-based process using green accounting spreadsheets and calculator tape to one based nearly exclusively on digital documents and materials. This case study examines electronic tax administration from the perspective of a recent review of technologies used by the Michigan Department of Treasury.

Overview of Tax Administration Technology in Michigan Background

The Michigan Department of Treasury (henceforth called Treasury was established by the Executive Organization Act of 1965, which merged the operations of the State Treasurer, Department of Revenue, Municipal Finance Commission, Board of Tax Appeals, State Tax Commission, and Auditor General (except state audit function). In later years, a number of state education finance functions were transferred into Treasury while others, including the Michigan Tax Tribunal and the Municipal Finance Commission, were transferred out or abolished. The State Treasurer is appointed by the governor and acts as principal advisor to the governor on tax and fiscal policy issues (Michigan Department of Treasury, 2005).

From an operational perspective, the Treasury is a relatively large and complex organization employing some 1,650 full-time-equated employees. The governor's recommended budget for the department for fiscal year 2005–2006 was $1.597 billion.

Treasury processes in excess of $18 billion a year in tax revenue collections and over $1 billion in tax refund payments each year.

Technology and Tax Administration

In 2000, the tax administration process in Michigan was substantially different than today. The Michigan Department of Treasury itself was structured organizationally to simply collect revenues by revenue type and did so in a manner that made sense with respect to the State's revenue system at the time. For example, the department maintained separate units serving payers of sales taxes, income taxes, business taxes, and so forth. Customers argued that Treasury staff did not communicate across units and provided relatively poor customer service.

While parts of the tax administration process were in need of attention, many others, including taxpayer communications, were not. Like many other governmental agencies, Treasury was just beginning to take advantage of powerful Internet technologies. It had a desire to improve tax administration and customer service and saw technology as a primary vehicle with which to accomplish this goal. Moreover, the massive amount of data available today combined with pervasive communication technology can and often does cause tax administrators and the public to be less able to make clear and efficient decisions.

To address these issues, in 2001 Treasury began a review of its communications, collection, and administration procedures via a consulting contract with Accenture Management Consulting (Michigan Department of Treasury, 2005). The process, still ongoing, was designed to be customer oriented. In the initial stages of the review, a number of customers were consulted about the services they desired from Treasury. These customers include:

- State and federal agencies
- Large businesses
- Small businesses
- Individual taxpayers
- Tax preparers

The needs of two specific groups—small businesses and tax preparers—are representative of what all five categories of clients identified as being important to them. The top need of the small businesses customers were:

- Ultimate security measures for taxpayer information on the Internet and e-mail
- No state sales tax levied on business on the Internet
- Increased use of electronic funds transfer
- Option to use credit cards for payments
- To correspond and conduct transactions via the Internet
- Accelerated phase out of single business tax

The leading needs to the tax preparers were:

- Ability to use credit and debit cards
- Ability to automate tax returns: Software should gather data that Treasury already has to help complete the form.
- E-mail notifications to customers and tax preparers
- Bank notification when direct deposit refund hits bank account
- More self service for preparers and customers

continues

- More e-mail and less paper
- One-stop shopping (Treasury Accenture, 2005)

Treasury and Accenture distilled these many stakeholder concerns into three basic objectives:

- Competence: Receiving accurate account and tax information
- Fairness in the administration of taxes and dealings with the department
- Respectful interactions

While Treasury was taking steps to enhance its information technology profile, many gaps remained. In a 2002–2003 performance audit, the Michigan auditor general found that:

1. The department's general controls over access to its mainframe information systems were not effective.
2. The department had not established effective organizational controls to support its critical information systems.
3. The department had not controlled access to its critical production system account. Access to the production system account can be used to gain unauthorized access to critical department information resources.
4. The department had not established effective access controls to its mainframe information system files.
5. The department had not established effective access controls to its production tax and other information systems.
6. The department had not established effective program and data change controls (Michigan Auditor General, 2003).

Tax Administration Elsewhere

States are examining the nature of the interaction of tax policy, administration, and technology (NCSL, 2005). Many of the issues faced by the Michigan Department of Treasury are being faced by other tax administration agencies, the private sector, and individuals. Light (2001) identified the following technology-oriented goals for tax administrators and tax preparers:

- Learn to adapt and transform themselves not once but constantly—at Internet speed.
- Become as flexible as the economy and people they serve.
- Make a commitment to creating complete transparency and providing more information formatted to customer needs—available quickly by phone, fax, or the Internet; communicated in plain English; and offered proactively rather than defensively.
- Guard the privacy of each customer's data from selected entities.
- Provide enterprise-wide data and services through accessible portals designed to meet customer needs.
- Work with other government agencies at all levels to provide one-stop shopping for all government services while safeguarding citizens' privacy.

The pressure for tax administration agencies like the Michigan Department of Treasury to develop sophisticated networking and data-transfer capability was driven largely by the development of advanced personal computers and the commercialization of the Internet. In the early to mid 1990s, the World Wide Web was becoming a primary business, industry, and governmental communications tool. At the same time, personal computer speed, memory, storage capacity, and communications capability was developing rapidly. High-speed modems, ISDN lines, and cable modems (a few years later) were becoming standard business tools.

In 1995, tax administration agencies were being encouraged to take advantage of modern networking technology. Electronic Data Interchange, a method used by companies for routine business transactions, such as ordering and invoicing, had been in place for over a decade (Levitan, Srinivasan, & Walter, 1995). EDI, deployed over wide area and IP networks, was seen as a tool with which tax administrators could communicate with customers. Clearly, tax administration agencies have been able to enhance customer service, compliance, and overall administration (Sorid, 2005) by using these new technologies. Finally, the emerging and widespread taxation of goods and services via the Internet is fundamentally changing tax administration, not just in the United States, but internationally as well (Nesbary & Garcia, 2005).

Adoption of these tools has led to some successes. In an examination of the Maryland Central Collection Unit, Randall (2002) found that the agency experienced an acceleration of revenue recovery directly correlated with the power of its collection system. The Maryland system, installed in 1988, saw increases in the collection of unrecoverable taxes of up to 34% annually. Moreover, today every state, including Michigan, allows for some level of electronic filing of individual income taxes (Federation of Tax Administrators, 2005). Clearly, "electronic tax administration no longer simply means filing tax returns" (Brand & Roberts, 2000).

How Did Treasury Respond to These Challenges?

Essentially, Treasury moved from a legacy system, which managed individual taxes separately, to a comprehensive integrated tax management system. These changes were made to the organization itself (modified organization chart and reporting responsibilities) and the acquisition of new technologies. In conjunction with Accenture, Treasury identified a three-year time frame during which the systems would be implemented. During this period, a wide variety of new technologies were made available to Treasury customers:

- Web-based customer self-help
- Web-based tax returns
- E-mail-based tax returns
- Integrated voice and data services
- Expanded interactive voice response system

The technology solutions were matched by administrative and management improvements, including the conversion from the "silo" model of tax administration (organizing staff by tax type) to a customer serviced based model.

Finally, Treasury implemented a customer service improvement project, designed to:

- Become the best tax customer service agency in the country.
- Institute continuous improvement as a work style.
- Become a central source of information on all tax customer service.

continues

- Celebrate excellence.
- Communicate regular updates, planning meetings, and ongoing learning.

External Views

The Michigan Department of Treasury reports some progress with respect to both customer satisfaction levels and tax-collection rates. While there is still progress to be made, the department appears to be well on the way to providing a comprehensive and secure transfer to a technology-based tax administration system.

Bill Bowerman, chief analyst and Department of Treasury analyst with the Michigan Senate Fiscal Agency since 1979, sees some progress and some challenges remaining for the department. Among the direct benefits to taxpayers that Bowerman sees are online filing and incentives offered by Treasury to tax preparers to file electronically via the Internet. He does, however, see electronic filing as a double-edged sword:

> I don't think that taxpayers should be required to pay to file electronically. As a taxpayer and an analyst, I don't see the time savings as being worth it (B. Bowerman, personal communication, May 25, 2005).

The Michigan auditor general conducted a follow-up to its 2003 audit to determine whether the Department of Treasury and the Department of Information Technology have taken appropriate corrective measures in response to the six material findings and six related recommendations found by the Michigan Auditor General (2005, p. 2). In his transmittal letter to the department, Michigan Auditor General Thomas H. McTavish reported that of the five recommendations related to the Department of Information Technology, it has complied with four recommendations and has partially complied with the fifth recommendation (dealing with control over access to mainframe information).

Future Considerations

The Michigan Department of Treasury is facing many of the same problems and issues faced by governmental agencies at all levels. Individuals, corporations, and government agencies are now often well schooled in advanced computer technology. They purchase goods and services via the Internet, pay taxes electronically, and have the ability via off-the-shelf software to file tax returns electronically. They rightly expect that their government tax administrators should be equally as advanced. The Michigan Department of Treasury is addressing all of these issues. All tax administration offices must be prepared to address these issues as well. Offices need to:

- Maintain a public web portal, available to taxpayers and the general public, capable of responding to a wide array of issues and capable of providing relevant information and self service capacity to these groups.
- Maintain a private web portal, available to internal governmental stakeholders (governmental agencies, legislative committees and staff, statute auditors, external governmental agencies) capable of responding to their needs, including self-service capacity.
- Ensure that online data transactions are equally as accurate as paper and earlier electronic reporting tools.
- Provide electronic or paper self notification capacity.
- Provide high levels of security to all data stored and all electronic communications tools, including web servers and taxpayer files.

References

Brand, P., & Roberts, L. (2000). E-commerce and tax administration. *The Tax Adviser, 31*(n5), 336–339.

Levitan, A., Srinivasan, S., & Walter, R. M. (1995). Tax filing and electronic data interchange. *The CPA Journal, 65,* 72–73.

Light, J. (2001). Bringing tax compliance into the information age. *The CPA Journal, 71*(v6), 10–11.

Michigan Department of Treasury: Customer Service Improvement Project. A joint project between the Michigan Department of Treasury and Accenture Corporation, February, 2005.

Michigan Department of Treasury Mission Statement. Retrieved May 11, 2005, from http://www. michigan.gov/treasury/0,1607,7-121-1755_2294—,00.html.

Michigan Department of Treasury: Constitutional and statutory responsibilities, Retrieved April 15, 2005, from http://www.michigan.gov/treasury/0,1607,7-121-1755-6311—,00.html.

Michigan Office of the Auditor General. (2003). Performance audit, automated information systems, Department of Treasury (Report Number 27-590-01). Lansing, MI: Author.

Michigan Office of the Auditor General. (2005). Performance audit, automated information systems, Department of Treasury, follow-up report (Report Number 27-590-01f). Lansing, MI: Author.

National Conference of State Legislatures. (2005). State Tax Study Commissions. Retrieved May 30, 2005, from http://www.ncsl. org/programs/fiscal/taxcomms.htm.

Nesbary, D., & Garcia, L. (2005). Internet tax policy: An international perspective. In G. D. Garson (ed.) *Handbook of public information systems* (2nd ed.). London Taylor and Francis Group.

Randall, B. (2002). Past due: Technology for revenue collection. *Government Finance Review, 18*(5), 43–45.

Sorid, D. (2005). Killer technology XBRL codifies gobbledygook. *The Courier Mail* (Queensland, Australia), Finance sec. p. 29.

Federation of Tax Administrators website. State Electronic Filing Programs for Individual Income Tax. Retrieved April 2, 2005, from http://www.taxadmin.org/fta/edi/PIT_snaps.html.

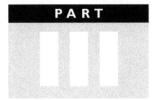

Management

The E-Government
Business Model

In the private sector a business model is the core strategy of a firm. It answers the question, "Why are we in business, and what is the overall design of our business?" The business model does not detail strategy. It is not the same as the firm's strategic plan. (Strategic planning is discussed in Chapter 11.) Rather, the business model sets forth the transactional architecture of the firm. It describes the basic process flow of the enterprise. The business model describes the business opportunity the firm is seeking to exploit, how the firm will interact with other organizations in the marketplace, and how it will enter into and process transactions. The transactional part of the business model shows how the firm provides value to consumers, how that value is delivered, and what the revenue stream will be that supports the enterprise. It includes a description of the business, its marketing, competition, operating procedures, personnel, business insurance, and financial data. Financial data in turn include loan applications, a capital equipment list, a balance sheet, breakeven analysis, income projections, and cash flow projections (SBA, 2001).

The public sector often tries to emulate the success of private-sector practices. Seeking to implement the concept of the business model is no exception. The great success of the American economy in the 1990s added compelling arguments to those who felt that what business models and e-commerce did for the private sector in the 1990s, business models and e-government could do for the public sector in the current decade. In requiring that federal agencies submit business plans for information technology (IT) projects, the Office of Management and Budget (OMB) was seeking to go beyond simple cost–benefit analysis. Instead it wanted to ensure that IT planning was guided by an overall vision and architecture that would promote the key business values of environmental scanning for opportunities, process reengineering to exploit opportunities, and creation of consumer-oriented delivery systems.

The business values and business models that the OMB sought to promote harmonized with certain intellectual trends within the public administration community, notably the "new public administration" (NPA) and the reinvention of government movement. As developed by H. George Frederickson (1980) and others, NPA advocated a citizen-oriented approach (consumer orientation) using decentralization and private-sector partnering and outsourcing to promote creative and innovative approaches to service delivery. NPA also advocated flatter organizational hierarchies, which IT facilitated. During the 1990s, NPA dovetailed with the reinvention movement associated with the National Performance Review of the Clinton–Gore administration, which advocated many of the same reforms, and subsequently with the Bush administration's President's Management Agenda (Fletcher, 2003). However, whereas the vision of the NPA upheld a positive vision of bureaucracy in the service of the public good, the tone of the reinvention movement was negative toward bureaucracy. This difference in vision and tone meant, in practice, that NPA's concept of partnering and contracting out became secondary under reinvention to an emphasis on massive downsizing and outsourcing to an extent that may threaten the capacity of agencies to effectively oversee and control their own business plans.

E-COMMERCE MODELS VS. E-GOVERNMENT MODELS

Because the vision of e-government takes inspiration from the private-sector practice of constructing business plans and from the e-commerce model of some of these plans, it is worth looking at what such plans and models are.

For instance, what is the business plan of the McDonald's fast food restaurant empire? In a nutshell, it is to meet the consumer demand for quick meals at convenient locations, featuring popular foods at low prices. The consumer may expect a stable, repeatable experience regardless of location, delivered in a branded, colorful circus-themed atmosphere through efficient, state-of-the-art performance methods. The vision is to maximize revenue under the slogan, "Convenience, Value, Execution."

Amazon.com provides an example of an e-commerce model. The model is to meet consumer demand for books, music, videos, and other products by offering consumers an extremely wide range of choices (greater than brick-and-mortar establishments). These choices are available online conveniently 24 hours a day, seven days a week. Online payments require consumers only to have to enter credit and shipping information one time to establish an account. Purchasing is made convenient through this one-time entry and through use of a shopping cart meta-phor already familiar to consumers.

In 2000, the General Services Administration (GSA) and *Government Computer News* hosted a government/industry Partners for Progress Executive Roundtable to explore strategies to leverage technology innovation. The GSA coordinator was Joan Steyaert, Deputy Associate Director, Office of Information Technology. Steyaert's (2002) roundtable report started from the observation that "Since 1990, the United States has reaped extraordinary economic growth from technology" based on such computer-enabled methodologies as just-in-time (JIT) manufacturing combined with direct-to-consumer sales, as with the Dell Computer model (pp. 2–3). The e-commerce business model "minimizes risk by pursuing only those technologies clearly demanded by its customers" (p. 3). E-commerce success stories have used a market-driven, results-oriented team approach uniting "employees with suppliers and partners globally" (p. 4). Most of all, the e-commerce model was willing to take and manage risks. For e-government to develop along e-commerce lines, Steyaert summarized, it would be necessary to support risk-taking investments using a portfolio approach to IT acquisitions and create standardized, enterprise-wide software applications (both discussed in Chapter 11), in addition to replacing paper processes with digital ones.

The vision by Steyaert and others of the e-government business model is of a public administration that is customer oriented, working in partnership with the private sector to deliver paperless JIT services using standardized hardware and software developed as part of a portfolio approach to IT investment, allowing greater risk-taking and greater payoffs. The hope is that e-government will do for the public sector what technology and e-commerce did for the private sector in the 1990s.

The Steyaert report, while typical of the thinking behind attempts to develop e-government business cases, raised as many questions as it answered. Were the economic good times of the 1990s due to technology and e-commerce? While it is true that the 1990s economy coincided with large investments in technology, economists are far from agreeing that these economic good times were the result of IT. Massive borrowing, Reagan or Clinton economic policies, the reorganization of the economy primarily to serve shareholders, the tripling of the balance of payments deficit, international trade considerations, and many other factors also played a role in this period of prosperity. Though technology is also among the growth factors, there is no simple IT investment equals prosperity equation. Government cannot blithely assume that IT investment "will do for government in the 2000s what it did for the private sector in the 1990s."

Equally, one may ask if JIT production will really provide a widely used model for public agencies? JIT inputs and outputs have less applicability in governmental organizations. Public agency budgets are often concentrated in personnel (public universities, for instance, may have over 90% of their budget in personnel lines), which makes agencies not very amenable to JIT procedures. The single largest agency, the Department of Defense, is illustrative of a range of agencies that must have prepositioned resources not delivered on demand. Another huge governmental component, the federal-state-local roads agencies, does not fit well with the notion of a "customer" appearing to "buy" a service that the agency then goes out and orders "just in time" and "delivers" to the customer. JIT methods can be a cost-saving aspect of e-government in certain circumstances but hardly with the impact JIT has had in the private sector.

How are public agencies to measure consumer demand in such areas as law enforcement, environmental protection, or homeland security? What is *customer satisfaction* in the public sector (taxpayers for the Internal Revenue Service (IRS)? patients for the Food and Drug Administration? soldiers for the Army?)? Would it really help matters if chief information officers in government were rated in terms of consumer satisfaction, at least where "customers" can be identified, such as by vacationers in state and national parks? Or should park administrators be guided less by the demands for more all terrain vehicle paths and more permissiveness about boomboxes, and guided more by environmental experts and their own professional training? When demand is low, should public agencies use market information to drop "slow movers" such as rural post offices? Up to now, the answer has been no. E-government can facilitate consumer feedback (though thus far agencies have been slow about soliciting public evaluation) but whereas customer-orientation in the private sector seeks to increase consumer demand, there is no corresponding simple purpose in the public sector.

Another centerpiece of the e-government business model, standardization of hardware and software, is a complex area in which the pendulum has swung back and forth several times. Economies of scale can be gained by standardization of hardware and software. On the other hand, interoperability requires less standardization of data formats and platforms than was the case 10 years ago. Also, past efforts at government-sanctioned standardization have frequently left agencies straightjacketed with outdated requirements and have prevented them from participating in the march of technology. The private-sector push for enterprise-wide software applications in the 1990s was often a record of failure. Currently the plans for a Department of Homeland Security (DHS), uniting dozens of agencies, has led OMB to freeze agency IT investments in anticipation of DHS-wide IT systems and standards. For instance, the Immigration and Naturalization Service (INS) has frozen its new financial system, which it is still running in tandem with its legacy system. Now INS faces the prospect of having to run both of these systems while trying to build toward some new unified DHS system. DHS systems for finance and other objectives not directly related to fighting terrorism may be lower in priority, meaning agencies like INS may be in IT limbo for years (Ryan, 2002). In the long run standardization may save money, but this aspect of the e-government business plan is not a sure thing and can even backfire.

Public-private partnerships are not a panacea either. Firms find it useful to model their products and services in real-world governmental settings so that they can subsequently better market to the public sector. Such seeding is part of a corporate business plan. However, while it should be taken advantage of when possible, such partnerships are problematic when proposed as part of a government business plan because of the conceptual mismatch involved. Partnering for firms is seeding, but it is proposed for e-government as a general strategy for jurisdictions across the board, glossing over the fact that when, say, the 100th law enforcement jurisdiction seeks to partner with a software firm to provide a model of data sharing, that agency is not apt to receive as warm a welcome as the early models so much discussed by e-government proponents. When the 100th jurisdiction comes along (and the United States has over 40,000 jurisdictions in law enforcement alone), "public-private partnership" means not corporate-subsidized projects but rather simply a cozy relationship with a vendor. The 100th jurisdiction would do much better to read the literature not on partnership but rather on effective procurement and contracting, particularly since the evaluations of outsourcing show a very mixed picture.

Portfolio management also involves some cautionary considerations. Portfolio management requires centralization of IT funding, making it more challenging to get agencies to feel they "own" the information processes that are addressed. It involves closer oversight of and performance standards for those lower in the IT chain of command, making it more difficult to maintain morale in an environment where the public sector is already at a personnel disadvantage. And while the portfolio manager can afford to take some risks (have losing projects), it is not clear the same can be said of the individual project managers and agencies saddled with high-risk projects. By definition, portfolio management has the potential to reap large rewards through large projects. Of course, the history of large IT projects in government is not a good one, though investment in e-government infrastructure promises to be one of the success stories. This, however, is not the same as saying that the portfolio management aspect of an e-government business plan will allow reduced budgets for agencies using that infrastructure. Initially at least, it will involve substantial increased costs, not actual dollar savings. Rather, the "savings" come from improved quality and quantity of transactions. This is quite in contrast to private-sector business plans, which are designed to raise actual dollar revenue.

E-government raises countless other questions. Would accountability suffer if agencies "went digital" and abolished paper trails? Would there be political support for monetary incentives and "share in savings" contracts for agencies and vendors who implemented more productive systems using technology? Because of the large number of policy issues, implementing e-commerce in the public sector was one of those areas of general agreement that quickly became embroiled in problems associated with devilish details. While there are aspects of business planning that can be imported into the public sector, Bozeman and Bretschneider (1986) remain correct that private sector and public management information systems operate under different dynamics. Ignoring these differences will undermine rather than enhance the long-range success of e-government.

In general, there are seven e-commerce models. Unfortunately, none of them are directly applicable to the public sector.

Auctions. This is the E-Bay model. The e-commerce firm makes money by charging a percentage of sales made by private parties who want to sell through the firm's online venue. Public agencies cannot set up online auctions to solicit private vendors in competition with E-Bay and other companies engaging in auctions and reverse auctions. This model conceivably could have some applicability as a way for public agencies to dispose of government surplus property more efficiently and profitably, but auctions do not provide a general model for e-government.

Virtual stores. Walmart.com, Sears.com, and thousands of other examples fit this model. The e-commerce firm makes money by selling its own line of products for profit, using an electronic analogy of displays, shopping carts, and checkout counters. While public agencies can and usually do establish websites, sometimes with provision for transactions, there are no profits from sales. In a few cases one may be able to actually raise revenue (perhaps online convenience will lead to more fishing licenses being sold, for instance), but usually this will be associated with increased costs of use (need for more Fish and Wildlife officers, more park maintenance costs). Most agencies can only hope there may be some transaction cost savings from doing agency business online. Others will find they have to offer online *and* brick-and-mortar venues, actually increasing their operating costs.

Online malls. Yahoo! Store is an example of this model. The e-commerce firm provides free customer services (e.g., search, mail, discussion group) to build up traffic, then charges third-party vendors for virtual space to sell their products. Services and sales may be integrated to add further value (when you search for *musk perfume*, perfume vendors who have paid a fee come up at the top of the search hit list). The public sector is prohibited from establishing this model in direct competition with the private sector. One could imagine a Department of Motor Vehicles (DMV) site, for instance, where certain transactions would bring up pitches from car insurance companies that have paid the DMV a fee. In reality, this is not done because in spite of all the talk of "partnering" in e-government, there is little public or political tolerance for the commercialization (as opposed to outsourcing) of public websites.

Sponsored advertising. A closely related model, used by AOL Online, Geocities, and many others, is simply selling advertising space on any high traffic web page. Some public sector precedents exist for this, such as advertising on city buses or, more controversially, commercial in-school advertising via Channel One, but governmental jurisdictions have not indulged in this potential revenue model. Again, as with "separation of church and state," there is a political culture supporting "separation of advertising and state."

Online brokerage. A fifth e-commerce model focuses on providing a forum where online sellers and online buyers may find one another, not as in a store or mall, but as in a place where negotiation can take place. An example is the online dynamic pricing system operated at http://www.ewinwin.com. The concept here is that the e-commerce firm sets up *deal rooms* where, under restricted access, buyers and sellers may negotiate (for example, buyers may get a lower price while the seller may negotiate a single shipment date). In the public sector, the concept of one set of "customers" (citizens) getting a different "deal" (government services) compared to another set is anathema to government as a universal and unbiased provider of services.

Information sales. There are any number of information-based corporations that sell access to their information online, ranging from the *New York Times* to the Gallup Poll organization to stock market analysis firms. This e-commerce model is one of the most compatible with the public sector, where many agencies amass a great deal of valuable information—weather data, geographic data, motor vehicle data, data on convicted felons, economic trend data, even digitized cultural images and sounds in the Smithsonian. In general, however, public sector agencies are either limited to a basic cost-recovery fee structure or prohibited from charging fees at all. Public domain law in the United States means that private data companies can appropriate expensive-to-amass public data (e.g., the TIGER line files that digitized all roads in the United States, at an expense of millions of dollars), provide added value (e.g., add roads in new housing developments), and resell the data to the public as if it were wholly their own product, while the originating agency (here, the U.S.

Census Bureau) can only recoup physical distribution costs, not development costs, let alone make a profit. Similarly, freedom of information laws and the tradition of right of access to government data mean that only in specialized circumstances can public agencies sell the information they collect. In most cases it remains public domain and freely available to all, and deviations from this would bring public outcry.

Direct sales. Finally, Dell Computers illustrates the direct sales e-commerce model. This is similar to the virtual stores model, but the concept is to eliminate middlemen altogether. Whereas the Sears virtual store is not intended to eliminate physical Sears stores, the Dell Computer model is to have no stores, but to sell computers directly to the end user. This cuts layers of costs and allows JIT production and inventory systems. While in the public sector there are some hopes that online direct transactions with citizens will eliminate the need for having quite as many brick-and-mortar agency locations, these hopes remain largely unfulfilled for a variety of reasons, including the obligation to provide services not deliverable via the web, the political drive to provide physical service presence in communities, and the fact that the digital divide means whole classes of citizens lack effective computer access in the first place.

In summary, it is tempting to talk about how e-commerce revolutionized business in the 1990s, bringing about a new economy, and to think that similarly, e-government might revolutionize the public sector in this decade, bringing about a new public administration. A closer inspection of the e-commerce models of the 1990s can have a sobering impact on such projections.[1]

In the private sector, business plans have a purpose: to convince investors that the firm has a vision of how to be profitable. Secondarily, they help the entrepreneur to think through what he or she is proposing to do. Because convincing investors is a central purpose, private-sector business plans often start with an upbeat review of profit history combined with evidence that the market is expanding or can be tapped in new ways. To gain trust, the plan emphasizes the experience and credibility of the management team. The plan includes a market analysis of leading competitors and outlines ways the firm can be differentiated from them, describing some competitive advantage that the firm enjoys (e.g., patents, special relations with suppliers, unique distribution channels). Empirical research is used to back up projections of consumer demand. There is always an advertising and market component to the business plan. There is a financial plan with sales forecasts, cash flow projections, and a forecast of relevant business ratios as growth occurs. Finally, a complete business plan outlines an exit strategy under which the investor can get out profitably after a few years, such as after a stock offering or merger that pushes up ownership values.

The nature of business planning in the public sector is quite different and any attempt to emulate it directly may fail. This is illustrated by the e-stamps program of the United States Postal Service (USPS). A Government Accountability Office (GAO) analysis of 2001 e-commerce efforts at the USPS found that whereas the USPS business plan projected $104 million in revenue, actual revenue was $1 million (Miller, 2002c). It found the Postal Service lost $10.4 million running its online payment services. E-Stamps Corporation, the first contractor, chose to sell its assets in 2001 after a disappointing sales record. A major problem was that most postal clients never became aware the USPS provided electronic bill payment, Internet fax services, certified e-mail, and online greeting cards, or never came to feel the e-stamp solution was a user-friendly, convenient way to buy postal services. The commission recommended the Postal Service get out of e-commerce, leaving it to commercial vendors (Miller, 2003s). With Microsoft incorporating e-postmark access into Office 2003 and XP, the USPS then hoped the hitherto little used e-stamp program would take off (Jackson, 2003e). However, though it is possible to print labels with postage on one's computer by using the Click-n-Ship feature of www.usps.com, it is instructive to note that the most recent USPS annual report at this writing (2004) chose not to highlight e-stamps as part of the transformational strategy outlining future development. While the e-stamp program may yet get back on track, the experience suggests that public-sector managers cannot expect the results of private-sector e-commerce models to be panaceas or even necessarily successful at all.

A different more successful e-government model, but one that raises policy questions, was the 2002 IRS offer that provided electronic tax filing services free to over half of American taxpayers. This deal represented a partnering with the nation's nine largest tax preparation firms, who agreed to offer the service to Americans making $25,000 per year or less in return for the federal government agreeing not to provide online tax preparation services. The Computer and Communications Industry Association (CCIA) touted the deal as a "huge victory" for business, consistent with the CCIA's push to stop government agencies from "sliding into e-commerce" (Matthews, 2002). That is, ironically, IRS partnering with the tax preparation industry was not so much a public-sector model of e-commerce as it was the opposite: using the threat of developing an e-commerce model to secure free private sector services in return for a pledge *not* to go the e-commerce route as the USPS had attempted to do.

To provide a different, more generalizable positive example, some of the greatest successes of the e-government model have occurred in agencies that have been able to reduce enormous printing and/or postage costs by making information available online. Between 1994 and 1996, the GAO put up its reports for free online, resulting in increased use of GAO reports accompanied by a one-third reduction in hard copy prints. Printing the *Commerce Business Daily* online through CBDNet reduced costs for business for notices from $18 to only $5 and saved an estimated $1.5 million per year in printing and distribution costs. The IRS, which began putting its forms and instructions online in the mid-1990s, estimated paper product savings of about $3 million per year. Digital recordkeeping and electronic access is one aspect of a business plan that GAO studies do show can reap substantial savings in the public sector (Schwartz, 2000). For paper- and postage-intensive agencies, e-government business plans often can present a sound self-funding strategy.

E-GOVERNMENT BUSINESS PLANNING TODAY

Congress has not been persuaded by e-government business plans. Between FY 2002, when the Bush administration called for $100 million for e-government over three years, and FY 2005 (that is, over four fiscal years), Congress has appropriated only $16 million dollars. In FY 2005, the Bush administration requested $5 million in directly appropriated funds, as well as authority to use $40 million in GSA federal agency fees. Congress chose to appropriate $3 million in direct funds and zero in GSA fees (Perera, 2004), less than the $4 million/year average for the three previous fiscal years. In addition, the House approved appropriations that would have banned the departments of the Interior and Energy and the Forest Service from spending more than $13 million of agency funds on four e-government projects, but this ban was overturned in the final version.

Mark Forman, former OMB head of e-government efforts, has taken the optimistic view that a separate $100 million fund was unnecessary and that e-government should be financed from savings brought about by abolition of the separate computer systems used in each of the various departments of an agency in favor of enterprise federal-wide integrated applications (Perera, 2004). Karen Evans, OMB's head of e-government and IT, has taken a similar upbeat view, holding that lack of e-government funding will help force departments to embrace enterprise applications.

At the departmental level, however, the absence of direct e-government funding and the prevalence of a pass-the-hat approach requiring agencies to find money in their own budgets has meant that agency officials have come to believe that e-government is not high on the Bush administration priority list. Worse, the pass-the-hat approach has given lead agencies for any given e-government effort a disincentive because they bear the burden of development costs—the incentive is not to be a lead agency in

e-government but to follow along afterwards and pick up successful initiatives after they are developed and proven by other agencies.

The OMB's push for IT business plans that buy into federal-wide or at
least multiagency application consolidation as well as meeting other
OMB-mandated standards has meant few departmental efforts have met
the mark. In 2004, Grants.gov was one of only 2 of the 25 Quicksilver lead
federal e-government projects judged by the OMB to have met its goals
(Mosquera, 2004).[2] With the OMB judging most e-government efforts not
to be successful, with OMB leaders saying that excess e-government
funding could remove department incentives for multiagency or federal-
wide applications consolidation (thought to be a major cost saver, unlike
most e-government efforts), and with the OMB seeking a separate innovation fund to pay for its lines-of-business consolidation projects (Miller,
2004k), little wonder that Congress did not rush to fund e-government,
particularly when massive IT spending for security became the number
one priority after the terrorist attack of September 11, 2001, thus displacing other priorities.

A GAO report in 2002 studied the business cases used to support the
Quicksilver initiatives that formed the centerpiece of Bush administration/
OMB e-government strategy (GAO, 2002a). The GAO found that the business cases had done little in the way of being based on citizen surveys or
other "customer orientation." "Fewer than half addressed collaboration
and customer focus, despite the importance of these topics to OMB's
e-government strategy and the President's stated goal: to 'champion citizen-
centered electronic government that will result in a major improvement
in the federal government's value to the citizen'" (p. 1). In the Quicksilver
business cases, the GAO found only 10 of 23 project cases linked to
strategic objectives, only 9 of 23 were linked to customer needs, and only
8 of 23 were linked to a collaboration strategy with other governmental
and nongovernmental agencies. Also, only 9 of the 23 projects developed
a funding strategy. That is, the clear implication of the 2002 GAO report
was that the Bush administration's e-government business cases did not
follow usual best practices for business plans and most, in fact, lacked
any market study of consumer need and demand.

The cause of e-government was not helped either when Rep. Adam
Putnam (R-FL) left the Committee on Government Reform in 2004 to
move to the more powerful House Rules Committee. David McClure,
vice president for e-government at the Council for Excellence in
Government, expressed concern that Putnam's replacement would not
be as intensely focused on IT issues. Putnam had held over 30 hearings
on IT subjects such as cybersecurity, enterprise architectures, and the
Quicksilver e-government initiatives. Often Putnam was the only law-
maker attending the hearings (Miller, 2004l). The January 2005 news

release reappointing Tom Davis as chair of the Committee on Government Reform stated "Davis plans to continue to focus the committee's vast oversight agenda on waste, fraud, abuse, and mismanagement in the federal government" (Committee on Government Reform, 2005). No mention was made of e-government, nor was this topic featured on the committee's website as of spring 2005.

Tom Davis (R, VA), chair of the House Committee on Government Reform (which oversees the procurement and use of IT), stated, "There is no political constituency pushing appropriators to allocate money (for e-government). They see no political benefit for putting money into e-gov and taking it from projects that they see as hometown accolades or campaign contributions" (*Government Computer News,* 2004).

At this writing, the FY 2006 budget is being drawn up with the OMB reviewing agency business cases for IT initiatives (Miller, 2004m). At the federal level, forecasts are for IT spending to increase at an annual rate of 5.3%. However, this is not because of the e-government vision but rather from a variety of other forces: increased costs of outsourcing IT, homeland security spending, the increased role of IT in the Department of Defense, and the OMB's drive for consolidated business platforms and enterprise applications (Kash, 2005). At the state and local level, IT spending for FY 2006 was increasing because of a growing demand for outsourced technical services driven by initiatives not for e-government but for advanced interoperable communications systems for coordinating law enforcement, border security, and homeland security (Welsh, 2005a).

SUMMARY

E-government business plans are intended to provide a framework for strategic planning, promoting the alignment of the agency's IT plans with its overall mission and encouraging clarification of roles and responsibilities for achieving desired results. Such results typically are to improve the availability, cost, and quality of public services, and to implement common IT standards in the hope of additional cost savings. As a form of results-oriented management, such public-sector business plans are intended to promote accountability at the individual and organizational levels.

While numerous business plan templates exist,[3] reliance on cookie-cutter templates may make for bland documents that fail to mobilize the agency internally or win support externally. Any number of pitfalls exist for the agency preparing such a plan. Common pitfalls include:

- Failure to tie the plan to the agency mission—The agency's business plan provides extensive justification for an IT project in technical or even economic terms, but fails to address how the project will help the agency achieve goals reflected in the agency's mission statement.
- Failure to differentiate the business plan from the agency budget—The budget document should reflect the plan, but the plan is not the budget. Rather, the business plan is based on an analysis of the needs of its clientele (customer orientation) and of forces in the environment (environmental scanning) such as market conditions and actions of related agencies (competitors).
- Failure to take risks—The purpose of portfolio management is to encourage agency risk taking. At the federal level, thinking too small is as bad as overreaching. The goal of the business plan is to manage risk in pursuit of substantial gains in agency effectiveness and efficiency.
- Poor risk management—Agencies should have explicit risk management procedures in place, and these should be reflected in business plans. Poor risk management may be evidenced by overly rigid plans that make no provision for deviation from plan assumptions, lack of attention to security risks, and by failure to analyze risk at all.
- Failure to research best practices—The business plan should show that the agency is aware of practices and standards in the field, the advice of experts, and best practices of lead agencies and jurisdictions.
- Inadequate human resource planning—A good business plan assigns key responsibilities to specific individuals and demonstrates that each is well qualified to inspire confidence that the IT project will be completed successfully.
- Inadequate reward structure—The plan should be designed so that all stakeholders are motivated to do their part on a continuing basis. In the private sector, incentive bonuses for managers and project teams as well as incentive clauses in vendor contracts are common. While the public sector is constrained in this regard, the plan should reward successful agencies and integrate a variety of incentives (bigger agency budgets, better equipment, training and development opportunities, professional recognition, increased discretion, etc.).
- Inadequate performance monitoring and evaluation—A good business plan sets forth performance measures as part of a feedback and evaluation plan that ensures the project has the ability for self-correction as unexpected or disappointing developments occur. These performance measures address the three success criteria of being on time, on budget, and with the desired functionality.

In summary, a good business plan is a strategic document that motivates employees and obtains external support for planning, measuring, and improving the effectiveness and efficiency of the agency.

Even when all pitfalls are avoided, however, public-sector business plans and models today face two major problems: (1) leading e-commerce business models have only limited applicability in the public sector, and (2) for a variety of reasons discussed above, the climate of political support for e-government has never materialized in the way envisioned and anticipated when such models were set forth in the mid-1990s. In fact, in many ways support has deteriorated. These dual difficulties mean that issues of partnering with the private sector (discussed next, in Chapter 10) and sound strategic planning (discussed in Chapter 11) are all the more critical to any effort to advance public-sector information systems.

DISCUSSION QUESTIONS

1. What is the main purpose of a business plan in the private sector? How is this similar to and different from a public-sector business plan?
2. The OMB's requirement that federal agencies submit business plans for IT projects was an effort to ensure that decisions were guided by an overall vision and architecture that would support key business values. What advantages and/or pitfalls do you see to this strategy?
3. Under what circumstances might just-in-time methods apply to the public sector?
4. What factors other than IT investment might account for the economic prosperity of the 1990s, according to economists?
5. What are the pros and cons of government-sanctioned standardization of software across agencies?
6. When are public-private partnerships most appropriate? Least?
7. Identify three reasons why e-business models might not work well at a broad level within the public sector.
8. Which e-business models have the most promise within the public sector?
9. How has the funding experience of e-government projects changed recently? What implications does this have for the future of e-government?
10. What is the risk of relying on cookie-cutter business plan templates? Even when good business models are employed, what challenges face the public sector?

GLOSSARY

Breakeven analysis: The calculation of fixed costs divided by revenue per unit minus variable costs per unit, with the result used to estimate the sales volume at which an organization starts making a profit.

Business model: A description of how an enterprise will operate, including service (or product) development, marketing, and revenues and expenses. A business model provides an overview of why the enterprise will be cost effective.

Business process: The set of activities that are designed to produce a specific output for a particular customer or market.

Cost–benefit analysis: A systematic comparison of the costs and benefits of a new system, often with a view to making an information technology investment decision or as part of program evaluation.

Enterprise resource planning: The creation of integrated information systems designed to tie together previously independent systems for human resources, budgeting, inventory, and other functions, including linkage to customers and vendors.

Fixed costs: Costs that are incurred even if no services or products are produced during the specified time period.

Portfolio management: Coordinated decision making for the enterprise-wide set of existing and proposed IT investments, as opposed to project-by-project decision making. Portfolio management typically involves a mix of higher-risk, higher-payoff projects and lower-risk, lower-payoff projects.

Quicksilver initiatives: A label given to two dozen e-government projects given high priority by the George W. Bush administration as part of the President's Management Initiative announced in 2001.

Strategic plan: A document that describes long-term goals of the organization and outlines how resources will be allocated toward fulfillment of those goals.

Variable costs: Costs that increase as the number of service events or products increases, usually but not exclusively due to the consumption of materials and/or labor time.

ENDNOTES

[1]The literature on public-sector business planning is relatively sparse, though there are a few resources available to guide the practitioner (Bean & Hussey, 1997; CIPFA, 2001).

[2]Grants.gov supports unified online application for $360 billion in annual federal grants dispensed by 900 programs, representing about 60% of all federal grantor agencies. In the first 12 months, grants.gov has grown to over 5 million views per month, received 1200 electronic grant applications, enrolled 3000 grant-seeking organizations to apply online, posted 1400 grant opportunity notices, and e-mailed 600,000 grant opportunity notices to interested parties weekly.

[3]For example, http://www.projectmanagement.tas.gov.au/pm_templates/pm 004_businessplanv1.0.htm. See also http://smallbusinessschool.org/webapp/ sbs/sbs/indexie.jsp?Size=1024&Speed=250&page=http%3A//smallbusiness school.org/webapp/sbs/Basics/hubp.jsp. One may also enter "government" OR "public sector" "business plan'" into a web search engine.

CASE STUDY
Digital Buildings: Transforming the Permitting Business Process

by Jennifer Kurtz, Purdue University

"Change is debilitating when done to us, but exhilarating when done by us."
—Rosabeth Moss Kanter, in World Class

Faced with the most severe of change management prospects—loss of mission—Indiana's Department of Fire and Building Services (DFBS) embarked on a remediation effort that has resulted in national recognition and institutional adoption of a "better living through e-processes" philosophy. Other returns on the 18-month investment of time are enhanced document version control, reduced costs for the agency and its constituents, increased staff productivity and morale, and improved revenue stream (permitting fee collection) for the state.

Indiana's DFBS reviews plans for all Class One public building projects in Indiana. When the review is complete, the state issues a Construction Design Release that allows local building departments to issue the appropriate building permits.

Government permitting processes tend to follow a black box model, with fixed roles and rules. Adherence to the form-laden procedural formula ultimately delivers the desired result: permit approval. In 1999, however, the Indiana building permitting process had slowed to the point that project documents were "filed" in grocery carts awaiting "check-out" for up to three months. Given Indiana's weather, excessive delays resulted in canceled projects. The Associated Builders and Contractors of Indiana trade group deplored the slow response time, and the Indiana General Assembly threatened with its own ultimatum: fix the broken process or lose the permitting franchise to local agencies. In addition to eliminating high-level oversight of construction standards across the state, this would have also eliminated an important source of revenue to the State Treasury ($3.5 million in 2000).

By teaming with its permitting stakeholder community, DFBS proved the viability of an alternative grassroots model for transforming government through technology. In this model, the commission management team allowed citizen scrutiny of the entire process and encouraged challenges to legacy standard operating procedures. Superfluous intermediate steps were eliminated. Advantage was taken of legislative changes that sanctioned the use of electronic signatures and corporate seals. The permit review process now takes 10 to 15 days.

The Paper Chase

When first identified as a problem, the DFBS processed about 8,000 projects annually. Each unique project requires multiple review feedback loops to accommodate architect/developer-originated design changes and Commission-directed revisions. Indiana does not count applications superceded by others in its weekly count. This means that one release can be associated with as many six different permits. The paperwork, including original and changed plans, can create files up to 150 pages long. The iterative and paper-driven process resulted in a chain of issues that affected document management and citizen service.

Document Mismanagement

A 12.5% increase in application filings during the 1999 construction boom and the coincidental resignation of four review staff members (from a roster of 14) aggravated inefficient file storage and retrieval problems. Files were assigned to grocery carts—literally. The all-paper system and poor project/document tracking system in place made it necessary for staff to find the actual paper files to determine filing status and respond to customer calls. Overworked staff misplaced and lost plans and fees that had been hand-carried or mailed. Manual input of formulaic information submitted on state forms introduced errors that complicated the resolution of customer inquiries. And, of course, increased processing delays led to even more customer complaints and inquiries, as staff attention was diverted to reactive tasks and away from processing through the application backlog. Employee morale suffered.

Citizen Disservice

The paper-based permitting process required construction and/or architectural firms to submit plans via postal or other package delivery service, or in-person by appearing at the DFBS in downtown Indianapolis. The mailing process itself added days and cost (especially given the number and size of construction plan documents) to the permitting process. To eliminate the time delay, submitters often sent staff to DFBS. Although not onerous to those within easy driving distance, firms could spend hundreds of dollars in lost staff productivity or in actual costs, if traveling from outlying areas of the state—or from out of state.

Perhaps less apparent than the business disservice to those who experienced delays in permit review was the financial disservice to Indiana citizens in general. The DFBS used expensive, pre-manufactured multi-carbon-copy State forms that could not be forwarded, completed, or stored electronically. In addition to printing costs, use of these forms incurred postal fees for the agency and its customers. DFBS staff mailed copies of the forms and plans to the submitters so that they could then take them to the appropriate local government entity for further processing—or back to the drawing board for revision prior to resubmission.

Each DFBS reviewer now processes more permits while enjoying more productive communication with applicants. As a consequence, higher permitting traffic is managed with a 30% reduction in the number of trouble calls and 65% reduction in application turn-around time.

Delays in depositing permit fees slowed revenue to the state and reduced interest accrual. The state receives its filing fees after an application is received, entered in the system, and an acknowledgment sent. In pre-digital days, fees were requested approximately 27 days after submission. These fees are now requested within 9 days.

Transforming the Permitting Business Process

DFBS management assembled a team to examine the process, rather than reassign the individuals involved or apply a quick technical fix. As Bill Franklin, who led the team as a state-trained facilitator, observed, "Processes get messy by trying to put band-aids on broken or inefficient processes." Besides, no funds were available to either augment staff or hire outside consultants.

Albert Einstein observed that, "No problem can be solved from the same consciousness that created it." Understanding that intuitively, Franklin brought together process stakeholders from both inside and outside state government. The effort was all-volunteer and would have foundered without the dedication of individuals from construction and architectural companies. Franklin also attributes some project success to the smaller and smarter structured methodology. Minutes of meetings were recorded and assignments and activities were tracked faithfully.

continues

Over a period of 18 months, the team identified extraneous steps in the review process and also realized that the sheer burden of paperwork needed to be addressed. During the first several months, the team met up to twice a month and established benchmarks to track progress. The groundwork included working within or changing plan review policies and rules. Although an eGovernment solution was not predicted at first, an e-filing system seemed a logical solution: to reduce the cost of mailing, storing and retrieving paper documents; to facilitate plan submissions from around the state and the country; and to streamline the review process. One potential bottleneck was payment method: legislation was introduced to allow DFBS to accept credit cards. Another potential bottleneck was concern from design professionals about protecting their intellectual property. Instructions for affixing an electronic seal and signature to designs and plans were defined and recorded in Indiana Code.

In the pre-digital building era, a DFBS input specialist received plans at the main counter, created a project number, calculated the cost, assigned the plan to a reviewer, and put the plan and project specifications in the reviewer's bin. This assignment process took from 15 to 20 working days. With electronic plan submissions, the reviewer receives the plans within four days or less. The plans include digitized seals to authenticate the submitter's license.

Not having the budget for a custom software system, the team identified off-the-shelf and shareware software that would support key system components. Products used included Adobe Acrobat Reader, Autoview Professional, Winzip compression and Microsoft Outlook, and Word.

Drawing files are accepted in a variety of file formats (DWF, PDF, TIFF) regardless of project size. Applications and other documents are sent as PDF, JPEG, TIFF, or Microsoft Word files. These files, sent as attachments to an e-mail message, are also zipped. By compressing the files, their transmission is made faster and more secure. Once at the agency, no drawing files are printed—only the application and cover page are. Environmental friendliness—less use of paper and ink—is a side benefit!

The low- or no-cost solution for the DFBS was not the only advantage to adopting this open software platform approach. It also increased flexibility for those submitting projects for review. The DFBS identified vendors who could digitize paper drawings for those architectural and building firms that did not use computer-aided design. Those submitting plans saved reams of paper when the DFBS eliminated the need to print out plans—and revisions to plans. In the future, it may be possible for applicants to send files directly from retail establishments that cater to homeowners.

Of course, most dramatically, the e-filing system has cured the project review backlog. The 17-member Commission staff received about 12,000 filings a year in 2003 and had to process 40 to 50 per day to stay current. Two-thirds of those filings were new projects. These require multiple filings, and thus, multiple reviews. In reporting the weekly applications number, however, Indiana does not count those superceded by others. One CDR can thus be associated with as many as six different permits.

User acceptance has been high, and more widespread use has helped the DFBS keep pace with increased workload. The Commission received between 75 to 100 electronic project filings per week in late 2004 or approximately 40% of permit applications. This is an increase of 25 to 67% over the number of electronic filings in early 2003, when approximately 60 filings a week (25%) were received electronically. When first launched, e-filing accounted for only about three submissions a week. Electronic submissions can be processed in three to ten days. Electronic seals are affixed to the filings, in accordance with electronic records legislation passed by the Indiana General Assembly during the 2000 session.

Digital Ease

The new process allows building permit applicants to submit their documentation electronically, on a 24x7 basis, from anywhere in the world. One architect based in Washington State estimated that electronic filing saved him $5,000 in travel costs and time. An in-state architect reduced his overhead costs because he no longer has to "float" the filing fees for his clients. (Formerly, this architect paid the application fee upon submitting the plan for review. Now the architect submits his client's credit card number online.) Priority shipping and copying costs for oversized building costs have been eliminated—a savings for both the agency and its clients. The DFBS has lowered its shipping costs by $100,000 and reduced its use of nonrenewable products: paper and ink (cartridges).

In one tangible economic development benefit, the small (2003 population: 10,607) Indiana community of Plymouth landed a project with Wal-Mart. The latter chose Plymouth over other sites in the United States because of the time- and cost-efficient electronic permitting available in Indiana. Another noteworthy client that has benefited from the e-government process is the Indianapolis Airport Authority, which used electronic filing for its new, almost $1 billion terminal.

The DFBS process transformation has served as a pilot project for other Indiana government jurisdictions. The City of Indianapolis now accepts an affidavit that plans submitted for its review are the same as those submitted to the state. The city now receives approximately one-third of the plans reviewed by the DFBS for the entire state. In the future, it should be possible to integrate the e-government permitting process at all levels, so that permits and approved plans can be forwarded electronically to the next appropriate level of government. A notice of transfer would then be sent electronically to the submitter as an update about the project's review status. The local government agency responsible for approving permits would benefit from:

- Web-based status update option for submitters (limiting the need to field routine inquiries)
- Reduced need to rekey formulaic information manually
- Assurance about integrity of approved plan (only the back page of paper plans is stamped, making it possible for submitters to substitute non-reviewed/unapproved pages)
- Generic application form for all jurisdictions (thus reducing submitter time to complete and clarifying communications between jurisdictions)

Other positive unintended consequences have been realized. Since electronic versions of the building plans are being transmitted to counties for their records, plans can then be linked to local 911 systems, including GPS. This means, for example, that a fire truck can have a copy of a building's layout loaded into a computer console so that crews know immediately where all stairwells, air ducts, and hazardous waste storage can be found.

The DFBS has continued to pursue process improvement for another area of responsibility: safety inspections. The DFBS is responsible for inspecting elevators and amusement park rides, in addition to ambulances, pressure vessels (e.g., hot water tanks), and construction site mobile trailers.

Eighteen inspectors examine approximately 15,000 elevators, 1,200 amusement park rides, and 60,000 pressure vessels around the state annually. The process was paper-intensive, redundant, and inefficient. Multiple carbon copies of reports had to be filed by building or ride owners, county officials, and the DFBS. Hand-written reports by inspectors were re-keyed by clerical staff for electronic records management. Report documentation did not travel with rides. Energized by the successful electronic permitting process, DFBS management explored the use of Radio Frequency Identification (RFID) technology for tracking emergency equipment so that the same information storage concept could be used for amusement rides.

Working with private industry firms from New York (SYSGEN) and Indiana (Northern Apex), the DFBS team developed an approach that is unique in the United States Inspectors equipped with a portable hand-held computer complete forms electronically and rewrite the data to the RFID tag affixed to amusement park rides since May 2002. They also use an infrared connection to print the inspection form to a belt-worn mobile printer for the ride owner. Through a dial-up modem connection, data on the hand-held computer is uploaded to the Commission's mainframe computer and new pertinent data are downloaded to the hand-held. Data integrity is maintained and re-keying tasks are eliminated. As a side benefit, inspectors can access e-mail messages from the field over the handheld devices.

Other states have expressed interest in the system. The public safety benefits are also clear: inspection reports are now affixed to rides and readily available, regardless of geographical location or ownership change. Again, a grass-roots e-government initiative to transform business processes through judicious use of technology has taken root.

Partnering, Outsourcing, Contracting, and Procurement

The rate of information technology (IT) project failure is high, and this is even more so in the public sector compared to the private (this is discussed further in Chapter 13 in the discussion of success and failure factors in implementation). Partnering with vendors, outsourcing IT functions to the private sector, and creating innovative forms of contract management such as performance and share-in-savings contracts with business providers of IT services are all responses to problems of IT failure. However, where panaceas exist in ideology, they do not exist in the pragmatic world of public management. Partnering, outsourcing, and contracting all create substantial problems, risks, and costs of their own, as decades of outrageous cost overruns in the defense sector have repeatedly shown.

To reveal the conclusion of this chapter at the outset, partnering, outsourcing, and contracting are not simple matters of turning IT (or other) governmental functions over to more efficient private-sector businesses. Simple-minded ideological forms of privatization can drive costs up rather than down and can easily undermine democratic accountability. As White and Korosec (2005, p. 429) note, "Contractual partnerships must have the enduring commitment and real involvement of management, as well as constant reinforcement and monitoring, to achieve realistic goals and expectations." More bluntly, partnering, outsourcing, and contracting require substantial investment in the performance-monitoring capabilities of the IT agency—costs that Congress, state legislatures, and other funders do not always wish to pay. When this is combined with the possibility that outsourcing can leave an IT agency with too few human resources to execute its contract oversight duties effectively, failure can ensue, as happened in 2004 when Florida had to cancel its MyFlorida Alliance IT outsourcing arrangements with Accenture and BearingPoint because the state found the program was not meeting public needs.

PARTNERING

Partnering is a very old tradition, going back at least to the Federalists' relationship with the nascent American financial community. Equally as old are criticisms of the mixing of the public and private spheres. On the one hand, Americans believe in free enterprise and think business methods would be superior to bureaucratic controls in the operation of government. When blue ribbon committees are formed to look into solutions for policy problems, the membership ranks are routinely populated by business representatives. On the other hand, Americans also acknowledge that business is run for profit, often short-term profit at the expense of other long-term values, and they know this can be inconsistent with the public interest. Americans want government to partner with the private sector, but they also want accountability in public policy and an avoidance of conflicts of interest.

A federal example of partnering is that between the U.S. Census Bureau and private sector firms for purposes of improving the accuracy of TIGER line files. TIGER files have been the basis for the digitization and mapping of the entire United States. Initiated with the 1990 census, by 2000 it had become apparent that inaccuracies in TIGER were preventing local governments from effectively meshing zoning, road, tax parcel, and other data with TIGER's street centerline map coordinates. The 1990 TIGER files had been accurate only to about 20 meters, far too little for many city spatial planning applications. For the 2000 census, the Census Bureau let out accuracy improvement contracts, seeking 7.6 meter accuracy or better. Geographic information system (GIS) contractors used proprietary software to integrate local and county government corrections to TIGER and also sent agents into the field to take global positioning system readings at road intersections. Contractors also used specialized vans loaded with GIS equipment to drive every road in a county when needed, gathering coordinate data. The bottom line: prior to partnering, Census TIGER data had been three times less accurate compared to after private-sector partners helped improve accuracy (Johnson & Kunz, 2005).

A local counterexample illustrates the advantages of not outsourcing IT. In largely rural Chatham County, North Carolina, only 65% of residents have a chance to access the Internet with a broadband connection, and only a fraction actually do so because many residents are low income and telecom companies charge monthly fees of $40 and up. Those interested in county economic development believed that providing low-cost broadband access would promote business, education, and community development. This is a typical situation that reflects the fact that compared to other countries, wireless broadband access in the United States, under control of private vendors, has provided "expensive and slow service, with limited availability" (Pauly, 2005). Some jurisdictions have sought to develop wireless broadband on a different model involving proactive government, including Carrboro, North Carolina. In a larger example, following a battle with the ComCast telecom company, the City of Philadelphia, is implementing a plan to provide residents with municipally owned wireless broadband for under $20 per month. Critics of outsourcing claim the practice routinely delivers poorer services at higher costs compared to government doing IT itself.

In matters of IT policy, the Industry Advisory Council (IAC) is at the pinnacle of intersector partnering efforts. It is used by the Office of Management and Budget (OMB), the federal chief information officer (CIO) Council, and other federal officials as a broker between government and IT vendors. In principle it operates as described by one IAC member: "Every time we [vendors and federal officials] get together we say there is a firewall" between the government and industry. "We cannot have a relationship that looks untoward" (Dizard, 2004c). Yet the reality is that the firewall breaks down from time to time, as happened in 2004 when Mark Emery, deputy CIO of the Homeland Security Department, endorsed William Errico of Lexmark Federal Systems and Bob Golas of Oracle Corp., in their run for the positions of chairman and vice chairman, respectively, of IAC's Homeland Protection Special Interest Group. While Emery had done nothing illegal, he was violating a tradition of separation of government and industry under which each partnering sector was supposed to be fully independent of the other.

There is a thin line between partnering on the one hand and sweetheart contracts and insider dealings on the other. In 1994, when Oracle was negotiating with the Department of Homeland Security and with the General Services Administration (GSA) officials for a new blanket contract, the governmental endorsement mentioned above was seen by many as a conflict of interest as well a form of governmental favoritism. At the state level, Oracle had been the private sector partner to California's Department of Information Technology, when suspect contracts led the state legislature to abolish the entire department.

Successful partnering is based on many contingencies, some of which are listed here. While not every contingency is a prerequisite to partnering success, the fewer that are present, the more the risk:

- The more the agency has a culture that is open to learning from the private sector, the more the likelihood partnering will work, contingent on the private-sector partner also being open to learning from the public sector and forgoing rigid implementation of business sector practices.
- The success of partnering is contingent on both the agency and the private-sector partner being willing to engage in a process of mutual problem solving and goal seeking.

- The success of partnering is contingent on the partnering agreement covering all aspects of the proposed system, including indirect ones. For example, the Advanced Traveler Information System was successfully created through a public–private partnership, but because the agreement failed to provide for marketing to citizens, it was underutilized (Lawther, 2004).
- Successful partnering is contingent on having an ongoing day-to-day mechanism for feedback, discussion between the parties, and resolution of conflicts.
- The more the partnering contract includes performance penalties as well as rewards for the private-sector partner, the more likely partnering will prove satisfactory, contingent on services rendered being cost-effective and competitive for both sides.
- The long-term success of partnering is contingent on the agency not becoming dependent on the partner, which requires that the agency retain core capacities that make effective contract oversight possible and, in the case of outsourcing, a capability of reentry by the public sector so as to maintain public–private sector competition if appropriate later on.
- The success of partnering is contingent on the private partner having the capacity to handle changes in the scale of services as needed.
- The success of partnering is contingent on accountability of the private-sector partner with regard not only to avoidance of unacceptable levels of profit taking, but also with respect to government requirements pertaining to privacy, security, and transparency.

There are, of course, many similar considerations for the public agency considering partnering as a solution. Many of these have to do with handling change. Does the partnering contract provide adequate notice to each party when the other party institutes changes? Are there provisions for termination of obligations without unreasonable costs to either party should a project prove not worth continuation? Is the partnering arrangement integrated with the agency's strategic planning process, including the setting of goals, objectives, and milestones with accompanying performance measures?

OUTSOURCING

Outsourcing of IT has become a national issue. News magazines and television media have carried headline stories about how IT jobs have been outsourced to India, Ireland, and other foreign countries. Outsourcing of federal jobs, though supported by the Bush administration, has become so controversial that bipartisan support has arisen to oppose it in some instances. In FY 2003, the Omnibus Appropriations bill prohibited the use of funds to impose outsourcing goals, targets, or quotas at federal agencies without thorough analysis. Similarly, the National Defense Authorization Act for FY 2004 placed Department of Defense (DOD) IT under the restrictions of the Buy American Act. The Defending American Jobs Act of 2004 sought to cut federal assistance to companies that fired American workers in the process of transferring jobs abroad but was not passed. In the same year, though, 28 state legislatures considered bills to ban offshore outsourcing in state contracts.

Outsourcing is not a new phenomenon. It raises issues in both the public and private sectors, and in the public sector it is not limited to the federal level. States and counties have outsourced whole IT business areas such as human relations and public welfare, motivated by budgetary constraints, problems arising from retirement of the first generation of IT specialists, and by the ideology of a new wave of business-oriented governors. San Diego County in 1999 signed a 7-year contract to outsource all county IT functions.[1] In 2003, the city of Minneapolis outsourced most city IT functions. In the state of Florida, under Governor Jeb Bush, the brother of President George W. Bush, Florida outsourced 138 programs and services, from food services to human relations (Peterson, 2004b).

San Diego's historic 1999 outsourcing contract with Computer Sciences Corporation (CSC) was judged by county officials to have improved the quality of IT services (better equipment, more integrated software, less downtime, better security), albeit at a higher cost. The San Diego path was bumpy. Initial transfer of public IT employees to a private vendor was protested. The vendor of the integrated tax system went bankrupt, forcing termination of that contract (Hanson, 2005). CSC went over contract by $10 million and 300 employees. Three years into the contract, San Diego had to send a letter to CSC charging it with breach of contract and not meeting numerous service-level agreements. CSC responded that performance standards in the contract needed to be lowered. Eventually, however, the county and CSC renegotiated performance expectations and by 2005, the country expressed limited satisfaction with CSC performance. A county official stated, "We were hoping that the outsourcing providers would bring new skill sets and application capabilities to our deal. But we haven't gotten to where we wanted to get yet" (Welsh, 2005b). At this writing, San Diego is seeking a second multiyear outsourcing contract, though it is not expected that CSC will bid. Gartner Group vice president John Kost noted that where once the San Diego experiment was expected to trigger other large-scale state and local outsourcing projects, in fact few have chosen to follow San Diego's example (Welsh, 2005b). Still, outsourcing is a hot topic in public IT management and many expect further growth of the practice.

Outsourcing, in principle, has several appeals:

- A contractor may be able to provide state-of-the-art technology that an agency could not hope to develop using internal IT resources.
- Outsourcers may be able to provide a technology less expensively, because they use system templates over and over for different clients.
- Agencies may receive hardware and software updates automatically as part of the contract.
- Large outsourcers are in a better position than most agencies to deal flexibly with scalability as it becomes necessary for projects to change in scope.
- Because the private sector can pay more for permanent and specialized or temporary labor, outsourcers may be able to bring superior human resources to bear.
- Agencies may be able to shed the burdens of training, help desks, maintenance, and other support services, enabling them to concentrate on their core missions.
- IT services are provided to the agency on a fixed and predictable budget, with no surprise costs.
- Competition among contractors in theory ensures high quality at the lowest cost.

The National Aeronautics and Space Administration (NASA) has been a showcase agency in terms of using outsourced contract services almost since its inception in 1958. In 1959, the GSA authorized NASA to use the Armed Services Procurement Regulations of 1947, which essentially exempted NASA from using the "low bidder" system to hire contract labor. Free of this impediment, NASA has been able to hire "the best and brightest" at competitive pay rates and has become a poster child for outsourcing in the public sector.

On the other hand, there are an equal or larger number of reasons for thinking that outsourcing might not always be in the public interest:

- Outsourcing of agency jobs can leave agencies with an impaired or even with no ability to oversee contractor performance standards.
- Agencies may lose the capacity to gather baseline performance data and no longer be able to conduct effective contract management.
- Outsourcing of public jobs may be and has been undertaken for conservative ideological reasons without meaningful cost–benefit analysis to ensure that the public interest is served and taxpayers are protected.
- Outsourcing may involve loss of local jobs, with attendant social, political, and labor problems. For the most part, these externalities do not fall on private-sector firms that outsource, but in the public sector, they involve real costs that governments must consider in cost–benefit calculations about outsourcing.

- Outsourcing may lower public agency morale and encourage turnover, which in turn increases costs and reduces quality of IT services.
- Outsourcing increases the possibility of favoritism, not just through outright corruption and kickbacks in contracts and overpricing of goods and services, but also the "revolving door" hiring of government officials by contractors and of vendor personnel by agencies, bringing conflicts of interest.
- Outsourcing is mainly done through large contractors who in turn subcontract to networks of vendors, making accountability difficult.
- Costs of effectively monitoring contracts for performance, privacy, security, and other agency objectives can be high. There is a tendency to underreport these costs, leading to lowered public accountability. (Note that the Chicago law firm of Gordon & Glickson LLC (2005) has published a useful manual on outsourcing contracts, published by the International City Management Association).
- Sometimes legislation forbids privatization (e.g., North Carolina county sheriffs cannot outsource jail functions).
- There is the possibility of expensive litigation with contractors.
- Outsourcing can hurt women and minorities if the public sector is a better equal opportunity employer than are outsourcers—a common situation.

In general, critics of outsourcing charge that the practice sharply reduces accountability and violates democratic principles under which public programs are carried out by agency personnel whose very jobs are directly dependent on officials elected by the people. Under outsourcing, it is said, transparency in government is replaced by corporate secrecy, and the possibility of democratic accountability is compromised. From a corporate viewpoint, outsourcing is mainly profitable when dealing with highly repeatable applications that can be sold across multiple jurisdictions, yet most jurisdictions want and demand customized features, hurting the profit margin (Welsh, 2005b).

Outsourcing has the potential to reduce the efficiency of federal government and to drive up government human resource costs because it can make working for the government less desirable. As Senator Kahikina Akaka (D, HI) stated in 2003, "We cannot expect young people to work for the government if they believe their work will be subject to outsourcing. Nor should we accept policies that will instill fear and distrust in current employees" (Akaka, 2003). Senator Akaka expressed fears that outsourcing jobs to the private sector was creating "a shadow government" that lacked democratic accountability. When combined with poor contract management, outsourcing may actually increase the cost of federal functions rather than lead to greater efficiency.

Factors that promote the success of outsourcing include the agency having clear objectives when the contract is made; measures of performance being well-defined; the contractor being motivated by hope of contract renewal; and existence of competition for the contract by multiple vendors. Factors that impede the success of outsourcing include lack of agency investment in the human capital needed for monitoring and oversight; lack of professional contract management skills in the agency; complex desired outcomes that are difficult to measure; and lack of knowledge of the relationship of inputs to outcomes in the system being contracted. The last constraining factor, inadequate input-output process knowledge, is particularly troubling for those considering outsourcing since it is so prevalent in the public sector.

Supporters and critics debate the impact of outsourcing on federal jobs. In 2004, IBM's Center for the Business of Government released the pro-outsourcing report, "Competitive Sourcing: What Happens to Federal Employees?" by Jacques S. Gansler, Defense Department undersecretary under President Clinton, and William Lucyshyn, a research director at the Defense Advance Research Projects Agency. Gansler and Lucyshyn analyzed over 65,000 DOD positions competed since 1995, finding only 5% lost their jobs involuntarily. However, John Threlkeld, legislative representative for the American Federation of Government Employees (AFGE), called the data "seriously flawed," noting the authors were well known as advocates of privatization and outsourcing of federal jobs and noting the Government Accountability Office (GAO) had three times criticized the DOD Commercial Activities Management System for having incomplete data about competitions, calling the data "inaccurate and incomplete." Colleen Kelley, president of the National Treasury Employees Union, said the facts were "wrong" and that the Treasury Department had seen no similar cost savings. Kelley noted that in two recent competitions, over 400 Internal Revenue Service (IRS) workers were displaced (Miller, 2004p). Even a low percentage would, over time, erode the federal work force and thereby weaken public-sector unions, which have on the whole leaned toward support of Democrats rather than Republicans. Some argue that outsourcing is a political strategy by Republicans for the unstated purpose of weakening the support basis of the opposition party.

Whichever side of the debate one is on, it is clear that promotion of outsourcing has been official policy under the Bush administration. Soon after President Bush took office, a March 2001 OMB Circular A-76 revision memo directed agencies to compete or outsource at least 5% of their FAIR Act jobs[2] in the ensuing fiscal year. The eventual goal for this directive was 50% of all eligible jobs to be considered under the competitive sourcing guidelines. These jobs were not restricted to IT positions, but IT departments were slated to receive close attention.

When the Bush administration forged ahead with the A-76 process of competing and outsourcing federal jobs in 2002, comments were solicited as required by law for any change of regulations. As would be expected, the comments fell largely into two categories: favorable comments from the private sector and administration officials on the one hand, and negative comments from unions and rank and file federal employees on the other. Negative comments focused on several factors:

Lowered security levels. Stephanie Zaiser, a DOD IT employee, wrote "It will cost more and more each year to contract these positions out, not to mention the security risks. The IT contracting world is too volatile to be depended upon for our defenses and in servicing our soldiers. The field changes greatly and, therefore, the private contractor's employees have proven themselves to be unstable at best" (Zaiser, 2002).

False claims of savings. Dave Nehring, a federal budget officer, wrote "Having been on the receiving end of the results of the A-76 process I find it very unsettling that no actual cost savings are ever shown. . . . The few studies that have been made public have shown that contracting is a disservice to the taxpayer. That holds true at my location where a transfer of functions to the contractor has given us less service for more money" (Nehring, 2002).

Questionable accounting procedures. Federal employee Charles Johnson noted that A-76 competitions had been marked by questionable accounting practices, stating "The argument that governmental property, facilities, and equipment used by governmental employees which is outdated, and in many cases obsolete, should be included in the costing is not fair and open competition" (Johnson, 2002). Johnson also observed that A-76 competitions failed to use full-cost accounting methods, making private bids seem lower in cost than total costs actually were.

Biased rules for competing jobs. Walter W. Pike, president of the National Association of Air Traffic Specialists, complained that the A-76 rules put the burden of proving federal jobs were not "commercial" on federal employees, rather than assuming federal jobs were governmental until proven "commercial" by private-sector challenges. Pike wrote, "Beginning from the initial presumption that all activities are presumed to be commercial, and ending with the confusing and poorly organized options for "best-value" procurements, this [A-76] revision puts too many restrictions on the federal agencies competing to retain their own work, especially considering that they are competing against industry firms well experienced in the development of proposals" (Grundmann, 2002; Pike, 2002; Stern, 2002).

Lack of adequate contract oversight. Andrew L. Stern, president of the Service Employees International Union (SEIU), representing 1.5 million members, and affiliated with the National Association of Government Employees and the International Brotherhood of Police Officers (both affiliate unions of SEIU), wrote to express deep concerns about Bush's A-76 policy. "Expanding the privatization of services before addressing necessary reforms to our nation's current system of contracting out is particularly alarming," he wrote. "Federal departments are currently unable to provide the necessary oversight of privatized public services" (Stern, 2002).

In the nonprofit sector concerns were also raised about the capacity and likelihood of private contractors to assume the costs of compliance with federal laws pertaining to women, minorities, the disabled, and other protected groups. For instance, Barbara Jackson LeMoine, legislative assistant for the American Foundation for the Blind, wrote that Bush administration guidelines for A-76 competitions "raise a variety of questions and concerns relative to the requirements of title V of the Rehabilitation Act, particularly section 508. We are concerned that there are not adequate protection processes to guarantee that persons with disabilities will obtain the comparable access provided for under section 508. . . . The federal government has made great strides in developing that expertise and knowledge in its establishment of internal management and compliant measures. . . . We are concerned that contractors will lack the knowledge, skills, and experience in providing appropriate accommodations for disabled persons" (LeMoine, 2002). In this vein, a GAO study found several contractors won contracts in spite of prior violations of labor, environmental, and health and safety laws (Stern, 2002).

Among the many comments to the OMB on Bush administration changes to accelerate A-76 outsourcing of federal jobs was one from Dave Baron (2002), who wrote, "I think the outsourcing should also apply to the OMB. Why should they not be included?" While humorous, Baron's comment got at the political element in A-76 competitions, also emphasized by Kerry Korpi, writing on behalf of the 1.4 million members of the American Federation of State, County and Municipal Employees. Korpi raised broader issues about A-76 outsourcing, writing that "There is a real danger of growing public cynicism about government, when contracting decisions appear to be political. . . . The revisions suggest that "best value" should replace lowest cost as the driving criteria for determining who should do the work of the federal government—the private sector or federal agencies. Because this principle is potentially very subjective, we fear that "best value" will be a smokescreen for political decision making to meet the underlying goal of privatization at all costs" (Korpi, 2002). Whereas some advocates of IT see it leading to enhancement of "human capital" in the public sector, IT investment has been coincident with an outsourcing policy well calculated to demoralize and literally decimate the public service. Reinforcement theorists would, of course, find further confirmation of their thesis that IT enhances market principles not so much for reasons of efficiency cited by systems theorists as much as for reasons of political power noted by critical theory.

The terrorist attack of September 11, 2001, distracted attention and drew priorities away from the outsourcing program temporarily, but by 2004 outsourcing was being pushed heavily again. Senator Akaka (D-HI) raised three central objections to the Bush administration's revision of the A-76 process for competing and outsourcing federal jobs after September 11 (Akaka, 2003):

1. Government work could be contracted out even if the work could be performed more efficiently by federal employees.
2. Unrealistic deadlines are set for conducting public–private competitions that could push government work out the door to the private sector as fast as possible and may not give federal workers a fair chance to compete.
3. Unlike the private sector, federal workers are required to compete for their jobs every five years and are prevented from competing for contracted out work.

In April 2004, the GAO further consolidated the Bush administration outsourcing drive by ruling that federal employees and their unions had no standing to file protests over public–private competitions under OMB Circular A-76, even though their jobs could be outsourced.

The GAO did suggest, however, that Congress amend the Competition in Contract Act of 1984 to allow such protests (Miller, 2004n). The Republican-controlled Congress, while sometimes resistant to the OMB policy of outsourcing government jobs, nonetheless did not take up this GAO suggestion. Adding a rider to the DOD's FY 2005 Authorization Act, Congress stipulated that federal employees did not have standing to contest A-76 competitions when 65 or fewer full-time positions were involved. A subsequent GAO final rule in 2005 held that for competitions over 65, only the agency head could contest a competition.

The effect of Congressional and Bush administration actions meant that union representatives such as the AFGE could not contest A-76 competitions even when they represented a majority of agency employees. This created a one-sided situation where the private sector was allowed to contest A-76 competitions but the public sector was effectively blocked, at least under a Republican administration intent on promoting the outsourcing of federal jobs. Nonetheless, there were exceptions, notably the protest by the Federal Aviation Administration after it awarded a $1.9 billion, 10-year contract to Lockheed Martin Corp. for automated flight services (Miller, 2005a).

The OMB claims success in the A-76 outsourcing/privatization program. It has stated that $1.1 billion was saved in 18,000 competitions for federal jobs in 2003, and another $1.35 billion in 12,000 competitions in 2004 (Miller, 2005d). However, many question the accounting practices used to come up with these numbers. For instance, John Threlkeld, legislative representative for the AFGE, said of these numbers, "These projected costs have not been realized and may never be. The appropriators we've talked to about privatization reviews said they see money shift from one part of the organization to the other, but the overall costs rarely diminish" (Miller, 2005c). Democratic critics of the administration noted that even if true, these figures would pale when compared to the $9 billion "missing because of corrupt contracting" in outsourced contracts for Iraq reconstruction alone (Move On PAC, 2005).

CONTRACT MANAGEMENT

The purpose of contract management is to obtain goods and services at an advantageous price, delivered on time and meeting functional specifications. At the federal level, improving contract management is an ongoing mission of the Contract Management Center (CMC) of the GSA's Federal Supply Service (FSS). The CMC assists contractors in understanding contract requirements, evaluates contractor performance, and is responsible for contract administration and industry relationship management, including within the IT sector. Located under the FSS is the Office of Acquisition Management (OAM), which develops acquisition policies to support the integration of contract policies for all acquisition programs within FSS. The OAM also develops and implements e-business strategies for acquisition systems within FSS. The OAM is composed of the CMC; the Acquisition Management Center, which is responsible for acquisition policy support and training; and the Systems Management Center, which is responsible for acquisition systems support.

The General Services Administration Modernization Act of 2005 (GSAMA), pending and expected to pass at this writing, merges the Federal Technology Service and FSS into a new Federal Acquisition Service. It also promotes partnering and outsourcing by allowing public- and private-sector acquisition staff to work in each other's organizations for a period of time. The GSAMA also makes permanent controversial share-in-savings contracting for IT, discussed later in this chapter. GSAMA also requires agencies to use commercially available online procurement services (e.g., reverse auctions).

White and Korosec (2005) have enumerated many of the problems with contracting IT out:

- Specification default—If the agency lacks clear goals and objectives, performance specification may default to vendor initiative. Vendors may run up profits by selling add-on features not justified on a cost-effectiveness basis.
- Requirements creep—As the agency begins to understand what the technology can do, it may ask for additional features. Because the vendor already has the contract, it may be in a position to impose undue charges for meeting requirements not in the original contract.
- Legacy maintenance—Vendors prefer to implement their own system templates rather than rework custom legacy systems that agencies may be using. While there may be merit to abandoning legacy systems, it is an expensive proposition and the risks of using vendor templates and commercial off-the-shelf software may not be understood at contract time by an agency that has never used these templates and software. Software developed for the private sector often requires customization for use by a public sector agency, leading to requirements creep. This can be true even for software that a vendor proposes to port from another public-sector organization.
- Integration risk—Vendors often propose and government increasingly seeks government-wide ("enterprise") software applications such that, for instance, the same financial system could be run in all agencies in a jurisdiction. However, the failure rate of enterprise resource planning applications in the private sector in the 1990s was high. Agencies may not factor in the increased risk of integrated software coming in over budget, behind time, and/or without the functionality desired by end users of one-size-fits-all software.

In response to these problems, agencies have pursued a number of strategies: professionalization of contract management positions, piloting before total acquisition, and writing more performance specifications and penalties into contracts.

Contract management has evolved into a full-fledged profession in its own right. Degree programs in public-sector contract management include courses on topics such as contracting fundamentals, contract formation, government contract law, facilities contracting, acquisition planning, procurement management, systems procurement, price analysis, contract pricing, cost analysis, and negotiation techniques. Office of Personnel Management (OPM) requirements for contract specialists stipulate a degree in either accounting, business, finance, law, contracts, purchasing, economics, industrial management, marketing, quantitative methods, or organization and management (OPM, 2000). Most agencies require contract management officers not only to be certified in skill areas such as these, but also to renew certification through continuing education.

Other topics with which a contract manager must become familiar include warranties, guarantees, contingent fees, proper and improper business practices, rescinding as well as awarding contracts, contract reporting, uniform procurement, contract competitions, proper release of contract information, acquisition from nonprofits, acquisition from Federal Prison Industries, vendor debarment and ineligibility, market research, developing requirement documents, performance schedules, payment procedures, sealed bidding, contracting by negotiation, award notifications, use of bid samples, fixed price contracts, incentive contracts, indefinite delivery contracts, time-and-materials contracts, labor-hour contracts, small business programs and set-asides, disadvantaged business programs, price evaluation adjustments for small disadvantaged business concerns, the Historically Underutilized Business Zone program, basic labor policies, the Walsh-Healey Public Contracts Act, Equal Employment Opportunity requirements, the Service Contract Act of 1965, employment of veterans and workers with disabilities, requirements for a drug-free workplace, occupational safety requirements, environmental requirements, requirements for the use of recovered materials, provision for freedom of information, privacy requirements, foreign acquisitions and the Buy American Act, compliance with the Balance of Payments Program, evaluating foreign offers, complying with trade sanctions, observance of patent and copyright law, knowledge of bonds and insurance, sureties for bonds, tax codes, compliance with guidelines from the Cost Accounting Standards Administration, handling payments, leasing, handling advance payments, contract funding, assignment of claims, electronic funds transfer, handling protests and appeals, administering federal supply schedules, dealing with cooperative purchasing, auditing procedures, handling bankruptcies, production surveillance and reporting, performance accounting, quality assurance, value engineering, acceptance testing, certification testing, and risk management—just to name a few dimensions of contract management!

There are several national organizations devoted to the professionalization of contract management. The National Contract Management Association is the largest of these associations. Others include the Society of Cost Estimating and Analysis, which serves both government and industry. The Association for the Advancement of Cost Engineering is an international organization of cost management professionals. The International Cost Engineering Council promotes cooperation between national and multinational cost engineering, quantity surveying, and project management organizations worldwide.

In spite of the professionalization of contract management, it does no good if elected officials choose to ignore best practices. Conflicts of interest are not uncommon in contract management. Rep. Henry A. Waxman noted several examples in 2004 testimony before the Government Reform Committee regarding Iraq War contracts:

- Prior to the Iraq War, the Bush Administration took the contract to feed U.S. troops in Iraq away from a Kuwaiti firm, giving it to Halliburton, an American company with close ties to Vice President Cheney. Halliburton then subcontracted the work back to the same Kuwaiti firm, tacking on a 40% middleman fee.
- Halliburton was selected by the Bush Administration to receive secret oil contracts for the redevelopment of Iraqi oil, and the selection was done by political appointees in the Bush Administration—not by procurement officials.
- The Parsons firm was hired to oversee its business partner Fluor in an Iraq reconstruction contract.
- Likewise, CH2M Hill was hired to oversee its business partner Washington Group International.

Waxman testified, "Our own investigation has exposed other examples of astoundingly bad contract management" (Waxman, 2004). Successful contract management requires political commitment at the top levels and a system of democratic accountability based on transparency in government financial operations.

Performance-Based Service Contracts (PBSC)

The GAO estimated in 2002 that federal agencies spent roughly $136 billion acquiring services ranging from clerical support to IT services, such as network support (GAO, 2002b). Some 85% of federal IT expenditures involve the use of a contractor. Congress and the executive branch have sought to achieve greater cost savings and better outcomes by requiring performance-based contracting. Under performance-based contracting, agencies are to specify in contracts only desired outcomes, leaving to vendors the methods of attaining those outcomes. A 2002 GAO study of 25 performance-based contracts at five major federal agencies—the Department of Energy, the Department of the Treasury, the DOD, NASA, and the GSA—found only that nine met all criteria for being performance based. In many cases, the GAO found, agencies specified outcomes but, for cost, technical, and safety reasons, also felt compelled to prescribe performance methods as well, some in more detail than others (GAO, 2002b), thus undercutting the spirit of performance contracting.

The difficulties of performance contracting in the IT sector have given rise to a new consulting business: helping agencies frame and manage performance contracts. The Performance Institute (PI), for example, advertises that "PI offers expert training and consulting in performance-based IT contracting, from identification of performance requirements to creation of innovative contracting vehicles. Moreover, PI will ensure that effective IT outsourcing strategy and contract management are integrated into the IT planning process, the budget, and that they are aligned with both the project and agency mission."[3] Use of performance contract consultants may be a strategy for greater agency oversight over performance contractors, or it can be outsourcing of oversight responsibilities in a way that diminishes public accountability, depending on how it is implemented.

For performance budgeting to work, the agency must have clear objectives that will not change for the life of the contract. It must have documented its baseline costs, equipment, and human capital prior to the start of the contract. The agency must have the time, staff, and resources necessary to effectively monitor performance. It must assess the risks of becoming dependent upon the contractor for information on performance. Because, unlike traditional fee-for-service contracts, performance-based contracts obligate the agency to pay the contractor when certain objectives are met, and since *when* this occurs may be more up to the contractor than the agency, a PBSC can dramatically affect an agency's cash flow. In general, performance contracting tends to be more successful when objectives are clear, quantifiable, and well understood, and there is an observable relationship between inputs and outputs.

Performance contracting is far from being a panacea and, in fact, is associated with a variety of pitfalls. One common problem is that higher authorities mandate performance contracting to save money, placing considerable pressure on the agency to achieve that objective by (1) writing the performance contract in terms that reduce services, particularly hard-to-quantify services, allowing the contracting firm to save on costs; or (2) failing to closely monitor performance results, particularly hard-to-quantify results, also obscuring the fact that savings came from effectively lowering service levels. As Fruth (2000) points out, agencies may also implicitly liquidate public assets as a way to obtain services at a discount. Long-term contractual agreements under performance contracting also can tie the hands of agency officials to be democratically responsive to changes in circumstances and public preferences. Elected officials and the public may find holding agencies accountable more difficult because performance contracting can involve "buck passing" between agency and contractor when things go wrong, and all the more so if there are multiple simultaneous performance contracts involved.

The larger the scope of activities, the more complex the performance contract. The more complex it is, the more difficult it is to monitor. Agencies face an inevitable trade-off: overly detailed specification of the contract undermines the flexibility of the private-sector contractor and undermines the intent of performance contracting. On the other hand, underspecification gives the contractor broad discretion and makes performance monitoring more difficult (and abuse more likely). Fruth (2000, p. 556) states, "This trade-off between losing control and providing too much specificity becomes particularly acute in projects to privatize information technology, because the contracts not only assign significant responsibility, but also encompass a large and complex set of services across many agencies." That is, performance contracting poses specific problems for IT management because IT is systems oriented and therefore intrinsically deals with complex sociotechnical relationships internal to the agency and with complex sociopolitical and socioeconomic relationships external to the agency.

Share-in-Savings Contracts (SISC)

SISC is a relatively recent, much-discussed contract management strategy for creating vendor incentives to deliver effective IT systems on time and within budget. Under SISC, contracts are written with provisions that award vendors a portion of savings brought about by systems they implement in the public sector. The theory is that the public sector will obtain goods or services with a lower up-front investment, while the vendor has the incentive to be efficient because the lower the cost in implementing the project, the greater the reward to the vendor. For instance, both defense and civilian agencies have long used SISC on energy and water conservation efforts for federal facilities. Energy and water conservation improvements are implemented by the vendor at the vendor's own cost (if both government and vendor agree), but the vendor receives a percentage of utility cost savings over the life of the contract (typically 10 years).

SISC was authorized by the E-Government Act of 2002,[4] which provided for 10 such contracts in both FY 2004 and FY 2005.[5] The Defense and Civilian Agency Federal Acquisitions Regulation Councils in July 2004 issued proposed rules for share-in-savings IT procurements and for proposed rules requiring expanded use of PBSC, including IT services. That is, agencies were instructed to specify to vendors only the desired results, not the methods of obtaining the results of SISCs. In IT, the distinction between methods and outcomes is not as sharp as politicians may suppose. By requiring performance-based contracting, pressure is brought upon agencies to be very precise in their specification of outcomes, restricting vendor discretion with regard to implementation (Cain, 2004).

Though at this writing, authority for SISC is scheduled to expire in September 2005, SISC has the strong support of the Bush Administration and the OMB. The Bush Administration view is that SISC represents the ultimate in performance-based budgeting and as such presents the best opportunity for procurement reform in IT and other arenas. Renewal of authority and expansion of SISC is anticipated.

In many cases, agencies have a disincentive to terminate problem SISCs because termination requires payoff of projected savings for the life of the contract. If a project is no longer required or has been superceded by other developments and programs, the agency can be left holding the liability of a substantial stream of costs years into the future. This, however, is a problem that in principle could be resolved by more stringent SISCs that make provision for agency cancellation of projects. However, for SISC to work at all, any cancellation provisions would still have to provide for vendor reimbursement of up-front investment costs plus a reasonable profit. Under SISC, the agency could be responsible for paying off up-front investment costs when a project is cancelled by a vendor.

SISC has many critics. Angela Styles, former head of the Office of Federal Procurement Policy (OFPP), in the newsletter of the American Bar Association, has charged that share-in-savings contracting uses "shady financing and accounting techniques" and moves federal IT purchases away from "public and congressional scrutiny" (Miller, 2004o). Styles warned that agencies may be tempted to use SISC to fund projects for which Congress has not appropriated funds, undermining democratic principles. For instance, a vendor implementing tax software for the IRS might create more vigorous and rigid enforcement and collection systems, raising unexamined policy issues. Moreover, the E-Government Act contains no limit on how much profit contractors can accrue from SISCs. Likewise, the E-Government Act places no limit on the monetary risk for the federal government. In essence, SISC as presently implemented would allow agencies "to mortgage billions of dollars in future spending," Styles observed (Miller, 2004o).

Evidence that SISC is a contract management practice in the public interest is weak at best. Styles attempted to provide a record of documented savings from SISC at federal, state, and local levels when she headed the OFPP, but found a lack of documentation.

PROCUREMENT

Procurement is one aspect of contract management, one which organizations would like to approach strategically. A strategic sourcing philosophy is emphasized by Accenture, among other large consulting firms that promote the concept. Strategic sourcing includes e-procurement, the use of requests for proposals (RFPs) instead of going directly to requests for bids (RFBs), enterprise-wide purchasing, tougher contracts, and ensuring that state-purchased systems can also be used by local governments (Harris, 2004). Criticisms of strategic sourcing include past practices of focusing on lowest price instead of best value, minimizing agency input below the enterprise level, and making contracts with smaller (minority, women-owned) firms more difficult.

In the IT sector as elsewhere, "best value" procurement has progressively eclipsed "lowest bid" procurement. Often requiring changes in state regulations and even legislation (as in New York, where best value contracting is mandated), best value procurement simply means that the agency can and should take more than lowest price into account when contracting goods and services. Other criteria introduced under best value procurement may include the vendor's record in terms of experience, the vendor's complaint history, consideration of qualitative rather than just quantitative factors, differences in risk assessment of alternative proposals, financial stability of the vendor, availability of technical support, costs of training, and total cost of ownership (all operational and replacement costs, not just acquisition costs).

Smart procurement may be a synonym for *best value* or it may refer to centralized purchasing at discount. The GSA's SmartBUY program was envisioned as a discount store for federal enterprise software license deals. However, by 2004 the GSA had managed to get agreements with only 2 of 25 top vendors of software used by government. By April 2005, SmartBUY licenses were still available only for ESRI, Manugistics, Novell, WinZip, and Prosight Project Portfolio Management. Oracle joined in SmartBUY in May. Part of the very slow diffusion of the SmartBUY program among private sector vendors has been due to poor or absent software inventories of federal departments, preventing the GSA from being able to state just what the federal government's software license needs are, in turn preventing making discount software deals through SmartBUY. Also, SmartBUY had been pushed politically by administration officials early on, but Larry Allen, executive director of the Coalition for Government Procurement, stated in 2004 that "There is no driving political force behind it anymore." Instead the GSA began reverting back to focusing on smaller deals from agencies with immediate licensing buying needs (Miller, 2004q).

To deal with strategic sourcing, SmartBuy, and related issues, procurement of IT falls under the OFPP, created by the Office of Federal Procurement Policy Act of 1974. Four years later, Public Law 95-507 established special provisions for the subcontracting of data systems. In 1970, the OFPP set up the Federal Procurement Data Center as a computerized repository of detailed information on all purchases over $25,000, and summary details of smaller ones. In 1982, administration of the OFPP was given to the GSA. The Clinger-Cohen Act of 1996 also gave the CIO Council an interest in procurement, and it plays an advisory role in the SmartBuy initiative. All these early laws and regulations lay the basis for moving procurement from a manual to an electronic basis in the 1990s and 2000s.

E-Procurement

Electronic procurement (e-procurement) began in the late 1990s when several startup software companies, led particularly by Ariba and Commerce One, began to develop a suite of applications that allowed vendors to create electronic catalogs. Later, under the George W. Bush administration, the OFPP became the cornerstone of e-procurement policy. Under 2002 regulations, if an agency wanted to procure an item over $25,000, it had to list the procurement opportunity with FedBizOpps.gov, which was the new portal for e-procurement. Further 2003 regulations stipulated that to receive a FedBizOpps.gov award, a contractor must register at the Central Contractor Registration, located on the web at http://www.ccr.gov. In 2004 the GSA began integrating many of the components of the Integrated Acquisition Environment e-government project, which was one of the Quicksilver initiatives (Miller, 2003u). The components were the following

- Business Partner Network
- Central Contractor Registration
- Intra Governmental Transactions Exchange
- Past Performance Information Retrieval System
- Federal Technical Data System
- Federal Procurement Data System

By the end of the first term of the George W. Bush administration, regulations and systems were in place forcing both agencies and vendors to use e-procurement, at least to a degree.

This is not to say that federal agencies were uniformly happy with e-procurement. FedBizOpps was the federal government's e-procurement portal. It came in over budget, at about $4.7 million/year. A DOD employee was quoted as saying, "We found out FedBizOpps cost more than anticipated, and we all got taxed for the extra funds. We had to go to our leadership and ask for more money, and every time we have to do that, it becomes a harder sell" (Miller, 2003t). At all levels of government, making e-procurement self-financing is an appeal to elected officials and a challenge for public administrators.

E-procurement also spread at the state level in the same period. In many cases, state statutes had to be revised to legalize online procurement. Success factors were thought to be having procurement rather than IT personnel design the system, partnering with the business community in design, and having the priority support of top state officials (Wong,

2004). Virginia committed to e-procurement in 2001, consolidating 171 separate agency-focused procurement systems. By 2004, the Virginia system was processing 220,000 orders totaling $1.71 billion for some 500 state agencies, local governments, and schools.

However, the state path to e-procurement has proved more than a little bumpy. South Carolina abandoned its e-procurement system in June 2002. Shortly afterwards vendor NIC Inc. announced it was quitting the e-procurement business, partly due to lack of government demand. The Virginia state auditor reported only 1.5% of the state's business was transacted through its state-of-the-art system, which cost $14.9 million. Pilot projects were shut down in 2002 in Massachusetts, Indiana, and Michigan. An April 2002 survey by the National Institute of Governmental Purchasing showed e-catalog purchasing by government actually decreased by 10% in 2002 compared to 2001 (Newcombe, 2002b). A more optimistic forecast by Input, Inc., estimated state and local e-procurement systems expenditures to double between 2003 and 2008. On the other hand, as of 2004, only six states had comprehensive e-procurement systems covering automated approvals and paying bills by direct deposit (Wong, 2004).

States have used a variety of e-procurement business models, most involving partnering. The Virginia system, contracted through American Management Systems (AMS), called on the state to guarantee AMS a minimum of $15 million in fees charged to suppliers, with possibilities of $25 million in revenue depending on system usage. Suppliers were charged $25 to register with the Virginia system, plus a 1% transaction cost, plus other fees for special services such as e-mail notification of business opportunities. A different financial model in Idaho involved the state paying low fees ($19,500 plus $1500/year support) to Sicommnet for e-procurement software, but allowing the vendor to sell subscription-based services to suppliers. Florida awarded a 5-year $92 million e-procurement contract to Accenture, paid for by a 1% transaction fee on companies that win state contracts. Massachusetts in the fall of 2003 contracted with BearingPoint for a $6.4 million upgrade to its e-procurement system, to be paid at least in part from subscription services to companies (like instant notification of business opportunities) (Wong, 2004).

A variety of obstacles to the spread of e-procurement emerged. Unlike e-procurement in the United Kingdom, the American variety was voluntary. Since it required firms to change their way of doing business, most opted not to do so. Suppliers balked at having to pay annual subscription or per-transaction fees imposed by states seeking to recover their costs of purchasing an e-procurement system from a software vendor. Then too, sometimes state financial woes in a weak economy meant lack of funding for new e-procurement initiatives in the first place. More broadly, it was believed that the slow adoption of e-procurement showed efficiency gains alone were not sufficient to ensure successful implementation. Traditional procurement principles such as separation of vendor and user, fixed price-fixed term contracting, and open access were all organizational culture factors constituting obstacles to adoption (MacManus, 2002).

SUMMARY

In terms of theories discussed in this book, perhaps reinforcement theorists would find the greatest support in this chapter, arguing that the march of IT outsourcing has been in support of powers that be, primarily large contractors in the private sector. They would argue that since much outsourcing has been done on ideological grounds, sometimes even at higher cost to the public, this disproves the systems theory assumption that the spread of IT proceeds on the basis of its rational efficiency. Technological determinists would perhaps be oblivious to this distinction, not caring which sector actually implemented IT, only observing that even outsourcing does not impede the seemingly inevitable drive toward more and greater technology. As for sociotechnical theorists, with their emphasis on human factors, team approaches to technology, and participation, they too might find the focus of this chapter on public versus private sector to be somewhat beside the point, insisting only that their human-centered theories and methods provide the most effective means to implementation regardless of sector. Still, since the reality is that outsourced and privatized implementation can mean less attention to such human factors as disabilities compatibility, minority participation, women's role, and the input of labor, there is some tension between trends outlined here and the expectations of sociotechnical theory.

Writing in the *Harvard Journal of Law & Technology*, David Fruth analyzed topics covered in this chapter (Fruth, 2000). His analysis concluded that "Privatizing public information technology will likely not generate the cost savings that governments expect, especially under a "whole-of-government" approach" (p. 549). Lack of significant cost savings were attributed to various structural and institutional constraints to privatizing complex government services. These included large transaction costs associated with managing the principle-agent relationship involved in partnering, outsourcing, and contract management. His survey of privatization trends and examples of privatization failures supported the argument that since government information services are complex, with rapidly changing goals, they are difficult to privatize.

The success of partnering, outsourcing, and contract management depends upon performance monitoring. As Forrest (1993, p. 51) notes, agencies are becoming transformed "from direct providers to monitoring, regulation, and contract-enforcing agencies." When IT services are no longer performed directly by public employees, but are instead delivered through interorganizational networks in the private sector, public managers can no longer use traditional hierarchical controls to direct the behavior of subordinates (Cohen & Eimicke, 2005). Tools of managerial power are lost, such as direct command, promotion and demotion, and even seeking to motivate employees through team spirit and enhancement of agency work culture. The public manager is challenged to replace these tools by creating new ones associated with performance measurement of the work of contracting organizations. However, elected officials who fund agencies may be so motivated by cost savings thought to be associated with partnering, outsourcing, and other forms of privatization that they are reluctant to face and fund the high cost of monitoring and contract management, not to mention third-party auditing.

Without substantial investment in the oversight capabilities of the IT or other agency, the agency is very apt to become dependent for performance information on data supplied by the contractor or vendor. There is a conflict of interest when those who gather and provide performance information are the same as those who implement the project and stand to reap benefits from any cost savings, as in the case of performance-based contracting. In more complex projects, as many in the IT field are, there are multiple system goals, many of them intangible. Share-in-savings contract principles emerged in and ride on examples from contracting for energy and water systems, where costs and savings are easily measured. When transferred to complex IT functions, such principles become problematic as very strong incentives are created to cut costs and increase profits through neglect of intangible performance factors, displacing externalities back onto the public sector, and outright juggling and misreporting of performance data.

DISCUSSION QUESTIONS

1. What motivates businesses to enter IT partnerships with government? What motivates agencies? In what ways are these motives consistent? Inconsistent?
2. Which do you think more typical—the Census TIGER example or the broadband access example at the beginning of this chapter?
3. On what contingencies does successful partnering depend in implementing public–private IT projects?

4. Considering that outsourcing federal IT (and other) jobs through A-76 competitions was a part of Bush administration policy, why do you think the Republican-dominated Congress sometimes opposed it?
5. What are the appeals of outsourcing? The problems? How should the public manager try to strike a balance?
6. What is *requirements creep* and why does it occur?
7. What do contract management professionals do? Would you want to be one? Why or why not?
8. What are performance-based service contracts? What are the pros and cons?
9. What are share-in-savings contracts? What are the pros and cons?
10. Why has e-procurement not spread faster?

GLOSSARY

A-76 competitions: In March 2001, an OMB Circular A-76 revision memo directed agencies to compete or outsource at least 5% of their FAIR Act jobs in the ensuing fiscal year. The eventual goal for this directive was 50% of all eligible jobs to be considered under the competitive sourcing guidelines. The effect of A-76 competitions is to privatize federal jobs.

Contract management: Contract management is the function of obtaining goods and services at an advantageous price, delivered on time and meeting functional specifications. More broadly, contract management refers to the professionalization of the contracting function in the public sector, including contract oversight as well as traditional procurement.

FAIR Act: The Federal Activities Inventory Reform Act of 1998 directs agencies to submit an annual inventory of activities that are "not inherently governmental." This inventory is, in essence, a list of federal jobs that are subject to outsourcing. Under the Bush administration, FAIR Act implementation has placed on agencies the burden of proving jobs are not commercial in nature.

Outsourcing: The transfer of elements of an agency's IT (or other) infrastructure, staff, processes, or applications to an external resource provider, generally one in the private sector.

Partnering: The establishment of working relationships between an agency and nongovernmental organizations, generally private-sector firms, for purposes of joint problem solving, teamwork, and implementing projects based on shared risks and rewards. Partnering does not necessarily assume privatization or outsourcing.

Performance contracts: A contractual agreement between an agency and a vendor that clearly specifies mutual performance obligations, with rewards for vendors meeting performance specifications and penalties for failing to do so.

Privatization: The transfer of governmental functions to the private sector. Where outsourcing usually connotes transfer of government processes to the private sector, retaining agency control and oversight through periodically renewed contracts, privatization usually refers to the transfer of broad functions with fewer controls. Privatization may involve abolition of former agencies, with control only through legislative and executive branch oversight agencies, not through substantive agencies.

Procurement: The purchasing, leasing, or renting of materials, services, and equipment in conformity with government regulations.

Share-in-savings contracts: Contracts under which an agency pays the contractor an amount equal to a portion of the savings developed by the agency, which is obligated to finance the up-front costs of the savings initiative (for example, finance improved networking services, thereby developing savings in personnel time).

RFB and RFP: RFPs are requests for proposals from vendors. Agencies gain information from RFPs and use this input to refine RFBs, which are more detailed and specific requests for bids.

ENDNOTES

[1] A 2004 audit, however, revealed inappropriate, excessive expenditures on entertainment and other items.

[2] FAIR was discussed in Chapter 2. The Federal Activities Inventory Reform Act of 1998 directs agencies to submit an annual inventory of activities that are "not inherently governmental." This inventory is, in essence, a list of federal jobs that are subject to outsourcing.

[3] Retrieved April 25, 2005, from http://www.performanceweb.org/consulting/e-government.html.

[4] Rep. Tom Davis (R, VA), chairman of the House Government Reform Committee, wrote the original share-in-savings provision of the E-Government Act.

[5] The Defense Department, NASA, and the Coast Guard are allotted the power to award five SISCs, while other agencies are to award the other five contracts per year.

CASE STUDY
Issues in IT Procurement, Contracting, and Partnerships: A Short Case Study from the Department of Information Systems and Services, Orange County, Florida

Ronnie L. Korosec, Department of Public Administration, University of Central Florida

Public organizations are indeed faced with formidable tasks. On one hand, they are charged with becoming more responsive and efficient in how they provide goods and services to the public—especially during economic downturns (Cohen & Eimicke, 2002; Osborne & Gaebler, 1992). On the other hand, they are expected to maintain stable organizations and limit exposure to risky behaviors (Vasu, Stewart, & Garson, 1998). At the end of the day, meeting these sometimes opposing interests can result in sizable accomplishments or considerable pain for public managers. How do governments maintain their foothold along this slippery slope? Increasingly, they are relying on new forms of information technology (IT) to enhance operations, streamline activities, and create higher quality, more responsive systems to meet both administrative and citizen-based needs (Heintz & Bretschneider, 2000; Holley, Dufner, & Reed, 2004; Landsbergen & Wolken, 2001). More and more, they are using IT to move toward a system of e-governance—or the online delivery of government information and public services, seven days a week, twenty-four hours a day (Brown, 2001; Norris & Moon, 2005).

This study focuses on one government, in particular—Orange County, Florida, and reviews the steps taken to initiate and support IT procurement, contracting, and partnership agreements. It uses the case study methodology and protocols suggested by Yin (1989, 2002)[1] to answer several key questions. How did the Orange County IT department create "business partners" in every department of the county?[2] What does their procurement process look like? Do they rely heavily on contractors for software or hardware? This case study examines these issues.

The Case for IT and E-Government in Orange County

Orange County is the fastest growing county in Florida, with a 32.3% growth rate between the years of 1990 and 2000 (Orange County Planning Division, 2005). Approximately one million people live in the cities and towns that make up Orange County, and several million more flock to this area each year to attend conventions and other tourist attractions in and around Orange County's most famous municipality, Orlando (Orlando/Orange County Convention and Visitors Bureau, 2004). Unlike neighboring municipalities that have faced budget cutbacks in the aftermath of September 11 (Conrad Cross, personal communication, March 18, 2005), Orange County has not faced the same issues. Thanks, in part, to taxes and other revenues collected through their booming tourism industry, a red-hot job market, and efforts to diversify the economy with more high-tech industry, Orange County's economy continues to be very strong (Crotty, 2005). The combination of a strong economy and growing population have enabled Orange County to fund advances in IT and implement an e-government system that is both unique and effective.

In the early 1990s, county leaders and administrators recognized the need to provide more efficient service delivery for citizens and tourists, as well as redesign service delivery functions within the county. In 1996, the county organized an IT department to launch its first website, and less than two years later, the site was host to more than 1500 web bases, searchable databases, and online forms (Orange County government website, 2005). Less than 10 years later, in 2005, the county's IT department (known as the Information Systems and Services or ISS department) now has evolved to a point where it processes more than 3 million phone calls and 4 million e-mails internally on a monthly basis, and hosts more than 3.5 million visitors per year on their website (Raphael Mena, personal communication, April 15, 2005). The website allows online access for citizens to pay fines, fees, and taxes; complete and submit permits and business licenses; request government records and have them delivered to the requestor; request services such as pothole repair; register for recreational facilities and activities; download forms such as voter registration forms and building permits; access GIS maps and data; access employment applications; read council agendas and minutes; view local ordinances and codes; view pets that are available for adoption at the county shelter; and access streaming video on current issues, among other things (Norris & Korosec, 2005; Orange County government website). This change toward a system of e-government (rather than traditional face-to-face interactions) required not only new types and applications of IT, but a new way of conducting business as well.

A Model for Partnerships

The model for IT development and implementation in Orange County is different from those in surrounding counties and cities (Norris & Korosec, 2005).[3] Part of the reason that Orange County has been so successful in implementing so many different aspects of IT and e-governance is that they have created a unique model of identifying and educating "business partners" within each department of the county. This includes finding individuals in each department to work with ISS and outside IT vendors, getting to know those individuals and how their businesses work, and then training and educating them on various aspects of IT and e-governance applications. For example, in the Public Works Department, there is an individual who has direct public works responsibilities (such as scheduling street repairs), but has received training on various IT applications and implementation, and thereby serves as the IT liaison for that department. This business partner works directly with ISS and outside vendors to communicate needs "on their terms and in their language," suggest changes in current applications or systems, craft new requests for hardware or software packages, and also to request funding for these new applications (Susan Hall, personal communication, April 15, 2005). This system serves a dual role, as the individual business partners are able to more effectively communicate their needs to ISS, and in return, ISS can produce more effective IT solutions to meet these business needs.

Through this partnership model, the county has effectively created an e-government system that has allowed them to change the role of staff members, reduce demands on departments, reduce administrative costs, improve local government communications with the public, enhance customer service, and reengineer business processes within the county (Norris & Korosec, 2005). Orange County CIO Raphael Mena has indicated that the biggest surprise he has encountered with expanding IT within the county has been "building an honest relationship with our business partners both internally and externally." He adds, "It's not about the technical aspects of the business, its about people and processes. We work with our business partners to define standards, consolidate structures, request funding, and build trust" (Mena, personal communication, April 15, 2005). The main thrust behind this system is to make each department more independent over time—to give it ownership of its own IT systems and data, and make it less reliant on ISS for administering these systems (Richarde, 2005). This is a good model, according to the CIO, but it is not without flaws (Mena). While many departments in

continues

Orange County were initially interested in new IT opportunities, few wanted to risk "giving up their people or their time" to support the partnership program when it was first developed (Hall, personal communication, April 15, 2005). Over time, however, ISS was able to prove to department managers that this cooperative program worked, and that it resulted in more efficiency in their departments. Now, the county has IT business partners in every one of the 20 departments in the county.

IT Procurement and Contracting

Orange County is also aware that the IT procurement process requires a delicate hand. The CIO meets with all department directors and business partners to determine requests, and then creates a centralized budget request based on these needs. There is a separate budget item under the ISS Department to support the e-government infrastructure, but e-governance efforts are all funded through general revenues (Mena, personal communication, April 15, 2005). "When we purchase, we don't reinvent the wheel. We define requirements of the system and the business team works on an RFP. We maintain that any proposal must meet at least 85% of our stated requirements for it to be considered viable. We try not to purchase tailored systems or software, as they tend to be more expensive to install and upgrade or more difficult to integrate with other existing systems" (Mena). Orange County must justify the purchase of any new or updated system or software through strict procurement rules and procedures.

In addition, while Orange County has started doing some e-procurement, they recognize that this is an area that they would like to expand. The CIO has indicated that there are about 20,000 attempts *per day* by hackers trying to infiltrate the website or related links, and that a large number of these are from overseas (Mena, personal communication, April 15, 2005). Because of concerns over Internet security and safety, the ISS is not only cautious about what they procure online, but also about the reliability of the hardware and software systems they use on a daily basis. Generally, most of their software and systems are developed in-house by any of the 165 ISS staff members (Norris & Korosec, 2005; Mena). Other applications and packages are developed by consultants or local government staff, and a small few are contracted out to IT vendors (Norris & Korosec, 2005). All website hosting, design, operations, and management, as well as the integration of websites with local government databases are all provided in-house by ISS staff (Norris & Korosec, 2005).

Safety and security are not the only reasons why the county is reluctant to outsource IT needs. The CIO has indicated that while "lots of vendors come into us and want to sell us their products," that each vendor provides "seemingly great solutions, but these solutions may not be 'great' for the county and its larger needs" (Mena, personal communication, April 15, 2005). The county prefers to purchase "plain vanilla packages" of hardware and software systems off the shelf, such as the Oracle, UNIX, and Microsoft systems they currently use (Mena). Only when there is a specific need that cannot be met by existing systems or software does the county consider purchasing specialized hardware or software applications (Hall, personal communication, April 15, 2005). Even then, they expect vendors to produce high-quality product and services—driven by the "best of the best standards" (Mena). Also, the county makes it clear that it will not purchase or create any IT applications that a specific department doesn't explicitly request—which is an effective tool in limiting unwanted solicitation from vendors. A large part of the success in IT in Orange County "is about control and ownership in each department" (Mena). "We won't roll anything out that our business partners haven't already asked for or don't expressly need" (Mena).

Challenges for the ISS

The Orange County experience in IT procurement, contracting, and partnerships is not without its share of opportunities and challenges. While this model has created new independence, flexibility, and efficiency in each partnership arrangement, it has also expanded the scope of work for ISS. "We are now involved in all types of business—from tracking dogs and cats, to tracking prisoners, inmates, and corpses. Every single business partner operates differently and independently, but our mission is to support them all" (Hall, personal communication, April 15, 2005). The work ISS is involved in is comprehensive and ranges "from initial concepts, to funding to final rollouts" (Hall). One of the biggest disappointments that ISS has faced is that some departments and agencies cannot (or are not willing to) communicate with one another to coordinate IT applications or e-government service delivery (Mena, personal communication, April 15, 2005). In addition, because the county relies on in-house staff for most IT needs, they have had to work to create an environment where different groups (such as software developers and web page artists) can speak the same language and get along with one another (Mena). In short, the size, scope, and diverse nature of issues that ISS is involved in sometimes can create obstacles for this group.

Conclusion

While it is a challenge to reduce the gap between available resources and business needs, IT provides governments with a wide array of tools to meet desired ends. Orange County, Florida, has found success in reducing this divide by organizing IT systems along individual business partnerships, and carefully fostering these relationships. They have attempted to keep the procurement process in line by using in-house IT staff to create new systems or applications, and have resisted pressures from vendors to contract out by working as teams, internally, to craft solutions to problems. Although there are limitations to this study,[4] the information contained in this case study is a useful beginning for understanding progression of IT and e-government in Orange County, as well as for learning more about some of the successes and limitations this county has faced. The county's IT efforts seem to be paying off. ISS has earned over 20 awards for its IT advances, including third place in the Digital Counties Survey in 2003, second place in the Digital Counties Survey in 2004 (Center for Digital Government, 2003, 2004), and a variety of other distinctions for excellence in online information service, including building permits, applicant tracking, consumer fraud, and corrections (Orange County government website, 2005). To this end, Orange County is a unique example for other municipalities to learn more about launching new e-government initiatives, creating new IT business partnerships, or rethinking the way they contract out or procure for IT.

Endnotes

[1]Yin (1989) suggests that case studies are applicable when we seek to answer the *how* and *why* questions associated with some phenomenon or issue, including how to explain complex causal links in real-life interventions, describe the real-life context in which interventions occur, describe the intervention itself, and explore those situations in which the invention being evaluated has no clear set of outcomes. Yin (2002) also indicates that there are at least six ways to collect data in a case study, including three used in this study: interviews, reviewing pertinent documents, and survey data.

[2]First, a questionnaire titled "Survey of Electronic Government Practices in Central Florida: 2005" was sent to the chief information officers (CIOs) for all municipalities in the Central Florida Metropolitan Statistical Area (including Orange County) in the Spring of 2005. The mailed survey

continues

contained various types of questions, including open-ended and closed-ended questions, and matrix questions. Questions on this survey were modeled after the ICMA (International City/County Management Association) "Electronic Government 2004" survey, and included items related to customer service and management, online procurement and contracting, barriers to IT development, and issues relating to partnerships and e-government, among others. The survey was conducted as part of a larger effort to find patterns of IT and e-government activity in the central Florida metropolitan statistical area (MSA). The targeted respondents for this survey were CIOs or similar, high-ranking managers. The list of these individuals was obtained by contacting each municipality in the MSA (as determined by U.S. Census data). Based on this information, the survey was mailed to the respondents. Once these responses were received, a follow-up interview was conducted with the Orange County CIO and his staff in April of 2005. In addition to this meeting, staff members from Orange County were invited to give commentary on IT and e-governance in a focus group late in April. Finally, public information and documents from several sources, including the "State of Orange County Address" and documents from the county website were also analyzed. Based on the information taken from the interview, focus group, and documents, several observations were recorded, and then used to suggest real-life contexts for the phenomenon observed.

[3]The "Survey of Electronic Government Practices in Central Florida: 2005" was conducted by the Dr. Donald Norris and Dr. Ronnie Korosec, Department of Public Administration at the University of Central Florida. This survey was sent to all cities and counties in the central Florida metropolitan statistical area (MSA) in February of 2005.

[4]First it should be noted that while every effort was made to collect objective data, the survey was based on the perceptions of the CIO and his staff—which may or may not reflect the opinions of others (such as elected officials or citizens). In addition, evidence was drawn from public records and documents. While expected to be accurate and objective, they may contain errors. In all, however, this study is still expected to provide quality information about IT and e-governance in Orange County.

References

Brown, M. (2001). The benefits and costs of information technology innovations: An empirical assessment of a local government agency. *Public Performance and Management Review, 24*(4), 351–366.

Center for Digital Government. (2003). Digital Counties Awards. Retrieved October 22, 2003 from http://www.centerdigitalgov.com.

Center for Digital Government. (2004). Digital Counties Awards. Retrieved November 6, 2004 from http://www.centerdigitalgov.com.

Cohen, S. & Eimicke, W. (2002). *The effective public manager: Achieving success in a changing government.* San Francisco, CA: Jossey-Bass.

Crotty, R. (2005). *State of the County Report 2005: In the Eye of the Hurricane.* Address given by Orange County Mayor Richard Crotty, May 11, 2005, Church Street Station Grand Ballroom, Orlando, FL.

Heintz, T., & Bretschneider, S. (2000). Information technology and restructuring in public organizations. Does adoption of informal technology affect organizational structures, communications, and decision making? *Journal of Public Administration Research and Theory, 10*(4): 801–830.

Holley, L., Dufner, D., & Reed, B. (2004). Strategic information systems planning in US county governments: Will the real SISP model please stand up? *Public Performance and Management Review, 27*(3), 102–126.

International City/County Management Association. (2004). Survey of Electronic Government 2004. Washington, DC: ICMA.

Landsbergen, D., & Wolken, G. (2001). Realizing the promise: Government information systems and the fourth generation of information technology. *Public Administration Review, 61*(2), 206–218.

Norris, D., & Korosec, R. (2005). Survey of Electronic Government Practices in Central Florida: 2005: Responses from Orange County. Orlando, FL: University of Central Florida, Department of Public Administration.

Norris, D., & Moon, J. (2005). Advancing e-government at the grassroots: Tortoise or hare? *Public Administration Review, 65*(1), 64–75.

Orange County. (2005). Orange County government website. Retrieved May 6, 2005 from http://www.organgecountyfl.net.

Osborne, D., & Gaebler, T. (1992). *Reinventing government: How the entrepreneurial spirit is transforming the public sector.* Reading, MA: Addison-Wesley.

Orange County Planning Division. (2005). *Your Local Government: At a Glance.* Orlando, FL: Author.

Orlando/Orange County Convention and Visitors Bureau. (2004). Annual Report, 2004. Orlando, FL: Author.

Richarde, K. (2005). IT Analyst, Orange County. Comments recorded during "IT and e-governance Focus Group" on April 28, 2005, at the University of Central Florida, Orlando, FL.

Vasu, M., Stewart, D., & Garson, D. (1998). *Organizational behavior and public management.* New York: Marcel Dekker.

Yin, R. (2002). *Applications of case study research.* Thousand Oaks, CA: Sage.

Yin, R. (1989). *Case study research: Design and methods.* Thousand Oaks, CA: Sage.

CHAPTER

Planning for Public Information Systems

In FY 2004, the federal government awarded $155 billion in information technology (IT) projects, $118 billion of it for the Department of Homeland Security (DHS), the Department of Defense (DOD), and the Army, Navy, and Air Force. This was a 60% increase over the previous year, reflecting the national investment in security through IT. Among the largest projects were DHS's $10 billion U.S. Visitor and Immigration Status Indication Technology System, the Air Force's $9 billion Network Centric Solutions program, and the Army's $7 billion Warfighter Information Network-Tactical System (Onley, 2004b). Historically, the larger the IT project, the greater the likelihood that it will be over budget, past deadline, and/or will not function to original intentions (Perlman, 2002). With unprecedented IT spending for massive systems, the need for IT planning has never been greater. Moreover, strategic IT planning is required of federal agencies by the Paperwork Reduction Act of 1995 and the Clinger-Cohen Act of 1996.

The need for IT planning was underlined by the terrorist attack on the World Trade Center on September 11, 2001. Dawes, Cresswell, and Cahan (2004) found that in the response to 9/11, data issues of quality, access, use, sharing, and security far outweighed technology problems and were harder to solve. Indeed, the naive belief held by some that technology "band-aids" could overcome underlying organizational and data quality problems was itself an obstacle to effective information sharing and integration. Other lessons included the need for more redundancy of systems, more planning for business recovery, the need to have well-designed security and privacy systems in place beforehand, the need for interoperability of systems used by responders, and in general the need for more planning.

THE ROLE OF THE FEDERAL CIO

At the dawn of federal computing in the 1960s and 1970s, IT planning was seen primarily as a matter of procurement and was handled as such by the General Services Administration. Later, the Office of Federal Procurement Policy played this role. It was not until the National Performance Review under President Clinton and Vice President Al Gore, in the 1990s, that new concepts such as *reinventing government, information resource management,* and *reengineering* came to the forefront, defining a new role for the heads of IT departments. Within IT as a profession, following the lead of the private sector, many called for the transformation of the support service role of the IT department head into the new role of chief information officer (CIO).

The rise of the federal CIO is part of the trend in the last decade to consolidate the administration of IT within the public sector. This applies not only to the federal level, but to the state level as well. In 2003 Virginia undertook a massive consolidation of agency IT departments into a single, centralized IT office. In 2004, New Mexico mandated a similar consolidation by executive order of the governor. Rhode Island, Texas, and Michigan were among other states moving toward some form of IT centralization in 2004. Centralization patterns at the federal level partly lead but also partly reflect general trends in the IT profession.

The vision of the federal CIO was that this officer would report directly to the head of the department and would play an inner-circle role in departmental planning, akin to the role of most chief financial officers. The Clinger-Cohen Act of 1996 reflected this new view of the role of the CIO as critical to strategic planning by the agency as well as reinvention of better, IT-supported governmental processes. In the late 1990s, the Federal CIO Council played the lead policy role in strategic IT planning, proposing and supporting what became FirstGov.gov, the nation's premiere e-government portal. Executive Order 13011, issued in conjunction with the Clinger-Cohen Act, supported the CIO Council and the Office of Management and Budget (OMB) by creating the Information Technology Resources Board as a staff agency providing recommendations on IT systems acquisitions.

The Clinger-Cohen Act had given primary IT planning oversight authority to the OMB and this political fact of life came to overshadow early visions of the paramount role of the CIO. In a few short years, the OMB largely displaced the CIO Council as the lead federal IT planning body. As *Government Computer News* executive editor Thomas Temin (2002) observed, "Currently the OMB is mandating enterprise architectures, cross-agency development, and capital planning. Agency people are being recruited repeatedly for short tours of duty at OMB. OMB is also strongly suggesting technical means for achieving e-government by actively pushing Web technologies. In the meantime, CIOs, whose roles have never fully matured as envisioned by the Clinger-Cohen Act, seem to be on the sidelines as OMB reaches out directly to program, technology, and financial managers."

Since 1998, the OMB and the CIO Council have jointly issued an annual strategic plan that sets goals (for example, "All citizens to be connected to the products, services, and information of their government."), breaks them down into objectives (such as, "Develop a single point-of-entry portal model to access government services."), which themselves are broken down into targets (for instance, "Support implementation of Firstgov.gov."), each with a time line for completion. The plan is meant to satisfy the requirements of the Paperwork Reduction Act of 1995 and Executive Order 13011 on Federal Information Technology. While the goal of the annual plan is to enhance the strategic focus of the CIO Council, this translates into the CIO Council helping spell out and embed into a plan priorities set by the OMB. OMB priorities, with departmental feedback, are mirrored in CIO Council strategic plans.[1] However, CIO Council strategic planning is not an effective independent check on the federal enterprise architecture (FEA) planning process implemented by the OMB and described below.

EO 13011 defined the CIO Council as a "forum," not a decision-making body. While it may make recommendations, it is primarily meant as a forum to share experiences, best practices, and ideas on how to implement the OMB's government-wide strategic plan. The sidelining of agency CIOs and the imposition of a largely top-down planning process by the OMB, described below, led Temin and others to speculate that in the long run, OMB strategic planning initiatives might not last unless the power of agency CIOs was restored. However, the OMB's control over the IT budget process combined with the Bush Administration presidential mandate to pursue cross-agency consolidation of IT has thus far proved more than adequate to keep the OMB ascendant, relegating the CIO Council to a secondary, advisory role.

CIOs are mandated to accept the OMB's vision of federal enterprise architecture for IT or suffer budgetary consequences. Rare is the CIO who publicly objects to the OMB-driven one-size-fits-all interagency consolidation of data structures, software applications, and information systems. Sometimes generic financial, human resource management, or other cross-agency software have been welcomed by agency CIOs, particularly if the agency provided the model for what was later applied to other agencies. In general, however, CIOs find themselves on the budgetary defensive, forced to finance OMB priorities even at the expense of the agency's own priorities and burdened with a new level of OMB planning paperwork for every innovation they propose. As a *Government Computer News* article explained, "Agencies are migrating to a number of e-government projects, such as E-Travel, E-Payroll and systems within the Integrated Acquisition Environment. Once they are fully utilizing the e-gov systems, OMB expects them to take down their internal systems" (Miller, 2005g).

In 2004 the Government Accountability Office (GAO) interviewed CIOs in 27 major departments and agencies. Among their findings was the fact that since the Clinger-Cohen Act, the average tenure of a CIO has been about two years, whereas both current CIOs and former agency IT executives most commonly cited three to five years as the minimal time required to be effective (GAO, 2004b). The GAO noted that high turnover was limiting the CIOs' ability to put their agendas into place. An illustration of agenda blocking is found in the 2005 criticism of the OMB by the Internal Revenue Service for underfunding its tax software initiatives (Miller, 2005e). High turnover is characteristic of stressful jobs in which responsibilities are not matched by power. The power displacement of CIOs by the OMB appears to be a possible underlying cause of high turnover.

In 2005, with e-government heavily downgraded in favor of security, the OMB changed course and announced that it wanted to be "the court of last resort in terms of execution" of e-government initiatives (Miller, 2005f). John Sindelar, project executive for OMB's Line of Business Consolidation effort and OMB staff member for the 25 e-government Quicksilver projects, stated, "We need to change the mind-set of letting OMB handle all the areas that need addressing," complaining that agencies were not "taking ownership" of the OMB-mandated projects. For their part, agencies reported dissatisfaction with the lack of an OMB master plan to bring enterprise architecture (EA), capital planning, and investment control together. Barry West, CIO for HSD's Emergency Preparedness and Response Directorate, observed, "Agencies do not have enough time or resources, and there are too many other political issues. Plus, most are looking at their own issues and cannot see the larger picture many times" (Miller, 2005f). In short, as of this writing, it appeared that the OMB might be having second thoughts about its role in e-government vis-à-vis agency CIOs.

STRATEGIC PLANNING

The heart of strategic planning is environmental scanning to perceive changes, then relating these changes to the organization's mission and goals. Strategic planning for IT involves seven steps: creating the planning structure, establishing an audit of information systems, defining goals, evaluating and prioritizing proposals, setting the time horizon and composing the annual plan, obtaining approvals, and implement-ing, evaluating, and revising the plan.[2] Ideally, these steps are not en-tirely sequential but rather are embedded in an iterative process with feedback.

- Creating the planning structure—Identifying stakeholders, securing the involvement and commitment of top management; establishing the need for planning, making sure the IT Department views its role as promoting partnerships and user-friendly cooperation; establishing a provisional planning structure involving top management and rep-resentatives from all units affected; making the mandate for planning the focus on outcomes, not outputs.
- Auditing information systems—Reviewing and clarifying the agency's mission (why what is done for whom and how); environmental scan-ning (assessing changes in stakeholders and their expectations, exam-ining planning assumptions, considering legislative mandates, noting competitors and changes in technology—all in relation to how such changes affect the mission); inventorying current systems, applica-tions, structures, staffing, and resources; assessing the gap between the current situation and the organizational mission and goals; iden-tifying obstacles and barriers to success, surveying critical success factors (discussed in Chapter 13).
- Defining goals—Developing a strategic vision statement using consensus-building methods; assessing IT technical and organizational system requirements needed to close the gap between current state and the goal state; reinventorying agency processes; determining the EA (data model ensuring interoperability, process model ensuring integrated flow, and a system model ensuring nonduplication); evaluating organizational units in terms of implementation of the architecture. In the usual schema, the mission is broken into strategic goals, goals into operational objectives, and objectives into activities with milestones and time lines.[3] Objectives should be specific, measurable, attainable, results oriented, and time bound (SMART). Moreover, each objective should have one or more per-formance indicators.
- Evaluating proposals—Developing options for the planning commit-tee, prioritizing proposals by impact on the agency mission and goals; investigating best practices; relating options to resources. In the con-text of FEA, discussed below, priorities favor agency-transforming proposals that support remote customer self-service, flatter organiza-tions, interagency systems sharing, faster processing, and outsourced handoffs of subprocesses.
- Composing the annual plan—Setting the time horizon, thinking ahead at least one year and preferably longer (often five years, with annual updates); implementing a governance plan to replace the provisional planning structure with a final one; setting timetables for decisions;

detailing who initiates, who approves agenda items; setting the relation of the planning structure to the budget process; drawing an organizational chart relating all plan participants; inventorying needed guidance documents for different classes of participants; consider differentiating the final executive board from a larger, more representative advisory board; establishing an implementation plan with goal roadmaps integrating broad goals, operationalizing objectives spelling out goals, identifying measurable milestones with time lines marking progress on objectives;[4] having a mobilization plan using some combinations of participatory methods (teams, focus groups, brainstorming, retreats, surveys, field trips to best practices, representative meetings, etc.); using off-site meetings and/or outside facilitators; creating a human resource plan, which maps the organization chart with plan responsibilities; having a training plan; having an evaluation plan with effectiveness measures; having efficiency measures; establishing baselines for measures as starting points for time series; establishing benchmarks for measures (peer agencies for comparison, best practices, professional standards, and other ways of defining performance expectations).

- Obtaining administrative and political approvals—Conformity to the EA of the federal government, the state, or other jurisdiction is typically part of the administrative approval process. Citation of the specific statutory authority for proposed goals and objectives is part of the political approval process.
- Implementing the plan, evaluating outcomes, revising the plan.

The GAO has identified 24 specific agency practices by which to evaluate the level of strategic planning:

1. Has the agency documented a strategic management process for IT, including assignment of responsibilities?
2. Has the agency documented its process to integrate IT management with organizational planning and budgeting? Is senior management given regular reports on IT projects as to cost, schedules, and performance?
3. Are information security management processes integrated with strategic planning processes?
4. Is the chief financial officer involved in accounting for IT investments?
5. Is the strategic plan enterprise-wide, relating IT projects to agency mission and goals, and identifying projects that are beyond budget, behind schedule, or under performance standards?
6. Does the plan describe how IT supports strategic goals, and does the plan relate this to the agency's capital asset plan?
7. Does the plan include methods of measuring progress?

8. Does the plan have goals that contribute to increased productivity and effectiveness?
9. Does the IT plan have e-government components? An antisoftware piracy component?
10. Does the plan have specific performance measures?
11. Is there an annual report on plan progress?
12. Are agency IT processes benchmarked against public and private sector processes?
13. Is there a formal IT investment management process?
14. Is there an agency-wide IT investment management board? Are its powers and responsibilities spelled out?
15. Does the agency maintain and keep current an inventory of its IT investments?
16. Is the IT asset inventory used in managerial decision making?
17. Have IT investments been justified in terms of being in-agency or outsourced to the private sector?
18. Is each IT investment backed up by having a business case that addresses costs, benefits, schedules, and risks?
19. Are all projects consistent with the FEA?
20. Is maximum use made of off-the-shelf software?
21. Is there a structured selection process for IT investments that sets priorities and guards against conflicts, overlaps, and redundancies? Is there a system of postimplementation review?
22. Are investments modularized to the maximum extent possible?
23. Are corrective actions taken on underperforming projects?
24. Are there formal processes for terminating projects when appropriate?

In general, strategic planning is not comprehensive planning. Rather it is planning for delimited, achievable success. Where comprehensive plans are liable to be filed away, unused, due to lack of resources and overambitious goals, true strategic plans are motivating because they are credible and doable, attracting support and building a planning culture within the organization. On the other hand, strategic plans do normally cover a range of policies, including not just technology policies but also human resource, data stewardship, privacy, and security policies as well.

Enterprise Resource Planning (ERP)

Enterprise resource planning (ERP) originated as a private sector software effort to consolidate financial, human resources, and other systems into a cost-saving, planning-enhancing supersystem. For the U.S. federal government, it is significant primarily as part of the ideational background to the FEA approach to planning implemented by the OMB and which is still the dominant framework for IT planning today. The FEA is discussed further in the section below.

Initial ERP efforts in the 1980s and 1990s were often corporate failures. Severe problems arose in the effort to impose standardized one-size-fits-all consolidated information systems with the particularistic requirements of individual enterprises (Peterson, 2004a). In spite of this record of private sector failure, a number of states (e.g., Pennsylvania and North Dakota) and cities (e.g., San Antonio, New Mexico) sought to apply ERP as a strategic planning and action strategy for IT in the 1990s.

Florida became a leader in ERP, to which it had turned after finding in the 1990s that its in-house attempt to create a comprehensive tax administration software system floundered. In 1999 the Florida Department of Revenue awarded SAP, Inc., a large award to create an ERP system for the state. Aware of past disasters with off-the-shelf ERP software products, SAP subcontracted with Deloitte Consulting to create a Florida-tailored version of ERP software. In following this path, Florida rejected the more common route of looking to public-sector-oriented software systems for tax management from companies like AMS or Accenture. Using the resulting ERP system, SUNTAX, Florida was able to get rid of aging legacy COBOL systems and reduce its IT staff. It also cut salaries by 15% to pay SAP for the new system (Peterson, 2004a). Florida was governed by the president's brother, and Florida ERP seemed to provide an illustration of the advantages of information system consolidation, which was to become a central focus of FEA.

The Federal Enterprise Architecture (FEA)

The Federal Enterprise Architecture (FEA, also called the Federal Enterprise Architecture Framework) is the primary planning system used by the OMB for purposes of IT planning and budgeting. Based on a survey by the GAO of best practices in the public and private sectors in the 1980s, the GAO advanced EA in the 1990s as a critical IT success factor. The OMB and the CIO Council collaborated with the GAO to develop EA guidance in the 1990s. The Clinger-Cohen Act of 1996 included a provision requiring agency CIOs to implement EAs in order to integrate agency goals and promote business processes with IT. In 1999 the CIO Council published the "Federal Enterprise Architecture Framework" as a way of encouraging common constructs in agency EA plans that were then emerging.[5] In 2002 the OMB formally initiated the FEA management system, drawing heavily from Zachman's (1987) framework as described in the *IBM Systems Journal,* a systems theory approach to IT.

The FEA framework is defined as a logical structure for classifying and organizing complex information. It is based on five reference models—

performance, business, technical, service, and data, described later in this section.[6] Each reference model is oriented toward supporting the identification of common data structures, software applications, and information systems that may represent patterns where cost savings may be achieved through cross-agency integration. That is, patterns are defined as frequently occurring combinations of business and technical elements that can be used to deliver reuseable business services across the enterprise and, by extension, across agencies. The practical import for an agency is that the OMB's FEA system pressures agencies to use generic cross-agency information systems rather than traditional systems customized to the agency. This may be perceived as good, bad, or neutral, depending on the agency. Then too, some agencies may find an advantage if their systems become the model for cross-agency integrated systems. OMB associate director for IT, Mark Forman, viewed having an FEA as the basis for attaining maximum interoperability and integration across federal agencies.

Starting in 2002, a $6 million federal CIO Council fund, contributed from agency budgets, was used by the OMB to develop the performance and business reference models. Later, the OMB requested a separate FEA budget (Miller, 2002c). The Federal Enterprise Architecture Program Management Office (FEAPMO) was created within the OMB to coordinate FEA efforts among the many agencies of the federal government.[7] In 2003, the OMB mandated that agencies support the interoperability and integration standards embedded in the FEA and warned agencies that noncompliance could be tied to cuts in their IT budgets.

OMB Circular A-11 in its 2004 version required all agency IT investment plans to support the President's Management Agenda, including emphasis on IT security, outsourcing of IT ("market-based government"), support for the President's e-government initiatives, and elimination of redundant IT activities (the focus of the FEA). In 2004, for FY 2005 planning, the OMB required agencies to consolidate their requests for "back-office applications" in just three business cases: office automation, infrastructure, and communications. The intended effect of this was to force agencies to make enterprise-wide rather than bureau-specific decisions about internal support applications used by agencies. This, in turn, was meant to structure agency budget requests for such applications in FEA terms, helping further identify patterns for cross-bureau and cross-agency integration and consolidation, thus centralizing IT (Miller, 2003m). For FY 2006 planning, the OMB required all agencies to identify opportunities for collaboration and consolidation as some agencies had already done, consistent with new EA (Housing and Urban Development, for instance, planned in 2004 to consolidate its 16 human resource systems into 1, and its 31 insurance support systems into 11) (Miller, 2003o).

Also in 2004, the OMB moved forcefully to promote the consolidation of IT in certain crucial lines of business—financial management, human resource management, health systems, case management, and grants management. Toward this end, the OMB issued requests for information to vendors and set up task forces to review vendor responses and draft recommendations with a view to finishing these consolidation projects in 2005 (Miller, 2004d). Its 2004 SmartBUY guidance required agencies to issue instructions to eliminate duplicative spending on projects over $2 million. It also demanded special agency justification proving nonduplication for any IT projects that were in any of the OMB's 25 e-government or "lines of business" consolidation initiatives (Miller, 2004f). Agencies were required to attest in writing on a quarterly basis that they were not planning or scheduling duplicate IT investments or acquisitions, with agencies to be held accountable in the quarterly President's Management Agenda evaluations. That is, in 2004 the OMB moved to take strong enforcement steps against agencies that might think about deviating from the OMB's plan to consolidate information systems in lines of business (e.g., financial systems) identified through FEA mechanisms described later.

The FEA's Performance Reference Model (PRM), released in 2003 (Version 1.0), described a set of outcomes and metrics by which agencies were to measure their performance against best business practices. The PRM outlined a set of performance measurement areas, such as mission and business results. Measurement areas were broken down into measurement categories, such as services for citizens. Each measurement category has generic measurement indicators, such as delivery time. The PRM also described processes by which agencies were to arrive at performance measures. In summary, the PRM is the basis for making the FEA a performance- or results-based management system. It addresses the problem identified by the GAO (2004d) that while most agencies have strategic plans and goals, these goals were not always linked to actual performance measures, in spite of agencies being required by the Paperwork Reduction Act of 1995 and the Clinger-Cohen Act of 1996 to develop performance measures.

The Business Reference Model (BRM) Version 1.0 was released in 2002 and 2.0 in 2003. The BRM 2.0 divided all federal government activity into four *Business Areas,* 39 *Lines of Business,* and 154 *Subfunctions.* This framework created a set of categories used by the OMB to cluster existing and proposed IT projects, to better consider which may be duplicative, and as a basis for creating cross-agency consolidated software systems in any given line of business. The BRM outlined four business areas. *Services for Citizens* included such lines of business as Economic Development, Homeland Security, Law Enforcement, Natural Resources, and General Science and Innovation. The *Mode of Delivery* business area included such lines of business as Direct Services for Citizens, Knowledge Creation and Management, and Credit and Insurance. *Support Delivery of Services* included lines of business such as Public Affairs, Revenue Collection, and Internal Risk Management. Finally, *Management of Governmental Services* included lines of business for Supply Chain Management, Human Resource Management, and Financial Management. Each line of business had associated subfunctions (e.g., Homeland Security had the subfunction of border and transportation security; Economic Development had the subfunction of financial sector oversight).

Agencies have had difficulty aligning their own functional classifications with the generic ones reflected in the BRM, particularly since the BRM categories kept being revised, at least in its first years. IT management, for instance, was in the Business Area of *Management of Governmental Services* in 2002 and in the different Business Area of *Support Delivery of Services* in 2003. Beyond the difficulty of some agencies in forcing their functional categories into BRM categories (e.g., community services in BRM 2.0 had to be mapped to the Community and Regional Development subfunction, even though they were not primarily oriented toward development), there was the broader issue that BRM was grouping by function. Other bases of grouping exist, such as grouping services by demographic target (e.g., African-Americans) or grouping by geographic region of delivery. Consolidation of IT by function (i.e., by lines of business) may mean that the resulting integrated systems will be different from what might evolve if demographic grouping or regional grouping were given priority instead. Specifically, BRM categories align well with OMB budget-driven initiatives but may not serve to promote alternative priorities and, indeed, may serve to inhibit them.

The Service Reference Model (SRM) involved identifying classes of software applications for enterprise licensing for cross-agency use.[8] The purpose was to promote reuse of software components across agencies. Applications were divided into seven domains: customer, process automation, business management, digital asset, business analytical, back office, and support services. These seven domains were broken down into 29 service types (for example, Customer Service has the service type customer relationship management; Business Analytical Services has the type analysis and statistics). The 29 service types were broken down into 168 components. Agencies must classify the applications they use in terms of the categories of the SRM, and when considering new systems, must consult the SRM to determine what similar applications are already in use by other agencies.

The Technical Reference Model (TRM) described technology used to support the delivery of service components of the architecture, including standards for implementing the technology. That is, the TRM was guidance for agencies to use in developing their technical architectures, describing standards, specifications, and technologies considered by the OMB to be consistent with the FEA and with which agencies should "align" their own architectures. The TRM organized this guidance into four core service areas: standards and specifications for service access and delivery, for service platform and infrastructure, for service components, and for service interface and integration (interoperability). The four service areas were broken down into more specific service categories, each with its own service standards, which in turn have service specifications. For example, the Service Access and Delivery core service area has the service category access channels, which in turn has the service standard Web browsers, which have the service specification Internet Explorer and Netscape Navigator. In essence, agencies must confine IT development to products and standards specified in the TRM guidance from OMB. The danger, of course, is that the guidance will fall behind technology change and will straightjacket innovation. Or put another way, there is an inevitable trade-off between standardization and innovation.

The Data Reference Model (DRM), released in November, 2004, is the fifth, last, and most critical for implementing FEA models. It mandated that agencies create common data definitions to categorize and exchange information. The DRM did not specify what the data structures and formats must be, but it called on agencies to agree on common data definitions, structures, and formats to promote sharing. The DRM also required that data to be collected and shared be related to and organized by lines of business and their subfunctions, with a view to data sharing among units engaged in the same subfunction. For instance, a 2003 DRM pilot project in the Department of Interior (DOI) applied the Data Reference Model to the DOI's Recreation One-Stop e-government project, to clarify what data to include and to share with regard to making reservations at state and national parks and to develop a Recreation Markup Language to support Recreation One-Stop (Miller, 2004c).

In addition to the five reference models of the FEA, there are various *overlays*. These are policy documents that affect all five FEA reference models. For instance, the Architecture and Infrastructure Committee of the Federal CIO Council in the fall of 2004 released two overlays on security and privacy, with a third planned at this writing.

The Federal Enterprise Architecture Assessment Framework from the OMB[9] (see Table 11-1) provides agencies with targets as they move from pre-implementation in stage 1 to FEA maturity in stage 5 (Table 11-1 is abbreviated to show just stages 3 and 5). Many elements of the assessment are based on the *Practical Guide to Federal Enterprise Architecture* from the Federal CIO Council, available from its website.[10] Levels 0 through 3 in the framework assess the content of an agency's EA program, while levels 4 and 5 assess the extent the agency integrates EA with the agency's IT investment decision-making process. At the time version 1.1 of the FEA was issued in April 2003, the OMB rated 76 of 96 agencies being at stage 1, with no structured FEA plans (Miller, 2003n). For the remaining four stages, the 2003 FEA version was more demanding of agencies than had been version 1.0 in 2002:

> *Stage 2:* An executive body is to be assigned to develop FEA, set metrics, and allocate resources. The 2002 version had only asked agencies to identify roles of the chief stakeholders. The OMB considered 10 agencies were at this level in 2003.
>
> *Stage 3:* Work is to have begun on implementing architecture products, and on tracking and measuring progress. The 2002 version had only asked for a transition plan. The OMB considered 10 agencies were at this level in 2003.
>
> *Stage 4.* A complete set of EA products is to have been approved by management and a maintenance policy in place. The 2002 version had only asked for approval, not a maintenance plan. The OMB considered that no agencies were at this level.
>
> *Stage 5.* Advanced performance metrics are to be in place; return on investment has been realized; security is integrated security with the FEA. The 2002 version had only asked for steering committee review of investments and a maintenance policy. The OMB considered only the Executive Office of the President was at this level in 2003.

Though there was some easing in 2004, considerable pressure was placed on CIOs by the OMB, which routinely rated FEA and e-government efforts of the departments to be at the lowest, unacceptable rung of the OMB's envisioned ladder of planning progress.

How is the FEA used for planning? In preparing their FY 2005 budgets, agencies had to relate proposed IT investments to the FEA performance reference model, defining performance metrics. This in turn enabled the OMB to spot where agencies share metrics. Shared performance metrics identified for the OMB areas of potential interagency collaboration, potential use of common software, and even potential use of common data structures. That is, a major driving force behind the FEA is enabling planners at the top to identify ways in which the local plans of con-

Table 11-1   OMB Enterprise Architecture Assessment Framework (Partial)

Agency:
Agency EA Date:
Evaluation Date:

	Level 3	Level 5
Change	EA is beginning to be operationalize across the enterprise (i.e., part of transition, CPIC, budget).	IT planning is optimized through the EA.
A. Architectural Approach	The transition plan describes some portions of the changes needed to transition from as-is to target; and information value chain model (operational views).	The EA demonstrates a relationship of the transition, target, and gap closure to investment planning and execution.
B. Strategic Direction	The EA defines a target architecture. EA defines change and risk management strategy or approach.	The EA demonstrates application of the EA for purposes of creating and maintaining investment programs. The EA demonstrates an implemented process for managing changes and updates to the EA.
Integration	EA is beginning to be operationalized across the enterprise (i.e., part of transition, CPIC, budget).	IT planning is optimized through the EA.

continues

	Level 3	Level 5
A. Interoperability	Interoperability standards are defined through patterns and are related to business functions. Business functions are aligned to components and services at the enterprise level.	Using common interoperability standards, the EA demonstrates the ability to link and integrate common technologies and business processes.
B. Data	Common and defined approach to integrating data with business processes and mission priorities is defined and used throughout the EA.	EA demonstrates its ability to increase integration and promote the reuse of data within the enterprise and across other agencies (linkage of data to common components, business functions (BRM).
C. Business Logic	Business rules are integrated and described throughout all portions of the architecture.	The EA demonstrates the results of viewing common business rules across the enterprise and across other agencies (integrated with the SRM).
D. Interface	Some form of a "node" diagram depicts inter-relationships between interfaces and business functions.	The EA demonstrates the establishment of common components that are integrated through well-defined interface requirements.
Convergence	EA is beginning to be operationalized across the enterprise (i.e., part of transition, CPIC, budget).	IT planning is optimized through the EA.

Table 11-1 *continued*

	Level 3	Level 5
A. Components	The EA uses services, components, and interoperability relationships to describe portions of the architecture.	The EA uses services, components, and interoperability relationships to describe transition and investment decision processes and to present a service/component-enabled target architecture.
B. Technical Platform	EA defines and integrates TRM with a view of services, which begins to show patterns.	EA links all artifacts to TRM and services and provides the ability to view redundancy across all EA products based on any TRM or service component.
C. Performance	EA defines detailed performance measures and links them to service and technical portions of the architecture.	EA defines detailed performance measures, links them to all technical and service layers, and integrates performance measures with transition and investment planning.
D. Security	Security standards are integrated within portions of the components, applications, and technologies.	Security standards are tightly defined and are presented as part of the transition planning and investment analysis portions of the EA.

stituent agencies may be reformulated in a strategic way to achieve cost savings through greater integration. For instance, the OMB used the FEA in conjunction with the fiscal year budgeting process to identify common financial management functions that could be shared across agencies. The identification process entails multiple rounds in which agencies progressively identify and build upon common definitions, reporting to the OMB.

This is not to say that the FEA planning process is an unmitigated success, even from the OMB viewpoint. For instance, for FY 2004, the OMB assessed over 1400 IT business cases representing $35 billion and found only 280 cases ($8 billion) were done correctly. Another 772 cases ($20.9 billion) failed to meet two of three criteria: (1) insufficient relation of budget to agency mission; (2) insufficient project management tracking cost goals and on-schedule goals, as well as mission-enhancement goals; and (3) inadequate security. Another 349 cases were so poor they were rejected outright (Miller, 2003l). Responding to criticism that the ever-changing FEA planning system was so inconsistent from year to year that agency expertise in business case planning was undercut by the OMB itself, in 2004 the OMB announced that FY 2006 planning would be stabilized to operate under the same guidance as FY 2005 (Miller, 2004e).

While cautiously supportive of OMB FEA efforts, the GAO has also questioned whether the FEA can even be considered an "enterprise architecture" as it had been envisioned in the 1990s. Of the FEA, the GAO (2004c p. 2) stated, "GAO's reading of its content suggests that it is more akin to a classification scheme for government operations than a true enterprise architecture. Further, OMB requires agencies to 'map' and 'align' their architectures with the FEA. However, since these terms are not well defined, GAO asks if the expected relationship between the FEA and the agencies' architectures is clear enough." By the OMB's measure of EA *maturity,* more agencies had gone backwards than forwards since 2001, while most agencies remained unchanged. That is, GAO reports bring into question the planning effectiveness of the FEA system. On the other hand, development of integrated information systems is going ahead for five lines of business that the OMB has targeted for elimination of duplication: human resource systems, financial systems, grants management, health, and case management.

The history of public sector IT is one that raises serious questions about the wisdom of very large IT systems. Such history had in the past led to the common view that "The larger the system, the more likely failure." The "Shall we super-size that?" approach to creating one-size-fits-all "McSystems" was contrasted with the "small is beautiful" view that success came from more limited, modular systems created by participative sociotechnical processes within agencies. The FEA is a bold systems theoretic policy to plan for comprehensive cross-agency systems. It is too early to tell what the ultimate outcome will be. What is clear, however, is that as a planning system, the FEA creates a presumption that government-wide information systems are good and agency-specific systems bear the burden of proving that they are justified.

PORTFOLIO MANAGEMENT

Portfolio management is an approach to managing IT investments and setting priorities among projects. It is considered a planning best practice and is required by the OMB. Traditional IT contract management was done on a project by project basis. While some prioritization of IT projects might occur in any given budget cycle, simply due to limited resources, the agency was not challenged to consider the entire set of projects as a whole in relation to strategic planning. Considering the entire set of projects was what was meant by managing IT investments as a *portfolio.*

Under traditional IT investment management, each project had been justified more or less separately, leading to a conservative policy in which risky projects were not funded. In a portfolio management approach, the public manager was encouraged to think in terms of a mix of less risky but lower-payoff projects *and* higher-risk but higher-payoff projects. Translated into specifics, the OMB and GAO hoped the portfolio approach would help promote large-scale e-government projects that involved reengineering agency work processes and that were higher in risk, but could be justified as part of a portfolio mix of investments.

Portfolio management requires top management support, buy-in by stakeholders, a strong evaluation/performance tracking component, attention to best practices in comparable organizations, and, eventually, a cross-agency approach that eliminates redundancy and seeks to reinvent government processes. It was first popularized by F. Warren McFarlan (1981) in an article in the *Harvard Business Review* and was later endorsed by the GAO, which outlined it in its 1994 publications, *Strategic Information Management Guide* and *Improving Mission Performance through Strategic Information Management.* The GAO's 1998 *Executive Guide: Measuring Performance and Demonstrating Results of Information Technology Investments* endorsed portfolio management and was widely influential. In 2000, the OMB's revision of Circular A-130 required agencies to maintain a portfolio of major information systems as part of their capital planning process. Also, OMB Circular A-11, Section 53, detailed agency portfolio reporting procedures, the reporting schedule, and the relation of the portfolio to the President's Management Agenda, which in turn was the basis for the FEA planning framework.

With the mandating of portfolio management, vendors raced in to provide software solutions for public managers. Portfolio management software proliferated, such as PlanView Portfolio Management (www.planview.com), ProSight Portfolios (www.prosight.com), and Niku Portfolio Manager (www.niku.com), to name a few (Essex, 2003). Other commercial software supported performance management and related aspects of assembling a business plan (Essex, 2005).

The portfolio management concept was embedded in the 2003 Investment Management Framework and its successor, the Information Technology Investment Management (ITIM) framework released by the GAO in 2004 (GAO, 2004e). The ITIM framework outlines five progressive stages of maturity of agency ITIM capabilities. To attain a higher stage, the agency must institutionalize all requirements for that stage and for all lower stages. ITIM's purpose is to be a roadmap for development of agency IT investment processes and planning:

- Stage 1 (Creating Investment Awareness)—Agency investments are selected in an unstructured, ad hoc manner. The agency is only beginning to create awareness of the investment process.
- Stage 2 (Building the Investment Foundation)—The foundation is laid for sound IT investment processes by formalizing investment control processes at the project level.
- Stage 3 (Developing a Complete Investment Portfolio)—The agency moves from project-centric processes to a portfolio approach, evaluating potential investments by how well they support the agency's missions, strategies, and goals.
- Stage 4 (Improving the Investment Process)—The agency implements formal evaluation techniques to improve its IT investment processes and its investment portfolio, including deselection of obsolete, high-risk, or low-value IT investments.
- Stage 5 (Leveraging IT for Strategic Outcomes)—IT investment processes are formally benchmarked against "best-in-class" organizations, and agencies look for breakthrough ITs that will enable them to transform their processes.

In practical terms, at Stage 2 agencies were expected to establish an investment review board and an EA board (Miller, 2003h).[11] The boards were supposed to work together and investments were supposed to be linked to the FEA, using a portfolio management approach.

RISK MANAGEMENT

Risk management (distinct from security management, discussed in Chapter 7) is a planning specialty that has become increasingly professionalized in the last two decades. While risk analysis audits may be performed by general IT staff, in larger agencies they are more likely to be performed by consultants and/or full-time in-house employees trained in risk management. The general purpose of the risk analysis audit is to divide potential risks into categories (physical, software, network, etc.), surveying risks in each category, assessing the magnitude and probability of each risk, identifying potential safeguards for each risk, and evaluating the costs of safeguards in terms of the estimated risk magnitudes and probabilities. The full costs of safeguards throughout their life cycle are estimated by including development or acquisition costs, installation and training costs, and ongoing operation and maintenance costs. Just as risk magnitudes are discounted by probability of risk occurrence, safeguard costs are discounted by estimated probability of safeguard effectiveness in preventing the risk. Multicriterion decision software and multiattribute utility models exist to help compare safeguards and calculate weighted values even for such diffuse risks as reputational harm. The result of the risk audit is a risk reduction recommendation to top management, prioritizing safeguard measures in terms of weighted, discounted costs and benefits.

Risk analysis can be broader than the type of risk audit described here. In its broad form, risk analysis is itself a form of strategic planning, surveying the agency's environment to consider risks from competing agencies, risks from the fiscal state of the government, risks from opposing stakeholders, risks from new technology, and so on. This more diffuse consideration of risks calls for more qualitative approaches. The simplest is perhaps using focus groups of stakeholders to discuss risks and fears. Scenario building is another qualitative approach, in which the risk analyst models hypothetical situations to assess possible outcomes, problems, and risks. War gaming in the DOD is perhaps the ultimate form of this, but it can be done on a smaller scale as when the National Park Service brainstorms ways in which tourists might have accidents in recreation settings.[12] Scenario building may be done on paper, by role playing, by computer simulation, or by some combination. Scenarios can also be developed from consideration of existing risk incidents, or by polling experts, as is done in the Delphi technique, which is an iterative process of surveys and feedback until experts reach consensus.

One form of IT risk is liability. Numerous examples exist. At a public hospital a machine used to administer radiation doses had a software malfunction that led to overdosing and the death of two patients in the early 1990s. The GAO once found that deficiencies in the Environmental Protection Agency's information system led to it failing to recognize potential birth defect hazards associated with a California chemical spill. Inaccurate computer-generated weather information from the National Weather Service was once held responsible for a ship's crew member washing overboard in a storm. In another case, erroneous elevations on a computer-generated map led a pilot to crash into a mountain, leading to lawsuits against the mapping agency. While risk management cannot prevent the unexpected, it can accomplish two things: (1) ensure that the agency has a risk abatement plan and has taken reasonable steps to identify and prevent mishaps, including having a process in place to identify, respond to, and adapt agency rules on the basis of mishaps; and (2) ensure that the agency has provided clients with appropriate risk information and disclaimers.

As outsourcing of IT functions occurs, risk increases. Part of risk management is actually a form of contract management, ensuring that contracts have a clear scope of work, with specified services each with clear acceptance criteria, due dates, officers designated to be responsible for sign-off, and a payment schedule including holdbacks not paid until acceptance points are reached or the project is completed. Risk management of contracts usually also provides for reduction of payments for failure to meet acceptance criteria on schedule, with the reduction increasing a certain percentage for each week late. A cap (e.g., 15% of total project costs) is usually placed on expense reimbursement to the contractor. The contractor may also be asked to sign warranties on staff (work force size and skill/experience levels) and performance quality of deliverables (e.g., 90-day warrantee). To avoid problem passing among different software, hardware, networking, and other vendors, the agency may well contract with a systems integrator who warrants the performance of the integrated system. Even with a systems integrator, however, the contact with the component (e.g., software) vendor should clearly specify the vendor's responsibility to identify the reasons for malfunctions. Also with software, the intellectual property status should be a written contract provision (i.e., a work for hire owned by the agency). Finally, risk managers will require that the contract specify the mechanisms for vendor–agency dispute resolution (i.e., mediation or arbitration). The larger the project, the more the agency should invest in professional risk management as vendor-supplied contracts generally provide little risk protection for the agency but instead often contain one-sided disclaimers of warranties, limitations on remedies, and limitations on liabilities.

Another particular category of risk management is dealing with the IT-related liability of workplace injury. For both public and private sector, the Bureau of Labor Statistics (BLS) estimates some 600,000 workers suffered serious workplace injury because of ergonomic hazards, including 28,000 with carpal tunnel syndrome, costing an average of $13,000 per case. Carpal tunnel syndrome is among the repetitive motion illnesses associated with keyboarding on computers. Based on BLS estimates, public managers can expect that about one in 500 office employees will suffer from repetitive motion disorder. Others put the rate higher. The

American Federation of Teachers, 95% of whose members use computers, says 26% of them have developed health problems from using computer-related equipment. Although Congress has repealed Clinton administration workplace rules on repetitive motion, public officials may still be liable in court if injury results and the agency has not taken reasonable steps to address ergonomic concerns (Newcombe, 2002a). Reasonable steps include health warnings, rest breaks, variation of tasks, and being responsive to employee needs for use of ergonomic keyboards, chairs, and other IT hardware and furniture.

RECORDS MANAGEMENT

Records are the agency memory that underpins all planning efforts. Moreover, good recordkeeping can save costs: the GAO has estimated that failure to create or maintain complete and accurate records has cost the government millions of dollars for goods and services never received (NARA, 1995, p. 2). Records are defined in the Federal Records Act, which states "Records include all books, papers, maps, photographs, machine-readable materials, or other documentary materials, regardless of physical form or characteristics, made or received by an agency of the United States Government under Federal law or in connection with the transaction of public business and preserved or appropriate for preservation by that agency or its legitimate successor as evidence of the organization, functions, policies, decisions, procedures, operations, or other activities of the Government or because of the informational value of the data in them."

Records management underlies e-government. It is instructive to note that certain African countries that have experimented with electronic access to records in financial information system, on the premise that greater information transparency would lead to greater governmental accountability, have found instead that corruption has not been checked. The reason, Barata and Cain (2001) found, was that for electronic access to records to lead to accountability, accurate record management must be established in the first place. This in turn requires accurate source data, realistic backup and storage, realistic targets and management of data collection, and payment of recordkeeping staff at a level adequate to maintain a good living standard without resort to corruption.

It is the obligation of public agencies to retain records. OMB Circular A-123 requires federal agencies to affirm the integrity of paper and digital electronic records. The National Archives and Records Administration's (NARA's) guidelines, *Agency Recordkeeping Requirements: A Management Guide* (NARA, 1995), provides this recordkeeping requirements checklist:

1. Has the agency provided guidance for all employees on the definition of federal records and nonrecord materials, including those created by office automation tools (word processing, electronic mail, spreadsheet, and database applications), and the ways in which they must be managed?

2. Does each office or program have written guidance on what records, including electronic records, are to be created and maintained and the format of each record copy?

3. Has the agency issued guidance and instructions for documenting policies and decisions, especially those decisions reached orally and for those communicated electronically?

4. Has the agency issued guidance on the record status of working papers or files and drafts?

5. Has the agency issued guidance on personal papers?

6. Has the agency implemented controls over the removal of documentary materials?

7. Do contracts identify which contractor-created records are federal records?

8. Do contracts specify the delivery of all records that may, in addition to the final product, have future value to the agency? Are contractors required to deliver background data and technical documentation along with electronic records?

The NARA guidelines require agencies to have a records management policy, but they do not spell out in detail just what must be retained and of that portion retained, how long it must be retained. In 2002, a NARA report admitted the agency had not been able to keep up with electronic recordkeeping, leading NARA to give departments more discretion over records disposal with fewer restrictions (Gellman, 2002a, 2002b). Records that are not disposed of but disseminated fall under OMB *Guidelines for Ensuring and Maximizing the Quality, Objectivity, Utility, and Integrity of Information Disseminated by Federal Agencies* (2001), which mandated that agencies have formal information quality control procedures.

Digital records are forcing a revolution in records management, if only because they are swamping NARA and its state counterparts. By 2003, some 80% of federal agencies had formal policies on managing electronic records and three quarters of agencies had converted records to digital formats (Walker, 2003b). NARA received more electronic files from the Clinton administration than it had in the previous three decades from all government departments. In 2003, NARA estimated it would need to archive 1 billion personnel files from DOD alone in the next 10 years. It also anticipated 40 terabytes (40 million megabytes) of information from the 2000 Census (Miller, 2003p).

Under interpretations of the Federal Records Act, e-mail communications are public records as noted in the previously mentioned NARA guide and in NARA regulations (36 CFR Chapter XII, Subchapter B). On the other hand, there is universal agreement that agencies should not waste taxpayer dollars archiving all e-mail—certainly not spam, for instance. This is an issue at state and local levels, not just federal. For instance, in 2002, the Associated Press and Lee Newspapers of Montana requested some 3500 e-mails from the governor in relation to an investigation by the Montana Department of Justice regarding improper use of state telephones for political fundraising. In the course of this controversy a number of issues emerged that have general import:

1. Freedom of Information Act and other public requests for access to e-mail is futile if the agency has a policy of short retention (Montana retained e-mail only 30 days).
2. Even if e-mail files for the past exist, they may be embedded in a disaster-recovery system that is not designed for easy, inexpensive retrieval of particular records.
3. Agency staff may have to read each e-mail to determine if there are privacy concerns regarding release of e-mail.
4. Montana maintained it was responsible for preserving only "official records," not all e-mail (not spam, for instance). While reasonable in principle, implementing this distinction requires either manual sorting (expensive) or use of a computer algorithm (subject to significant erroneous classification).

It also emerged in the Montana case that the state did not have a records management policy and system for e-mail. Noting that agencies had lost 50% of their electronic records, including e-mail from the governor, key legislators, as well as policy drafts shedding light on the origin of key decisions, in 2002 Washington launched the first State Government Digital Archives in the United States (Brown, 2002). At the federal level, NARA requires that agencies have a policy for all digital records, including e-mail, but agency compliance has not been given high priority.

Data structures are also a significant problem for records management. Also in 2003, NARA estimated that federal agencies used some 4800 different data formats. By 2007 NARA hopes to have developed an archiving system that will be hardware- and software-independent and that will reproduce documents and data in their original format and preserve context (the relation of records to each other) (Miller, 2003p). In the meantime, the U.S. government lacks an information system adequate to the needs of governmental records management.

Records management can raise issues of federalism. State open-records laws may conflict with federal laws that prohibit distribution of data.

For instance, after the 9/11 terrorism attack, the American Civil Liberties Union (ACLU) sued Passaic and Hudson counties in New Jersey to get a list of detainees under a state law that stipulates that the names and the dates of entry of all inmates in county jails, without exception, "shall be open to public inspection." The Immigration and Naturalization Service claimed that since detainees were federal prisoners, even though held in county jails under contract, information could not be released. The ACLU claimed county jail records were purely state records, not federal. The state court sided with the ACLU.

Another federalism issue pertaining to records management arose when Congress passed a law (23 USC 409) stating that accident victims could not use state-collected records on which intersections are most hazardous. Congress wanted to limit the use of such data to support for state requests for federal highway funds. The Washington State Supreme Court, however, holding Congress had infringed on 10th Amendment states' rights, said plaintiffs could indeed use state traffic hazard records in lawsuits (Hammitt, 2002). In the case of *Pierce County v. Guillen* (2003), the U.S. Supreme Court overturned the state court and upheld Congress's right to withhold intersection fatality data, reasoning that forcing the withholding of state records could reasonably be believed to result in more diligent reporting and improved public road safety.[13]

The digital revolution in information records has the potential to diminish rather than increase accountability. While in simple systems with limited information, rules may be manually applied or if embedded in computer-sorting algorithms the rules are still easily identifiable. In a complex information system handling records on a massive basis, and which has evolved over a long period of time, perhaps through one or more outsourced contractors, Meijer (2001) noted the "logic" of outcomes is not easily deciphered in thousands of lines of code. Since system implementation often differs from system documentation, effectively rules may become untraceable and accountability lost.[14]

SUMMARY

In good times, organizations engage in planning to achieve objectives that further the organization's goals and fulfill its mission. In economically adverse times, the reality of planning tends to be more defensive, serving the prime directive of all organizations—survival. At this writing, President Bush's FY 2005 budget proposal has asked Congress for only a 1% increase in IT funding, the lowest in a decade. It is even lower, taking inflation into account. Moreover, the greatly increased budgetary bite of security-related IT in the post-9/11 world has meant that mission-oriented IT finds itself struggling. Strategies for planning in adverse times favor alignment (agency plans emphasize the priorities of the president, governor, or other chief political officer), core continuity (plans prioritize core agency functions over innovative expansions), and cost savings (plans give priority to revenue-producing or cost-cutting systems).

In this challenging environment, public management leadership is critical. A study of successful federal e-commerce projects by Shi (2002) found that IT success was associated with "transformational leadership" and with strategic planning by public managers. Ultimately, planning is about organizational transformation, and leaders who recognize this are in the best position to contribute to their agencies. This may seem a mere generalization, but leaders who cast planning as an exercise in budget cutting or as a top-down passing on of the current party line from on high are not apt to create the culture of planning that mobilizes the entire agency for progressive change. Leaders who cast planning as an exercise in organizational transformation are positioned to relate the agency's mission to a vision of change. To paraphrase scripture, without a vision, the agency fails.

Sociotechnical theory would seem to have the most to contribute to the concept of transformational leadership in strategic planning. The sociotechnical school has focused on information systems as human systems requiring stakeholder motivation and participatory buy-in to the vision of organizational change. However, the reality of strategic planning as implemented by the OMB and GAO is much closer to systems theory, on which it is explicitly based, with its emphasis on comprehensive integration of information systems. In the arena of planning, reinforcement theorists would probably find their views confirmed by the use of technology to centralize power in the OMB, even to the point of sidelining departmental CIOs. And as to technological determinist theory, planning has been less technology driven than it has been politically driven by a presidential management agenda that sees the application of what it thinks are business enterprise methods to the public sector as the best way forward.

DISCUSSION QUESTIONS

1. What lessons for IT can one draw from the terrorist attacks of September 11, 2001?
2. What was the vision of the position of CIO at the federal level? How has the OMB's primary authority in IT planning oversight impacted the position of CIO?
3. In your own words, describe the process of strategic planning for IT. What essential actions must occur in order for a strategic plan to succeed?

4. What is the Federal Enterprise Architecture? What "incentives" exist to encourage agency adherence to FEA standards?
5. The FEA's Performance Reference Model includes a set of outcomes and metrics that agencies can use to measure their performance against best business practices. How does this model fit or not fit into existing agency frameworks?
6. What are the five FEA reference models? What is their overall purpose? What overlays exist?
7. What criticism has been brought against the OMB's FEA efforts?
8. How does a portfolio management approach to managing IT investments differ from the traditional approach? How does the GAO's ITIM framework work?
9. How is risk management a form of contract management?

GLOSSARY

Business Reference Model: The BRM is that component of the Federal Enterprise Architecture that categorizes all government activities into business areas, lines of business, and subfunctions.

Data structures: Data structures are codified configurations of information or data organized in a classification system for access in a particular manner.

Enterprise architectures: An enterprise architecture is a framework for IT decision making. It consists of a logically consistent set of principles, policies, models, standards, and guidelines that seek to ensure that IT systems will likely be interoperable and efficient.

Environmental scanning: Environmental scanning is the organization's process for examining external factors that may impact the organization, positively or negatively.

Ergonomics: Ergonomics is the study of human environments (work, leisure, home) and tools and their physiological impact on humans.

Performance indicators: Performance indicators are statistical measures used to assess progress toward goals and objectives.

Performance Reference Model: The PRM is that component of the Federal Enterprise Architecture that defines outcomes and metrics by which agencies are to measure their performance against best business practices.

Project success: In an IT context, a project is successful if it is implemented on time, within budget, and with the specified performance capabilities.

Repetitive motion injury/illness: An injury or illness caused by stress on the body from the repetitious nature of a movement, such as prolonged typing at a keyboard or prolonged viewing of a computer monitor.

Software Reference Model: The SRM is that component of the Federal Enterprise Architecture that identifies classes of software applications for enterprise licensing for cross-agency use, with a view to promote the reuse of software components across agencies.

Technical Reference Model: The TRM is that component of the Federal Enterprise Architecture (FEA) that provides guidance to agencies regarding interoperable technical standards, specifications, and technologies considered by the OMB to be consistent with the FEA.

ENDNOTES

[1]The 2004 CIO Council Strategic Plan is available at http://www.cio.gov/documents/CIO_Council_Strategic_Plan_FY04.pdf.

[2]This description of strategic planning steps is partly based on the *Guidelines for Strategic Planning* from the U.S. Department of Energy (1996).

[3]Strategic planning vocabulary varies and some schema are more elaborate than others. For instance, some call for a vision statement as well as a mission statement. Some refer to the activities that implement objectives as *strategies,* while others prefer to preserve that term for use in relation to strategic goals. Some label these activities *key efforts.* Large organizations may have program missions and program goals as well as department/agency/organizational mission and goals.

[4]While the common form of planning breaks the organization mission down into strategic goals, then into targets or objectives, some agencies use other schemes. The GAO, for instance, in its *GAO Performance and Accountability Report 2004,* breaks the mission into strategic goals, then goals into strategic objectives, then these into performance goals, which in turn are broken into key efforts.

[5]The first EA plan was from the National Institute of Standards in 1989, followed by EA plans in DOD and Treasury.

[6]The five models were documented at http://www.feapmo.gov/, as of December, 2004.

[7]In 2004, FEAPMO issued FEA best practices guidance to agencies.

[8]In 2002, the OMB named the IBM Grid Computing Platform and also the Microsoft. NET with Extensible Markup Language platform as two acceptable platforms for the Bush Administration's 24 e-government Quicksilver initiatives.

[9]Retrieved December 4, 2004, from http://www.feapmo.gov/resources/OMB%20Enterprise%20Architecture%20Assessment%.

[10]The website is at http://www.cio.gov/index.cfm?function=documents&section=Enterprise%20Architecture&subsection=archives.

[11]In Stage 3, agencies were expected to relate investments to agency mission as well as to architecture, and to do return on investment analyses.

[12]See http://www.nps.gov/riskmgmt/lessons1/issue1.html.

[13]The opinion is available at http://www.supremecourtus.gov/opinions/02pdf/01-1229.pdf.

[14]Meijer's conclusions were based in part on a Delphi survey of 30 experts.

CASE STUDY
Platforms and Planning:
Pennsylvania's Transition to Enterprise Computing

Steve Sawyer, The Pennsylvania State University
Charles Christopher Hinnant, The University of Georgia
Tracey Rizzuto, Louisiana State University

In this case study, we report on the Commonwealth of Pennsylvania's ongoing efforts to pursue enterprise computing. In doing this we make two contributions. First, we focus explicitly on the enterprise perspective of computing (Bernard, 2004). We characterize the Commonwealth of Pennsylvania's government as an enterprise and focus on its computing changes over the past decade to provide examples of the move from organizational to enterprise perspectives (Fountain, 2001). Our second contribution is to focus explicitly on the role of information and communications technologies (ICT) planning, again using Pennsylvania's efforts as the source of examples, highlighting both strategic alignment (Henderson & Venkatraman, 1993) and platform (Ciborra, 1996) perspectives. The strategic alignment perspective helps focus on making explicit the ICT decisions that will best support achieving desired organizational goals. The platform perspective helps focus on the potential for the uses of ICT to lead to unexpected activities and second-order effects: those that were not at first imagined, but become possible only by having a particular ICT in place and used (Sproull and Kiesler, 1991).

While organizations in both the public and private sector continue to seek administrative rationalization and increased operational effectiveness (albeit often using different measures to define success), we know that public sector organizations differ from private sector in their take up and uses of ICT (Boyne, 2002; Bozeman & Bretschneider, 1986; Danziger, Dutton, Kling, & Kraemer, 1982; Rainey & Bozeman, 2000). In particular, the concept of enterprise computing, the arrangement of computing assets in a rationalized and strategically compliant way and embodied in approaches such as enterprise architecture (Bernard, 2004; NASCIO, 2003), has been taken up at the U.S. federal and state levels to some degree (see, for example, www.feams.gov). In contrast, the take up and use of enterprise systems such as those sold by SAP, Oracle, and others, and often known as enterprise resource planning or ERP systems, has been a dominant computerization activity in the global Fortune 1000 companies over the past 15 years (and is now a focal activity of many small to medium enterprises).

Enterprise Computing

Enterprise computing marries the selection, development, and deployment of ICT tightly with organizational structure and operations (Bernard, 2004). This is done via semi-automating key organizational processes; aggregating data and information; standardizing operating systems, applications, and physical devices; integrating workers using common systems; and demanding a rationalized set of operational policies and procedures. This is typically depicted as a "stack" or "layered" model—known as an *enterprise architecture* (Spewak, 1993). In these models, computing elements are arranged by functionality with lower levels focused on transporting data and information, and higher

This research was supported in part by a grant from the IBM Endowment for the Business of Government.

We thank Sara Reagor, Ryan Horne, and Sharoda Paul for their efforts in collecting data as part of this work.

levels engaging issues of people and organizational needs. In the five-tiered enterprise computing model, the first layer includes the transportation media, protocols, and devices as the base. Operating systems, systems software, and data structures are at the second level, above which are the devices, applications, and interdependencies that are demanded of software (third level) followed by the fourth level, which includes work processes and procedures, that are both guided by and integrated into the policies, procedures, and strategies being pursued by the enterprise that are laid out in the fifth tier. In this way enterprise computing links functionally based computer applications and strategic planning.

In contrast, an enterprise system often has a number of integrated modules that share access to a common set of data that can be accessed via coherently designed uniform screens. These screens are often web based (i.e., a personal computer can gain access using a simple browser such as Netscape or Firefox). One difference between workgroup office suites and enterprise systems is scale. For example, SAP's R/3 software (one of the most common and comprehensive enterprise systems and the one chosen by Pennsylvania) is based on 1980s programming and innovations in creating a client-and-server architecture. The SAP R/3 system has four major elements: an integrated database; a set of development tools (ABAP); a means to encode, apply, and manage business; and workflow rules that guide the operations and the collection of business modules. These modules are typically grouped into four elements: finance, human resources, manufacturing (and logistics), and sales. Within each of these elements is a range of modules (e.g., sales can include customer relationship management and distribution modules).[1]

The Pennsylvania Enterprise Computing Efforts: 1995–2004

We focus on the Commonwealth of Pennsylvania's efforts in enterprise computing for three reasons. First, states are complex enterprises and serve the purpose of being a revelatory case for this exploration (Yin, 1989). The U.S. federal government is too large to engage as a singular enterprise, while regional or county-level enterprise activities are still relatively rare. Second, Pennsylvania was one of the first states to attempt an enterprise systems implementation (engaging SAP in 1999) and did so by first engaging enterprise computing principles. Third, since 2003, Pennsylvania has been actively pursuing enterprise architecture as a means to realize the values of enterprise computing and their investment in an enterprise system.

Pennsylvania Context

In the early 1990s Pennsylvania government was composed of approximately 152,000 employees (FTE), supporting an estimated population of 12 million citizens. State government revenues totaled approximately $36.7 billion (U.S. Census Bureau, 1992). Pennsylvania's economy was still dependent on traditional manufacturing-based industries, and Pennsylvania was ranked 47th in job growth rate. Not surprisingly, even before January 1995, when Governor Tom Ridge and his administration took office, there was a widely perceived need to move the state economy and labor force toward new forms of economic development that were less likely to focus on traditional blue-collar manufacturing jobs. Beginning in 1995, Pennsylvania engaged seven strategic actions in regards to state government IT investment (IMPACCT, 1996):

- Reexamine agency policies regarding the sharing of information.
- Alter personnel policies in order to improve compensation for IT managers and staff.

---

[1]For more information on enterprise systems, see www.cio.com/research/erp.

- Move toward off-the-shelf application procurement instead of in-house development.
- Create an inventory for reuse of packages already developed by the Commonwealth.
- Select common software engineering tools for developing new custom applications.
- Move toward the development of relational databases.
- Revise procurement to meet required standards, improve competition, and reduce prices.

In early 1996, at about the same time the IMPACCT report was released, Governor Ridge created the Office for Information Technology (OIT) within Commonwealth's Office of Administration (OA is the administrative arm of Pennsylvania state government). The deputy secretary of OIT became Pennsylvania's chief information officer (CIO). The CIO was charged with engaging the recommendations of the IMPACCT report, as laid out in their 1997 strategic plan (Office of Administration, 1996).

Enterprise Computing in Pennsylvania

The OIT staff were encouraged to innovate using ICT. They worked to take on big ideas, to learn from mistakes, and to pursue a range of projects tied to either economic development or educational excellences. The combination of clear and active issue advocacy from senior executives, the legitimization that access to both budget and senior cabinet counsel provided, the combination of innovative ideas with analytic approach to taking on ICT projects, and the willingness to take risks all reflect both the administration's commitment to engaging ICT and the important role the OIT played in establishing both a vision for computing and standards for the commonwealth. In doing this, OIT exemplified the enterprise computing perspective.

The OIT played a critical role in developing an enterprise perspective. Its very presence—coming from nothing to a thriving organization housed in the Office of Administration with direct access to the Governor—and willingness to engage in formal and informal actions to establish enterprise computing oversight across Pennsylvania state government made it a central player.

The OIT's guiding principles were set out in a short (six-page) document. These principles depicted ICT as a lever to enable economic development, reflected private-sector sophistication in developing ICT combined with public-sector ideals of service delivery and access, and laid out general principles for what ICT and the computing architecture of Pennsylvania would be. This larger view provided a guiding frame, and not a detailed specification, for how to take on ICT. These principles helped OIT focus on leveraging interests of constituents and emphasized negotiation and consensus. The OIT staff took an analytic orientation when engaging this work: focusing on getting evidence and using it to make their points. Their ability to develop (and provide) evidence, and their pursuit of computing tied to the guiding principles, became a potent force pushing the enterprise computing agenda.

In Table 11-2 we highlight seven projects undertaken by OIT to engage enterprise computing. These seven projects represent a subset of the more than 30 initiatives undertaken wholly or in part by OIT during 1995–2005.[2] They reflect the projects that have substantial enterprise computing components and our intent in highlighting these is to make two points:

[2]We do not include the public safety radio initiative and Justice Network (JNET) system development. While these are enterprise wide, they are also focused in the specific areas of public safety and criminal justice/homeland security. The nine projects we highlight engage the entire Commonwealth of Pennsylvania government.

Table 11-2   Pennsylvania's Enterprise Computing Projects Timeline (1995–2004)

Year	Selected Pertinent Events
1995	• January—Tom Ridge (R) sworn in as governor of PA • October—PA is 48th state in US to have a website
1996	• Spring—IMPACCT report published
1997	• July—**Data PowerHouse Project** (data center consolidation) announced • August—**Commonwealth Connect** (desktop/office and e-mail standardization) discussions begun
1998	• Summer—**Technology Incentive Plan (TIP)** fund created • June—Contract with Microsoft finalized for **Commonwealth Connect**
1999	• Spring—Began processes to select vendors for ERP and systems integrators for **Imagine PA** (the enterprise system effort) • October—**PA Open for Business** portal site launched
2000	• June—Contract with SAP finalized for **Imagine PA** software vendor • August—Continuous enrollment begins in **Invitation to Qualify (ITQ),** a procurement and vendor registration program • October—Full transition to **Data PowerHouse** complete • October—Official launch of the **PA PowerPort** website
2001	• Early—**Imagine PA** project team created • March—Contract with KPMG Consulting (with IBM as partner) finalized as system integrator for **Imagine PA** (SAP implementation) • July—All Pennsylvania agencies' PCs (40,000 total) standardized on **Commonwealth Connect** desktop software • December—Lt. Gov. Mark Schweiker becomes governor (Tom Ridge becomes first secretary of Homeland Security)
2002	• July—Beginning of implementation of **Imagine PA** software (SAP) • November—Ed Rendell (D) elected to be governor of PA • End of year—The majority of all agencies' PCs (60,000) standardized on **Commonwealth Connect** desktop software and e-mail network
2003	• January—Most of migration to mySAP to be complete for **Imagine PA** project • August—OIT creates office of Enterprise Integration • September—OIT gets oversight to agency IT budget/planning and input on hiring agency-level CIOs
2004	• July—SAP (ERP) software to be fully implemented for Enterprise Integration (aka/Imagine PA) project

1. Technological development of Pennsylvania's enterprise computing is inseparable from the organizational and policy developed to guide and support this work.
2. Enterprise computing efforts made by Pennsylvania and the OIT across 10 years (1995 to 2004) represent a consistent planning focus that reflects both a platform approach and strategic alignment principles.

These seven projects include the effort to consolidate across the nearly 60,000 personal computers into a common desktop software and e-mail standard (and, when Pennsylvania did this, they became the first state to partner with Microsoft with a statewide licensing agreement). Second, they consolidated the data centers and telecommunications. Third, they developed a streamlined ICT procurement process (ITQ). Fourth, they embarked on several government-to-business web portals (PA Open for Business) and developed a state portal providing a range of services (PA Powerport). Fifth, many of these projects were funded in part by an innovative technology investment program (TIP) that allowed the CIO to fund initiatives that embodied or enabled economic development or educational excellence. The money from TIP and the leadership by OIT staff made this (new) office a central node in e-government. Sixth, beginning in the Ridge administration and continuing into the Rendell administration, Pennsylvania pursued an enterprise systems implementation effort, focusing on SAP R/3 as a statewide administrative operational platform. Seventh, early in the Rendell administration, OIT engaged in three related efforts to consolidate IT decision making for the Commonwealth of Pennsylvania. First, they opened a statewide office to support enterprise architecture. Second, OIT was able to gain authority to both review and approve the other state agency's IT planning and funding requests. And, the deputy secretary of OIT was given some input on hiring for the 43 agency CIO positions, providing formal oversight to a process that had relied on informal interaction for the first 10 years of the OIT work.

Planning and Pennsylvania Enterprise's Computing Activities

Across 10 tumultuous years, the Commonwealth of Pennsylvania's political and IT leadership made a series of decisions that showcase a pattern of enterprise thinking around the value and uses of computing. These decisions transcend three governors, two administrations, four CIOs, the rapid rise and bursting of the dot.com boom, terrorist attacks, and a host of less visible but significant events. The evidence is compelling: Pennsylvania has made substantial progress.

This 10-year trajectory provides evidence of an enterprise computing perspective. As we laid out at the beginning, enterprise computing is the most recent and most visible effort to engage the symbiotic relationships among an institution's structures and functions and the ensemble of computing and communications technologies (Bernard, 2004). We also reflect on this 10-year effort from platform and strategic alignment perspectives. These represent fundamentally different approaches to planning: platform perspectives highlight bottom-up, and strategic alignment focuses on top-down engagement (Ciborra, 1997; Saaksjarvi, 1997).

Planning: An Enterprise Computing Perspective

The literature suggests that public sector organizations engage in computing differently than do private sector organizations (Boyne, 2002; Bozeman & Bretschnieder, 1986; Heintz & Bretschneider, 2000). The level of red tape, purposes for use, and funding models make it more difficult for public sector organizations to realize the value of computing. Evidence suggests that managing public-sector IT efforts is also different from private sector in that it is even more difficult to engage in process reengineering (Cats-Baril & Thompson, 1995; Shalala, 1998).

More recently, enterprise computing has become a focal point in the practice of public-sector IT (Fountain, 2001; NASCIO, 2003). Enterprise computing provides a layered and integrated view and focuses on ordering the strategic and operational elements of an organization with the applications, data, and infrastructure to support them.

Seen in this light, the combination of policy decisions to establish IT oversight with OIT, the rationalization of the telecommunications, desktop and data centers, and the move toward an enterprise system reflects steady progress in pursuit of a coherent enterprise computing architecture. The more recent efforts by the OIT Office of Enterprise

Architecture to establish standards for development environments, middleware applications, and information sharing indicate that the efforts are cohering.

Planning: A Platform Perspective

Empirical evidence on the take-up and uses of computing in organizations indicate that many new systems do not lead to the effects intended, and often lead to unintended consequences (Leonard-Barton, 1988; Sproull & Goodman, 1989; Sproull & Kiesler, 1991). Ciborra (1996, 2000) builds on this, arguing that new IT serves as a platform for innovation. This innovating and learning can only happen once the system is in place, which leads to a bottom-up view of planning: planning for IT can only take the organization to a certain point, then bricolage (learning and doing) takes over. This results in an indeterminate IT planning approach that requires extensive coordination and communication to engage.

The evidence from Pennsylvania's efforts over the past 10 years to more effectively engage computing can also support the bricolage argument. There have been many changed directions: the Microsoft licensing deal was not renewed, the vendor providing telecommunications has nearly failed, the ERP effort took two years longer than expected, and many of the intended benefits have yet to be realized. One limitation of the bricolage view of bottom-up learning is that, over time, organizations can learn—they adapt (Leonard-Barton, 1988) and the tumult of days and weeks in transition can give way to subsequent years of viable operations.

For those who advocate for bottom-up planning, the evidence from Pennsylvania suggests that organizations that pay attention to constituents, by creating forums and vehicles to engage people, can learn. OIT set a model example of how to engage in their seeking to innovate, focusing on gathering data and building a business case, and providing both financial support and internal expertise in project management and contracts.

Planning: A Strategic Alignment Perspective

The strategic alignment model posits that there is a complex relationship among the components of business strategy, functional operations, and the deployment and uses of computing (Avison et al., 2004; Grant, 2003; Henderson & Venkatraman, 1993). Strategic alignment is a dynamic, top-down approach, where organizational leaders seek to match strategic intent with the proper development and deployment of an IT infrastructure and processes. Critics point to its complexity and see it as a static or notional view (Ciborra, 1997), though current evidence suggests that strategic alignment is situated and always ongoing (Grant, 2003).

The nominal position in the strategic alignment model is that an organization's strategic vision should align with its strategic vision for computing and this should drive the selection and deployment of the computing infrastructure. If decisions about the computing infrastructure drive strategic decisions, there may be alignment. This leads to where tactical decisions are forcing strategic choices, known as *reactive planning*. A third approach to strategic alignment is that operational pressures of the organization could lead to making operational choices in computing. That is, operational decisions presuppose any strategic decisions. In practice, this resembles the strategic drift Ciborra (1996, 2000) argues occurs too often in contemporary organizations.

The evidence from 10 years of work by Pennsylvania and its OIT suggests that they have been able to move from operationally led decision making toward a strategic alignment model. The ability to see through projects, such as telecommunications infrastructure rationalization, common desktop standards, streamlined IT procurement, the

TIP (to support strategic initiatives), and the recent oversight controls for agency CIO and IT planning, suggests steady progress toward increased alignment between the commonwealth's strategic vision and the ability of its computing investments to support these visions.

The lengthy and difficult implementation of the SAP ERP suggests that process-level changes across the commonwealth government are slow to realize. This is not all that different from the findings from the private sector (Avison et al., 2004; Grant, 2003). Given the differences in how computing is engaged in public-sector organizations, and some of the differences between private- and public-sector organizations, it may be that process changes will be the most difficult to realize (Boyne, 2002; Rainey & Bozeman, 2000).

The 10 years of evidence shows that Pennsylvania's state-level government has been able to engage in strategic alignment. The effort is not without its struggles, and the timescale suggests that alignment change is neither quick nor direct. The evidence does suggest that an enterprise's strategic intent can be mapped to the development, deployment, and uses of computing assets. Furthermore, this alignment can be carried on across substantial organizational and environmental change. The scale and scope of Pennsylvania's government helps to make clear that organizational size, while a considerable influence, is not a barrier to such change.

What is also clear at this time is that infrastructural alignment is easier than process alignment. However, this is a relative comparison: the efforts to align the telecommunications, desktop standards, and procurement and funding approaches to computing are complex, difficult, and expensive. As Pennsylvania's state government embarks on efforts to leverage its substantial investment in an ERP, the focus will be on business process change. From both the strategic alignment and enterprise perspectives, this focus is also the link between strategy and infrastructure. Given the steady progress made to develop a coherent enterprise computing architecture and to engage in strategic alignment, Pennsylvania is well positioned to engage this next stage in computing.

For those who seek examples and evidence for how to engage enterprise computing and pursue strategic alignment, Pennsylvania's efforts from 1995 to 2004 provide both a viable template and practical lessons. For those who seek to characterize the take-up and uses of computing as bricolage and drift, or to focus on the role of platforms for postimplementation innovation, there is extensive evidence from Pennsylvania's efforts to engage computing.

References

Avison, D., Jones, J., Powell, P., & Wilson, D. (2004). Using and validating the strategic alignment Model. *Journal of Strategic Information Systems, 13*(3), 223–246.

Bernard, S. (2004). *An introduction to enterprise architecture.* Washington, DC: Enterprise Institute.

Boyne, G. (2002). Public and private management: What's the difference? *Journal of Management Studies, 39*(1), 97–122.

Bozeman, B., & Bretschneider, S. (1986). Public management information systems: Theory and prescription. *Public Administration Review, 46*, 475–487.

Cats-Baril, W., & Thompson, R. (1995). Managing information technology projects in the public sector. *Public Administration Review, 55*(6), 559–566.

Ciborra, C. (1996). The platform organization: Recombining strategies, structures, and surprises. *Organization Science, 7*(2), 103–118.

Ciborra, C. (1997). De profundis? Deconstructing the concept of strategic alignment. *Scandinavian Journal of Information Systems, 9*(1), 67–82.

Ciborra, C. (2000). *From Control to drift: The dynamics of corporate information infrastructure.* Oxford, England: Oxford University Press.

Danziger, J., Dutton, W., Kling, R., & Kraemer, K. (1982). *Computers and Politics: High Technology in American Local Governments*. New York: Columbia University Press.

Fountain, J. (2001). *Building the virtual state: Information technology and institutional change*. Washington, DC: Brookings Institution Press.

Grant, G. (2003). Strategic alignment and enterprise systems implementation: the case of Metalco. *Journal of Information Technology, 18*(3), 159–175.

Heintz, T., & Bretschneider, S. (2000). IT and restructuring in public organizations: Do IT-related structural changes improve organizational performance? *Journal of Public Administration Research and Theory, 10*(3), 801–830.

Henderson, J., & Venkatraman, N. (1993). Strategic alignment: Leveraging information technology for transforming organizations. *IBM Systems Journal, 32*(1), 472–484.

Hughes, T. (1986). *Networks of power*. Baltimore: The Johns Hopkins University Press.

IMPACCT. (1996). *Improve Management and Cost Control Task Force, Final Report*. Harrisburg, PA: Commonwealth of Pennsylvania Governor's Office of Administration.

Kling, R., & Scacchi, W. (1982). The web of computing: computer technology as social organization. *Advances in Computers, 21*, 1–90.

Leonard-Barton, D. (1988). Implementation as a mutual adaptation of technology and organization. *Research Policy, 17*, 251–267.

Markus, M., Majchrzak, A., & Gasser, L. (2002). "A design theory for systems that support emergent knowledge processes." *MIS Quarterly, 26*(3), 179–212.

NASCIO. (2003). Enterprise Architecture Maturity Model. Retrieved May 20, 2000 from http://www.nascio.org/publications/index.cfm.

Office of Administration. (1996). *Breaking through barriers: A new direction*. Harrisburg, PA: Commonwealth of Pennsylvania Governor's Office of Administration. Retrieved from www.oit.state.pa.us.

OMB (2001). Guidelines for ensuring and minimizing the quality, objectivity, unity and integrity of information disseminated by federal agents. Washington, DC: Federal Register notes.

Rainey, H., & Bozeman, B. (2000). Comparing public and private organizations: Empirical research and the power of a priori. *Journal of Public Administration Research and Theory, 10*(2), 447–465.

Saaksjarvi, M. (1997). About top down and bottom-up perspectives on strategic alignment. *Scandinavian Journal of Information Systems, 9*(1), 83–84.

Shalala, D. (1998). Are large public organizations manageable? *Public Administration Review, 65*, 284–289.

Spewak, T. (1993) *Enterprise architecture planning*. Boston: QED.

Sproull, L., & Goodman, P. (1989). Technology and organizations: Integration and opportunities. In P. Goodman, & L. Sproull (Eds.), *Technology and organizations* (pp. 254–266). New York: Jossey-Bass.

Sproull, L., & Kiesler, S. (1991). *Connections: New ways of working in the networked organization*. Cambridge, MA: MIT Press.

U.S. Census Bureau. (1992). Census of Governments. Washington, DC: Government Printing Office.

Yin, R. (1989). *Case study research: Design and methods*. Beverly Hills, CA: Sage.

Needs Assessment and Project Management

As discussed in the previous chapter, strategic information technology (IT) planning identifies objectives that serve goals implementing the organization's mission. To translate objectives into projects, however, two other things are needed: a lower level of planning that identifies the gap between the present and the desired future (needs assessment), and a system for implementing projects designed to fill that gap (project management).

A needs assessment is a report to management that analyzes a problem and that may seek to provide solutions to this problem. A business process analysis (BPA) may be related to the needs assessment, serving to analyze work processes with a view to designing new processes that may use new technologies. If solutions are proposed, then a feasibility study may be associated with the needs assessment, analyzing the organization's capacity in terms of technical and human resources needed to implement and maintain the proposed solution. Particularly for IT projects, needs assessments help avoid costly mistakes, where systems might be implemented to meet performance standards that do not conform to the actual needs of end users. Well-documented needs assessments avoid this and are also part of most project funding proposals.

Once a project is funded, project management supports it through an administrative role charged with organizing a project in a logical and cost-effective manner so that the tasks involved with implementation are sequenced appropriately, clear responsibilities are assigned to tasks, lines of authority are delineated, and systems of accountability are established to ensure completion of a project on time, within budget, and to performance standards. Increasingly, project management is a professionalized function. Project proposals are more likely to receive approval when project management expertise can be documented, thereby demonstrating organizational capacity to follow through with what is planned.

NEEDS ASSESSMENT

Needs assessments serve to identify organizational problems (both internal and arising from the organization's environment), to investigate opportunities for change, and to document and defend projects that are proposed to address problems. IT needs assessments assure that information technology projects are directed to real problems faced by the organization rather than wasting scarce resources introducing innovations based on vendors' claims, "leading edge" novelties in the field, the practices of other jurisdictions that may differ in critical ways, or on other false premises.

Properly implemented, a good needs assessment can reenergize an organization, providing hope that something fresh and constructive is being done about long-recognized shortcomings or problems faced by the organization. Needs assessments let participants specify the functions they want technology to have and the needs technology is supposed to meet. By creating awareness of needs, assessments help create the momentum for change. Needs assessments can be vehicles for involving stakeholders in the process of organizational transformation, particularly if implemented in a participatory way that gives members a feeling of ownership of what is being proposed.

Needs are not wants, and conducting a needs assessment is not compiling a wish list. An agency may want to upgrade to wireless computing, for instance, but this is not a need unless it can be shown that wireless computing will allow the agency to achieve its objectives more effectively. It is not a priority need unless the gain in effectiveness is of greater value than gains from other proposed improvements. Even a priority need must be shown to be feasible in terms of the organizational resources identified in the needs assessment process.

Although there are obvious benefits to conducting a needs assessment, it is not unusual to encounter staff resistance as well. Staff may feel that they are already familiar with what the organization needs and may feel that needs assessment is an unnecessary bureaucratic burden dreamed up by out-of-touch superiors. Resistance may be all the more pronounced when the needs assessment is implemented by outside consultants, whom staff may see as know-it-alls who do not understand the organization. Those who implement needs assessments must recognize the reality that staff do know more about the organization than anyone and that needs assessments may require months of work that compete for valuable staff time. These realities in turn mean that resistance is unlikely to be overcome unless the prospective outcome of the needs assessment process will be an environment that improves the quality of working life for the participants.

The mandate for needs assessment generally comes from the top management of the organization, who identify the general area of IT inquiry (e.g., "Should the agency establish a Web portal? Should the agency link data with other agencies?"). Needs assessments can be conducted by in-house staff or by outside consultants. Numerous guides are readily available (Altschuld & Witkin, 2000; Strock & Adkins, 1989). Consultants are particularly appropriate when there is intraorganizational conflict over work processes, since such third parties may be better able to make all stakeholders feel their input has been listened to impartially and without conflict of interest.

Whether in-house or by consultants, the general IT needs assessment process is implemented in four stages:

1. Collecting information
2. Identifying and prioritizing problems
3. Researching alternative possible solutions
4. Seeking consensus on a proposed solution

Where there is doubt about the capacity of the organization's financial, technical, and human resource ability to support a proposed solution, a feasibility study (discussed in a later section) may need to be undertaken in parallel with the needs assessment process. An explicit financial analysis may need to accompany the needs assessment or feasibility study. The financial analysis is not an audit, though past audits may be consulted. Rather, a financial analysis is focused on gauging the organization's economic resources to undertake, implement, and maintain proposed changes associated with the needs assessment.

Information Collection

In the preassessment phase, a needs assessment committee and leader are established. Among the initial steps is an examination of past needs assessments as well as the strategic plan. Past assessments help identify baseline data. Past assessments also help identify which data need to be updated. The strategic plan helps identify what information needs to be collected, if some data collected in the past is now unnecessary, and if new data are needed to throw light on new objectives.

The information collection phase of needs assessment typically encompasses multiple methods, some of which are policy review of existing legislation, regulations, and resolutions; archival research on organization records (policy statements, job descriptions, operating manuals);

analysis of records of organizational transactions; interviews of key staff and stakeholders about actual and desired practices; brainstorming by the needs assessment committee; Delphi method iterative interviewing of experts; organizational surveys of all employees; focus groups of staff and client groups; electronic discussion groups; participant observation by needs assessment staff; and in the case of certain agencies, forums or public hearings.

Focus groups are a particularly common needs assessment tool because they gather representative data but usually require far less in the way of organizational resources than do surveys. Feedback from focus groups can help avoid costly IT mistakes. For instance, Dan Combs, former Iowa director of digital government, found a new e-government real estate licensing initiative was underutilized by agents and traced the problem to the fact that users had not been consulted. It was found users disliked the one-at-a-time licensing of the e-government application, which lacked capacity for batch processing. To avoid similar problems with future development projects, Iowa now uses focus groups of end users (*State Tech,* 2003, p. 25). The state of Kansas also uses focus groups as a matter of policy in IT implementation.

To be effective, focus groups must be led by a neutral party who has strong people skills, is energetic and upbeat, is a good active listener, knows how to be supportive to all sides, knows how to encourage participation, and who does not present him- or herself as an expert who already knows the answers but rather as someone sincerely seeking information and ideas from members of the group. At the same time, focus group leaders must have leadership skills, particularly the ability to probe participants with follow-up questions for reactions and comments, the ability to keep conversation on topic, and the ability to function as a good summarizer. Sometimes having participants report and comment on findings of organizational surveys is a useful starting point for focus group discussions. Often there are two focus group facilitators— one to lead the meeting and one who acts as recorder/observer. Sometimes focus group sessions are taped as well, but care is usually taken to ensure participants will not be identified by full name or affiliation in the official record of the focus group.

Organizational surveys are even more common as a needs assessment tool than are focus groups. The Clinger-Cohen Assessment Survey (CCAS) from the Federal Chief Information Officer's Council (CIO Council, 2003) provides both an illustration of an agency survey and also an inventory of areas upon which a needs assessment may focus, especially in the area of needed IT competency development. The CCAS is used by the CIO Council to fulfill the 1996 Clinger-Cohen Act's requirement that an annual IT work force assessment be done and to prioritize IT investments by agency mission and objectives, to satisfy similar 2004 requirements of the Office of Management and Budget (OMB), and to fulfill the E-Government Act's requirement in Section 209 that an IT personnel needs assessment be conducted. The CCAS has items that survey general IT competencies such as contracting and procurement (knowledge of various types of contracts, techniques for contracting or procurement, and contract negotiation and administration), technical competencies such as business process reengineering (knowledge of methods, metrics, tools, and techniques of BPR), and skill areas such as data analysis or biometrics. Because the general and technical competencies as well as IT skills surveyed by the CCAS come as close as anything to an inventory of areas that a comprehensive IT needs assessment might cover, they are reproduced in the appendix to this chapter.

As a second example of the use of organizational surveys, the Federal CIO Council provides a spreadsheet-based online readiness assessment (found at www.cio.gov/archive/smpratc_tool_oct_2000.xls) that allows users to rate their organization in eight areas:

1. Strategy
2. Business focus
3. Leadership
4. Capital planning and investment control
5. Project management
6. Performance management
7. Technology acquisition
8. Architecture

Filling out the online form leads to an instant automated evaluation of organizational readiness to implement IT projects.

Finally, the information collection stage should survey resources outside the organization as well as within. Depending on the agency and its objectives, this may range from identifying community resources to considering prospective international partners. The needs assessment team may list all resources that already exist within the agency's environment, including human resources, financial resources, equipment resources, and organizational allies, and may consider how each relates to problems that are identified or to proposed solutions. At a minimum, the needs assessment team will define and profile the stakeholders in the possible change process, including focusing on what incentives would be needed to get stakeholders to participate in proposed IT solutions.

Problem Identification and Prioritization

Among the benefits of needs assessment is that the data gathered in the information collection stage form a baseline measurement against which improvement may be measured. If needs assessment is conceived as an ongoing activity, the organization may benefit from time series data on performance. However, the needs assessment process does not stop with information gathering. As information is gathered, problems are identified and the process of prioritizing needs begins.

The needs assessment analyst or facilitator functions to identify needs based on information revealing the gap between current practice and desired levels of performance; clustering needs into categories (e.g., needs related to increasing client convenience of use); and assisting stakeholders to rank problems in terms of their importance in relation to the agency's mission. This is a sort of "triage" process, dividing needs into those the meeting of which is essential to the survival of the agency in the long run, those that are merely "wants" but do not appreciably increase organizational performance, and those in the middle that the agency would do well to implement but only after those in the top category are dealt with.

In the problem identification stage, the focus for IT is on whether technology can help serve to meet priority needs and especially on what stakeholders wish technology systems could do for them. The focus is not on selecting a technology but rather on defining the specifications that are desired. At the same time, the needs assessment facilitator must be careful that unrealistic expectations are not raised by the problem identification process. Excessive optimism about proposed systems can be as damaging to implementation success as can employee resistance to change.

The culmination of the needs identification phase is typically a statement of technology needs. This is not a wish list, nor is it a survey of leading-edge technologies that may be coming into use. Rather the needs statement is grounded in documentation of needs articulated by stakeholders and by participants in the needs assessment process, and in documentation of how needs were prioritized in relation to the agency's mission and objectives. The needs statement is not a strategic plan, though it could be a supporting document for one. A good IT needs statement will present a convincing case that there are problems to be addressed, that some problems are more significant than others, and that problems might be ameliorated through introduction of new information systems with general specifications emerging from needs assessment information collection efforts. That is, the needs statement contains general parameters for technology solutions, but it is not as technical as a request for proposals (RFP) or a request for bids will be later in the implementation process.

Researching Solutions

When researching possible technological solutions as part of the needs assessment process, a number of routes are possible. First, there may be mandated information architectures (e.g., from the OMB) that dictate to the agency the range of permitted solutions. Federal or state purchasing regulations may be in place that constrain the agency to select solutions from approved vendor lists. Professional associations, such as the CIO Council, may recommend "best practices" in a given area, such as security. Associations such as the International City Management Association also are a resource for identifying jurisdictions that have implemented best practices in a given functional area. IT journals such as *Government Computer News* and *Government Technology* are among those giving annual awards for technology innovation, and award-winning jurisdictions are also models for best practices.

Vendor conferences are a possible avenue for researching technology solutions. The needs statement can be the basis for feedback from vendors who may be quite willing and even anxious to have a venue where they can suggest how their products may dovetail with identified agency needs. Statements from vendors may help needs assessment analysts to refine the general specifications of what emerges as recommendations from the needs assessment. Vendor conferences can also help needs assessment staff and participants explore dimensions such as security, privacy protection, and interoperability issues.

The stage of researching solutions may have as its result a *functional specifications document*. This document spells out in greater detail than the needs statement what the capabilities and outcomes of a proposed information system should be (e.g., system storage/retrieval capabilities, processing capabilities and scalability, reporting capabilities, networking capabilities). Various specific technologies may be capable of achieving the named outcomes. A good functional specification document is vendor independent, does not use proprietary process models or other proprietary intellectual property, and is useful for comparing technical solutions across vendors. It should also be relatively free from jargon and accessible to the participants in the needs assessment process. Finally, to the extent that the agency's sunk IT investments require continuity with legacy information systems, compatibility with these systems is a common functional specification.

It should be emphasized that the "researching solutions" stage of needs assessment is purposely plural. It is rarely wise to research and document one technical solution for an organizational problem. Rather, the needs assessment analysis is to support a broader decision-making process, such as strategic planning. In this context it is almost always more useful to decision makers if the needs assessment effort results in alternatives for decision, not simply the case for "the one best way" as seen by the needs assessment analysts.

Seeking Consensus

Needs assessment is a social marketing method, not just a decision support effort. That is, a good IT needs assessment is consumer focused, even for public agencies. The information gathered, problems identified, and proposed solutions investigated and prioritized are all intended to help the agency more effectively meet the needs of its ultimate target audience—its consumers. The needs assessment process is not just meant to uncover data about problems, though some managers wrongly treat it as such. A good needs assessment process goes beyond this to build group consensus, a sense of participation and self-investment in change, and increased commitment to the organization's mission. That is, a good needs assessment is a form of organization development.

Not the least of the concerns of the needs assessment team is selling the needs assessment recommendations to top management at the end of the process, which is really just the beginning of implementation. The more the needs assessment has focused on the nexus between the organization's mission and specific proposed IT changes, the easier it is for the assessment team to convince top management that what has emerged from the needs assessment process deserves organizational priority. Management wants to know not just what needs are perceived, but also how identified needs relate to the agency's mission and objectives. For this reason, the needs assessment report must be framed as a planning document, not as a technical evaluation.

Development of prototype IT systems can be an aid to building consensus. By allowing users to experience directly the "look and feel" of new systems, even though prototypes are not fully functional and may be limited to use of artificial data, prototypes can allay fears and even inspire enthusiasm. On the other hand, prototypes can at times elicit negative user feedback, leading the needs assessment team to "go back to the drawing board" to alter and refine proposals. Either way, prototyping, while expensive in time and resources, can be well worth its cost.

An alternative to prototyping is controlled implementation of the project at pilot sites. Pilot sites can be convincing examples for other units, and personnel from the pilot site can be used as a cadre of peer-level trainers for units entering later in the technology adoption process. The pilot strategy is also useful for obtaining end-user feedback on proposed systems as well as on metrics for measuring the performance of those systems.

BUSINESS PROCESS ANALYSIS

BPA is not the same as needs assessment, nor necessarily even associated with it. BPA is a long-established planning process for undertaking organizational innovations that involve reengineering tasks and, often, doing so by introducing new technologies. Though not limited to such situations, BPA is often used where the organization is aware that existing business processes are inefficient or outdated, and it wants to identify ways to change. BPA focuses on workflow analysis both within an agency and among agencies. Workflows are categorized into *processes* (e.g., the budget development process, the procurement process). Each process is associated with a named *process owner,* who participates in the BPA analysis, that draws together the range of organizational staff and stakeholders involved with the process(es) being studied. BPA uses iterative methods to consider how the process might be reengineered and to arrive at a consensus on proposed solutions. Sometimes, however, BPA is used in reverse, where the organization has identified or even has acquired new technology (e.g., Web portal technology mandated by the OMB) but has given insufficient planning attention to how that technology is to serve organizational work processes.

As practiced by the U.S. Department of State, business process analysis organizes process team discussions around a checklist of 15 questions:

1. What is the process called?
2. How does this process contribute to the mission of the organization?
3. Identify business drivers, e.g., laws and regulatory guidance, event statutes and other constraint guides, and controls.
4. What types, when, and how often are the information and other input used and transformed by the process to produce one or more products or services?
5. What types of resources, including technologies, data, applications, people, and facilities are used to perform the process?
6. What activities are included in this process?
7. Define each activity.
8. What sequence of steps is required to perform each activity?
9. What triggers the performance of each activity?
10. What output does each of the activities produce? Who uses it? How?
11. What types and sources of data are used to perform activity?
12. Develop target or "to-be" processes based on the process improvement method.
13. Consider reusing technology by sharing and standardizing to minimize your requirements.
14. Perform gap analysis to support new process requirements.
15. Develop requirement document for inclusion in our project plan.

The BPA facilitator must identify processes, process owners, and stakeholders, as well as organize the process analysis team. The team must identify mission-related activities and opportunities, prioritize process needs, describe current processes, and prepare a document describing the "to-be" business process, including a market survey based on process requirements and a study of compatibility of reengineered processes with existing agency architectural IT assets (U.S. Department of State, 2004).

The U.S. Patent and Trademark Office (PTO) provides a case illustration of the BPA process. In 1995, the PTO head decided to initiate a BPA process to address the problem that, at that time, new patent processing times averaged 19 months. The initiative was placed in the hands of Jerry Russomano, director of the PTO's Office of BPR, whose mandate was to reduce processing time to 60 days. Russomano selected 150 PTO staff members and divided them into 12 BPA teams. Spending two days a week on BPA activities, team members assessed five areas: technology, quality, customer relations, culture, and process. Over a period of a few months, teams developed "as-is" and "to-be" pictures of the PTO (Reengineering Resource Center, 1996).

Later in the BPA process at the PTO, teams focused on fleshing out the "to-be" model, which centered on using technology to speed workflow and reduce costs. New work processes were designed around new technologies such as optical scanning and optical disk storage, "electronic cabinets," sorting using artificial intelligence, and introduction of new workflow software. Much of the BPA effort centered on organizational development and creating employee readiness for new work processes, using techniques ranging from customer feedback cards to new performance measures to hands-on meetings and internal networks. In the course of the change process, employee resistance appeared. PTO union representatives argued that the new digital system would make the examiner's job more difficult than under the old paper document system, and that the old individual patent examiner process was superior to the new team approach. PTO management persisted in the face of union opposition, but unlike many BPR efforts, it initially adopted an incremental approach to introducing change, partly due to limited funds. Later, however, the reengineering effort gained momentum as part of more general IT initiatives at the federal level.

Work at the PTO based on BPA was one of the models reflected in the 1997 Department of Defense's (DOD's) "Design Criteria Standard for Electronic Records Management Applications." This standard, known as DOD 5015.2-STD or just as the 5015.2 standard, is the current federal standard for the design criteria to be used to identify, mark, store, and dispose of electronic records. A 2002 revision in the standard added requirements for access control, declassification, and classified markings. The 5015.2 standard is required within the DOD and is recommended by a 2003 National Archives and Records Administration (NARA) bulletin for all federal agencies considering implementation of electronic records management (ERM) systems. Not only the PTO, but also the Department of Education, the Environmental Protection Agency, Department of Energy, the Federal Deposit Insurance Corporation, the Social Security Administration, and many other federal agencies now require 5015.2 certification for implementation of ERM applications. NARA ERM guidance is integral to the e-government initiatives of the President's Management Agenda (NARA, 2004). The current 2004–2009 strategic information plan of the PTO commits the agency to the electronically based team-oriented reengineering of agency work processes that originated in the BPA processes a decade earlier (U.S. Patent and Trademark Office, 2004).

FEASIBILITY STUDIES

What is needed may not be feasible, and what is feasible may not be needed. This logic would seem to be the basis for clearly differentiating needs assessments and feasibility studies into separate categories. In reality, however, needs assessments tend not only to assess needs but also to identify possible solutions and to evaluate their feasibility. When used in this way, feasibility studies are a component of comprehensive needs assessments. However, feasibility studies may be undertaken in their own right, to look more carefully into proposals emerging from strategic planning, legislative inquiry, executive mandate, or from whatever source. Either way, IT feasibility studies are more delimited than are needs assessments, concentrating on identifying obstacles to implementation and what is needed to overcome these obstacles. Feasibility studies normally are undertaken only after the organization has identified and defined a proposed IT systems project, and has a written requirements analysis and a general design statement for it.

In general, a feasibility study analyzes a business problem. It has three broad dimensions: operational (will the proposed IT system, in fact, work?), economic (do benefits exceed costs?), and technical (can we integrate the proposed system with existing technology?). In commissioning an IT feasibility study, top management is looking for a distant early warning signal that can be used as a go/no-go decision support factor before the organization has committed its time, energy, and resources to the development of a proposed system. The higher the risk of the project, based on formal risk assessment procedures, the greater the need for a feasibility study.

What does a feasibility report look like? To take one example, the feasibility study format employed by the Department of Housing and Urban Development (HUD, 2004) requires the analyst to enter general, management, and system information. The general information section of the feasibility report includes a statement of purpose, an outline of the scope of the study, an overview of the system under study, project references, a list of acronyms and abbreviations used in the study, a list of contacts that may be needed by the document user for informational and troubleshooting purposes, and a list of organizations that require coordination between the project and its specific functions. The management summary section describes the organizational environment, organizations involved, inputs and outputs of the organization, how the organization processes the flow of demands and services, how security is handled, interaction between the system and other systems, factors in the physical environment, current functional procedures, performance objectives, assumption and constraints, and evaluation criteria used to assess the system. The final section on the proposed system describes the proposed system; enumerates improvements the proposal makes over the present system; details time and resource costs; and assesses system impacts, including equipment, software, organizational, operational, developmental, site and facility, security, and privacy impacts. There may be additional system sections comparing alternative proposed systems.

Another example is provided by the Federal Highway Administration's guidelines for state agencies considering feasibility studies (FHWA, 2003). The FHWA defines feasibility as the degree to which a given proposal is economically justified; the degree to which it is considered preferable from an environmental or social perspective; and the degree to which its eventual implementation and operation can be financed and managed. The FHWA feasibility study guidelines recommend convening an advisory committee to provide review and to assist in management of the study. The committee divides the study into discrete tasks that build upon one another. Examples of tasks would be documentation of existing conditions; forecasts of future demand (e.g., travel forecasts in the case of highway projects); preliminary economic justification and assessment of financial feasibility; engineering and environmental feasibility studies; evaluation of alternative modes of implementation; management strategies; and design of levels and locations for the project. Feasibility studies should, at least initially, consider a wide range of alternatives based on inputs from interested groups and the public. The assessment team must study constraining considerations such as legislative statute or legal restrictions on the use of funds, or constraints imposed by natural or man-made factors.

FHWA guidelines also call for public involvement activities, focusing primarily on near-term, reasonably implementable projects. There must also be an economic justification with a cost-benefit analysis, nonmonetary but quantifiable considerations, and nonquantifiable considerations. Feasibility studies should also present sensitivity tests for costing under different assumptions (e.g., different interest rates), comparing projected results based on different assumptions. Beyond economic justifications, the feasibility study must discuss the degree to which proposed alternatives are preferable from an environmental or social perspective. Finally, financial feasibility must be analyzed: the degree to which eventual construction and operation of the proposed project can be financed and managed. This aspect of the feasibility study quantifies resources needed for construction and operation; identifies funding and personnel sources; and in general, lays the groundwork for financial planning documents related to project implementation. The final feasibility report should include a description of existing conditions, summary of public input, economic study of proposed alternatives, analysis of noneconomic but quantifiable costs and benefits, discussion of nonquantifiable considerations, and an executive summary.

Feasibility studies can also be understood in terms of what they are not. Feasibility studies are different from strategic planning and do not ensure that projects match agency mission, or if they do, that they do so more effectively than other projects competing for priority. Therefore, feasibility studies are not normally stand-alone efforts independent of agency strategic planning. Feasibility studies are different from needs assessments and do not establish need. Feasibility studies are not intended to support or supplement ongoing projects. Feasibility studies are not a way of proving a preconceived project proposal is right. Feasibility studies are not final proven results, merely estimates. In fact, the track record for feasibility studies is that they are often not accurate when viewed with the benefit of hindsight, and they should be viewed not as static analyses on a particular date, but rather they should be employed as a form of dynamic analysis illuminating costs, benefits, and risks for alternative proposed project options. In this way, feasibility studies bridge the distance between strategic planning and needs assessment on the one hand and the practical concerns of the project manager on the other.

THE ROLE OF THE PROJECT MANAGER

The OMB has documented a tremendous need for improved project management. In its FY 2004 budget process, the OMB sampled IT projects and found cost growth overbudget of 10 to 225%. In one DOD project, $126 million was spent over seven years before terminating an IT project as a failure. Cost overruns were blamed on poor or absent project management. To address this problem, OMB associate director for e-government, Mark Forman, said the federal government had an immediate need to find 1400 trained project managers (Miller, 2003q). This may be considered an understatement in view of the fact that risk management principles call for each critical project to have a trained alternate project manager as well.

The IT project manager is like the sergeant on the front lines of the implementation battle. What is the job description? Everything to do with the project, and everything that's not in anyone else's job description! One pair of authors described the job in terms of 10 broad tasks:

1. Setting clear goals for the project
2. Setting clear objectives for the project
3. Establishing specific checkpoints, activities, relationships, and timelines
4. Scheduling tasks for the project
5. Developing the project team and the individuals in it
6. Motivating team members
7. Keeping all stakeholders informed
8. Managing project risks creatively
9. Negotiating agreements with all internal and external groups involved with the project
10. Negotiating enough power for the project manager, commensurate with responsibility (Randolph & Posner, 1992). Other authors describe nine basic knowledge areas that project managers and project teams must apply (Duncan, 1996), or the five stages of reengineering (Frame, 1995), or the business workflow model (Sanders, 1995), and other frameworks (Verma, 1995).

Whether described in terms of 5, 9, 10, or more dimensions, it is clear that the role of the project manager is comprehensive. Little wonder that the job of project manager has become increasingly professionalized in the last two decades, backed up by an array of federal, state, and academic training programs. The OMB has been pushing agencies to hire professionally certified public managers, and the Office of Personnel Management (OPM) has issued guidance to agencies in the document, *Interpretive Guidance for Project Manager Positions*.[1] In response, a number of training programs have emerged in recent years. The Project Management Institute of Philadelphia (PMI at pmi.org) is the most widely recognized certification authority for project managers. Fields of study for certification include overseeing cross-functional teams of designers, coders, systems architects, and others; Web services; critical path tracking; risk management; task leveling; and much more.[2]

Project management certification programs are now sponsored by the Department of Energy, the Department of Agriculture, the Department of Health and Human Services, and other units of the federal government. Project management training is also offered by the OPM,[3] which conducts training on-site as well as at OPM Management Development Centers. The OPM's courses in 2004 included Managing Complex Projects, Managing Project Teams, Managing Projects, Project Management Principles, Leading Successful Projects, Optimizing Project Performance, Managing Successful Information Systems Projects, and Managing Project Managers. The OPM curriculum allows managers to sit for the PMI's Project Management Professional Certification exam. Project management training is also offered by GoLearn.gov, which has launched some 30 IT project management courses developed by HUD and by OPM.

Today many professional associations support project management, including the International Project Management Association, the International Association of Project and Program Management, the Association for the Advancement of Cost Engineering, the PMI, the Association of Project Management, and the American Society for the Advancement of Project Management.

Because a significant role of project managers is overseeing the acquisition of software, hardware, and services related to the project, part of the training of project managers should involve mastering knowledge of the acquisition process and familiarity with contract management. The Federal Acquisition Institute has published a guide, "Contract Specialists' Training Blueprints," listing acquisition-related functions for project managers.[4]

Among the universal skill requirements for project managers is project scheduling. While partly a matter of defining and sequencing key elements of tasks involved in the project, familiarity with specific estimating and diagramming techniques is a learning objective of the OPM curriculum in project management. One such technique is the programming evaluation and review technique (PERT), a common management systems tool for sequencing and diagramming project tasks and task dependencies, including PERT charting of task schedules and even schedules for individual employees and for use of specific agency resources. The OPM curriculum also teaches work breakdown structure analysis as a means to organize project tasks. Other specific skills in the OPM curriculum include cost-benefit analysis as a strategy for establishing performance metrics; establishing baseline costs; using the nominal group technique or multicriteria rating methods in support of project decision making; and knowledge management techniques for project documentation and support of organizational memory for future projects.

Not all agency managers entirely accept the OMB call for project management certification, believing in-house experience to be more important to project success. A survey of 100 IT systems managers by *Government Computer News* in 2003 found that 51% felt there was no shortage of qualified, in-house project managers at their agency. Correspondingly, 58% said their agency had no formal program to recruit, train, and retain qualified project managers. Some 69% rated the quality of project management at their agency to be good or excellent. While 48% supported the OMB's push to require commercial certification of project managers, only 39% rated it as one of the most important qualifications for a project manager to have (Walker, 2003c). Notwithstanding this element of skepticism, project management is increasingly a formal profession in the public sector.

PROJECT MANAGEMENT PROTOCOLS

A project is a temporary management effort undertaken to launch a product, service, or process. Project management is the organization and oversight of that effort, from receiving the mission, goals, and objectives from agency authorities at the beginning to transfer of the project to operational management at the end of the project. Projects have a clear beginning and end and are not ongoing operations, support services, or program maintenance initiatives. The project manager is an individual who is often formally trained in project management as a profession. The project manager's role is to meet or exceed the requirements established by a needs assessment of stakeholders and reflected in the agency's strategic plan. The project manager in larger agencies may be housed in and have the support of a projects office, which functions to provide leadership, support, and mentoring for project initiation, planning, execution, control, and operationalization.

A project plan involves several elements. It has a mission statement, which gives an overview of the project. The mission is broken down into clear goals and objectives. The plan describes the governance of the project, including the composition and responsibilities of the project management team and the project leader, and it spells out when and which authorities must sign off on which elements of the project (e.g., the chief financial officer must sign off on the preliminary budget prior to the first purchases being made, and must sign off on all budget line changes over $10,000). The project plan also describes the general project management approach and the evaluation procedures to be used.

Actual project management protocols vary from informal ones used by some local governments to the extremely detailed, as in many units of the U.S. Army.[5] To take an example, the National Aeronautics and Space Administration's Goddard Space Flight Center project management checklist divides tasks into 10 categories: tasks related to the project team itself, communications, mission requirements, costing and scheduling, systems engineering, validation and verification, risk management, independent and peer reviews, documentation, and transition to operations. Each category is then broken down into subtasks for the project manager:

- Tasks related to the project team itself
  - Ensuring stakeholder elements are adequately represented on the project team
  - Defining and clarifying roles and responsibilities
  - Making sure each team member understands the importance of his or her individual contributions
  - Making sure staffing is adequate for the project size
  - Making sure the right people are selected for staff positions
  - Setting overtime guidelines to prevent burnout
- Communications
  - Establishing and communicating an open communications policy
  - Encouraging all team members to report problems
  - Ensuring good communications between the project and affected organizations
  - Soliciting concerns and reviewing and acting on top concerns weekly
- Mission requirements
  - Full and minimum mission success criteria are established at the outset
  - Ensuring that mission requirements are agreed upon by all parties
  - Ensuring all team members are aware of and comply with all pertinent laws and regulations
- Costing and scheduling
  - Developing the project budget based on "bottoms up" methods
  - Establishing a task schedule for the project
  - Ensuring cost reserves are adequate and schedule slack is available to solve problems that may arise
  - Ensuring that schedule has been coordinated to ensure the right skills are available when needed
  - Defining metrics to quantitatively measure meeting cost and on-time targets
- Systems engineering
  - Establishing a mission architecture consistent with agency IT architecture
  - Defining metrics to quantitatively measure meeting performance targets
  - Defining acceptable margins around targets
  - Putting in place a formal process to incorporate lessons learned from previous projects
  - Putting in place a formal system to investigate causes of project failures to meet targets

- Validation and verification
  - Establishing processes/facilities for prototype simulation, verification, and validation
  - Arranging for independent validation and verification
  - Repeating tests after configuration changes
  - Testing and sign-off is conducted by affected units
  - Mission-critical software is identified
- Risk management
  - Define mission risk at the outset with buy-in at all management levels
  - Establish a system for actively tracking and managing risk
  - Identify and model potential failure scenarios
  - Identify backups and establish contingency plans for known risks
  - Utilize risk assessment tools (e.g., failure modes and effects analysis, fault tree analysis, probabilistic risk assessment)
  - Ensure that project risk plans address dependencies affecting other projects
- Independent and peer reviews
  - Establish a project review plan
  - Conduct extensive peer reviews
  - Report peer review results to higher-level reviews
  - Identify lay technical experts to review
  - Identify and obtain commitment from line organizations to provide the right people for sustained support of reviews
- Documentation
  - Document and communicate all design decisions and limitations
  - Ensure that documentation is adequate to support unanticipated personnel changes
  - Document externally imposed budget/schedule changes and their impacts
- Transition to operations
  - Establish a development-to-operations transition plan
  - Complete nominal and worst case network loading analyses for various levels of system demand
  - Integrate the operations team into the development effort
  - Ensure that a sufficient number of core people transition to operations to ensure continuity
  - Validate and test contingency plans with operations staff
  - Formulate and document standard operating procedures

In general, project management involves clearly specifying goals and objectives, identifying stakeholders, securing top management support, breaking the project into tasks, establishing a project schedule for the tasks, maintaining ongoing interaction with stakeholders and end users, staffing the project with qualified personnel, assigning task responsibilities, responding to demands for routine trouble-shooting, conducting peer review and arranging independent review, and transitioning to operational launch of the completed project.

The comprehensive project management protocol described above, it should be noted, is not always followed in full. Especially when the project manager has been trained in software engineering rather than project management, the protocol is apt to reflect a model such as the Software Engineering Institute's software capability maturity model (CMM). The CMM conceptualizes project processes in terms of six procedures: requirements management, software project planning, software project tracking and oversight, software subcontract management, software quality assurance, and software configuration management, defined as follows:

1. Requirements management: Defining, validating, and prioritizing requirements, including performance specifications and delivery dates
2. Software project planning: Developing estimates for tasks, obtaining commitments, and defining the work plan
3. Software project tracking and oversight: Tracking and reviewing software results against commitments and plans and adjusting plans based on actual results
4. Software subcontract management: Selecting and overseeing qualified contractors
5. Software quality assurance: Reviewing and auditing software systems to ensure they comply with the prevailing standards and procedures
6. Software configuration management: Selecting project specifications and reporting change activity for these specifications

The CMM is most appropriate when the projects at hand are repeatable software-oriented undertakings in which technical resources are more salient than human resources in overall system design. When applied to projects where work systems are reinvented or where system outputs are nontechnical and diffuse in nature, the CMM model may not be an adequate framework for project management because it was conceived for purposes of software development projects and not for general project management.

There are as many project management protocols and models as there are consultants and academic experts. Many of the protocols are proprietary products of consulting firms that have copyrighted forms, software, survey instruments, and even terminology associated with their own brand of project management support system. Many other protocols are simply logical checklists of considerations for managing projects, based on past experience. Such useful checklists, such as that used by the California Department of Finance,[6] may include questions in the following areas:

- Planning—Is there a detailed project plan with tasks, milestones, dates, and estimated hours by task, and is it loaded into project management software? Is there a formal staffing plan?
- Tracking—Are two or more estimation methods used to refine estimates? Are actual costs recorded and compared to budgeted costs?
- Procurement—Do all solicitation documents have a detailed written scope of work for all services? For large-scale outsourcing, is qualified legal counsel obtained?
- Risk management—Is there a written risk management plan? Does the management team review risks at least monthly?
- Communication—Is there a written communication plan? Is there regular stakeholder involvement in major project decisions?
- System engineering—Are end users involved in requirements specification and testing? Is a formal system development life cycle methodology employed?

In the Internet age, project managers can now assemble their own customized project management protocols based on a synthesis of the most applicable elements drawn from the wide variety protocols and checklists employed by agencies for widely varied projects.

SUMMARY

Needs assessments, business process analyses, feasibility studies, and project management protocols form the management bridge between strategic IT planning and actual implementation. These tools serve to establish needs and opportunities, relate proposals to agency mission, and prioritize competing projects. By the time a proposal comes under project management, there is not only a generalized plan, but likely also a resource management plan, a human resource plan, a cost management plan, a procurement plan, a quality assurance plan, a risk management plan, a communications plan, and an organizational development/mobilization plan. Though new IT may provide the focal leverage for agency change, those responsible for needs assessment and project management will spend much more time on human factors than on technical ones, contrary to the image suggested by technological determinist theory, which would predict managers would have no choice but to spend their energies coping with the march of sheer technology.

To some extent, the methods discussed in this chapter are extensions of systems theory, with its focus on inventorying inputs and relating them to outputs, with a view to optimal structuring of work processes. Some of the methodologies, like needs assessment, are likely to involve the kind of stakeholder processes emphasized by sociotechnical theory, which focuses on human factors and participatory approaches to organizational change. Even business planning analysis, which is explicitly rooted in systems theory, nonetheless begins with broad stakeholder involvement. All the methods discussed in this chapter operate based on assumptions provided to the needs assessment, business planning analysis, feasibility study, or project management team by management, perhaps based on strategic planning but also possibly based on executive or legislative fiat.

Commentators who like to emphasize reinforcement theories of IT can rightly observe that the management methodologies discussed in this chapter are intended to reflect top management values, assumptions, and goals. Needs assessments, for instance, might establish strong employee needs for improved quality of working life—a major value of the sociotechnical school. Yet if these needs cannot be related to service to agency missions, they are given short shrift in the management methodologies discussed here. This was the case, for instance, with employee and union objections to BPA-based reforms at the PTO, as discussed above. Although needs assessments, project management, and related methodologies may bring to light unexpected findings that may lead top management to reevaluate plans, fundamentally these methods are not designed to and are not likely to bring about organizational democratization or other radical visions of the cyberfuture. Such methodologies could serve such radical ends only if top management did also. By themselves they are tools and as such serve and reinforce the purposes of the powers that be.

DISCUSSION QUESTIONS

1. In your own words, what is the purpose of a needs assessment? What are pitfalls to avoid?
2. What are four basic steps in an IT needs assessment? Pick one and describe why it is necessary for a successful needs assessment and what would happen if it were omitted.
3. What is a functional specifications document and how does it relate to vendors?
4. What is a BPA? Is there a generally accepted standard for IT-related BPAs?
5. What are feasibility studies used for? When are they generally undertaken?
6. What is the role of the project manager? Why might an agency reject calls for using a professional project manager?
7. Use the Internet to find the OMB's "Interpretive Guidance for Project Manager Positions." Describe the knowledge, skills, and abilities associated with IT project management.
8. What is a project management protocol?
9. What is the capacity maturity model? When is this model most appropriately used?
10. In what way can the methods discussed in this chapter be considered extensions of systems theory?

GLOSSARY

Business process analysis: A business process analysis (BPA) is a systematic, iterative, group method of analyzing work processes with a view to designing new processes that may use new technologies.

Feasibility study: A feasibility study analyzes the organization's capacity in terms of technical and human resources needed to implement and maintain an already-proposed solution.

Focus groups: Focus groups are a common needs assessment tool used to gather feedback from representative stakeholders in order to avoid costly IT mismatches between systems design and actual user needs.

Functional specifications document: This document details what the specific capabilities and outcomes of a proposed information system should be (e.g., system storage/retrieval capabilities, processing capabilities and scalability, reporting capabilities, networking capabilities).

JAD: Joint application development.

Needs assessment: A needs assessment is a report to management that analyzes a problem and that may seek to provide solutions to this problem.

PERT: PERT is the programming evaluation and review technique, which is a common management systems tool for sequencing and diagramming project tasks and task dependencies, including charting of task schedules and even schedules for individual employees and for the use of specific agency resources.

Project management: Project management is an administrative role charged with organizing a project in a logical and cost-effective manner so that tasks are sequenced appropriately, clear responsibilities are assigned to tasks, lines of authority are delineated, and systems of accountability are established to ensure completion of a project on time, within budget, and to performance standards

RAD: Rapid application development.

Triage: Sorting and acting upon based on level of need.

Appendix 12-A
Clinger-Cohen Assessment Survey (CCAS) by the Federal Chief Information Officer's Council: General Competencies, Technical Competencies, and Skills

GENERAL COMPETENCIES

1. Administration and management—Knowledge of planning, coordination, and execution of business functions, resource allocation, and production
2. Contracting/procurement—Knowledge of various types of contracts, techniques for contracting or procurement, and contract negotiation and administration
3. Customer service—Works with clients and customers (that is, any individuals who use or receive the services or products that the work unit produces, including the general public, individuals who work in the agency, other agencies, or organizations outside the government) to assess their needs, provide information or assistance, resolve their problems, or satisfy their expectations; knows about available products and services; is committed to providing quality products and services
4. Decision making—Makes sound, well-informed, and objective decisions; perceives the impact and implications of decisions; commits to action, even in uncertain situations, to accomplish organizational goals; causes change
5. Financial management—Prepares, justifies, and/or administers the budget for program areas; plans, administers, and monitors expenditures to ensure cost-effective support of programs and policies; assesses financial condition of an organization
6. Influencing/negotiating—Persuades others to accept recommendations, cooperate, or change their behavior; works with others toward an agreement; negotiates to find mutually acceptable solutions
7. Interpersonal skills—Shows understanding, friendliness, courtesy, tact, empathy, concern, and politeness to others; develops and maintains effective relationships with others; may include effectively dealing with individuals who are difficult, hostile, or distressed; relates well to people from varied backgrounds and different situations; is sensitive to cultural diversity, race, gender, disabilities, and other individual differences

8. Leadership—Influences, motivates, and challenges others; adapts leadership styles to a variety of situations

9. Legal, government, and jurisprudence—Knowledge of laws, legal codes, court procedures, precedents, legal practices and documents, government regulations, executive orders, agency rules, government organization and functions, and the democratic political process

10. Managing human resources—Plans, distributes, coordinates, and monitors work assignments of others; evaluates work performance and provides feedback to others on their performance; ensures that staff are appropriately selected, utilized, and developed, and that they are treated in a fair and equitable manner

11. Oral communication—Expresses information (for example, ideas or facts) to individuals or groups effectively, taking into account the audience and nature of the information (for example, technical, sensitive, controversial); makes clear and convincing oral presentations; listens to others, attends to nonverbal cues, and responds appropriately

12. Organizational awareness—Knows the organization's mission and functions, and how its social, political, and technological systems work and operate effectively within them; this includes the programs, policies, procedures, rules, and regulations of the organization

13. Planning and evaluation—Organizes work, sets priorities, and determines resource requirements; determines short- or long-term goals and strategies to achieve them; coordinates with other organizations or parts of the organization to accomplish goals; monitors progress and evaluates outcomes

14. Problem solving—Identifies problems; determines accuracy and relevance of information; uses sound judgment to generate and evaluate alternatives and to make recommendations

15. Public safety and security—Knowledge of the military, weaponry, and intelligence operations; public safety and security operations; occupational health and safety; investigation and inspection techniques; or rules, regulations, precautions, and prevention techniques for the protection of people, data, and property

16. Strategic thinking—Formulates effective strategies consistent with the business and competitive strategy of the organization in a global economy; examines policy issues and strategic planning with a long-term perspective; determines objectives and sets priorities; anticipates potential threats or opportunities

TECHNICAL COMPETENCIES

1. Accessibility—Knowledge of tools, equipment, and technologies used to help individuals with disabilities use computer equipment and software

2. Artificial intelligence—Knowledge of the principles, methods, and tools used to design systems that perform human intelligence functions

3. Business process reengineering—Knowledge of methods, metrics, tools, and techniques of business process reengineering

4. Capacity management—Knowledge of the principles and methods for monitoring, estimating, or reporting actual performance or the performance capability of information systems or components

5. Capital planning and investment assessment—Knowledge of the principles and methods of capital investment analysis or business case analysis, including return on investment analysis

6. Computer forensics—Knowledge of tools and techniques used in data recovery and preservation of electronic evidence

7. Computer languages—Knowledge of computer languages and their applications to enable a system to perform specific functions

8. Configuration management—Knowledge of the principles and methods for planning or managing the implementation, update, or integration of information systems components

9. Cost-benefit analysis—Knowledge of the principles and methods of cost-benefit analysis, including the time value of money, present value concepts, and quantifying tangible and intangible benefits

10. Data management—Knowledge of the principles, procedures, and tools of data management, such as modeling techniques, data backup, data recovery, data dictionaries, data warehousing, data mining, data disposal, and data standardization processes

11. Database administration—Knowledge of the principles, methods, and tools for automating, developing, implementing, or administering database systems

12. Database management systems—Knowledge of the uses of database management systems and software to control the organization, storage, retrieval, security, and integrity of data

13. Distributed systems—Knowledge of the principles, theoretical concepts, and tools underlying distributed computing systems, including their associated components and communication standards

14. Electronic commerce (e-commerce)—Knowledge of the principles, methods, and tools for conducting business online, including electronic data interchange

15. Embedded computers—Knowledge of specifications and uses of specialized computer systems used to control devices (for example, automobiles, helicopters), including the appropriate programming languages

16. Encryption—Knowledge of procedures, tools, and applications used to keep data or information secure, including public key infrastructure, point-to-point encryption, and smart cards

17. Hardware—Knowledge of specifications, uses, and types of computer or computer-related equipment

18. Hardware engineering—Knowledge of the principles, methods, and tools for designing, developing, and testing computer or computer-related equipment

19. Human factors—Knowledge of the principles, methods, and tools used to identify and apply information about human behavior, abilities, limitations, and other characteristics to the design of tools, machines, systems, tasks, jobs, and environments for effective human use

20. Information assurance—Knowledge of methods and procedures to protect information systems and data by ensuring their availability, authentication, confidentiality, and integrity

21. Information resources strategy and planning—Knowledge of the principles, methods, and techniques of information technology (IT) assessment, planning, management, monitoring, and evaluation, such as IT baseline assessment, interagency functional analysis, contingency planning, and disaster recovery

22. Information systems security certification—Knowledge of the principles, methods, and tools for evaluating information systems security features against a set of specified security requirements; includes developing security certification and accreditation plans and procedures, documenting deficiencies, reporting corrective actions, and recommending changes to improve the security of information systems

23. Information systems/network security - Knowledge of methods, tools, and procedures, including development of information security plans, to prevent information systems vulnerabilities, and provide or restore security of information systems and network services

24. Information technology architecture—Knowledge of architectural methodologies used in the design and development of information systems, including the physical structure of a system's internal operations and interactions with other systems

25. Information technology performance assessment—Knowledge of the principles, methods, and tools (for example, surveys, system performance measures) to assess the effectiveness and practicality of information technology systems

26. Information technology research and development—Knowledge of scientific principles, methods, and tools of basic and applied research used to conduct a systematic inquiry into a subject matter area

27. Infrastructure design—Knowledge of the architecture and typology of software, hardware, and networks, including LANS, WANS, and telecommunications systems, their components and associated protocols and standards, and how they operate and integrate with one another and with associated controlling software

28. Knowledge management—Knowledge of the value of collected information and the methods of sharing that information throughout an organization

29. Logical systems design—Knowledge of the principles and methods for designing business logic components, system processes and outputs, user interfaces, data inputs, and productivity tools (for example, CASE)

30. Modeling and simulation—Knowledge of mathematical modeling and simulation tools and techniques to plan and conduct test and evaluation programs, characterize systems support decisions involving requirements, evaluate design alternatives, or support operational preparation

31. Multimedia technologies—Knowledge of the principles, methods, tools, and techniques of developing or applying technology using text, audio, graphics, or other media

32. Network management—Knowledge of the operation, management, and maintenance of network and telecommunication systems and linked systems and peripherals

33. Object technology—Knowledge of the principles, methods, tools, and techniques that use object-oriented languages, analysis, and design methodologies

34. Operating systems—Knowledge of computer network, desktop, and mainframe operating systems and their applications

35. Operations support—Knowledge of procedures to ensure production or delivery of products and services, including tools and mechanisms for distributing new or enhanced software

36. Organizational development—Knowledge of the principles of organizational development and change management theories, and their applications

37. Process control—Knowledge of the principles, methods, and procedures used for the automated control of a process, including the design, development, and maintenance of associated software, hardware, and systems

38. Product evaluation—Knowledge of methods for researching and analyzing external products to determine their potential for meeting organizational standards and business needs

39. Project management—Knowledge of the principles, methods, or tools for developing, scheduling, coordinating, and managing projects and resources, including monitoring and inspecting costs, work, and contractor performance

40. Quality assurance—Knowledge of the principles, methods, and tools of quality assurance and quality control used to ensure a product fulfills functional requirements and standards

41. Requirements analysis—Knowledge of the principles and methods to identify, analyze, specify, design, and manage functional and

infrastructure requirements; includes translating functional requirements into technical requirements used for logical design or presenting alternative technologies or approaches

42. Risk management—Knowledge of methods and tools used for risk assessment and mitigation of risk

43. Software development—Knowledge of the principles, methods, and tools for designing, developing, and testing software

44. Software engineering—Knowledge of software engineering design and development methodologies, paradigms, and tools; the software life cycle; software reusability; and software reliability metrics

45. Software testing and evaluation—Knowledge of the principles, methods, and tools for analyzing and developing software test and evaluation procedures

46. Standards—Knowledge of standards that either are compliant with or derived from established standards or guidelines

47. System testing and evaluation—Knowledge of the principles, methods, and tools for analyzing and developing systems test and evaluation procedures and technical characteristics of IT systems, including identifying critical operational issues

48. Systems integration—Knowledge of the principles, methods, and procedures for installing, integrating, and optimizing information systems components

49. Systems life cycle—Knowledge of systems life cycle management concepts used to plan, develop, implement, operate, and maintain information systems

50. Technical documentation—Knowledge of procedures for developing technical and operational support documentation

51. Technology awareness—Knowledge of developments and new applications of information technology (hardware, software, telecommunications), emerging technologies and their applications to business processes, and applications and implementation of information systems to meet organizational requirements

52. Telecommunications—Knowledge of transmissions, broadcasting, switching, control, and operation of telecommunications systems

53. Web technology—Knowledge of the principles and methods of Web technologies, tools, and delivery systems, including Web security, privacy policy practices, and user interface issues

SKILLS

1. Fourth-generation language
2. Animation

3. Authentication
4. Biometrics
5. Broadband media
6. Browsers
7. Cabling
8. Client-server
9. Collaboration software
10. Communications software
11. Cryptology
12. Data analysis
13. Data entity-relationship diagramming
14. Data flow diagrams
15. Debugging tools
16. Desktop publishing software
17. Desktop services
18. Develop functional specifications
19. Development system analysis
20. Development toolkits
21. Document management
22. Electronic mail
23. Encryption/decryption algorithms
24. Enterprise directory services
25. Enterprise portal development
26. Enterprise resource planning
27. Federal/OMB enterprise architecture
28. File systems
29. Firewalls
30. Flowcharts
31. FTP servers
32. Groupware
33. HTML
34. HTTP (generic)
35. Internet browsers
36. JAD
37. Low-level language
38. Mainframe
39. Midlevel language
40. Network architecture and design
41. Network configuration and implementation
42. Network protocols
43. Network troubleshooting
44. Network voice/data integration
45. Network topology (general)
46. Object-oriented languages
47. Personal digital assistants

48. PKI
49. Portal development
50. Process design
51. Programming concepts
52. Project management software
53. Prototyping
54. RAD
55. Records management
56. Reusable modules
57. Scripting
58. SEI capability maturity models
59. Sound editing
60. Spreadsheet software
61. SQL (generic)
62. Statistical software
63. Storage devices
64. Structured analysis
65. Structured design
66. Systems security and user administration
67. Systems security applications
68. Telephony
69. Test acceptance testing
70. UML
71. Understanding and translating user requirements
72. UNIX (generic)
73. Video imaging
74. Virtual reality
75. Web design
76. Web-editing software
77. Web graphics design
78. Web site management
79. Wireless technologies
80. Word-processing software

Source: CIO Council, 2003, pp. 59–67.

ENDNOTES

[1]Available at http://www.opm.gov/fedclass/html/whatsnew.asp.

[2]PMI has government initiatives at pmi.org/prod/groups/public/documents/info/ gmc_governmentsig.asp.

[3]For more information on OPM's Project Management Curriculum as well as other courses offered by the OPM Management Development Centers, visit http://www.leadership.opm.gov/courselist.cfm.

[4]Available at http://www.fai.gov/policies/contract.htm.

[5]For example, see http://www.atimp.army.mil/reeng/rem.asp.

[6]Available at http://www.dof.ca.gov/HTML/IT/Oversight/Appendix%20F.doc.

CASE STUDY
Improving Public Sector Needs Analysis in a Small City

Paul K. Dezendorf and Tracy Leigh Jenkins, Winthrop University

Introduction: A Changing Environment

The City of Rock Hill covered approximately 32 square miles and included 56,114 residents in 2005. The city operates under a council–manager form of government with an elected at-large mayor and six council members elected by ward with 4-year staggered terms. Overall, the city's stability (the last four city managers served an average of 12 years each) and ability to deliver services is reflected in 103 separate annexations in the past 20 years despite some of the most restrictive annexation laws in the country. The city is located in the Charlotte, North Carolina, metropolitan area about 25 miles south of city center with easy access to one of the busiest airports in the United States and the corridor of development running from Atlanta, Georgia, to Raleigh, North Carolina.

The traditional culture of small towns, personal relationships, and slow pace of life of this area changed in the past generation with the loss of historic industries, such as textiles, and the transition to the economy of the New South as national and international companies relocated here to benefit from lower wages, low taxes, mild climate, good transportation, and a probusiness environment. Newcomers arrived with a higher level of formal education, greater expectations of public sector services, and accustomed to modern IT. In addition, the conservative political environment in South Carolina that encouraged low and limited services was intensified by the increased economic challenges of the dot.com bust, 9/11, and the overall conservative trend in the country. All told, the City of Rock Hill was typical of many metropolitan fringe small cities throughout the United States.

Entrepreneurial Response

By the early 1990s, the changing environment for the City of Rock Hill resulted in the adoption of a consciously entrepreneurial business approach to running the city, a focus on basic services, and using needs assessments to better understand residents (e.g., citywide telephone surveys and questionnaires aimed at specific programs) (Greene, 1997). Resulting initiatives included construction of fire and police substations, road construction, improved water infrastructure, and so on. Other efforts at better understanding needs included innovations such as an automated voice response system for reporting utility problems. These changes were accompanied by increased attention to customer service; in 1989, the city started customer service training programs for all employees; by 1995, the city moved from an individual-based service orientation to a community-based service delivery approach, including community policing and neighborhood empowerment programs. At present, the city employs a five-person call center focused on maintaining top-quality customer responsiveness.

Better understanding needs and focusing on customers was accompanied by a managed competition approach to providing service, meaning the city would develop an RFP and cost-benefit analysis and place the targeted service either in-house, contract it out, or partially contract it, or eliminate the service. This approach was accompanied by benchmarking and performance data analysis that started in 1994. Although oriented to innovation, the city's attention to bottom line is evident from the fact that the percentage of IT expenses compared with general revenues varies by less than a tenth of a percent over the 15-year period of 1990–2005, despite Y2K, major mainframe projects, initiation of a geographic information system (GIS), and other IT initiatives. Overall, the city's efforts focused on providing a vision, communicating change, involving the entire organization, taking risks, learning from others, but always focusing on the bottom line (Greene, 1997).

Foundations of E-Government

The city's management made strategic use of IT to realize those entrepreneurial objectives and began to deliver government services via IT, created cross-cutting internal services, encouraged interaction across traditional bureaucratic boundaries, and developed a flatter organization with decentralized authority and delegated decision making; thus, the City of Rock Hill moved toward "e-government" (Schelin, 2003). This shift was accomplished without many of the common political consequences of the growth of IT in government noted by Rocheleau (2003). Rather than turf disputes, the city's response was characterized by coordination across departments, openness to innovation, designing IT around the user rather than the IT professional, and consultative IT support.

Overall, three sets of changes aided the e-government transition. The first set of changes was a succession of IT developments related to core services and in particular the utilities area. Utilities provide roughly 65% of general revenues; the costs to the city plus worry about national changes such as privatization and utility deregulation increased the city's efforts to use technology to reduce costs and improve effectiveness while increasing the ability of the city to understand the needs of the citizens. On the operational level, expensive paper-and-pencil recordkeeping and work order systems were replaced by automated work orders. Process activities, such as new residential construction, were integrated by IT and deviance from plan, such as review of plans taking longer than specified, triggers automatic e-mails to department heads. The city also provided a system to allow employees with typical desktop skills to directly publish a form to the Web.

A second set of activities was the development of cross-cutting efforts; perhaps the most fundamental was the development of GIS. Rather than pursue separate IT initiatives, midlevel managers from 10 city departments agreed in the early 1990s to develop an accurate database foundation of street addresses and parcel numbers and thus allow integrated databases for application areas due to their understanding of the cross-cutting nature of GIS (Carr, 2003). Top-down support came in the form of resources to develop the system and constantly update the database long before benefits came back from GIS. The present GIS system supports several hundred separate layers above the foundation of street addresses and parcel numbers; GIS provides a common database for use in managing data, analysis, and then reporting, e.g., "School Locator" with information for parents keyed to specific street addresses.

Another major cross-cutting factor has been development of a management information system (MIS) department that focuses on supporting departmental needs rather than data as a result of top management's willingness to delegate responsibility and authority, support of innovation (such as introducing Internet protocol (IP) telephony in 2002 and installing 38 miles of fiber-optic backbone to two dozen remote locations) and flexibility in allowing changes in purchasing to meet changes in technology. Innovations to improve needs assessment include beginning a network of video cameras and experimenting with low-power transceivers to allow radio frequency (RF) meter reading, tracking of vehicles, and so on.

The third set of activities has been a move toward public engagement. For example, the city was far behind regarding Web use despite moving rapidly ahead in other IT areas. In 1998, there was only a Front Page site with a department list and several PDF planning files. The city contracted out public engagement via Web sites in July of 2002 and by January of 2005, the URL http://www.ci.rock-hill.sc.us/ was drawing over 30,000 unique visitors a month to a city of 56,114 residents.

Better Understanding of Needs

Those three sets of activities (focusing on core services, developing cross-cutting efforts, and moving toward public engagement) resulted in an increased needs analysis ability for the city. The first of the three sets of activities, focus on core services, provided the motivation and cash flow. The cross-cutting elements, in particular GIS and MIS, provided improved tools. The third set, public engagement, increased stakeholder support. As a result of all three sets working together, needs analysis was improved regarding neighborhood empowerment, economic development, and policy making.

These IT changes greatly improved the city's understanding of residents' needs regarding public safety, housing stock, street maintenance, utilities, and school services. This understanding focused on usage of service, demand for service, customer satisfaction, and projecting growth and changes. The improved understanding supported analysis on a neighborhood basis and thus reinforced the city's move to a neighborhood orientation. These quantitative measurements themselves did not "empower" neighborhoods; empowerment is still principally centered on face-to-face activities and developing in-person groups despite discussion of the use of IT for empowerment. However, the value of survey research to the public sector (Vasu & Vasu, 2003) has motivated city efforts throughout the period discussed to directly measure citizen perceptions. This effort has continued as a university within Rock Hill began in 2002 to perform computer-assisted telephone interviewing surveys for both the city and county.

In economic development, a better understanding of needs resulted from the greatly increased information from utilities, better understanding of growth patterns and land use from GIS, and increased information regarding development interests via Web interface. Further, economic development's public engagement activities, encouraging enquiries and communicating to prospects, are well developed.

The benefits of IT development for policy making have centered on expositions regarding specific projects; for example, the ability to examine land use information and projected data regarding growth to develop plans for federal community development block grants. Policy makers can receive sophisticated reports regarding city services such as crime reports. However, the city's large regional databases are not integrated into policy making as Carr (2003) suggests is possible. The city's IT and organizational changes appear to move in the direction of what Musso, Weare, and Hale (2000) called *good management* rather than *good democracy*.

Conclusions

The City of Rock Hill started the period 1990–2005 at a low level of IT sophistication but by 2005 had developed numerous public sector IT applications because of a conscious shift to a business entrepreneurship model, greatly improved core services technology applications, cross-cutting efforts in GIS and MIS, and increased attention to public engagement; these improvements supported a great increase in needs analysis capability. The city's success appears to confirm the critical success factors of top management support, stakeholder involvement, communications, end-user involvement, qualified staff, adequate financial support, cross-functional teams, strategic planning, use of rewards, and political support reported by Schelin and Garson (2004). Overall, the city is an example of good long-term returns from technology investment during a challenging

continues

time period. Among the questions still to be answered, however, are whether the *good management* using IT may be accompanied at some point by IT-supported *good democracy* (Shi & Scavo, 2000).

References

Carr, T. R. (2003). Geographic information systems in the public sector. In G. D. Garson (Ed.), *Public information technology: Policy and management issues* (pp. 252–270). New York: Marcel-Dekker.

Greene, J. Jr. (1997). Entrepreneurial government in Rock Hill: A case study. *South Carolina Policy Forum, 8,* 30–40.

Musso, J., Weare, C., & Hale, M. (2000). Designing Web technologies for local government reform: Good management or good democracy? *Political Communication, 17*(1), 1–19.

Rocheleau, B. (2003). Politics, accountability, and government information systems. In G. D. Garson (Ed.), *Public information technology: Policy and management issues* (pp. 20–52). New York: Marcel-Dekker.

Schelin, S. H. (2003). E-government: An overview. In G. D. Garson (Ed.), *Public information technology: Policy and management issues* (pp. 120–137). New York: Marcel-Dekker.

Schelin, S., & Garson, G. D. (2004). *Humanizing information technology: Advice from experts.* Hershey, PA: CyberTech.

Shi, Y., & Scavo, C. (2000). Citizen participation and direct democracy through computer networking. In G. D. Garson (Ed.), *Handbook of public information systems* (pp. 247–264). New York: Marcel-Dekker.

Vasu, M. L., & Vasu, E. S. (2003). Survey research, focus groups, and information technology in research and practice. In G. D. Garson (Ed.), *Public information technology: Policy and management issues* (pp. 221–251). New York: Marcel-Dekker.

Implementation

Implementation Success Factors

Information technology (IT) has great public relations. The public and even elected officials believe that technology is the engine of administrative efficiency and progress. IT's dirty secret, however, is that IT projects very often are either late, over budget, do not achieve original functional objectives, or are simply canceled. While this is not unique to the public sector, the public sector's greater emphasis on accountability and lower acceptance of taking risks makes failure particularly a concern for public managers. Moreover, since in recent years governments have given priority to larger and larger projects of a more comprehensive nature, the costs of failure have risen correspondingly. As Nelson (2005, p. 93), writing about the increasing number and size of governmental IT projects, has noted, "These large-scale IT projects are particularly prone to failure . . . increasing commitment to success yields subsequent project iterations that are both increasingly costly and increasingly less likely to succeed." Ironically, according to Nelson, failure in large-scale projects often actually leads not to project cancellation but rather to greater commitment.

IT organizations such as the Gartner Group, Meta Group, and the Standish Group have long reported astonishing rates of IT failure in both public and private sectors. A study of Fortune 500 firms found over half of their users either underused or had entirely abandoned the software that was supposed to increase their productivity on the job (Watt, 1989). Similarly, back in 1990 the Gartner Group's study of Fortune 500 companies found that 40% had experienced runaway or near-runaway IT projects (Mehler, 1991). In 1994, the Standish Group (1994) consulting firm found that more than 80% of IT projects were late, over budget, lacking in functionality, or never delivered; 3 of 4 projects were late with schedule overruns averaging above 200%; 2 of 3 projects ended without implementing originally scheduled features/functions; 3 in 10 projects were cancelled; and cost overruns averaged nearly 200%. The Standish Group study estimated that some $75 billion was wasted through IT project failure in a recent year. A 1999 study of enterprise resource planning software projects found that fully 90% wound up late or over budget (Fryer, 1999).

In a 2000 update, the Standish Group (2001) found that the average IT project success rate was still only 28%, though up from 16% in 1994. While cost overruns averaged 45% in 2000, this was better than the 69% found by the Standish Group in 1998 and the 189% found in 1994. Likewise, time schedule overruns dropped from 222% in 1994 to 63% in 2000, and the number of projects coming in with the required features rose from 61% in 1994 to 67% in 2000. In summary, in 2000, coming in late was the most common problem (63%), with 45% of projects not coming in on or under budget, and 33% not coming in with originally specified features and functionality. In 2000, some 23% of IT projects were canceled outright.

There is evidence that the problem of IT failure is worse in the public sector. The 1994 Standish Group study found that the IT success rate varied from 59% in retail establishments, 32% in financial sector firms, 27% in manufacturing, but was only 18% in government—well below the all-sectors success rate of 26%. In the 2000 Standish Group update, considering federal, state, and local governments, the success rate had increased from 18% to 24%, an improvement but well below the 40% success rate in the private sector. Fully half of all government IT projects were either late, over budget, or did not meet required features. About one in four (26%) of government projects were rated failures, not meeting any of the three criteria, compared to only 16% in the private sector. The Standish Group (2001) estimated that as of 2000, IT contract failures cost government from $7.8 billion to $11.7 billion annually. In the same vein, the Gartner Group reported that 60% of all e-government initiatives fail (Harris, 2002).

Office of Management and Budget (OMB) ratings tend to point up the same problem with public-sector IT failure. Over half of 1400 major federal IT initiatives were identified on OMB's "At Risk List" in the president's FY 2004 budget. Many of these initiatives were at risk because of their inability to demonstrate their value consistent with the principles of performance management and measurement. Numerous scholars have noted the high level of IT failure and risk in the public sector (Brown, 2000). A majority (17 of 26) federal agencies evaluated received the failing rating of "red" on Budget and Performance Integration in the President's Management Agenda scorecard (Federal Enterprise Architecture Program Management Office, 2003). Likewise, in 2004 because of problems with their annual business cases, the OMB put 621 projects (55% of all IT projects), with budgets totaling $22 billion, on its "watch list" (Miller, 2004h). The FY 2006 rate fell to 31% as OMB accepted more business cases for agency IT proposals, but this still represented $15 billion in investment spread out over 342 federal IT projects.

WHY INFORMATION TECHNOLOGY PROJECTS FAIL

The failure of public-sector IT projects is neither new nor rare. For instance, in the 1990s many states (e.g., Washington) invested in Wang document imaging systems. When Wang went out of the word-processing business, agencies that had purchased their proprietary solutions became unable to retrieve agency data. This debacle reinforced the lesson that systems must be open and platform independent. To take another example of public-sector IT failure, James (1997) has reported that the Internal Revenue Service (IRS) cost taxpayers $50 billion a year (mainly in lost revenue) due to a series of IT project failures, in spite of $8 billion invested. In the same period the Food and Drug Administration's CANDA electronic document program had to be essentially abandoned (Williams, Canfield, & Ritondo, 1997). Later, in 2003, the IRS Oversight Board noted that all of that agency's seven major IT projects were behind schedule and over budget. The central effort, the Customer Account Data Engine, designed to replace the old tape-based system for taxpayer records, was then two years behind schedule and $30 million over budget (Lais, 2003). The IRS was hardly alone. For example, the Transportation Department's Inspector General criticized the Federal Aviation Administration in June 2003 due to a $4.3 billion cost overrun in 20 of the agency's major projects. Similarly, in 2004 the Justice Department's Inspector General flagged the Federal Bureau of Investigation's (FBI's) Virtual Case File case management systems project as a $170 million failure.

Failure can characterize whole genres of systems. It is estimated that one-third of customer relationship management implementations, for instance, yield no return and another third yield only minor benefits (Coffee, 2001). A large number of applications are purchased and not used. The Navy-Marine Corps Intranet program inventoried 36,713 applications in 2002 to see which were security compliant. The survey revealed that some 20% to 30% of applications were not being used by anyone (Onley, 2002c).[1]

Similarly, at the state level, IT failure is common. For instance, NYeNET was a $42 million effort of the New York State Office for Technology to unify, streamline, and reduce costs of telecommunications for state and local agencies. An audit found it had "done little to improve services for New Yorkers." Only three of six networks scheduled to be replaced by NYeNET had made the transition. No formal plans exist to expand beyond the six. Widely used networks such as the Health Department's Medicaid Payment System or the Labor Department's Unemployment Insurance System were not included. Local governments were found to have "waited years" just to get information on the NYeNET system. Auditors blamed poor management, failure to use project management techniques, failure to perform a feasibility study, and failure to set measurable objectives (Dizard, 2003c).

Of course, failure is not unique to the United States. Heeks (2002) has reported many total or partial failures of aid agencies that spent vast sums on health information systems (IS) in South Africa, IS projects in China, and World Bank funded projects in Africa. In his book *Software Failure,* Flowers (1996) described the London Ambulance Service's computerized dispatch system, which after a week "slowed down and then locked up altogether. Attempts to reboot the system failed to correct the problem and, when the backup system failed to cut in, the control room staff had no alternative but to revert to a fully manual paper-based system" (p. 74). Flowers also described the United Kingdom case of the Wessex Regional Information Systems Plan, which failed after spending over £40 million, only to become a national scandal thought to have lost a decade of systems development by the National Health Service, making the phrase "another Wessex" synonymous with IT failure.

A classic instance of IT failure centered on the Therac-25 radiation machine used in hospitals. Due to poorly written software, excessive dosages of radiation were given, leading to several deaths. A detailed report compiled by Leveson and Turner (1993) revealed that minor errors in data entry by technicians could lead to major misapplications of radiation. As the Therac-25 was frequently used in high-stress situations under time pressure, the possibility of such errors was predictable, but software engineers had been untrained in anticipating such possibilities. Although initially blamed on poor programming and failure to trap errors and confirm choices via software, the blame for the Therac disaster actually could be allotted to a variety of factors:

- The programmers, for faulty software
- The vendor, for not adequately testing and recalling a defective product
- The government regulators, for deferring to vendors and not independently testing and ensuring safety of the machine
- The hospital managers, for continuing to use the Therac-25 even after problems appeared

- The Therac-25 operators, for not providing human judgment to balance reliance on the machine

Each group had excuses and could cite mitigating circumstances, but the case as a whole points out that software problems are not merely technical in nature but are enmeshed in sociopolitical systems. It is the integration (or lack of it) of the technical and the human that determines ultimate success or failure.

Chiles' (2001) study of engineering disasters from the Titanic to Chernobyl shows system failure is not unique to IT, but is rooted in common factors. His eight common reasons why IT projects fail are described in the following sections.

Complexity

IT projects may fail because they become too large and complex. The executive vice president for the Standish Group, which has studied failure rates in government IT programs since 1994, was quoted as saying, "We have seen a little bit of improvement over that time, but not a lot. We see smaller projects today than there were seven years ago, and our research shows smaller projects have a greater chance of success than larger projects" (Dizard, 2001). Larger projects have more stakeholders, and the greater the number of stakeholders, the more complex the requirements and the higher the risk of project failure (Kristensen & Buhler, 2001).

Commitment Failure

IT projects may fail because of lack of commitment from the organization's stakeholders. Because of this, the project manager must spend most of his or her time mobilizing the stakeholders, leaving IT issues largely to the tech team. Time is spent, for instance, getting agency leadership to figure out what they really want and to assess whether they have the time or resources to do it. The organization's executive leadership is the prime stakeholder, whose active support is critical to implementation success. Flowers (1996) asserts that IT projects commonly fail because senior management lacks understanding not only of the technology but also of the general systemic nature of their organizations, and particularly they lack an understanding that technological change means change of the organizational culture. Involvement of top management and stakeholders requires participation in IT planning and implementation. Lack of the required participative approach is commonly cited as a cause of IT failure. Without participation, IT initiatives often fail to capture important social relationships that may undermine the technical logic of the IT system (Montealegre, 1996). Absence of participation is associated with failure to build trust, which is necessary for commitment (Kristensen & Buhler, 2001).

Planning Failure

IT projects may fail because of poor business plans. To be sustainable, an IT project must make economic sense to the principal stakeholders. Thus there must be an economic model that accompanies the technology model. Project managers must focus on business needs first, technology second. When the solution is selected solely on technological grounds, ignoring business requirements, failure often ensues. The Gartner Group has found that as many as three quarters of all corporate IT projects fail because of poor planning. Failure to conduct needs assessments, failure to have written design plans, and failure to familiarize the program team with plans is at the core of failed software development, according to Griffith (2004). Failure to invest in real organizational planning for the project and instead buying a prepackaged outside "solution" is one of Flowers' (1996) four leading reasons for IT failure. (The other three are lack of management understanding, time pressure, and lack of a participative approach.)

Vision Failure

IT projects may fail because the underlying assumptions about a program are unrealistic. It is essential that agency leaders understand and clearly visualize the gap between present practice and the desired state (Heeks, 2003). Vendors and consultants hype their products and services in order to sell them to agencies, but this very marketing can raise unrealistic expectations that distort the agency's vision and that create severe implementation problems down the road. Having realistic goals serves to control both expectations and implementation costs (Andrews & Johnson, 2002). Common managerial mistakes cited by Andrews (2002) are expecting perfection of the project team, being unwilling to delegate implementation details to the project team, reluctance to make or even admit that change involves trade-off choices, and inability to admit to uncertainty and to build a project organization that is flexibly adaptive. Perhaps even more important than any of these forms of vision failure comes when management keeps changing the vision, as for instance, when the FBI's ill-fated Virtual Case File system came to grief in 2004 partly because managers allowed the case file project to stray into new missions such as evidence management that fell outside the original goals for the system (Dizard, 2005b). Incremental visions are more apt to succeed than grandiose ones. Reduced scope also reduces the risk that IT designs will already be obsolete when implemented.

Inappropriate Methods

IT projects may fail because conventional methods that are traditional to the organization but that are inappropriate to the IT project are forcibly used in new IT initiatives. The project manager must not adopt cutting-edge technologies simply to be cutting edge when in fact the organization might benefit from older, more stable technologies. The project manager should not change the problem to fit the preconceived technology solution. Because of the temptation to do so, it may be wise to assign the responsibility for setting and monitoring project goals and for technology implementation to separate officials and groups, so as to avoid conflicts of interest.

Short Time Horizon

The old "Rome was not built in a day" adage applies in the IT world as well. IT projects may fail because of unrealistically short time horizons (Kristensen & Buhler, 2001). This is sometimes encouraged by IT consultants who seek or need to close and go on to new projects. It may also occur in the public sector because expending an agency's entire budget before the end of the fiscal year is a common pattern, designed to demonstrate need so as to ensure the following year's budget will be at least as large. This strategy, however, can result in undue acceleration of IT projects. This is compounded when the strategy is implemented at the end of the year, under an even more compressed time schedule (Flowers, 1996).

Turbulent Environments

The more rapid the rate of change in the environment, the more disordered and uncoordinated the implementation of technology initiations, the more likely the system failure. Unfortunately, large-scale change is often what it takes to trigger the launching of management initiatives that restructure the way the agency does business. Successful IT implementation in turbulent environments requires a management team that is adept at change management. Turbulent environments may call for a different leadership style that is more proactive, mobilization oriented, partnering oriented, and flexible in comparison with traits needed to administer stable processes (Hamel, 2002; Hamel, Prahalad, Thomas, & O'Neal, 1998). When turbulence strikes, the proper form of leadership may not be in place and implementation may suffer.

Failure to Support End Users

IT projects may fail because of inadequate support, training, and incentives for end users. Lack of user input may lead to an inappropriate technology design from the start. An important part of IT implementation is mobilization at the workgroup level. This may involve participative planning, training, and individual and/or group rewards for IT success. Lack of communication and understanding between top management, the technology team, and end users is a major factor in the failure of IT projects. Without strong support for end users, buy-in by those who ultimately are the actual implementers of an IT project will not occur. Unfortunately, top management is often more apt to give priority to hardware and software investments in a project than it is to investing in human capital.

Beyond these eight reasons for IT failure, a system of organizational myths can create a failure-prone culture. Dale and Goldfinch (2002) studied the collapse of the Integrated National Crime Investigation System (INCIS) in New Zealand. INCIS was a highly ambitious system to be based on over 3000 personal computers linking all police stations to each other and to a national crime database. The project, which had been developed through business process analysis methods discussed in the previous chapter, was abandoned in 1999 after incurring a cost of NZ$100 million. In analyzing the reasons for failure, Dale and Goldfinch emphasized what they called the "Four Enthusiasms of IT Apocalypse," reflected in Figure 13-1.

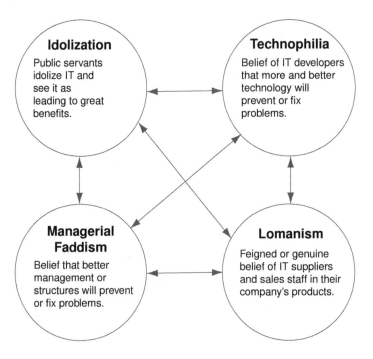

Figure 13-1   Four Enthusiasms of IT Apocalypse. *Source:* Reprinted by permission of the authors, Tony Dale and Shaun Goldfinch, from their article, "Pessimism as an information system management tool in the public sector: Lessons from the INCIS fiasco in the New Zealand Police Force" (2002).

These four "enthusiasms" each are mostly common and reasonable belief sets held by stakeholders in IT change projects: top managers thinking that IT-based new structures will fix problems, public officials seeing IT as a near panacea, their IT staff believing in technological fixes, and vendors enthusiastically selling their system solutions. Together, however, these belief sets can encourage an uncritical drive toward implementation that pushes realities aside, only to find the implementation is unrealistic and doomed to failure at the end.

INTERNAL SUCCESS FACTORS

When considering what factors may lead to IT implementation success, there are numerous problems. As Rocheleau (2000) has observed, public managers looking for IT "lessons" have four sources, all of them problematic. The "best practices" literature provides recommendations that are too general. The empirical research literature on public sector IT is sparse and contradictory in prescription. Benchmarking studies are underdeveloped and subject to corruption. The problem/disaster case literature is unrepresentative of most failures. The success factors literature is largely based on surveys of IT managers' perceptions of what is important, case studies of particular agencies, and anecdotal observations. This literature names dozens of success factors—so many that the practitioner may feel it is not helpful. Nonetheless, it is clear that some factors are cited as being critical much more often than others. These factors are described in the following sections.

Management Support

The active involvement and attention of top management is almost invariably at the top of the list in studies in the success factor literature (GAO, 2001b, p. 10; Northrop, 2002; Poon & Wagner, 2001; Schelin & Garson, 2004). IT implementation is associated with revitalized management practices (West & Berman, 2001) sponsored by a strong top leadership (Miller, 2002b). Projects benefit from a high-level champion who appreciates what technology can do and makes the case to the rest of top management (Fletcher, Bretschneider, Marchand, Rosenbaum, & Bertot, 1992). The type of management involvement needed is not merely the passive receiving of project information, but rather active management leadership and advocacy for the project. Obtaining support is facilitated if management makes a conscious "sales" effort, which IT staff then market to end users and stakeholders through visits, forums, newsletters, user support groups, seminars, executive briefings, tours, demonstrations, hotlines, surveys, and other outreaches. Support must not be a one-time announcement; it requires active, ongoing involvement and follow-up. A management that has fostered a proactive and flexible culture of change is better than one that rigidly values convention and organizational tradition. Finally, success is tied to leadership that has the managerial and technical skills needed to establish credibility with stakeholders in the IT project.

Stakeholder Motivation

IT systems are more likely to be implemented successfully when top management has worked with the project manager to ensure that a well-considered motivation system is in place so that all stakeholders receive benefits from successful implementation (Metz, 1986; Schelin & Garson, 2004). Reward systems reinforce project goals and foster teamwork as stakeholders work together to achieve benefits (Milis & Mercken, 2002). Although typical employee attitudes are resistant to change, if new technology is seen as bringing desired benefits, then attitudes will adapt (Larwood, 1984). Promoting collegiality among stakeholders through workshops, site visits, and public meetings, as the Bureau of Land Management did in creating its National Integrated Land System, was seen by the Industry Advisory Council (2002) as a key success factor. Although securing stakeholder motivation may seem obvious, in fact stakeholder analysis is often neglected in planning IT projects on the false assumption that technology alone will determine implementation success. Stakeholding may account for findings that managers and professionals are significantly more positive in their perceptions of computer projects than are rank-and-file employees (Safayeni, Purdy, & Higgins, 1989). This is because the former are much more likely to be accorded a formal stake in IT projects than are the latter.

Stakeholder motivation begins with needs assessment, which ties the planning processes discussed with respect to goal clarity with motivational considerations. Stakeholder motivation is difficult at best when systems are not designed for stakeholder needs. Systems where, for instance, all cost savings of the new system are garnered by the state legislature or other outside body are less likely to succeed than those where the affected agency and its staff receive some of the savings back in the form of increased budgets. The usual array of motivators applies to IT projects: remuneration, awards, publicized recognition, opportunities for travel, better equipment, better working conditions, opportunities for networking with superiors, professional prestige with peers, greater task control, more training, upgraded job descriptions, and so on. Perhaps an even more important motivator than any of these is a compelling vision set forth by a charismatic leadership (Harvard Policy Group, 2001a; Industry Advisory Council, 2002). In fact, some authors feel visioning and planning are the most important success factors (Al-Mashari, Al-Mudimigh, & Zairi, 2003).

Goal Clarity

Early research quickly discovered that lack of a plan or inadequate definition of project scope were the most important causes of implementation failure (Keider, 1984). It is difficult to be successful when you do not know where you are going. Top management involvement is often a prerequisite to achieving goal clarity. One of the key tasks of the project manager is to involve top management and the organization generally in a process of clearly relating the mission to goals, goals to objectives, and objectives to measurable milestones (Industry Advisory Council, 2002; Miller, 2002b). Milestones and deadlines create a "pressure for progress" (Harvard Policy Group, 2001a) and were found to be the fifth most important success factor by Schelin and Garson (2004) in a survey of public and private sector chief information officers (CIOs). Clarifying what the system *won't* do limits unrealistic expectations. It is important that the goals of IT initiatives are consistent across departments of the organization. If the organization has an enterprise architecture to guide project decision making, success may be more likely also. Finally, if the organization is used to long-term, strategic planning rather than operating in a short-term reactive mode, goal clarity is enhanced and planning for IT projects will be reinforced by the agency strategic plans they serve.

Support for Organizational Culture

Implementing IT projects is an exercise in shifting organizational culture, though even leading models of IT implementation often neglect this (Baker, 1991). That is, successful project managers understand that cognitive change issues arise in implementation. The more implementation changes organizational culture, the more resistance. Ho and Ni (2004) identified perceived staff resistance as the key driver accounting for variance in e-government diffusion and innovation. However, the more the IT initiative can retain and even reinforce the existing organizational culture, the less resistance and the more likely it is to succeed. This leads to considerations such as these: Is the existing authority structure reflected in the implementation? Does the initiative reflect the traditional chain of command, or does it disrupt it? Are the organization's logos, language, and other symbols integrated in the design? Does implementation minimize the need for employees to express themselves in new concepts, categories, and vocabulary? Does the implementation attempt to preserve traditional cultural values in the organization (e.g., pride in craftsmanship, personal service)?

Participatory Implementation

Employee resistance to the implementation of IT projects is as old as computing itself, having been explored since the 1970s by organizational psychologists such as Chris Argyris (1971) and management scientists such as Henry C. Lucas (1975). In Argyris's work, participation aided in "organizational health," while Lucas showed the importance of employee participation in bringing IT implementation to a successful conclusion. By the 1980s a large literature on dealing with resistance to IT had arisen (Majchrzak, 1988), the majority of it supporting the concept of participatory IT design as a critical success factor because of its role in blunting employee resistance that arises when top-down implementation strategies are used.

Participation increases motivation and stakeholder buy-in because individuals invest themselves in the decision-making processes leading to project initiation and implementation (Harvard Policy Group, 2001a; Monnickendam & Eaglestein, 1993). Participation also brings cross-functional collaboration to the project effort, particularly in forcing useful interaction between IT and operating elements (Milis & Mercken, 2002; Teo & Ang, 1999). Formation of collaborative teams representing diverse affected interests for project planning and implementation is a staple of successful project management (Ang, Sum, & Yeo, 2002). Naturally, end users are key members of any such collaboration.

Mantei and Teorey (1988) carefully cost out the use of participative methods, finding a major direct savings in the form of reduced training costs, error reduction costs, and savings from avoidance of last-minute IT design changes. They also found intangible benefits in the form of greater adoption of time-saving IT features, avoiding system sabotage problems, and enhancing the ability of employees to solve problems using the software system. The implication is that the project manager must recognize that part of implementation is organization development (OD), and formal or informal OD methods can and should be used to mobilize team spirit behind implementation. This success factor is tied to management support, since participation in planning and implementation is hollow if management is not listening to feedback. Pseudo-participation can backfire, raising and then frustrating expectations, and leaving cynicism toward all IT projects in its wake.

User Friendliness

Stakeholder motivation is increased by the user friendliness of the application, and user friendliness is more likely to emerge from participatory forms of project implementation. To take a negative example, excessive use of numeric activity codes was a significant factor leading to the failure of a New York City (NYC) welfare management system. Social workers were asked by the system to enter hard-to-remember codes for case attributes, often for activities not directly relevant to their own contributions. As a result, entered data were frequently erroneous or missing, sabotaging the system. Northrop (2002) cited a similar example, where a court system required users to memorize 2000 codes, thereby multiplying training time and resulting in an error-fraught system which proved frustrating and unsatisfactory. Likewise, ergonomics and the human–machine interface should not be ignored.

Adequate Budgeting and Time Horizon

Doing IT "on a shoestring" can be a recipe for failure. Adequate funding is an outgrowth of top management involvement, the primary success factor (Milis & Mercken, 2002). Senior management must ensure that sufficient resources are assigned to the planning, implementation, and evaluation stages of IT implementation. Adequate budgeting of time is as important as budgeting of money. An unrealistic time frame may require end users to absorb too much too quickly, and releasing IT systems before they are ready can cause clients to reject them, even if later "fixes" are made to correct problems arising from rapid deployment. A longer time frame also allows for testing out new systems through prototyping, a strategy that has also been tied to project success (Hong & Kim, 2002).[2]

Phased Implementation

Phased implementation is an extension of goal clarity, closely related to the idea of milestones as clear, measurable targets. Testing and piloting of projects should precede the first phase of actual implementation, so as to allow for the system to adapt to realities discovered in the field. Then dividing the overall project into separable steps that may be implemented in phases has been identified as a key success factor (Miller, 2002b). Success breeds success, and successful projects are designed with phased implementation so the early phases deliver demonstrable successes that motivate stakeholders in later phases (GAO, 2001a, p. 34). Modularization also makes implementation more manageable and protects the project from shifts in budgetary and other forms of resource support (Harvard Policy Group, 2001a).

Process and Software Reengineering

Outdated legacy systems create major implementation challenges, as was the case in overhauling New York State's central accounting system (CTG, 2000a). Homeowners know it is often easier to install plumbing in a new structure than to repair it in an old one. Similarly, the millions of lines of COBOL and other ancient computer code that still exist can be a major obstacle to maintaining efficient systems. Though IT has diffused widely in the public sector, large old-technology systems hamper public sector IT progress and lead to high failure rates. As a case study of human relations software in Vermont has shown, process reengineering must precede task automation or IT will be geared to inefficient or obsolete procedures (Cats-Baril & Thompson, 1995). In spite of the engineering label to this success factor, success is more likely when reengineering is headed by a project manager of broad vision rather than a narrowly trained technician (GAO, 2001a, p. 27). Technicians have less understanding of business processes and thus are more likely to automate what exists rather than creating new, better processes.[3] They are also less effective in the trust-building activities needed to mobilize stakeholders (CTG, 2000b). Finally, a major reengineering effort requires major investments, so this is also a budget resource issue as well as one requiring top management support, as previously discussed.

Project Management

Professional project management has been found to be among implementation success factors. More generally, it is important that the project manager and project consultants be perceived as having credibility. Credibility is associated with past implementation success, prestigious professional credentials, and/or affiliation with prestigious entities. The higher the project manager is placed in the organizational hierarchy, the more likely the success of the project. Perhaps the most essential skill needed by project managers is demonstrated skill in negotiation (Industry Advisory Council, 2002).

Other Success Factors

A wide variety of other factors have been found to be helpful to implementation success and are described here (Industry Advisory Council, 2002):

- Good communications—Having an effective internal communications system in place helps apprise all participants of the progress and benefits of IT systems being implemented (Garson, 1987; Hartman & Ashrafi, 2002; Industry Advisory Council, 2002). Good communications was the third most important critical success factor in the study by Schelin and Garson (2004), after top management support and stakeholder involvement.
- Measuring performance—Having good measures to prove performance and having an evaluation plan helps the project ward off criticism, promotes support, and helps secure resources (assuming performance is indeed good). Performance measures should be based on outcomes (effectiveness), not outputs (efficiency) (Industry Advisory Council, 2002).

- IT skill levels—High computer literacy and general skill levels within the agency promote acceptance of IT changes and reduce the learning curve.

- IT staff expertise and reputation—The perceived quality of the IT staff is a major determinant of attitudes toward IT implementation (Thomas, 1990). It helps if implementation is based on established, respected theories and models and if the IT project measures itself against the practices of the best in the field. The 2002 International City/County Management Association (ICMA) E-Government survey indicated that lack of technology/Web staff and expertise were two of the leading challenges to successful e-government implementation (Schelin & Garson, 2004, p. 8). Schelin and Garson (2004) found high staff qualifications to be the sixth most important success factor out of 14 studied.

- CIO position—A number of studies suggest that locating the CIO high in the organizational chart, reporting directly to top management, is a success factor (Dickson & DeSanctis, 2001; GAO, 2001b; Harvard Policy Group, 2001a). Presumably this is because such CIOs are better able to ensure top management support for the project. However, other research concludes CIO position is among the less important success factors (Schelin & Garson, 2004).

- Customer orientation—Integration of customer orientation into organizational norms, including collection and analysis of customer data, helps organizations identify IT needs as a basis for realistic systems planning. The Industry Advisory Council (IAC) (2002) cited securing customer-oriented project leadership as a key success factor, contrasting this with technology-minded leadership.

- Cyclical timing—Intermixing periods of pressure toward deadlines with periods of relief and stability is more conducive to long-term success than is continuous pressure for change (Harvard Policy Group, 2001a).

- Standardization—Some degree of standardization characterizes success projects (Industry Advisory Council, 2002). Two-thirds of the 50 runaway systems tackled by a leading consulting firm specializing in righting out-of-kilter computer projects had to do with botched attempts of systems integrators unable to make subsystems with different standards work together (Mehler, 1991, pp. 20–21).

- Formal data-sharing agreements—Data sharing is required by interagency and cross-jurisdictional projects, and the IAC's e-government shared interest group has noted that data sharing is facilitated when there are formal data agreements overseen by a supportive interunit committee (Miller, 2002b). Due to privacy and other types of legislation, having attorney support on the project team may be critical for cross-jurisdictional IT efforts.

When it comes to success factors for IT project implementation, it seems everything helps! However, some factors are more salient than others. Management support, goal clarity, and stakeholder motivation are almost always among the most important factors cited, along with training, discussed next.

THE ROLE OF TRAINING

The amount of attention and resources devoted to training has frequently been found to be among the top factors behind successful IT projects (Dickson & DeSanctis, 2001; Harvard Policy Group, 2001a; Northrop, 2002); yet training is perpetually seen by management as a "soft" factor not meriting the priority given to hardware and software and sometimes not budgeted at all.[4] From the system vendor's viewpoint, training is a cost factor to be minimized or even eliminated in the list of deliverables. Even from end users the demand for training may be low because it tends to be seen as a time-costly distraction from regular work, or a burdensome add-on to it. Why then does the General Accounting Office (GAO) recommend that an increasing percentage of the IT budget be devoted to training (GAO, 2001a, p. 51)?

Training should make staff feel and be competent in using new IT systems. As such, the trainees must perceive benefits to using the new system. That is, training is not just a matter of conveying technical information in an operating manual. Good training is enmeshed in the overall motivational design of the project, a design that must give each stakeholder benefits for participation. Training spells out these benefits and then shows participants how they can use the new system to gain these benefits.

Training requires time, almost always taken from existing tasks. For this reason, it is important that management make clear that this displacement of time is approved and that successful completion of training is valued by managers and by the organization. One way in which management value can be attached to training is when managers are trained in the new system, they train midlevel managers, who train the next level down, and so on in a ripple effect throughout the agency. In other situations, training can be tied to coaching and mentoring systems already in place to support career development within the organization. Value also can be conveyed through performance evaluations, issuance of certificates signed by top management, and by publicity in internal agency newsletters. At the very least, training should not be implemented as a burden on individual employees (not requiring training time to be made up later, not requiring long travel to off-site training locations, not causing employees to pay for training expenses out of pocket).

Training is for managers too. Public managers must act as project advocates before city councils, with the governor's office, or for the OMB at the federal level. Unfamiliarity with the systems they are supposed to advocate for undermines the leadership contribution of managers. Not having benefited themselves from training, top managers may not see the importance of holding middle management accountable for providing appropriate training for their staff. More broadly, long-term lack of training of managers reduces their ability to envision the kinds of contributions IT might make, and this in turn may mean that strategic planning in the agency does not adequately consider how IT can leverage process changes to do old things in new, more efficient and effective ways.

Timing is important in training. If training is too early, employees may not remember enough to feel successful when it is time to actually use the system. If too late, rushed training can equally easily be ineffective, creating needless frustration along with personal and organizational failure. A phased implementation of training is sometimes best, training the in-agency trainers earlier, then having them train end users. This tiered approach creates desirable redundancy in training resources, making training not dependent upon a single individual. Timing becomes less critical when it is conceived as an ongoing endeavor, not a one-time experience. This is the better way for training to be budgeted in any event, because training is continually needed for newly hired individuals and employees shifting positions, and simply because refresher courses help the individual and the experienced individual is in a better position to give feedback to trainers.

Developing supportive information culture is often a goal of training programs. This is recognized, for instance, in the U.S. General Services Administration's (GSA's) Trail Boss program, to enhance the professional level core competencies in IT services. This program resulted in over a thousand graduates. The purpose of training is to inculcate a sense of cooperation and common vision, something more effective than specifying policies in detailed regulations. The GSA found that the success of the Trail Boss program is directly dependent on the agency's organizational culture. By the same token, successful Trail Boss programs have contributed substantially to fostering supportive information cultures in participating agencies.

In summary, reliance on end-user mutual support alone is a recipe for failure (Swider, 1988) and lack of investment in training and support personnel is an important cause of failure in IT implementation (Richter, 1993).

EXTERNAL SUCCESS FACTORS

The agency's environment can be a major determinant of project success. For instance, success is more likely if the organization and its resources are growing, which, for public sector organizations, has primarily to do with external factors in the agency's political environment. Also, there is more likely to be follow-through and success in IT implementation if there are competitive pressures to adopt technology to keep up with rival agency, supplier group, or client group use of IT. Simply being in a dynamic environment promotes IT innovation. If the environment is changing in terms of suppliers, clients, and or governmental regulations, these uncertainties create a receptivity to change (Matheson, 1993). Conversely, if the organization is successful in a stable uncompetitive environment, then the "if it ain't broke, don't fix it" mentality tends to undermine change efforts, including IT implementation.

Partnerships with Vendors and Other Strategic Partners

Even large agencies often lack the IT resources available to large software firms who conduct massive research and development efforts, nor with large consulting firms who may well have much greater experience implementing public networks, e-government portals, data transaction systems, and the like. Partnering can tap into knowledge resources that would be very difficult to develop in-house. Short of formal partnering, some of the same benefits can be gained by holding vendor conferences prior to specifying systems to be bid upon. Vendor input at such conferences can help agencies frame specifications that are up to date in technology and that take advantage of past outside experience. Agencies may also wish to engage strategic partners throughout the planning and implementation process through formation of representative advisory groups (CTG, 2000a). Partnering is cited as a governmental IT success factor by industry groups (Industry Advisory Council, 2002). The OMB urges agencies at the very least to become aware of and benefit from best practices in private industry (McVay, 2004) and, indeed, this is required of federal agencies by the Clinger-Cohen Act of 1996.

Independence from Vendors

Project implementation is more likely to be successful if the agency is not dependent upon the vendor. If outsourcing to vendors shrinks the agency's IT staff to the point where contracts cannot be independently evaluated due to lack of in-house expertise, the likelihood of project failure is increased. The GAO recommends agencies always keep core IT competencies in-house (GAO, 2001, p. 46). Whereas in the private sector, businesses may seek close strategic alliances to cover an entire "value chain" in a marketing area, public-sector agencies rarely seek integration with suppliers or distributors, nor are they likely to be concerned with branding, product pricing, or cross-marketing of products with allies. Rather, public agencies are much more likely to be concerned with being captives of suppliers.

Public administration literature has frequently focused on the desirability of policy decision making taking place within issue networks characterized by many competing interests, as opposed to "iron triangles" with incestuous relationships among agencies, legislative committees, and vendors or other forms of excessive special interest group influence (Industry Advisory Council, 2002). An extreme case example was provided by the excessive reliance on the Oracle Corporation by IT officials representing the state of California, leading to a 2002 contractual scandal that caused the state legislature to terminate the Department of Information Technology, leaving California temporarily as the largest state in the nation without a central IT agency (Peterson, 2002b).

Accountability to the Political Layer

Unlike the private sector, the public sector must be concerned with accountability to city councils, state legislatures, and Congress, as well as to mayors, governors, and the president, depending on agency level. Such accountability is a success factor. Projects are more likely to be successful if their long-term funding is secure, and this may well depend upon their ability to justify their business plans and IT investment strategies and performance. Agencies do not "like" accountability and may resist reporting performance measures to funding bodies. Nonetheless, in the long run tracking and reporting IT performance not only to agency management but also to political funders is a sound strategy that is more conducive to success than is neglecting performance data and not being able to demonstrate results. In this sense, effective project evaluation is a parallel success factor.

SUMMARY

Since the appearance of the modern computer, managers, politicians, and the public have become accustomed to believe that investment in IT is the automatic path to success and progress. It is now a fundamental notion in management literature that nations and organizations that know how to take advantage of IT will gain a competitive edge over others. Writers such a Peter Drucker, F. Warren McFarlan, Lynda Applegate, James Cash, Michael Porter, and others pioneered this view of IT, writing extensively in the *Harvard Business Review* and other influential publications. It is clear that computers can crunch a lot of numbers, process a lot of words, and print endless forms, but these efficiencies may not translate into genuine organizational effectiveness in fulfilling the goals, values, and mission of the agency.

Original enthusiasm has given way in academia to empirical assessment. It became no longer assumed that IT investments equaled automatic success. In early research, Noonan (1991, p. 25) found that for white-collar work, introduction of new office technology was associated with 20% longer workweeks and an actual decline in white-collar productivity. One reason for lowered productivity was suggested by Schellhardt (1990), whose research showed that middle managers spent an increasing proportion of their time on activities formerly performed by secretaries and support personnel (typing, document composing, mailing). In fact, Schellhardt found that after the introduction of IT, middle managers spent only 27% of their time on actual management tasks.

IT investment then and now had been justified on optimistic cost-cutting grounds. After implementation, there can be considerable pressure to cut costs through staff reductions—even when productivity gains do not warrant this. Such face-saving cuts can hurt organizational effectiveness and productivity, as illustrated by the case of the Customs Service. Customs used investment in its automation projects (e.g., identification of high-risk illicit cargos) to justify significant staff reductions even though many, including the GAO, found the automated systems were largely useless and even though investment in staff more than paid for itself in recovered revenues (Grimm, 1988, p. 12).

Whereas productivity effects were often debatable, there was rarely any arguing with the fact that computerization tended to lead to rising demands for computer services and to a rising total volume of work. Computers created new employee and client demands for hardware, software, training, maintenance, telecommunications, and other forms of support. The talk in the early 1980s of the coming "paperless society" gave way to the empirical realization in the 1990s that actual consumption of paper had grown faster than gross domestic product in the new computer era. Because computerization makes mass mailing easy, for instance, more organizations did more mass mailings more frequently. Because it was easy and convenient, managers found themselves reading exponentially more e-mail than old-style postal mail. In Frantzich's study of Congress, for instance, computerized mail meant per-letter efficiency, but overall greater costs were incurred as Congressional representatives mailed many more letters (Frantzich, 1987). Because computerization made reporting easier, more organizations had more reports more often for more managers. And on the client side, more forms could be filled out more easily and more information could be accessed more frequently, increasing the convenience of citizens but not necessarily lowering costs as most agencies found most brick-and-mortar services had to be maintained in parallel with new electronic forms.

Several factors limit the success of IT in the public sector. Limiting factors include goal-setting problems, subjectivity problems, complexity problems, cost problems, motivation problems, human resource problems, and human error factor problems.

Goal-Setting Limits

IT can only yield productivity in relation to organizational goals, yet goal-setting is intrinsically political—a dimension computers cannot resolve. An IT system designed to promote the maximization of one goal may do so at the expense of another. In particular, many IT systems track quantitative performance indicators, creating incentives to work to increase what is measured and neglect what is not measured. In the context of a government agency, there may be political differences about such goals as maximizing service, minimizing costs, achieving service equity, maximizing client satisfaction, maximizing public satisfaction, maximizing the satisfaction of legislators, and so on. Thus an IT system may improve the goal of job satisfaction but not the goal of economic productivity, or may increase the quantity of communications with clients but not increase the number of clients served (Frederickson & Riley, 1985). The IT literature agrees that implementation success depends upon managers agreeing on goals, including the indicators to be tracked and maximized. The reality is that managers themselves may disagree, be unable to resolve goal conflicts, may shift goal priorities frequently, or may draw back from even attempting to settle goal-setting issues. All these tendencies constitute a limit of the effectiveness of IT solutions.

Subjectivity Limits

A second limit to computing has to do with managerial subjectivity. Individual styles of decision making lead different administrators to follow different courses, yet they may arrive at equally effective results. In particular, managers who rely on intuition, hunches, and practice wisdom may find IT decision-support systems, relying on more quantitative inputs, arrive at solutions inconsistent with those arrived at by subjective factors. IT-based solutions may prevail in spite of the fact that managers may have been selected for top positions of authority precisely because it was believed that their subjective judgment would guide the agency to success. Moreover, if such a manager tries to adopt an IT-based decision-making pattern that is not appropriate for him or her, poor results may follow. Managers often find computer tools do not fit their management style. Although there has been some attempt in the area of expert systems and decision support software to take account of cognitive and personality differences of managers in decision making, the subjective element in productivity is a significant obstacle in many computer applications in management, most of which assume all managers can appropriately use identical software.

Complexity Limits

The complex contingencies of decision making are a third obstacle to achieving productivity through IT. IT can support decisions only to the extent that decisions can be modeled. The more the salience of unpredictable factors, the less computers can outperform human judgment. Since management decision making depends frequently on political and subjective factors, this is no small limitation. Although some believe that expert systems and artificial intelligence will overcome these limitations, current evidence is that such software is most useful for routine expertise on well-understood problems. Contrary to public belief that the sentient robots of Hollywood are near at hand or perhaps already exist in military laboratories, progress toward "thinking machines" capable of wrestling with subjective complexity is slow and may be impossible.

Cost Limits

Fourth, there are obvious financial limits to IT. To be truly productive, computing must not only provide savings that pay for new technology but also for training, technical support, employee time, and a host of human factors. An agency may suddenly find it needs additional positions in technical support, hardware maintenance, training, networking, data management, and more. In social work, for instance, "most agencies have restricted budgets that are controlled by outside funding agencies, [so] the massive expenditures required to computerize social work practice as well as questions about the effectiveness of such a move deter agency administrators from supporting such an innovative initiative (Cnaan, 1989, p. 6). Even at the federal level, the hundreds of millions in e-government funding envisioned at the start of the Bush administration in 2000 almost immediately dwindled to a tiny fraction of the original promise, and much of that had to be squeezed from existing departmental budgets, making other priorities suffer.

Motivation Limits

Limitations pertaining to human motivation constitute a fifth obstacle to IT productivity. For instance, when computers were introduced for word processing, there was an opportunity to replace the inefficient typewriter-like QWERTY keyboard with a more efficient one. This would have significantly increased the efficiency of almost all computer operations everywhere, but "no one was willing to face the resistance of tens of millions of secretaries, typists, and others who had learned to type on a QWERTY keyboard" (Westrum, 1991, p. 206). In general, information is a public good and suffers the problems of other public goods—what is in the good of all may not be in any particular person's interest. Managerial motivation is also a frequent limit. Managers receive status and even compensation from the size of their budgets and number of personnel they supervise, giving them strong incentives not to turn productivity gains into reduced budgets or reduced labor requirements. Finally, the control uses of computing can also undermine employee motivation. "When computer technology is used as an electronic whip to make people work faster, to intrude on their personal privacy, to judge them on subjective criteria, and to single out and punish substandard performance, good organizational results are hard to imagine" (Piturro, 1990, p. 31). Such control systems may represent an organizational reversion to top-down, authoritarian ("Theory X") types of leadership rejected decades ago as less effective than bottom-up, participative ("Theory Y") leadership.

Human Resource Limits

Human resource limitations of various types are a sixth obstacle to IT success. End users frequently lack training for computer use or lack a sense of efficacy, which leads to computer avoidance. IT technicians are often narrowly trained and therefore ignorant of the substantive functions of the organization (e.g., strategic planning) to be able to mobilize IT systems effectively. Managers, often themselves ill trained in the possibilities and challenges of IT, may be reluctant to invest the large sums required for retraining or restaffing but instead often seek to cut corners by imposing IS on unready users.

Human Error Limits

Even when no other obstacle exists, people are prone to make mistakes. Vendors routinely encourage organizations to overinvest in IT. Decisions based on computer simulation are not infrequently flawed because the state of the art of knowledge is insufficient. In the crash of Northwest Flight 255 that killed 156 people, it was later found that a crucial warning indicator worked correctly in the simulator but not in the actual aircraft. The collapse of the Salt Lake City Shopping Mall was due to failure of the computer model to take into account extreme conditions. The selection of an inappropriate computer model also led to incorrect beam connections that led to the collapse of the Hartford Civic Center Coliseum. The more turbulent the agency environment, the greater the likelihood of error in providing inputs to an IT system. The more the fiscal duress of the agency, the lower the investment in training, quality control, and factors that would reduce error. The more diffuse the objectives of the agency, the greater the likelihood of inappropriate and erroneous application of IT solutions to complex problems. In the end, IS are only as good as the data and the algorithms humans supply for the solution of problems, and humans err.

How do the four general theoretical approaches to public IS bear on the topic of failure and success factors in IT project implementation? Of course, by and large those who research these factors tend to be empiricists, much more concerned with uncovering pragmatic advice for the practitioner than contributing to theory. Of the four approaches, the sociotechnical school has been by far the most active in success factor research, documenting their central theme: IT failure comes when human factors such as management support, stakeholder motivation, and especially participation in planning and execution are neglected. This is the core of their central argument against the technological determinists. In this arena, it is difficult to argue that technology is paramount. If anything, the success factors literature finds that not only is technology subordinate to human factors, but it is dangerous to place technology-oriented people in charge of implementation projects, which often require enterprise-wide generalist knowledge and people-oriented negotiation skills. Reinforcement theory, in contrast, finds support in general agreement on the fact that implementation success hinges most heavily on top management support, but as most success factors do not focus on power issues, this perspective is largely off to the side in the success factors literature. Likewise, systems theory does not particularly direct our attention to the success factors enumerated in this chapter. While its overall concept of evolution toward more comprehensive and integrated systems with better feedback finds expression in some success factors research, such as the need for good communications channels, systems theory is also more off to the side as well, though not rebutted as is the case with technological determinism.

DISCUSSION QUESTIONS

1. What is/should be the definition of *success* in terms of IT project implementation?
2. There are eight common reasons why IT projects fail. Select two of these reasons and explain how the situation could be addressed.
3. Choose two main internal success factors and explain how their presence or absence might affect project implementation.
4. Why is training often a low priority for both vendors and management? How should training be approached (for whom, timing, etc.)?
5. What are external success factors? Can an IT project be successfully implemented solely on the basis of internal support factors?

DISCUSSION QUESTIONS continued

6. What should be the role of top management with regard to the implementation of IT projects?
7. What are the general findings of the sociotechnical school for IT implementation?
8. Have you ever observed the implementation of an IT project within your organization? Was it successful? Name the strengths/weaknesses that affected its outcome. What were the most important factors?

GLOSSARY

External success factors: External implementation success factors are those in the environment of the organization that contribute to the level of IT project implementation success but that are generally not controlled by the organization (e.g., politics that impacts funding). External success factors include independence from vendors, accountability to the political layer, and partnerships with strategic partners.

Internal success factors: Internal implementation success factors are those within the organization itself and thus largely controlled by the organization. Some internal success factors include management support, stakeholder motivation, and good communication systems.

Legacy systems: Legacy systems refer to old and outdated computing software in which the organization may have a large investment but that may be incompatible with current enterprise architecture or may simply be difficult to maintain.

Paperless society: At the advent of the "computing age," one of the benefits of incorporating computers into the workplace was thought to be the conversion of paper transactions and records to digital format, thereby eliminating paper. In reality, the computer era has also led to increased paper consumption, not its elimination.

QWERTY: These letters refer to the traditional layout of keys (letters) on a keyboard. Q, W, E, R, T, and Y are the first six keys on the first row of a keyboard. QWERTY keyboards are less efficient than some other layouts but are still prevalent because so many people learned keyboarding on them and prefer to use them rather than have to relearn keyboarding skills.

Theory X: Theory X is a theory of human motivation that views workers as inherently lazy and thus requiring strict oversight and control by managers to accomplish goals. This theory was critiqued in Douglas McGregor's *The Human Side of Enterprise* (1960).

Theory Y: Theory Y is a theory of human motivation that assumes workers are ambitious and eager to take on responsibilities, and as such require minimal oversight by managers to reach goals. This theory was advocated in Douglas McGregor's *The Human Side of Enterprise* (1960).

ENDNOTES

[1]The NMCI has subsequently adopted a new policy requiring command officials to account for each software application it owns and to provide the names of commands that use each one.

[2]Schelin and Garson (2004) found prototyping to be the 13th most important success factor of 14 studied, reflecting CIO rankings.

[3]A survey of the top 500 information systems companies found "What began in the transistor age as a 'techie' career is now frequently the domain of executives whose understanding of economics and business plans exceeds their knowledge of MIPS and throughput. Companies are looking for renaissance men (and women) then, and not technical wizards for IT jobs" (*InformationWeek*, September 19, 1989, 113, 120).

[4]Schelin and Garson (2004) found training to be rated by CIOs as only the 7th most important implementation success factor of 14 studied, though this may merely reflect the fact the tendency to underrate the true importance of training.

CASE STUDY
Success Factors of the Homeless Information Management System (HIMS)

by Jennifer Powers

SUNY-Albany

The Homeless Information Management System (HIMS) was a shared database created to improve services to the 37,000 homeless in New York City and surrounding areas. Quite often clients receive a variety of services from different homeless service providers, but providers have traditionally been reluctant to share data unless required to do so. And yet, the New York State Bureau of Shelter Services (BSS, now called the Bureau of Homeless Services) saw sharing information among providers as a way of streamlining services and reducing recidivism. HIMS was then prototyped through a collaborative effort of state, county, city, and private providers in New York City and the surrounding areas. This study identifies the success factors and challenges involved in creating a network of organizations to plan a shared database. For instance, the participating organizations were drawn in by the two-way flow of communication between the state and the participants, as opposed to traditional relationships that were defined by one-way mandates. Trust then began to develop between and among the members because of their open communication and fairly regular meetings and interactions. Many of the participants also realized that it would serve them better if they got involved in the planning rather than waiting for the state to mandate its use. Ultimately, the state had power and everyone was aware of it, even if it was not used explicitly. This case study focuses on communication, development of trust, and recognition of power as factors for successfully cultivating the network of organizations involved in developing HIMS.

The following case study was developed through interviews with members of the network of organizations developing HIMS. All participation was voluntary. A complete account of the research is documented in "Homeless Information Management System: A Case Study of Information Sharing Among Government Agencies and Private Homeless Service Providers in New York State."

Background

Traditionally, both private and public homeless service providers are responsible for administering services, managing their own budgets and technology, and reporting on the services rendered to their funding bodies, such as the state BSS. BSS mandates what data need to be reported and when. As BSS collects those data, they can do very little with it to determine recidivism and effectiveness of particular services because of the overwhelming amount and variety of data. Sometimes those data are so dissimilar, it is like comparing apples to oranges. Furthermore, they do not share the data with the providers themselves. The flow of information is one-way: up to the funding source.

At one point, the New York City Department of Homeless Services, another funding agency, mandated that every NYC homeless service provider that reported to them report their data using a consistent case management information system called ANCHoR. The homeless service providers were uncomfortable with the system for a variety of reasons, the foremost being that case managers traditionally kept their case notes confidential. Yet ANCHoR required these case notes to be entered into the system. Additionally, the mandated information system forced the service providers to provide the data in different ways than they originally collected it. Finally, the service providers felt that it was one more mandate that reinforced the one-way information flow. Eventually, the opposition to ANCHoR grew so strong that the project was scrapped.

A New Approach

BSS realized that there is real value in the sharing of information. If they could collect data in such a way that made comparisons and aggregate analysis possible, they could also turn around and share the data with the providers themselves. Together, BSS and the providers could begin to streamline services and be more effective and efficient with their limited budgets and services. HIMS, while not developed beyond prototype into an actual product, was created as a part of the Using Information in Government Project at the Center for Technology and Government in Albany, New York.

While the intent was to address the one-way flow of information problem, BSS also recognized that the homeless providers needed reassurance that this was not another attempt at an ANCHoR-like project. For this reason, participation was not mandatory. This could not be one more thing that a funding agency mandated service providers do, especially with little or no explanation. Furthermore, HIMS did not require data that the service providers themselves were not comfortable sharing. Confidential data would stay confidential and would not be shared with other service providers. These initial efforts to make the providers feel comfortable with the process set the HIMS participants on a course for open communication and budding trust.

The following sections examine in more detail communication and trust as success factors, as well as one of the challenges—power—that led to a successful collaboration in developing the HIMS prototype.

continues

Communication

As previously mentioned, the homeless providers were understandably wary of the idea of HIMS, which followed closely on the heels of the ANCHoR debacle. Unlike the mandate of ANCHoR, however, participation in the development of HIMS was voluntary, yet encouraged through the director of BSS actively recruiting potential members through personal contacts and phone calls. As providers began to express "What's in it for me?" concerns, BSS made it a priority to promote the benefits to the providers, such as improving and streamlining their own services as well as developing a larger understanding of the problem of homelessness in NYC overall. The organizations that did participate later explained their participation as due to the repeated reassurances by BSS that their input would be greatly valued. To encourage input from all providers, communication was developed through regular meetings in person and online. Much of the input mentioned most by those involved in developing HIMS was the type and format of data to be input. Some explained that they participated so that HIMS would be in line with the information system they already used; others explained that it was such a unique opportunity to be in on the ground level of a government project, they could not turn it down.

In addition to regular meetings, one of the first things the service providers asked for—and BSS provided—was reassurance that their confidential data would stay confidential. BSS gave the providers strong assurance that confidential data would remain confidential and that HIMS would not require anything that was not part of the current inspection process in the form of a signed letter by the commissioner. This is another indication of the communication—both about what the providers needed and what BSS was willing to provide—that contributed to the success of HIMS.

Trust

Because of BSS's willingness to work with the homeless service providers, both in the development of HIMS and in allaying the providers' concerns, a level of trust developed. The HIMS project was created so that it would be a mutually beneficial process and the participants interviewed realized that. Likewise, the process itself was rewarding for the members. One interviewee explained that it was an "ambitious vision, and [we] broke it down and got from point A to point B." Cooperation and the feeling that it was a win-win situation can be attributed to this process.

Participants began to feel that this was really something special and they could actually get a great deal out of sharing information through HIMS. A shared context—all the providers are trying to help individuals and families succeed on their own—led to a feeling of "it's a small universe," which also led to a sense of trust among the service providers themselves. That is, while they were still competing for the same grants and so on, they also realized that a greater good could be served by working together on HIMS. One interviewee explained that even though the New York City providers were competitors with each other for funding, they "put that aside because they are there [part of HIMS] for a higher reason." He stressed that "collaboration in the city is key" to serving their clients.

Power

Of course, the fact that BSS was still the funding agency for these providers was on the minds of the providers. While no interviewee indicated that there was an explicit risk or penalty to be suffered if they did not participate, there was a feeling among some of the providers that they must participate: "being out of the loop is a big thing."

Some providers acknowledged that BSS is a regulatory agency, and even if they did not intend to use HIMS participation as a barometer of sorts, "All providers have an interest in meeting the state's needs." While they may not always do what the state asks, they do usually give the state what they want. Furthermore, once the state determines what data it wants, "it will become the industry standard." This interviewee clarified that "These are not the rules, it's unsaid, not official, intangible, not legal, but . . . it's the way it is. This is just the way organizations work." While BSS worked very hard to develop a culture of communication and trust, the recognition that power was still an issue helped providers keep perspective on the project. Just as communication and trust were essential to the success of the collaborative effort, so too was the recognition that power was an issue.

Conclusions

This case study found that consistent communication, the development of trust, and a recognition of power were critical success factors in the development of a shared information system by a network of organizations. The homeless service provider culture had traditionally been defined by one-way information flow, overt power, mandates, and working in isolation. HIMS, however, offered an opportunity to develop relationships and work together on a common goal—serving the homeless effectively and efficiently. Although HIMS as a product was not developed due to financial constraints, lessons can be learned regarding the development of a network of organizations to share information and the key factors involved.

Reference

Powers, J. G. (2001). Homeless information management system: A case study of information sharing among government agencies and private homeless service providers in New York State. Unpublished doctoral dissertation.

Evaluation of Public Information Systems

For top management, evaluation is integral to making smart information technology (IT) choices. Portfolio management (discussed in Chapter 11) requires evaluation in order to select among IT alternatives and manage the agency's investment portfolio. To operating managers, evaluation is central to making the case for particular IT projects and for justifying budgets. Evaluation provides the ammunition the chief information officer (CIO) needs when he or she goes to decision makers seeking money. Under conditions of budgetary austerity—all too common in the public sector—the demand for evaluation rises in importance. Thus a headline in *Government Computer News* reads, "OMB to agencies: Justify that budget" (Miller, 2003w), quoting Office of Management and Budget (OMB) director Mitchell Daniels saying that "much of the $60 billion" in the FY 2004 federal IT budget was misspent. The article noted, "OMB found while preparing the budget request that the greatest problem for agencies is identifying how systems perform when compared against cost, schedule, and mission improvement goals" (p. 12). With cost overruns ranging from 10% to 225%, the OMB was demanding agencies adopt an earned-value management system based on private-sector practices. But are private-sector IT evaluation methods the best answer for public managers?

Evaluation is a key element in preparation of the business case for an IT project, discussed in Chapters 9 and 11. Business plans include discussion of costs and benefits, performance measures, progress milestones, assessment of risk, cost estimates for alternatives, and general justification for the advocated alternative. Approaches to evaluation range from the qualitative and general (e.g., "hopes and fears exercises," which guide stakeholders from problem identification to consensus on priorities) to the quantitative and specific (e.g., cost-benefit studies of prototypes). Evaluation activities may include comparisons of the agency with best practices, development of performance measures and benchmarks, and cost-performance analysis (Dawes et al., 2003).

IT projects cannot be evaluated if objectives cannot be articulated clearly. "Improving public safety" is too general for evaluation purposes, but "reduction in auto thefts per 1000 registered vehicles" can be assessed. The challenge in constructing evaluation systems is to identify a set of performance objectives that are not only specific and measurable, but also representative of the desired outcomes. Representativeness is crucial because people tend to work to standard, raising the strong possibility of performance distortion. That is, if in an employment office IT system, for example, performance is measured by job placements, employment counselors may seek to maximize what is measured (job placements) by minimizing or even abandoning what is not measured (e.g., job counseling, appropriateness/permanency of placement). Only if the evaluation system has measures for the full range of desired outcomes will job distortion be held to acceptable levels. This is more easily said than done, often requiring modification of evaluation systems over a period of years.

STRATEGIES FOR EVALUATING PUBLIC INFORMATION TECHNOLOGY

Given the many issues that arise in measuring the diffuse costs and benefits of public IT initiatives, it is hardly surprising that in the public sector there has been less support than in the private sector for undertaking this task at all. Forrer and Anderson (2001) used survey data from both sectors to show that whereas almost 90% of private managers said return on investment (ROI) projections had a moderate or high impact on IT-related organizational decisions, 40% of public managers perceived little or no impact. Some 61% of private managers felt that measuring ROI was a good way to analyze IT investments. The corresponding figure for public managers was a mere 10%, presumably in no small part because ROI methodology is associated with traditional financial models that normally ignore intangible, subjective, potential, and controlled costs and benefits, all of which are important in the public sector.

Public IT's ability to use quantitative evaluation techniques not only suffers from lack of a public-sector counterpart to "bottom line" profits in the private sector, but also because public IT projects tend to generate indirect second- or third-level benefits. In the private sector, launching an online catalog can directly lead to higher revenue—a first-level benefit. But a government health agency launching an online Web page about health needs of infants will lead to a benefit (lower county hospital costs due to better parenting of infants) only if the parent/citizen chooses to act on the advice. A school Web page may even be a third-level benefit, helping influence the parent to influence the student.

In general, public-sector IT initiatives are more likely than private to focus on service and information sharing rather than on a product. Some information services, such as National Oceanic and Atmospheric Administration (NOAA) weather alerts to airlines, enjoy an active base of direct users who translate information into benefit. Other agencies have a relatively inactive user base (e.g., public health information services regarding smoking) or users who do not generate dollar revenues or savings (Federal Election Commission [FEC] reports on campaign funding). Agency officials in the public health service or the FEC would feel their IT initiatives are as valuable as those of NOAA, but would state that the nature of their end user base differs due to second-level considerations inherent in the subject matter with which they deal.

Both in the methodology for measuring benefits and in the methodology for measuring costs, a wide variety of questions arise. The problem of indirect benefits has its counterpart in the problem of intangible costs (e.g., harm to agency reputation).

Questions Regarding Measurement of Benefits

- Often there are different evaluative criteria for benefits (degree of consistency with the organization's mission, improvement in satisfaction with service, increased revenues, increased usage, and so on). What are the criteria to be? Are they to be weighted, such that some criteria are counted as more beneficial than others?
- Should intangible benefits be "guess-timated" into dollar terms? Traditional financial models do not look at intangible benefits, but if they do, they convert to dollar terms.
- Should dollar benefits be expressed in terms of net present value (NPV), such that the further in the future a benefit of a given size, the less dollar value it has today? Traditional financial models use NPV.
- How far into the future should the benefit stream be measured? Traditional financial models typically examine a short period such as 2–5 years.
- Should "potential value" be included in benefits? Potential values are benefits that are contingent on future factors. If potential values are included, should they be discounted by multiplying by the probability of occurrence of the contingent factors? Traditional financial models do not look at potential values.
- Should benefits be discounted by control factors representing other parallel causes of the benefit? If a benefit has multiple causes besides the IT initiative being evaluated, ideally a statistical path diagram linking causes to benefit effects could be constructed and the effect partitioned among paths leading from various causes. The path weight for the IT initiative as a cause could be used to discount the benefit

(to establish the share of the benefit attributable to the IT initiative). In reality, causal models may be unknown and even where known, variables in the model may be intangible, unmeasured, or measured with error. Should discounting benefits for control factors be "guesstimated" when ideal statistical control is impossible to attain? Traditional financial models do not look at control factors.

- Are benefits that are solely internal to the agency, such as employee satisfaction, "real" benefits that should be counted in ROI? Traditional financial models do not look at internal benefits.
- In view of the problem with objective measures of benefits, should subjective measures be used as, for example, whether managers, clients, experts, or some other group *thinks* the IT intervention has been beneficial, perhaps on a subjective scale from 1 to 10? Traditional financial models do not look at subjective measures.

Questions Regarding Measurement of Costs

- Will measurement be in terms of total cost or marginal cost? For instance, an IT project might take no additional equipment and require no hiring of additional personnel, having a zero marginal cost, yet if machine cycles and personnel hours were costed proportionately, there might be considerable cost.
- Will costs be discounted over time, as with applying NPV to benefits?
- How much of agency infrastructure is to be allocated as cost to the IT project, and by what formula?
- Are life-cycle maintenance costs included?
- Are training costs included? Costs of upgrading personnel lines?
- Is depreciation of facilities, equipment, or even software included?

Life-cycle costing is an important aspect of cost evaluation. Ownership costs, operations and maintenance costs, and disposition costs can consume as much as 80% of a project's total life-cycle costs (OMB, 1997, p. 79). Ownership and maintenance costs include such items as hardware upgrades, software upgrades, software modifications, and ongoing user training.

THE PRIVATE SECTOR MODEL: RETURN ON INVESTMENT

From a managerial perspective, IT investment tends to shift from an initial "honeymoon period" to a later period of "competitive realism." In the early period, IT investments are not expected to make an immediate profit, perhaps not even for years. Rather, the purpose of investment is to build the digital infrastructure of the enterprise, to gear up both human and technological capital, and to bring the firm to the cutting edge where, it is hoped, it can exert advantage over its competitors. Later, however, there is a tendency for top management to ask IT to justify its investments on the same empirical basis as other organizational investment projects. IT funding requests become institutionalized and subjected to scrutiny of routine budget analysis. For their part, IT managers come to feel that their budgetary survival depends upon their ability to demonstrate ROI.

ROI traditionally focuses on tangible benefits:

- Increased revenue
- Lower operational costs (e.g., staff time savings)
- Higher worker productivity
- Faster time to delivery
- Earlier problem detection
- Reduced postage or phone cost
- Reduced printing and paper cost
- Reduced travel costs
- Reduced consulting costs
- Reduced manually handled information queries
- Reduction in redundant records
- Increased volume or traffic
- Faster, more reliable inventory
- Increase in grant support

In the private-sector model, one begins by identifying market forces that may be opportunities for the firm, then proceeds to devise strategies to take advantage of these opportunities, managing IT investments and justifying them through quantitative performance indicators. Measures might involve such indicators as minutes per order fulfillment, order capacity per day per staff person, or orders fulfilled accurately the first time.

ROI would involve calculations such as Stoiber (1999) mentions: "If the department currently processes 2000 orders per day, the same department could process 2600 orders using the new software. Assuming each order specialist earns roughly $40,000 annually . . . that translates into an annual cost savings of $240,000" for a staff of 20, not counting the savings of recruitment and training costs not incurred by not having to hire six additional staff to reach the higher capacity level. Using the NPV function of any spreadsheet, figuring an initial investment cost of $500,000, a cost of money discount rate of 5%, and a 3-year life for the software, the ROI expressed as NPV would be $146,266. The software could cost as much as $653,590, and the IT project would still break even in NPV.

Private-sector managers not infrequently choose not to measure intangible benefits when undertaking ROI analysis. Not only are intangible benefits difficult to measure, but even among tangible benefits there are problems because some, such as faster time to delivery or increased traffic, do not necessarily directly affect revenue or costs. However, while it is plausible in many private-sector settings to make decisions largely on the basis of direct tangible benefits such as the value of increased orders in the example above, doing so in the public sector can lead to poor choices. The Harvard Policy Group (2001b, p. 2) noted, "When budget analysis focuses almost exclusively on whether front-end costs can be covered by downstream savings, governments may underinvest in nonfinancial benefits."

Intangible benefits can be as important as tangible ones, especially in the public sector:

- Client and citizen awareness
- Client and citizen satisfaction
- Policy consistency
- Upholding democratic accountability and transparency
- Staff morale
- Improving citizen choices regarding public health, the environment, and so on
- Improved information sharing in the federal system
- More nonhierarchical communication
- Higher organizational reputation
- More effective targeting of services
- Enhancing organizational capacity for the future

Some intangible benefits can be measured, as with surveys of citizen satisfaction. But then how are survey satisfaction points to be compared to dollar costs to get ROI? Moreover, the state of the art of social science is not adequate to model many intangible benefits. For instance, so many factors affect health choices of citizens besides public health agency educational projects that it is controversial at best to attribute such choices to specific agency investments.

EVOLUTION OF A PUBLIC-SECTOR MODEL FOR IT EVALUATION

In public administration, efforts to improve evaluation go back half a century. The Kennedy administration, for instance, introduced management techniques pioneered in the automobile industry. Under Secretary of Defense Robert McNamara, program planning and budgeting systems (PPBS) were mandated in the Department of Defense and later spread to other departments. Later, under the Reagan administration and in response to budgetary austerity, interest in performance measurement in government again became a major managerial concern.

Over the years, a very wide variety of performance measures for IT have been practiced or advocated, many of them enumerated in a literature review by Specht (2000). Performance measures have included IT fit to strategy, ratio of IT expenses to total operating expenses, economic benefits, system usage, user satisfaction, value of information generated, sustained competitive advantage, revenue attributable to the IT Department, timeliness, impact on organizational reputation, user acceptance, increase in managerial control, penetration of the technology with the organization, and many more. Many of these measures pertained to efficiency rather than effectiveness. Over time, the focus of IT evaluation efforts in the public sector has shifted more and more toward measures of effectiveness in mission fulfillment.

Performance measures were mandated for federal agencies by a variety of pieces of legislation in the 1990s:

- The Chief Financial Officers (CFO) Act of 1990 required improved financial reporting practices in government agencies:
  (a) 31 USC 902(a)(3): Agency chief financial officers (CFOs) must develop and maintain integrated agency accounting and financial management systems for reliable, consistent, and timely information, including cost information and including systematic measurement of performance.
- The Government Performance and Results Act (GPRA) of 1993 required agencies to adopt a strategic planning process based on measurable program performance indicators related to the agency's goals, objectives, and mission; agencies were specifically required to identify gaps between actual and desired performance levels:
  (a) 31 USC 1115: Agency head must prepare annual performance plans for each budgeted program category. Plans must include performance goals in objective, quantifiable, and measurable form. There must be performance indicators to measure outputs, service levels, and outcomes for each program activity.
  (b) 31 USC 1116: Agency heads must submit annual program performance reports to the president and to Congress, comparing actual program performance against performance goals.
- The Federal Acquisition Streamlining Act of 1995 required agencies to define cost and performance goals for all federal acquisitions, including for IT projects, and to monitor programs accordingly
  (a) Title V: Agencies must define cost, schedule, and performance goals for all federal IT and other acquisition programs. Programs must be monitored to ensure they remain within prescribed tolerances.
- The Paperwork Reduction Act Amendments of 1995 called on agencies to utilize information resources to improve agency efficiency:
  (a) 44 USC 3506(a)(4): Agency heads, in consultation with agency CIOs and CFOs, must define program information needs.

(b) 44 USC 3506(b)(2): Agency heads must develop agency information resource management (IRM) plans. The agency plan must include plans to reduce the information burden placed on the public, to increase public access, and to meet the technology needs of government.

(c) 44 USC 3506(b)(3)(c): Agency heads must establish IRM goals and methods for measuring progress toward achieving each goal.

(d) 44 USC 3514(a)(2)(D): The OMB director must report to Congress annually on the extent to which agencies have improved performance and the accomplishment of agency missions through IRM.

- The Clinger-Cohen Act of 1996 called on agencies to implement results-oriented IT management, including implementing processes to assess and manage IT risks:

(a) Section 5112(b): The OMB director has responsibility to improve the productivity, efficiency, and effectiveness of federal programs.

(b) Section 5112(c): In support of the president's annual budget, the OMB director must submit to Congress a report on net program performance benefits achieved as a result of agencies' major capital investments, including describing how benefits relate to the achievement of agency goals. The OMB director must develop a process for analyzing, tracking, and evaluating risks and results for all major IT investments by federal agencies. Analysis must cover the life cycle of each system and must measure projected and actual costs, benefits, and risks of each investment.

(c) Section 5113(b)(5): To enforce these functions, the OMB director is given the authority to recommend increases or decreases in agency IT budgets, to restrict agency IT funds, and to designate an executive agent to contract with private sources for the agency's acquisition and management of IT resources.

(d) Section 5122: Agency heads are required to implement a process to assess and manage the risks of their IT acquisitions. The process must include quantitative net risk-adjusted ROI and must include quantitative and qualitative criteria for prioritizing alternative IT projects. Criteria must cover requirements, timeliness, and cost.

(e) Section 5123(3): Agency heads must ensure that performance measures are prescribed for IT used within the agency.

(f) Section 5125(c)(2): Agency CIOs must monitor the performance of IT programs of the agency using performance measures, on the basis of which the CIO will advise the agency head about project continuation, modification, or termination.

(g) Section 5126: Financial and program performance data must be provided to agency financial systems on a reliable, consistent, and timely basis.

(h) Section 5127: In the agency IRM plan (required by the Paperwork Reduction Act), the agency head must identify IT programs that have deviated significantly from cost, schedule, or performance goals.

In addition, OMB guidance documents spelled out performance measurement and evaluation obligations of agencies. OMB Circular A-94 contained a checklist for conducting cost-benefit and cost-effectiveness analysis, including how to discount costs and benefits over time. OMB Circular A-123 provided guidance on establishing management structures and controls for accountability. OMB Circular A-130 prescribed uniform, government-wide IRM policies as required by the PRA. This circular's Section 8b(1) spelled out agency obligations with respect to IT project evaluation and performance measurement, including life-cycle cost-benefit analysis, and mandated postimplementation reviews of information systems to validate estimated benefits. Section 8b(3) mandated information system oversight mechanisms that would ensure each information system met agency mission requirements, holding the IT program administrator accountable for this.

In summary, by the turn of the century, performance measurement had become well established as a major and permanent function of public organizations (Poister & Streib, 1999). In this environment it was inevitable that public IT projects came under governmental mandates to implement ROI and other evaluation techniques.

Traditional Value-Ranking Methods

Traditional public-sector evaluations establish value categories. Each category is broken down into specific criteria. Points are associated with criteria. The evaluation consists of summing all the points for all criteria for all values. The alternative with the highest point value is the highest ranked alternative. The Office of Management and Budget (OMB, 1997, pp. 98–103) has provided the following example. Five value areas are defined: strategic alignment (25 points), benefit-cost impact (25 points), mission effectiveness (20 points), risk (20 points), and organizational impact (20 points):

A. Strategic Alignment
   1. Business model (7 of 25 points): Zero points if the project does not support products/services/processes identified in the business model; 1 or 2 points if the project supports the business model but is not in the agency IRM plan; 3 or 4 points if the project does both; 5 to 7 points if it does both and has been coordinated with all appropriate offices.

2. Level of interest (12 of 25 points): Zero points if there is no documented support by Congress or by senior managers; 12 points for documented strong support by Congress, departmental senior managers, and/or the agency head.

3. Business process redesign (6 of 25 points): Zero points if the system automates an existing process with little improvement; 6 points if the system implements a significant improvement in the way the agency conducts its business.

B. Benefit-Cost Impacts

1. Benefit/cost ratio (0 to 25 points): Zero points for a ratio less than 1.0 (costs exceed benefits); 1 point for a ratio of 1.0; 5 points for 1.5 to 1.75; 10 points for 1.76 to 1.99; 15 points for 2.0 to 2.99; 20 points for 2.0 to 3.99; 25 points for a benefit/cost ratio of 4.0 or higher.

C. Mission Effectiveness

1. Improving internal program services (10 of 20 points): Zero points if the system does not appear to meet a problem defined by an internal customer; little improvement of timeliness, quality, or availability of agency services/products is expected; 10 points for a significant, quantified improvement in timeliness, quality, and/ or availability with regard to a problem defined by customers.

2. Improved service to the public (10 of 20 points): Zero points if the system appears to provide little or no direct improvement in service to the public; there may be small improvements in timeliness, quality, or availability, but there is no documented need for such improvements; 10 points if the system significantly improves service to the public where need is demonstrated and supports the mission of the agency.

D. Risk

1. Schedule risk (4 of 20 points): Zero points if the project is very risky and is likely to slip (indicators are contract not awarded in time, inadequate staffing, unrealistic time frame); 4 points for low-risk projects.

2. Cost sensitivity (4 of 20 points): Zero points if cost estimates require refinement (scrutiny required for complex projects or ones where software development exceeds 50% of project predicted cost); 4 points where cost estimates are well supported and little software development is required.

3. Technical risk (4 of 20 points): Zero points where hardware and/ or software does not conform to organizational architecture and/or the organization has little or no experience with the given technology and/or custom software must be developed rather than using commercial off-the-shelf software and support; 4 points if the system conforms to established architecture, the organization is experienced with the technology, and hardware/software/support are commercially available.

4. Organizational risk (4 of 20 points): Zero points if system implementation requires significant organization change, process redesign, and/or retraining and the project has not incorporated risk-reduction steps to forestall associated problems; 4 points where the system has little impact on the organization or the project mitigates this risk through training and/or investment in business process redesign efforts building commitment to the system.

5. Risk of not doing it (4 of 20 points): Zero points if the project is an incremental improvement to an existing system and impacts can be achieved by other means; 4 points if failure to implement the project will mean the organization will fail to meet customer demands in the near future.

E. Organizational Impact

1. Personnel and training (3 of 10 points): Zero points if the system requires significant new skills but has not incorporated appropriate training, changes in rating qualifications, etc.; 3 points if the system requires relatively little new skill and/or knowledge to operate and support, or if required, the project mitigates this risk by incorporating appropriate training and planning for rating qualification changes.

2. Scope of beneficiaries (4 of 10 points): Zero points if the system affects a single office in a single area or district; 4 points for systems serving a number of offices, areas, and/or districts, and/or may be used by the public.

3. Quality of work life (3 of 10 points): Zero points if there is little or no positive impact on the quality of work life, or may increase workloads (e.g., additional data entry); 3 points if the project makes positive contributions to work life, as through increasing job satisfaction.

Traditional ranking systems of evaluation have the advantage of being relatively straightforward and simple to use. Their disadvantage is that they do not deal well with value conflicts (e.g., trade-offs between scope of beneficiaries and technical risk, or between job satisfaction and organizational risk). Also, they do not allow different decision makers to weight different criteria differently. They lend themselves to an evaluation done by an evaluation expert but not to participative evaluations that seek to use the evaluation process to motivate and mobilize employees in the process of organizational change.

Value-Measuring Methodology (VMM)

Attempts have been made to systematize value-measuring or ranking methodology to achieve broader purposes. Among these attempts, value-measuring methodology (VMM) has been recommended by the CIO Council as a best practice in evaluation (CIO Council, 2002). It was developed by Jerry Mechling, a strategic computing and telecommunications specialist at Harvard University's John F. Kennedy School of Government, and by e-government experts at the consulting company Booz Allen Hamilton, under a $220,000 grant from the Social Security Administration and the General Services Administration (GSA) in 2002. VMM was subsequently used in the GSA's E-Authentication and E-Travel initiatives, and in the Social Security Administration's Check Your Benefits and Deferred Application Process initiatives.

VMM drew heavily on the Analytic Hierarchy Process (AHP), a multicriterion decision-making methodology that had been around for many years. AHP was developed in the 1970s by Dr. Thomas Saaty at the Wharton School of Business. Under AHP, complex decisions are reduced to a series of pairwise comparisons, enabling comparative ranking and development of overall scores based on the application of multiple, often subjective criteria by multiple decision makers. Criteria may be political, social, even aesthetic, in addition to the usual economic criteria.

In 1983, Saaty joined Ernest Forman, a professor of management science at George Washington University, to cofound Expert Choice (www. expertchoice.com). Expert Choice software structures decision making and allows multiple decision makers to rank policy alternatives, after which the software calculates an integrated decision score for all decision makers. The Department of Housing and Urban Development has used Expert Choice to help select investments for its IT portfolio, based on rankings of its senior executives. In a second round, the Expert Choice tool is used again to optimize the portfolio to mirror strategic priorities reflected in Congressional appropriations.

Under VMM, cost dimensions are detailed in a Cost Element Structure (CES). The sum of CES values is the total cost. Value is assessed in terms of direct customer value (e.g., increased access), social value (e.g., increased trust in the agency), operational value (e.g., improved infrastructure), strategic or political value (e.g., fulfilling agency missions), and financial values (e.g., reduced cost of correcting errors). Risk analysis includes identifying risks and establishing the agency's risk tolerance levels. Risk scores reflect the impact of the identified risk and its probability of occurrence.

VMM is organized into four basic steps:

1. Developing a decision framework: Values, risks, and costs are defined in a structured manner.
2. Analyzing alternatives: Alternatives are identified, values are attached to benefits and costs, and risk is analyzed.
3. Integrating information: Value, cost, and risk scores are calculated for each alternative, as is ROI.
4. Communicating decisions: Results are reported to stakeholders, and a budget justification document is prepared.

Where ROI focuses primarily on cost, VMM looks equally at value and risk, creating value scores that allow alternative projects to be rated on a comparable basis even though they may involve indirect benefits and intangible costs (Miller, 2003v).

The Program Assessment Rating Tool (PART)

OMB developed the Program Assessment Rating Tool (PART) to assess and improve program performance through a formal review process that was meant to identify a program's strengths and weaknesses. A PART review includes assessment of program purpose and design, performance measurement, traditional evaluation, strategic planning documents, program management analyses, and reportage of program results over time. The intention is that by making PART reviews standardized, programs may be compared. Completing a PART review is considered by the OMB to constitute compliance with the GPRA. Put another way, the OMB was trying to breathe life into the GPRA by mandating PART reviews for about 20% of federal agencies each year, with all programs slated to be "PART-ed" by FY 2008.

PART is a 25- to 30-part questionnaire, used by OMB in FY 2005 to review about 40% of federal programs. PART evaluation forms came in seven formats, one for each type of federal program (direct federal programs such as the National Weather Service, competitive grant programs, block/formula grant programs, regulatory-based programs, capital asset and service acquisition programs, credit programs, and research and development programs). Most PART items appear in all seven forms. Several PART items deal with the quality of a program's long-term and annual performance goals and measures, assessing whether they were meaningful, employed sound methodology, and could be verified with reliable data. OMB and agencies have to agree on appropriate measures early in PART reviews, involving relevant stakeholders, as required by the GPRA.

Is PART actually important in political decision making? The picture is mixed. On the one hand, President Bush did recommend eliminating some 13 programs that rated poorly in PART performance evaluations in FY 2005. On the other hand, a low PART rating did not necessarily bring a budgetary penalty and, indeed, some such programs actually received funding increases. PART has the support of many in Congress, some of whom want to institutionalize it, including Rep. Todd Platts R-PA), whose bill, the Program Assessment and Results Act is pending in the House as of fall 2005.

Opposing PART, many at the agency level regard it as one more form of burdensome analysis, duplicative of the GPRA, and likely to disappear once the Bush administration leaves office. *OMB Watch* said of PART, "As with cost-benefit analysis and risk assessments, the PART is yet another complicated and highly technical tool in which potentially controversial political judgments are embedded in faux-objective formulae. With 10 percent of the total score depending on cost-effectiveness and improved 'efficiencies,' the PART may be yet another vehicle for pushing the agencies to treat industry compliance costs as an equal counterweight to the public interest" (*OMB Watch,* 2005).

The Performance Reference Model (PRM)

Shortly after VMM was released, the OMB in September 2003 released its "performance reference model" (PRM), a major component of strategic planning based on enterprise architecture, as discussed in Chapter 11 (Daukantas, 2003b). Acknowledging that performance metrics for the public sector cannot be directly borrowed from the private sector, the PRM called on agencies to use four types of evaluation measures:

1. Mission and business results, particularly measures of conformity with GPRA strategic planning requirements
2. Customer results, particularly measures of accessibility and timeliness of services
3. Processes and activities, particularly measures dealing with finances, productivity, security, privacy, and innovation
4. Measures dealing with IT quality, efficiency, standardization, reliability, and effectiveness

Later PRM versions also include human resources measures and fixed capital measures.

For each type, the PRM provides a framework for categorizing operational evaluation measures. For instance, for the "mission and business results" type, evaluation measures were broken into 31 subcategories, including administrative management, community and social services, controls and oversight, correctional activities, defense and national security, disaster management, economic development, financial management, and more. Financial management, in turn, was broken down into accounting, budget and finance, payments, collections and receivables, and asset and liability management measurement categories. However, the measurement categories did not contain operational examples, only the injunction that "As agencies use the PRM for their specific IT initiatives they will create the inventory of operationalized indicators."

The OMB sees the PRM as part of a "balanced scorecard" approach to evaluation. The balance reflects inputs not only from operational PRM measures to be developed by agencies, but also from agency business cases and PART evaluations and in general, by agency compliance with the GPRA (Arveson, 2003).

Other Models

There are, of course, an almost infinite variety of evaluation models employed in the public sector around the world. To illustrate the variety, just one will be described here: the factor radar chart model as applied to United Kingdom local government by Les Worrall of the Management Research Center, University of Wolverhampton (Worrall, Remenyi, & Money, 2000). This model is survey based and focuses on highlighting the gap between *is* and *ought to be* factors in IT projects. Although the survey employs a relatively large number of items, it is simple to administer and can be analyzed statistically with graphical presentation of results on a perceptual map.

In this factor radar chart methodology, respondents at various levels of the organization are asked to rank the importance of a large number (38) of attributes, such as "ease of access for users," "fast response time," and "participation in the planning of system requirement." Each attribute rated has in terms of the importance the attribute actually has in the organization, and then again in terms of what the importance of that attribute ought to be. By simple subtraction, the difference of *is* and *ought* scores provides a *gap score*. Thus every attribute can be ranked in terms of its actual importance score, ideal importance score, and gap score.

After scores are obtained, data space is reduced by factor analysis. That is, for the data in the authors' example, the 38 attributes were reduced to eight underlying factors: systems support (five attributes, such as promptness in processing requests), training and service monitoring (three attributes, such as extent of user training), support staff (three attributes, including user confidence in systems), being up to date (two attributes, one for hardware, the other for software), enhancing personal effectiveness (three attributes, including cost-effectiveness), job enrichment and control (two attributes, including degree of personal user control), confidentiality and security (three attributes, including provision for disaster recovery), and system responsiveness (two attributes, including system response time).

Factor analysis of evaluation attributes allows each UK municipality to receive a factor score on each of the eight underlying evaluation dimensions. Factor regression allows the evaluators to see the relation of evaluation dimensions to desired outcomes. For instance, for the example data, the authors found that overall satisfaction with the IT Department depended primarily on only two of the eight factors (support staff and system responsiveness).

The primary output of this evaluation model is a radar diagram depicting the relative performance of each of the eight local government authorities studied. Arranging the eight factors as eight points on a compass, with lines from the origin outward toward these points, dots are plotted on these eight axis lines proportional to the factor scores of the local governments. The higher the factor score on, say, the support staff factor, the further that jurisdiction's point is plotted on the support staff axis. For any given jurisdiction, a different color line connects that jurisdiction's dots on all eight axes, forming a closed irregular octagon (of course the number of axes would vary according to factor analysis results for different data).

In the factor radar plot, the highest-performing local governments have the largest octagons (their lines are furthest from the origin), while the worst-performing jurisdictions have small octagons closer to the origin of the radar plot. In fact, there can be three such plots—one for *actual* data, one for *ought to be* data, and one for *gap* data. The factor radar plot allows evaluators or decision makers to spot at a glance which jurisdictions are performing best or worst, or have the longest way to go, on multiple dimensions of IT efforts. In the example data, for instance, the Banton local government authority was found to be the worst-performing on all IT dimensions except training and monitoring. Many other conclusions can be derived from application of such a model, including assessing user involvement, assessing managerial needs, and evaluating overall user satisfaction.

EVALUATION OF GOVERNMENTAL WEBSITES

Special evaluation methodologies have been developed to assess governmental Web sites, which are, of course, central to e-government and to public information systems. A very general but now common form of evaluation involves categorizing Web sites according to their position in a five-stage progression reflected in a report by the United Nations Division for Public Economics and Public Administration and the American Society for Public Administration (Ho, 2002; UN & ASPA, 2002):

1. Emerging Web presence: Limited one-way information access
2. Enhanced Web presence: Some forms, e-mail, links to other agencies
3. Interactive Web presence: Portal (gateway) concept with links to many agencies at various levels of government; more forms; first online transactions
4. Transactional Web presence: Many transactions and forms, support for digital signatures and public key infrastructures (PKI) security
5. Seamless Web presence: Full portal status, mirrors all traditional brick-and-mortar services, single user input brings multiagency response

In practice, most agencies today are at stage three or four, with none fully implementing stage 5, which is a distant goal. The UN/ASPA report established benchmarks for e-government, societal in level, including personal computers per 100 population, Internet hosts per 10,000 population, percent of population online, telephone lines per 100 population, and so on.

In terms of more detailed evaluation of governmental websites, McClure, Sprehe, and Eschenfelder (2000), writing on contract for the Defense Technical Information Center, the Energy Information Administration, and the U.S. Government Printing Office, have usefully summarized a broad spectrum of work on website evaluation. The authors divided Web assessment measures into five types:

1. Extensiveness measures: Number of user sessions, ratio of unique to repeat user sessions, number of document downloads, etc.
2. Efficiency measures: Website cost per user session, percent website downtime, full-time employee maintenance time per Web page, savings in diminished print publications/mailings, etc.
3. Effectiveness measures: Proportion of agency publications and press releases online; timeliness of Web publication; permanency of Web publication; measures of outreach to new audiences, such as Hispanic, etc.
4. Service quality: Mean time between online user requests and agency responses, number of user complaints, user success rate in finding specific information in a given time period, help desk availability, courtesy and helpfulness of survey measures, etc.
5. Usefulness measures: User satisfaction measures, number of referrals from other websites, user comments from surveys and focus groups—especially regarding impact on user productivity, etc.

In addition, McClure, Sprehe, and Eschenfelder provided checklists of questions evaluators might ask regarding federal websites. Many checklist questions focused on management and infrastructure factors, including questions on technology management (Is there adequate bandwidth for acceptable response time? Is there 24/7 availability? Are there provisions for disaster recovery? Is the budget adequate to achieve the goals of the website?) And on technology standards (Is the website consistent with the World Wide Web Federal Consortium's Home Page Guidelines? Is there access control over posting to the website? Is there a formal quality control process? Is the site registered with search engines and appropriate portals? Is there staffing for user support? Are there regular website evaluations?

Additional checklist questions included ones on privacy (Does the website carry a privacy notice? Are cookies avoided? Is collection of information from children screened?); access (Does the website post Freedom of Information Act (FOIA) procedures for obtaining agency information? Is there an electronic reading room, as per FOIA? Is there compliance with the 1997 presidential directive on access for children?); copyright (Does the website screen for copyright violation? Does the website post policies allowing maximum reuse of contents consistent with copyright?); disabilities (Is the website compliant with Section 508 of the Rehabilitation Act?); security (Is the website secure? Does the website permit support digital signatures?); OMB compliance (Does the site comply with the Paperwork Reduction Act? With the Government Information Locator Service's indexing?); and records management (Are website publications made available to the Federal Depository Library Program? Is there provision for transferring website records to agency record archiving systems?).

McClure, Sprehe, and Eschenfelder also provide a valuable listing, with key excerpts, of applicable federal legislation pertinent to performance evaluation of websites, including coverage of the Privacy Act of 1974; Rehabilitation Act of 1973, Section 508 (added by the Rehabilitation Act Amendments of 1986; the GPRA; OMB Circular No. A-11, Part II, Preparation and Submission of Strategic Plans, Annual Performance Plans, and Annual Program Performance Reports; Setting Customer Service Standards (Executive Order 12862), 1993; the Federal Records Act of 1994; the Paperwork Reduction Act of 1995; the FOIA as amended; the Information Technology Management Reform (Clinger-Cohen) Act of 1996; the Electronic Freedom of Information Act Amendments of 1996; the Computer Security Act of 1987; the Government Paperwork Elimination Act of 1998; the Digital Millennium Copyright Act of 1998; and the President's Memorandum on Electronic Government, December 17, 1999. The authors also list and excerpt relevant OMB guidance documents and court opinions. Such a legislative and judicial review of mandates and compliance with them is an essential part of a full governmental website evaluation.

Any number of other Web assessment instruments have been developed. Some evaluation surveys have focused primarily on openness and transparency measures (the Cyberspace Policy Research Group; see Demchak, Friis, & LaPorte, 2000). Brown University's Center for Public Policy has emphasized usage features and transactional capabilities of websites (West, 2000, 2003a, 2003b, 2004). Others have focused on user friendliness indicators such as graphical, navigation, and usability features (Ceaparu & Shneiderman, 2002). Organization for Economic Co-operation and Development member country website evaluation practices surveyed by van Gils (2002) included indicators on cost savings, accessibility, satisfaction, interoperability, and service improvement. Lee (2004) has developed a survey instrument focused on e-reporting of agency documents and information. And, of course, there are special assessment instruments for evaluating websites for disability access ("Bobby analysis,"[1] see Stowers, 2002). For a general survey of e-government performance measures, see Stowers (2004).

In June 2004, the OMB's Interagency Committee on Government Information issued recommended guidelines for all federal websites. These guidelines encompassed seven criteria, all given in very concrete detail in the report, but only summarized below (OMB, 2004):

1. Identifiability: Federal public websites must use government domains, show U.S. sponsorship, and make clear when citizens are linking to other sites from an agency site.
2. Customer orientation: Content must be organized to make sense to the public (not primarily for agency employees); customer satisfaction and usability of federal websites must be measured.
3. Accessibility: Federal websites should use plain language, have consistent navigation, have a search engine, and use standard metadata; document access must be in widely used file formats.
4. Integration: Federal websites should link to FirstGov.gov and other appropriate portals, and should avoid duplication; agencies should collaborate in development of portals.
5. Timeliness: Federal websites should be current and should establish a schedule for posting their content, complying with the E-Government Act of 2002, Section 207(f)2.
6. Compliance: Federal websites must comply with a broad range of legislative requirements, including those related to privacy, freedom of information, security, information quality, paperwork reduction, records management, digital rights, performance results, and the No Fear Act, to name a few.
7. Standardization: The committee recommended that the OMB establish a Web Content Advisory Council to approve common content and links and to coordinate cross-agency portals, requiring agencies to report compliance with standard Web content policies and requirements.

Under these guidelines, Web evaluation processes were to include usability testing, customer satisfaction surveys, focus groups, contacts with the public (e-mail, phone, letter), interviews with intended audience members, and analysis of Web statistics (e.g., page hits, search terms). At this writing, the OMB has not yet established the Web Content Advisory Council, but the other recommendations above became official OMB policy in December 2004, and are available at the Federal Web Manager's Toolkit page at http://www.firstgov.gov/webcontent/.

In spite of the many evaluation instruments and official policies pertaining to the evaluation of public websites, as LaVigne (2001, p. 1) has noted, "The costs of e-government initiatives are almost always underestimated." The hardware and software costs typically measured are less important than five other factors LaVigne studied: the cost of building and maintaining relationships behind the portal, the cost of reinventing processes to take full advantage of Web technology, the cost of training and relearning, the cost of coordinating the interdependent tasks needed for e-governance, and the cost of data integration itself. That is, as in other public-sector arenas, evaluation of governmental websites must give great attention to indirect and sometimes intangible costs and benefits.

SUMMARY

There is no one best way to evaluate public-sector IT projects. Nonetheless, there is some consensus on principles that must underlie an evaluation effort (Specht, 2000). Projects must be evaluated primarily in terms of achievement of the agency's mission, goals, and objectives. Measures of processing efficiency, outreach, user satisfaction, and the like, are important only when related to mission, goals, and objectives. Because costs and benefits may change, evaluation measurement must be ongoing, gathering data at many points in time. Greater complexity of goals in the public sector calls for multiple measures addressing multiple levels of the organization. These multiple measures must address indirect, intangible, and long-term benefits, not just immediate dollar costs and gains. Overall, the evaluation system should be integrated with PPBS, and it should involve affected staff and stakeholders in a way that allows them to understand the benefits of IT systems and take ownership of them.

In overseeing evaluation processes in federal agencies, the OMB asks three sets of questions (OMB, 1997, p. 13):

- Does the agency have decision-making and management processes in place to select IT projects and systems, to control and monitor these projects throughout their life cycle, and to evaluate results and revise the processes based on lessons learned?
- Are IT decisions being driven by cost, risk, and benefit information, and are project justifications updated as funding is spent and interim benefits assessed?
- Most important, is the organization making decisions that maximize benefits while minimizing risks? Are the selected projects being monitored and controlled, and are actions being taken to address problems as they are identified?

Specifically, the OMB expects all projects

should have complete and accurate project information—cost and benefit data, risk assessments, links to business/program goals and objectives, and performance measures, as well as up-to-date project-specific data, including current costs, implementation plans, staffing plans, and performance levels. In addition, the organization should have qualitative and quantitative project requirements and decision criteria in place to help screen IT projects, assess and rank projects, and control and evaluate the projects as they move through the various phases of their life cycle (OMB, 1997, p. 15).

In other words, agencies should integrate planning and evaluation. In the OMB's terminology, "the information gained from PIRs" (postimplementation reviews for evaluation purposes) "is critical for improving how the organization selects, manages, and uses its IT resources" (OMB, 1997, p. 70). Evaluation information should come from measures of mission fulfillment, customer satisfaction surveys, assessments of information product (accuracy, timeliness, adequacy, and appropriateness of information), compliance with enterprise architecture, workforce competency, and employee satisfaction. Evaluation outputs should include costs broken down by category, measures of benefits, a comparison matrix of actuals to estimates, and performance effectiveness measures.

The foregoing seemingly neutral and reasonable consensus on public-sector IT evaluation masks many policy and even political considerations. These considerations may be summarized by the question, "Performance for what?" Quite apart from the problematic issue of developing sound performance indicators, there is the broader issue of what top officials want to track in the first place. For a conservative administration, for instance, weight may be given to outsourcing of formerly public functions as an indicator of "good performance." When evaluation is embedded in a top-down management control system and tied to the budgetary club, the "neutral" idea of integrating planning and evaluation in a balanced scorecard approach to evaluation can seem heavy-handed and very partisan. However, the theory of representative democracy sanctions precisely this total control of bureaucracy by elected officials.

As noted in Chapter 11, strategic planning and evaluation as implemented by the OMB and General Services Administration is based on systems theory, with its emphasis on comprehensive integration of information systems. Current evaluation practice would seem to confirm also the views of reinforcement theorists who believe technology serves those at the top and who in the evaluation area would point to the use of technology to further centralize power in the OMB. Technological determinists might find support in the embedding of evaluation in computerized data systems, though in truth these systems are driven by political and managerial trends, not technology in its own right. PART evaluation, for instance, is widely seen as a Bush administration innovation likely to be abandoned by future presidencies. However, it is true that at a very general level, evaluation and data systems will always go hand in hand in the future. As to sociotechnical theory, the participative element is even weaker in evaluation than it is in planning, though it is true that the GPRA requires stakeholder involvement in evaluation. Still, it is hard to characterize contemporary IT evaluation processes as much concerned with human relations and organization development priorities emphasized by sociotechnical theorists.

DISCUSSION QUESTIONS

1. If you were a top manager, what role would you give to qualitative factors in evaluation?
2. Is quantitative return on investment (ROI) analysis useful in the public sector?
3. What is performance distortion, and how does it relate to evaluation?
4. Compare evaluation in the public and private sectors. Similarities? Differences?
5. How participative should evaluation processes be? What are the pro and con arguments?
6. How should the manager decide how far into the future to measure benefit streams or cost factors?
7. Are benefits that are solely internal to the agency, such as employee satisfaction, "real" benefits that should be counted in return on investment?
8. Should "potential benefits" be considered in evaluation, even if they are contingent on future developments?
9. Why is the Government Performance and Results Act (GPRA) considered to be particularly important to public IT evaluation?
10. Can IT evaluation be neutral? Why or why not?

GLOSSARY

Baselining: Obtaining data on the current process that provide the metrics against which to compare improvements and to use in benchmarking.

Benchmarking: A structured approach for identifying the best practices from industry and government, and comparing and adapting them to the organization's operations to identify more efficient and effective processes for achieving intended results. Benchmarks are used to suggest ambitious goals for program output, service quality, and process improvement.

Best practices: The processes, practices, or systems identified in public and private organizations that performed exceptionally well and are widely recognized as improving the organization's performance and efficiency in specific areas.

Business case: A structured proposal for business improvement that functions as a decision package for organizational decision makers. It includes an analysis of process performance and associated needs or problems, proposed alternative solutions, and a risk-adjusted cost-benefit analysis.

Cost-benefit analysis: A technique used to compare the various costs associated with an investment with the benefits that it is expected to return. Both tangible and intangible factors may be addressed.

Discount rate: The interest rate used to calculate the net present value of benefits and costs over time.

Information resource management (IRM):   The process of managing information resources to accomplish agency missions, including managing personnel, funds, and information technology as well as information itself.

Life-cycle cost: The overall estimated cost for a particular program alternative over the life of the program, including direct and indirect initial costs plus continuing operation and maintenance costs.

Net present value: The future stream of benefits and costs converted into equivalent values today by assigning monetary values to benefits and costs, discounting future benefits and costs using an appropriate discount rate, and subtracting the sum of discounted costs from the sum of discounted benefits.

Return on investment (ROI):   Either annual benefit divided by initial investment cost, or life-cycle benefits divided by life-cycle investment costs.

ENDNOTE

1See http://www.wcet.info/resources/publications/guide1003/guide/%7BBBFDC 751D-C83E-11D3-9309-005004AD2ACC%7D_2028_1487.htm.

CASE STUDY
Evaluating City Websites Using Focus Groups

By Alana Northrop, University of California–Fullerton

Introduction

Websites for U.S. cities are still quite new endeavors (Moon, 2002; Norris & Moon, 2005). Many cities find that they need to reconsider their sites and add, modify, and delete features. But how to know whether the overall design works? A city could survey its citizens or Web visitors. A city could also analyze e-mail comments about the website, or a city could use a focus group for feedback. This case study reports on the use of a focus group, which can be more efficient than a survey and can also offer valuable feedback.

If a city wants to use a focus group, it has to decide who will make up that group. A group of citizens or municipal employees might be likely choices. But it may be advantageous to use Masters of Public Administration students for several reasons. MPA students learn about formal evaluation methods and thus can take on the whole task and could even do it as a course project. They also can see websites from the two sides, one as citizen and one as government official or department. In contrast, a group of citizens would have to be given or walked through the goal specification and measurement steps. They would also come with their own biases because they live in the city. As for municipal employees of the city under review, they would likely be too close to the issue at hand to see the weaknesses of the site and likely would also be biased.

This case study reports on the use of 12 MPA students[1] as a focus group that evaluated four Southern California city websites. The task took two $2\frac{1}{2}$ hour meetings and about 30 to 40 minutes for each student to collect the data from the four websites. From the start, the focus group's aim was defined as evaluating the city websites from a private citizen's perspective. Taking on the city visitor or business perspective would require a separate meeting and focus and was omitted from the aim of this group's task.

Defining and Prioritizing the Goals

The students met in a $2\frac{1}{2}$-hour brainstorming session where all city website goals were inventoried on a whiteboard. The students had no input from city officials or consultants. The group then went through the extensive list and rephrased the goals, dropping goals that were identical but differently phrased.

Next the students prioritized the goals. These were the results:

Priority One
- Budget savings in terms of staff time balanced against cost of maintaining site
- Increased public awareness by providing information

Priority Two
- Easy accessibility

Priority Three
- Increased public satisfaction with city government

Priority Four
- Increased public involvement in local government affairs

The focus group agreed that similar to private businesses, cities are highly motivated to see websites as a way to reduce personnel costs or at least stem their increase. The group also felt that cities equally viewed their websites as a means of providing information to their citizens. In fact, the two priority one goals can be seen as complementary because if a citizen gets a question answered by going to the website that likely is thought to mean that no phone call or personal visit to city hall was made to get the information.

Second in priority is making the website accessible, because without ease of use priority one goals may not be achieved. This priority two goal is thought to be the means to achieving priority one goals. Still, easy accessibility is not the same as increased awareness nor does it necessarily result in increased awareness. So it is an end in itself but not as important as increased public awareness by providing information.

The focus group all agreed that increased public satisfaction with city government had to be an end goal of a city website but initially disagreed as to its priority or importance from city hall's perspective. Some felt that it was so distant from the direct pay-off intended by establishing websites that it might be hard to measure. In the end, the vagueness of the goal was seen as a weak and thus third priority measure of the effectiveness of the city website. It was considered more a summary impression by citizens of their overall experience and reaction to the website. It could be a reaction that could add fuel to the fire if the citizen were already displeased with his or her government or one that could grudgingly eliminate a little of the hostility. From the perspective of a happy citizen, a good website visit was thought to polish the halo and a bad one to tarnish it a bit. In essence, a city's website was thought to be only one small piece in an already established view of local government.

Finally, increased public involvement is currently an extremely rare goal of city websites (Norris & Moon, 2005; West, 2004), and thus it had the lowest priority.

What to Measure?

The focus group could not measure the priority one goal of budget savings. That goal must be determined internally by referencing the relevant cost estimates. In addition, the focus group felt that because the priority four goal of increased public involvement is so rarely emphasized in websites and is likely a very long-term goal, that it should not be an evaluative goal. It is rare for cities to allow citizens to, for example, register to vote or even vote or send messages to officials via the websites (Northrop, 2005).

That left three goals to measure. The next task was deciding how to measure awareness, accessibility, and satisfaction. The following were the agreed-upon measures of each of those three goals.

Priority One: Increased Public Awareness by Providing Information

- Was there any old or out-of-date material on the home page or other pages visited? (yes/no)
- How up to date was the Web page? (daily, weekly, monthly, unknown)
- Was there a calendar? (yes/no)
- Did you learn at least two things that you didn't know from the home page? (yes/no)

Priority Two: Easy Accessibility

- Number of clicks to find out the answers to each of the following five common city website questions: job postings, city council meeting time, how to contact the city clerk, finding out about building permits, and about recreation classes. The focus group first generated a list of 10 common information requests and then selected these 5 from the list.
- Was there a clear link to a search function? (yes/no)
- Was there a drop-down menu on the home page links? (yes/no)
- Did the visitor ever encounter any unavailable pages? (yes/no)

Priority Three: Increased Public Satisfaction with City Government

- An overall impression of the website visit (A to F rating)

continues

Data Collection

The focus group agreed on a date and time for each of them to visit the four city websites, which were Brea, Long Beach, Santa Ana, and Upland, California. It was thought it would take over two hours to collect the data, but the experience of each of the focus group members and the leader was that it took a total of 30 to 40 minutes. It was important that all members visited the sites on the same day and relative time period because some sites are updated daily and thus information or format can change.

Analysis and Issues of Measurement

In another $2\frac{1}{2}$-hour meeting, the focus group turned their scores for each city on each measure into group scores on each measure.

Priority One: Increased Public Awareness by Providing Information—Four Indicators

Out-of-date material and presence of a calendar were yes/no scores and were unanimously scored the same. How up to date the website was also was scored unanimously as either indicated on the page or left unknown. Whether a focus group member learned two new things from the home page was scored yes or no but, as one could guess, varied by the person as well as due to the vagueness of the indicator. It was recommended that a clearer definition of learning new things be used in a future evaluation or else drop this goal indicator.

Based on the group scores, the overall goal evaluation was expressed as a pass or fail with pluses and minuses allowed. So, for example, one city had only one student learning two new things, the website was quite old with much out of date material, but there was a calendar. That city got a Fail score overall. Another city's website was updated daily and had a calendar, everyone learned two new things, and only two of the students encountered old material. This city got a Pass+.

Priority Two: Easy Accessibility—Four Indicators

The first indicator was the number of clicks to find out the answers to five common city website questions such as the meeting time of the city council. Unlike three of the indicators of the priority one goal, here was the possibility of different or nonunanimous ratings. It was discussed whether to use the mean, median, or modal response of the focus group. Because some of the focus group's members never found some of the answers, they had no clicks to report. It was decided to use the median number of clicks to recognize those members who never found the answers; using the mean or mode would have had to ignore those members and actually lose valuable information in the evaluation of the website. The focus group produced five median scores for the number of clicks to answer the five questions. Still it needed an overall rating standard. Members of the focus group thought that three or less clicks to find each piece of information was excellent or high pass, and four clicks was good or pass performance. No city scored a median of 5 or higher, which would have been in the low pass and fail range.

The focus group members were in agreement on whether or not there was a clear link to a search function and whether there was a drop-down menu on the home page. Cities either got a pass or fail on these two indicators.

The fourth indicator was also scored pass/fail although a minus score was allowed when, for example, one or two students encountered pages unavailable. Intriguingly, two cities did get a high pass or excellent on number of clicks and then fail the latter three indicators. So the need for multiple indicators of accessibility was warranted and would be useful feedback information.

Priority Three: Increased Public Satisfaction with City Government

Students were not unanimous in their A to F ratings and split between two or three letter grades. Much discussion took place trying to reconcile earlier scores on accessibility and providing information with overall impression, resulting in a consensus of the grade. It was clear that the initial grades did not always mesh with the same student's overall impression of the website. It was decided that this happened because of the student emphasizing one indicator more than another and also in one case especially liking a graphic. This experience might indicate that it is likely that little, subtle, even idiosyncratic things may be important in a citizen's overall impression of the website independent of accessibly and information issues.

Reports to Cities

Clearly the focus group had evaluative comments to pass on to the cities. For instance, cities could either be told that they lack search and drop-down menus and had out-of-date information on their websites or that they had all or most of the key indicators. Areas for improvement would be obvious. Still, aside from such specific comments, what else should the focus group report? It was decided that cities would find it useful to get an actual grade, such as B+. Cities could relate to such a score easily because beaches and restaurants in the area are scored that way in terms of health issues. So, just as consumers and restaurant owners use an A to F rating as a way to compare eating establishments, the same could be done by cities in comparing their website with other cities' websites.

For example, one city's report card:

Increased public awareness	Pass+
Updated—daily	
Old information—yes for 2/12	
Calendar—yes	
Learn two new things—yes	
Easy accessibility	Pass+
Number of clicks—less than 4	
Search link—yes	
Drop-down menu—yes	
Unavailable pages—yes for 7 /12	
Satisfaction with city government	B+
Overall	B+

What else to include in the reports to cities? Any biases or contamination issues? The focus group admitted that they had ignored visuals on the websites and might want to include a relevant indicator in another evaluation. In addition, the focus group acknowledged that they are highly educated, interested, and very knowledgeable about local government and the Internet so their ability to surf the websites was probably not typical. Therefore, their accessibility ratings were probably inflated. Moreover, because focus group members do not work or live in the cities, they are not representative of the citizenry, and their overall satisfaction ratings may lack the local political and social context even if it is related to the actual website experience.

Finally, if a city wanted to use a similar focus group, it might be advantageous to also convey the city's intended goals behind providing a website. Still, the city needs to be open to the focus group adding unintended goals as well as other goals from their perspective of website visitors that may not have been considered or emphasized by the city.

continues

Some Evaluative Comments on City Websites in General

Focus group members also asked five people each their reactions to city websites they had visited. This nonrandom and small sample was meant to broaden the insights of the focus group. One thing was clear from the informal interviews: the respondents talked in terms of finding the information they wanted and how easy the website was to navigate. It appeared that the focus group was correct in its definition and priority of goals for a website. Another common reaction was that the respondents tended to be surprised and pleased with how much information was on the websites and especially pleased if they could register for recreation classes or pay bills or buy event tickets online. Interestingly, while the 60 interviewees were generally surprisingly pleased with city websites, this did not necessarily translate to overall impression of the city and the services offered. This was particularly true of the youngest respondents who may take a lot for granted and may have very high technical standards when it comes to the Internet. A final interesting reaction was that the younger respondents, while finding the information interesting on the website, had little use for what was on the website and thought they would probably not revisit.

References

Moon, M. J. (2002). The evaluation of e-government among municipalities: rhetoric or reality? *Public Administration Review, 62*, 424–433.

Norris, D. F., & Moon, M. J. (2005). Advancing e-government at the grassroots: Tortoise or hare? *Public Administration Review, 65*, 64–75.

Northrop, A. (2005). E-government: The URBIS cities revisited. In G. D. Garson (Ed.), *Handbook of public information systems*. New York: Marcel Dekker.

West, D. M. (2004). E-government and the transformation of service delivery and citizen attitudes. *Public Administration Review, 64*, 15–27.

Endnote

[1]Adriana A. Badillo, academic counselor for Gear Up Anaheim; Angela Carr, program director for Boys & Girls Clubs of Fullerton; Jason Chan, project manager for Social Science Research Center; Ray A. Childers, systems analyst; Kortney Dodd, police detective; David Green, UCI Extension Housing coordinator; David J. Kowalski, LAPD sergeant; Gloria Lujan, workers compensation specialist; Tom Philip, senior accountant; Fabian Villenas, senior management analyst; Nelida M. Yanez, paralegal; and Edgar J. Yu, victim specialist for the Victim Witness Assistance Program.

Public Information Technology, Organization Behavior, and Organization Theory

Organization Behavior and Organization Theory

Optimism has abounded in the discussion of the relationship of information technology (IT) to organization theory and organization behavior. Vannevar Bush, science advisor to Franklin Delano Roosevelt, was one of the early utopians. His 1945 *Atlantic Monthly* article, "As We May Think," envisioned a desk-sized "memex" which would give access to vast archives of books. In the 1960s, Marshall McLuhan (1964) popularized computer technology and telecommunications as forces that were creating a "global village" uniting everyone, everywhere, to everything. By 1980, when Alvin Toffler wrote *The Third Wave* about how telecommunications was creating an "infosphere," the utopian vision of computing as a democratizing and empowering force was well established. The vision of a "democratic information society" or "electronic democracy" has since been set forth for three decades by many other writers.

Matching democratic theses about the role of IT has been critical theory. This perspective could be traced back to fears about how totalitarian societies might consolidate their power through technology, as in George Orwell's famous novel, *1984*. More recently, Manuel Castells (1996, 1997, 1998) has presented a grand theory, backed by an enormous diversity of historical and empirical research. He wrote, "The rise of informationalism in this end of the millennium is intertwined with rising inequality and social exclusion throughout the world" (Castells, 1998, p. 70). International inequalities grow, particularly at the extremes, and groups are systematically denied the resources for meaningful survival of their cultural identity. "Black holes of information capitalism" appear, from which there is no empirically evident means to escape poverty and deidentification. Castells' theory is not far from those of Marxist and critical thinkers collected in McChesney, Wood, and Foster (1998), where the argument is made that the contradictions of capitalism are revealed in the growing tension between the democratic potential of info-tech and economic demands for profit that ultimately override this potential.

In this chapter we attempt to find a middle ground between optimism and pessimism by approaching organization theory and organization behavior empirically, first looking at the alleged effects of IT on organization structure and then on organization behavior. Does IT truly flatten organization structures by shrinking middle management? Does IT deterritorialize organizations through remote work? Is its long-run tendency centralizing or decentralizing? And perhaps most important, does IT tend to reinforce or erode existing organizational power structures? On terms of organization behavior, does IT intensify social networking and thus build social capital? Does IT really improve managerial decision making? In terms of organizational change, does IT promote the diffusion of innovation? Is IT linked to organizational evolution toward the consolidation of control? After investigating these key questions that relate IT to organization theory and organization behavior, the summary to this chapter relates the answers to these questions to the four theories that have been a theme to this book: technological determinism, reinforcement theory, sociotechnical theory, and systems theory.

EFFECTS OF IT ON ORGANIZATIONAL STRUCTURE

Flattening Organizational Structures by Shrinking Middle Management?

One of the most common structural predictions regarding IT is that it would have the effect of flattening organizations by cutting the ranks of middle management. This effect would come about because by using IT, top management could oversee lower ranks more easily. Automated feedback from the bottom would support top-level resource decisions without the need for middle echelons of supervisory interpreters of data from the rank and file. At the same time, it was argued, IT would facilitate increased decision-making authority among lower-level employees, eroding middle management from the bottom.

Flattening of organization structures has been reported to have been central to American private-sector productivity increases in the 1990s—increases fed by IT investment. A similar trend toward flatter organizational structures has been reported in the nonprofit sector (Clolery, 2000). What often happened was not so much wholesale elimination of a middle management layer but rather the absorption of some middle management tasks by IT and the reconstruction of new job descriptions and positions for tasks not automated. Command and control layers in the old structure became replaced by problem-oriented teams in the new, more flexible structure. Lower-level employees and teams took on added responsibilities, accounting for an estimated 25% decrease in the number of layers between chief executive officers and the shop floor (Ellis, 2003). While there is no doubt that organizational flattening has become a central reform strategy in the private sector and that IT enabled greater decision making at lower levels, what occurred was not a simple IT investment-organizational flattening cause and effect. Rather, regression analysis of private-sector organizational flattening data suggests that, if anything, flattening was tied to private-sector organizations becoming more human capital intensive and elevating the role of the human resource director (Ellis, 2003), with IT serving as a facilitating factor.

The private sector model of organizational flattening envisions that engineers, technicians, factory employees, and members of the sales force would work together in teams to develop new products in response to changing consumer demand. In doing so, these teams would organize themselves, assign work responsibilities, make decisions, and set goals in ways formerly the responsibility of a bygone layer of middle managers. Each point of this model is difficult to translate into the public sector. Consumer demand is much less volatile and is expressed more indirectly. Expert staff and operational managers are not empowered to do things in new ways on their own authority. Work responsibilities are usually circumscribed by civil service systems. Lower-level goal setting conflicts with the principles of democratic accountability embedded in legislation. In the public sector, the traditional layer of middle managers remains in place. And even were some agency to implement the private-sector model of organizational flattening, the reward structure providing incentive to do so is generally absent in the public sector.

Thus it is unsurprising that overall in the public sector there is little evidence that IT is changing organizational structure in the same way. Heintz and Bretschneider (2000) studied the use of IT in relation to restructuring in public organizations, asking if adoption of IT affected organizational structures, communications, and decision making. They found there was little empirical relationship between IT adoption and subsequent agency restructuring in the public sector. In the cases where restructuring occurred, managers reported only minimal effects on performance. While IT may improve performance directly, it is far less clear whether IT alters public organizational structure.

Public-sector research has supported the idea that IT is indeed associated with the downsizing of middle management—but only for centralized structures. If management is decentralist, IT may not reduce the ranks of middle management (Kraemer & Dedrick, 1997). Thus, in the centralized environment of the U.S. military, when the North American Defense Command installed the SAGE system of computer-controlled warning functions, the number of levels of management was reduced from five to four. More recently, the Coast Guard has made an organizational commitment to a flatter organizational structure, in part enabled by improved IT (Moody, 2004). Indeed, much of the strategic thinking about the modern "electronic battlefield" is based on Department of Defense (DOD) plans to combine highly centralized IT-based command and control with highly flexible combat teams having greater information and greater discretion to use it.

The popularity of imitating the supposed private-sector model has recently led under the Bush Administration to top-down quota-like mandates to reduce manager-to-employee ratios, as in the administration of the EPA Superfund. However, these sometimes successful efforts at organizational flattening are only peripherally driven by IT. The driver seems more to be the political power of myths and symbols drawn from the private sector, providing a rationale for governmental outsourcing and downsizing as a way of imitating the productivity gains of the private sector in the 1990s.

Deterritorializing Organizations Through Telework?

Early proponents of telecommuting believed IT would radically alter organizational structures in the future, creating "boundaryless organizations" that would have flatter hierarchies and operate in more flexible and reconfigurable ways no longer dependent on brick-and-mortar locations or even geographic territories.

Again, the private sector has provided the inspiration. Telework has proliferated in the private sector. By 1998, the Bureau of Labor Statistics reported that some 21 million Americans worked at home, though about half of these were merely bringing unpaid office work home. Using different measures, the International Telework Association and Council (ITAC) estimated 23.5 million Americans teleworked in 2003 (Joch, 2004). The progress of telework in the public sector has been slower. A 2002 Department of Labor report put private-sector telecommuting at 10% of the private-sector work force, compared to a 2% rate in the public sector.

Nonetheless, almost from the start, Congress has been sympathetic to the concept of telework, believing its spread would reduce the sizable costs of capital construction of office space. Congress had established the federal telecenter program in 1993. Initially there had been three telecenters (used by the Equal Employment Opportunity Commission, Interior, and Agriculture), all confined to the DC area. By 2002 there were 17 telecenters in the DC area and a few more elsewhere. Also in 2002, Congress appropriated $5.8 million to fund the Telework Consortium, which worked with General Services Administration (GSA) telecenters to test teleworking technology and with the Treasury Department to develop evaluation and measurement tools for telework projects.

Congress mandated that by 2003, 50% of federal workers be given the opportunity to telework. In response to a 2003 General Accounting Office (GAO) report criticizing federal agency telework plans as uncoordinated and inconsistent (GAO, 2003c), the Office of Personnel Management (OPM) and the GSA in 2003 launched a $500,000 effort to promote telework in 20 federal agencies. The Web portal www.telework.gov was redesigned as part of this promotional effort. A 2003 OPM survey of 77 federal agencies, found an increase, with 5% of the federal civilian work force teleworking. Teleworking ranged from 40.6% in the OPM, 31.7% in the Federal Deposit Insurance Corporation, and 30.6% in the Department of Education, down to 8% in Energy, only 1.4% in the State Department and 1.2% in the Department of Justice (Miller, 2003r). A GAO report found only about half of agencies would meet the 2003 deadline of offering telework to half their employees.

Congress turned the heat up in the FY 2005 appropriations bills, specifying that if Commerce, Justice, State, the Small Business Administration, the Securities and Exchange Commission, and the federal judiciary appropriations bills did not offer every eligible worker the opportunity to telecommute by mid-to-late January, 2005, they would lose $5 million under a provision passed as part of the fiscal 2005 Omnibus spending bill (Miller, 2004i). A subsequent study by CDW Government Inc. found only 1% more federal employees became involved in telework as a result, however (Miller, 2005h). Hoping to move telework into the fast lane in spite of mediocre progress, in 2005 federal and private-sector officials established the Telework Exchange to promote the benefits of teleworking. The exchange was endorsed by the Office of Management and Budget (OMB), the OPM, and the chairman of the House Government Reform Committee, and was sponsored by Intel, Citrix Systems, CDW-G, and other industries.

From a management viewpoint, telework promises increased productivity, greater ability to attract and maintain personnel who may value the flexibility of telecommuting, and when telework is implemented on a large scale, management may reap lower costs of office space. When telework is implemented through decentralized telecenters in various regions or neighborhoods, citizens may also perceive agencies to be "closer to the people." ITAC has estimated that organizations sponsoring telework cut turnover 30%, increased productivity 22%, and cut absenteeism 60%. Moreover, ITAC also estimated a well-equipped home office costs $3500 and setting up a telework program costs $25,000 in consulting and training—very modest investment costs compared to capital construction of office space (Joch, 2004).

However, telework has unattractive as well as attractive features. Historically, "cottage industries," where workers labored at home on piece work, constituted a system that oppressed workers and that was fought by labor unions. Unions remain skeptical toward such systems, including telework. Feminists also have critiqued telework as a form of return to the home for women (Zimmerman, 1990). Employees fear that working from home or even remotely can lead to isolation from the organization (Forester, 1989). Also, employees may feel that they will lose social interactions with other employees, which is generally a source of job satisfaction. Particularly for individuals with children, role conflict and role ambiguity may increase. For individuals suffering from workaholism, telework exacerbates the tendency to sacrifice normal dimensions of life for work tasks (Kaplan, 1996).

For their part, managers often feel telework eliminates direct "line of sight" supervision and requires the rethinking of supervisory roles, which can be threatening (Ellison, 2000). Telework poses much greater security problems for managers as well as networking issues. Sometimes it is a cost, not a savings, and agencies may resent paying "double overhead" for slots at federal telework centers. Moreover, in the public sector, managers may well find that any productivity savings revert to the department level, not the agency level, giving agency managers little incentive to promote telework.

In summary, the powerful forces for and against deterritorialization of organizational structures through telework mean that one may expect this to be a continuing trend, but one slow to spread and far from the revolution earlier predicted.

Centralizing or Decentralizing Organizational Structure?

The microcomputer revolution of the 1980s led many social scientists to associate IT with decentralization. Democratization and decentralization theories of IT foresaw a dramatic broadening of the span of control, shrinkage of middle management, and overthrow of Fordist hierarchy in favor of problem-centered teams. Workers, citizens, and consumers would gain control due to vastly increased access to information. Increased information would lead to greater market efficiency. Passive television viewing would yield to interactive and participatory forms of media. More time would be spent in online communication and groups, rebuilding social capital (Cohill & Kavanaugh, 1997), and education would become more accessible, widespread, and appropriate when delivered online. Nations that wanted to compete would democratize because information societies thrive in democratic settings. Even more idealistically, increased information would lead to greater international harmony in the global village while domestically, electronic communication would reinvigorate democracy and increase social capital, reversing, among other things, the long-time decline in voting levels. In a fast-changing world, the future would lie with multidisciplinary problem-oriented team organization designed to be rapidly responsive and operating by and through IT (Tapscott & Caston, 1992).

In the field of public administration, G. N. Reschenthaler and Fred Thompson (1996) applied democratization and decentralization theory to their concept of "new public management." If increased levels of information made markets more efficient, they reasoned, then increased information would lessen the need to regulate the economy. For instance, regulation of airlines and other industries would become unnecessary because such things as landing rights (or pollution rights in industry) could be securitized and government regulation could be replaced by the self-regulation of the market. This "new public management" perspective believed that IT could make New Zealand-type government possible, where the public sector shrank and was handled more by electronic markets.

Early IT offices were centralized. Centralization was seen as bringing economies of scale, less redundancy, more integration of databases, and better ability to serve strategic goals. However, the personal computing revolution in the 1980s and early 1990s was marked by the rise of "end-user computing" and reliance on distributed networks. A 1993 public-sector survey by Danziger, Kraemer, Dunkle, and King (1993) showed end users to be just as happy with decentralized department-level computing services as with centralized IT units that had hitherto been dominant. By the late 1990s, however, the pendulum swung back toward recentralization (Kraemer & Dedrick, 1997), which in the 2000s flowered under the banners of "enterprise architecture" and "standardization."

Illustrative of centralization trends was the decision of the e-Rulemaking project for all federal agencies to opt for a centralized docket system for regulations rather than a decentralized agency-centric one. The project team estimated the centralized system would cost $20 million whereas the decentralized one would cost $80 million. They also estimated it would take one year to build the centralized system but three years to build a decentralized one (Miller, 2004j). Likewise, in 2005 the GSA was calling for the centralization of all government purchases except weapons systems, based on new IT capacities for central purchasing and based explicitly on the OMB's "enterprise" strategy for government-wide applications (Miller, 2005b). In 2005, the Defense Intelligence Agency (DIA) moved to centralize and take over operational and budgetary control of 10 unified combatant commands, making some 800 military and civilian workers across the military services DIA employees (Onley, 2005a). Even the National Aeronautics and Space Administration, usually a poster child for IT matters, was criticized by its Inspector General for "fragmented organization" of its IT organizational structure, prompting calls for centralization (Wait, 2005). Throughout the federal government, the central OMB and DOD agendas for IT was similar: achieve economies through centralized, federal-wide (or at least consolidated) IT initiatives.

The federal drive toward centralization was paralleled at the state level. In the late 1990s and into the 2000s, financial austerity led states to transfer IT personnel from operating departments back into the central IT office, reversing some of the earlier decentralization. For instance, in 2002 the state of Virginia created the Virginia Information Technologies Agency, which consolidated state IT functions in a single agency, eliminating three prior IT agencies and two IT oversight boards, all prompted by that state's $6 billion budget shortfall. In 2003, the state of New Hampshire transferred 315 IT employees from nine state agencies into its new Office of Information Technology, with the goal of saving money through standardization of operating systems, software, and purchasing. Also in 2003, the state of Texas, as part of its health and human services consolidation, also consolidated IT functions (McKeith, 2004).

Although it is true that recent centralization is consistent with some degree of distributed processing, from the viewpoint of bureaucratic structure, the centralization was real. Power really did shift from department chief information officers (CIOs) to central IT authorities in the OMB. Departments were taxed in real dollars shifted from other objectives to support centralized Quicksilver e-government and security initiatives. Agencies had to give up custom applications in favor of one-size-fits-all enterprise applications. Lower-level IT investment priorities increasingly had to follow central priorities, shifting, for example, from e-government toward IT security after 9/11. Throughout the federal government, any new large-scale investment in IT had to be justified in business plans that demonstrated conformity to centralized federal-wide enterprise planning.

Ironically, the present era of IT centralization is rooted in antibureaucratic ideas about managing by results and about reengineering government processes to achieve those results. In the United States, the concept of results-oriented government has morphed into an elaborate OMB system for performance tracking and forcing agencies to develop OMB-sanctioned business plans. Innate to this process is the transfer of discretion from departmental CIOs in the periphery to OMB administrators at the center. There is a direct link from the concepts of managing by results, eliminating duplication, and leveraging IT to the contemporary reality of recentralization, enterprise architecture, and other forms of large-scale IT-based consolidation.[1] The National Performance Review under Clinton in the 1990s started with the rejection of traditional bureaucracy, but in the 2000s the emergent centralized IT reality strayed very far from this starting point—yet was connected to it by the inner logic that results must be embedded in information systems designed and enforced from the center.

Reinforcing or Eroding Organizational Power Structures?

The power structure issue is, of course, the focus of reinforcement theory. With many exceptions, most research on the effect of IT on power structure has suggested that IT reinforces existing power arrangements, whether they be centralized or decentralized, authoritarian or autocratic (Coyne & Wiszniewski, 1999; Kolleck, 1993; Kraemer & King, 1986). Hood (2000), for instance, found that IT was unlikely to change organizational control patterns, except insofar as different cultures use IT differently. Agre (2002) found reinforcement (amplification) theory to be a better explanatory model than technological determinism, concluding that the Internet is rapidly amplifying existing political relationships, not overthrowing them. This research is in line with that of other researchers going back to the 1970s, including the noted work of Kraemer and his associates, which consisted of a study of local governments that found that information and communication technologies' (ICT) decisions tended to amplify the political power of the dominant coalition within the organization (Danziger, Dutton, Kling, & Kraemer, 1982; Kraemer & Dedrick, 1997).

Some have gone beyond reinforcement theory to argue that IT confers power not on the powers-that-be, but on a new class of technocrats. Illustrative of this argument is the work of Steven Vallas (2000), who studied how automation of a paper pulp plant altered organizational power structure. Sensors and statistical quality control replaced human judgment and workers' upward mobility in the organization became closed as engineering credentials became necessary even for foremanlike positions. Process rules became embedded in computer programs that regulated work and that workers could not alter. Vallas thus found automation was a control strategy for process engineers, who used IT to restrict the role of skilled workers to ensure the supremacy of technocratic control over craftsmanship in regulating processes within the plant. Whereas some (Zuboff, 1988) had argued that IT would be a democratizing force that would overturn the hierarchical, Fordist pattern of work, Vallas found that IT was used to consolidate the power and privilege of professional, technical, and managerial employees at the expense of less educated workers.

By supporting Rifkin (1995) and other critical theorists in this way, Vallas was arguing that in the process of IT implementation, technocrats wield cultural capital that is socially defined as legitimate, and they could use this to invoke a technical vocabulary whose power reflected its symbolic value in achieving power. Vallas's thesis was that IT systems have to do with the construction of subculture boundaries within an organization. In the case he studied, technocrats wanted to define manual workers as illegitimate and backward and also wanted to show that engineering knowledge was essential and that they alone could supply it. This thesis was supportive of the "power-process approach" articulated by Robert J. Thomas (1994). Power-process theory, a variant of control theory, argued that while on the surface IT interventions are based on rational efficiency/effectiveness factors, in reality, process innovations are driven by underlying patterns of conflict and struggle for power.

Some research emphasizes how information access can confer power on new participants in the decision-making process (Innes, 1988) and open up organizational power structures (Kraemer & Dedrick, 1997, p. 106) even to nontechnocrats. In the private sector it is clear that e-commerce based on IT has brought major challenges to traditional brick-and-mortar firms (Gereffi, 2001). In the public sector, however, even for technocrats the trend has been for increased outsourcing of IT functions, diminished control by CIOs, and increased centralized power through the OMB. While some efforts toward organizational flattening do increase lower-level discretion (the Army platoon in the "electronic battlefield" for instance), this has been accompanied by an increased centralization of command and control and, indeed, that is integral to the very concept of organizational flattening. Lower-level team discretion rarely represents an erosion of top-level control and may very well reflect consolidation of traditional power structure under new forms.

In terms of historical precedent, writers such as Mosco (1998, p. 58) have drawn analogies to radio, which in its early days was also touted as a two-way technological revolution destined to bring radical democratization through creation of virtual communities in the ether—but which, in fact, saw the market forces of commercialism become overwhelmingly dominant, leaving the vision of democratic community through amateur radio a socially peripheral curiosity. Critical theory emphasizes that the boundaries of information openness can be controlled from the top down and can be circumscribed in ways inconsistent with democratization/empowerment visions of the future "information society." As Singapore demonstrates, and Northrop and Kraemer (2000) acknowledge, it is entirely possible to "leap into the Information Age" while suppressing civil liberties, freedom of the press, and democratization. Kraemer's study of the Internet in eight nations comes to the conclusion, "Computers and information technology actually reinforce the existing power structure. The Internet may increase the 'digital divide,' not decrease it" (Kraemer, 2004). Power may be defined, as the famous political scientist, Harold Lasswell, did, in terms of "who gets what." By this criterion, the Gini index of wealth and income inequality has grown markedly more unequal in the United States and elsewhere during the last quarter century of massive IT investment, suggesting reinforcement rather than erosion of traditional power structures (Parayil, 2005). This finding supports the conclusions of May (2002), who found IT was not particularly associated with new labor conditions or new social relations.

EFFECTS OF IT ON ORGANIZATIONAL BEHAVIOR

Does IT Weaken Organizational Norms Through Deindividuation?

Deindividuation is the process of alienation of the individual from social norms. It has been linked to IT through the argument that the absence of visual and social cues and absence of close physical proximity in computer-mediated communication (CMC) undermines processes of identification with social norms (Lea & Spears, 1991). Also, from a control viewpoint, when employees are not observable, it is difficult for managers to hold them accountable for their contributions to team tasks. This in turn can lead to peer perceptions of effort inequality and to further undermining of group cohesion. In this argument, if social order rests on cultural enchantment, computer use is said to lead to disenchantment in the Weberian sense. Kiesler, Siegel, and McGuire (1991), for instance, found that CMC removed the contextual salience of social norms, weakening conformity to them. Likewise, Loch and Conger (1996) linked computer use to deindividuation and degradation of social norms pertaining to computer use.

It should be noted, however, that much of the research on deindividuation and alienation from social norms has been conducted not on employees using CMC, but rather has focused on groups such as computer hackers, whose aggression is seen to be facilitated by anonymity and by social distance from their victims (Kabay, 1998) or on similar groups, such as "flamers" in anonymous group support networks (Reinig & Mejias, 2004). Nonetheless, workplace deindividuation can exist. In a study for the RAND Corporation, Wainfan and Davis (2004) observed increased polarization, deindividuation, and disinhibition in CMC environments, with individuals becoming more extreme, less sensitive to interpersonal aspects of their messages, but more honest and candid. Overall, Wainfan and Davis found that CMC can reduce efficiency (as measured in time to solution) of work processes even as it broadens the range of inputs and ideas.

In the workplace, CMC is apt to supplement face-to-face interactions, not replace them, and anonymity is typically not present, greatly lessening the possibility of deindividuation. While there is some research demonstrating the existence of deindividuation in workgroup settings (Clarke, 2002), research suggests that even in CMC environments, proper design of virtual spaces can eliminate problems suggested by early deindividuation theory (Shachaf & Hara, 2002). This corroborates earlier sociotechnical theory research that suggested that deindividuation depends upon the specific manner of implementation of IT within the organization and is not intrinsic to IT per se (Mantovani, 1994).

Does IT Intensify Social Networking and Thus Build Social Capital?

Social capital may be defined as those resources inherent in social relations that facilitate collective action. Social capital resources include trust, norms, and networks of association representing any group that gathers consistently for a common purpose. A norm of a culture high in social capital is reciprocity, which encourages bargaining, compromise, and pluralistic politics. Another norm is belief in the equality of citizens, which encourages the formation of cross-cutting groups.

Social capital theory points almost in the opposite direction from de-individuation theory. Because IT increases the level of horizontal and vertical communication within organizations, it is argued that social networking is also intensified. These arguments are all part of a broader argument that interactive networking leads to the accumulation of social capital, which has been declining in the face of technologies such as passive television (Putnam, 1995a, 1995b), but which may be rebuilt through new interactive information media (Calabrese & Borchert, 1996). Thus Blanchard and Horan (2000) surveyed a California community and found citizen interest by at least two out of three respondents in developing virtual communities around education, community activities, and government and politics. They interpreted this as an indication that technology may be leading people into an era that reverses the decline of social capital as represented by lower levels of civic interest. Numerous other studies emphasize the capacity of the Internet to promote political organizing and mobilization, even when organizers have few resources by traditional standards (Bimber, 1998).

Of course, as Kraemer and Dedrick (1997, pp. 103–104) observe, the increased communication can have both positive (more information sharing) and negative (more performance monitoring) effects from the point of view of the individual employee. Moreover, other scholars (Alexander & Pal, 1998) have reasoned that the Internet could actually increase levels of civic disinterest and accelerate social fragmentation and the decline of social capital. The substitution of Internet and cable news consumption for readership of locally owned newspapers, the replacement of face-to-face public hearings with e-mail feedback under e-regulation, and the substitution of mass Internet mobilization of political contributions for traditional ward organization of neighborhoods are all strong arguments that local-level social capital may be diminished in the modern information age.

The role of IT with respect to social capital is bidirectional. High levels of social capital, such as preexisting strong nonelectronic networks, constitute a success factor in establishment of electronic-based networks (Fukuyama, 1995). At the same time, the spread of IT creates networking infrastructure that encourages the formation of social capital (Calabrese & Borchert, 1996). As discussed earlier, IT can also have an anonymizing, deindividuating effect that eats away at social norms and erodes social capital.

Does IT Improve Managerial Decision Making?

Because IT increases the level of information in the organization, one could conjecture that it would improve managerial decision making. Many information systems are designed for just this purpose, such as executive information systems (EIS), decision support systems, expert systems, computer models, and performance tracking systems. These uses of IT force managers to be explicit about goals and objectives, and goal clarity has been thought to be a prerequisite to effective managerial decision making.

In spite of potential benefits to managerial decision making, there is little evidence that such an effect actually occurs. Kraemer and Dedrick speculate that there may be more effect at the operational level than at the managerial level because operating management deals more directly with information systems (Kraemer & Dedrick, 1997, pp. 104–105). Use of IT to improve decision making is reflected in the spread of expert systems and their use to displace time spent by human managers. Expert systems have spread most where processes are stable and predictable, involve quantitative inputs and outputs, and answers to management decisions can be reduced to agreed-upon algorithms. For instance, expert systems have reduced some management positions in the insurance industry. Without reducing the ranks of management, expert systems have become common in such arenas as agricultural allocation of fertilizers and medical diagnosis of symptoms. However, expert systems are rare in the corporate boardroom or in meetings of agency policy boards.

At times, greater information can reduce the quality of managerial decision making. Research on "groupthink" and "decision by committee" suggests that judgments made after group discussion will be more extreme in the same direction as the average of individual judgments made prior to discussion, due to the tendency of participants to conform to perceived group orientations. Greater IT-facilitated group discussion can intensify attitudes, beliefs, attitudes, polarizing judgments. To the extent that e-mail and other forms of IT communicate average judgments more quickly, a premature consensus may emerge that squelches the innovative as well as the deviant, yet may itself represent polarized thinking. Improved group decision making is associated with a nonjudgmental leadership that encourages all views to be made known, lessens the pressure for social conformity, and reduces the risks of expressing innovative views. These factors are independent of use or nonuse of IT.

There is a large literature on IT and decision making, reflected for instance in the *International Journal of Information Technology and Decision Making*, but almost all of it focuses on research and case studies on specific IT-based decision-making techniques without ever assessing the larger question of whether IT has actually improved the overall level and quality of managerial decision making. IT may provide greater and better information at higher levels of decision making, but whether qualitatively different and better decisions emerge as outcomes is simply uncharted research territory.

IT AND THEORIES OF ORGANIZATIONAL CHANGE

Does IT Promote the Diffusion of Innovation?

Organization members' acceptance of innovations can be associated with a variety of motives. Managerial desire for control can lead to seeking out innovations that augment control, as many information systems do (Bugler & Bretschneider, 1993). Likewise, the organization's need for information sharing, aided by IT, can lead to innovation as managers seek to fulfill their missions in an increasingly interdependent world (Bugler & Bretschneider, 1993). Then too, there is the tendency of middle managers to push technology if only as a way to demonstrate new contributions to the organization, contributions that may be recognized through advancement (Caudle, 1990). Innovation is also encouraged through force of example and peer learning as managers encounter innovations at professional gatherings and in peer networks (Kraemer & Dedrick, 1997, pp. 91–93). Finally, simple training transmits innovations from academia and best practices from the field, making these innovations seem to be part of professionalization for the manager and professional status for the organization (Northrop, Dunkle, Kraemer, & King, 1994).

Innovation is change, and IT has a disruptive aspect that has promoted change on a large scale. As Lyytinen and Rose (2003) have shown with regard to private-sector systems development organizations, at times the advent of IT in forms such as the Internet can have pervasive, radical, disruptive effects on organizational processes. Disruption itself creates necessary but not sufficient conditions for subsequent innovation. The rise of the international New Economy is based on an IT-driven sharp drop in communications costs, which in turn has promoted specialized production networks involving producers in many countries. The ensuing intense competition in quality, price, and delivery has disrupted traditional patterns of commerce and forced a rapid pace of innovation among multinational firms.

Not all strategies for linking IT to innovation are equally effective. Research on IT's role in diffusion of innovation has included study of technology push versus market pull patterns. In general, it has been found that projects that seek to promote innovation through top-down introduction of technology are less likely to be successful than bottom-up strategies that are driven by local demand. Jansen (1995) found, for instance, that a Norwegian program for introducing technology to rural areas had little impact because it did not tie general development strategies to local market forces. Market-pull forces, Jansen found, could be more easily be adapted to local conditions and needs and lay a better basis for implementation success. Baark and Heeks (1998) similarly found inattention to market pull forces underlay limited impact of technology diffusion projects they studied in China. In contrast, market pull dynamics characterize the rise of the New Economy discussed above. The New Economy innovation system is led by large retailing superstores that group central facilities to meet consumer demand, reaching out to final consumers, constantly monitoring the level and nature of demand, and converting this into demand on their own suppliers and ultimately into online transactions and delivery to the market.

IT does not always lead to innovation. For instance, expectations in the late 1990s that e-government would lead federal agencies to "reinvent" themselves are now acknowledged to have fallen far short (Gerin, 2005). Likewise, Mossberger's (2000) study of an IT innovation in the educational sector led to the finding that IT-driven ease of access to best practices information may not lead to innovation diffusion but may instead increase information overload decision-making paralysis. Information systems development may be thwarted by cultural differences among the parties to implementation, as in the failure of an automated record retrieval system at the U.S. Bureau of Land Management (Rivera & Casias, 2001; Rivera & Rogers, 2004). Moore and Benbasat (1991), based on the work of Everette Rogers (1962), identified eight factors that condition the diffusion of innovations. These are relative advantage of an innovation compared to present processes, compatibility with the prevailing organization, ease of use, result demonstrability, image (potential to increase the status of the organization and system users), visibility, trialability (opportunity to experiment), and voluntariness. In fact, all of the factors discussed in Chapter 13 on success and failure factors could mean IT will not lead to innovation in a specific setting.

In Rogers' (2003) influential theory of the diffusion of innovation, emphasis is placed on the role of early adopters in promoting imitation and eventually leading to a "tipping point," after which innovation spreads rapidly, following an S-shaped curve. A succession of groups make the innovation decision, starting with the innovators and followed in turn by early adopters, the early majority, the late majority, and laggards. In Rogers' description, a critical group is the early adopters, who include opinion leaders who gain status because of their reputation for making careful decisions based on assessment of costs and benefits. While not itself based on the study of information systems, an implication of Rogers' theory of innovation is that for the diffusion of innovation to occur in any large-scale IT undertaking, emphasis must be placed on reaching out to organizational and community opinion leaders. Innovation diffusion efforts must be carefully targeted toward separate adopter groups, not undertaken in a sweeping one-size-fits-all marketing effort (Jurison, 2000). The literatures on market-pull forces and on success factors in IT implementation both link successful diffusion of innovation to what sociotechnical theorists have long emphasized—participative involvement of leading stakeholders in the proposed technology project.

Is IT Linked to Organizational Evolution Toward the Consolidation of Control?

Systems are created for control. Current trends toward centralization and enterprise architecture have given renewed plausibility to control theories of IT and organizational change. At the heart of control theory is the belief that the inner telos of information technology is a drive toward ever more effective systems control. In control theory, systems are selected primarily for their control functionality and only secondarily for their efficiency. Translated into practical terms, control theory predicts that business, government, the military, and other elites will use IT to increase surveillance and control over employees and internal processes, and insofar as they can, to regulate their external environments as well. Thanks to IT, surveillance is at an unprecedented level not accessible in the past even to totalitarian societies, albeit in a more benign manner. Control theory finds democratization theory simply wrong: Singapore demonstrates it is entirely possible to be an "information society" while suppressing free speech and free press and not being democratic.

The core tenets of control theory may be supplemented with optional, more controversial corollaries:

1. Within the workplace, technocratic elites displace unions of workers. Systems knowledge replaces craft knowledge. The counterbalancing of management and union within the organization is replaced by the alliance of management and technocracy.
2. In each sphere of activity, IT leads interactions to become depersonalized. Social workers treat clients categorically rather than individually. Doctors become driven by computerized scheduling and cost-accounting. Military officers are distanced from destruction and death, and so on.
3. IT supports a global economy of multinational corporations able to shift resources across borders to defeat unions, smaller competitors, and even governments.

4. Between nations, the international digital divide reinforces a form of permanent technological apartheid, supporting unequal terms of trade between rich and poor nations.

In the more far-reaching version of control theory, John Kenneth Galbraith's mid-20th century notion of "countervailing powers" is replaced by a 21st-century monism of "private government" by multinationals in what Manuel Castells (1996, 1997, 1998) has called "informational capitalism." Global politics ceases to be about competing national economies and becomes about national and subnational pockets of resistance, where local and regional struggles attempt to preserve cultural identity by resisting multinationalization (Barber, 1992).

The literature supporting control theory is extensive. For example, a study of the use of EIS by Vandenbosch (1999) found that control and power largely drive the perceptions of benefits associated with using management information in organizations. Similarly, Henman and Adler (2003) studied the Social Security Administration and found that computerization had generally increased management control over both staff and claimants, contrary to democratization theory notions about how IT empowers employees.

The central argument against the concept of IT leading to consolidation of control comes from the sociotechnical systems school, whose advocates believe that IT projects often fail precisely due to top-down methods of implementation. What is needed, they say, are participative approaches that seek to adapt technology to human relationships and patterns of interaction (Trist, 1973; Trist & Murray, 1990; Trist, Emery, Murray, & Trist (1997). Sociotechnical theory predicted that in the long run, genuinely participatory IT design processes would win out over centralized planning. The Tavistock Institute and other centers of sociotechnical systems (STS) consulting prescribed meaningful user involvement in system design, planning for skills upgrading rather than deskilling, having an incentive system that rewarded stakeholders, and in general avoiding top-down implementation (Emery & Trist, 1960). However, as centralization overrides agency control, any forms of participation in systems design become subservient to rationalization of enterprise architecture. The course of centralization of IT in the last decade has shown the ability of implementation principles antithetical to STS to move ahead quite effectively.

A recent version of sociotechnical theory is the "technology enactment theory" put forward by Jane Fountain (2001) in her book, *Building the Virtual State*. As Carl Grafton (2003) has observed, this is a restatement and updating of the sociotechnical viewpoint. Technology enactment theory holds that technological possibilities are enacted into technological realities in ways strongly affected by organizational, political, and cultural environments, with nondeterministic results that cannot be predicted from technological considerations alone. Technology enactment theory is consistent with the fact that large-scale public sector IT projects often fail, with neglect of human factors commonly found to be at the root of the problem (Garson, 1995).

The relative importance of human factors over narrowly technological factors had been the central thrust of sociotechnical theory since the 1960s (Emery & Trist, 1965) and subsequently of Ken Kraemer and his associates on the urban information system (URBIS) studies (Kraemer & King, 1986), which focused on the relative importance of political factors over narrowly technological factors in public information systems. Similar concepts of the embeddedness of technology decisions in the group culture are at the heart of the theory of the social construction of technology, developed by Bijker and his associates (Bijker, 1995; Bijker, Hughes, & Pinch, 1987; Pinch & Bijker, 1986). Gascó (2003) similarly has developed "new institutionalism" theory, explicitly following Fountain, arguing that technology creates perceived win-win situations for all actors, prompting organizational change, but the direction of change may be positive or negative, depending on technological, managerial, and political variables. "Governance theory" likewise is a loose, currently popular constellation of ideas in the sociotechnical tradition, holding that the process of governing transcends the institutions of government and that the enhancement of democratic governance rests in part on leveraging ICT choices in creative ways that are not technologically determined.

At the global level, the drive toward control and centralization takes the form of what has sometimes gone under the label of "global integration theory" (Garson, 2000, pp. 601–603). Northrop and Kraemer (2000) have demonstrated the close link between computerization in a society and its level of socioeconomic development. Broad diffusion of computing is associated not only with advanced industrialization, but also with provision of mass education, the permeation of all forms of "information society," such as widespread use of telephones and television, and with provision of open access to information. Some go so far as to argue that information society requires information openness, for which democratization is a prerequisite (Kedzie, 1995). The clear implication is that nations that want to compete must democratize as well as computerize, and that democratization and computerization are mutually reinforcing processes.

Somewhat along the lines of Fountain's technology enactment theory, global integration view emphasizes that if the powers that be do not take purposeful remedial actions, the global digital divide will become permanent (Ferguson, 1998). Without government regulatory actions, world financial markets will become dangerously susceptible to manipulation of multinational corporations (Soros, 1998). Without government protocols on technology, multinational corporations will monopolize technology to create worldwide dependencies. Without affirmative steps by government to protect cultural identities, multinational (but heavily American) domination of media and information flow will overwhelm local cultures. And of course, in the military sector, the U.S. government itself (not multinationals) is well along the road to monopolizing the means of global military integration (Golden, 1998).

As infrastructure becomes more complicated and resources become more interdependent, communication levels increase exponentially. In such an environment, organizations respond by seeking to implement information systems that will restore reliability, integration, and control with respect to the flow of information. For instance, in the private sector, leading Japanese and U.S. software firms have largely rejected reengineering corporate organization and have avoided large-scale outsourcing. Instead their strategy has emphasized maintaining control over purchasing and development (Rapp, 2002). Management is forced to reinvent structure as the organization's size and complexity increase. Managers seek new structures that will allow delegation of decision making without abdicating control of the organization (Fletcher & Taplin, 2001).

The consolidation of control is about integration, not about centralization. Based on a study of 70 global corporations, Beaman and Guy (2005) found that both organizations that start centralized (often due to applying a domestic organizational model to the global environment) and those that start decentralized (often due to acquisitions), over time evolve toward distributed networks that are optimal for efficiency and effectiveness. In the public sector, the evolution of strategic planning for IT, discussed in Chapter 11, is all about government-wide integration and control, yet distributed networks are promoted for purposes of access to data and to computer tools. The discussion of centralization versus decentralization that was so prominent in the 1980s and early 1990s has given way to a realization that distributed integration is the synthesis that allows organizations to pursue control over their internal and external environments.

SUMMARY

Systems theory focuses on the drive toward ever more comprehensive and integrated systems involving greater control for decision makers but also better feedback from the bottom. Systems theorists often believe that IT can allow a wider span of control at the top, allowing the flattening of organizational structures and working to undergird a telework revolution. System theorists focus on the integrating effects of IT, which are seen to transcend centralization and decentralization. Their analysis tends to be apolitical, but systems analysts in practical administration see their role as consulting to and for top management. They are not uncomfortable with the concept that their work reinforces the goals, values, and mission articulated by powers at the top. They tend to see employee resistance as irrational and temporary. They see IT ultimately as a force to strengthen organizational norms, not weaken them. Systems theorists emphasize networking and see networking as a primary way to build up organizational resources, consistent with social capital theory. Improving management decision making is a prime goal of systems theories and analysts, who also see IT as the carrier of innovation. They are more apt to see successful systems implementations as increasing control at all levels than consolidating control at the top. They prefer apolitical descriptions of information systems that minimize broader social, political, and international impacts of information systems on society.

Though technological determinist theory tends to be scorned in the academic literature, it is alive and well among popularizers and detractors of the potential of IT. Technological determinists predict more and more IT, marching forward with little resistance, carried by force of example. Though both utopian and dystopian varieties of technological determinism exist, they unite in predicting sweeping impacts of IT. They agree that IT will flatten organizational structures, but utopians focus on this leading to greater efficiency while dystopians focus on it leading to greater employee surveillance and control. Technological determinists agree telework will deterritorialize organizations, but utopians see this as a new era of employee choice and freedom whereas dystopians see it as a revival of nineteenth-century piecework, characterized by worker isolation and exploitation. With regard to effects on power structure, the utopian determinists are polar opposites of their dystopian colleagues. The former believe IT will usher in a revolution of democratization and decentralization and the latter foresee new forms of electronic serfdom. Both the utopians and dystopians tend to agree IT will reinforce organizational norms, and both believe information networking will become the ubiquitous basis for economic and governmental activity. The utopian determinists are inclined to believe that more information will translate more or less directly into better managerial decision making, whereas the dystopians are apt to see IT making the same old decision-making machinery run better, perhaps using the symbolic power of IT to legitimate what would have been done anyway. It follows that the utopians see innovation spreading everywhere, and the dystopians see instead the consolidation of information capitalism with the primary innovation being the deepening of social control over rank-and-file employees and over citizens at large.

The central message of sociotechnical theorists is that without participatory attention to human factors, information systems will fail to fulfill their promise. They emphasize the free will of systems designers. Will middle management be eliminated? Will telework displace conventional work? Will the organization centralize? Decentralize? Alter in its power structure? It is all open for choice. Enlightened managers will choose to invest heavily in human capital and make technology subservient to human factors. Through participatory, enlightened management of IT projects, employee identification with the organization will become much stronger. Through the good experiences with IT that sociotechnical planning brings, networks will fulfill human needs and the social capital of the organization will increase. By delegating great discretion to the bottom, where the factors of operation are better known, operational decision making will improve while at the same time top management decisions, freed from excessive operational detail, will also be better targeted and will become more effective. The role of top management is to unleash the creativity of the bottom, letting innovation proliferate, often with the aid of IT. The evolution of the organization is not so much toward ever more integrated control from the top as it is toward ever more dynamic and creative marshaling of the organization's human resources to utilize technology to better fulfill the mission of the organization.

Reinforcement theory, finally, operates under the premise that organizational conflict and the struggle for power are the natural focus of organizational life. IT is a tool and like all tools may be used by the power structure "ins" and as well as by the "outs," by top management and by unions, by technocrats and by rank-and-file employees. However, the power structure "ins" are in a better position to have more IT tools, more resources to deploy IT operations, more ability to make technocrats their "hired guns," and, often, more experience in playing the game of power. Reinforcement theorists are most at home in discussing how IT reinforces organizational power structures and how IT serves in the process of organizational evolution toward the consolidation of control (which is not necessarily centralization). They agree with the sociotechnical theorists that whether organizational structures are flattened or organizations are deterritorialized through telework are matters of choice. They predict the choices will be made that increase or at least preserve control from the top, and managers' perceptions of what is in the interest of their own power may vary from setting to setting. Top management will disagree, for instance, on whether telework increases or decreases their control. Top management will not assume, as technological determinists often seem to do, that IT is an automatic engine of innovation and progress. Rather they will require proposed IT innovations to submit business plans that prove their advantage to those who control the reins of organizational power. Top managers are cognizant of the power implications of proposed IT systems and at the end of the day, they choose systems that reinforce their own power advantage.

Each of these four theoretical viewpoints (systems theory, technological determinism, sociotechnical theory, reinforcement theory) arose and remain popular to this day because each contains truths. Each is able to explain certain aspects of the topics covered in this book. Systems theory is at its best in understanding the logic of and drive for integration illustrated, for instance, in the IT guidance provided by the OMBC, which draws explicitly from systems analysis. Technological determinism is most compelling in its predictions about the spread of IT in the public sector, in e-government for example, and in accounting for the fact that managers frequently feel they do not have the freedom of choice other theories emphasize but instead in the long run feel compelled to follow the path of technology. The central contribution of sociotechnical theory is emphasizing that information systems first and foremost rest on human resources, not technology, and thus IT failures are generally traced to human factors problems and IT success rests on prior investment in human capital. Reinforcement theory extends this recognition of the importance of human factors to bring into the explanation an appreciation of the role of conflict over control and power, seeing IT efforts not as sanitized technical systems but rather as organizational moves in a strategic chess game centered on winning power.

Likewise, each of these four theoretical perspectives has difficulty explaining some aspects of IT. Systems theorists attempt to incorporate human factors but on the whole, its central logic of rational integration leads in the direction of one-size-fits-all implementation from the top. Technological determinists are not very good at explaining why superior technologies may lose out to inferior ones (beta to VHS, for instance) or at explaining the slow growth of superior technologies (Linux versus Windows), or for that matter, why technology spreads more rapidly in one setting than in another. Sociotechnical theorists have much to contribute about IT implementation, but their common assumption that there is a consensual basis for all stakeholders to an IT effort sometimes is less useful than reinforcement theory's understanding that different stakeholders may have different interests and are locked in a struggle for power. Finally, reinforcement theory has difficulty accounting for the fact that IT does lead to substantial changes in organizational structure (the New Economy for instance) that are not well explained by notions that IT reinforces existing power arrangements.

In this chapter we have discussed the relative lack of correlation between IT investment on the one hand and organizational restructuring on the other. While not highly correlated with IT investment, nonetheless we are seeing some of the predictions of IT development, such as organizational flattening and teleworking, make slow inroads into the public sector. These developments are clearly dependent upon IT investment. Although the research is not conclusive, it appears likely that investment in human capital and the development of social capital may explain these facts and both play much larger roles than either systems theory or technological determinism have suggested but which have been pointed to by sociotechnical theory. It also appears that reinforcement theory has much to contribute in emphasizing control considerations in explaining the course of telework: the slowness of its spreading does seem due in large part to managerial fears of loss of control, while at the same time addressing these concerns seems key to successful implementation.

This chapter has also discussed the recentralization of IT operations, the tendency of IT to reinforce structures of power, and the tendency of organizations to evolve toward consolidation of control, albeit using distributed networks. Networks do seem to develop social and organizational capital, but to what end? If one theorizes that that end is in support of the mission, goals, and values of those who hold power in organizations, one would expect the outcome to be a form of elite cultural hegemony. A melding of social capital theory, network theory, and reinforcement theory would explain the relative absence of deindividuation, the technocratic drive toward centralization of IT operations on an enterprise-wide basis, and the fact that outcomes such as e-government are implemented in ways that generally do not enact the radical and participatory potential of information and communications systems.

It has been outside the scope of this book to do more than point out the relation of prevailing theories (systems theory, technological determinism, sociotechnical theory, reinforcement theory) to major topics and trends in public-sector information systems. No "unified field theory" of public information systems has been presented. However, the practical world of IT does have theoretical implications. One's theoretical perspective will guide how one goes about interpreting the potential and promise of IT and will inform the choices one makes about its direction. Those who claim to be "practical" and "have no theory" inevitably make assumptions about the nature and direction of IT. Not infrequently these assumptions become those of technological determinism, assuming the inevitable march forward by the force of sheer technology. It is better to be explicit about theoretical assumptions, to examine them critically, and to be open to the synthesis of ideas. That synthesis must be cognizant of certain basic facts about the evolution of IT: that it involves political choices over policy, power, and control.

DISCUSSION QUESTIONS

1. How has IT investment in private and nonprofit organizations affected middle management? What structural changes have occurred? Is this unique to public organizations?
2. What conflicting viewpoints exist with respect to teleworking? What action has Congress taken to promote telework? What is the usual managerial view of telework?
3. What are the organizational benefits of a centralized IT office? What are the costs? How does this relate to an organization's management system?
4. Describe reinforcement theory's traditional view of IT with respect to power structure.
5. How is IT related to deindividuation? Can you think of a firsthand observation or experience?
6. How do you think IT affects social networking? Is IT likely to increase social capital in an agency? Why or why not?
7. How has the process of organizational decision making changed with IT? Is IT likely to improve the quality of decisions? Why or why not?
8. IT and innovation do not always go hand in hand. What attributes enhance the diffusion of IT innovations?
9. An "information society" does not guarantee a democratic society. How might IT be used to reinforce nondemocratic trends in an organization? In a society?
10. Does IT tend to change organizational structure?

GLOSSARY

Countervailing powers: John Kenneth Galbraith, an American economist, set forth this theory to explain how the success of American democracy rested on the balancing relationship among business, government, and organized labor.

Fordist hierarchy: A reference to Henry Ford's system of assembly line system of mass production, which provided greater managerial control over workers' performance.

New economy: The current, highly competitive, global business environment in which the speed of communication has dramatically increased due to technological advancement and an evolving class of technological knowledge-based employees.

Organizational behavior: A field of management studies that emerged in the 1940s, centering on what people do, think, and feel within organizations. Individual, team, and structural characteristics of an organization are important levels of organizational behavior.

Organization theory: Theories of how organizations function in relation to interpersonal relations, processes, politics, power, structure, motivation, organizational culture, leadership style, and environmental factors.

Telecenter: A location, other than an organization's main office, that provides technological, media, or other aid to employees so they may function at a remote location but with all the conveniences of the office where they work.

Telework: Conducting work from some location other than a traditional office setting. This is also known as telecommuting, remote work, work from home, etc.

URBIS: Urban Information Systems; URBIS is a set of research studies conducted under the leadership of Ken Kraemer and others, which investigated the use of IT within local governments, with a focus on political implications.

ENDNOTE

[1]The archetype of large-scale IT-based consolidation is the creation of the gigantic Department of Homeland Security and its corresponding consolidated information systems. This "mother of all bureaucracies" has been ironically established by a political party ideologically opposed to bureaucracy.

CASE STUDY
Communities of Practice—An Australian Case Study: Leveraging Knowledge by Complementing Technology with Social Participative Learning

Sandra Jones and Owen Lockwood
Royal Melbourne Institute of Technology, Australia

About Communities of Practice

ICT provides multiple opportunities to share—as distinct from discover—explicit (observable) knowledge. Some commentators claim that increased knowledge development and sharing is inherent in the technology itself. McDermott summarizes this succinctly:

> IT . . . led many companies to imagine a new world of leveraged knowledge . . . these companies believe that if they could get people to simply document their insights and draw on each other's work they could create a web of global knowledge that would enable their staff to work with greater efficiency and effectiveness (McDermott, 2000, p. 22).

However, the effectiveness by which data is turned into useful knowledge requires greater emphasis on the role played by people in an organization as they participate in the development and sharing of that new knowledge (Davenport & Prusak, 1998). This is particularly important when considering the tacit knowledge or experience residing within people's minds (Leonard-Barton, 1995; Nonaka, 1998; Nonaka & Takeuchi, 1995).

In this environment, communities of practice are increasingly being seen as a very effective means of knowledge discovery, development, and sharing. They have been defined as "collections of individuals bound by informal relationships that share similar work roles and a common context" (Snyder [1997] quoted in Lesser & Prusak 2000, p. 125). Wenger (2000, p. 3) goes further and describes them as "providing the capacity to create and use organizational knowledge through informal learning and mutual engagement." Communities differ in diverse ways from the teams or work groups previously hailed as the best approach to community work. Lesser and Prusak (2000, p. 125) state that teams or work groups "have a task orientation, are often launched for a specific purpose, and have formal requirements for membership . . . communities of practice, by contrast, have an informal membership that is often fluid and self-organizing in nature." Specifically, such communities are driven by the value of sharing interests or practices to discover new knowledge that evolves from the ongoing collective process, as compared to teams driven under a defined charter, with the value measured by results delivered. The knowledge domain or practice that defines the community may change organically over time with the focus being on making connections between issues—compared to teams that are task defined by clear boundaries in which individual contribution is made according to a work plan.

In summary, communities of practice operate more independently than teams or work groups, are less easily managed, and their output is less easy to measure. Consequently, defining a step-by-step approach to establish a community is not an easy task. Wenger, McDermott, and Snyder (2002) argue that communities of practice need to be first acknowledged, and then supported and fully integrated into the operation of organizations in a way that does not disrupt the informality, collegiality, self-organization and internal leadership of these communities. The underpinning need when developing communities Wenger argues, is to "build capacity through mapping knowledge needs and build a social learning system through developing communities and connecting across boundaries" (Wenger, 2000, pp. 5–6). Designing an effective communication strategy requires a communal approach that links technology to people, and nurtures a willingness to share knowledge in a trusting environment.

The Australian Context

The Australian system of government has public sector departments at federal (whole of Australia) and state levels that implement government policy and programs. Both the federal government and public sector recognize that Australia needs an e-government knowledge strategy to produce a knowledge economy. Similarly, the Victorian state government and public sector know that the escalating take-up of ICT in society is having significant impact on the workplace and service delivery. To function effectively in this changing and often ambiguous environment, departments must capitalize on the value of their knowledge repositories. This means not only codifying, storing, and retrieving known explicit information but critically, uncovering, sharing, and applying the tacit knowledge residing within employees' heads.

It is examining how a community of practice encourages the uncovering, transfer and leverage of tacit knowledge as part of an e-government strategy that sets the purpose for this case study.

Case Study

This first-time-shown case study is set in the Department of Justice, one of 10 departments in the Victoria public sector. Having a budget of AUS$800 million, the Department comprises 43 business units and 53 associated agencies and statutory authorities. One of the three largest state government departments, it deploys 15,500 permanent staff and 5500 volunteers in six core program areas; Police and Emergency Services, Attorney-General (including courts and tribunals), Corrections, Consumer Affairs, Gaming, and Racing.

In 1999, the then Departmental Secretary Peter Harmsworth,[1] saw "Limited cooperation between people, no visible leadership, and poor performance metrics as being significant inhibitors to sharing tacit knowledge." On analyzing the Australian Quality Council's Australian Business Excellence Framework (ABEF), Harmsworth embedded its 12 leadership and management principles in the embryonic business improvement strategy emerging on his watch. In launching the strategy, Harmsworth used the ABEF Organizational Self Assessment (OSA), a performance diagnostic tool, to evaluate departmental performance at corporate level. Acting on OSA findings, Harmsworth approved a comprehensive program to design an integrated knowledge management (KM) strategy aligned with organizational goals and focussing on core business practices and processes. The corporate intent was that learning, through collaborative networks and enabling ICT systems, would be part of everyday life.

The then chief knowledge officer, Philip Hind,[2] knew ICT as a necessary, but in itself not sufficient, element of an effective KM strategy. In May 2002, following two years of intense knowledge mapping and analysis, Hind, in launching the resulting KM Strategy, Deployment & Change Model emphasized, "We . . . are drowning in a sea of information and documents . . are failing to tap the potential of our people." An element of the strategy was "The formation and operation of communities of practice where they make appropriate contributions to overall corporate objectives, as well as to personal development goals." Here was recognition that communities "can play a crucial role in sharing knowledge expertise across functional boundaries." In this context, Hind defined a community of practice as "A network of people who share an interest in a similar subject area and who agree to work together in sharing knowledge, developing expertise or solving problems."

continues

Establishing a Business Excellence Community of Practice

Synthesizing and giving practical form to the business improvement and KM strategies, Harmsworth created and sponsored the Business Excellence Network (BEN) as a community of practice which, in 2005, is the exemplar for public-sector participative social learning. Managers across the department nominated interested persons to join the BEN, of which 15 were trained in the OSA diagnostic and tasked with facilitating OSAs at business unit level.

Harmsworth describes this organizational development initiative as "giving people permission to group" and recalls his vision for the BEN was:

> To stimulate discussion and experimentation of continuous improvement initiatives across the department . . . to build a new staff empowerment culture . . . to demonstrate the power of communities of practice, and to spawn other communities.

Importantly, Harmsworth appreciated the ABEF as being more than a business improvement model, he also understood its value in increasing intellectual and social capital:

> The framework is a great device for getting people to engage, not just within, but also across boundaries . . . it helps break up silo behaviors . . . it is a platform for building trust, and trust is essential to open and willing exchange and transfer of knowledge . . . it's about making new friendships while exploring new territory.

Realizing Harmsworth's objective of fostering "innovative free thought and comments and open discussion," the BEN was self-organizing, professionally facilitated, met regularly, initiated dialogue with persons of interest, and shared learning about organizational self-assessment and improvement.

Having a knowledge domain, practice, and community, the BEN was a community of practice as described by Wenger, McDermott, and Snyder (2002). The domain was business excellence, practice was implementation of the ABEF principles, and participation was voluntary. The core element of practice allowed members to openly communicate and explore issues, and to actively promote, initiate, and facilitate business excellence activities within their sphere of influence. To further increase personal learning and knowledge networks, members were encouraged to contribute to a broad spectrum of improvement activities, and to recruit and mentor newer members.

The rapid, unqualified success of the BEN is evidenced in part by the fact that, 18 months after forming, increasing interest in the community and demand for its knowledge saw membership increase by a factor of 4 to more than 65. In 2001, however, it was realized that the BEN had grown too large, and the skills of members too diverse, for ongoing development and resourcing of the network to be viable.

Responding to this crisis of expansion, the inaugural 20 person Business Excellence Strategy Group (BESG) community of practice was created by, and from, BEN members. This group receives focused training around business excellence disciplines and tools, and is highly involved in business excellence work, while the BEN, having completed its major work of the Departmental OSA, evolved to being a community of interest.

Experience of Business Excellence Communities of Practice

Marie Syrjanen, a BEN-BESG foundation member, is the manager of organizational development at the Victorian Institute of Forensic Medicine, part of the Department of

Justice. Having for six years been immersed in the business excellence experience, Marie is sure and articulate in describing four factors critical to community success.

First, Syrjanen insists, Peter Harmsworth's belief, vision, and support were absolutely essential, "There must be a high-level champion to clear the way, to inspire, and to provide material support." This ensured managerial backing at lower levels, particularly in releasing members to join organizational improvement activities, in funding members to attend events and study tours, and participation in a peer support learning and development program.

Second, ongoing training is essential as it empowers through knowing the "how to do" as well as the "what to do." Syrjanen's experience is that "When new people with different understandings of business excellence came on board, there is a risk of them being overwhelmed and not continuing." Consequently, community members "would spend valuable social time with new people in introducing them to what it was all about."

Third, nurturing and trust building is vital to the exchange of ideas, information, and knowledge. As Syrjanen explains:

"We observe the Chatham House rule . . . frank discussion does not go outside the network and that is a real trust builder, a belief thing . . . if the rule was broken, I think it would be the end."

Fourth, there must be open access and flexibility rather than rigid structure—this means focus on the value of community practice and peer support rather than structure. Syrjanen recalls:

"There was a period during which the practice became very structured and adopted more a meeting style. During this time people lost energy . . . the group lost momentum . . . but people who were committed were not going to be deterred."

Benefits of Business Excellence Communities

Syrjanen firmly believes that the business excellence community benefits members, business entities, the Department of Justice, and Victorian government.

First, members gain from developing close relationships within the community. "You grow personally and professionally, develop and bond with these people . . . you can share, you understand each other." This leads to leveraging other people's information. Contacts are made across the department that provide quick access to where knowledge resides, and who may have what information is shared between the members as trust develops. "I have never had anyone say I haven't got time—everyone will help." Trust increases as relationships grow: "You can talk to people confidentially." Finally, Syrjanen comments "To experience this and not come out a different person wouldn't happen . . . it's only logical to join because of the networks that are created . . . and the knowledge gained by being part of the group."

Second, gains to the department are many. Knowledge sharing leads to shorter learning time, quicker problem solving, improved service delivery, reduced costs, and greater employee satisfaction. Syrjanen notes that the shared learning led to "Beliefs in the value of sharing knowledge migrating back into the workplace . . . this led to a more holistic framework." This in turn increased promotion of the ABEF principles across the department which increased support for organizational improvement initiatives. This in turn led to enhanced employee relationship practices, and improved planning and project management processes. Harmsworth stated that the benefits he observed were that ideas and learning were traded between people as they became mutually sup-

continues

porting, leading to "fermenting change at the operational level." He described the whole process as "letting one thousand flowers bloom," in which it became normal practice to constantly "scan the environment." Harmsworth also stated that in his view the experience of the business excellence community helped to:

> Change the department and improve its ability to develop partnerships, to continually work on improving the Justice system, to build an inclusive planning process to achieve a vision and gain staff buy-in, to develop better performance measures, and to develop capabilities to achieve a vision.

Third, there were also benefits for the Victorian government. Both Harmsworth and Syrjanen believe that the BEN-BESG experience has increased information and knowledge sharing across departments resulting in greater interdepartmental collaboration. The Department of Justice learning is being used to model a broader Victorian public-sector approach to communities contributing to quality improvement and KM. Furthermore, communities of practice have since been adopted as part of a whole-of-government strategy that aims to "Develop active communities that will be of value to the e-government programs, citizens, departments, e-government projects, and individual members."

Lessons for Communities of Practice as an E-Government Strategy

A number of lessons can be learned from this case study in assisting communities of practice to become an effective element of an e-government strategy.

First, ensure that communities have high-level sponsorship. This is especially important given that resources are needed to ensure that they are able to function effectively.

Second, and related to the above, members must be able to demonstrate the (often intangible) benefits of communities to senior decision makers and potential members. This is a particular challenge as quantitative measures are not always applicable or appropriate in demonstrating the degree to which community practice benefits the organization. As Syrjanen notes "It is important to make the wins high profile, communicate them in many ways, provide updates of what is happening to the Secretary and all levels of management."

Third, communities must be very visible to the general work force. For Syrjanen this also means "Keeping the language simple and not using management jargon."

Fourth, communities must be allowed to grow organically, and although some structure is required, allow members to experiment with new ways of working, to decide on the degree of formality they desire, and not to overformalize engagement.

Fifth, continually focus on keeping the community relevant and fresh to ensure that members see value in participating, and as Harmsworth has it, to "constantly seek ways to embed new learning into mainstream operations." This means having a workplace culture in which innovation and experimentation are encouraged in discovering new ideas and approaches.

Sixth, knowledge sharing in communities is a highly effective, low-cost activity that complements and adds value to ICT systems as knowledge repositories.

Conclusion

This case study shows that communities of practice are important to government in improving service delivery to society. Such communities are a means by which trusting personal relationships can grow into reliable and responsive networks in which the discovery, transfer, and leverage of existing and new knowledge—especially tacit knowledge—can occur. It illustrates that very successful e-government strategies provide a social as well as an ICT vector for change.

References

Davenport, T,. & Prusak, L. (1998). Working knowledge. Boston: Harvard Business School Press.

Lesser, E., & Prusak, L. (2000). Communities of practice: Social capital and organisational knowledge. In E. Lesser, M. Fontaine, & J. Slusher (Eds.), *Knowledge and communities* (pp. 123–132). Massachusetts: Butterworth-Heinemann.

Leonard-Barton, D. (1995). Wellsprings of knowledge: Building and sustaining the sources of innovation. Boston: Harvard Business School Press.

McDermott, R. (2000). Why information technology inspired but cannot deliver knowledge management. In E. Lesser, M. Fontaine, & J. Slusher (Eds.), *Knowledge and communities* (pp. 21–35). Massachusetts: Butterworth-Heinemann.

Nonaka, I. (1998). *The knowledge-creating company* (pp. 24–44). Boston: Harvard Business Review on Knowledge Management.

Nonaka, I., & Takeuchi, H. (1995). *The knowledge creating company*. Oxford, England: Oxford University Press.

Snyder, W. (1997). Communities of practice: Combining organizational learning and strategy insights to create a bridge to the 21st century. Academy of Management Conference.

Wenger, E. (2000). Communities of practice: The key to knowledge strategy. In E. Lesser, M. Fontaine, & J. Slusher (Eds.) *Knowledge and communities* (pp. 3–20). Massachusetts: Butterworth-Heinemann.

Wenger, E., McDermott, R., & Snyder, W. (2002). *Cultivating communities of practice*. Boston: Harvard Business School Press.

Correspondence

Dorothy Krajewski, immediate past Manager—Continuous Improvement, Department of Justice, Victoria, e-mail 29.03.05.

Philip Hind, Chief Knowledge Officer—Australian Taxation Office, e-mail 29.03.05.

Endnotes

[1]Now inaugural Chairman and CEO of the Victorian State Services Authority.

[2]Now Chief Knowledge Officer—Australian Taxation Office.

References

ABC News. (2000). ABC News Poll January 21–26, 2000. N=1,006 adults nationwide. Retrieved April 7, 2004, from http://www.pollingreport.com/computer.htm.

About.com. (2003, September 3). The digital divide is still wide. *Race Relations Blog*. Retrieved September 30, 2004, from http://racerelations.about.com/b/a/023411.htm.

Accenture, Inc. (2003). CRM in government. Bridging the gaps. Retrieved August 6, 2005, from http://www.accenture.com/xdoc/en/industries/government/insights/crm_bridging.pdf.

ACLU. (2002, November 15). Stop the plan to mine our privacy. Retrieved November 19, 2002, from www.aclu.org/Privacy/Privacy.cfm?ID=11323&c=130.

ACLU. (2004, May 20). ACLU unveils disturbing new revelations about MATRIX surveillance program. Retrieved December 14, 2004, from http://www.aclu.org/Privacy/Privacy.cfm?ID=15834&c=130.

Agre, Philip E. (2002). Real-time politics: The Internet and the political process. *The Information Society, 18*(5), 311–331.

Agre, Philip E., & Rotenberg, Marc (Eds.). (1998). *Technology and privacy: The new landscape*. Cambridge, MA: MIT Press.

Akaka, Kahikina. (2003). *Then and now: An update on the administration's competitive sourcing initiative: Hearing of the Subcommittee on the Oversight of Government Management, the Federal Workforce, and the District of Columbia*. July 24, 2003. Washington, DC: Government Printing Office.

Alderman, Ellen, & Kennedy, Caroline. (1997). *The right to privacy*. New York: Vintage.

Alexander, Cynthia J., & Pal, Leslie A. (Eds.). (1998). *Digital democracy: Policy and politics in the wired world*. New York: Oxford University Press.

Al-Mashari, Majed, Al-Mudimigh, Abdullah, & Zairi, Mohamed. (2003). Enterprise resource planning: A taxonomy of critical factors. *European Journal of Operational Research, 146*, 352–364.

Altschuld, James W., & Witkin, Belle Ruth. (2000). *From needs assessment to action: Transforming needs into solution strategies*. Thousand Oaks, CA: Sage.

American Gaming Association. (2004). Industry information. Retrieved November 26, 2004 from http://www.americangaming.org/Industry/factsheets/issues_detail.cfv?id=17.

Amnesty International. (2004, January 1). China: Controls tighten as Internet activism grows [Press release]. 1/28/2004. Retrieved September 15, 2004, from http://news.amnesty.org/index/ENGASA170052004.

Anderson, James G. (2004). Consumers of e-health: Patterns of use and barriers. *Social Science Computer Review, 22*(2), 242–248.

Andrews, David H. (2002, November 1). Management can spur IT success. *Internet World Magazine*. Retrieved January 11, 2005, from http://www.iw.com/magazine.php?inc=110102/11.01.02ceo.html.

Andrews, David H. J., & Johnson, Kenneth R. (2002). *Revolutionizing IT: The art of using information technology effectively.* New York: John Wiley and Sons.

Ang, James S. K., Sum, Chee-Chuong, & Yeo, Lei-Noy. (2002). A multiple-case design methodology for studying MRP success and CSFs. *Information and Management, 39*, 271–281.

Argyris, Chris. (1971). Management information systems: The challenge to rationality and emotionality. *Management Science, 17*(6), B275–B292.

Arveson, Paul. (2003). The convergence of strategy, performance, and enterprise architecture in the U.S. federal government. Retrieved June 4, 2005, from http://www.balancedscorecard.org/bscit/prm.html.

Atkinson, Steven D., & Hudson, Judith. (1990). *Women online.* Binghamton, NY: Haworth Press.

Baark, Erik, & Heeks, Richard. (1998). Evaluation of donor-funded information technology transfer projects in China: A lifecycle approach. [*Working Papers Series*, Paper No. 1.] Manchester, UK: Institute for Development Policy and Management, University of Manchester.

Baase, Sara. (1974, April 4–10). IBM: Producer or predator? *Reason.* Retrieved November 16, 2004, from http://www-rohan.sdsu.edu/faculty/giftfire/ibm.html.

Baase, Sara. (1996). *A gift of fire: Social, legal and ethical issues in computing.* Englewood Cliffs, NJ: Prentice Hall.

Badagliacco, Joanne M. (1990). Gender and race differences in computing attitudes and experience. *Social Science Computer Review, 8*(1), 42–62.

Bagalawis, Jennifer. (2001, January 1). How IT helped to topple a president. *Computer World.* Retrieved October 8, 2004 from http://wireless.itworld.com/4273/CW_13101_it/page_1.html.

Baker, Juli Ann. (1991). *Processes of change: An anthropological inquiry into resistance to technological changes in an organization.* Unpublished doctoral dissertation. Boulder, CO: University of Colorado-Boulder.

Balas, Janet. (1990). The people's electronic exchange. *Computers in libraries, 10*(1), 30–32.

Barata, Kimberly, & Cain, Piers. (2001). Information, not technology, is essential to accountability: Electronic records and public-sector financial management. *The Information Society, 17*(4), 247–258.

Barber, Benjamin R. (1992). Jihad vs. McWorld. *Atlantic Monthly, 269*(3), 53–65.

Baron, Dave. (2002). A-76 comments to the OMB. Washington, DC: Office of Management and Budget. Retrieved March 19, 2005, from http://www.whitehouse.gov/omb/circulars/a076/comments/a76-140.pdf.

Baum, Christopher, & Di Maio, Andrea. (2000). Gartner's four phases of e-government model [TU-12-6113.]. Stamford, CT: Gartner Group.

Beaman, Karen V., & Guy, Gregory R. (2005, July). Organizational evolution in the global age. Fifth International Conference on Knowledge, Culture, and Change in Organizations. Rhodes, Greece: University of the Aegean.

Bean, Jennifer, & Hussey, Lascelles. (1997). *Business planning in the public sector.* London: HB.

Becker, Shirley Ann. (2004). E-government visual accessibility for older adult users. *Social Science Computer Review, 22*(1), 11–23.

Berman, Jerry, & Bruening, Paula. (2001). Is privacy still possible in the twenty-first century? *Social Research, 68*. Retrieved November 30, 2004, from http://www.cdt.org/publications/privacystill.shtml.

Bhambhani, Dipka. (2002). Michigan lawmakers give birds-eye view of sessions. *Government Computer News*, 10.21.02: 32.

Bijker, Weibe E. (1995). *Of bicycles, bakelites, and bulbs: Toward a theory of sociotechnical change.* Cambridge, MA: MIT Press.

Bijker, Weibe, Hughes, Thomas P., & Pinch,Trevor (Eds.). (1987). *The social construction of technological systems: New directions in the sociology and history of technology.* Cambridge, MA: MIT Press.

Bimber, Bruce. (1998). The Internet and political mobilization: Research note on the 1996 election season. *Social Science Computer Review, 16*(4), 391–401.

Blanchard, A., & Horan, T. (2000). Virtual communities and social capital. In G. David Garson (Ed.), *Social dimensions of information technology: Issues for the new millenium* (pp. 6–22). Hershey, PA: Idea Group Press.

Blanchette, Jean-François, & Johnson, Deborah G. (2002). Data retention and the panoptic society: The social benefits of forgetfulness. *The Information Society, 18*(1), 33–45.

Bloomfield, Brian P., & Coombs, Rod. (1992). Information technology, control and power: The centralization and decentralization debate revisited. *Journal of Management Studies, 29*(4), 459–484.

Borrus, Michael, & Zysman, John. (1997). Globalization with borders: The rise of Wintelism and the future of global competition. *Industry and Innovation, 4*(2), 141–166.

Bozeman, Barry, & Bretschneider, Stuart. (1986). Public management information systems: Theory and prescription. *Public Administration Review, 46*, 475–487.

Bozeman, Barry, & Pandey, Sanjay K. (2004). Public management decision making: Effects of decision content. *Public Administration Review, 64*(5), 553–565.

Brasch, Walter. (2005). *America's unpatriotic acts: The federal government's violation of constitutional and civil rights.* New York: Peter Lang.

Brin, David. (1999). *The transparent society: Will technology force us to choose between privacy and freedom?* New York: Perseus.

Brown, Justine K. (2002). Slipping through electronic cracks. *Government Technology*, October, 56–58.

Brown, Mary Maureen. (2000). Mitigating the risk of information technology initiatives: Best practices and points of failure for the public sector. In G. David Garson (Ed.), *Handbook of public information systems* (pp. 153–164). NY: Marcel Dekker.

Brown, Ronald H., Irving, Larry, Prabhakar, Arati, & Katzen, Sally. (1994). *The global information infrastructure: Agenda for cooperation.* Washington, DC: National Telecommunications and Information Administration. Retrieved November 1, 2004, from http://www.ntia.doc.gov/reports/giiagend.html.

Brown University. (2004, September 27). Fourth annual urban e-government study. [News release.] Providence, RI. Retrieved October 19, 2004, from http://www.brown.edu/Administration/News_Bureau/2004-05/04-030.html.

Brunker, Mike. (2001, April 10). Online gambling goes global: International players seek piece of the pie. MSNBC. Retrieved November 23, 2004, from http://msnbc.msn.com/id/3071032/.

Bruce, Donald, Deskins, John, & Fox, William F. (2004). Has Internet taxation affected Internet use? *Public Finance Review, 32*(2), 131–147.

Brzezinski, Matthew. (2004). *Fortress America: On the frontlines of homeland security—an inside look at the coming surveillance state.* NY: Bantam Books.

Bugler, Daniel T., & Bretschneider, Stuart. (1993). Technology push or program pull: Interest in new information technologies within public organizations. In Barry Bozeman (Ed.), *Public management: The state of the art* (pp. 275–293). San Francisco: Jossey-Bass.

Bush, Vannevar. (1945). As we may think. *Atlantic Monthly, 176*(1), 101–108. Retrieved from http://www.theatlantic.com/unbound/flashbks/computer/bushf.htm.

Business Journal. (2004, January 14). UCLA: Internet has a gender gap. *Silicon Valley/San Jose Business Journal.* Retrieved September 26, 2004, from http://sanjose.biz journals.com/sanjose/stories/2004/01/12/daily33.html

Cain, Jonathon. (2004). Infotech and the law: If the shoe fits, it still may not be for you. *Washington Technology, 19*(9). Retrieved April 15, 2005 from http://www.washingtontechnology.com/news/19_9/infotech-cain/24140-1.html.

Calabrese, Andrew, & Borchert, Mark. (1996). Prospects for electronic democracy in the United States: Rethinking communications and social policy. *Media, Culture, and Society, 18*, 249–268.

Carlile, Jennifer. (2004). In Britain, somebody's watching you: CCTV used to fight crime, terror in most-monitored nation in world. MSNBC News. Retrieved October 31, 2004, from http://www.msnbc.msn.com/id/5942513/.

Carr, Kathleen, & Duffy, Daintry (2004a, July). Federal withholding. *CSO: The resource for security executives.* Retrieved October 19, 2004, from http://www.csoonline.com/read/070104/briefing_fed.html.

Castells, Manuel. (1996). *The rise of the network society, the information age: Economy, society and culture* (Vol. I). Cambridge, MA: Oxford, UK: Blackwell.

Castells, Manuel. (1997). *The power of identity, the information age: Economy, society and culture* (Vol. II). Cambridge, MA: Blackwell.

Castells, Manuel. (1998). *The end of the millennium, the information age: Economy, society and culture* (Vol. III). Cambridge, MA: Blackwell.

Castells, Manuel. (2001). *The internet galaxy. Reflections on the Internet, business and society.* New York: Oxford University Press.

Cats-Baril, William, & Thompson, Ronald. (1995). Managing information technology projects in the public sector. *Public Administration Review, 55*(6), 559–566.

Caudle, Sharon L. (1990). Managing information resources in state government. *Public Administration Review, 50*(5), 515–524.

CDT. (2005). Federal ID proposals for U.S. citizens and others grow in number and scope. *CDT Policy Post, 11*(1). Center for Democracy and Technology.

Ceaparu, Irina, & Shneiderman, Ben (2002). Improving Web-based civic information access: A case study of the 50 U.S. states. *Proceedings of the IEEE International Symposium on Technology and Society* (pp. 275–285, IEEE Document No. 0-7803-7824-0/02/).

Center for Digital Government. (2004). *Digital legislatures survey, 2003.* Retrieved September 18, 2004, from http://media.centerdigitalgov.com/CDG04_RPRT_DigLegBOB.pdf.

CERT. (2004). 2004 e-crime watch survey shows significant increase in electronic crimes. Pittsburgh, PA: CERT Coordination Center, Software

Engineering Institute, Carnegie-Mellon University. Retrieved November 6, 2004, from http://www.cert. org/about/ecrime.html.

Chalk, Peter, & Rosenau, William. (2004). *Confronting "the enemy within": Security intelligence, the police, and counterterrorism in four democracies.* Santa Monica, CA: RAND.

Chen, Milton. (1986). Gender and computers: The beneficial effects of experience on attitudes. *Journal of Educational Computing Research, 2*(3), 265–282.

Chiles, James R. (2001). *Inviting disaster: Lessons from the edge of technology.* New York: HarperBusiness.

Cho, Yong Hyo, & Choi, Byung-Dai. (2004). E-government to combat corruption: The case of Seoul metropolitan government. *International Journal of Public Administration, 27*(10), 719–735.

Chomsky, Noam. (1992). *Deterring democracy.* New York: Hill and Wang.

Chomsky, Noam. (1994). *World orders old and new.* New York: Columbia University Press.

Chomsky, Noam. (1996). *Class warfare.* Pluto Press.

CIO Council. (2002, October). *Value measuring methodology: Highlights.* CIO Best Practices Committee, Federal CIO Council. Retrieved April 18, 2003, from http://www.cio.gov/documents/ValueMeasuring_Highlights_Oct_2002. pdf.

CIO Council. (2003). *Clinger-Cohen assessment survey.* Federal CIO Council. Retrieved December 22, 2004, from http://www.cio.gov/documents/CCA Survey_2003_Analysis_Report.pdf.

CIPFA. (2001). *Managing activities in the public sector—the use of business planning techniques—ideas from the United Kingdom.* London: Chartered Institute of Public Finance and Accountancy.

Clarke, P. (2002, September). Human-computer interaction: A cognitive intervention approach. Paper presented to the ECPPM 2002, "Conference on eWork and eBusiness in AEC." Portoro, Slovenia. Retrieved February 27, 2005, from http://2002.ecppm.org/data/papers/robots/229.htm.

Clolery, Paul. (2000, February). NPT salary survey. *The Nonprofit Times.* Retrieved February 14, 2004, from http://www.nptimes.com/Feb00/00salaries.html.

Cnaan, Ram A. (1989). Social work practice and information technology—an unestablished link. *Computers in Human Services, 5*(1/2), 1–15.

CNN. (2000, December 14). 'Cyberwarriors' hit Philippine impeachment trial. Retrieved September 8, 2004, from http://www. cnn.com/2000/TECH/ computing/12/14/philippines.estrada.reut/.

Coe, Roland J., & Broucek, Eric F. (2000). Intellectual property for public managers. In G. David Garson (Ed.), *Handbook of public information technology.* New York: Marcel Dekker.

Coffee, Peter. (2001). E-CRM: Making the customer king? *eWeek, 18*(20), 39.

Cohen, Julie. (2003). DRM and privacy. *Communications of the ACM. 46*(4), 47–49.

Cohen, Steven, & Eimicke, William. (2005). Using strategic information systems to improve contracted services and assess privatization options. In G. David Garson (Ed.), *Handbook of public information systems* (2nd edition). Boca Raton, FL: CRC Press.

Cohill, Andrew M., & Kavanaugh, Andrew L. (Eds.). (1997). *Community networks: Lessons from Blacksburg, Virginia.* Boston: Artech House.

Collins, Graham. (2002). *USA local government IT observations.* Retrieved September 22, 2004, from http://www.asiapacific.geac.com/object/mgmtittrends_GESPAC.html.

ComData News. (2002). The electronic legislature. *ComData News* 4(1). January. Retrieved September 18, 2004, from http://www.comdata.com/cn0401-sap.html.

Commission of the European Communities. (2003). *Communication from the Commission: Compliance with the rules of the common fisheries policy.* Brussels, 11.06.2003 COM(2003)344 final. Retrieved September 22, 2004, from http://europa.eu.int/comm/fisheries/doc_et_publ/factsheets/legal_texts/doscom/en/com_03_344_en.pdf.

Committee on Government Reform. (2005). Davis Reappointed Chairman of House Government Reform Committe [News release]. Washington, DC: U.S. House of Representatives. Retrieved March 25, 2005, from http://reform.house.gov/pdfs/010605109thchairmanrelease.pdf.

Compaine, Benjamin M. (Ed.). (2001). *The digital divide: Facing a crisis or creating a myth?* Cambridge, MA: MIT Press.

Computer Science and Telecommunications Board. (2002). *Cybersecurity today and tomorrow: Pay now or pay later.* Washington, DC: National Academy Press.

Continuity Central. (2004, June 30). 2004 E-Crime Watch survey shows significant increase in electronic crimes. Retrieved November 27, 2004, from http://www.continuitycentral.com/news01338.htm.

Cooper, Mark S. (2002). Does the digital divide still exist? Bush administration shrugs, but the evidence says yes. Consumer Federation of America. Retrieved September 30, 2004, from http://www.consumerfed.org/DigitalDivideReport 20020530.pdf.

Cooper, Joel, & Weaver, Kimberlee D. (2003). *Gender and computers: Understanding the digital divide.* Mahwah, NJ. Lawrence Erlbaum Associates.

Council for Excellence in Government. (2003). The new e-government equation: Ease, engagement, privacy & protection. Retrieved May 28, 2003, from http://www.excelgov.org/usermedia/images/uploads/PDFs/egovpoll2003.pdf.April 2003.

Council for Excellence in Government. (2004). Hart-Teeter poll. Retrieved April 7, 2004, from http://www.comcast.net/News/DOMESTIC/XML/1110_AP_Online_Regional___National__US_/85ec8b88-6d0a-4127-bf0a-10d47d779e8c.html.

Coyne, Richard, & Wiszniewski, Dorlan. (1999). Technical deceits: Critical theory, hermeneutics and the ethics of information technology. Proceedings of the Second International Workshop on Philosophy of Design and Information Technology: Ethics in Information Technology Design, December 9–10, Saint-Ferréol, Toulouse, France, pp. 35–44. Retrieved November 11, 2003, from http:// www.caad.ed.ac.uk/~richard/FullPublications/TechnicalDeceits.pdf.

Cragon, Harvey G. (2003). *From fish to Colossus: How the German Lorenz cipher was broken at Bletchley Park.* Dallas, TX: Cragon Books.

Cronin, Blaise, & Davenport, Elisabeth. (2001). E-Rogenous zones: Positioning pornography in the digital economy. *The Information Society, 17*(1), 33–48.

CRS. (2004). *Congressional Research Service, Annual Report, FY 2003.* Retrieved September 18, 2004, from http://www.loc.gov/crsinfo/CRS03_AnnRpt.pdf.

Crutchfield George, Lynch, Barbara, P., & Marsnick, Susan J. (2001). U.S. multinational employers: Navigating through the "Safe Harbor" principles to comply with the EU Dat Privacy Directive. *American Business Law Journal, 38*(4), 735–783.

CTG. (2000a). Listen before you leap: Revitalizing the New York State central accounting system. Albany, NY: Center for Technology in Government. Retrieved April 20, 2003, from http://www.ctg.albany.edu/guides/usinginfor/ Cases/osccas_case.htm.

CTG. (2000b). Building trust before building a system: The making of the Homeless Information Management System. Albany, NY: Center for Technology in Government. Retrieved April 20, 2003, from http://www.ctg.albany.edu/ guides/usinginfor/Cases/bss_case.htm.

Dale, Tony, & Goldfinch, Shaun. (2002). Pessimism as an information system management tool in the public sector: Lessons from the INCIS fiasco in the New Zealand Police Force. Retrieved December 26, 2003, from http://www. cosc.canterbury.ac.nz/research/reports/TechReps/2002/tr_0202.pdf.

Danziger, James N. (1986). Computing and the political world. *Computers and the Social Sciences, 2*(4), 183–200.

Danziger, James N., & Andersen, Kim Viborg. (2002). Impacts of information technology on public administration: An analysis of empirical research from the "golden age" of transformation. *International Journal of Public Administration, 25*(5), 591–627.

Danziger, James N., Dutton, William H., Kling, Rob, & Kraemer, Kenneth L. (1982). *Computers and politics: High technology in American local governments.* New York: Columbia University Press.

Danziger, James N., Kraemer, Kenneth L., Dunkle, Debora E., & King, John Leslie. (1993). Enhancing the quality of computing service: Technology, structure and people. *Public Administration Review, 53*(2), 161–169.

Database Searcher. (1988). Librarians battle for electronic freedom. *Database Searcher,* 4(7), 37.

Daukantas, Patricia. (2003a). Chiefs resign, PCs "lost" at energy lab. *Government Computer News.* January 13, 2003: 16.

Daukantas, Patricia. (2003b). OMB releases final version of Performance Reference Model. *Government Computer News,* September 23, 2003: 8.

Davis, Charles N. (2003). Electronic access to information and the privacy paradox: Rethinking practical obscurity and its impact on electronic freedom of information. *Social Science Computer Review, 21*(1), 15–25.

Dawes, Sharon S., Cresswell, Anthony M., & Cahan, Bruce B. (2004). Learning from crisis: Lessons in human and information infrastructure from the World Trade Center response. *Social Science Computer Review, 22*(1), 52–66.

Dawes, Sharon S., Pardo, Theresa A, Simon, Stephanie, Cresswell, Anthony M., LaVigne, Mark F., Andersen, David F., et al. (2003). *Making smart IT choices: Understanding value and risk in government IT* (2nd ed). Albany, NY: SUNY-Albany, Center for Technology in Government.

Dean, John W. (2004). *Worse than Watergate: The secret presidency of George W. Bush.* New York: Little, Brown.

DeGroat, Bernie. (2004, February 19). Detroit's digital divide not due to race. University of Michigan News Service. Retrieved September 30, 2004, from http://www.umich.edu/news/?Releases/2004/Feb04/r021904a.

Demchak, Chris C., Friis, Christian, & LaPorte, Todd M. (2000). Webbing governance: National differences in constructing the face of public organizations. In

G. David Garson (Ed.), *Handbook of public information systems* (pp. 179–190). New York: Dekker.

Demetrulias, Diana M., & Rosenthal, Nina R. (1985). Discrimination against females in microcomputer advertising. *Computers and the Social Sciences, 1,* 91–95.

Department of Defense. (1985). *Department of Defense trusted computer system evaluation criteria* [DoD 5200.28-STD.] Washington, DC: DOD. Retrieved November 9, 2004, from http://csrc.ncsl.nist.gov/secpubs/rainbow/std001.txt. The original 1983 publication was CSC-STD-001-83.

Dickson, Gary W., & DeSanctis, Gerardine (Eds.). (2001). *Information technology and the future enterprise.* Upper Saddle River, NJ: Prentice Hall.

Divis, Dee Ann, & Horrock, Nicholas M. (2002). A National ID? *Insight on the News,* April 18. Retrieved October 30, 2004, from http://www.insightmag.com/main.cfm/include/detail/storyid/239956.html.

Dizard, Wilson P., III. (2001). CIOs labor over contracting crisis. *Government Computer News, 7*(11). Retrieved January 8, 2005, from http://www.gcn.com/state/7_11/news/16778-1.html.

Dizard, Wilson P., III. (2002a). BIA systems are in limbo. *Government Computer News,* August 26: 46.

Dizard, Wilson P., III. (2002b). The case of the routinely disappearing notebook PCs. *Government Computer News,* September 9: 17.

Dizard, Wilson P., III. (2003a). GAO finds flaws in DHS' latest data-sharing plans. *Government Computer News,* September 15: 10.

Dizard, Wilson P., III. (2003b). Terror center sparks Hill skepticism. *Government Computer News,* March 10: 16.

Dizard, Wilson P., III. (2003c). Auditors criticize New York intranet construction. *Government Computer News,* September 22: 22.

Dizard, Wilson P., III. (2004a). GAO identifies nearly three dozen networks supporting homeland security. *Government Computer News,* October 19. Retrieved October 20, 2004, from http://www.gcn.com/vol1_no1/daily-updates/27648-1.html.

Dizard, Wilson P., III. (2004b). Judge again orders Interior to take systems offline. *Government Computer News,* March 22: 12.

Dizard, Wilson P., III. (2004c). Federal official's endorsement of IAC officials rankles members. *Government Computer News,* November 12. Retrieved November 15, 2004, from http://www.gcn.com/vol1_no1/daily-updates/27886-1.html.

Dizard, Wilson P., III. (2005a). Exodus from DHS' upper tier accelerates. *Government Computer News,* January 20. Retrieved January 13, 2004, from http://www.gcn.com/vol1_no1/daily-updates/34807-1.html.

Dizard, Wilson P., III. (2005b). Senate probes FBI case file project. 01/25/05. *Government Computer News,* January 25. Retrieved February 9, 2005, from http://www.gcn.com/vol1_no1/daily-updates/34901-1.html.

Dizard, Wilson P., III. (2005c). Justice Web site to unify sex offender tracking. *Government Computer News,* May 20. Retrieved May 24, 2005, from http://www.gcn.com/vol1_no1/daily-updates/35879-1.html.

Dizard, Wilson P., III, & Gail Repsher Emery. (2003). DHS plans threefold attack on cyberthreats. *Government Computer News,* September 9, 13.

Downing, John D. H. (1989). Computers for political change: PeaceNet and public data access. *Journal of Communication, 39*(3), 154–162.

Drori, Gili S., & Jang, Yong Suk. (2003). The global digital divide: A sociological assessment of trends and causes. *Social Science Computer Review, 21*(2), 144–161.

Duncan, George T., & Stephen F. Roehrig (2003). Mediating the tension between information privacy and information access: The role of digital government. In G. David Garson (Ed.), *Public information technology* (pp. 94–119). Hershey, PA: Idea Group.

Duncan, William R. (1996). *A guide to the project management body of knowledge* (2nd ed). Upper Darby, PA: Project Management Institute.

Dutton, William H. (1992). Political science research on teledemocracy. *Social Science Computer Review, 10*(4), 505–522.

Dutton, William H., Blumler, Jay G., & Kraemer, Kenneth L. (Eds.). (1987). *Wired cities: Shaping the future of communications.* Boston: G. K. Hall and Co.

Eastman, Beva. (1991). Women, computers, and social change. *Computers in Human Services, 8*(1), 41–53.

EDRI-news. (2004). *EDRi-news Digest, 14*(1).

Edwards, Roger & Englehardt, K. G. (1989). Microprocessor-based innovations and older Americans: AART survey results and their implications for service robotics. *International Journal of Technology and Aging, 2*(1), 43–55.

Eger, John M. (1997, October 26). Cyberspace and cyberplace: Building the smart communities of tomorrow. *San Diego Union-Tribune,* October 26. Retrieved October 30, 2005, from http://www.smartcomm_unities.org/pub_cyberplace.htm.

Elgan, Mike. (1999). The legacy data disaster. *TechWeb,* October 8. Retrieved October 26, 2004, from http://www.winmag.com/columns/bigpicture/1999/1008.htm.

Ellis, Caroline. (2003). The flattening corporation. *Sloan Management Review 44*(4), 5.

Ellison, Nicole. (2000). Researching telework: Past concerns and future directions. In G. David Garson (Ed.), *Social dimensions of information technology* (pp. 255–276). Hershey, PA: Idea Group.

Emery, Fred E., & Trist, Eric L. (1960). Sociotechnical systems. In C. W. Churchman, & M. Verhulst, (Ed.), *Management science models: Management and techniques* (pp. 83–97). New York: Pergamon.

Emery, Fred E., & Trist, Eric L. (1965). The causal texture of organizational environments. *Human Relations, 18*(1), 21–32.

Emery, Gail Repsher. (2002). Fortress America. *Washington Technology, 17*(5). Retrieved October 7, 2004, from http://www.washingtontechnology.com/news/17_5/federal/18325-1.html.

Emery, Gail Repsher. (2003). Latest cybersecurity report card finds few agencies made the grade. *Government Computer News,* December 15; 8.

Erdman, Harold P., & Foster, Sharon W. (1988). Ethical issues in the use of computer-based assessment. *Computers in Human Services, 3*(1/2), 71–87.

Essex, David. (2003). Software tools can help you get with the program and put your agency's IT investments in order. *Government Computer News Management,* September, 38–39.

Essex, David. (2005). Assembling a business case. *Government Computer News, 24*(10). Retrieved June 2, 2005, from http://www.gcn.com/24_10/buyers_guide/35686-1.html.

Etzione, Amitai. (2000). *The limits of privacy*. NY: Basic Books.

Executive Office of the President. (1993). Executive Order 12862: Setting customer service standards. Washington, DC: Author. Retrieved September 21, 2005, from http://www.blm.gov/nhp/news/regulatory/EOs/eo_12862.html.

Fang, Kunsheng. (2004). *Boosting productivity of delinquent collections: A proposal for improving delinquent collection practices in utility billing services in the city of Raleigh, North Carolina*. Raleigh, NC: North Carolina State University, Public Administration Program.

Farrar, Charles. (2004). Somebody is looking at all that e-porn. *AVN Magazine*, April 5. Retrieved November 22, 2004, from http://www.avn.com/index.php? Primary_Navigation=Articles&Action=View_Article&Content_ID=79466.

Federal Enterprise Architecture Program Management Office. (2003). *The Performance Reference Model Version 1.0*. Retrieved October 17, 2003, from http://www.feapmo.gov/resources/fea_prm_release_document_rev_1_vol_1. pdf.

Federal Reserve. (2000, February 29). Outsourcing of information and transaction processing [Memorandum]. Washington, DC: Board of Governors, Federal Reserve. Retrieved October 26, 2004, from http://www.federalreserve.gov/board docs/srletters/2000/sr0004.htm.

Federal Trade Commission. (1999, July 13). *Self-regulation and privacy online. Statement before the Subcommittee on Telecommunications, Trade, and Consumer Protection of the Committee on Commerce, United States House of Representatives, Washington, D.C.* Retrieved October 28, 2004, from http://www.ftc.gov/os/1999/07/pt071399.htm.

Federal Trade Commission. (2000). *Online profiling: A report to Congress, June 2000*. Washington, DC: FTC. Retrieved October 28, 2004, from http://www.ftc.gov/os/2000/06/onlineprofilingreportjune2000.pdf.

Federation of American Scientists. (2004, October 21). *Secrecy News*. FAS project on government secrecy (92). Retrieved October 24, 2004, from http://www.fas.org/sgp/news/secrecy/2004/10/102104.html.

Ferguson, Kerry. (1998). World information flows and the impact of new technology. *Social Science Computer Review, 16*(3): 252–267.

FGIPC. (2003). *High payoff in electronic government: Measuring the return on e-government investments*. Intergovernmental Advisory Board Federation of Government Information Processing Councils. Retrieved September 22, 2004, from http://www.gsa.gov/gsa/cm_attachments/GSA_DOCUMENT/High-Payoff-finalreport_R2F-aQX_0Z5RDZ-i34K-pR.doc.

FHWA. (2003). Procedural guidelines for highway feasibility studies. Federal Highway Administration. Original document 1998; last modified March 25, 2003. Retrieved January 5, 2004, from http://www.fhwa.dot.gov/hep10/corbor/feastudy.html.

Finel, Bernard I., & Lord, Kristin M. (2002). *Power and conflict in the age of transparency*. New York: Palgrave MacMillan.

Fletcher, Douglas S., & Taplin, Ian M. (2001). *Understanding organizational evolution: Its impact on management and performance*. Westport, CT: Quorum Books.

Fletcher, Patricia. (2003). Portals and policy: Implications of electronic access to U.S. federal government information and services. In Alexei Pavlichev & G. David Garson (Eds.), *Digital government* (pp. 52–62). Hershey, PA: Idea Group.

Fletcher, Patricia, Bretschneider, Stuart, Marchand, Donald, Rosenbaum, Howard, & Bertot, John Carlo (1992). *Managing information technology: Transforming county governments in the 1990s.* Syracuse, NY: Syracuse University, School of Information Studies.

Flowers, Stephen. (1996). *Software failure, management failure: Amazing stories and cautionary tales.* New York: John Wiley.

Forester, Tom. (1989). The myth of the electronic cottage. In T. Forester (Ed.), *Computers in the human context* (pp. 213–227). Cambridge, MA: MIT Press.

Forrer, Donald A., & Anderson, Terry A. (2001). The dichotomy of measurement: Information technology return on investment in the public sector. Paper presented at the Professional Operations Management Society Conference, March 31–April 2. Orlando, FL.

Forrest, Ray. (1993). Contracting housing provision: Competition and privatization in the housing sector. In P. Taylor-Goodby & R. Lawson (Eds.), *Markets and managers: New issues in the delivery of welfare.* Buckingham, UK: Open University Press.

Fountain, Jane. (2001). *Building the virtual state: Information technology and institutional change.* Washington: Brookings Institution Press.

Fox, Susannah (2004). *Older Americans and the Internet.* Pew Internet and American Life Project. Washington. Retrieved September 30, 2004, from http://www.pewinternet.org/pdfs/PIP_Seniors_Online_2004.pdf.

Fox News. (2000). FOX News/Opinion Dynamics Poll. June 7–8, 2000. N=900 registered voters nationwide. Retrieved April 7, 2004, from http://www.pollingreport.com/computer.htm.

Frame, J. Davidson. (1995). Managing projects in organizations: How to make the best use of time, techniques, and people. Revised ed. San Francisco: Jossey-Bass.

Frantzich, Stephen E. (1987). The use and implications of information technologies in Congress. In Karen B. Levitan (Ed.), *Government infostructures: A guide to the networks of information resources and technologies at federal, state and local levels* (Ch. 2). New York: Greenwood Press.

Fredell, Eric. (1987). California tries electronic democracy. *Government Computer News, 6*(22), 24–25.

Frederickson, H. George. (1980). *New public administration.* University, Alabama: The University of Alabama Press.

Frederickson, Lee W., & Riley, Anne W. (Eds.). (1985). *Computers, people, and productivity.* New York: Haworth Press.

Frenkel, Karen A. (1988). Computers and elections. *Communications of the ACM, 31*(10), 1176–1183.

Fridman, Sherman. (2000). Report: Money, not race, underlies digital divide. *Newsbytes,* June 19. Retrieved September 30, 2004, from http://www.computeruser.com/news/00/06/19/news18.html.

Fruth, Darrell A. (2000). *Harvard Journal of Law & Technology, 13*(3), 549–657.

Fryer, Bronwyn. (1999). The ROI challenge. *CFO,* 915(9), 85–90.

Fujii, Yusaku, Yoshiura, Noriaki, & Ohta, Naoya. (In press). Creating a worldwide community security structure using individually maintained home computers: The e-JIKEI network project. *Social Science Computer Review,* 23.

Fukuyama, Francis. (1995). *Trust: The social virtues and the creation of prosperity.* New York: Free Press.

Funds for Learning. (2004, October 5). Senate Commerce Committee probes e-rate funding suspension. *E-Rate News*, Retrieved October 14, 2004, from http://www.fundsforlearning.com/cgi-bin/NewsList.cgi?cat=News&rec=559&cat=E-rate.

Furger, Roberta. (1989). The growth of the home office. *InfoWorld,* October 9, 45–49.

Gamble Tribune. (2004a). Online gambling regulation to boost economy. *Gamble Tribune*, September 24. Retrieved November 23, 2004, from http://www.gambletribune.org/article1003.html.

Gamble Tribune. (2004b). Attorney General John Ashcroft summoned to answer online gambling free speech complaint. *Gamble Tribune*, August 27. Retrieved November 23, 2004, from http://www.gambletribune.org/article1003.html.

Gamble Tribune. (2004c). Challenge to ban on Internet gambling upheld. *Gamble Tribune*, April 5. Retrieved November 23, 2004, from http://www.gambletribune.org/article1003.html.

Ganley, Gladys D. (1991). Power to the people via personal electronic media. *Washington Quarterly, 14*(2), 5–22.

GAO. (1997). *Assessing risks and returns: A guide for evaluating federal agencies' IT investment decisions* (GAO/AOMD=10.1.13). Washington, DC: Government Printing Office.

GAO. (1998). *Executive guide: Information security management: Learning from leading organizations* (GAO/AIMD-98-68). Washington, DC: Government Printing Office.

GAO. (2001a). *Record linkage and privacy: Issues in creating new federal research and statistical information* (GAO-01-126SP). Washington, DC: Government Printing Office.

GAO. (2001b). *Maximizing the success of chief information officers* (GAO-01-376G). Washington, DC: Government Printing Office.

GAO. (2002a). *Electronic government: Selection and implementation of the Office of Management and Budget's 24 initiatives.* Report to the Committee on Governmental Affairs, U.S. Senate (GAO-03-229). Washington, DC: Government Printing Office.

GAO. (2002b). *Contract management: Guidance needed for using performance-based service contracting. Report to the Chairman, Subcommittee on Technology and Procurement Policy, Committee on Government Reform, House of Representatives* (GAO-02-1049). Washington, DC: Government Accountability Office.

GAO. (2003a). *Electronic rulemaking: Efforts to facilitate public participation can be improved* (GAO-03-901). Washington, DC: Government Printing Office.

GAO. (2003b). *Homeland security: Information sharing responsibilities, challenges, and key management issues: Statement of Robert F. Dacey, Director, Information Security Issues, and Randolph C. Hite, Director, Information Technology Architecture and Systems Issues* (GAO-03-715T). Washington, DC: Government Printing Office.

GAO. (2003c). *Human capital: Further guidance, assistance and coordination can improve federal telework* (GAO-03-679). Washington, DC: Government Printing Office.

GAO. (2004a). *Federal chief information officers: Responsibilities, reporting relationships, tenure, and challenges* (GAO-04-823). Washington, DC: Government Printing Office.

GAO. (2004b). *Electronic government initiatives sponsored by the Office of Management and Budget have made mixed progress* (GAO-04-561T). Washington, DC: Government Printing Office.

GAO. (2004c). *Information technology: The federal enterprise architectures are still maturing* (GAO-04-798T). Washington, DC: Government Printing Office.

GAO. (2004d). *Information technology management: Improvements needed in strategic planning, performance measurement, and investment management governmentwide* (GAO-04-478T). Washington, DC: Government Printing Office.

GAO. (2004e). *Information technology investment management: A framework for assessing and improving process maturity* (GAO-04-394G). Washington, DC: Government Printing Office.

GAO. (2004f). *OMB and Department of Homeland Security investment reviews* (GAO-04-323). Washington, DC: Government Printing Office.

GAO. (2005a). *Information security: Internal Revenue Service needs to remedy serious weaknesses over Taxpayer and Bank Secrecy Act data* (GAO-05-482). Washington, DC: Government Printing Office.

GAO Management News. (2004). Success story: Gathering data with web-based surveys. *GAO Management News, 31*(29). Retrieved September 17, 2004, from http://www.gao.gov/qpl/mn3129qpl.htm.

Gardner, William. (2004). Compelled disclosure of scientific research data. *The Information Society, 20*(2), 141–146.

Garfinkel, Simson. (2001). *Database nation: The death of privacy in the 21st century.* Sebastopol, CA: O'Reilly.

Garson, G. David. (1987). *Computers in public employee relations.* Alexandria, VA: International Personnel Management Association.

Garson, G. David. (1995). *Computer technology and social issues.* Hershey, PA: Idea Group Press.

Garson, G. David. (2000). Information systems, politics, and government: Leading theoretical perspectives. In G. David Garson (Ed.), *Handbook of public information technology* (pp. 331–357). New York: Marcel Dekker.

Gascó, Mila. (2003). New technologies and institutional change in public administration. *Social Science Computer Review, 21*(1), 6–14.

Gattiker, Urs E. (2001). *The Internet as a diverse community: Cultural, organizational, and political issues.* Mahwah, NJ: Lawrence Erlbaum.

Gattiker, Urs E, & Nelligan, Todd W. (1988). Computerized offices in Canada and the United States: Investigating dispositional similarities and differences. *Journal of Organizational Behavior, 9*(1), 77–96.

Geary, Bob. (2005, January 19). Who won? Who knows? *The Independent* (Raleigh, NC): 15.

Gellman, Robert. (2002a). National Archives lacks a records management policy. *Government Computer News,* September 17: 41.

Gellman, Robert. (2002b). NARA makes another half-hearted attempt at policy. *Government Computer News,* September 23: 33.

Gellman, Robert. (2002c). Perspectives on privacy and terrorism: All is not lost—yet. *Government Information Quarterly, 19,* 255–264.

Gellman, Robert. (2003a). Are e-gov act's privacy reviews a hollow demand? *Government Computer News,* January 13: 28.

Gellman, Robert. (2003b). Flap is brewing over federal Web privacy policies. *Government Computer News,* March 10: 32.

Gereffi, Gary. (2001). Shifting governance structures in global commodity chains, with special reference to the Internet. *American Behavioral Scientist, 44*(10), 1616–1637.

Gerin, Roseanne. (2005, April 7). Accenture: E-gov yet to live up to its potential. *Government Computer News*. Retrieved May 4, 2005, from http://www.gcn.com/vol1_no1/daily-updates/35478-1.html.

Glasner, Joanna. (2002, October 3). Wana bet? Feds say not so fast. *Wired News*. Retrieved March 22, 2003, from http:///www.wired.com/news.business/0,1367,55510,00.html.

Gold, J. R. (1991). Fishing in muddy water: Communication media, homeworking and the electronic cottage. In S. D. Brunn, & T. R. Leinbach (Eds.), *Collapsing Space and Time* (pp. 327–341). London: Harper Collins.

Golden, James R. (1998). *Economics and national strategy in the information age: Global networks, technology policy, and cooperative competition*. New York: Praeger.

Golden, Tim. (2004, October 24). After terror, a secret rewriting of military law. *New York Times*. Retrieved October 24, 2004, from http://www.nytimes.com/2004/10/24/international/worldspecial2/24gitmo.html.

Gordon & Glickson LLC. (2005). *Information technology outsourcing: A handbook for government* (2nd ed.). Washington, DC: International City Management Association.

Government Computer News. (2004). Interview with Rep. Tom Davis. *Government Computer News,* January 12: 11.

Government Reform Minority Office. (2004). *Secrecy in the Bush Administration*. U.S. House of Representatives, Committee on Government Reform, Minority Office. Retrieved October 24, 2004, from http://democrats.reform.house.gov/ features/secrecy_report/index.asp.

Government Technology. (2003). Workplace email issues. *Government Technology*, September: 14.

Grafton, Carl. (2003). "Shadow Theories" in Fountain's theory of technology enactment. *Social Science Computer Review, 21*(4), 411–416.

Graham, Lawrence D. (1999). *Legal battles that shaped the computer industry*. New York: Quorum Books.

Grant-Lewis, Suzanne, & Wood, Julie M. (2000). Gender trends: The statistics. *Exploring Gender and Technology*. Retrieved September 25, 2004, from http://www.gse.harvard.edu/~wit/exploring/gender.htm.

Greenwatch Today. (2004, June 23). Bush administration secrecy imperils environment and public health. *Greenwatch Today*. Washington, DC: Environmental Media Services. Retrieved October 24, 2004, from http://www.bushgreenwatch.org/mt_archives/000142.php.

Griffith, Arthur. (2004). *How to fail at software development*. Anchorage, AK: Anchor Point.

Griffiths, Mark D., & Park, Jonathon. (2002). The social impact of Internet gambling. *Social Science Computer Review, 20*(3), 312–320.

Grimm, Vanessa Jo. (1988). Union leader assails Customs automation plans. *Government Computer News*, May 13: 12.

Griswold, Peter A. (1985). Differences between education and business majors in their attitudes about computers. *AEDS Journal, 18*(3), 131–138.

Grundmann, Susan. (2002). A-76 comments to the OMB. Washington, DC: Office of Management and Budget. Retrieved March 19, 2005, from http://www.whitehouse.gov/omb/circulars/a076/comments/a76-187.pdf.

Gutek, Barbara A., & Bikson, T. K. (1985). Differential experience of men and women in computerized offices. *Sex Roles, 13*, 123–136.

Hamel, Gary. (2002). *Leading the revolution: How to thrive in turbulent times by making innovation a way of life.* New York: Plume Books.

Hamel, Gary, Prahalad, C. K., Thomas, Howard, & O'Neal, Don, (Eds.). (1998). *Strategic flexibility: Managing in a turbulent environment.* New York: John Wiley and Sons.

Hammitt, Harry. (2000). The legislative foundation of information access policy: Balancing access against privacy and confidentiality. In G. David Garson (Ed.), *Handbook of public information systems* (pp. 27–40). NY: Dekker.

Hammitt, Harry. (2002). Disclosure debate. *Government Technology,* September: 60–61.

Hanson, Wayne. (2005). San Diego County nears completion of 7-year outsourcing contract, prepares for next steps. *Government Technology,* February 11. Retrieved April 30, 2005, from http://www.govtech.net/news/news.php?id=93060.

Harris, Blake. (2002). E-government failures reflect changing workforce needs. *Government Technology*, May. Retrieved September 17, 2002, from http://www.govtech.net/magazine/channel_story.phtml?channel=10.0&id=3030000000008.

Harris, Blake. (2004). Strategic sourcing: Smart procurement practices save governments a bundle. *Government Technology, 17*(5), 40–44.

Harris, Scott. (2000). 'Nader Traders' may have affected outcome in Florida. CNN.com, November 17. Retrieved September 7, 2004, from http://www.cnn.com/2000/TECH/computing/11/17/nader.traders.help.gore.idg/.

Hart, Jeffrey A., & Kim, Sangbae. (2002). Explaining the resurgence of U.S. competitiveness: The rise of Wintelism. *The Information Society, 18*(1), 1–12.

Hartman, Francis, & Ashrafi, Rafi A. (2002). Project management in the information systems and information technologies industries. *Project Management Journal, 33*(3), 5–15.

Harvard Policy Group. (2001a). *Eight imperatives for leaders in a networked world: Imperative 3—utilize best practices for implementing IT initiatives.* Cambridge, MA: JFK School of Government.

Harvard Policy Group. (2001b). *Eight imperatives for leaders in a networked world: Imperative 4—Improve budgeting and financing for promising IT initiatives.* Cambridge, MA: JFK School of Government.

Hastings Group. (2003). Privacy news: U.S. public supports biometrics, with privacy safeguards [E-mail newsletter]. January 7.

Hattie, John, & Fitzgerald, Donald. (1987). Sex differences and attitudes, achievement, and use of computers. *Australian Journal of Education, 31*(1), 3–26.

Heeks, Richard. (2002). *Failure, success and improvisation of information system projects in developing countries.* Manchester, UK: Institute for Development Policy and Management.

Heeks, Richard. (2003). Most eGovernment-for-Development projects fail: How can risks be reduced? Manchester, UK: Institute for Development Policy and

Management. Retrieved May 4, 2005, from http://www.eldis.org/static/DOC 14447.htm.

Heeks, Richard, & Bhatnagar, Subhash. (1999). Understanding success and failure in information age reform. In Richard Heeks (Ed.), *Reinventing government in the information age.* New York: Routledge.

Heintz, Theresa, & Bretschneider, Stuart. (2000). IT and restructuring organizations: Do IT-related structural changes improve organizational performance? *Journal of Public Administration Research and Theory, 10*(4), 801–830.

Henman, Paul, & Adler, Michael. (2003). Information technology and the governance of Social Security. *Critical Social Policy, 23*(2), 139–164.

Higgins, Steve. (1992). 'Electronic democracy' wins votes. *PC Week, 9*(20), 19.

Hiltz, Roxanne Starr, & Turoff, Murray. (1978). *The network nation: Human communication via the computer.* Reading, MA: Addison Wesley.

Hiltz, Roxanne Starr, & Turoff, Murray. (1993). *The network nation* (rev. ed.). Cambridge: MIT Press.

Hinsley, Francis H., & Stripp, Alan. (2001). *Codebreakers: The inside story of Bletchley Park* (rev. ed.). New York: Oxford University Press.

Ho, Alfred Tat-Kei. (2002). Reinventing local government and the e-government initiative. *Public Administration Review, 62*(4), 434–444.

Ho, Alfred Tat-Kei, & Ni, Anna Y. (2004). Explaining the adoption of e-government features: A case study of Iowa county treasurers' offices. *American Review of Public Administration, 34*(2), 164–180.

Holcomb, Briavel. (1991). Socio-spatial implications of electronic cottages. In S. D. Brunn & T. R. Leinbach (Eds.), *Collapsing space and time* (pp. 342–353). London: Harper Collins.

Holden, Stephen H. (2003). OMB's e-authentication policy isn't fully baked. *Government Computer News,* October 13: 75.

Hong, Yung-Kwon, & Kim, Young-Gul. (2002). The critical success factors for ERP implementation: An organizational fit perspective. *Information and Management, 40,* 25–40.

Hood, Christopher. (2000). Where the state of the art meets the art of the state: Traditional public-bureaucracy controls in the information age. *International Review of Public Administration* (South Korea), *5*(1), 1–12.

Horan, Thomas A. (2000a). *Digital places: Building our city of bits.* Washington, DC: The Urban Land Institute.

Horan, Thomas A. (2000b). Planning digital places: A new approach to community telecommunications planning and deployment. In G. David Garson (Ed.), *Handbook of public information systems.* New York: Marcel Dekker.

HUD. (2004). *Guidelines for the feasibility study checklist.* Department of Housing and Urban Development. Retrieved December 22, 2004, from http://www.hud.gov/offices/cio/sdm/devlife/tempchecks/fschecklist.doc.

Hunter, Christopher. (2002a). Political privacy and online politics: How e-campaigning threatens voter privacy. *First Monday, 7*(2). Retrieved September 17, 2004, from http://www.firstmonday.dk/issues/issue7_2/ hunter/.

Hunter, Richard. (2002b). *World without secrets: Business, crime and privacy in the age of ubiquitous computing.* New York: Wiley.

Ibrahim, F. A. (1985). Human rights and ethical issues in the use of advanced technology. *Journal of Counseling and Development, 64,* 134–135.

Industry Advisory Council. (2002). *Cross-jurisdictional e-government imple-mentations.* Fairfax, VA: Federation of Government Information Processing Councils, Industry Advisory Council, eGovernment Shared Interest Group. Retrieved September 16, 2003, from http://www.edevlet.net/raporveyayinlar/X-Juris_eGov2002.pdf.

Information Today. (1989). Library awareness program. *Information Today,* December: 7.

Innes, Judith. (1988). Effects of data requirements on planning: Case studies of environmental impact assessment and community development block grants. *Computers, Environment, and Urban Systems,* 12, 77–88.

Irvine, Cynthia E. (2000). Security issues for automated information systems. In G. David Garson (Ed.), *Handbook of public information technology* (pp. 231–246). New York: Marcel Dekker.

ITU. (2003). *Guidance on the regulatory framework.* International Telecommunication Union. Document No. 1B/TEMP/1-E. Retrieved September 22, 2004, from http://ntiacsd.ntia.doc.gov/ussg1/temp/wp1b/R03-WP1B-031030-TD-0001!!MSW-E.doc.

Jackson, Derrick Z. (2002, July 17). President shrugs at the digital divide. *Boston Globe,* Retrieved September 25, 2004, from http://www.commondreams.org/views02/0717-02.htm.

Jackson, Kelly. (1988). Virus alters networking. *Communications Week,* November 14: 1, 75.

Jackson, William. (2002a). NIST identifies good and bad points of biometrics. *Government Computer News,* August 26: 7.

Jackson, William. (2002b). DNS attacks could be a warning shot. *Government Computer News,* November 4: 7.

Jackson, William. (2003a). Privacy enforcement tool could become a TIA boon. *Government Computer News,* August 4: 32.

Jackson, William. (2003b). TIA swaps "terrorism" for "total." *Government Computer News,* June 2: 14.

Jackson, William. (2003c). Feds plan for common IDs by 2006. *Government Computer News,* October 27: 12.

Jackson, William. (2003d). Is HHS certifiable? Department keyed up to make the leap to widespread e-authentication. *Government Computer News,* November 10: 1, 15.

Jackson, William. (2003e) USPS strives to attract users to E-Postmark app. *Government Computer News,* November 10: 9.

Jackson, William. (2004a). Some security analysts cast a "no" vote on Defense's online absentee voting system. *Government Computer News,* February 9: 8.

Jackson, William. (2004b). Internet threats take on new hue. *Government Computer News,* September 20. Retrieved September 21, 2004, from http://www.gcn. com/vol1_no1/daily-updates/27353-1.html.

Jackson, William. (2004c). Fingerprint ID systems have the edge, NIST finds. *Government Computer News,* August 9: 46.

Jackson, William. (2005a). Cyber Eye: National ID standards could create "ID theft kit." *Government Computer News, 24*(7). Retrieved April 28, 2005, from http://www.gcn.com/24_7/tech-report/35391-1.html.

Jackson, William. (2005b). Agencies say standards needed for assessing FISMA compliance. *Government Computer Review,* April 7. Retrieved May 9, 2005, from http://www.gcn.com/vol1_no1/daily-updates/35481-1.html.

Jackson, William, & Miller, Jason. (2003). E-authentication is ready to go live. *Government Computer News,* April 21: 7.

James, Geoffrey. (1997). IT fiascoes . . . and how to avoid them. *Datamation,* November: 84–88.

Jansen, Arilde. (1995). Rural development through diffusion of information technology. *Scandinavian Journal of Information Systems, 7*(1), 99–120.

Jasperson, J., Carte, T. A., Saunders, C. S., Butler, B., Croes, H. J. P., & Zheng, W. J. (2002). Review: Power and information technology research: A metatriangulation review. *MIS Quarterly, 26*(4), 397–459.

Jayakar, Krishna P. (2003). Cross-sectoral differences in intellectual property enforcement in developing countries: The role of state-industry linkages. *The Information Society, 19,* 155–169.

Jefferson, David, Rubin, Aviel D., Simons, Barbara, and Wagner, David. (2004). *A security analysis of the Secure Electronic Registration and Voting Experiment (SERVE).* Retrieved February 2, 2004, from http://www.servesecurityreport.org/paper.pdf.

Joch, Alan. (2004). Bringing the office home. *State Tech,* Spring: 18–22.

Johnson, Charles. (2002). A-76 comments to the OMB. Washington, DC: Office of Management and Budget. Retrieved March 19, 2005, from http://www.white house.gov/omb/circulars/a076/comments/a76-126.pdf.

Johnson, Shawana P., & Kunz, J. Edward. (2005). Private sector makes Census Bureau's TIGER roar. *Geospatial Solutions, 15*(5), 28–32.

Jurison, Jaak. (2000). Perceived value and technology adoption across four end user groups. *Journal of End User Computing, 12*(4), 21–28.

Kabay, Mitch E. (1998). Anonymity and pseudonymity in cyberspace: Deindividuation, incivility and lawlessness versus freedom and privacy. Paper presented at the Annual Conference of the European Institute for Computer Anti-virus Research (EICAR). March 1998, 16–18, Munich, Germany. Retrieved February 14, 2005, from http://www2.norwich.edu/mkabay/overviews/anon pseudo.htm.

Kakabadse, Andrew, Kakabadse, Nada K., & Kouzmin, Alexander. (2003). Reinventing the democratic project through information technology: A growing agenda for debate. *Public Administration Review, 63*(1), 44–60.

Kaplan, Karen. (1996). For workers, telecommuting hits home. *Los Angeles Times,* July 29: D7.

Kash, Wyatt. (2005). Forecast sees federal IT spending on the rise. *Government Computer News,* March 29. Retrieved March 31, 2005, from http://www.gcn.com/vol1_no1/daily-updates/35375-1.html.

Katz, Peter. (1993). *New urbanism: Toward an architecture of community.* New York: McGraw-Hill.

Kay, Robin H. (1989). Gender differences in computer attitudes, literacy, locus of control and commitment. *Journal of Research on Computing in Education 21*(3), 307–316.

Kedzie, Christopher R. (1995). Democracy and network interconnectivity. RAND Paper. Santa Monica, CA: RAND.

Keider, Stephen P. (1984). Managing systems development projects. *Journal of Information Systems Management, 1*(3), 31–36.

Kent, Stephen T., & Millett, Lynette I. (Eds.). (2002). *IDs—not that easy: Questions about nationwide identity systems.* Washington, DC: National Academy Press.

Kettl, Donald F. (2002). *The transformation of governance.* Baltimore: Johns Hopkins University Press.

Kiesler, Sara, Siegel, Jane, & McGuire, T. W. (1991). Social psychological aspects of computer-mediated communication. In C. Dunlop & R. Kling (Eds.), *Computerization and controversy: Value conflicts and social choices.* San Diego, CA: Academic Press.

Kling, Rob, & Iacono, Suzanne. (1988). The mobilization of support for computerization: The role of computerization movements. *Social Problems, 35*(3), 226–243.

Kolleck, Bernd. (1993). Computer information and human knowledge: New thinking and old critique. In Marcos Leiderman, Charles Guzetta, Leny Struminger, and Menachem Monnickendam (Eds.), *Technology in people services: Research, theory, and applications.* New York: Haworth Press.

Korpi, Kerry. (2002). A-76 comments to the OMB. Washington, DC: Office of Management and Budget. Retrieved March 19, 2005, from http://www.whitehouse.gov/omb/circulars/a076/comments/a76-258.pdf.

Kraemer, Kenneth L. (2004, June). Globalization of IT fails to close gap between rich and poor. *Today@UCI Tipsheet.* Retrieved March 2, 2005, from http://today.uci.edu/news/tipsheet_detail.asp?key=85.

Kraemer, Kenneth L., & Dedrick, Jason. (1997). Computing and public organizations. *Journal of Public Administration Research and Theory, 7*(1), 89–112.

Kraemer, Kenneth L., & King, John Leslie. (1986). Computing and public organizations. *Public Administration Review, 46* (Special Issue), 488–496.

Kraemer, Kenneth L., & King, John Leslie. (1987). Computers and the Constitution: A helpful, harmful, or harmless relationship? *Public Administration Review, 47*(1), 93–105.

Krause, Micki, & Harold F. Tipton. (1998). *Handbook of information security management.* New York: Auerbach Publications/CRC Press.

Kraut, Robert E. (1987). Predicting the use of technology: The case of telework. In R. Kraut (Ed.), *Technology and the transformation of white-collar work* (pp. 113–134). Hillsdale, NJ: Lawrence Erlbaum Associates.

Krill, Paul. (2004). Legislation may be needed to fix open source IP issues: SCO battles raise legal questions. *Infoworld,* March 18.

Kristensen, Jens, & Buhler, Bernd. (2001, March). The hidden threat of e-government: Avoiding large government IT failures. Paris: OECD. Public Management Policy Brief 8. Retrieved May 4, 2005, from http://www.oecd.org/dataoecd/19/12/1901677.pdf.

Lais, Sami. (2002). EPA views web posting of data in a new light. *Government Computer News,* August 26: 5.

Lais, Sami. (2003). Can major efforts avoid more slip-ups? *Government Computer News,* December 15: 12.

Landay, Jonathon S. (2005). U.S. eliminates annual terrorism report. *Seattle Times,* April 16. Knight-Ridder Press Service. Retrieved April 23, 2005, from http://seattletimes.nwsource.com/html/nationworld/2002243262_terror16.html.

Lane, Frederick S. III. (2003). *The naked employee: How technology is compromising workplace privacy.* New York: AMACOM.

Larrison, Christopher R., Nackerud, Larry, Risler, Ed, & Sullivan, Michael. (2002). Welfare recipients and the digital divide: Left out of the new economy? *Journal of Technology in Human Services, 19*(4), 1–12.

Larsen, Elena, & Rainie, Lee. (2002a). *The rise of the e-citizen: How people use government agencies' web sites.* Washington, DC: Pew Internet & American Life Project.

Larsen, Elena, & Rainie, Lee. (2002b). *Digital town hall: How local officials use the Internet and the civic benefits they cite from dealing with constituents online.* Washington, DC: Pew Internet & American Life Project.

Larwood, Laurie. (1984). *Organizational behavior and management.* Boston: Kent.

LaVigne, Mark. (2001). Underestimating e-government costs proves costly: Traditional approaches are not enough. Albany, NY: Center for Technology in Government, SUNY-Albany. Retrieved February 24, 2003, from http://www.netcaucus.org/books/egov2001/pdf/egovtcos.pdf.

Lawther, Wendell. (2004). Public outreach for public-private partnerships: The case of Advanced Traveler Information Systems. *Public Works Management & Policy, 9*(2), 120–131.

Lea, Martin, & Spears, Russell. (1991). Computer-mediated communication, de-individuation, and group decision-making, *International Journal of Man Machine Studies, 34,* 283–301.

Lee, Mordecai. (2004, February). *E-reporting: Strengthening democratic accountability.* Washington, DC: IBM Center for The Business of Government.

Leitschuh, Jan. (1989, June 7). Electronic age links students to Chinese protests: Computers now a key tool of revolution. *News and Observer* (Raleigh, NC), 1D, 3D.

LeMoine, Barbara Jackson. (2002). A-76 comments to the OMB. Washington, DC: Office of Management and Budget. Retrieved March 19, 2005, from http://www.whitehouse.gov/omb/circulars/a076/comments/a76-640.pdf.

Lemos, Robert. (2004). Online attack puts 1.4 million records at risk. *CNET News.com.* October 20. Retrieved October 24, 2004, from http://news.zdnet.com/2100-1009_22-5420149.html?tag=default.

Leveson, N. G., & Turner, C. S. (1993). An investigation of the Therac-25 accidents. *IEEE Computer, 25*(7), 18–41.

Levy, Steven. (2002). Glitterati vs. geeks: Two heavyweights, Hollywood and Silicon Valley, take the fight over content to the Supremes. *Newsweek,* October 14, 40–42.

Levy, Steven. (2003). Can snooping stop terrorism? *Newsweek,* October 13: 65.

Levy, Sydelle B., & Gordon, Arlene R. (1988). Age-related vision loss: Functional implications and assistive technologies. *International Journal of Technology and Aging, 1*(2), 116–125.

Leyden, John. (2004). U.S. cybersecurity czar quits. *The Register,* October 4. Retrieved November 15, 2004, from http://www.theregister.co.uk/2004/10/04/cybersecurity_czar_quits/.

Lewis, Jeremy R. T. (2000a). FOIA and the emergence of federal information policy in the 1980s and 1990s. In G. David Garson (Ed.), *Handbook of public information systems* (pp. 41–52). New York: Dekker.

Lewis, Jeremy R. T. (2000b). Electronic access to public records. In G. David Garson (Ed.), *Handbook of public information systems* (pp. 197–214). New York: Dekker.

Lipowicz, Alice. (2005). New cyberterrorism security center opens. *Government Computer News.* April 22. Retrieved April 26, 2005, from http://www.gcn. com/vol1_no1/daily-updates/35632-1.html.

Livingston, Brian. (2000, June 16). New web tracking service raises old privacy concerns. *C/Net News.com.* Retrieved October 28, 2004, from http://news. com.com/2010-1071-281326.html.

Loch, Karen D., & Conger, Sue. (1996). Evaluating ethical decisions and computer use. *Communications of the ACM, 39*(3), 48–60.

Lucas, Henry C., Jr. (1975). *Why information systems fail.* New York: Columbia University Press.

Lyman, Jay. (2004). Open source winning in federal government, slowly. *NewsForge,* July 28. Retrieved November 21, 2004, from http://www.news forge.com/article.pl?sid=04/07/23/2335201.

Lyon, David. (1994). *The electronic eye: The rise of surveillance society.* Minneapolis, MI: University of Minnesota Press.

Lyon, David. (2002). *Surveillance as social sorting: Privacy, risk and automated discrimination.* London: Routledge.

Lyons, Daniel J. (1989). Modems, technology empower Chinese fighting for reform. *PC Week,* June 19: 71–72.

Lyytinen, Kalle, & Rose, Gregory M. (2003). The disruptive nature of information technology innovations: The case of Internet computing in systems development organizations. *MIS Quarterly, 27*(4), 557–595.

MacManus, Susan A. (2002). Understanding the incremental nature of e-procurement implementation at the state and local levels. *Journal of Public Procurement, 2*(1), 5–28.

Majchrzak, Ann. (1988). *The human side of factory automation.* San Francisco: Jossey-Bass.

Malina, Anna. (1999). Perspectives on citizen democratisation and alienation in the virtual public sphere. In Barry N. Hague, & Brian D. Loader (Eds.), *Digital democracy: Discourse and decision-making in the information age.* London: Routledge.

Mallory, Jim. (1991). Public libraries go online. *Link-Up, 8*(5): 1, 12.

Mantei, Marilyn M., & Teorey, Toby J. (1988). Cost/benefit analysis for incorporating human factors in the software lifecycle. *Communications of the ACM, 31*(4), 428–439.

Mantovani, Guiseppe. (1994). Is computer-mediated communication intrinsically apt to enhance democracy in organizations? *Human Relations, 47*(1), 45–62.

Marshall, Jon C., & Bannon, Susan. (1988). Race and sex equity in computer advertising. *Journal of Research on Computing and Education, 21*(1), 15–26.

Matheson, A. Duncan. (1993). Innovative use of computers for planning in human service organizations. In Marcos Leiderman, Charles Guzetta, Leny Struminger, & Menachem Monnickendam (Eds.), *Technology in people services: Research, theory, and applications* (pp. 383–395). New York: Haworth Press.

Matthews, William. (2002). IRS deal cools debate about online services. *Government Computer News,* August 5. Retrieved August 21, 2005, from http://www. fcw.com/fcw/articles/2002/0805/news-tax-08-05-02.asp.

May, Christopher. (2002). *The information society: A sceptical view.* Cambridge, UK: Polity Press.

Mazarr, Michael J. (Ed.). (2002). *Information technology and world politics.* New York: Palgrave Macmillan.

McCarthy, Shawn P. (2002). Spam nearly at the tipping point: 50% of Net traffic. *Government Computer News,* September 16: 32.

McCarthy, Shawn P. (2004a). Government shouldn't break its privacy promises. *Government Computer News, 23*(2), 38.

McChesney, Robert W., Wood, Ellen Meiksins, & Foster, John B. (Eds.). (1998). *Capitalism and the information age: The political economy of the global communication revolution.* New York: Monthly Review Press.

McClure, Charles R., J. Sprehe, Timothy, & Eschenfelder, Kristen (2000). *Performance measures for federal agencies: Final report.* Washington, DC: Defense Technical Information Center, the Energy Information Administration, and the U.S. Government Printing Office.

McCormick, John. (2003). "Naked" federal sites are open to attack. *Government Computer News,* February 24: 1, 10.

McCullagh, Declan. (2004a). National IDs—politics as usual? *CNET News.com,* October 4. Retrieved October 24, 2004, from http://news.zdnet.com/2100-1009_22-5395638.html?tag=default.

McCullagh, Declan. (2004b). Judge disarms Patriot Act proviso. Bush stumps for Patriot Act extension. *CNET News.com,* September 29. Retrieved October 24, 2005, from http://news.zdnet.com/2100-1009_22-5388764.html?tag=default.

McCullagh, Declan. (2004c). CIA funds chatroom surveillance. *ZDNet UK,* November 25. Retrieved November 28, 2004, from http://news.zdnet.co.uk/internet/security/0,39020375,39175016,00.htm.

McDonald, A. (2002). Planning the digital library: A virtual impossibility? *Serials: The Journal for the Serials Community, 15*(3), 237–244.

McFarlan, F. Warren. (1981). Portfolio approach to information systems. *Harvard Business Review, 59*(5), 142–150.

McGarr, Sheila M. (2000). Snapshots of the Federal Depository Library Program. Updated from *Administrative Notes, 15*(11), 6–14. Retrieved September 6, 2004, from http://www.access.gpo.gov/su_docs/fdlp/history/snapshot.html.

McGirk, Tim. (1999). Wired for warfare. *Time, 154*(15). Retrieved September 8, 2004, from http://www.globalpolicy.org/globaliz/cvlsocty/zapatis.htm.

McGraw, Tim. (1988). Board hashes out proposal for FBI's NCIC system. *Government Computer News,* January 1.

McGregor, Douglas. (1960). *The human side of enterprise.* New York: McGraw-Hill.

McKay, Jim. (2004a). Pass on privacy? *Government Technology News, 17*(4), 3841.

McKay, Jim. (2004b). Internet takedown. *Government Technology News, 17*(6), 25–28.

McKeith, Tom. (2004). Squeeze play: More and more states look at consolidation to minimize IT spending and get the most out of scarce resources. *Government Technology,* January: 29–33.

McLuhan, Marshall. (1962). *The Gutenberg galaxy.* London: Routledge & Kegan Paul.

McLuhan, Marshall. (1964). *Understanding media: The extensions of man.* New York: McGraw-Hill.

McLuhan, Marshall, Fiore, Quentin, & Agel, Jerome. (1967). *The medium is the message: An inventory of effects.* New York: Bantam Books.

McLuhan, Marshall, & Powers, Bruce R. (1989). *The global village: Transformations in world life and media in the 21st century.* Oxford: Oxford University Press.

McNamara, Joel. (2003). *Secrets of computer espionage: Tactics and counter-measures.* New York: John Wiley & Sons.

McVay, William H. (2004). *Critical success factors for effectively using CCA.* Washington, DC: Office of Management and Budget, Office of Information and Regulatory Affairs. Retrieved September 14, 2004, from http://www.cio.gov/documents/omba11_csf_0410.ppt.

Mehler, Mark. (1991). Reining in runaway systems. *InformationWeek, 351,* 20–24.

Mehta, Michael D. and Éric Darier. (1998). Virtual control and disciplining on the Internet: Electronic governmentality in the new wired world. *The Information Society, 14*(2), 107–116.

Menke, Susan M. (2003). Putnam: Tighten cybersecurity or face legislation. *Government Computer News,* November 23: 12.

Menke, Susan M. (2004a). GPO's permanent press. *Government Computer News, 23*(28). Retrieved September 18, 2004, from http://www.gcn.com/23_28/news/27322-1.html.

Menke, Susan M. (2004b). Military struggles for secure collaboration. *Government Computer News,* November 8. Retrieved November 8, 2004, from http://www.gcn.com/23_32/news/27834-1.html.

Menke, Susan M. (2004c). Insecure credentials worry states, feds. *Government Computer News,* December 3: 1.

Mercuri, Robecca. (2003). Abstract of a lecture delivered at North Carolina State University, November 13, 2003.

Metz, Edmund J. (1986). Managing change toward a leading edge information culture. *Organizational Dynamics,* 15.

Michael, Sara. (2004). Agencies cut paper. *Federal Computer Week,* March 11. Retrieved September 21, 2004, from http://www.fcw.com/fcw/articles/2004/0308/web-gpea-03-11-04.asp.

Milis, Koen, & Mercken, Roger. (2002). Success factors regarding the implementation of ICT investment projects. *International Journal of Production Economics, 80,* 105–117.

Miller, Jason. (2002a). Agency IT investments will have to line up with architecture standards. *Government Computer News,* September 16: 7.

Miller, Jason. (2002b). Study finds e-gov success factors. *Government Computer News,* October 21: 21.

Miller, Jason. (2002c). USPS plans business model makeover. *Government Computer News,* April 15.

Miller, Jason. (2003a). Despite mixed results, feds make GPEA a priority. *Government Computer News,* March 24: 7.

Miller, Jason. (2003b). Agencies submit privacy plans. *Government Computer News,* September 22: 20.

Miller, Jason. (2003c). OMB issues IT systems, web site privacy policy. *Government Computer News,* September 30. Retrieved October 3, 2003, from http://www.gcn.com/vol1_no1/daily-updates/23729-1.html.

Miller, Jason. (2003d). OMB sets new data privacy regulations. *Government Computer News,* October 13: 1, 104.

Miller, Jason. (2003e). GSA to roll out smart cards in 2004. *Government Computer News,* September 8. Retrieved September 10, 2003, from http://www.gcn.com/vol1_no1/daily-updates/23445-1.html.

Miller, Jason. (2003f). GSA gives gateway app a push. *Government Computer News,* September 22: 1, 16.

Miller, Jason. (2003g). Davis: Why the delay on e-authentication? *Government Computer News,* October 15. Retrieved October 16, 2003, from http://www.gcn.com/vol1_no1/daily-updates/23881-1.html.

Miller, Jason. (2003h). GAO preps investment advice. *Government Computer News,* May 5: 46.

Miller, Jason. (2003i). Central authentication gateway plan is history. *Government Computer News,* October 27: 1, 12.

Miller, Jason. (2003j). New authentication plan takes shape. *Government Computer News,* November 10: 1, 10.

Miller, Jason. (2003k). OPM emphasizes security training. *Government Computer News,* September 12. Retrieved September 15, 2003, from http://www.gcn.com/vol1_no1/daily-updates/23523-1.html.

Miller, Jason. (2003l). OMB to agencies: Justify that IT spending. *Government Computer News,* February 10: 1, 12.

Miller, Jason. (2003m). OMB tightens screws on business cases. *Government Computer News,* May 5: 1, 15.

Miller, Jason. (2003n). GAP: Agencies toddle toward EA maturity. *Government Computer News,* December 15: 14.

Miller, Jason. (2003o). Agencies expect enterprise efforts to bear fruit in '04. *Government Computer News,* December 15: 14.

Miller, Jason. (2003p). Digital records swamp NARA: Agency struggles to keep afloat amid sea of data. *Government Computer News,* January 20: 1, 8.

Miller, Jason. (2003q). Many agencies fall short on project management. *Government Computer News,* May 19: 48.

Miller, Jason. (2003r). Agencies make telework gains: Barriers remain. *Government Computer News,* March 24: 20.

Miller, Jason. (2003s). Presidential panel questions postal IT efforts. *Government Computer News*, August 18: 9.

Miller, Jason. (2003t). E-gov projects advance, fund models stand still. *Government Computer News*, September 29: 8.

Miller, Jason. (2003u). GSA will link many pieces of e-procurement. *Government Computer News,* October 27: 5.

Miller, Jason. (2003v). Taking measure of e-gov projects. *Government Computer News,* October 27: 48.

Miller, Jason. (2003w). OMB to agencies: Justify that IT spending. *Government Computer News*, February 10: 1, 12.

Miller, Jason. (2004a). GSA to test authentication. *Government Computer News,* May 3: 1, 44.

Miller, Jason. (2004b). GPO gets a grip on its glut. *Government Computer News.* April 5: 1, 12.

Miller, Jason. (2004c). OMB releases much-anticipated data model. *Government Computer News, 23*(32). Retrieved November 8, 2004, from http://www.gcn.com/23_32/news/27832-1.html.

Miller, Jason. (2004d). E-gov efforts moving forward? Depends who you ask. *Government Computer News*, April 5: 8.

Miller, Jason. (2004e). OMB to make biz cases a bit easier. *Government Computer News*, May 17: 7.

Miller, Jason. (2004f). OMB to agencies: No duplicate IT projects? Prove it. *Government Computer News*. December 3. Retrieved December 7, 2004, from http://www.gcn.com/vol1_no1/daily-updates/28028-1.html/.

Miller, Jason. (2004g). Agencies lag in assessing the impact of systems upgrades. *Government Computer News*, May 17: 1, 12.

Miller, Jason. (2004h). OMB to demand more detailed business cases. *Government Computer News*, March 8: 8.

Miller, Jason. (2004i). Congress OKs $5 million penalty for telecommuting shortfalls. *Government Computer News*, November 24. Retrieved November 28, 2004, from http://www.gcn.com/vol1_no1/daily-updates/28000-1.html.

Miller, Jason. (2004j). E-rulemaking goes for central system. *Government Computer News*, April 19: 12.

Miller, Jason. (2004k). OMB may seek a "loan" to pay for lines-of-business projects. *Government Computer News*, October 26. Retrieved October 27, 2004, from http://www.gcn.com/vol1_no1/daily-updates/27740-1.html.

Miller, Jason. (2004l). With Putnam's move, federal IT loses an advocate. *Government Computer News, 23*(30). Retrieved October 12, 2004, from http://www.gcn.com/23_30/news/27591-1.html.

Miller, Jason. (2004m). Agencies setting up lines-of-business management structure. *Government Computer News*, November 18. Retrieved November 22, 2004, from http://www.gcn.com/vol1_no1/daily-updates/27946-1.html.

Miller, Jason. (2004n). GAO: Workers have no role in A-76 protests. *Government Computer News*, April 26: 5.

Miller, Jason. (2004o). Former OFPP head warns agencies about risks of share-in-savings contracts. *Government Computer News*, November 12. Retrieved November 15, 2004, from http://www.gcn.com/vol1_no1/daily-updates/27887-1.html.

Miller, Jason. (2004p). IBM's competitive sourcing report draws ire of unions. *Government Computer News*, October 29. Retrieved November 1, 2004, from http://www.gcn.com/vol1_no1/daily-updates/27770-1.html.

Miller, Jason. (2004q). GSA reinvents SmartBuy—again. *Government Computer News, 23*(30). Retrieved October 12, 2004, from http://www.gcn.com/23_30/news/27578-1.html.

Miller, Jason. (2005a). GAO finalizes rule giving feds A-76 protest rights. *Government Computer News*, April 15. Retrieved April 18, 2005, from http://www.gcn.com/vol1_no1/daily-updates/35552-1.html.

Miller, Jason. (2005b). GSA head supports consolidating most procurement. *Government Computer News*, April 25. Retrieved April 26, 2005, from http://www.gcn.com/vol1_no1/daily-updates/35640-1.html.

Miller, Jason. (2005c). OMB report leads union to question why feds can't improve without A-76 competitions. *Government Computer News*, January 28. Retrieved March 4, 2005, from http://www.gcn.com/24_2/inbrief/34855-1.html.

Miller, Jason. (2005d). OMB report says A-76 is still paying off. *Government Computer News, 24*(2). Retrieved March 4, 2005, from http://www.gcn.com/24_2/inbrief/34864-1.html.

Miller, Jason. (2005e). IRS funding slows IT modernization, former commissioner says. *Government Computer News*, May 24. Retrieved May 24, 2005, from http://www.gcn.com/vol1_no1/daily-updates/35899-1.html.

Miller, Jason. (2005f). Agencies still not owning up to e-government projects. *Government Computer News*, May 25. Retrieved May 26, 2005, from, http://www.gcn.com/vol1_no1/daily-updates/35907-1.htm.

Miller, Jason. (2005g). OMB looking to shut down systems that duplicate e-gov projects. *Government Computer News*, May 4. Retrieved May 11, 2005, from http://www.gcn.com/vol1_no1/daily-updates/35739-1.html.

Miller, Jason. (2005h). New group to promote telework. *Government Computer News*, April 5. Retrieved April 18, 2005, from http://www.gcn.com/vol1_no1/daily-updates/35461-1.html.

Miller, Stuart. (2003). Pornographers hijack home computers. *The Guardian*, June 13. Retrieved June 30, 2003, from http://www.guardian.co.uk/uk_news/story/0.3604.976332.00.html.

Mitchell, William J. (1996), *City of Bits: Space, place, and the infobahn.* Cambridge: MIT Press.

Mizrahi, Terry, John Downing, Rob Fasano, Patricia McCullough, & Jeremy Shapiro. (Eds.). (1991). *Computers for social change and community organizing.* Binghamton, NY: Haworth Press.

Monnickendam, Menachem, & A. Solomon Eaglestein. (1993). Computer acceptance by social workers: Some unexpected research findings. *Computers in Human Services, 9*(3/4), 409–424.

Montealegre, Ramiro. (1996). What can we learn from the implementation of the automated baggage-handling system at the Denver International Airport? Retrieved December 27, 2003, from http://hsb.baylor.edu/ramsower/ais.ac.96/papers/monteal.htm.

Moody, Bruce. (2004). Deepwater. Homeland Defense Radio. Retrieved March 1, 2005, from http://www.homelanddefenseradio.com/special_reports/reports_125.shtml.

Moore, Gary C., & Benbasat, Izak. (1991). Development of an instrument to measure the perceptions of adopting an information technology innovation. *Information Systems Research, 2*(3), 173–191.

Morahan-Martin, Janet, Alan Olinsky, & Phyllis Schumacher. (1992). Gender differences in computer experience, skills, and attitudes among incoming college students. *Collegiate Microcomputer, 10*(1), 1–8.

Morano, Lou. (2002). Propaganda: Remember the Kuwaiti babies? *United Press International,* February 26. Retrieved October 26, 2004, from http://www.propagandacritic.com/articles/examples.osi.html.

Mosco, Vincent. (1998). Myth-ink links: Power and community on the information highway. *The Information Society, 14*(1), 57–62.

Mosquera, Mary. (2004). Grants.gov marks first anniversary. *Government Computer News*, October 27. Retrieved October 28, 2004, from http://www.gcn.com/vol1_no1/daily-updates/27758-1.html.

Mossberger, Karen. (2000). Information and public organizations—a brave new world? *Public Administration & Management: An Interactive Journal, 5*(4), 157–160.

Move On PAC. (2005). $82 billion more for Iraq. Retrieved May 4, 2005, from http://www.moveonpac.org/iraq/.

Moynihan, Daniel Patrick. (1998). *Secrecy: The American experience.* New Haven: Yale University Press.

Moynihan, Donald P. (2004). Building Secure Elections: E-voting, Security and Systems Theory. *Public Administration Review 64*(5), 515–528.

Muris, Timothy J. (2003). Prepared statement of the Federal Trade Commission before the Subcommittee on Commerce, Justice, State, the Judiciary and Related Agencies of the Committee on Appropriations United States House of Representatives. Washington, D.C. April 9, 2003. Retrieved November 23, 2004, from http://www.ftc.gov/os/2003/04/030409testimony.htm.

Nakashima, Ellen. (2002, March 3). Bush view of secrecy is stirring frustration. Disclosure battle unites right and left. *Washington Post,* A04.

NARA. (1994). *Electronic records management guidance on methodology for determining agency-unique requirements.* National Archives and Records Administration. Retrieved January 5, 2005, from http://www.archives.gov/records_management/policy_and_guidance/requirements_guidance.html.

NARA. (1995). *Agency recordkeeping requirements: A management guide.* National Archives and Records Administration. Retrieved October 14, 2003, from http://www.archives.gov/records_management/policy_and_guidance/agency_recordkeeping_requirements.html.

NARA. (1998). Bulletin 98-02: Disposition of electronic records. Washington, DC: National Archives and Records Administration.

NARA. (2004). Electronic records management guidance on methodology for determining agency-unique requirements. Washington, DC: National Archives and Records Administration. Retrieved October 14, 2005, from http://www.archives.gov/records-mgmt/policy/requirements-guidance.html.

National Center for Education Statistics. (2003). *Internet Access in U.S. Public Schools and Classrooms: 1994-2002.* Washington: U.S. Department of Education, Institute of Education Sciences (NCES 2004-011). Retrieved October 14, 2004, from http://nces.ed.gov/pubs2004/2004011.pdf.

National Urban League. (2004). *The State of Black America 2004.* New York: National Urban League. Retrieved September 30, 2004, from http://www.nul.org/pdf/soba exec.pdf.

Nehring, Dave. (2002). A-76 comments to the OMB. Washington, DC: Office of Management and Budget. Retrieved March 19, 2005, from http://www.white house.gov/omb/circulars/a076/comments/a76-26.pdf.

Nelson, Mark R. (2005). Understanding large-scale IT project failure: Escalating and de-escalating commitment. In G. David Garson (Ed.), *Handbook of public information systems* (2nd ed., pp. 93–105). Boca Raton, FL: CRC Press.

Nesbary, Dale. (2000). The taxation of Internet commerce. *Social Science Computer Review, 18*(1), 17–39.

Newcombe, Tod. (2002a). The price of progress? *Government Technology, 16*(1), 10–11, 42.

Newcombe, Tod. (2002b). Can ERP save e-procurement? *Government Technology,* October: 10–11, 60.

Nielsen NetRatings. (2003). More than 10 million African-Americans are online [News release]. Retrieved September 30, 2004, from http://phx.corporate-ir.net/phoenix.zhtml?c=82037&p=irol-newsArticle&ID=538994&highlight.

Noonan, Dana E. (1991). Information technology: Promises remain unfulfilled. *Computerworld,* February: 18, 25.

Norris, Pippa, Bennett, W. Lance, & Entman, Robert M. (Eds.). (2001). *Digital divide: Civic engagement, information poverty, and the Internet worldwide.* New York: Cambridge University Press.

Northrop, Alana (2002). Lessons for managing information technology in the public sector. *Social Science Computer Review, 20*(2), 194–205.

Northrop, Alana, Dunkle, Debora, Kraemer, Kenneth L., & King, John Leslie. (1994). Computers, police, and the fight against crime: An ecology of technology, training, and use. *Information and the Public Sector, 3,* 21–45.

Northrop, Alana, & Kraemer, Kenneth L. (2000). The information age: Which nations will benefit? In G. David Garson (Ed.), *Handbook of public information systems.* New York: Marcel Dekker

Novotny, Patrick. (2002). Local television, the World Wide Web, and the 2000 presidential election. *Social Science Computer Review, 20*(1), 58–72.

NRC. (2002). *Making the nation safer: The role of science and technology in countering terrorism.* Washington, DC: National Academies Press for the Committee on Science and Technology in Countering Terrorism, National Research Council.

NTIA. (1992). A Nation Online: How Americans Are Expanding Their Use of the Internet. Washington, DC: U.S. Department of Commerce, Economics and Statistics Administration and the National Telecommunications and Information Administration. February.

NTIA. (1995). Falling through the Net: A survey of the "have nots" in rural and urban America. Washington, DC: U.S. Department of Commerce, National Telecommunications and Information Administration. Retrieved September 20, 2005, from http://www.ntia.doc.gov/ntiahome/fallingthru.html.

NTIA. (1998). Falling through the Net II: New data on the digital divide. Washington, DC: U.S. Department of Commerce, National Telecommunications and Information Administration. Retrieved September 20, 2005, from http://www.ntia.doc.gov/ntiahome/net2.

NTIA. (1999). Falling through the Net: Defining the digital divide. Washington, DC: U.S. Department of Commerce, National Telecommunications and Information Administration. Retrieved September 20, 2005, from http://www.ntia.doc.gov/ntiahome/digitaldivide.

NTIA. (2002). A nation online: How Americans are expanding their use of the Internet. Washington, DC: U.S. Department of Commerce, National Telecommunications and Information Administration. Retrieved September 20, 2005, from http://www.ntia.doc.gov/ntiahome/dn/nationonline_020502.htm.

NUA. (2003a). Global Internet audience increases. *Internet Surveys.* Retrieved October 2, 2003, from http://www.nua.com/surveys/index.cgi?f=VS&art_id=905358729&rel=true.

NUA. (2003b). Africa. *Internet Surveys.* Retrieved October 2, 2003, from http://www.nua.com/surveys/index.cgi?f=VS&art_id=905358408&rel=true.

NUA eMarketer. (2001). Almost all US schools now online. NUA Internet surveys. *eMarketer,* May 21. Retrieved October 2, 2003, from http://www.nua.com/surveys/index.cgi?f=VS&art_id=905356783&rel=true.

NUA eMarketer. (2002). NUA Internet surveys. *eMarketer.* Retrieved October 2, 2003, from http://www.nua.com/surveys/index.cgi?f=VS&art_id=905358143&rel=true.

Nyce, James M., & Kahn, Paul. (1991). *From memex to hypertext: Vannevar Bush and the mind's machine.* San Diego, CA: Harcourt Brace Jovanovich.

OECD. (1980). *OECD guidelines on the protection of privacy and transborder flows of personal data.* Brussels, Belgium: OECD. Retrieved November 1, 2004, from http://www.oecd.org/document/18/0,2340,en_2649_34223_1815186_1_1_1_1,00.html.

Office of the Press Secretary. (2004). Fact sheet: President Bush signs anti-spam law, [White House Press release]. December 16, 2003. Retrieved October 24, 2004, from http://www.whitehouse.gov/news/releases/2003/12/20031216-4.html.

Ogozalek, Virginia Z. (1991). The social impacts of computing: Computer technology and the graying of America. *Social Science Computer Review, 9*(4), 655–666.

Oliver, Richard E. (2004). *What is transparency?* New York: McGraw Hill.

Olsen, Florence. (2004). FISMA compliance: Money misspent? *Federal Computer Week*, May 21. Retrieved November 16, 2004, from http://www.fcw.com/fcw/articles/2004/0517/web-fisma-05-21-04.asp.

OMB. (1997). Information technology investment evaluation guide. Assessing risks and returns: A guide for evaluating federal agencies' IT investment decision-making. GAO/AIMD-10.1.13.

OMB. (2001). *The president's management agenda, FY 2002* (S/N 041 –001 –00568). Washington, DC: Superintendent of Documents, Government Printing Office.

OMB. (2002). E-Government Strategy. February 27. Retrieved July 30, 2005 from http://www.whitehouse.gov/omb/inforeg/egovstrategy.pdf.

OMB. (2003a). *Implementing the President's Management Agenda for e-government.* Retrieved September 3, 2004, from http://www.whitehouse.gov/omb/egov/2003egov_strat.pdf.

OMB. (2003b). Regulations.gov to transform U.S. rulemaking process and save nearly $100 million. Office of Management and Budget. Retrieved September 13, 2004, from http://www.whitehouse.gov/omb/pubpress/2003-03.pdf.

OMB. (2004). *Recommended policies and guidelines for federal public websites: Final report of the Interagency Committee on Government Information.* June 9. Retrieved December 3, 2004, from http://www.cio.gov/documents/ICGI/web-guide lines.html.

OMB Watch. (2005). House bill calls for agency performance ratings. Retrieved June 5, 2005, from http://www.ombwatch.org/article/articleview/2621/1/308?TopicID=1.

O'Neil, Dara V., & Baker, Paul M. A. (2003). The role of institutional motivations in technological adoption: Implementation of DeKalb County's Family Technology Resource Centers. *The Information Society, 19*(2), 305–314.

O'Neil, Michael J., & Dempsey, James X. (2000). Critical infrastructure protection: Threats to privacy and other civil liberties and concerns with government mandates on industry. *DePaul Business Law Journal, 12,* 97. Retrieved August 30, 2003, from http://www.cdt.org/publications/lawreview/2000depaul.shtml#1.

Onley, Dawn S. (2002a). DARPA's plans for data mining draw criticism. *Government Computer News,* December 16: 36.

Onley, Dawn S. (2002b). Army investigates breaches. *Government Computer News,* August 26: 14.

Onley, Dawn S. (2002b). What if they installed an app and nobody used it? *Goverment Computer News.* August 19: 41.

Onley, Dawn S. (2003). Defense pushes smart-card rollout into spring. *Government Computer News,* November 10: 18.

Onley, Dawn S. (2004a). DOD to vendors: Join PKI system or take a hike. *Government Computer News,* March 22: 1, 16.

Onley, Dawn S. (2004b). Report: Spending on IT contracts surges in 2004. *Government Computer News,* December 3. Retrieved December 7, 2004, from http://www.gcn.com/vol1_no1/daily-updates/28030-1.html.

Onley, Dawn S. (2005). DIA will centralize IT management, *Government Computer Quarterly,* April 26. Retrieved April 28, 2005, from http://www.gcn.com/vol1_no1/daily-updates/35656-1.html.

Ono, Hiroshi, & Zavodny, Madeline. (2002). Gender and the Internet. Federal Reserve Bank of Atlanta, *Working Paper Series.* June 24, 2002. Retrieved September 26, 2004, from http://www.findarticles.com/p/articles/mi_m0KXF/is_2002_June_24/ai_90305995/pg_1.

OPM. (2000). *Operating manual: Qualification standards for general schedule positions: Individual occupational requirements for GS-1102: Contract specialist.* U.S. Office of Personnel Management. January 1. Retrieved February 10, 2005, from http://www.opm.gov/qualifications/sec-iv/b/gs1100/1102r.htm#Revised_1102_Qual_Stnd.

OTA. (1986). *Federal government information technology: Management, security, and Congressional oversight.* Retrieved September 18, 2004, from http://www.wws.princeton.edu/cgi-bin/byteserv.prl/~ota/disk2/1986/8611/861103. PDF.

Packer, George. (2003). Smart mobbing the war. *New York Times,* March 9. Retrieved September 8, 2004, from http://www.nytimes.com/2003/03/09/magazine/09ANTIWAR.html?ex=1095134400&en=4f8343d07d084627&ei=5070&page wanted=print&position=top.

Parayil, Govindan. (2005). Digital divide and increasing returns: Contradictions of informational capitalism. *The Information Society, 21*(1), 41–51.

Parenti, Christian. (2003). *The soft cage: Surveillance in America from slavery to the war on terror.* New York: Basic Books.

Pauly, George. (2005). Wireless Internet in Chatham aims to offer access to all. *Chatham County Line, 3*(3), 1, 7.

Perera, David. (2004). Congress cuts e-gov funds—again. *Federal Computer Week,* December 6. Retrieved March 28, 2005, from http://www.fcw.com/fcw/articles/2004/1206/news–egov–12–06–04.asp.

Perlman, Ellen. (2002). Contract hoops and lopholes. *Governing, 15*(10), 53–60.

Perritt, Henry H., Jr. (1995). Executive Summary. *Electronic dockets: Use of information technology in rulemaking and adjudication: Report to the Administrative Conference of the United States.* Retrieved September 21, 2004, from http://www.kentlaw.edu/classes/rstaudt/internetlaw/casebook/Downloadsexecutiv.htm.

Perry, Gail. (2004). Naming and shaming: States fight tax delinquency online. *Accounting Today. 18*(5), 3.

Peterson, Shane. (2002a). Digital legislature. *Electronic Government, 3*(3), 8–12.

Peterson, Shane. (2002b). End of the line. *Government Technology,* October, 18–24, 62–64.

Peterson, Shane. (2003). Something for nothing? Tight finances prompt agencies to take a hard look at open source software. *Government Technology, 16*(5), 27–32, 64–65.

Peterson, Shane. (2004a). Evolving ERP: Enterprise resource planning takes on unconventional tasks. *Government Technology, 17*(5), 19–24.

Peterson, Shane. (2004b). Outside in. *Government Technology, 17*(10), 19–22, 50.

Pike, Walter W. (2002). A-76 comments to the OMB. Washington, DC: Office of Management and Budget. Retrieved March 19, 2005, from http://www.white house.gov/omb/circulars/a076/comments/a76-222.pdf.

Pinch, Trevor, & Bijker, Weibe. (1986). Science, relativism and the new sociology of technology: Reply to Russell. *Social Studies of Science, 16*, 347–360.

Piturro, Marlene. (1990). Electronic monitoring. *Information Center, 6*(7), 26–31.

Platter, Adele. (1988). Computer experiences of young adults: An empirical analysis. *Social Indicators Research, 8*(3), 291–302.

Poister, Ted H., & Streib, Gregory. (1999). Performance measurement in municipal government. *Public Administration Review, 59*(4), 325–335.

Poon, PoPo, & Wagner, Christian. (2001). Critical success factors revisited: Success and failure cases of information systems for senior executives. *Decision Support Systems, 30*, 393–418.

Popper, Karl R. (1945). *The open society and its enemies.* London: George Routledge & Sons.

Porter, Charlene. (2003). A new way of governing in the digital age. *Global Issues,* November. Retrieved September 22, 2004, from http://usinfo.state.gov/journals/itgic/1103/ijge/gj05.htm.

Privacy International. (2004). *Mistaken identity: Exploring the relationship between national identity cards & the prevention of terrorism.* London and Washington: Privacy International.

Privacy Journal. (2004). Tips for individuals and organizations. Retrieved November 1, 2004, from http://www.privacyjournal.net/bio.htm.

Prysby, Charles L., & Prysby, Nicole D. (2003). Electronic mail in the public workplace: Issues of privacy and public disclosure. In G. David Garson (Ed.), *Public information technology* (pp. 271–298). Hershey, PA: Idea Group.

Public Citizen. (2004). Freedom of Information Act. Washington, DC: Public Citizen. Retrieved October 24, 2004, from http://www.bushsecrecy.org/Page Index.cfm?ParentID=2&CategoryID=2&PagesID=15.

Public Management. (1989). The electronic democracy. *Public Management, 71*(Nov.), 2–13.

Putnam, Robert D. (1995a). Bowling alone: America's declining social capital. *Journal of Democracy, 6*, 65–78.

Putnam, Robert D. (1995b). Tuning in, tuning out: The strange disappearance of social capital in America. *Political Science and Politics, 28*, 664–683.

Randolph, W. Alan, & Posner, Barry Z. (1992). *Getting the job done! Managing project teams and task forces for success.* Englewood Cliffs, NJ: Prentice-Hall.

Rapp, William V. (2002). *Information technology strategies: How leading firms use IT to gain an advantage.* New York: Oxford University Press.

Reengineering Resource Center. (1996). Progress report: Pushing ahead at the Patent and Trademark Office. Retrieved January 4, 2005, from http://www.reengineering.com/articles/mar96/patent.htm.

Reinig, Bruce A., & Mejias, Roberto J. (2004). The effects of national culture and anonymity on flaming and criticalness in gss-supported discussions. *Small Group Research, 35*(6), 698–723.

Reisman, Jane. (1990). Gender inequality in computing. *Computers in human services, 7*(1/2), 45–63.

Reporters Committee for Freedom of the Press. (1998). Clinton, Gore push stricter federal privacy policies. June 1. Retrieved October 28, 2004, from http://www.rcfp.org/news/1998/0601f.html.

Reporters' Committee for Freedom of the Press. (2002). Reporters committee warns of severe restrictions in homeland security bill. November 19. Retrieved October 21, 2004, from http://rcfp.org/news/releases/view.php?2002_11_19_homeland.txt.

Reschenthaler, G. B., & Thompson, Fred. (1996). The information revolution and the new public management. *Journal of Public Administration Research and Theory, 6*(1), 125–143.

Reuters. (2003). Privacy group calls for JetBlue prosecution. Reuters Press Agency. September 22. Retrieved October 24, 2004, from http://news.zdnet.com/2100-1009_22-5080334.html.

Rheingold, Howard. (1991). Electronic democracy: The great equalizer. *Whole Earth Review, 71*(Summer), 4–12.

Richards, Evelyn. (1989). Proposed FBI crime computer system raises questions on accuracy, privacy. *Washington Post*. February 13. Reprinted in C. Dunlop and R. Kling, *Computerization and controversy* (pp. 436–438). New York: Academic Press.

Richardson, William. (1990). Earth day 1990 online. *Database Searcher, 6*(4), 14–19.

Richter, Michael J. (1992). Turning a technological innovation into an empty promise. *Governing, 5*(4), 65.

Rifkin, Jeremy. (1995). *The end of work: The decline of the global labor force and the dawn of the post-market era*. New York: Putnam.

Rivera, Mario A., & Casias, Robert A. (2001). Resource constraints in information systems development: A land management case study. *International Journal of Public Administration, 24*(6), 521–547.

Rivera, Mario A., & Rogers, Everett M. (2004). Evaluating public sector innovation in networks: Extending the reach of the National Cancer Institute's web-based Health Communication Intervention Research Initiative. *The Innovation Journal: The Public Sector Innovation Journal, 9*(3). Retrieved March 14, 2005, from http://www.innovation.cc/volumes-issues/vol9-iss3.htm.

Rivero, Victor. (2004). The Dean dream: The 2004 presidential campaign may mark the beginning of a new era of Internet campaigning. *Government Technology News, 17*(5), 30–38.

Roberts, Nancy. (2004). Public deliberation in an age of direct citizen participation. *American Review of Public Administration, 34*(4), 315–353.

Roberts, Vanessa Jo. (2004). GAO: Homeland security lacks big picture on IT. *Government Computer News, 23*(30). Retrieved October 19, 2004, from http://www.gcn.com/23_30/news/27593-1.html.

Rocheleau, Bruce. (2000). Prescriptions for public-sector information management: A review, analysis, and critique. *American Review of Public Administration, 30*(4), 414–435.

Rogers, Everett M. (2003). *Diffusion of Innovations* (5th ed.). New York: The Free Press.

Ronen, Joiwind Williams. (2000). E-government, the next American revolution. Washington, DC: Council for Excellence in Government. In Congressional Internet Caucus (2001). *E-Government Briefing Book.* Available from http://www.netcaucus.org/books/egov2001/pdf/Bluecove.pdf.

Ronfeldt, David F., & Arquilla, John. (1998). The Zapatista social netwar in Mexico. Retrieved September 8, 2004, from http://www.rand.org/publications/MR/MR994/.

Rosen, Jeffrey. (2001). *The unwanted gaze: The destruction of privacy in America.* New York: Vintage Books.

Rosen, Jeffrey. (2004). *The naked crowd: Reclaiming security and freedom in an anxious age.* New York: Random House.

Ruberg, Laurie F. (1989). Human services on cable: A case study of a data retrieval system designed for public access. *Computers in Human Services, 4*(3/4), 233–241.

Ryan, Stephen M. (2002). Homeland agencies will be wards of OMB. *Government Computer News,* September 9: 42.

Safayeni, Frank R., Purdy, R. Lyn, & Higgins, Christopher A. (1989). Social meaning of personal computers for managers and professionals: Methodology and results. *Behaviour & Information Technology, 8*(2), 99–107.

Sanders, Robert L. (1995). Finishing what we start: A lesson for functional managers from project management and automated workflow. *Records Management Quarterly,* April: 48, 50–55.

Sandvig, Christian. (2003). Public Internet access for young children in the inner city: Evidence to inform access subsidy and content regulation. *The Information Society, 19*(2), 171–183.

Santosus, Megan. (2004). E-democracy: The lowdown on e-voting. *CIO,* June 1. Retrieved September 13, 2004, from http://www.cio.com/archive/060104/evote.html.

SBA. (2001). *The business plan—road map to success.* Washington, DC: Small Business Administration. Retrieved October 16, 2002, from http://www.sba.gov/starting/indexbusplans.html.

Schelin, Shannon, & Garson, G. David. (2004). *Humanizing information technology: Advice from experts.* Hershey, PA: CyberTech.

Schellhardt, Timothy D. (1990, November 28). Middle managers get mired in the mundane. *Wall St. Journal,* B1.

Schmitt, Christopher H., & Pound, Edward T. (2003). Keeping secrets: The Bush administration is doing the public's business out of the public eye. *U.S. News and World Report,* December 22: 18–22, 24, 27–29.

Schölvinck, Johan. (2001). Bridging the digital divide: The role of the United Nations. New York: United Nations Online Network in Public Administration and Finance (UNPAN). Retrieved October 15, 2004, from http://unpan1.un.org/intradoc/groups/public/documents/UN/UNPAN000698.pdf.

Schonfield, Erick. (2003). Total information delusion. *Business 2.0,* February 3. Retrieved February 3, 2003, from http://www.business2.com/articles/web/0,1653,46876,00.html.

Schwartau, Winn. (2002). *Pearl Harbor dot com.* New York: Thunders' Mouth Press/Avalon.

Schwartz, Ari. (2000). Cost. Washington, DC: Center for Technology and Democracy. Retrieved October 15, 2002, from http://www.netcaucus.org/books/egov2001/pdf/cost.pdf.

Seifert, Jeffrey W. (2003). *A primer on e-government: Sectors, stages, opportunities, and challenges of online governance.* Washington, DC: Congressional Research Service. Retrieved September 4, 2004, at http://www.fas.org/sgp/crs/RL31057.pdf.

Shachaf, Pnina, & Hara, Norio. (2002). Ecological approach to virtual team effectiveness. [Working Paper WP-02-08]. Bloomington, IN: Center for Social Informatics Retrieved February 29, 2005, from http://www.slis.indiana.edu/CSI/WP/WP02-08B.html.

Shah, Anup. (2004). Creation of an official propaganda office. Globalissues.org/Geopolitics/WarOnTerror/Media. April 4. Retrieved August 6, 2005, from http://www.globalissues.org/Geopolitics/WarOnTerror/Media.asp?p=1#Creationofan OfficialPropagandaOffice.

Sharlot, Lady. (2004). *How to be an Internet pornographer.* Topeka, KS: Tassel.

Shattuck, John. (1996). Computer matching is a serious threat to individual rights. In Rob Kling (Ed.), *Computerization and controversy: Value conflicts and social choices* (2nd ed.). New York: Academic Press.

Shelley, Mack, Thrane, Lisa, Shulman, Stuart, Lang, Evette, Beisser, Sally, Larson, Teresa, et al. (2004). Digital citizenship: Parameters of the digital divide. *Social Science Computer Review, 22*(2), 256–269.

Shi, Wenbo. (2002). Contribution of organizational factors in the success of electronic government commerce. *International Journal of Public Administration, 25*(5), 629–657.

Shields, Mark. (1985). Gender, computing experience, and attitudes toward computing: A survey of Brown University undergraduates. Paper presented at, IBM University Advanced Education Projects Conference, June 23–26.

Siegel, Lenny. (1986). Microcomputers: From movement to industry. *Monthly Review, 38*(3), 110–117.

Smith, Ralph Lee. (1972). *The wired nation: Cable TV—The electronic communications highway.* New York: Harper and Row.

Smith, Robert Ellis. (2002). *A national ID card: A license to live.* Providence, RI: Privacy Journal.

Smith, Robert Ellis. (2004a). *Compilation of state and federal privacy laws (2002)* with *2004 Supplement.* Providence, RI: Privacy Journal.

Smith, Robert Ellis. (2004b). Ranking of states in protections. Retrieved October 31, 2004, from http://www.privacyjournal.net/events.htm.

Smith, William E. (1993). Journalism students' attitudes toward and experience with computers: A longitudinal study. *New Computing Journal, 8*(4), 9–18.

Snyder, J. (1988). Early career achievements of National Science Foundation graduate fellows, 1967–1976. Washington, DC: OSEP, NRC.

Sofaer, Abraham D, & Cuellar, Mariano-Florentino. (2001). *The transnational dimension of cyber crime and terrorism.* Hoover National Security Forum Series. Stanford, CA: Hoover Institution.

Solove, Daniel J., & Rotenberg, Marc. (2003). *Information privacy law.* New York: Aspen.

Soros, George. (1998). The crisis of global capitalism. *Newsweek,* December 7: 78–86.

Soto, Carlos A. (2003). Beware: Hackers are lurking in public places. *Government Computer News,* October 13: 16–17.

Specht, Pamela Hammers. (2000). The impact of IT investment on orgnization performance in the public sector. In G. David Garson (Ed.), *Handbook of public information systems* (pp. 141–151). New York: Dekker.

Standish Group. (1994). *CHAOS Report*. The Standish Group. Retrieved January 8, 2005, from http://www.standishgroup.com/sample_research/chaos_1994_1.php.

Standish Group. (2001). *Extreme CHAOS*. The Standish Group. Retrieved January 8, 2005, from http://www.standishgroup.com/sample_research/PDFpages/extreme_chaos.pdf.

Stanley, Laura D. (2003). Beyond access: Psychosocial barriers to computer literacy. *The Information Society, 19*(5), 407–416.

State Tech. (2003). If you build it, will they come? *StateTech,* Fall: 24–25.

State Tech. (2004). Types on cyber attacks and abuse detected in 2003. *State Tech,* Spring: 37.

Stern, Andrew L. (2002). A-76 comments to the OMB. Washington, DC: Office of Management and Budget. Retrieved March 19, 2005, from http://www.whitehouse.gov/omb/circulars/a076/comments/a76-274.pdf.

Sternstein, Aliya. (2004). Interior's Internet disconnect. *Federal Computer Week,* October 11. Retrieved October 8, 2004, from http://www.fcw.com/fcw/articles/2004/1011/pol-interior-10-11-04.asp.

Steyaert, Joan. (2002). Public and private sector innovation risk and return in information technology. *Government Computer News,* October 14. Retrieved October 14, 2002, from http://www.gcn.com/partners/partners.html.

Stoiber, John R. (1999). Maximizing IT investments. *CIO,* July 15. Retrieved October 2, 2002, from http://www.cio.com/archive/enterprise.071599_checks_con tent.html.

Stolfi, Francesco, & Sussman, Gerald. (2001). Telecommunications and transnationalism: The polarization of social space. *The Information Society, 17*(1), 49–62.

Stone, Amey. (2003). The digital divide that wasn't. *Business Week Online,* August 19. Retrieved September 30, 2004, from http://www.businessweek.com/technology/content/aug2003/tc20030819_4285_tc126.html.

Stowers, Genie N. L. (2002). *The state of federal websites: The pursuit of excellence*. Arlington, VA: The PricewaterhouseCoopers Endowment for The Business of Government.

Stowers, Genie N. L. (2004). *Measuring the performance of e-government*. Washington, DC: The IBM Center for The Business of Government.

Strock, Barry, & Dave Adkins. (1989). *The municipal computer systems handbook*. Rensselaerville, NY: Rensselaerville Systems.

Sweeney, Jim. (2002). Study uncovers more security on Web sites. *Government Computer News,* September 23: 5.

Sweeney, Jim. (2003). Filters block porn sites—federal sites too. *Government Computer News,* January 13: 5.

Swider, Gaile. (1988). Ten pitfalls of information center management. *Journal of Information Systems Management, 5*(1), 22–28.

T1. (2004). Internet governance has become a non-issue. *Circle ID,* September 23. Retrieved November 21, 2004, from http://www.circleid.com/article/768_0_1_0_C/.

Tapscott, Don, & Caston, Art. (1992). *Paradigm shift: The new promise of information technology*. New York: McGraw-Hill.

Temple, Linda, & Lips, Hilary M. (1989). Gender differences and similarities in attitudes toward computers. *Computers in Human Behavior, 5*(4), 215–226.

Temin, Thomas R. (2002). OMB-centric world. *Government Computer News,* September 23: 28.

Teo, Thompson S. H., & Ang, James S. K. (1999). Critical success factors in the alignment of IS plans with business plans. *International Journal of Information Management, 19,* 173–185.

The Economist. (2003a). Rich nations reject IT fund for poor nations. *The Economist,* December 11.

The Economist. (2003b). Governments like open-source software, but Microsoft does not. *The Economist,* September 11.

Thomas, Arthur Peach. (1990). *A study of cognitive factors affecting the successful implementation of end-user information technology,* unpublished doctoral dissertation. Buffalo, NY: State University of New York at Buffalo.

Thomas, Douglas, & Loader, Brian D. (Eds.). (2000). *Cybercrime: Law enforcement, security, and surveillance in the information age.* London: Sage.

Thomas, Robert J. (1994). *What machines can't do: Technology and politics in the industrial enterprise.* Berkeley, CA: University of California Press.

Thornburgh, Dick, & Lin, Herbert S. (Eds.). (2002). *Youth, pornography, and the Internet.* Washington, DC: National Academy Press.

Toffler, Alvin. (1980). *The third wave.* New York: Harper Collins.

Tonn, Bruce E., Zambrano, Persides, & Moore, Sheila. (2001). Community networks or networked communities? *Social Science Computer Review, 19*(2), 201–212.

TopTenReviews, Inc. (2004). Pornography industry revenue statistics. *Internet Filter Review.* Retrieved November 22, 2004, from http://www.internetfilter review.com/internet-pornography-statistics.html.

Tracy, Rick. (2003). Wake up before FISMA kicks you out of bed. *Government Computer News,* October 27: 27.

Transportation Security Administration. (2004). Privacy impact assessment: Secure Flight test phase. Washington, DC: Department of Homeland Security, Transportation Security Administration (TSA-2004-19160). Retrieved November 4, 2004, from http://www.tsa.gov/public/interweb/assetlibrary/Secure_Flight_PIA_Notice_9.21.04.pdf.

Treasury Board of Canada Secretariat. (2002). *Privacy impact assessment guidelines: A framework to manage privacy risks.* Ottawa, Canada: Treasury Board. Retrieved October 22, 2003, from http://www.tbs-sct.gc.ca/pubs_pol/ciopubs/pia-pefr/paipg-pefrld_e.asp.

Trist, Emery L. (1973). *Organizations and technical change.* London: Tavistock Institute of Human Relations.

Trist, Emery L. (1981, June). The evolution of sociotechnical systems: A conceptual framework and an action research program (Occasional Paper No. 2). Toronto: Ontario Quality of Working Life Center.

Trist, Emery L., Emery, Fred, Murray, Hugh, & Trist, Beul (Eds.). (1997). *The social engagement of social science: A Tavistock anthology, Vol. 23: The socio-ecological perspective.* Philadelphia, PA: University of Pennsylvania Press.

Trist, Emery, & Murray, Hugh. (1990). *The social engagement of social science: A Tavistock anthology, Vol. 2: The socio-technical perspective.* Philadelphia, PA: University of Pennsylvania Press.

Turoff, Murray. (1985). Information, value, and the internal marketplace. *Technological Forecasting and Social Change, 27*(1985), 357–373.

Turoff, Murray, Hiltz, Roxanne Starr, & Mills, Miriam. (1989). Telecomputing: Organizational impacts. In *Research Annual on Social Sciences and Computers*, (Vol. 2, Ch. 9) Greenwich, CT: JAI Press.

UCLA. (2003). *The UCLA Internet Report: Surveying the Digital Future Year Three*. Los Angeles: UCLA Center for Communication Policy.

UN and ASPA. (2002). Benchmarking E-Government: A Global Perspective—Assessing the UN Member States. Washington, DC: American Society for Public Administration and the United Nations. Retrieved September 4, 2004, from: http://www.unpan.org/egovernment2.asp.

U.S. Department of Commerce. (2000). *Falling through the net: Toward digital inclusion*. National Telecommunications and Information Administration. Executive Summary. Retrieved September 26, 2004, from http://www.ntia.doc.gov/ntiahome/digitaldivide/execsumfttn00.htm.

U.S. Department of Energy. (1996). *Guidelines for strategic planning*. (DOE/PO-0041). USDOE, Office of Strategic Planning, Budget, and Program Evaluation. Retrieved June 14, 2003, from http://www.orau.gov/pbm/links/sp-guide.pdf.

U.S. Department of Justice, Civil Rights Division, Disability Rights Section. (2003). *Accessibility of state and local government websites to people with disabilities*. Washington, DC: USGPO.

U.S. Department of State. (2004). *Managing department of state projects* (5 FAH-5 H-210). Retrieved January 4, 2005, from http://foia.state.gov/masterdocs/05 FAH05/ITS0210.PDF.

U.S. Patent and Trademark Office. (2004). Strategic information technology plan, FY 2004–FY 2009. Office of the Chief Information Officer, USPTO. Retrieved January 5, 2005, from http://www.uspto.gov/web/offices/cio/sitp/ 2004/ocio-sitp-fy 2004-final.pdf

Vallas, Steven. (2000). Manufacturing knowledge: Technology, culture, and social inequality at work. In G. David Garson (Ed.), *Social dimensions of information technology* (pp. 236–254). Hershey, PA: Idea Group.

Vance, Faith. (1991). HandsNet links advocates. *Link-Up, 8*(6), 28.

Vandenbosch, Betty. (1999). An empirical analysis of the association between the use of executive support systems and perceived organizational competitiveness. *Accounting, Organizations and Society, 24*(1), 77–92.

van Dijk, Jan, & Hacker, Kenneth. (2003). The digital divide as a complex and dynamic phenomenon. *The Information Society, 19*(4), 315–326.

van Gils, Diane. (2002, September). Examples of evaluation practices used by OECD member countries to assess e-government. Brussels, Belgium: OECD. Retrieved August 7, 2003, from http://www.tbm.tudelft.nl/modulemateriaal/voltijd/tb393/Zenc. vanGils.htm.

Vasishtha, Preetha. (2002a). Next year, tax forms will talk. *Government Computer News*, September 23: 20.

Vasishtha, Preeti. (2002b). HUD site changes for users. *Government Computer News*, September 16: 50.

Vasishtha, Preeti. (2002c). IG report calls IRS' tracking of its PCs shoddy. *Government Computer News*. August 26: 5.

Verma, Vijay K. (1995). *Organizing projects for success: The human aspects of project management (Vol. 1)*. Upper Darby, PA: Project Management Institute.

Vernon, Robert, & Lynch, Darlene. (2003). Consumer access to agency websites: Our best foot forward? *Journal of Technology in Human Services, 21*(4), 37–52.

Wagner, Jim. (2004). Spam spikes this holiday season. New York: MessageLabs. Retrieved February 6, 2005, from http://www.messagelabs.com/news/virus news/detail/ default.asp?contentItemId=1231&region.

Wainfan, Lynne, & Davis, Paul. (2004). Challenges in virtual collaboration: Videoconferencing, audioconferencing, and computer-mediated communications. Santa Monica, CA: RAND Corporation. Retrieved December 14, 2004, from http://www.rand.org/pubs/monographs/2004/RAND_MG273. pdf.

Wait, Patience. (2005). NASA inspector general critical of IT structure. *Government Computer News*, April 12. Retrieved April 18, 2005, from http://www. gcn.com/vol1_no1/daily-updates/35494-1.html.

Walker, Richard W. (2003a). Managers fret about security for wireless units. *Government Computer News,* October 13: 24.

Walker, Richard W. (2003b). Paperless office?: Check the writing on the wall. *Government Computer News*, March 24: 26.

Walker, Richard W. (2003c). Experience is key to a project manager's success. *Government Computer News,* August 18: 26.

Walsh, Trudy. (2003a). Security experts give e-voting a thumbs down. *Government Computer News,* August 18: 7.

Walsh, Trudy. (2003b). California city tracks workers' Internet use. *Government Computer News,* March 10: 5.

Ware, Mary C., & Stuck, Mary F. (1985). Sex-role messages vis-a-vis microcomputer use: A look at the pictures. *Sex Roles, 13*(3–4), 205–214.

Warschauer, Mark. (2003). Dissecting the "digital divide": A case study in Egypt. *The Information Society, 19*(2): 297–304.

Wartell, Julie, & J. McEwan, Thomas. (2001). *Privacy in the information age: A guide for sharing crime maps and spatial data* (NCJ 188739). Washington, DC: U. S. Department of Justice, Office of Justice Programs, National Institute of Justice. Available from http://www.ncjrs.org/pdffiles1/nij/188739.pdf.

Watt, Peggy. (1989). Study shows workers underuse software. *InfoWorld, 27,* March: 17.

Waxman, Henry A. (2004). Statement before the Government Reform Committee, June 15, 2004. Retrieved March 16, 2005, from http://www.democrats.reform. house.gov/Documents/20040826161707-44655.pdf.

Wayne, L. (2000, September 9). Voter profiles selling briskly as privacy issues are raised. *New York Times,* A1.

Weisman, Shulamith. (1983). Computer games for the frail elderly. *The Gerontologist, 23*(4), 361–363.

Weiss, Rick. (2004). "Data Quality" law is nemesis of regulation. *The Washington Post, 127*(255), A1, 6–7.

Weissberg, Robert. (2003). Technology evolution and citizen activism: The Net and the rebirth of limited government. *Policy Studies Journal, 31*(3), 385–395.

Welsh, William. (2005a). State and local IT spending on the rebound. *Government Computer News,* March 30. Retrieved March 31, 2005, from http://www. gcn.com/vol1_no1/daily-updates/35387-1.html.

Welsh, William. (2005b). Despite a bumpy first ride, San Diego goes for a second-generation outsourcing deal. *Government Computer News, 24*(7). Retrieved April 30, 2005, from http://www.gcn.com/24_7/outsourcing/35432-1.html.

West, Darrell M. (2000). *Assessing e-government: The Internet, democracy, and service delivery by state and federal governments.* Providence, RI: Taubman Center for Public Policy, Brown University. Retrieved October 1, 2002, from http://www.insidepolitics.org/egov/egovtreport00.html.

West, Darrell M. (2003a). *Achieving e-government for all.* Providence, RI: Taubman Center for Public Policy, Brown University. Retrieved October 30, 2003, from http://www.benton.org/publibrary/egov/access2003.html.

West, Darrell M. (2003b). *Global E-Government, 2003.* Providence, RI: Taubman Center for Public Policy, Brown University. Retrieved October 10, 2004, from http://www.insidepolitics.org/egovt03int.html.

West, Darrell M. (2004). *Fifth annual state and federal e-government study: Press release.* Retrieved September 12, 2004, from http://www.insidepolitics.org/PressRelease 04us.html.

West, J. P., & Berman, Evan M. (2001). The impact of revitalized management practices on the adoption of information technology: A national survey of local governments. *Public Performance and Management Review, 24*(3), 254–269.

Westrum, Ron. (1991). *Technologies and society: The shaping of people and things.* Belmont, CA: Wadsworth.

Whitaker, Reg. (2000). *The end of privacy: How total surveillance is becoming a reality.* New York: New Press.

White, Jay D., & Korosec, Ronnie. (2005). Issues in contracting and outsourcing information technology. In G. David Garson (Ed.). *Handbook of public information systems* (2nd ed). New York: Taylor & Francis.

Wilhelm, Anthony G. (2003). Leveraging sunken investments in communications infrastructure: A policy perspective from the United States. *The Information Society, 19*(4), 279–286.

Williams, Joseph Kip Canfield, & Ritondo, Michele. (1997). IT lessons learned from the Food and Drug Administration's CANDA program. *Failure & Lessons Learned in Information Technology Management, 1*, 39–47.

Williams, Sarah. (2003). Internet weblogs soar due to recent presidential campaigns. Retrieved September 16, 2004, from http://www.jhunewsletter. com/vnews/display.v/ART/2003/11/21/3fbd41b9ce719?template=pda.

Wilson, Ernest J., III (2004). *The information revolution and developing countries.* Cambridge, MA: MIT Press.

Wilson, Kenneth R., Wallin, Jennifer S., & Reiser, Christa. (2003). Social stratification and the digital divide. *Social Science Computer Review, 21*(2), 133–143.

Winston-Salem/Forsyth County Public Schools. (2001). *Winston-Salem/Forsyth County Public Schools Technology Plan, 2001–2005.* Retrieved October 14, 2004, from http://mts.admin.wsfcs.k12.nc.us/admin/techplan/Techplan.pdf.

Wong, Wylie. (2004). Taking the e-procurement plunge. *State Tech,* Spring: 14–16.

Wood, Patricia. (2000). People, politics, and technology: Public service in the 21st century. National Capital Area Chapter, American Society for Public Administration Spring Conference, May 12. Retrieved November 30, 2004, from http://govinfo.library.unt.edu/accessamerica/docs/feed81.html.

World Bank. (2002). *The right to tell: The role of mass media in economic development.* Washington, DC: World.

Worrall, Les, Remenyi, Dan, & Money, Arthur. (2000). A methodology for evaluating the effectiveness of the delivery of IT services: A comparative study of six UK local authorities. In G. David Garson (Ed.), *Handbook of public information systems* (pp. 501–520). New York: Dekker.

Wright, Tom. (1996). Towards a culture of openness. *IPC Perspectives,* 5(2). Retrieved October 26, 2004, from http://www.ipc.on.ca/scripts/index_.asp?action=31&P_ID=11343&N_ID=1&PT_ID=11351&U_ID=0#1.

Wulf, William A. (2000). *The declining percentage of women in computer science: An academic view. Who will do the science of the future?: A symposium on careers of women in science.* Office of Scientific and Engineering Personnel (OSEP). Retrieved September 25, 2004, from http://books.nap.edu/books/0309071852/html/31.html.

Zachman, John A. (1987). A framework for information systems architecture. *IBM Systems Journal, 26*(3), 276–292.

Zaiser, Stephanie. (2002). A-76 comments to the OMB. Washington, DC: Office of Management and Budget. Retrieved March 19, 2005, from http://www.whitehouse.gov/omb/circulars/a076/comments/a76-227.pdf.

Zimmerman, J. (1990). Some effects of the new technology on woment. In M. D. Ermann, M. Williams, and C. Gutierrez (Eds.), *Computers, ethics, and society.* New York: Oxford University Press.

Zuboff, Shoshanna. (1988). *In the age of the smart machine.* New York: Basic Books.

Index

Page numbers followed by *t* or *f* denote tables or figures.